The Complete France FC 1904-2020

Dirk Karsdorp

British Library Cataloguing in Publication Data
A catalogue record for this book is available from the British Library

ISBN 978-1-86223-462-8

Copyright © 2021, SOCCER BOOKS LIMITED. (01472 696226)
72 St. Peter's Avenue, Cleethorpes, N.E. Lincolnshire, DN35 8HU, England

www.soccer-books.co.uk

All rights are reserved. No part of this publication may be reproduced, stored in a retrieval system or transmitted, in any form or by any means, electronic, mechanical, photocopying, recording, or otherwise, without the prior written permission of Soccer Books Limited.

Manufactured in the UK by Severn

FOREWORD

Thirteen years ago we published a series of books about the international games played by the Home Nations – England, Scotland, Wales, Northern Ireland and the Republic of Ireland. These books contained full line-ups (including that of the opponents) and statistics for every game played by each country covered and proved very popular. So popular, in fact, that the 3rd edition of each of these books was published in 2020, bringing the statistics up to date.

We have decided to extend this series to cover a number of other European countries and this book covers every official match played by the French national team from their very first game against Belgium in 1904, through to the end of 2020. Other books also available in this series cover matches played by the Belgian national team 1904 to 2020, the Netherlands national team from 1905 to 2020, the Italian national team from 1910 to 2020 and the Spanish National team from 1920 to 2020.

1. 01.05.1904   Évence Coppée Trophy
BELGIUM v FRANCE 3-3 (1-2)
Stade du Vivier d'Oie, Brussels
Referee: John C. Keene (England)   Attendance: 1,500
BELGIUM: Alfred Verdyck, Albert Friling, Edgard Poelmans, Guillaume Vanden Eynde, Charles Cambier, Camille Van Hoorden, Max Tobias, Alex Wigand, Georges Quéritet, Pierre-Joseph Destrebecq, Charles Vanderstappen.
FRANCE: Maurice Guichard, Fernand Canelle, Joseph Verlet, Georges Bilot, Jacques Davy, Charles Bilot, Louis Mesnier, Marius Royet, Georges Garnier, Gaston Cyprès, Adrien Filez.   Manager: Robert Guérin
Goals: Georges Quéritet (7, 50), Pierre-Joseph Destrebecq (65) / Louis Mesnier (12), Marius Royet (13), Gaston Cyprès (87)

2. 12.02.1905
FRANCE v SWITZERLAND 1-0 (0-0)
Parc des Princes, Paris
Referee: John Lewis (England)   Attendance: 500
FRANCE: Maurice Guichard, Fernand Canelle, Joseph Verlet, Charles Wilkes, Pierre Allemane, Eugène Nicolai, Louis Mesnier, Marius Royet, Georges Garnier, Gaston Cyprès, Adrien Filez.   Manager: Robert Guérin
SWITZERLAND: Alfred Uster, Fritz Bollinger, Eric Mory, Alfred Mégroz, Jean Forestier, Robert Studer, Eugen Dütschler, Hans Billeter, Eduard Garonne, Hans Kämpfer, Hermann Kratz.
Goal: Gaston Cyprès (60)

3. 07.05.1905
BELGIUM v FRANCE 7-0 (3-0)
Stade du Vivier d'Oie, Brussels
Referee: Rodolphe William Seeldrayers (Belgium) then John Lewis (England) after 16 minutes   Attendance: 300
BELGIUM: Robert Hustin, Edgard Poelmans, Ernest Moreau de Melen, Hector Raemaekers, Henri Dedecker, Camille Van Hoorden, Max Tobias, Laurent Theunen, Gustave Vanderstappen, Pierre-Joseph Destrebecq, Charles Vanderstappen.
FRANCE: Georges Crozier, Fernand Canelle, Henri Moigneu, Eugène Nicolai, Marius Royet, Charles Wilkes, Raymond Gigot, Louis Mesnier, Georges Garnier, Gaston Cyprès, Adrien Filez.   Manager: Robert Guérin
Georges Crozier left the field after 65 minutes because he needed to catch the train to return to his army barracks. France finished the game with 10 players.
Goals: Camille Van Hoorden (15, 70), Pierre-Joseph Destrebecq (19, 55, 86), Laurent Theunen (30, 80)

4. 22.04.1906
FRANCE v BELGIUM 0-5 (0-3)
Stade de La Faisanderie, Saint-Cloud
Referee: Jack Wood (England)   Attendance: 515
FRANCE: Georges Crozier, Joseph Verlet, Henri Moigneu, Julien Du Rhéart, Pierre Allemane, Louis Schubart, Albert Jouve, Louis Mesnier, Marius Royet, Gaston Cyprès, Adrien Filez.   Manager: Robert Guérin
BELGIUM: Robert Hustin, Roger Piérard, Edgard Poelmans, Guillaume Vanden Eynde, Charles Cambier, Camille Van Hoorden, Alphonse Wright, René Feye, Robert Deveen, Pierre-Joseph Destrebecq, Hector Goetinck.
Goals: René Feye (30, 35), Camille Van Hoorden (40), Robert Deveen (58, 60)

5. 01.11.1906
FRANCE v ENGLAND (Amateurs) 0-15 (0-5)
Parc des Princes, Paris
Referee: Alexandre Guillon (Belgium)   Attendance: 1,500
FRANCE: Zacharie Baton, Fernand Canelle, Henri Moigneu, Charles Wilkes, Pierre Allemane, Louis Schubart, Émile Sartorius, Marius Royet, André François, Gaston Cyprès, Julien Verbrugghe.   Manager: Robert Guérin
ENGLAND: Ernest Proud, Fred Milnes, Herbert Smith, Colin McIver, Percy Farnfield, Bob Hawkes, James Raine, Sammy Day, Vivian Woodward, Stanley Harris, Harold Hardman.
Goals: Stanley Harris (15, 18, 43, 49, 51, 57, 83), Vivian Woodward (39, 63, 65, 73), Sammy Day (41, 76), James Raine (80), Percy Farnfield (87)
Vivian Woodward missed a penalty kick (66)

6. 21.04.1907
BELGIUM v FRANCE 1-2 (1-1)
Stade du Vivier d'Oie, Brussels
Referee: Herbert James Willing (Netherlands)   Attendance: 2,000
BELGIUM: Robert Hustin, Marcel Feye, Edgard Poelmans, Guillaume Vanden Eynde, Charles Cambier, Camille Van Hoorden, Alphonse Wright, René Feye, Robert Deveen, Clément Robyn, Hector Goetinck.
FRANCE: Zacharie Baton, Fernand Canelle, Victor Bentall-Sergent, Paul Zeiger, Pierre Allemane, Henri Moigneu, André Puget, Marius Royet, André François, Georges Bon, René Camard.   Manager: Robert Guérin
Goals: Charles Cambier (18) / Marius Royet (41), André François (72)

7. 08.03.1908
SWITZERLAND v FRANCE 1-2 (1-0)
Parc des Sports, Geneva
Referee: Herbert Patrick Devitte (Switzerland)
Attendance: 3,500
SWITZERLAND: Ivan Dreyfus, Louis Artigue, Oskar Kihm, Alfred Mégroz, Daniel Hug, Emil Hasler, Ernst Walter, Jacques Reich, Adolf Frenken, Georges Lang, Hans Kämpfer.
FRANCE: Zacharie Baton, Joseph Verlet, Victor Bentall-Sergent, Maurice Vandendriessche, Pierre Allemane, Henri Moigneu, Émile Sartorius, Albert Jenicot, André François, Paul Mathaux, Gabriel Hanot.   Manager: Robert Guérin
Goals: Adolf Frenken (41) /
Émile Sartorius (60), André François (70)

8. 23.03.1908
ENGLAND (Amateurs) v FRANCE 12-0 (6-0)
Royal Park Ground, London
Referee: Thomas Kyle (England)   Attendance: 6,000
ENGLAND: Horace Peter Bailey, Watty Corbett, Albert Edward Scothern, Kenneth Hunt, Evelyn Lintott, Bob Hawkes, James Raine, Vivian Woodward, Willie Jordan, Arthur Berry, Gordon Wright.   Manager: Alfred Davis
FRANCE: André Renaux, Victor Bentall-Sergent, Henri Moigneu, Maurice Vandendriessche, Pierre Allemane, Julien Denis, Émile Sartorius, Marius Royet, André François, Paul Mathaux, Gabriel Hanot.   Manager: Robert Guérin
Goals: Bob Hawkes (9), Willie Jordan (16, 32, 40, 48, 58, 89), V. Woodward (23, 52, 66), Arthur Berry (25), James Raine (75) /

9. 12.04.1908
FRANCE v BELGIUM 1-2 (0-2)
Stade du Matin, Colombes
Referee: James P. Stark (Scotland)   Attendance: 498
FRANCE: Zacharie Baton, Joseph Verlet, Victor Bentall-Sergent, Charles Wilkes, Pierre Allemane, Henri Moigneu, Émile Sartorius, Marius Royet, Albert Jenicot, Paul Mathaux, Gabriel Hanot.   Manager: Robert Guérin
BELGIUM: Henri Leroy, Roger Piérard, Edgard Poelmans, Guillaume Vanden Eynde, Charles Cambier, Camille Van Hoorden, Max Tobias, Maurice Vertongen, Robert Deveen, Louis Saeys, Edgard Van Boxtaele.
Goals: Joseph Verlet (76 pen) / Robert Deveen (22, 29)

10. 10.05.1908
NETHERLANDS v FRANCE 4-1 (2-0)
Stadion Prinsenlaan, Rotterdam
Referee: Joseph Brauburger (Belgium)   Attendance: 3,000
NETHERLANDS: Reiner Beeuwkes, Karel Heijting, Guus van Hecking Colenbrander, Kees Bekker, Bok de Korver, Noud Stempels, Caius Welcker, Edu Snethlage, Jack Akkersdijk, Jan Thomée, Mannes Francken.   Manager: Cees van Hasselt
FRANCE: Maurice Tilliette, Fernand Canelle, Henri Moigneu, Julien Du Rhéart, Julien Denis (55 Victor Denis), Marius Royet, René Eucher, Louis Mesnier, André François, Paul Mathaux, Gabriel Hanot.   Manager: Robert Guérin
Goals: Edu Snethlage (18, 76), Jan Thomée (22), Jack Akkersdijk (60) / André François (74)

11. 22.10.1908   IV Olympic Games Final Tournament
1908 – Semi-final
DENMARK v FRANCE 17-1 (6-1)
White City Stadium, London (England)
Referee: Thomas P. Campbell (England)   Attendance: 1,000
DENMARK: Ludvig Drescher, Charles Buchwald, Harald Hansen, Harald Bohr, Kristian Middelboe, Nils Middelboe, Johannes Gandil, August Lindgren, Sophus Nielsen, Vilhelm Wolfhagen, Bjørn Rasmussen.   Manager: Charles Williams
FRANCE: Maurice Tilliette, Ursule Wibaut, Jean Dubly, Georges Bayrou, Charles Renaux, Louis Schubart, Émile Sartorius, George Albert, André François, Gaston Cyprès, René Fenouillère.   Manager: Robert Guérin
Goals: Sophus Nielsen (3, 4, 7, 39, 46, 48, 52, 64, 66, 76), August Lindgren (18, 37), Vilhelm Wolfhagen (60, 72, 82, 89), Nils Middelboe (68) / Émile Sartorius (16)

12. 09.05.1909
BELGIUM v FRANCE 5-2 (2-0)
Stade du Vivier d'Oie, Brussels
Referee: James R. Schumacher (England)   Attendance: 1,500
BELGIUM: Robert Hustin, Émile Andrieu, Joseph Robyn, Hector Raemaekers, Charles Cambier, Camille Van Hoorden, Georges Pootmans, Fernand Goossens, Robert Deveen, Laurent Theunen, Edgard Van Boxtaele.
FRANCE: Juste Tessier, Ernest Tossier, Henri Guerre, Jean Rigal, Raymond Gouin, Jean-Marie Barat, Maurice Meunier, Henri Bellocq, Félix Julien, Alfred Compeyrat, Henri Mouton.
Goals: Robert Deveen (30, 41, 80), Camille Van Hoorden (83), Laurent Theunen (85) / Henri Mouton (60), Jean Rigal (89)

13. 22.05.1909
FRANCE v ENGLAND (Amateurs) 0-11 (0-6)

Stade de la FGSPF (Fédération Gymnastique et Sportive des Patrinages de France), Gentilly

Referee: Joseph Brauburger (Belgium)   Attendance: 390

FRANCE: Juste Tessier, Gilbert Brébion, André Sollier, Jean Rigal, Raymond Gouin, Jean-Marie Barat, Victor Hitzel, Henri Bellocq, Henri Mouton, Félix Julien, Marcel Louis Pacot.

ENGLAND: Dr. Ron Brebner, Albert Edward Bell, Herbert Smith, Fred Fayers, Fred Chapman, Bob Hawkes, James Raine, Vivian Woodward, Harry Stapley, Chris Porter, Gordon Wright. Manager: Alfred Davis

Goals: Vivian Woodward (4), Harry Stapley (??, 24), Chris Porter (1 in the 1st half and 2 in the 2nd half), Gordon Wright (1 in the 1st half), Fred Fayers (1 in the 1st half and 1 in the 2nd half), James Raine (2 in the 2nd half)

14. 03.04.1910
FRANCE v BELGIUM 0-4 (0-1)

Stade de la FGSPF (Fédération Gymnastique et Sportive des Patrinages de France), Gentilly

Referee: James B. Stark (Scotland)   Attendance: 956

FRANCE: Juste Tessier, Daniel Mercier, André Sollier, Jean Rigal, Jean Ducret, Eugène Petel, Maurice Olivier, Henri Bellocq, Henri Mouton, Étienne Jourde, Joseph Delvecchio.

BELGIUM: Pierre Kogel, Paul Bouttiau, Émile Andrieu, Prosper Braeckman, Charles Cambier, Fernand Goossens, Hector Goetinck, Alphonse Six, Robert Deveen, Louis Saeys, Désiré Paternoster.   Manager: William Sturrock Maxwell

Goals: Alphonse Six (27, 70, 85), Robert Deveen (73)

15. 16.04.1910
ENGLAND (Amateurs) v FRANCE 10-1 (6-0)

Goldstone Ground, Brighton and Hove

Referee: Christiaan Jacobus Groothoff (Netherlands)
Attendance: 3,500

ENGLAND: Frank Leese, Harry Boardman, William Martin, Fred Fayers, Fred Chapman, Kenneth Hunt, Arthur Berry, Lionel Louch, William Steer, Tom Wilson, Arthur Kerry.

FRANCE: Juste Tessier, Daniel Mercier, André Sollier, Jean Rigal, Jean Ducret, Henri Vascout, Maurice Olivier, Henri Bellocq, Henri Mouton, Étienne Jourde, Auguste Tousset.

Goals: Tom Wilson (9, 10, 70, 82), Arthur Berry (18), Fred Chapman (27), William Steer (35, 43, 53, 84) / Auguste Tousset (87)

16. 15.05.1910
ITALY v FRANCE 6-2 (2-0)

Arena Civica, Milano

Referee: Henry Goodley (England)   Attendance: 4,500

ITALY: Mario De Simoni, Franco Varisco, Francesco Calì, Attilio Trerè, Virgilio Fossati (I), Domenico Capello, Enrico Debernardi, Giuseppe Rizzi, Aldo Cevenini, Pietro Lana, Arturo Boiocchi.   Manager: Umberto Meazza

FRANCE: Juste Tessier, Daniel Mercier, André Sollier, Jean Rigal, Jean Ducret, Henri Vascout, Maurice Olivier, Henri Bellocq, Henri Mouton, Henri Sellier, Étienne Jourde.

Goals: Pietro Lana (13, 59, 89 pen), Virgilio Fossati (20), Giuseppe Rizzi (66), Enrico Debernardi (82) / Henri Bellocq (49), Jean Ducret (62)

17. 01.01.1911
FRANCE v HUNGARY 0-3 (0-2)

Stade du Cercle Athlétique de Paris, Charenronneau

Referee: Charles Barette (Belgium)   Attendance: 2,032

FRANCE: Henri Beau Coulon, Alfred Gindrat, André Sollier, Jean Rigal, Jean Ducret, Julien Du Rhéart, Pol Morel, Henri Bellocq, Eugène Maës, Ernest Gravier, Julien Verbrugghe.

HUNGARY: Ernö Sipos, Béla Révész, Oszkár Szendrö, Gyula Bíró, Izidor Kürschner, Dániel Takács, Ferenc Weisz, Jenö Károly, Károly Koródy, Imre Schlosser, Gáspár Borbás. Manager: Frigyes Minder

Goals: Imre Schlosser (10, 30, 49)

Sent off: André Sollier (66)

18. 23.03.1911
FRANCE v ENGLAND (Amateurs) 0-3 (0-1)

Stade de Paris, Saint-Ouen

Referee: René Wolters (Belgium)   Attendance: 1,638

FRANCE: Henri Beau Coulon, Alfred Gindrat, Alfred Compeyrat, Jean Rigal, Jean Ducret, Henri Vascout, Pol Morel, Louis Mesnier, Eugène Maës, Ernest Gravier, Julien Verbrugghe.

ENGLAND: William McKee, Thomas Burn, Arthur Knight, Charles Tyson, Bill Stapley, Joe Dines, Arthur Berry, Dick Healey, William Steer, Gordon Hoare, Gordon Wright.

Goals: Dick Healey (30), Gordon Hoare (60, 75 pen)

19. 09.04.1911
FRANCE v ITALY 2-2 (2-1)

Stade de Paris, Saint-Ouen

Referee: Charles Barette (Belgium)   Attendance: 1,532

FRANCE: Henri Beau Coulon, Charles Bilot, Joseph Verlet, Jean Rigal, Jean Ducret, Henri Vascout, Louis Mesnier, Émilien Devic, Eugène Maës, Ernest Gravier, Julien Verbrugghe.

ITALY: Mario De Simoni, Angelo Binaschi, Renzo De Vecchi, Guido Ara, Giuseppe Milano (I), Virgilio Fossati (I), Pietro Antonio Gavinelli, Giuseppe Rizzi, Aldo Cevenini, Carlo Rampini (I), Arturo Boiocchi.   Manager: Umberto Meazza

Goals: Eugène Maës (14, 40) /
Carlo Rampini (33), Arturo Boiocchi (81)

20. 23.04.1911
SWITZERLAND v FRANCE 5-2 (4-0)

Parc des Sports, Geneva

Referee: Herbert Patrick Devitte (Switzerland)
Attendance: 4,000

SWITZERLAND: Ernst Flückiger, Louis Würsten, Heinrich Müller, Konrad Ehrbar, Marcel Henneberg, Maurice Henneberg, Ernst Weiss, Ernst Rubli, Paul Wyss, Edouard Sydler, Pierre Collet.

FRANCE: Henri Beau Coulon, Charles Bilot, Lucien Gamblin, Jean Rigal, Jean Ducret, Henri Vascout, Georges Géronimi, Louis Mesnier, Eugène Maës, Ernest Gravier, Marcel Triboulet.

Goals: Edouard Sydler (5), Ernst Rubli (22, 26), Paul Wyss (31, 57) / Louis Mesnier (69), Eugène Maës (70)

21. 30.04.1911
BELGIUM v FRANCE 7-1 (3-0)

Rue de Forest, Brussels

Referee: James B. Stark (Scotland)   Attendance: 3,000

BELGIUM: Henry Leroy, Émile Andrieu, Gaston Hubin, Hector Raemaekers, Camille Nys, Camille Van Hoorden, Jean Bouttiau, Fernand Nisot, Robert Deveen, Louis Saeys, Joseph Musch.   Manager: William Sturrock Maxwell

FRANCE: Henri Beau Coulon, Charles Bilot, Alfred Compeyrat, Jean Rigal, Gaston Barreau, Henri Vascout, Louis Mesnier, Émilien Devic, Eugène Maës, Ernest Gravier, Étienne Jourde.

Goals: Robert Deveen (20, 38, 42, 67, 86), Louis Saeys (48), Jean Bouttiau (60) / Eugène Maës (75)

22. 29.10.1911
LUXEMBOURG v FRANCE 1-4 (1-2)

Stade Racing Club, Luxembourg City

Referee: Raphaël Van Praag (Belgium)   Attendance: 2,400

LUXEMBOURG: Alphonse Weicker, François Lang, Joseph Michaux, Henri Schwartz, Michel Ungeheuer, Joseph Faber, Albert Elter, Emile Kuborn, Jemmy Becker, Victor Kauth, Zénon Bernard.

FRANCE: Pierre Chayriguès, Maurice Bigué, Paul Romano, Gaston Barreau, Jean Ducret, Henri Vascout, Maurice Olivier, Louis Mesnier, Henri Vialmonteil, Ernest Gravier, Francis Vial.

Goals: Albert Elter (15) / Henri Vialmonteil (26), Louis Mesnier (32 , 80 pen), Ernest Gravier (85)

23. 28.01.1912
FRANCE v BELGIUM 1-1 (0-0)

Stade de Paris, Saint-Ouen

Referee: James B. Stark (Scotland)   Attendance: 1,980

FRANCE: Pierre Chayriguès, Alfred Gindrat, Charles Bilot, Jean Rigal, Jean Ducret, Gaston Barreau, Émile Lesmann, Louis Mesnier, Eugène Maës, Henri Vialmonteil, Marcel Triboulet.

BELGIUM: Henry Leroy, Émile Andrieu, Gaston Hubin, Charles Bauwens, Guillaume Vanden Eynde, Joseph Thys, Pierre Vergeylen, Alphonse Six, Robert Deveen, Louis Saeys, Joseph Musch.   Manager: William Sturrock Maxwell

Goals: Eugène Maës (75) / Gaston Hubin (89 pen)

24. 18.02.1912
FRANCE v SWITZERLAND 4-1 (0-0)

Stade de Paris, Saint-Ouen

Referee: Charles Barette (Belgium)   Attendance: 2,626

FRANCE: Pierre Chayriguès, Alfred Gindrat, Paul Romano, Maurice Bigué, Jean Ducret, Gaston Barreau, Maurice Olivier, Louis Mesnier, Eugène Maës, Henri Vialmonteil, Marcel Triboulet.

SWITZERLAND: Ernst Maurer, Louis Würsten, Albert Schmid, Konrad Ehrbar, Maurice Henneberg, Paul Neumeyer, Ernst Weiss, Paul Kaiser, Paul Wyss, Karl Koblet, Theo Kobelt.

Goals: Louis Mesnier (50), Marcel Triboulet (60), Eugène Maës (70), Henri Vialmonteil (83) / Paul Wyss (86)

25. 17.03.1912
ITALY v FRANCE 3-4 (1-2)
Campo di Piazza d'Armi, Torino
Referee: James B. Stark (Scotland)   Attendance: 5,000
ITALY: Vittorio Faroppa, Marco Sala, Renzo De Vecchi, Guido Ara, Giuseppe Milano (I), Felice Milano, Pietro Leone (I), Felice Berardo, Aldo Cevenini, Carlo Rampini (I), Edoardo Mariani.   Manager: Umberto Meazza
FRANCE: Pierre Chayriguès, Émile Fiévet, Paul Romano, Maurice Bigué, Jean Ducret, Gaston Barreau, Fernand Faroux, Louis Mesnier, Eugène Maës, Henri Vialmonteil, Étienne Jourde.
Goals: Carlo Rampini (I) (24, 58), Aldo Cevenini (47) / Eugène Maës (10, 38, 66), Louis Mesnier (52)

26. 12.01.1913
FRANCE v ITALY 1-0 (1-0)
Stade de Paris, Saint-Ouen
Referee: Herbert James Willing (Netherlands)
Attendance: 3,600
FRANCE: Pierre Chayriguès, Lucien Letailleur, Gabriel Hanot, Auguste Tousset, Jean Ducret, Gaston Barreau, Ferdinand Rochet, Louis Mesnier, Eugène Maës, Henri Vialmonteil, Abel Lafouge.
ITALY: Piero Campelli, Attilio Trerè (46 Carlo Galletti), Modesto Valle, Guido Ara, Virgilio Fossati (I), Pietro Leone (I), Felice Milano, Giuseppe Rizzi, Aldo Cevenini, Carlo Rampini (I), Amedeo Varese.   Manager: Umberto Meazza
Goal: Eugène Maës (35)

27. 16.02.1913
BELGIUM v FRANCE 3-0 (2-0)
Stade du Vivier d'Oie, Brussels
Referee: James R. Schumacher (England)   Attendance: 6,000
BELGIUM: Jules Mayné, Dominique Baes, Gaston Hubin, Joseph Thys, Oscar Bossaert, Prosper Braeckman, Louis Bessems, Fernand Nisot, Sylvain Brébart, Joseph Musch, Clément De Meyer.   Manager: William Sturrock Maxwell
FRANCE: Pierre Chayriguès, Victor Bentall-Sergent, Gabriel Hanot, Maurice Bigué, Jean Ducret, Gaston Barreau, Henri Lesur, René Jacolliot, Eugène Maës, Henri Vialmonteil, Raymond Dubly.
Goals: Fernand Nisot (21, 31), Louis Bessems (52)

28. 27.02.1913
FRANCE v ENGLAND (Amateurs) 1-4 (0-2)
Stade du Matin, Colombes
Referee: Maurice Goossens (Belgium)   Attendance: 2,500
FRANCE: Pierre Chayriguès, Fernand Massip, Lucien Gamblin, Maurice Bigué, Jean Ducret, Gaston Barreau, Henri Lesur, André Poullain, Henri Bard, Ernest Guéguen, Raymond Dubly.
ENGLAND: Horace Bailey, Fred Ansell, Arthur Knight, Albert Barclay, Jimmy Harrold, Joe Dines, Arthur Berry, Sam Sanders, George Gemmell, Gordon Hoare, Reg Callender.
Goals: André Poullain (75) / Arthur Berry (16, 64), Gordan Hoare (40, 54)

29. 09.03.1913
SWITZERLAND v FRANCE 1-4 (1-2)
Parc des Sports, Geneva
Referee: Herbert Patrick Devitte (Switzerland)
Attendance: 5,000
SWITZERLAND: Joseph Navarro, Heinrich Müller, Otto Fehlmann, Jean Steinemann, Victor Adamina, Christian Albicker, Ernst Weiss, Otto Märki (46 Eugen Leuner), Ernst Siegrist, Pierre Collet, Ernst Rubli.
FRANCE: Louis Bournonville, Jean Degouve, Charles Dujardin, Charles Montagne, Jean Ducret, Gaston Barreau, Henri Lesur, André Poullain, Albert Eloy, Paul Chandelier, Raymond Dubly.
Goals: Ernst Rubli (7) / Charles Montagne (13), Albert Eloy (16, 83), Raymond Dubly (67)

30. 20.04.1913
FRANCE v LUXEMBOURG 8-0 (2-0)
Stade de Paris, Saint-Ouen
Referee: Hubert Istace (Belgium)   Attendance: 3,000
FRANCE: Pierre Chayriguès, Lucien Gamblin, Gabriel Hanot, Charles Montagne, Jean Ducret, Gaston Barreau, Paul Voyeux, André Poullain, Eugène Maës, Felice Romano, Raymond Dubly.
LUXEMBOURG: Robert Stümper, François Lang, François Krebs, Henri Schwartz, Michel Ungeheuer, Joseph Faber, Emile Thill, Jean Massard, Victor Kauth, Adolphe Reckinger, Eugène Becker.
Goals: Eugène Maës (28, 56, 68, 86, 88), André Poullain (30), Felice Romano (78), Jean Ducret (83)

31. 25.01.1914
FRANCE v BELGIUM 4-3 (3-3)
Stade Victor Boucquey, Lille

Referee: Herbert Mortimer (England)   Attendance: 4,813

FRANCE: Pierre Chayriguès, Lucien Gamblin, Gabriel Hanot, Émilien Devic, Jean Ducret, Gaston Barreau, Henri Lesur, Henri Bard, Étienne Jourde, Paul Chandelier, Raymond Dubly.

BELGIUM: Henri Leroy, Oscar Verbeeck, Gaston Hubin, Joseph Thys, Fernand Nisot, Maurice De Coster, Joseph Musch, Fernand Wertz, Sylvain Brébart, Jean Van Cant, Georges Hebdin.   Manager: Charles Bunyan

Goals: Gabriel Hanot (16 pen), Henri Bard (24), Étienne Jourde (37), Raymond Dubly (65) / Jean Van Cant (6), Sylvain Brébart (8), Joseph Thys (41)

32. 08.02.1914
LUXEMBOURG v FRANCE 5-4 (2-3)
Stade Racing Club, Luxembourg City

Referee: Maurice Goossens (Belgium)   Attendance: 3,000

LUXEMBOURG: Eugène Didier, Thomas Schmit, Bernard Wirtz, Joseph Faber, Jean-Pierre Voelker, Henri Hoffmann, Emile Thill, Jean Massard, Zénon Bernard, Auguste Rizzi, Victor Kauth.

FRANCE: Jean Loubière, René Bonnet, Jean Degouve, Émilien Devic, Jean Ducret, Maurice Olivier, Maurice Gastiger, Henri Bard, Albert Eloy, Charles Géronimi, Marcel Triboulet.

Goals: J. Massard (4 pen, 20 pen, 46, 81), Zénon Bernard (47) / Henri Bard (13), J. Ducret (22 pen), Charles Géronimi (41), Marcel Triboulet (85)

33. 08.03.1914
FRANCE v SWITZERLAND 2-2 (0-1)
Stade de Paris, Saint-Ouen

Referee: John Thomas Howcroft (England)
Attendance: 4,000

FRANCE: Pierre Chayriguès, Lucien Gamblin, Gabriel Hanot, Maurice Bigué, Jean Ducret, Albert Jourda, Maurice Gastiger, Étienne Jourde, Émilien Devic, Albert Schaff, Raymond Dubly.

SWITZERLAND: Edmund Bieri, Edouard Duriaux, Otto Fehlmann, Ernst Kaltenbach, Paul Neumeyer, Oskar Neumeyer, Oskar Merkt, Georges Schreyer, Fritz Bollinger, Christian Albicker, Pierre Collet.

Goals: Émilien Devic (46), Maurice Gastiger (85) / Georges Schreyer (39), Christian Albicker (88)

34. 29.03.1914
ITALY v FRANCE 2-0 (0-0)
Campo di Piazza d'Armi, Torino

Referee: Charles Barette (Belgium)   Attendance: 15,000

ITALY: Giovanni Innocenti, Modesto Valle, Renzo De Vecchi, Luigi Barbesino, Virgilio Fossati (I), Biagio Goggio, Felice Berardo, Angelo Mattea, Aldo Cevenini, Amedeo Varese, Carlo Corna (I).   Manager: Umberto Meazza

FRANCE: Albert Parsys, Lucien Gamblin, Gabriel Hanot, Maurice Bigué, Jean Ducret, Albert Jourda, Henri Lesur, Jules Dubly, Jean Picy, Paul Chandelier, Raymond Dubly.

Goals: Felice Berardo (46), Aldo Cevenini (89)

35. 31.05.1914
HUNGARY v FRANCE 5-1 (1-1)
Üllöi út, Budapest

Referee: Heinrich Retschury (Austria)   Attendance: 6,000

HUNGARY: Karoly Zsák, Gyula Rumbold, Imre Payer, Béla Kiss, Jenö Károly, Zoltán Blum, Györö Rácz, Sándor Bodnár, Mihály Pataki, Imre Schlosser, Gáspár Borbás.
Manager: Ede Herczog

FRANCE: Pierre Chayriguès, Maurice Mathieu, Gabriel Hanot, André Allègre, Gaston Barreau, Albert Jourda, Henri Lesur, Juste Brouzes, Étienne Jourde, Émile Dusart, Marcel Triboulet.

Goals: Sándor Bodnár (20, 81, 87), Imre Payer (59 pen), Mihály Pataki (76) / Juste Brouzes (1)

36. 09.03.1919
BELGIUM v FRANCE 2-2 (1-0)
Stade du Vivier d'Oie, Brussels

Referee: Christiaan Jacobus Groothoff (Netherlands)
Attendance: 25,000

BELGIUM: Henry Leroy, Armand Swartenbroeks, Oscar Verbeeck, Joseph Musch (46 Louis Van Hege), François Moucheron, Joseph Thys, Louis Bessems, Robert Coppée, Honoré Vlamynck, Georges Michel, Georges Hebdin.

FRANCE: Raymond Frémont, Maurice Mathieu, Lucien Gamblin, Albert Mercier, François Hugues, Émilien Devic, Paul Faure, Gabriel Hanot, Henri Bard, Louis Darques, Marcel Triboulet.

Goals: Georges Michel (5), Lucien Gamblin (75 og) / Gabriel Hanot (80, 89)

37.   18.01.1920
ITALY v FRANCE 9-4 (4-3)
Velodrome Sempione, Milano
Referee: John Forster (Switzerland)   Attendance: 14,000
ITALY: Angelo Arturo Cameroni, Giuseppe Ticozzelli, Renzo De Vecchi, Guido Ara, Carlo Carcano, Cesare Lovati, Felice Berardo, Ermanno Aebi, Guglielmo Brezzi, Luigi Cevenini, Augusto Bergamino.   Manager: Nino Resegotti
FRANCE: Maurice Cottenet, Pierre Mony, Alexis Mony, Émilien Devic, Louis Olagnier, Louis Mistral, Jules Dewaquez, Albert Rénier, Paul Nicolas, Henri Bard, Raymond Dubly.   Manager: Gaston Barreau
Goals: Luigi Cevenini (7, 19), Ermanno Aebi (18, 62, 70), Guglielmo Brezzi (38, 52, 84), Carlo Carcano (72) / Paul Nicolas (24), Henri Bard (28, 44), Raymond Dubly (87)

38.   29.02.1920
SWITZERLAND v FRANCE 0-2 (0-1)
Parc des Sports, Geneva
Referee: Giovanni Mauro (Italy)   Attendance: 15,000
SWITZERLAND: Alfred Berger, Otto Fehlmann, Gustav Gottenkieny, Paul Schmiedlin, Oskar Neumeyer, Jakob Schneebeli, Werner Huber, Paul Funk, Paul Wyss, Kurt Friedrich, Raymond Keller.
FRANCE: Albert Parsys, Alfred Roth, Édouard Baumann, Philippe Bonnardel, François Hugues, Louis Mistral, Jules Dewaquez, Louis Darques, Paul Nicolas, Henri Bard, Raymond Dubly.   Manager: Gaston Barreau
Goals: Jules Dewaquez (43), Paul Nicolas (78)

39.   28.03.1920
FRANCE v BELGIUM 2-1 (1-1)
Parc des Princes, Paris
Referee: Henry R. Child (England)   Attendance: 13,000
FRANCE: Albert Parsys, Marcel Vanco, Lucien Gamblin, Charles Montagne, François Hugues, Maurice Gravelines, Jules Dewaquez, Maurice Gastiger, Paul Nicolas, Henri Bard, Raymond Dubly.   Manager: Gaston Barreau
BELGIUM: Léon Vandermeiren, Armand Swartenbroeks, Oscar Verbeeck, Joseph Musch, Émile Hanse, Auguste Fierens, Louis Van Hege, Robert Coppée, Honoré Vlamynck, Georges Michel, Georges Hebdin.   Manager: William Sturrock Maxwell
Goals: Paul Nicolas (16, 79) / Honoré Vlamynck (4)

40.   05.04.1920
FRANCE v ENGLAND (Amateurs) 0-5 (0-1)
Stade des Bruyères, Rouen
Referee: Charles Barette (Belgium)   Attendance: 14,500
FRANCE: Maurice Cottenet, Marcel Vanco, Lucien Gamblin, Jean Batmale, François Hugues, Philippe Bonnardel, Jules Dewaquez, Maurice Mercery, Paul Nicolas, Émilien Devic, Raymond Dubly.   Manager: Gaston Barreau
ENGLAND: Ernest Herbert Coleman, Lambert Golightly, Arthur Knight, Kenneth Hunt, George Atkinson, Charlie Harbidge, Fred Nicholas, Miles Howell, Wesley Harding, Dick Sloley, Kenny Hegan.
Goals: Kenny Hegan (22), Dick Sloley (46), Wesley Harding (60, 67), Fred Nicholas (63)

41.   29.08.1920   VII Olympic Games Final Tournament 1920 – Quarter-final
FRANCE v ITALY 3-1 (2-1)
Olympisch Stadion, Antwerp (Belgium)
Referee: Henri Christophe (Belgium)   Attendance: 10,000
FRANCE: Albert Parsys, Léon Huot, Édouard Baumann, Jean Batmale, René Petit, François Hugues, Jules Dewaquez, Jean Boyer, Paul Nicolas, Henri Bard, Raymond Dubly.   Manager: Gaston Barreau
ITALY: Giovanni Giacone, Antonio Bruna, Renzo De Vecchi, Enrico Sardi, Mario Meneghetti, Cesare Lovati, Pio Ferraris, Adolfo Baloncieri, Guglielmo Brezzi, Aristodemo Emilio Santamaria, Giustiniano Marucco.   Manager: Giuseppe Milano (I)
Goals: Jean Boyer (10), Paul Nicolas (14), Henri Bard (54) / Guglielmo Brezzi (33 pen)

42.   31.08.1920   VII. Olympic Games Final Tournament 1920 – Semi-final
CZECHOSLOVAKIA v FRANCE 4-1 (1-0)
Olympisch Stadion, Antwerp (Belgium)
Referee: Johannes Mutters (Netherlands)
Attendance: 12,000
CZECHOSLOVAKIA: Rudolf Klapka, Antonín Hojer, Karel Steiner, Frantisek Kolenatý, Karel Pesek, Emil Seifert, Josef Sedlácek, Antonín Janda, Jan Vaník, Otakar Skvajn Mazal, Jan Placek.
FRANCE: Albert Parsys, Léon Huot, Édouard Baumann, Jean Batmale, René Petit, François Hugues, Jules Dewaquez, Jean Boyer, Paul Nicolas, Henri Bard, Raymond Dubly.   Manager: Gaston Barreau
Goals: Otakar Skvajn Mazal (18, 75, 87), Karel Steiner (70) / Jean Boyer (79)

43. 08.02.1921
**FRANCE
v REPUBLIC OF IRELAND (Amateurs) 1-2** (0-2)
Parc des Princes, Paris

Referee: Raphaël Van Praag (Belgium)   Attendance: 15,000

FRANCE: Maurice Beaudier, Maurice Meyer, Lucien Gamblin, Marcel Vanco, François Hugues, Philippe Bonnardel, Jules Dewaquez, Louis Darques, Paul Nicolas, Paul Bloch, Raymond Dubly.   Manager: Gaston Barreau

REPUBLIC OF IRELAND: Nathaniel Adams, John O.McCarthy, Robert Mills, John Harris, Francis Heaney, Harold Risk, Samuel Jackson, Alexander Steele, James Chambers, Patrick O'Flaherty, John Carey.   Manager: C.Harris

Goals: François Hugues (65) /
James Chambers (35), Alexander Steele (38)

44. 20.02.1921
FRANCE v ITALY 1-2 (1-0)
Stade de l'Huveaune, Marseille

Referee: John Forster (Switzerland)   Attendance: 10,000

FRANCE: Maurice Beaudier, Eugène Langenove, Lucien Gamblin, Jean Batmale, François Hugues, Philippe Bonnardel, Jules Dewaquez, Émilien Devic, Paul Nicolas, Henri Bard, Raymond Dubly.   Manager: Gaston Barreau

ITALY: Piero Campelli, Virginio Rosetta, Renzo De Vecchi, Pietro Genovesi, Carlo Carcano, Luigi Burlando, Enrico Migliavacca, Adolfo Baloncieri, Luigi Cevenini, Aristodemo Emilio Santamaria, Augusto Bergamino.
Manager: Giuseppe Milano (I)

Goals: Émilien Devic (22) /
Luigi Cevenini (53), Aristodemo Emilio Santamaria (63)

45. 06.03.1921
BELGIUM v FRANCE 3-1 (0-0)
Parc Duden, Vorst

Referee: Johannes Mutters (Netherlands)
Attendance: 20,000

BELGIUM: Jean De Bie, Armand Swartenbroeks, Oscar Verbeeck, François Moucheron, André Fierens, Joseph Musch, Louis Van Hege, Ivan Thys, Mathieu Bragard, Rik Larnoe, Désiré Bastin.   Manager: William Sturrock Maxwell

FRANCE: Maurice Beaudier, Eugène Langenove, Lucien Gamblin, Albert Jourda, François Hugues, Philippe Bonnardel, Jules Dewaquez, Antoine Rouchès, Paul Nicolas, Henri Bard, Raymond Dubly.   Manager: Gaston Barreau

Goals: Mathieu Bragard (52, 75), Louis Van Hege (60 pen) /
Jules Dewaquez (63)

46. 05.05.1921
FRANCE v ENGLAND (Amateurs) 2-1 (1-1)
Stade Général John Joseph Pershing, Vincennes

Referee: Henri Christophe (Belgium)   Attendance: 30,000

FRANCE: Maurice Cottenet, Marcel Vanco, Lucien Gamblin, François Hugues, Albert Jourda, Philippe Bonnardel, Jules Dewaquez, Jean Boyer, Paul Nicolas, Henri Bard, Raymond Dubly.   Manager: Gaston Barreau

ENGLAND: Ernest Coleman, Joseph Payne, Alfred Bower, Albert Read, A. Cox, Frederick Spiller, L. Partridge, John Prince, E. Farnfield, C. Wise, A. Grant.

Goals: Jules Dewaquez (6), Jean Boyer (67) / E. Farnfield (9)

47. 13.11.1921
FRANCE v NETHERLANDS 0-5 (0-1)
Stade Général John Joseph Pershing, Vincennes

Referee: Charles Barette (Belgium)   Attendance: 15,000

FRANCE: Maurice Cottenet, Marcel Vanco, Lucien Gamblin, Louis Mistral, Albert Jourda, Philippe Bonnardel, Jules Dewaquez, Louis Darques, Édouard Macquart, Henri Bard, Raymond Dubly.   Manager: Gaston Barreau

NETHERLANDS: Henk van Tilburg, Fons Pelser, Piet Stevens, Henk Hordijk, Harry Dénis, Herman Legger, Max Tetzner, Harry Rodermond, Jan van Gendt, Hein Delsen, Jan de Natris.   Manager: Frederick Warburton

Goals: Jan van Gendt (30, 52, 87), Harry Rodermond (69, 85)

48. 15.01.1922
FRANCE v BELGIUM 2-1 (0-1)
Stade Olympique Yves-du-Manoir, Colombes

Referee: William John Edwards (England)
Attendance: 18,000

FRANCE: Émile Friess, Marcel Vanco, Édouard Baumann, Maurice Gravelines, François Hugues, Albert Courquin, Jules Dewaquez, Robert Accard, Paul Nicolas, Louis Darques, Raymond Dubly.   Manager: Gaston Barreau

BELGIUM: Jean De Bie, Armand Swartenbroeks, Oscar Verbeeck, Fernand Caremans, Émile Hanse, Jacques Vandevelde, Louis Bessems, Joseph Musch, François Dogaer, Pierre Braine, Georges Michel.
Manager: William Sturrock Maxwell

Goals: Louis Darques (50), Jules Dewaquez (67) /
Georges Michel (35)

49. 30.04.1922
FRANCE v SPAIN 0-4 (0-4)
Stade Sainte-Germaine, Le-Bouscat
Referee: Raphaël Van Praag (Belgium)   Attendance: 10,000
FRANCE: Émiele Friess, Marcel Vanco, Marcel Domergue, Grégoire Berg, Philippe Bonnardel, Jules Dewaquez, Paul Nicolas, André Ryssen, Jean Boyer, Raymond Dubly, François Hugues.   Manager: Gaston Barreau
SPAIN: RICARDO ZAMORA Martínez, Pedro VALLANA Jeanguenat, Domingo CAREAGA Achalandabaso "Monacho", Josep "JOSÉ" SAMITIER Vilalta, MANUEL MEANA Vallina, Anacleto JOSÉ MARÍA PEÑA Salegui, José ECHEVESTE Galfarsoro, FÉLIX SESÚMAGA Ugarte, Manuel López Llamosas "TRAVIESO", PAULINO ALCÁNTARA Riestrá, Domingo Gómez-ACEDO Villanueva.
Goals: PAULINO ALCÁNTARA Riestrá (20, 27), Manuel López Llamosas "TRAVIESO" (33, 35)

50. 28.01.1923
SPAIN v FRANCE 3-0 (2-0)
Estadio Municipal de Atoche, San Sebastián
Referee: Charles Barette (Belgium)   Attendance: 22,000
SPAIN: RICARDO ZAMORA Martínez, Pedro VALLANA Jeanguenat, Domingo CAREAGA Achalandabaso "Monacho", Josep "JOSÉ" SAMITIER Vilalta, MANUEL MEANA Vallina, Anacleto JOSÉ MARÍA PEÑA Salegui, VICENTE PIERA Pañella, José Luis ZABALA Arrondo, Juan MONJARDÍN Callejón, CARMELO Goyenechea Urrusolo, Domingo Gómez-ACEDO Villanueva.
FRANCE: Pierre Chayriguès, Pierre Mony, Lucien Gamblin, Robert Joyaut, François Hugues, Philippe Bonnardel, Jules Dewaquez, Juste Brouzes, Paul Nicolas, Henri Bard, Raymond Dubly.   Manager: Gaston Barreau
Goals: Juan MONJARDÍN Callejón (11, 83), José Luis ZABALA Arrondo (42)

51. 25.02.1923
BELGIUM v FRANCE 4-1 (2-0)
Parc Duden, Vorst
Referee: Claude Newman (England)   Attendance: 28,757
BELGIUM: Jean De Bie, Armand Swartenbroeks, Oscar Verbeeck, Georges Verlinde, Florimond Vanhalme, Achille Schelstraete, Louis Bessems, Maurice Gillis, Rik Larnoe, Joseph Musch, Désiré Bastin.
Manager: William Sturrock Maxwell
FRANCE: Pierre Chayriguès, Pierre Mony, Maurice Depaepe, Robert Joyaut, François Hugues, Philippe Bonnardel, Gérard Isbecque, Raymond Wattine, Jean Boyer, Louis Darques, Raymond Dubly.   Manager: Gaston Barreau
Goals: Maurice Gillis (28, 77), Rik Larnoe (36, 61) / Gérard Isbecque (57)

52. 02.04.1923
NETHERLANDS v FRANCE 8-1 (4-0)
Het Nederlandsch Sportpark, Amsterdam
Referee: Einar Ulrich (Denmark)   Attendance: 30,000
NETHERLANDS: Fred van der Poel, Harry Dénis, Eb van der Kluft, André Le Fèvre, Evert van Linge, Frits Kuipers, Ber Groosjohan, Wim Roetert, Jaap Bulder, Wim Addicks, Dick Sigmond.   Manager: Frederick Warburton
FRANCE: Charles Berthelot, Pierre Mony, Robert Coat, Robert Joyaut, François Hugues, Philippe Bonnardel, Jules Dewaquez, André Caillet, Paul Hoenen, Jean Boyer, Henri Bard.   Manager: Gaston Barreau
Goals: Wim Roetert (1, 18), Evert van Linge (15, 55), Jaap Bulder (44, 86), Wim Addicks (53, 81) / Henri Bard (82)

53. 22.04.1923
FRANCE v SWITZERLAND 2-2 (1-2)
Stade Général John Joseph Pershing, Vincennes
Referee: William Musther (England)   Attendance: 20,000
FRANCE: Pierre Chayriguès, Paul Baron, Lucien Gamblin, Robert Joyaut, François Hugues, Philippe Bonnardel, Jules Dewaquez, Louis Darques, Paul Nicolas, Henri Bard, Raymond Dubly.   Manager: Gaston Barreau
SWITZERLAND: Hans Pulver, Gustav Gottenkieny, Edmond De Weck, Paul Fässler, Auguste Mayer, Aron Pollitz, Paolo Sturzenegger, Jean Haag, Robert Afflerbach, Max Abegglen, Marcel Katz.
Goals: Raymond Dubly (37), Paul Nicolas (61) / Robert Afflerbach (17, 27)

54. 10.05.1923
FRANCE v ENGLAND 1-4 (0-2)
Stade Général John Joseph Pershing, Vincennes
Referee: Charles Barette (Belgium)   Attendance: 30,000
FRANCE: Pierre Chayriguès, Pierre Mony, Lucien Gamblin, Louis Mistral, François Hugues, Philippe Bonnardel, Jules Dewaquez, Louis Darques, Marcel Dangles, Henri Bard, Raymond Dubly.   Manager: Gaston Barreau
ENGLAND: John Alderson, Warney Cresswell, Harry Jones, Seth Plum, James Seddon, Percy Barton, Frank Osborne, Charlie Buchan, Frederick Norman Creek, Frank Hartley, Kenneth Hegan.
Goals: Jules Dewaquez (89) / Kenneth Hegan (9, 84), Charlie Buchan (35), Frederick Norman Creek (55)

Frank Hartley left the pitch injured after 60 minutes.

55. 28.10.1923
FRANCE v NORWAY 0-2 (0-2)
Parc des Princes, Paris
Referee: Robert Walton (England)   Attendance: 12,000
FRANCE: Maurice Cottenet, Marcel Vanco, Ernest Gravier, Louis Mistral, François Hugues, Marcel Domergue, Jules Dewaquez, Louis Darques, Jean Boyer, Henri Bard, Raymond Dubly.   Manager: Gaston Barreau
NORWAY: Hugo Hofstad, Martin Johansen, Thaulow Goberg, Jacob Berner, Sverre Eika, Gunnar Andersen, Einar Wilhelms, Harald Strøm, Bjarne Johnsen, Finn Berstad, Herbert Lunde.
Goals: Einar Wilhelms (12), Finn Berstad (18)

56. 13.01.1924
FRANCE v BELGIUM 2-0 (1-0)
Stade Buffalo, Montrouge
Referee: Thomas Small (Scotland)   Attendance: 27,000
FRANCE: Pierre Chayriguès, Édouard Baumann, Bernard Lenoble, Michel Dupoix, Marcel Domergue, Philippe Bonnardel, Gérard Isbecque, Jean Boyer (25 Robert Accard), Albert Rénier, Ernest Gross, Raymond Dubly.   Manager: Gaston Barreau
BELGIUM: Jean De Bie, Armand Swartenbroeks, Oscar Verbeeck, André Fierens, Florimond Vanhalme, Achille Schelstraete, Cornelius Elst, Maurice Gillis, Rik Larnoe, Ivan Thys, Désiré Bastin.   Manager: William Sturrock Maxwell
Goals: Ernest Gross (43), Albert Rénier (49)

57. 23.03.1924
SWITZERLAND v FRANCE 3-0 (2-0)
Parc des Sports, Geneva
Referee: Umberto Meazza (Italy)   Attendance: 15,000
SWITZERLAND: Hans Pulver, Adolphe Reymond, Rudolf Ramseyer, August Oberhauser, Paul Schmiedlin, Aron Pollitz, Edmond Kramer, Robert Pache, Walter Dietrich, Max Abegglen, Charles Bouvier.   Manager: Teddy Duckworth
FRANCE: Pierre Chayriguès, Édouard Baumann, Bernard Lenoble, Ernest Clère, François Hugues, Philippe Bonnardel, Gérard Isbecque, Robert Accard, Jean Boyer, Ernest Gross, Raymond Dubly.   Manager: Gaston Barreau
Goals: Edmond Kramer (8), Walter Dietrich (9), Robert Pache (60)

58. 17.05.1924
FRANCE v ENGLAND 1-3 (0-2)
Stade Général John Joseph Pershing, Vincennes
Referee: Willem Eijmers (Netherlands)   Attendance: 20,000
FRANCE: Pierre Chayriguès, Édouard Baumann, Ernest Gravier, Antoine Parachini, Marcel Domergue, Philippe Bonnardel, Jules Dewaquez, Jean Boyer, Paul Nicolas, Ernest Gross, Raymond Dubly.   Manager: Gaston Barreau
ENGLAND: Ted Taylor, Tommy Lucas, Thomas Mort, Freddie Ewer, George Wilson, George Blackburn, George Thornewell, Stanley Earle, Vivian Gibbins, Harry Storer, Fred Tunstall.
Goals: Jules Dewaquez (58) /
Vivian Gibbins (25, 40), Édouard Baumann (83 og)

59. 27.05.1924   VIII Olympic Games Final Tournament 1924 – Round of 16
FRANCE v LATVIA 7-0 (3-0)
Stade de Paris, Saint-Ouen (France)
Referee: Henri Christophe (Belgium)   Attendance: 5,145
FRANCE: Pierre Chayriguès, Édouard Baumann, Antoine Parachini, Marcel Domergue, Édouard Crut, Jean Boyer, Philippe Bonnardel, Paul Nicolas, Ernest Gravier, Jules Dewaquez, Raymond Dubly.   Manager: Gaston Barreau
LATVIA: Arvīds Jurgens, Kārlis Asmanis, Aleksandrs Roge, Ceslavs Stanciks, Kārlis Bone, Pauls Sokolovs, Arkādijs Pavlovs, Valdis Plade, Edvīns Bārda, Arvīds Bārda, Rūdolfs Bārda.   Manager: Juris Rēdlihs
Goals: Édouard Crut (17, 28, 55), Paul Nicolas (25, 50), Jean Boyer (71, 87)
Sent off: Édouard Baumann (35)

60. 01.06.1924   VIII Olympic Games Final Tournament 1924 – Quarter-final
FRANCE v URUGUAY 1-5 (1-2)
Stade Olympique de Colombes, Colombes (France)
Referee: Per Andersen (Norway)   Attendance: 30,868
FRANCE: Pierre Chayriguès, Marcel Domergue, Ernest Gravier, Antoine Parachini, Jean Batmale, Philippe Bonnardel, Jules Dewaquez, Jean Boyer, Paul Nicolas, Édouard Crut, Raymond Dubly.   Manager: Gaston Barreau
URUGUAY: Andrés MAZALI, José NASAZZI Yarza, Pedro ARISPE, José Leandro ANDRADE, Juan Alfredo ZIBECHI Rossi, Alfredo Juan GHIERRA, José NAYA, Héctor Pedro SCARONE Beretta, Pedro PETRONE Schiavone, José Pedro CEA, Alfredo Ángel ROMANO.   Manager: Ernesto FIGOLI
Goals: Paul Nicolas (12) / Héctor Pedro SCARONE (3, 35), Pedro PETRONE Schiavone (59, 85), Alfredo ROMANO (86).

61. 04.06.1924
FRANCE v HUNGARY 0-1 (0-1)

Stade de la Cavée Verte, Le Havre

Referee: Félix Herren (Switzerland)   Attendance: 5,000

FRANCE: Maurice Cottenet, Léon Huot, Jacques Canthelou, Albert Jourda, Marcel Domergue, Jean Batmale, Jules Dewaquez, Édouard Crut, Albert Rénier (46 Pierre Chesneau), Ernest Gross, Robert Dufour.   Manager: Gaston Barreau

HUNGARY: Ferenc Kropacsek, Károly Fogl, Dezsö Grósz, Vilmos Kertész, Henrik Nádler, Zoltán Blum, József Fogl, György Molnár, Zoltán Opata, József Eisenhoffer, Rudolf Jeny. Manager: Ödön Holits

Goal: József Eisenhoffer (25)

62. 11.11.1924
BELGIUM v FRANCE 3-0 (1-0)

Stade à Molenbeek-Saint-Jean, Brussels

Referee: Ruben Gelbord (Sweden)   Attendance: 27,000

BELGIUM: Jean De Bie, Armand Swartenbroeks, François Demol, Edouard Morlet, Joseph Augustus, Pierre Braine, Léopold Dries, Gustaaf Van Goethem, Georges De Spae, Maurice Gillis, Désiré Bastin.
Manager: William Sturrock Maxwell

FRANCE: Maurice Cottenet, Ernest Gravier, Jacques Canthelou, René Dedieu, François Hugues, Philippe Bonnardel, Gérard Isbecque, Serge Denis, Albert Rénier, Louis Bloquel, Raymond Sentubéry.   Manager: Gaston Barreau

Goals: Pierre Braine (2), George De Spae (47, 52)

63. 22.03.1925
ITALY v FRANCE 7-0 (1-0)

Stadio di Corso Marsiglia, Torino

Referee: Heinrich Retschury (Austria)   Attendance: 15,000

ITALY: Gianpiero Combi, Umberto Caligaris, Renzo De Vecchi, Ottavio Barbieri (25 Carlo Bigatto), Antonio Fayenz, Leopoldo Conti, Adolfo Baloncieri, Giovanni Moscardini, Luigi Cevenini, Fulvio Bernardini, Virgilio Felice Levratto.

FRANCE: Maurice Cottenet, Urbain Wallet, Marcel Vignoli, Maurice Thédié, Paul-Émile Bel, Philippe Bonnardel, André Liminana, Robert Accard, Charles Bardot, Louis Bloquel, Félix Pozo.   Manager: Gaston Barreau

Goals: Leopoldo Conti (4), Adolfo Baloncieri (47, 59), Virgilio Felice Levratto (52, 88), Giovanni Moscardini (65, 78)

64. 19.04.1925
FRANCE v AUSTRIA 0-4 (0-3)

Stade Général John Joseph Pershing, Vincennes

Referee: Antonio Scamoni (Italy)   Attendance: 25,000

FRANCE: Maurice Cottenet, Pierre Lienert, Jacques Canthelou, Robert Dauphin, François Hugues, Philippe Bonnardel, André Liminana, Guillaume Lieb, Paul Nicolas, Ernest Gross, Julien Buré.   Manager: Gaston Barreau

AUSTRIA: Rudolf Aigner, Karl Rainer, Josef Blum, Karl Kurz, Leopold Resch, Leopold Nitsch, Wilhelm Morocutti, Fritz Gschweidl, Ferdinand Swatosch, Gustav Wieser, Otto Fischer. Manager: Hugo Meisl

Goals: Ferdinand Swatosch (11, 27), Gustav Wieser (22), Wilhelm Morocutti (84)

Paul Nicolas missed a penalty kick (82).

65. 21.05.1925
FRANCE v ENGLAND 2-3 (0-1)

Stade Olympique de Colombes, Colombes

Referee: Theodorus (Theo) van Zwieteren (Netherlands) Attendance: 35,000

FRANCE: Pierre Chayriguès, Marcel Domergue, Marcel Vignoli, Robert Dauphin, François Hugues, Philippe Bonnardel, Jules Dewaquez, Guillaume Lieb, Paul Nicolas, Jean Boyer, Raymond Dubly.   Manager: Gaston Barreau

ENGLAND: Freddie Fox, Tom Parker, William Felton, Thomas Magee, Billy Bryant, George Green, George Thornewell, Frank Roberts, Vivian Gibbins, Billy Walker, Arthur Dorrell.

Goals: Jean Boyer (62), Jules Dewaquez (75) / V. Gibbins (23), Philippe Bonnardel (46 og), Arthur Dorrell (50)

Vivian Gibbins left the pitch injured after 35 minutes.

Freddie Fox left the pitch injured after 75 minutes.

66. 11.04.1926
FRANCE v BELGIUM 4-3 (3-0)

Stade Général John Joseph Pershing, Vincennes

Referee: Albert James Prince-Cox (England)   Att: 23,000

FRANCE: Maurice Cottenet, Urbain Wallet, Jacques Canthelou, Georges Moulène, Marcel Domergue, Alexandre Villaplane, Jules Dewaquez, Guillaume Lieb, Edmond Leveugle, Édouard Crut, Maurice Gallay (46 Raymond Sentubéry).   Manager: Gaston Barreau

BELGIUM: Jean De Bie, Auguste Ruyssevelt, François Demol, Pierre Braine, Florimond Vanhalme, Henri van Averbeke, Raymond Braine, Michel Vanderbauwhede, Gérard Devos, Ivan Thys, Jan Diddens.   Manager: William Sturrock Maxwell

Goals: Jules Dewaquez (17), Édouard Crut (33, 59), Edmond Leveugle (40) / Michel Vanderbauwhede (60), Ivan Thys (82), Gérard Devos (89)

67. 18.04.1926
FRANCE v PORTUGAL 4-2 (2-1)

Stade des Ponts Jumeaux, Toulouse

Referee: Edmond Dizerens (Switzerland)   Att: 16,000

FRANCE: Maurice Cottenet, Urbain Wallet, Jacques Canthelou, René Dedieu, Marcel Domergue, Alexandre Villaplane, Jules Dewaquez, Henri Salvano, Fernand Brunel, Édouard Crut, Georges Bonello.   Manager: Gaston Barreau

PORTUGAL: ANTÓNIO Fernandes ROQUETE, ANTÓNIO PINHO, JORGE Gomes VIEIRA, Raul Soares de Figueiredo "TAMANQUEIRO", AUGUSTO da SILVA, CÉSAR Rodrígues DE MATOS, JOSÉ RAMOS, JOÃO dos SANTOS, JORGE Gonçalves TAVARES, José Carlos DELFIM Santos, Manuel da FONSECA e CASTRO.
Manager: António RIBEIRO DOS REIS

Goals: Henri Salvano (16), Fernand Brunel (40, 65), Georges Bonello (56) / AUGUSTO da SILVA (35), JOÃO dos SANTOS (86)

68. 25.04.1926
FRANCE v SWITZERLAND 1-0 (1-0)

Stade Olympique de Colombes, Colombes

Refereee: Bruno Bellini (Italy)   Attendance: 15,000

FRANCE: Maurice Cottenet, Urbain Wallet, Jacques Canthelou, Robert Dauphin, Marcel Domergue, Alexandre Villaplane, Jules Dewaquez, Guillaume Lieb, Paul Nicolas, Édouard Crut, Georges Bonello.   Manager: Gaston Barreau

SWITZERLAND: Hans Pulver, Oskar Hürzeler, Rudolf Ramseyer, August Oberhauser, Albert Schnorf, Paul Fässler, Karl Ehrenbolger, Max Brand, Raymond Passello, Max Abegglen, Jean-Pierre Martenet.
Manager: Teddy Duckworth

Goal: Paul Nicolas (12)

69. 30.05.1926
AUSTRIA v FRANCE 4-1 (1-1)

Simmeringer Sportplatz, Vienna

Referee: Frantisek Cejnar (Czechoslovakia)
Attendance: 25,000

AUSTRIA: Rudolf Aigner, Johann Tandler, Josef Blum, Johann Richter, Leopold Resch, Josef Schneider, Wilhelm Morocutti, Rudolf Hanel (46 Robert Juranic), Fritz Gschweidl, Gustav Wieser, Ferdinand Wesely.   Manager: Hugo Meisl

FRANCE: Maurice Cottenet, Urbain Wallet, Jacques Canthelou, René Dedieu, Marcel Domergue, Alexandre Villaplane, Désiré Gosselin, Guillaume Lieb, Raymond Sentubéry, Édouard Crut, Maurice Gallay.
Manager: Gaston Barreau

Goals: Rudolf Hanel (16), Ferdinand Wesely (61, 89), Robert Juranic (65) / Édouard Crut (11)

Josef Schneider missed a penalty kick (43).

70. 13.06.1926
FRANCE v YUGOSLAVIA 4-1 (3-1)

Stade Olympique de Colombes, Colombes

Referee: Paul Putz (Belgium)   Attendance: 12,000

FRANCE: Maurice Cottenet, Urbain Wallet, Jacques Canthelou, René Dedieu, Marcel Domergue, Alexandre Villaplane, Jules Dewaquez, Guillaume Lieb, Paul Nicolas, Robert Accard, Maurice Gallay.   Manager: Gaston Barreau

YUGOSLAVIA: Dragutin Fridrih, Stjepan Vrbancic, Milutin Ivkovic, Mare Marjanovic, Danijel Premerl, Mirko Bonacic, Ljubomir Bencic, Antun Bonacic, Dusan Petkovic, Slavin Cindric, Franjo Giler.   Manager: Ante Pandakovic

Goals: Maurice Gallay (16), Paul Nicolas (17, 37, 61) / Mirko Bonacic (25)

71. 20.06.1926
BELGIUM v FRANCE 2-2 (1-1)

Stade à Molenbeek-Saint-Jean, Brussels

Referee: John William Lucas (England)   Attendance: 35,000

BELGIUM: Jean Caudron, Armand Swartenbroeks, François Demol, Georges Ditzler, Émile Hanse, Pierre Braine, Maurice Gillis, Ferdinand Adams, Raymond Braine, Ivan Thys, Jan Diddens.   Manager: William Sturrock Maxwell

FRANCE: Maurice Cottenet, Léon Huot, Jacques Canthelou, René Dedieu, Marcel Domergue, Alexandre Villaplane, Jules Dewaquez, Guillaume Lieb, Paul Nicolas (16 Georges Stuttler), Robert Accard, Maurice Gallay.   Manager: Gaston Barreau

Goals: Maurice Gillis (32), Ferdinand Adams (71) / Robert Accard (3), Jules Dewaquez (89)

72. 16.03.1927
PORTUGAL v FRANCE 4-0 (2-0)

Estádio do Lumiar, Lisboa

Referee: Luis Colina Álvarez (Spain)   Attendance: 15,000

PORTUGAL: ARTUR Augusto CAMOLAS Júnior, JORGE Gomes VIEIRA, Raul Soares de Figueiredo "TAMANQUEIRO", AUGUSTO da SILVA, Manuel Gonçalves "VARELA" (10 CÉSAR Rodrígues DE MATOS), LIBERTO dos Santos, JOÃO dos SANTOS, Francisco Da SILVA MARQUES, José Manuel Soares "PEPE", JOSÉ Manuel MARTINS, ANTÓNIO PINHO.
Manager: CÂNDIDO Plácido Fernandes DE OLIVEIRA

FRANCE: Jacques Dhur, Urbain Wallet, Jacques Mairesse, Louis Cazal, Philippe Bonnardel, Jacques Wild, André Hurtevent, Charles Bardot, Julien Sotiault, Édouard Crut, Georges Bonello.   Manager: Gaston Barreau

Goals: José Manuel Soares "PEPE" (7, 44), JOSÉ Manuel MARTINS (49, 74)

73. 24.04.1927
FRANCE v ITALY 3-3 (1-2)
Stade Olympique de Colombes, Colombes
Referee: Albert James Prince-Cox (England)
Attendance: 35,000

FRANCE: Maurice Cottenet, Urbain Wallet, André Rollet, Robert Dauphin, François Hugues, Jacques Wild, Jules Dewaquez, Julien Sotiault, Georges Taisne, André Maschinot, Maurice Gallay.   Manager: Gaston Barreau

ITALY: Gianpiero Combi, Virginio Rosetta, Umberto Caligaris, Dario Martin, Antonio Janni, Mario Sperone, Leopoldo Conti, Adolfo Baloncieri, Julio Libonatti, Gino Rossetti, Virgilio Felice Levratto.   Manager: Augusto Rangone

Goals: Georges Taisne (16, 52), Julien Sotiault (89) / Julio Libonatti (29, 36), Leopoldo Conti (75)

74. 22.05.1927
FRANCE v SPAIN 1-4 (1-2)
Stade Olympique de Colombes, Colombes
Referee: Arthur Henry (Harry) Kingscott (England)
Attendance: 25,000

FRANCE: Maurice Cottenet, Urbain Wallet, André Rollet, Louis Cazal, Robert Dauphin, Jacques Wild, Jules Dewaquez, Guillaume Lieb, Julien Sotiault, Jean Boyer, Maurice Gallay (46 Marcel Langiller).   Manager: Gaston Barreau

SPAIN: RICARDO ZAMORA Martínez (49 Manuel VIDAL Hermosa), Antonio ARRILLAGA Izaguirre, Domingo ZALDÚA Anabitarte, Manuel PRATS Guerendiáin "Pachuco", Francisco GAMBORENA Hernandorena, Anacleto José María PEÑA Salegui, Manuel SAGARZAZU Martínez, LUIS REGUEIRO Pagola, José María YERMO Solaegui, FÉLIX PÉREZ Marcos, LUIS OLASO Anabitarte.

Goals: Jean Boyer (22) / Domingo ZALDÚA (23 pen, 75 pen), José María YERMO Solaegui (27), LUIS OLASO (68)

75. 26.05.1927
FRANCE v ENGLAND 0-6 (0-2)
Stade Olympique de Colombes, Colombes
Referee: Henri Maeck (Belgium)   Attendance: 25,000

FRANCE: Alexis Thépot, Urbain Wallet, André Rollet, Robert Dauphin, François Hugues, Jacques Wild, Marcel Langiller, Guillaume Lieb, Julien Sotiault, Georges Taisne, Maurice Gallay.   Manager: Gaston Barreau

ENGLAND: John Henry Brown, Roy Goodall, Herbert Jones, Willis Edwards, Jack Hill, Sidney Bishop, Joe Hulme, George Brown, Dixie Dean, Arthur Rigby, Louis Page.

Goals: George Brown (4, 50), Dixie Dean (24, 75), André Rollet (55 og), Arthur Rigby (87)

Julien Sotiault left the pitch injured after 70 minutes.

76. 12.06.1927
HUNGARY v FRANCE 13-1 (6-0)
Üllöi út, Budapest
Referee: Heinrich Retschury (Austria)   Attendance: 28,000

HUNGARY: Ferenc Weinhardt, József Fogl, Károly Fogl, László Pesovnik, János Köves, Béla Rebró, János Schmidt, József Takács (87 Zoltán Opata), György Orth, György Skvarek, Vilmos Kohut.   Manager: Gyula Kiss

FRANCE: Maurice Cottenet, Urbain Wallet, André Rollet (28 Jean Fidon), Aimé Durbec, Jacques Wild, Jules Dewaquez, Guillaume Lieb, Julien Sotiault, Georges Taisne, Maurice Gallay, René Dedieu.   Manager: Gaston Barreau

Goals: J. Takács (17, 41, 51, 60, 83, 85), G. Orth (25, 26), György Skvarek (30, 88), Vilmos Kohut (32, 62), Jules Dewaquez (78 og), / Jules Dewaquez (80)

77. 21.02.1928
FRANCE v NORTHERN IRELAND (Amateurs) 4-0 (3-0)
Stade Buffalo, Montrouge
Referee: Paul Ruoff (Switzerland)   Attendance: 27,000

FRANCE: Alexis Thépot, Urbain Wallet, Marcel Domergue, Jacques Wild, Robert Dauphin, Alexandre Villaplane, Georges Ouvray, Guillaume Lieb, Paul Nicolas, Pierre Seyler, Victor Farvacque.   Manager: Gaston Barreau

NORTHERN IRELAND: Edward McCracken, Robert Thompson, Robert Patrick Fulton, William Pollock, George Moorhead, James McGuire, Hugh Blair, James Ferris, Samuel Curran, John Doherty, John Harold McCaw.
Manager: Hugh Tanner

Goals: Paul Nicolas (8, 27, 35), Georges Ouvray (88)

78. 11.03.1928
SWITZERLAND v FRANCE 4-3 (3-0)
Stade Olympique de La Pontaise, Lausanne
Referee: Johannes Mutters (Netherlands)
Attendance: 18,000

SWITZERLAND: Frank Séchehaye, John Dubouchet, Rudolf Ramseyer, Henry Nicole, Walter Weiler, Gustave Heine, Robert Afflerbach, Willy Jäggi, Jacques Romberg, Max Abegglen, Ernesto Fink.   Manager: Teddy Duckworth

FRANCE: Alexis Thépot, Urbain Wallet, Jacques Wild, Augustin Chantrel, Marcel Domergue, Alexandre Villaplane, Jules Dewaquez, Guillaume Lieb, Paul Nicolas, Pierre Seyler, Maurice Gallay.   Manager: Gaston Barreau

Goals: Willy Jäggi (18, 22, 49), Jacques Romberg (40) / Guillaume Lieb (61), Pierre Seyler (80), Paul Nicolas (89)

79. 15.04.1928
FRANCE v BELGIUM 2-3 (1-2)
Stade Olympique Yves-du-Manoir, Colombes
Referee: Albert James Prince-Cox (England)
Attendance: 25,000
FRANCE: Laurent Henric, Urbain Wallet, Marcel Domergue, Augustin Chantrel, René Kenner, Alexandre Villaplane, Jules Dewaquez, Charles Bardot, Marcel Langiller, Paul Nicolas, Maurice Gallay.   Manager: Gaston Barreau
BELGIUM: Jean Caudron, Jules Lavigne, Nikolaas Hoydonckx, Pierre Braine, Florimond Vanhalme, Gustave Boesman, Bernard Voorhoof, Gérard Devos, Raymond Braine, Jacques Moeschal, Jan Diddens.   Manager: Viktor Löwenfeld
Goals: Charles Bardot (44, 66) /
Bernard Voorhoof (5), Raymond Braine (26, 73)

80. 29.04.1928
FRANCE v PORTUGAL 1-1 (1-1)
Parc des Princes, Paris
Referee: Stanley Frederick Rous (England)
Attendance: 25,000
FRANCE: Alexis Thépot, Urbain Wallet, Jacques Canthelou, Augustin Chantrel, Robert Dauphin, Alexandre Villaplane, Jules Dewaquez, Juste Brouzes, Paul Nicolas, Henri Pavillard, Marcel Langiller.   Manager: Gaston Barreau
PORTUGAL: ANTÓNIO Fernandes ROQUETE, CARLOS ALVES Júnior, JORGE Gomes VIEIRA, Raul Soares de Figueiredo "TAMANQUEIRO", AUGUSTO da SILVA, CÉSAR Rodrígues DE MATOS, VALDEMAR Mota da Fonseca, José Manuel Soares "PEPE", VÍTOR Marcolino da SILVA, ARMANDO da Silva MARTINS, JOSÉ Manuel MARTINS.   Manager: CÂNDIDO Plácido Fernandes DE OLIVEIRA
Goals: Paul Nicolas (44) /
ARMANDO da Silva MARTINS (24)

81. 13.05.1928
FRANCE v CZECHOSLOVAKIA 0-2 (0-1)
Stade Olympique Yves-du-Manoir, Colombes
Referee: Henri Christophe (Belgium)   Attendance: 19,000
FRANCE: Alexis Thépot, Urbain Wallet, Marcel Domergue, Augustin Chantrel, Robert Dauphin, Alexandre Villaplane, Jules Dewaquez, Juste Brouzes, Paul Nicolas, Henri Pavillard, Marcel Langiller.   Manager: Gaston Barreau
CZECHOSLOVAKIA: Frantisek Plánicka, Antonín Hojer, Antonín Perner, Ferdinand Hajný, Karel Pesek, Antonín Carvan, Jaroslav Srba, Frantisek Svoboda, Josef Silný, Antonín Puc, Josef Kratochvíl.   Manager: Rudolf Hencl
Goals: Antonín Puc (2, 57)

82. 17.05.1928
FRANCE v ENGLAND 1-5 (1-3)
Stade Olympique Yves-du-Manoir, Colombes
Referee: Dr. Adolf Miesz (Austria)   Attendance: 40,000
FRANCE: Alexis Thépot, Jacques Canthelou, Urbain Wallet, Robert Dauphin, Marcel Domergue, Alexandre Villaplane, Jules Monsallier, Juste Brouzes, Charles Bardot, Henri Pavillard, Marcel Langiller.   Manager: Gaston Barreau
ENGLAND: Benjamin Olney, Roy Goodall, Ernest Blenkinsop, Willis Edwards, Vincent Matthews, George Green, John Bruton, David Jack, Dixie Dean, George Stephenson, Leonard Barry.
Goals: Marcel Langiller (2) / George Stephenson (21, 80), David Jack (23), Dixie Dean (27, 64)

83. 29.05.1928   IX Olympic Games Final Tournament 1928 – First round
ITALY v FRANCE 4-3 (3-2)
Olympisch Stadion, Amsterdam (Netherlands)
Referee: Henri Christophe (Belgium)   Attendance: 2,509
ITALY: Giovanni De Prà, Virginio Rosetta, Umberto Caligaris, Silvio Pietroboni, Fulvio Bernardini, Antonio Janni, Enrico Rivolta, Adolfo Baloncieri, Elvio Banchero, Gino Rossetti, Virgilio Felice Levratto.   Manager: Augusto Rangone
FRANCE: Alexis Thépot, Urbain Wallet, Marcel Domergue, Augustin Chantrel, Robert Dauphin, Alexandre Villaplane, Jules Dewaquez, Juste Brouzes, Paul Nicolas, Henri Pavillard, Marcel Langiller.   Manager: Peter Farmer
Goals: Gino Rossetti (19), Virgilio Felice Levratto (39), Elvio Banchero (43), Adolfo Baloncieri (60) /
Juste Brouzes (15, 17), Robert Dauphin (61)

84. 24.02.1929
FRANCE v HUNGARY 3-0 (3-0)
Stade Olympique Yves-du-Manoir, Colombes
Referee: Paul Ruoff (Switzerland)   Attendance: 20,000
FRANCE: Laurent Henric, Urbain Wallet, Marcel Bertrand, Augustin Chantrel, Maurice Banide, Alexandre Villaplane, Jules Dewaquez, Guillaume Lieb, Paul Nicolas, Émile Veinante, Marcel Galey.   Manager: Gaston Barreau
HUNGARY: Mihaly Beneda, Károly Fogl, Gyula Dudás, Ferenc Borsányi, Márton Bukovi, Elemér Berkessy, Albert Ströck, József Takács, Jenõ Kalmár, Ferenc Hirzer, Pál Titkos.   Manager: István Tóth-Potya
Goals: Maurice Banide (23), Paul Nicolas (25), Guillaume Lieb (33 pen)

85. 24.03.1929
FRANCE v PORTUGAL 2-0 (0-0)
Stade Olympique Yves-du-Manoir, Colombes
Referee: Raphaël Van Praag (Belgium)   Attendance: 25,000
FRANCE: Laurent Henric, Urbain Wallet, Marcel Bertrand, Manuel Anatol, Guillaume Lieb, Maurice Banide, Alexandre Villaplane, Paul Nicolas, Jules Dewaquez, Émile Veinante, Marcel Galey.   Manager: Gaston Barreau
PORTUGAL: ANTÓNIO Fernandes ROQUETE, CARLOS ALVES Júnior, ANTÓNIO PINHO, Raul Soares de Figueiredo "TAMANQUEIRO", AUGUSTO da SILVA, MARTINHO Andrade de OLIVEIRA, RAUL JORGE da Silva, José Manuel Soares "PEPE", VÍTOR Marcolino da SILVA, ARMANDO da Silva MARTINS, ALFREDO RAMOS.
Manager: CÂNDIDO Plácido Fernandes DE OLIVEIRA
Goals: Paul Nicolas (49), Marcel Galey (80)

86. 14.04.1929
SPAIN v FRANCE 8-1 (2-0)
Estadio de Torrero, Zaragoza
Referee: Albert James Prince-Cox (England)
Attendance: 15,000
SPAIN: RICARDO ZAMORA Martínez, Félix QUESADA Mas, JACINTO Francisco Fernández de QUINCOCES López de Arbina, Manuel PRATS Guerendiáin "Pachuco", Martín MARCULETA Barbería, Anacleto José María PEÑA Salegui, Jaime LAZCANO Escolá, Severiano "Seve" GOIBURU Lopetegui, GASPAR RUBIO Meliá, Francisco "PACO" BIENZOBAS Ocáriz, Mariano YURRITA Llorente.
Manager: José María MATEOS Larrucea
FRANCE: Laurent Henric, Urbain Wallet, Marcel Bertrand, Robert Dauphin, Maurice Banide, Alexandre Villaplane, Raoul Dutheil, Guillaume Lieb, Paul Nicolas, Émile Veinante, Marcel Galey.   Manager: Gaston Barreau
Goals: Francisco "PACO" BIENZOBAS Ocáriz (6, 60 pen), GASPAR RUBIO Meliá (40, 56, 77, 81), Severiano "Seve" GOIBURU Lopetegui (73, 80) / Émile Veinante (86)

87. 09.05.1929
FRANCE v ENGLAND 1-4 (0-1)
Stade Olympique Yves-du-Manoir, Colombes
Referee: Louis Baert (Belgium)   Attendance: 35,000
FRANCE: Alexis Thépot, Manuel Anatol, Marcel Bertrand, Yvon Segalen, Robert Dauphin, Alexandre Villaplane, Jules Dewaquez, André Cheuva, Paul Nicolas, Edmond Delfour, Maurice Gallay.   Manager: Gaston Barreau
ENGLAND: Ted Hufton, Ernest Blenkinsop, Tommy Cooper, Fred Kean, Jack Hill, John Peacock, Hugh Adcock, Edgar Kail, George Camsell, Joe Bradford, Leonard Barry.
Goals: Jules Dewaquez (54) / Edgar Kail (35, 68), George Camsell (59, 86)

88. 19.05.1929
FRANCE v YUGOSLAVIA 1-3 (0-2)
Stade Olympique Yves-du-Manoir, Colombes
Referee: Paul Ruoff (Switzerland)   Attendance: 15,000
FRANCE: Alexis Thépot, Manuel Anatol, Marcel Bertrand, Yvon Segalen, Robert Dauphin, Alexandre Villaplane, Jules Dewaquez, André Cheuva, Paul Nicolas, Edmond Delfour, Maurice Gallay.   Manager: Gaston Barreau
YUGOSLAVIA: Maksimilijan Mihalcic, Milutin Ivkovic, Milos Beleslin, Milorad Arsenijevic, Kolnago Ferante, Branko Kunst, Blagoje Marjanovic, Ivan Hitrec, Vladimir Lajnert, Janos Horvat, Franjo Giler (18 Ivan Pavelic).
Manager: Ante Pandakovic
Goals: André Cheuva (63) / Ivan Hitrec (25), Blagoje Marjanovic (39), Vladimir Lajnert (75)

89. 26.05.1929
BELGIUM v FRANCE 4-1 (2-0)
Stade Vélodrome de Rocourt, Liège
Referee: René Mercet (Switzerland)   Attendance: 20,000
BELGIUM: Louis Somers, Jules Lavigne, Nikolaas Hoydonckx, Henri van Averbeke, Florimond Vanhalme, Gustave Boesman, Pierre Braine, Michel Vanderbauwhede, Raymond Braine, Jacques Moeschal, Désiré Bastin.
Manager: Viktor Löwenfeld
FRANCE: Charles Allé, Manuel Anatol, Jacques Wild, Yvon Segalen, Robert Dauphin, Alexandre Villaplane, Jules Dewaquez, Edmond Delfour, Jean Boyer, Henri Pavillard, Maurice Gallay.   Manager: Gaston Barreau
Goals: Michel Vanderbauwhede (6), Raymond Braine (10), Désiré Bastin (49, 74) / Jules Dewaquez (81)

90. 23.02.1930
PORTUGAL v FRANCE 2-0 (1-0)
Campo do Ameal, Porto
Referee: Johannes Julianus (John) Langenus (Belgium)
Attendance: 20,000
PORTUGAL: ANTÓNIO Fernandes ROQUETE, CARLOS ALVES Júnior, MARTINHO Andrade de OLIVEIRA, Raul Soares de Figueiredo "TAMANQUEIRO", Francisco Da SILVA MARQUES, CARLOS RODRIGUES, António ABRANTES MENDES, Waldemar "VALDEMAR" MOTA da Fonseca, ACÁCIO Pereira de MESQUITA, José Manuel Soares "PEPE", JOSÉ LUIS.   Manager: LAURINDO GRIJÓ
FRANCE: Antonio Lozes, Manuel Anatol, André Chardar, Louis Cazal, Jean Gautheroux, Alexandre Villaplane, Ernest Libérati, Lucien Laurent, Gustave Dubus, André Maschinot, Pierre Korb.   Manager: Gaston Barreau
Goals: José Manuel Soares "PEPE" (44, 70)

91.   23.03.1930
FRANCE v SWITZERLAND 3-3 (2-2)
Stade Olympique Yves-du-Manoir, Colombes
Referee: Stanley Frederick Rous (England)
Attendance: 20,000
FRANCE: Antonio Lozes, Manuel Anatol, André Chardar, Louis Cazal, Alexandre Villaplane, Henri Pavillard, Ernest Libérati, André Cheuva, Paul Nicolas, André Maschinot, Pierre Korb.   Manager: Gaston Barreau
SWITZERLAND: Charles Pasche, Max Weiler, Rudolf Ramseyer, Paul De Lavallaz, Adolfo Spiller, Charles Regamey, Adolf Stelzer, Willy Baumeister, Jacques Romberg, August Lehmann, René Grimm.   Manager: Teddy Duckworth
Goals: André Cheuva (17), Manuel Anatol (34), Ernest Libérati (58) /
August Lehmann (10, 13), Jacques Romberg (68)

92.   13.04.1930
FRANCE v BELGIUM 1-6 (1-5)
Stade Olympique Yves-du-Manoir, Colombes
Referee: Paul Ruoff (Switzerland)   Attendance: 18,000
FRANCE: Antonin Lozes, Manuel Anatol, Marcel Capelle, Henri Pavillard, Maurice Banide, Alexandre Villaplane, Ernest Libérati, André Cheuva, Gustave Dubus, Lucien Laurent, Pierre Korb.   Manager: Gaston Barreau
BELGIUM: Arnold Badjou, Theodoor Nouwens, Nikolaas Hoydonckx, Pierre Braine, Florimond Vanhalme, Jean De Clercq, Louis Versyp, Bernard Voorhoof, Michel Vanderbauwhede, Ferdinand Adams, Désiré Bastin.   Manager: Viktor Löwenfeld
Goals: Gustave Dubus (44) / Louis Versyp (12, 36), Ferdinand Adams (14), Michel Vanderbauwhede (16, 32, 83)

93.   11.05.1930
FRANCE v CZECHOSLOVAKIA 2-3 (2-2)
Stade Olympique Yves-du-Manoir, Colombes
Referee: Johannes Julianus (John) Langenus (Belgium)
Attendance: 28,000
FRANCE: Alexis Thépot, Manuel Anatol, Marcel Capelle, Jean Laurent, Maurice Banide, Louis Cazal (15 Célestin Delmer), Marcel Kauffmann, Henri Pavillard, Marcel Pinel, Edmond Delfour, Pierre Korb.   Manager: Gaston Barreau
CZECHOSLOVAKIA: Frantisek Plánicka, Ladislav Zenísek, Antonín Hojer, Antonín Vodicka, Antonín Carvan, Adolf Simperský, Frantisek Junek, Josef Kostálek, Frantisek Svoboda (27 Antonín Puc), Josef Silný, Karel Sokolár
Manager: Josef Fanta
Goals: Pierre Korb (25 pen), Edmond Delfour (30) /
Josef Kostálek (6), Josef Silný (17), Frantisek Junek (76)

94.   18.05.1930
FRANCE v SCOTLAND 0-2 (0-1)
Stade Olympique Yves-du-Manoir, Colombes
Referee: Raphaël Van Praag (Belgium)   Attendance: 25,000
FRANCE: Alexis Thépot, Manuel Anatol, Marcel Capelle, Jean Laurent, Maurice Banide, Augustin Chantrel, Marcel Kauffmann, Henri Pavillard, Marcel Pinel, Edmond Delfour, Pierre Korb.   Manager: Gaston Barreau
SCOTLAND: John Thomson, James Nelson, James Crapnell, Peter Wilson, George Walker, Frank Hill, Alexander Jackson, Alec Cheyne, Hughie Gallacher, George Stevenson, Jimmy Connor.
Goals: Hughie Gallacher (42, 85)

95.   25.05.1930
BELGIUM v FRANCE 1-2 (1-1)
Stade du Pont d'Ougrée, Ougrée
Referee: Gustaf Ekberg (Sweden)   Attendance: 11,000
BELGIUM: Jean De Bie, Theodoor Nouwens, Nikolaas Hoydonckx, Pierre Braine, Florimond Vanhalme, Jacques Moeschal, Louis Versyp, Bernard Voorhoof, Michel Vanderbauwhede, Ferdinand Adams, Désiré Bastin.   Manager: Viktor Löwenfeld
FRANCE: Alexis Thépot, Étienne Mattler, Marcel Capelle, Louis Cazal (22 Jean Laurent), Célestin Delmer, Augustin Chantrel, Marcel Kauffmann, Henri Pavillard, Marcel Pinel, Edmond Delfour, Marcel Langiller.
Manager: Gaston Barreau
Goals: Bernard Voorhoof (21) / Marcel Pinel (26, 72)

96.   13.07.1930   FIFA World Cup Final Tournament – Group 1
FRANCE v MEXICO 4-1 (3-0)
Estadio Pocitos, Montevideo (Uruguay)
Referee: Domingo Lombardi (Uruguay)   Attendance: 4,444
FRANCE: Alexis Thépot, Augustin Chantrel, Marcel Capelle, Alexandre Villaplane, Marcel Pinel, Ernest Libérati, Edmond Delfour, André Maschinot, Lucien Laurent, Marcel Langiller, Étienne Mattler.   Manager: Raoul Caudron
MEXICO: Óscar BONFÍGLIO Martínez, Rafael GARZA Gutiérrez, Manuel ROSAS Sánchez, Efraín AMÉZCUA, Alfredo Viejo SÁNCHEZ, Felipe ROSAS Sánchez, Hilario LÓPEZ García, José RUIZ, Dionisio MEJÍA Vieyra, Juan CARREÑO Lara, Luis PÉREZ González.
Manager: Juan LUQUE De Serrallonga
Goals: Lucien Laurent (19), Marcel Langiller (40), André Maschinot (43, 87) / Juan CARREÑO Lara (70)

Alexis Thépot left the pitch injured after 26 minutes and was replaced by Augustin Chantrel.

97.   15.07.1930   FIFA World Cup Final Tournament – Group 1
ARGENTINA v FRANCE 1-0 (0-0)
Estadio Gran Parque Central, Montevideo (Uruguay)
Referee: Gilberto Leonel de Almeida Rêgo (Brazil)
Attendance: 23,409
ARGENTINA: Ángel Bossio, José Della Torre, Ramón Alfredo Muttis, Pedro Bonifacio Suárez Pérez, Luis Felipe Monti, Juan Evaristo, Natalio Perinetti, Francisco Antonio Varallo, Manuel Ferreira, Roberto Eugenio Cherro, Marino Evaristo.   Managers: Juan José Tramutola & Francisco Olazar
FRANCE: Alexis Thépot, Étienne Mattler, Marcel Capelle, Marcel Pinel, Augustin Chantrel, Ernest Libérati, Edmond Delfour, André Maschinot, Lucien Laurent, Marcel Langiller, Alexandre Villaplane.   Manager: Raoul Caudron

Goal: Luis Monti (81)

98.   19.07.1930   FIFA World Cup Final Tournament – Group 1
CHILE v FRANCE 1-0 (0-0)
Estadio Centenario, Montevideo (Uruguay)
Referee: Aníbal Tejada (Uruguay)   Attendance: 2,000
CHILE: Roberto CORTÉS González, Ernesto CHAPARRO Esquivel, Guillermo RIVEROS Conejeros, Arturo TORRES Carrasco, Guillermo SAAVEDRA Tapia, Casimiro Luis TORRES Valdés, Tomás OJEDA Álvarez, Guillermo SUBIABRE Astorga, Eberardo VILLALOBOS Schad, Carlos VIDAL Lepe, Carlos Alberto SCHNEEBERGER Lemp.
Manager: Györgi Orth
FRANCE: Alexis Thépot, Étienne Mattler, Marcel Capelle, Augustin Chantrel, Célestin Delmer, Alexandre Villaplane, Ernest Libérati, Edmond Delfour, Marcel Pinel, Émile Veinante, Marcel Langiller.   Manager: Raoul Caudron

Goal: Guillermo SUBIABRE Astorga (67)

Guillermo SAAVEDRA Tapia missed a penalty kick (30).

99.   07.12.1930
FRANCE v BELGIUM 2-2 (1-1)
Stade Buffalo, Montrouge
Referee: René Mercet (Switzerland)   Attendance: 20,000
FRANCE: Alexis Thépot, André Chardar, Étienne Mattler, Louis Finot, Célestin Delmer, Augustin Chantrel, Ernest Libérati, Edmond Delfour, Marcel Pinel, Henri Pavillard, Hervé Marc.   Manager: Gaston Barreau
BELGIUM: Arnold Badjou, Theodoor Nouwens, Nikolaas Hoydonckx, Alfons Mertens, August Hellemans, Pierre Braine, Louis Versyp, Bernard Voorhoof, Michel Vanderbauwhede, Joseph Van Beeck, Désiré Bastin.   Manager: Hector Goetinck

Goals: Marcel Pinel (3, 67) /
Joseph Van Beeck (7), Bernard Voorhoof (64)

100.   25.01.1931
ITALY v FRANCE 5-0 (3-0)
Stadio Littoriale, Bologna
Referee: Paul Ruoff (Switzerland)   Attendance: 48,000
ITALY: Gianpiero Combi, Virginio Rosetta, Umberto Caligaris, Attilio Ferraris, Fulvio Bernardini, Alfredo Pitto, Renato Cattaneo, Renato Cesarini, Giuseppe Meazza, Giovanni Ferrari, Raimundo Orsi.   Manager: Vittorio Pozzo
FRANCE: Alexis Thépot, Étienne Mattler, Marcel Capelle, Louis Finot, Célestin Delmer, Augustin Chantrel, Ernest Libérati, Edmond Delfour, Joseph Alcazar, Henri Pavillard, Pierre Korb.   Manager: Gaston Barreau

Goals: Giuseppe Meazza (21, 34, 40), Renato Cesarini (51), Renato Cattaneo (73)

101.   15.02.1931
FRANCE v CZECHOSLOVAKIA 1-2 (1-1)
Stade Olympique Yves-du-Manoir, Colombes
Referee: Johannes Julianus (John) Langenus (Belgium)
Attendance: 28,000
FRANCE: Alexis Thépot, Manuel Anatol, Étienne Mattler, Louis Finot, Célestin Delmer, Raoul Diagne, Raymond Durand, Edmond Delfour, Paul Nicolas, Henri Pavillard, Marcel Langiller.   Manager: Gaston Barreau
CZECHOSLOVAKIA: Frantisek Plánicka, Jaroslav Burgr, Antonín Novák, Antonín Vodicka, Karel Pesek, Frantisek Tyrpekl, Frantisek Junek, Jindrich Soltys, Frantisek Svoboda, Josef Silný, Karel Sokolár.   Manager: Josef Fanta

Goals: Marcel Langiller (23 pen) /
Antonín Novák (5 pen, 84 pen)

102.   15.03.1931
FRANCE v GERMANY 1-0 (1-0)
Stade Olympique Yves-du-Manoir, Colombes
Referee: Thomas Crewe (England)   Attendance: 40,076
FRANCE: Alexis Thépot, Manuel Anatol, Étienne Mattler, Louis Finot, Joseph Kaucsar, Pierre Hornus, Jules Monsallier, Edmond Delfour, Roger Rolhion, Lucien Laurent (40 Pierre Korb), Marcel Langiller.   Manager: Gaston Barreau
GERMANY: Willibald Kreß, Franz Schütz, Heinrich Weber, Reinhold Münzenberg, Ludwig Leinberger, Georg Knöpfle, Josef Bergmaier, Sigmund Haringer, Heinrich Hergert, Ludwig Hofmann (31 Hans Welker), Richard Hofmann.
Manager: Otto Nerz

Goal: Reinhold Münzenberg (14 og)

103. 14.05.1931
FRANCE v ENGLAND 5-2 (3-1)
Stade Olympique Yves-du-Manoir, Colombes
Referee: Johannes Julianus (John) Langenus (Belgium) Attendance: 35,000
FRANCE: Alexis Thépot, Marcel Capelle, Étienne Mattler, Louis Finot, Joseph Kaucsar, Pierre Hornus, Ernest Libérati, Edmond Delfour, Robert Mercier, Lucien Laurent, Marcel Langiller.   Manager: Gaston Barreau
ENGLAND: Hugh Turner, Tommy Cooper, Ernest Blenkinsop, Alfred Strange, Thomas Graham, Joseph Tate, Sammy Crooks, George Stephenson, Thomas Waring, Harry Burgess, Eric Houghton.
Goals: Lucien Laurent (15), Robert Mercier (18, 76), Marcel Langiller (29), Edmond Delfour (57) / Sammy Crooks (10), Thomas Waring (71)

104. 29.11.1931
FRANCE v NETHERLANDS 3-4 (1-4)
Stade Olympique Yves-du-Manoir, Colombes
Referee: Paul Ruoff (Switzerland)   Attendance: 25,000
FRANCE: Alexis Thépot, André Chardar, Étienne Mattler, Louis Finot, Joseph Kaucsar, Pierre Hornus, Marcel Kauffmann, Émile Veinante, Robert Mercier, Lucien Laurent, Marcel Langiller.   Manager: Gaston Barreau
NETHERLANDS: Gejus van der Meulen, Mauk Weber, Sjef van Run, Jaap Paauwe, Wim Anderiesen sr., Puck van Heel, Frank Wels, Law Adam, Wim Lagendaal, Jaap Mol, Joop van Nellen.   Manager: Robert Glendenning
Goals: Robert Mercier (7), Émile Veinante (53, 68) / Wim Lagendaal (12, 24, 26), Jaap Mol (23)

105. 20.03.1932
SWITZERLAND v FRANCE 3-3 (2-1)
Stadion Neufeld, Bern
Referee: Stanley Frederick Rous (England) Attendance: 18,000
SWITZERLAND: Frank Séchehaye, Severino Minelli, Max Weiler, Albert Hintermann, Otto Imhof, Gabriele Gilardoni, Gaston Tschirren, André Abegglen, Alessandro Frigerio, Max Abegglen, Alfred Jäck.   Manager: Teddy Duckworth
FRANCE: Alexis Thépot, Manuel Anatol, André Chardar, Jules Cottenier, Joseph Kaucsar, Émile Scharwath, Ernest Libérati, Lucien Laurent, Charles Bardot, Émile Veinante, Marcel Langiller.   Manager: Gaston Barreau
Goals: Max Abegglen (22), André Abegglen (36, 87) / Ernest Libérati (15), Émile Veinante (69), Charles Bardot (71)

106. 10.04.1932
FRANCE v ITALY 1-2 (1-1)
Stade Olympique Yves-du-Manoir, Colombes
Referee: René Mercet (Switzerland)   Attendance: 45,000
FRANCE: André Tassin, Manuel Anatol, André Chardar, Émile Scharwath, Joseph Kaucsar, Jean Laurent, Ernest Libérati, Charles Bardot, Lucien Laurent, Marcel Langiller, Adolphe Touffait (15 Edmond Delfour).
Manager: Gaston Barreau
ITALY: Gianpiero Combi, Virginio Rosetta, Luigi Allemandi, Alfredo Pitto, Attilio Ferraris, Luigi Bertolini, Raffaele Costantino, Renato Cesarini, Angelo Schiavio, Mario Magnozzi, Raimundo Orsi.   Manager: Vittorio Pozzo
Goals: Ernest Libérati (11) / Mario Magnozzi (43), Raffaele Costantino (52)

107. 01.05.1932
BELGIUM v FRANCE 5-2 (3-0)
Stade du Jubilé (Centenaire), Brussels
Referee: Heinrich Retschury (Austria)   Attendance: 28,779
BELGIUM: Louis Vandenbergh, Jules Lavigne, Henri De Deken, Charles Simons, Émile Stijnen, Jean Claessens, Louis Versyp, Jean Brichaut, Jean Capelle, Joseph Van Beeck, Stanley Vanden Eynde.   Manager: Hector Goetinck
FRANCE: André Tassin, Manuel Anatol, André Chardar, Émile Scharwath, Joseph Kaucsar, Jean Laurent, Ernest Libérati, Émile Veinante, Jean Sécember, Henri Pavillard, Marcel Langiller.   Manager: Gaston Barreau
Goals: Jean Brichaut (23), Stanley Vanden Eynde (25, 61), Jean Capelle (38), Joseph Van Beeck (46) / Henri Pavillard (48), Jean Sécember (82)

108. 08.05.1932
FRANCE v SCOTLAND 1-3 (1-3)
Stade Olympique Yves-du-Manoir, Colombes
Referee: Albino Carraro (Italy)   Attendance: 8,000
FRANCE: Alexis Thépot, Manuel Anatol, André Chardar, Émile Scharwath, Joseph Kaucsar, Jean Laurent, Ernest Libérati, Joseph Alcazar, Robert Mercier, René Gérard, Marcel Langiller.   Manager: Gaston Barreau
SCOTLAND: Jack Harkness, James Crapnell, Joseph Nibloe, Alex Massie, Robert Gillespie, John Miller, James Crawford, Alec Thomson, Neil Dewar, Bob McPhail, Alan Morton.
Goals: Marcel Langiller (43 pen) / Neil Dewar (14, 27, 40)

109. 05.06.1932
YUGOSLAVIA v FRANCE 2-1 (1-1)
Stadion Beogradski S.K., Beograd
Referee: Frantisek Cejnar (Czechoslovakia)
Attendance: 8,000

YUGOSLAVIA: Jovan Spasic, Slavko Zagorac, Dragomir Tosic, Milorad Arsenijevic, Danijel Premerl, Andjelko Marusic, Aleksandar Tirnanic, Svetislav Glisovic, Slavko Milosevic, Franjo Giler, Dobrivoje Zecevic. Manager: Bosko Simonovic

FRANCE: André Tassin (46 Raoul Chaisaz), André Chardar, Jacques Mairesse, Émile Scharwath, Joseph Kaucsar, Jean Laurent, Ernest Libérati, Jacques Delannoy, Roger Rolhion, Joseph Alcazar, Pierre Korb. Manager: Gaston Barreau

Goals: Svetislav Glisovic (26, 59) / Joseph Alcazar (1)

110. 09.06.1932
BULGARIA v FRANCE 3-5 (0-4)
Stadium Yunak, Sofia
Referee: Josip Fabris (Yugoslavia)   Attendance: 6,000

BULGARIA: Todor Dermonski (40 Radi Maznikov), Nikola Kalkandzhiev, Todor Mishtalov, Hristo Minkovski, Dimitar Baykushev, Borislav Gabrovski, Lubomir Angelov, Velcho Stoyanov, Mihail Lozanov, Asen Peshev, Asen Panchev. Manager: Pavel Grozdanov

FRANCE: André Tassin (62 Raoul Chaisaz), André Chardar, Georges Houyvet, Émile Scharwath, Joseph Kaucsar, Jean Laurent, Ernest Libérati, Joseph Rodriguez, Jean Sécember, Joseph Alcazar, Pierre Korb. Manager: Gaston Barreau

Goals: Asen Panchev (55, 66, 77 pen) / Joseph Rodriguez (1), Jean Sécember (6, 16, 28, 47)

Sent off: Joseph Alcazar (75)

111. 12.06.1932
ROMANIA v FRANCE 6-3 (3-0)
Stadionul Oficiul National de Educatie Fizica, Bucharest
Referee: Mihály Iváncsics (Hungary)   Attendance: 10,000

ROMANIA: Stefan Czinczer, Rudolf Bürger, Gheorghe Albu, Adalbert Hrehuss, Petre Steinbach, Ladislau Raffinsky, Andrei Glanzmann, Alexandru Schwartz, Rudolf Wetzer, Iuliu Bodola, Elemer Kocsis (42 Stefan Dobay). Manager: Constantin Radulescu

FRANCE: André Tassin, André Chardar, Jacques Mairesse, Émile Scharwath, Joseph Kaucsar, Jean Laurent, Ernest Libérati, Joseph Rodriguez (43 Roger Rolhion), Jean Sécember, Joseph Alcazar, Pierre Korb. Manager: Gaston Barreau

Goals: Iuliu Bodola (10, 81), Rudolf Wetzer (17, 68), Alexandru Schwartz (20, 46) / André Chardar (52 pen), Roger Rolhion (75, 77)

112. 12.02.1933
FRANCE v AUSTRIA 0-4 (0-0)
Parc des Princes, Paris
Referee: Johannes Julianus (John) Langenus (Belgium)
Attendance: 37,459

FRANCE: Robert Défossé, Jules Vandooren, Jacques Mairesse, Augustin Chantrel, Joseph Kaucsar, Edmond Delfour, Marcel Kauffmann, René Gérard, Jean Nicolas, Roger Rio (26 Robert Mercier), Marcel Langiller. Manager: Gaston Barreau

AUSTRIA: Rudolf Hiden, Karl Rainer, Karl Sesta, Karl Gall, Josef Smistik, Walter Nausch, Karl Zischek, Franz Weselik, Matthias Sindelar, Anton Schall, Adolf Vogl. Manager: Hugo Meisl

Goals: Matthias Sindelar (65), Karl Zischek (69), Franz Weselik (70), Adolf Vogl (83)

113. 19.03.1933
GERMANY v FRANCE 3-3 (2-1)
Deutsches Stadion, Berlin
Referee: Thomas Crewe (England)   Attendance: 45,000

GERMANY: Hans Jakob, Sigmund Haringer, Josef Wendl, Rudi Gramlich, Heinrich Hergert, Hugo Mantel, Erich Fischer (I), Ludwig Lachner, Oskar Rohr, Willi Lindner (40 Richard Hofmann), Stanislaus Kobierski. Manager: Otto Nerz

FRANCE: Robert Défossé, Jules Vandooren (9 André Chardar), Étienne Mattler, Augustin Chantrel, Joseph Kaucsar, Edmond Delfour, Ernest Libérati, René Gérard, Jean Nicolas, Roger Rio, Marcel Langiller. Manager: Gaston Barreau

Goals: Oskar Rohr (28, 45), Ludwig Lachner (65) / Roger Rio (22), René Gérard (81, 83)

114. 26.03.1933
FRANCE v BELGIUM 3-0 (1-0)
Stade Olympique Yves-du-Manoir, Colombes
Referee: Stanley Frederick Rous (ENG)   Attendance: 30,000

FRANCE: Robert Défossé, Jules Cottenier, Étienne Mattler, Paul Poirier, Joseph Kaucsar, Edmond Delfour, Robert Mercier, René Gérard, Jean Nicolas, Roger Rio, Marcel Langiller. Manager: Gaston Barreau

BELGIUM: Louis Vandenbergh (82 Robert Braet), Henri De Deken, Nikolaas Hoydonckx, Joseph Van Ingelghem, August Hellemans, Jean Claessens, Louis Versyp, Bernard Voorhoof, Joseph Desmedt, François Vanden Eynde, Stanley Vanden Eynde. Manager: Hector Goetinck

Goals: Roger Rio (34), Marcel Langiller (74), Jean Nicolas (81)

115. 23.04.1933
FRANCE v SPAIN 1-0 (1-0)

Stade Olympique Yves-du-Manoir, Colombes

Referee: William Bangerter (Switzerland)
Attendance: 45,010

FRANCE: Robert Défossé, Jules Vandooren (37 Jules Cottenier), Étienne Mattler, Raoul Diagne, Joseph Kaucsar (27 Georges Verriest), Edmond Delfour, Robert Mercier, René Gérard, Jean Nicolas, Roger Rio, Marcel Langiller. Manager: Gaston Barreau

SPAIN: RICARDO ZAMORA Martínez, CIRIACO Errasti Suinaga, JACINTO Francisco Fernández de QUINCOCES López de Arbina, Leonardo CILAURREN Uriarte, Miguel AYESTARÁN Elizalde, Martín MARCULETA Barbería, José PRAT Ripollés "Pitus", LUIS Pagola REGUEIRO "CORZO", Julio Antonio ELÍCEGUI Cans, José GONZALO DÍEZ GALÉ "Chalo" (37 Severiano "Seve" GOIBURU Lopetegui), Cristanto BOSCH Espín "Tin". Manager: JOSÉ MARÍA MATEOS Larrucea

Goal: Jean Nicolas (32)

116. 25.05.1933
FRANCE v WALES 1-1 (0-0)

Stade Olympique Yves-du-Manoir, Colombes

Referee: Raphaël Van Praag (Belgium)   Attendance: 25,000

FRANCE: Robert Défossé, Jules Vandooren, Étienne Mattler, Célestin Delmer, Georges Verriest, Edmond Delfour, Albert Polge, Noël Liétaer, Jean Nicolas, Roger Rio, Marcel Langiller. Manager: Gaston Barreau

WALES: Roy John, Bob John, Sid Lawrence, Jimmy Murphy, Tom Griffiths, Charlie Jones, Thomas Jones, Leslie Jones, Thomas Bamford, Walter Robbins, Frederick Warren.

Goals: Jean Nicolas (78) / Tom Griffiths (57)

117. 10.06.1933
CZECHOSLOVAKIA v FRANCE 4-0 (1-0)

Letenský Stadion, Praha

Referee: Andrzej Rutkowski (Poland)   Attendance: 18,000

CZECHOSLOVAKIA: Frantisek Plánicka, Jaroslav Burgr, Josef Ctyroký, Josef Kostálek, Stefan Cambal, Jan Knobloch, Frantisek Junek, Karel Hes, Antonín Puc (39 Frantisek Svoboda), Josef Silný, Oldrich Nejedlý.   Manager: Karel Petru

FRANCE: Robert Défossé, Roger Rolhion, Étienne Mattler, Célestin Delmer, Georges Verriest, Edmond Delfour, Albert Polge, René Gérard, Émile Veinante, Roger Rio, Marceau Lherminé. Manager: Gaston Barreau

Goals: Antonín Puc (20), Frantisek Junek (47), Frantisek Svoboda (59), Oldrich Nejedlý (63)

118. 06.12.1933
ENGLAND v FRANCE 4-1 (3-0)

White Hart Lane, London

Referee: Johannes Julianus (John) Langenus (Belgium)
Attendance: 17,097

ENGLAND: Harry Hibbs, Roy Goodall, David Fairhurst, Alfred Strange, Arthur Rowe, Wilf Copping, Sammy Crooks, Arthur Thomas Grosvenor, George Camsell, Willie Hall, Eric Brook.

FRANCE: Robert Défossé, Jules Vandooren, Étienne Mattler, Célestin Delmer, Maurice Banide, Edmond Delfour, Roger Courtois, René Gérard, Jean Nicolas, Roger Rio, Émile Veinante.   Manager: Gaston Barreau

Goals: George Camsell (14, 41), Eric Brook (21), Arthur Thomas Grosvenor (53) / Émile Veinante (78)

119. 21.01.1934
BELGIUM v FRANCE 2-3 (2-2)

Stade du Jubilé (Centenaire), Brussels

Referee: Walter James Lewington (England)
Attendance: 35,826

BELGIUM: Arnold Badjou, Philibert Smellinckx, Albert Heremans, Frans Peeraer, August Hellemans, Jean Claessens, André Saeys, Jean Brichaut, Jean Capelle, Bernard Voorhoof, Stanley Vanden Eynde.   Manager: Hector Goetinck

FRANCE: Robert Défossé, Jules Vandooren, Étienne Mattler, Louis Finot, Maurice Banide, Émile Scharwath, Ernest Libérati, Joseph Alcazar, Jean Nicolas, Émile Veinante, Albert Polge.   Manager: Gaston Barreau

Goals: Bernard Voorhoof (8), Stanley Vanden Eynde (11) / Jean Nicolas (3, 54), Émile Veinante (37)

120. 11.03.1934
FRANCE v SWITZERLAND 0-1 (0-1)

Parc des Princes, Paris

Referee: Rinaldo Barlassina (Italy)   Attendance: 25,000

FRANCE: Alexis Thépot, Jules Vandooren, Étienne Mattler, Max Charbit, Joseph Kaucsar, Noël Liétaer, Alfred Aston, Joseph Alcazar, Jean Nicolas, Roger Rio, Pierre Korb.   Manager: Gaston Barreau

SWITZERLAND: Frank Séchehaye, Severino Minelli, Max Weiler, Albert Guinchard, Hans Liniger, Ernest Lörtscher, Alexander Laube, Raymond Passello, Leopold Kielholz, André Abegglen, Giuseppe Bossi.   Manager: Heinrich Müller

Goal: Leopold Kielholz (35)

121. 25.03.1934
FRANCE v CZECHOSLOVAKIA 1-2 (1-1)
Stade Olympique Yves-du-Manoir, Colombes
Referee: Walter James Lewington (England)
Attendance: 27,931

FRANCE: Alexis Thépot, François Vasse, Étienne Mattler, Max Charbit, Célestin Delmer, Noël Liétaer, Alfred Aston, Edmond Delfour, Jean Nicolas, Émile Veinante, Pierre Korb. Manager: Gaston Barreau

CZECHOSLOVAKIA: Frantisek Plánicka, Frantisek Nejedlý, Vilhelm Náhlovský, Josef Kostálek, Jaroslav Boucek, Ludovít Rado (40 Stefan Cambal), Ladislav Mráz, Frantisek Svoboda, Jirí Sobotka, Oldrich Nejedlý, Antonín Puc. Manager: Karel Petru

Goals: Pierre Korb (6) /
Frantisek Svoboda (37), Jirí Sobotka (89)

122. 15.04.1934   FIFA World Cup Qualification – Group 8
LUXEMBOURG v FRANCE 1-6 (0-2)
Stade Municipal, Luxembourg City
Referee: Marc Turfkruyer (Belgium)   Attendance: 18,000

LUXEMBOURG: Camille Leger, Henri Reiners, Victor Majerus, Gaston Theis, Arnold Kieffer (46 Eugène Kremer), Ernest Mengel, Florian Mengel, Mathias Becker, Théophile Logelin, Théophile Speicher, Joseph Fischer. Manager: Paul Feierstein

FRANCE: Alexis Thépot, Georges Rose, Étienne Mattler, Edmond Delfour, Célestin Delmer, Noël Liétaer, Ernest Libérati, Joseph Alcazar, Jean Nicolas, Roger Rio, Alfred Aston. Manager: Gaston Barreau

Goals: Théophile Speicher (47) / Alfred Aston (3), Jean Nicolas (26, 67, 85, 89 pen), Ernest Libérati (80)

123. 10.05.1934
NETHERLANDS v FRANCE 4-5 (4-4)
Olympisch Stadion, Amsterdam
Referee: Rudolphe Wittwer (Switzerland)
Attendance: 35,000

NETHERLANDS: Gerrit Keizer, Mauk Weber, Sjef van Run, Henk Pellikaan, Toon Oprinsen, Puck van Heel, Frank Wels, Leen Vente, Beb Bakhuys, Kick Smit, Jaap Mol. Manager: Robert Glendenning

FRANCE: Alexis Thépot, Jacques Mairesse, Étienne Mattler, Jules Cottenier, Georges Verriest, Noël Liétaer, Fritz Keller, Joseph Alcazar, Jean Nicolas, Roger Rio, Alfred Aston. Manager: Gaston Barreau

Goals: Leen Vente (4), Beb Bakhuys (7, 12), Kick Smit (31) / Fritz Keller (13), Jean Nicolas (21, 25, 73), Joseph Alcazar (38)

124. 27.05.1934   FIFA World Cup Final Tournament – First round
AUSTRIA v FRANCE 3-2 (1-1, 1-1) (AET)
Stadio Municipal Benito Mussolini, Torino (Italy)
Referee: Johannes Franciscus van Moorsel (Netherlands)
Attendance: 16,000

AUSTRIA: Peter Platzer, Franz Cisar, Karl Sesta, Franz Wagner, Josef Smistik, Johann Urbanek, Karl Zischek, Josef Bican, Matthias Sindelar, Anton Schall, Rudolf Viertl. Manager: Hugo Meisl

FRANCE: Alexis Thépot, Jacques Mairesse, Étienne Mattler, Edmond Delfour, Georges Verriest, Noël Liétaer, Fritz Keller, Joseph Alcazar, Jean Nicolas, Roger Rio, Alfred Aston. Manager: George Kimpton

Goals: M. Sindelar (44), Anton Schall (93), Josef Bican (109) / Jean Nicolas (18), Georges Verriest (116 pen).

125. 16.12.1934
FRANCE v YUGOSLAVIA 3-2 (1-1)
Parc des Princes, Paris
Referee: Louis Baert (Belgium)   Attendance: 37,000

FRANCE: Alexis Thépot, Manuel Anatol, Étienne Mattler, Louis Gabrillargues, Georges Verriest, Noël Liétaer, Fritz Keller, Roger Courtois, Jean Nicolas, Roger Rio, Marcel Langiller. Manager: Gaston Barreau

YUGOSLAVIA: Franjo Glaser (13 Bartol Culic), Milutin Ivkovic, Jozo Matosic, Bozidar Petrovic (38 Zvonko Jazbec), Ivan Gajer, Gustav Lechner, Svetislav Glisovic, Blagoje Marjanovic, Aleksandar Zivkovic, Djordje Vujadinovic, Dobrivoje Zecevic.

Goals: Jean Nicolas (12, 86), Roger Courtois (88) / Blagoje Marjanovic (44), Djordje Vujadinovic (84)

126. 24.01.1935
SPAIN v FRANCE 2-0 (1-0)
Estadio Chamartín, Madrid
Referee: Walter James Lewington (England)
Attendance: 22,000

SPAIN: RICARDO ZAMORA Martínez, Pedro Pablo ARESO Aramburu, Serafin AEDO Renieblas, Leonardo CILAURREN Uriarte, José MUGUERZA Anitúa, Martín MARCULETA Barbería, Leal Ramón De la Fuente "LAFUENTE", LUIS Pagola REGUEIRO "Corzo", Isidro LÁNGARA Galarraga, Juan Marrero Pérez "HILARIO", Guillermo GOROSTIZA Paredes. Manager: AMADEO GARCÍA de Salazar Luco

FRANCE: Alexis Thépot, Jules Vandooren, Étienne Mattler, Louis Gabrillargues, Georges Verriest, Maxime Lehmann, Roger Courtois, Joseph Alcazar, Jean Nicolas, Roger Rio, Marcel Langiller. Manager: Gaston Barreau

Goals: LUIS Pagola REGUEIRO "Corzo" (13), Juan Marrero Pérez "HILARIO" (78)

127. 17.02.1935
ITALY v FRANCE 2-1 (2-1)
Stadio Nazionale del P.N.F., Roma
Referee: Louis Baert (Belgium)   Attendance: 23,000
ITALY: Carlo Ceresoli, Eraldo Monzeglio, Ernesto Mascheroni, Mario Montesanto, Attilio Ferraris, Mario Varglien, Enrique Guaita, Alejandro Scopelli Casanova, Giuseppe Meazza, Giovanni Ferrari, Pietro Ferraris. Manager: Vittorio Pozzo
FRANCE: René Llense, Jules Vandooren, Étienne Mattler, Louis Gabrillargues, Georges Verriest, Edmond Delfour, Fritz Keller, Yvan Beck, Roger Courtois, Pierre Duhart, Alfred Aston. Manager: Gaston Barreau
Goals: Giuseppe Meazza (5, 15) / Fritz Keller (26)

128. 17.03.1935
FRANCE v GERMANY 1-3 (0-1)
Parc des Princes, Paris
Referee: Louis Baert (Belgium)   Attendance: 38,483
FRANCE: Alexis Thépot, Jules Vandooren, Étienne Mattler, Louis Gabrillargues, Georges Verriest, Edmond Delfour, Alfred Aston, Yvan Beck, Jean Nicolas, Pierre Duhart, Aimé Nuic (37 Jean Sécember).   Manager: Gaston Barreau
GERMANY: Hans Jakob, Paul Janes, Wilhelm Busch, Rudi Gramlich, Reinhold Münzenberg, Paul Zielinski, Ernst Lehner, Karl Hohmann, Edmund Conen, Otto Siffling, Stanislaus Kobierski.   Manager: Otto Nerz
Goals: Pierre Duhart (59) / Ernst Lehrer (36), Stanislaus Kobierski (51), Karl Hohmann (88)

129. 14.04.1935
BELGIUM v FRANCE 1-1 (0-1)
Stade du Jubilé (Centenaire), Brussels
Referee: Rudolphe Wittwer (Switzerland)
Attendance: 40,500
BELGIUM: Arnold Badjou, Robert Paverick, Philibert Smellinckx, Pierre Dalem, Émile Stijnen, Jean Claessens, François De Vries, Bernard Voorhoof, Raymond Braine, Hendrik Isemborghs, Joseph Van Beeck. Manager: Gyula Jules Turnauer
FRANCE: René Llense, Raoul Diagne, Étienne Mattler (43 Jules Vandooren, 46 Étienne Mattler), Georges Verriest, Edmond Delfour, Alfred Aston, Yvan Beck, Roger Courtois, Émile Veinante, Marcel Langiller, Max Charbit. Manager: Gaston Barreau
Goals: Joseph Van Beeck (63) / Roger Courtois (20)

Étienne Mattler was replaced by Jules Vandooren due to an thigh injury. As Belgian officials protested during the half-time (FIFA allowing replacements until the 40th minute only), Mattler was obliged to return to the pitch and Vandooren had to withdraw.

130. 19.05.1935
FRANCE v HUNGARY 2-0 (1-0)
Stade Olympique Yves-du-Manoir, Colombes
Referee: Walter James Lewington (England)
Attendance: 25,000
FRANCE: René Llense, Jules Vandooren, Étienne Mattler, Max Charbit, Georges Verriest, Edmond Delfour, Alfred Aston, Yvan Beck, Roger Courtois, Lucien Laurent, Fritz Keller. Manager: Gaston Barreau
HUNGARY: József Pálinkás, József Vágó, Sándor Bíró, Antal Szalay, György Szücs (30 József Turay), Gyula Lázár, Mátyás Korányi, Jenö Vincze, György Sárosi, László Cseh, Pál Titkos. Manager: Károly Dietz
Goals: Roger Courtois (37, 72)

131. 27.10.1935
SWITZERLAND v FRANCE 2-1 (1-1)
Stade des Charmilles, Geneva
Referee: Walter James Lewington (England)
Attendance: 25,000
SWITZERLAND: Gustav Schlegel, Severino Minelli, Hans Stalder, Francis Defago, Walter Weiler, Eduard Müller, Adolf Stelzer, André Abegglen, Willy Jäggi, Jacques Spagnoli, Alfred Jäck.   Manager: Heinrich Müller
FRANCE: René Llense, Jules Vandooren, Étienne Mattler, Marcel Desrousseaux, Louis Gabrillargues, Edmond Delfour, Émile Zermani, André Cheuva, Roger Courtois, Pierre Duhart, Alfred Aston.   Manager: Gaston Barreau
Goals: André Abegglen (41), Willy Jäggi (56) / Walter Weiler (4 og)

132. 10.11.1935
FRANCE v SWEDEN 2-0 (1-0)
Parc des Princes, Paris
Referee: Arthur Barton (England)   Attendance: 26,905
FRANCE: René Llense, Raoul Diagne, Étienne Mattler, Louis Gabrillargues, Georges Verriest, Edmond Delfour, Robert Mercier, André Cheuva, Roger Courtois, Ignace Kowalczyk, Édouard Wawrzeniak.   Manager: Gaston Barreau
SWEDEN: Sven Bergqvist, Nils Axelsson, Valter Sköld, Fritz Berg, Harry Johansson, Einar Karlsson, Curt Bergsten, Erik Persson, Sven Jonasson, Karl-Erik Grahn, Axel Nilsson. Manager: John Pettersson
Goals: Fritz Berg (33 og), Roger Courtois (70)

133. 12.01.1936
FRANCE v NETHERLANDS 1-6 (0-4)
Parc des Princes, Paris
Referee: George Reginald Rudd (England)   Attendance: 30,000
FRANCE: René Llense, Raoul Diagne, Étienne Mattler, Louis Gabrillargues (26 Maurice Banide), Georges Verriest, Edmond Delfour, Jules Monsallier, André Cheuva, Roger Courtois, Émile Veinante, Aimé Nuic (23 Alfred Aston). Manager: George Kimpton
NETHERLANDS: Leo Halle, Mauk Weber, Bertus Caldenhove, Bas Paauwe, Wim Anderiesen sr., Puck van Heel, Frank Wels, Daaf Drok, Beb Bakhuys, Kick Smit, Joop van Nellen. Manager: Robert Glendenning
Goals: Roger Courtois (64) / Beb Bakhuys (5, 40, 41), Frank Wels (35), Daaf Drok (85), Joop van Nellen (87)

134. 09.02.1936
FRANCE v CZECHOSLOVAKIA 0-3 (0-3)
Parc des Princes, Paris
Referee: Pedro Escartín Morán (Spain)   Attendance: 40,138
FRANCE: Laurent Di Lorto, Jules Vandooren, Étienne Mattler, Louis Gabrillargues, Georges Verriest, Edmond Delfour, Roger Courtois, Roger Rio, Jules Bigot, Ignace Kowalczyk, Ali Benouna. Manager: George Kimpton
CZECHOSLOVAKIA: Frantisek Plánicka, Jaroslav Burgr, Josef Ctyroký, Josef Kostálek, Jaroslav Boucek, Erich Srbek, Václav Horák, Vojtech Bradác, Oldrich Zajícek, Oldrich Nejedlý, Antonín Puc. Manager: Jaroslav Bezecný
Goals: Antonín Puc (14), Jaroslav Boucek (20), Oldrich Nejedlý (25)

135. 08.03.1936
FRANCE v BELGIUM 3-0 (1-0)
Stade Olympique Yves-du-Manoir, Colombes
Referee: Dr. Peter Joseph (Peco) Bauwens (Germany)
Attendance: 30,000
FRANCE: Laurent Di Lorto, Joseph Gonzalés, Charles Zehren, Edmond Delfour, Raymond François, Maxime Lehmann, Edmond Novicki, Pierre Duhart, Roger Courtois, Roger Rio, Ali Benouna. Manager: Gaston Barreau
BELGIUM: Robert Braet, Robert Paverick, Philibert Smellinckx, Pierre Dalem, Émile Stijnen, Jean Claessens, Louis Versyp, Bernard Voorhoof, Marius Mondelé, John Lodts, François De Deken. Manager: John Dennis Butler
Goals: Roger Coutois (37, 54), Roger Rio (48)

136. 13.12.1936
FRANCE v YUGOSLAVIA 1-0 (1-0)
Parc des Princes, Paris
Referee: Rinaldo Barlassina (Italy)   Attendance: 32,903
FRANCE: Robert Défossé, Jules Vandooren, Georges Beaucourt, Matthieu André, Jean Gautheroux, Émilien Méresse, Alfred Aston, Pierre Duhart, Roger Courtois, Oscar Heisserer, Fritz Keller. Manager: Gaston Barreau
YUGOSLAVIA: Franjo Glaser, Bernard Higl, Jozo Matosic, Milorad Arsenijevic, Iva Stevovic, Momcilo Djokic, Aleksandar Tirnanic, Blagoje Marjanovic, Aleksandar Tomasevic, Branislav Sekulic, Dobrivoje Zecevic. Manager: Nikola Simic
Goal: Fritz Keller (19)

137. 24.01.1937
FRANCE v AUSTRIA 1-2 (1-1)
Parc des Princes, Paris
Referee: Arthur Barton (England)   Attendance: 37,898
FRANCE: René Llense, Maurice Dupuis, Raoul Diagne, Michel Payen, Louis Gabrillargues, Matthieu André, Edmond Novicki, Roger Rio, Jean Nicolas, Georges Janin, Bernard Antoinette. Manager: Gaston Barreau
AUSTRIA: Rudolf Raftl, Karl Sesta, Willibald Schmaus, Karl Adamek, Leopold Hofmann, Walter Nausch, Franz Riegler, Josef Stroh, Franz Binder, Camillo Jerusalem, Rudolf Viertl. Manager: Hugo Meisl
Goals: Edmond Novicki (42) / Josef Stroh (39 pen), Franz Binder (83)

138. 21.02.1937
BELGIUM v FRANCE 3-1 (1-1)
Stade du Jubilé (Centenaire), Brussels
Referee: Hans Samuel Boekman (Netherlands)
Attendance: 37,668
BELGIUM: Robert Braet, Robert Paverick, Constant Joacim, Pierre Dalem, Émile Stijnen, Alphonse De Winter, Léon Torfs, Arthur Ceuleers, Bernard Voorhoof, Raymond Braine, Stanley Vanden Eynde. Manager: John Dennis Butler
FRANCE: René Llense, Maurice Dupuis, Raoul Diagne, Michel Payen, François Bourbotte, Matthieu André, Fritz Keller, Roger Rio, Roger Courtois, Pierre Duhart, Bernard Antoinette. Manager: Gaston Barreau
Goals: Raymond Braine (43), Arthur Ceuleers (65), Stanley Vanden Eynde (78) / Roger Rio (12)

139. 21.03.1937
GERMANY v FRANCE 4-0 (2-0)
Adolf Hitler Kampfbahn, Stuttgart
Referee: Rinaldo Barlassina (Italy)   Attendance: 72,000
GERMANY: Hans Jakob, Paul Janes, Reinhold Münzenberg, Rudolf Gellesch, Ludwig Goldbrunner, Albin Kitzinger, Ernst Lehner, Otto Siffling, August Lenz, Fritz Szepan, Adolf Urban. Manager: Sepp Herberger
FRANCE: Laurent Di Lorto, Maurice Dupuis, Raoul Diagne, Michel Payen, François Bourbotte, Edmond Delfour, Jules Bigot, Roger Rio, Jean Nicolas, Ignace Kowalczyk, Fritz Keller. Manager: Gaston Barreau
Goals: Ernst Lehner (26), Adolf Urban (31, 76), August Lenz (87)

140. 23.05.1937
FRANCE v IRISH FREE STATE 0-2 (0-0)
Stade Olympique Yves-du-Manoir, Colombes
Referee: Gustav Krist (Czechoslovakia)   Attendance: 16,688
FRANCE: Laurent Di Lorto, Abdelkader Ben Bouali, Raoul Diagne, François Bourbotte, Georges Meuris, Edmond Delfour, Michel Lauri, Ignace Kowalczyk, Roger Courtois, Michel Frutuoso, Alfred Aston. Manager: Gaston Barreau
IRISH FREE STATE: Tommy Breen, William O'Neill, John Feenan, Joe O'Reilly, Charlie Turner, Con Moulson, Jackie Brown, David Jordan, Jimmy Dunne, Paddy Farrell, Willie Fallon.
Goals: David Jordan (51), Jackie Brown (58)

141. 10.10.1937
FRANCE v SWITZERLAND 2-1 (1-0)
Parc des Princes, Paris
Referee: Johannes Julianus (John) Langenus (Belgium)   Attendance: 36,730
FRANCE: Laurent Di Lorto, Héctor Cazenave, Étienne Mattler, François Bourbotte, Marcel Desrousseaux, Edmond Delfour, Curt Keller, Yvan Beck, Roger Courtois, Émile Veinante, Marcel Langiller. Manager: Gaston Barreau
SWITZERLAND: Renato Bizzozero, Severino Minelli, August Lehmann, Hermann Springer, Sirio Vernati, Ernest Lörtscher, Alfred Bickel, Paul Aebi, Eugen Rupf, Genia Walaschek, Georges Aeby. Manager: Karl Rappan
Goals: Émile Veinante (41, 82) / Eugen Rupf (66)

142. 31.10.1937
NETHERLANDS v FRANCE 2-3 (0-1)
Olympisch Stadion, Amsterdam
Referee: James Harry Wiltshire (England)   Attendance: 44,000
NETHERLANDS: Leo Halle, Mauk Weber, Bertus Caldenhove, Henk Pellikaan, Wim Anderiesen sr., Bas Paauwe, Frank Wels, Leen Vente, Kick Smit, Puck van Heel, Ko Bergman. Manager: Robert Glendenning
FRANCE: Laurent Di Lorto, Héctor Cazenave, Étienne Mattler, François Bourbotte, Charles Fosset, Edmond Delfour, Roger Courtois, Oscar Heisserer, Jean Nicolas, Émile Veinante, Marcel Langiller. Manager: Gaston Barreau
Goals: Kick Smit (56, 86) / Jean Nicolas (13), Marcel Langiller (48), Roger Courtois (73)

143. 05.12.1937
FRANCE v ITALY 0-0
Parc des Princes, Paris
Referee: Hans Wüthrich (Switzerland)   Attendance: 39,046
FRANCE: Laurent Di Lorto, Héctor Cazenave, Étienne Mattler, François Bourbotte, Charles Fosset, Edmond Delfour, Roger Courtois, Oscar Heisserer, Jean Nicolas, Émile Veinante, Marcel Langiller. Manager: Gaston Barreau
ITALY: Aldo Olivieri, Eraldo Monzeglio, Pietro Rava, Pietro Serantoni, Michele Andreolo, Ugo Locatelli, Egidio Capra, Giuseppe Meazza, Silvio Piola, Giovanni Ferrari, Pietro Ferraris. Manager: Vittorio Pozzo

144. 30.01.1938
FRANCE v BELGIUM 5-3 (2-2)
Parc des Princes, Paris
Referee: Arthur James Jewell (England)   Attendance: 39,000
FRANCE: René Llense, Héctor Cazenave, Étienne Mattler, François Bourbotte, Auguste Jordan, Marcel Marchal, Roger Courtois, Ignace Kowalczyk, Jean Nicolas, Oscar Heisserer, Émile Veinante. Manager: Gaston Barreau
BELGIUM: Arnold Badjou, Robert Paverick, Philibert Smellinckx, Pierre Dalem, Frans Gommers, Alphonse De Winter, Charles Vanden Wouwer, Bernard Voorhoof, Jean Capelle, Raymond Braine, Stanley Vanden Eynde. Manager: John Dennis Butler
Goals: Roger Courtois (8), Émile Veinante (41, 51), Oscar Heisserer (47), Ignace Kowalczyk (78) / Raymond Braine (22), Bernard Voorhoof (28), Stanley Vanden Eynde (76)

145.   24.03.1938
FRANCE v BULGARIA 6-1 (2-0)
Parc des Princes, Paris

Referee: Walter James Lewington (England)
Attendance: 28,512

FRANCE: Laurent Di Lorto, Héctor Cazenave, Étienne Mattler, François Bourbotte, Auguste Jordan, Raoul Diagne, Alfred Aston, Oscar Heisserer, Jean Nicolas, Emmanuel Aznar, Émile Veinante.   Manager: Gaston Barreau

BULGARIA: Todor Dermonski, Nikola Nikolov, Georgi Balakchiev, Borislav Gabrovski, Dimitar Baykushev, Liubomir Petrov, Krum Milev, Lubomir Angelov, Mihail Lozanov, Borislav Kamenski, Vuchko Yordanov.
Manager: Stanislav Toms

Goals: Jean Nicolas (6, 87), Alfred Aston (29, 52), Emmanuel Aznar (79), Émile Veinante (83) / Mihail Lozanov (67)

146.   26.05.1938
FRANCE v ENGLAND 2-4 (2-3)
Stade Olympique Yves-du-Manoir, Colombes

Referee: Louis Baert (Belgium)   Attendance: 45,168

FRANCE: Laurent Di Lorto, Héctor Cazenave, Étienne Mattler, François Bourbotte, Auguste Jordan, Raoul Diagne, Roger Courtois, Michel Brusseaux, Jean Nicolas, Oscar Heisserer, Alfred Aston.   Manager: Gaston Barreau

ENGLAND: Victor Woodley, Bert Sproston, Eddie Hapgood, Ken Willingham, Alf Young, Stan Cullis, Frank Broome, Stanley Matthews, Ted Drake, Len Goulden, Clifford Bastin.

Goals: Auguste Jordan (32), Jean Nicolas (36) / Frank Broome (6), Ted Drake (34, 40), Clifford Bastin (85 pen)

147.   05.06.1938   FIFA World Cup Final Tournament – First Round
FRANCE v BELGIUM 3-1 (2-1)
Stade Olympique Yves-du-Manoir, Colombes (France)

Referee: Hans Wüthrich (Switzerland)   Attendance: 30,454

FRANCE: Laurent Di Lorto, Héctor Cazenave, Étienne Mattler, Jean Bastien, Auguste Jordan, Raoul Diagne, Alfred Aston, Oscar Heisserer, Jean Nicolas, Edmond Delfour, Émile Veinante.   Manager: Gaston Barreau

BELGIUM: Arnold Badjou, Robert Paverick, Cornelius Seys, Jan John Van Alphen, Émile Stijnen, Alphonse De Winter, Charles Vanden Wouwer, Bernard Voorhoof, Hendrik Isemborghs, Raymond Braine, Fernand Buyle.
Manager: John Dennis Butler

Goals: Émile Veinante (1), Jean Nicolas (12, 69) / Hendrik Isemborghs (20)

148.   12.06.1938   FIFA World Cup Final Tournament – Quarter-final
FRANCE v ITALY 1-3 (1-1)
Stade Olympique Yves-du-Manoir, Colombes (France)

Referee: Louis Baert (Belgium)   Attendance: 58,455

FRANCE: Laurent Di Lorto, Héctor Cazenave, Étienne Mattler, Jean Bastien, Auguste Jordan, Raoul Diagne, Alfred Aston, Oscar Heisserer, Jean Nicolas, Edmond Delfour, Émile Veinante.   Manager: Gaston Barreau

ITALY: Aldo Olivieri, Alfredo Foni, Pietro Rava, Pietro Serantoni, Michele Andreolo, Ugo Locatelli, Amedeo Biavati, Giuseppe Meazza, Silvio Piola, Giovanni Ferrari, Gino Colaussi.   Manager: Vittorio Pozzo

Goals: Oscar Heisserer (8) /
Gino Colaussi (9), Silvio Piola (52, 72)

149.   04.12.1938
ITALY v FRANCE 1-0 (1-0)
Stadio Giorgio Ascarelli, Napoli

Referee: Johannes Julianus (John) Langenus (Belgium)
Attendance: 40,000

ITALY: Aldo Olivieri, Alfredo Foni, Pietro Rava, Pietro Serantoni, Michele Andreolo, Ugo Locatelli, Amedeo Biavati, Attilio Demaría, Silvio Piola, Giovanni Ferrari, Gino Colaussi.   Manager: Vittorio Pozzo

FRANCE: René Llense, Jules Vandooren, Étienne Mattler, François Bourbotte, Auguste Jordan, Raoul Diagne, Alfred Aston, Haj Abdelkader Larbi Ben M'barek, Jean Nicolas, Oscar Heisserer, Émile Veinante.   Manager: Gaston Barreau

Goal: Amedeo Biavati (32)

150.   22.01.1939
FRANCE v POLAND 4-0 (2-0)
Parc des Princes, Paris

Referee: Walter Jordan (Switzerland)   Attendance: 35,000

FRANCE: René Llense, Jules Vandooren, Étienne Mattler, François Bourbotte, Auguste Jordan, Roland Schmitt, Alfred Aston, Haj Abdelkader Larbi Ben M'barek, Mario Zatelli, Oscar Heisserer, Émile Veinante.   Manager: Gaston Barreau

POLAND: Adolf Krzyk, Wladyslaw Szczepaniak, Edmund Twórz, Wilhelm Góra, Erwin Günter Nytz, Edwald Dytko, Leonard Piatek, Jerzy Wostal, Michal Matyas, Ernest Wilimowski, Gerard Wodarz.   Manager: Józef Kaluza

Goals: Émile Veinante (16, 57), Oscar Heisserer (41), Mario Zatelli (70)

Erwin Günther Nytz former known as Edward Piotr Nyc.
Ernest Wilimowski was born as Ernest Otto Prandella.

151. 16.03.1939
FRANCE v HUNGARY 2-2 (1-1)
Parc des Princes, Paris

Referee: Walter James Lewington (England)
Attendance: 27,367

FRANCE: Julien Darui, Jules Vandooren, Étienne Mattler, François Bourbotte, Auguste Jordan, Raoul Diagne, Alfred Aston, Haj Abdelkader Larbi Ben M'barek, Roger Courtois, Oscar Heisserer, Edmond Weiskopf.
Manager: Gaston Barreau

HUNGARY: Antal Szabó, Lajos Korányi, Sándor Bíró, Gyula Lázár, Béla Sárosi, István Balogh, József Szántó, Gyula Zsengellér, Ferenc Kolláth, István Kiszely, László Gyetvai.
Manager: Károly Dietz

Goals: Haj Abdelkader Larbi Ben M'barek (15), Oscar Heisserer (87) / István Kiszely (17, 56)

152. 18.05.1939
BELGIUM v FRANCE 1-3 (0-1)
Stade du Jubilé (Centenaire), Brussels

Referee: Alexander Sidney Donaldson (England)
Attendance: 35,793

BELGIUM: Arnold Badjou, Robert Paverick, Georges Van Calenberg, Jan John Van Alphen, Émile Stijnen, Paul Henry, Jean Fiévez, Robert Lamoot, Jean Capelle, Hendrik Isemborghs, Raymond Braine. Manager: John Dennis Butler

FRANCE: Julien Darui, Jules Vandooren, Étienne Mattler, François Bourbotte, Auguste Jordan, Raoul Diagne, Jules Bigot, Haj Abdelkader Larbi Ben M'barek, Désiré Koranyi, Oscar Heisserer, Jules Mathé. Manager: Gaston Barreau

Goals: Robert Lamoot (62) / Désiré Koranyi (28, 85), Jules Mathé (48)

153. 21.05.1939
FRANCE v WALES 2-1 (2-0)
Stade Olympique Yves-du-Manoir, Colombes

Referee: Laurent Franken (Belgium)   Attendance: 23,064

FRANCE: Julien Darui, Jules Vandooren, Étienne Mattler, François Bourbotte, Auguste Jordan, Raoul Diagne, Jules Bigot, Oscar Heisserer, Désiré Koranyi, Émile Veinante, Jules Mathé.
Manager: Gaston Barreau

WALES: George Poland, Bert Turner, Billy Hughes, George Green, Jackie Williams, Harry Hanford, Dai Astley, Charles Jones, Donald Dearson, Jack Warner, Seymour Morris.

Goals: Jules Bigot (10), Désiré Koranyi (13) / Dai Astley (53)

154. 28.01.1940
FRANCE v PORTUGAL 3-2 (2-0)
Parc des Princes, Paris

Referee: Edward Bainbridge (England)   Attendance: 18,083

FRANCE: Rudolf Hiden, Jules Vandooren, Étienne Mattler, François Bourbotte, Auguste Jordan, Raoul Diagne, Roger Courtois, Henri Hiltl, Désiré Koranyi, Oscar Heisserer, Émile Veinante. Manager: Gaston Barreau

PORTUGAL: JOÃO Mendonça AZEVEDO, JOSÉ Ribeiro SIMÕES Costa, Álvaro GASPAR PINTO, Mariano Rodrigues AMARO, CARLOS Jesus PEREIRA, FRANCISCO FERREIRA "Xico", Adolfo Albino MOURÃO, ALBERTO Luis GOMES, FERNANDO Baptista de Seixas PEYROTEO de Vasconcelos, ARMANDO Félix FERREIRA, JOÃO Pedro Da CRUZ.
Manager: CÂNDIDO Plácido Fernandes DE OLIVEIRA

Goals: Oscar Heisserer (17), Désiré Koranyi (23, 75) / FERNANDO PEYROTEO de Vasconcelos (83, 85)

155. 08.03.1942
FRANCE v SWITZERLAND 0-2 (0-2)
Stade Vélodrome, Marseille

Referee: Pedro Escartín Morán (Spain)   Attendance: 36,000

FRANCE: Julien Darui, Jules Vandooren, Henri Roessler, François Bourbotte, Auguste Jordan, Roland Schmitt, Alfred Aston, André Simonyi, Désiré Koranyi, Maurice Dupuis, Henri Arnaudeau. Manager: Gaston Barreau

SWITZERLAND: Erwin Ballabio, Severino Minelli, August Lehmann, Hermann Springer, Sirio Vernati, Franz Rickenbach, Alfred Bickel, Lauro Amadò, Fritz Knecht, Genia Walaschek, Rodolfo Kappenberger. Manager: Karl Rappan

Goals: Lauro Amadò (14), Rodolfo Kappenberger (23)

156. 15.03.1942
SPAIN v FRANCE 4-0 (2-0)
Estadio de Nervión, Sevilla

Referee: António dos Santos Palhinhas (Portugal)
Attendance: 40,000

SPAIN: Alberto MARTORELL Otzet, Ricardo TERUEL García, Isaac OCEJA Oceja (35 Salvador ARQUETA Echevarría), Ramón GABILONDO Alberdi, GERMÁN Gómez Gómez, Ángel Andrés MATEO Vilches, Epifanio "EPI" Fernández Berridi, Jesús "Chus" ALONSO Fernández, Edmundo "MUNDO" Suárez de Trabanco, Francisco CAMPOS Salamanca, José BRAVO Domínguez.
Manager: EDUARDO TEUS López-Navarro

FRANCE: Julien Darui, Jules Vandooren, François Mercier, François Bourbotte, Auguste Jordan, Henri Roessler, Alfred Aston, André Simonyi, Désiré Koranyi, Maurice Dupuis, Henri Arnaudeau. Manager: Gaston Barreau

Goals: Francisco CAMPOS Salamanca (4, 68), Edmundo "MUNDO" Suárez de Trabanco (38), Epifanio "EPI" Fernández Berridi (85)

157. 24.12.1944
FRANCE v BELGIUM 3-1 (2-0)

Parc des Princes, Paris

Referee: Paul Tréhou (France)   Attendance: 24,095

FRANCE: Alfred Dambach, André Frey, Jean Swiatek, Jean Baratte, Jules Bigot, Jean Bastien, Félix Pironti, Henri Hiltl, Alfred Aston, André Simonyi, Henri Arnaudeau. Manager: Gaston Barreau

BELGIUM: Henri Meert, Robert Gérard, Joseph Pannaye, Antoine Puttaert, Marcel Vercammen, John Van Alphen, François De Wael, Désiré Van Den Audenaerde, Arsène Vaillant, Fernand Voussure, Fernand Buyle. Manager: François Demol

Goals: André Simonyi (38), Henri Arnaudeau (42), Alfred Aston (79) / François De Wael (83)

158. 08.04.1945
SWITZERLAND v FRANCE 1-0 (0-0)

Stade Olympique de La Pontaise, Lausanne

Referee: Pierre Georges Louis Capdeville (France)   Attendance: 25,000

SWITZERLAND: Erwin Ballabio, Rudolf Gyger, Willi Steffen, Joseph Courtat, Franco Andreoli, Gabriel Pégaitaz, Alfred Bickel, Genia Walaschek, Numa Monnard, Hans-Peter Friedländer, Lauro Amadò.   Manager: Karl Rappan

FRANCE: Julien Darui, André Frey, Maurice Dupuis, Lucien Jasseron, Auguste Jordan, Jules Bigot, René Bihel, Alfred Aston, André Simonyi, Ladislas Smid, Ernest Vaast. Manager: Gaston Barreau

Goal: Hans-Peter Friedländer (59)

Ladislas Smid was also known as László Sikló.

159. 26.05.1945
ENGLAND (amateurs) v FRANCE 2-2 (1-1)

British Empire Exhibition Stadium, London

Referee: George Reader (England)   Attendance: 60,000

ENGLAND: Bert Williams, Laurence Scott, George Hardwick, Frank Soo, Neil Franklin, Joe Mercer, Stanley Matthews, Horatio Carter, Tommy Lawton, Robert Brown, Leslie Smith.

FRANCE: Julien Darui, Maurice Dupuis, Jean Swiatek, Jean-Claude Samuel, Auguste Jordan, Lucien Jasseron, Alfred Aston, Oscar Heisserer, René Bihel, Ladislas Smid, Ernest Vaast. Manager: Gaston Barreau

Goals: Horatio Carter (10), Tommy Lawton (79) / Ernest Vaast (44), Oscar Heisserer (90)

160. 06.12.1945
AUSTRIA v FRANCE 4-1 (2-1)

Praterstadion, Vienna

Referee: Jean Lutz (Switzerland)   Attendance: 55,000

AUSTRIA: Walter Zeman, Gustav Gerhart, Karl Bortoli, Leopold Mikolasch, Ernst Sabeditsch, Siegfried Joksch, Franz Riegler, Karl Decker, Franz Binder, Camillo Jerusalem, Leopold Neumer.   Manager: Eduard Bauer

FRANCE: Julien Darui, Maurice Dupuis, Marcel Salva, Jean-Claude Samuel, Auguste Jordan, Jean Bastien, Alfred Aston, Ladislas Smid, Émile Bongiorni, Haj Abdelkader Larbi Ben M'barek, Ernest Vaast.   Manager: Gaston Barreau

Goals: Karl Decker (14, 16, 79), Leopold Neumer (68) / Émile Bongiorni (8)

161. 15.12.1945
BELGIUM v FRANCE 2-1 (2-0)

Stade Oscar Bossaert, Brussels

Referee: Alfred Emiel (Aad) van Welzenes (Netherlands)   Attendance: 23,576

BELGIUM: François Daenen, Robert Paverick, Joseph Pannaye, Antoine Puttaert, Marcel Vercammen, René Devos, Victor Lemberechts, Joseph Mermans, Léon Gillaux, Désiré Van Den Audenaerde, François Sermon. Manager: François Demol

FRANCE: Julien Darui, Maurice Dupuis, Marcel Salva, Jean-Claude Samuel, Gabriel Braun, Marcel Ourdouillié, Alfred Aston, Ladislas Smid, Émile Bongiorni, Haj Abdelkader Larbi Ben M'barek, Ernest Vaast.   Manager: Gaston Barreau

Goals: François Sermon (19, 33) / Alfred Aston (77)

162. 07.04.1946
FRANCE v CZECHOSLOVAKIA 3-0 (1-0)

Stade Olympique Yves-du-Manoir, Colombes

Referee: Eugen Adolf Scherz (Switzerland)   Attendance: 52,242

FRANCE: Julien Darui, André Grillon, Antoine Cuissard, Marcel Salva, Lucien Leduc, Jean Prouff, Alfred Aston, Oscar Heisserer, René Bihel, Haj Abdelkader Larbi Ben M'barek, Ernest Vaast.   Manager: Gaston Barreau

CZECHOSLOVAKIA: Karel Finek, Vlastimil Luka, Karel Senecký, Ladislav Koubek, Rudolf Smejkal, Jiří Hanke, Vladimír Perk, Ferdinand Plánický, Viktor Tegelhoff, Josef Bican, Jiří Zmatlík. Manager: Karel Myska

Goals: Ernest Vaast (15, 75), Oscar Heisserer (83)

163. 14.04.1946
PORTUGAL v FRANCE 2-1 (1-0)
Estádio Nacional do Jamor, Oeiras

Referee: George Reader (England)   Attendance: 62,000

PORTUGAL: JOÃO Mendonça AZEVEDO, ALVARO CARDOSO da Silva, SERAFIM Das NEVES, Mariano Rodrigues AMARO, António FELICIANO, FRANCISCO FERREIRA "Xico", RAFAEL António CORREIA, Antonio De ARAÚJO, FERNANDO Baptista de Seixas PEYROTEO de Vasconcelos, ARTUR Da Silva QUARESMA, ROGÉRIO Lantres de CARVALHO "Pipo".
Manager: João Joaquim TAVARES DA SILVA

FRANCE: Julien Darui, André Grillon, Marcel Salva, Jean Prouff, Antoine Cuissard, Lucien Leduc, Alfred Aston, Oscar Heisserer, René Bihel, Haj Abdelkader Larbi Ben M'barek, Ernest Vaast.   Manager: Gaston Barreau

Goals: Antonio De ARAÚJO (39), FERNANDO Baptista de Seixas PEYROTEO de Vasconcelos (72) / Ernest Vaast (68)

164. 05.05.1946
FRANCE v AUSTRIA 3-1 (0-1)
Stade Olympique Yves-du-Manoir, Colombes

Referee: Paul von Wartburg (Switzerland)
Attendance: 57,205

FRANCE: Julien Darui, André Grillon, Marcel Salva, Jean Prouff, Antoine Cuissard, Lucien Leduc, Alfred Aston, Oscar Heisserer, René Bihel, Haj Abdelkader Larbi Ben M'barek, Ernest Vaast.   Manager: Gaston Barreau

AUSTRIA: Walter Zeman (87 Josef Spale), Franz Pavuza, Engelbert Smutny, Leopold Gernhardt, Ernst Sabeditsch, Siegfried Joksch, Ernst Melchior, Karl Decker, Josef Stroh, Wilhelm Hahnemann, Karl Kerbach.
Manager: Eduard Bauer

Goals: E. Vaast (66), Oscar Heisserer (83), Lucien Leduc (86) / Wilhelm Hahnemann (23)

165. 19.05.1946
FRANCE v ENGLAND (Amateurs) 2-1 (0-0)
Stade Olympique Yves-du-Manoir, Colombes

Referee: Eugen Adolf Scherz (Switzerland)
Attendance: 58,481

FRANCE: Julien Darui, André Grillon, Marcel Salva, Jean Prouff, Antoine Cuissard, Lucien Leduc, Alfred Aston, Oscar Heisserer, Pierre Sinibaldi, Haj Abdelkader Larbi Ben M'barek, Ernest Vaast.   Manager: Gaston Barreau

ENGLAND: Bert Williams, Joseph Bacuzzi, George Hardwick, Billy Wright, Neil Franklin, Herbert Johnsson, Stanley Matthews, Horatio Carter, Tommy Lawton, James Hagan, Leslie Smith.   Manager: Walter Winterbottom

Goals: Jean Prouff (54), Ernest Vaast (78) / James Hagan (80)

166. 23.03.1947
FRANCE v PORTUGAL 1-0 (1-0)
Stade Olympique Yves-du-Manoir, Colombes

Referee: Cyril John (Jack) Barrick (England)
Attendance: 57,791

FRANCE: Julien Darui, André Grillon, Roger Marche, Antoine Cuissard, Jean Swiatek, Jean Prouff, Roger Courtois, Oscar Heisserer, René Bihel, Haj Abdelkader Larbi Ben M'barek, Michel Jacques.   Manager: Gaston Barreau

PORTUGAL: JOÃO Mendonça AZEVEDO, ALVARO CARDOSO da Silva, SERAFIM Das NEVES, Mariano Rodrigues AMARO, António FELICIANO, FRANCISCO FERREIRA "Xico", António JESUS CORREIA, Antonio De ARAÚJO, FERNANDO Baptista de Seixas PEYROTEO de Vasconcelos, JOSÉ António Barreto TRAVASSOS, ROGÉRIO Lantres de CARVALHO "Pipo".
Manager: João Joaquim TAVARES DA SILVA

Goal: René Bihel (41)

167. 03.05.1947
ENGLAND v FRANCE 3-0 (0-0)
Highbury Stadium, London

Referee: Louis André Baert (Belgium)   Attendance: 54,389

ENGLAND: Frank Swift, Laurie Scott, George Hardwick, Billy Wright, Neil Franklin, Eddie Lowe, Tom Finney, Raich Carter, Tommy Lawton, Wilf Mannion, Robert Langton.
Manager: Walter Winterbottom

FRANCE: Julien Darui, Jean Swiatek, Roger Marche, Antoine Cuissard, Jean Grégoire, Jean Prouff, Ernest Vaast, Boleslaw Tempowski, Émile Bongiorni, Oscar Heisserer, Jean Lechantre.
Manager: Gaston Barreau

Goals: Tom Finney (50), Wilf Mannion (64), Raich Carter (77)

168. 26.05.1947
FRANCE v NETHERLANDS 4-0 (1-0)
Stade Olympique Yves-du-Manoir, Colombes

Referee: Stanley Boardman (England)   Attendance: 38,215

FRANCE: Julien Darui, Joseph Jadrejak, Sauveur Rodriguez, Antoine Cuissard, Jean Grégoire, Jean Prouff, Georges Dard, Jean Baratte, René Alpsteg, Roger Carré, Ernest Vaast.
Manager: Gaston Barreau

NETHERLANDS: Piet Kraak, Jeu van Bun, Henk van der Linden, Gerrie Stroker, Hennie Möring, Arie de Vroet, Guus Dräger, Faas Wilkes, Wim Roosen, Kees Rijvers, Ko Bergman.
Manager: Jesse Carver

Goals: René Alpsteg (17), Jean Baratte (60, 86), Georges Dard (75)

169.   01.06.1947
FRANCE v BELGIUM   4-2 (1-1)
Stade Olympique Yves-du-Manoir, Colombes
Referee: Jan Beneda (Czechoslovakia)   Attendance: 35,176
FRANCE: Julien Darui, Joseph Jadrejak, André Grillon, Antoine Cuissard, Jean Grégoire, Charles Heiné, Georges Dard, Jean Baratte, René Alpsteg, Oscar Heisserer, Ernest Vaast.   Manager: Gaston Barreau
BELGIUM: François Daenen, Léon Aernaudts, Joseph Pannaye, Hendrik Coppens, Jules Henriet, Fernand Massay, Victor Lemberechts, Joseph Mermans, Albert De Cleyn, Léopold Anoul, René Thirifays.   Manager: William Joseph Gormlie
Goals: E. Vaast (13, 84), Jean Baratte (77), Georges Dard (83) / Albert De Cleyn (17), Hendrik Coppens (76)

170.   08.06.1947
SWITZERLAND v FRANCE 1-2 (1-2)
Stade Olympique de La Pontaise, Lausanne
Referee: George Reader (England)   Attendance: 34,000
SWITZERLAND: Erwin Ballabio, Rudolf Gyger (53 René Maillard), André Belli, Olivier Eggimann, Roger Bocquet, Alfred Bickel, Walter Fink, Jean Tamini, Lauro Amadò, Jacques Fatton, Willi Steffen.   Manager: Karl Rappan
FRANCE: Julien Darui, Joseph Jadrejak, André Grillon, Jean Prouff, Jean Grégoire, Antoine Cuissard, Charles Heiné, Jean Baratte, René Alpsteg, Oscar Heisserer, Ernest Vaast.   Manager: Gaston Barreau
Goals: Jacques Fatton (16) / René Alpsteg (36), Jean Baratte (44)

171.   23.11.1947
PORTUGAL v FRANCE   2-4 (1-0)
Estádio Nacional do Jamor, Oeiras
Referee: Paul von Wartburg (Switzerland)
Attendance: 70,000
PORTUGAL: JOÃO Mendonça AZEVEDO, Octávio Dos Santos BARROSA, SERAFIM Das NEVES, Mariano Rodrigues AMARO, António FELICIANO, Francisco MOREIRA, António JESUS CORREIA, Antonio De ARAÚJO, FERNANDO Baptista de Seixas PEYROTEO de Vasconcelos, JOSÉ António Barreto TRAVASSOS, ALBANO Narciso Pereira.
Manager: VIRGÍLIO PAULA
FRANCE: Julien Darui, André Grillon, Roger Marche, Jean Prouff, Jean Grégoire, Louis Hon, René Alpsteg, Oscar Heisserer, Jean Baratte, Haj Abdelkader Larbi Ben M'barek, Ernest Vaast.   Manager: Gaston Barreau
Goals: FERNANDO Baptista de Seixas PEYROTEO de Vasconcelos (32), Antonio De ARAÚJO (71) / E. Vaast (47, 51, 77), Haj Abdelkader Larbi Ben M'barek (84)

172.   04.04.1948
FRANCE v ITALY   1-3 (0-3)
Stade Olympique Yves-du-Manoir, Colombes
Referee: Arthur Edward Ellis (England)
Attendance: 60,074
FRANCE: Marcel Domingo, André Grillon, Roger Marche, Antoine Cuissard, Robert Jonquet, Jean Prouff, René Alpsteg, Oscar Heisserer, Jean Baratte, Haj Abdelkader Larbi Ben M'barek, Ernest Vaast.   Manager: Gaston Barreau
ITALY: Valerio Bacigalupo, Aldo Ballarin, Alberto Eliani, Carlo Annovazzi, Mario Rigamonti, Giuseppe Grezar, Romeo Menti, Ezio Loik, Guglielmo Gabetto, Valentino Mazzola, Riccardo Carapellese.   Manager: Vittorio Pozzo
Goals: Jean Baratte (71 pen) / Riccardo Carapellese (31, 38), Guglielmo Gabetto (36)

173.   23.05.1948
FRANCE v SCOTLAND   3-0 (0-0)
Stade Olympique Yves-du-Manoir, Colombes
Referee: Karel Louis van der Meer (Netherlands)
Attendance: 46,032
FRANCE: Julien Darui, Guy Huguet, Roger Marche, Antoine Cuissard, Jean Grégoire, Jean Prouff, Georges Sésia, Jean Baratte, Émile Bongiorni, Haj Abdelkader Larbi Ben M'barek, Pierre Flamion.   Manager: Gaston Barreau
SCOTLAND: James Cowan, John Govan, David Shaw, William Campbell, George Young, Archibald MacAulay, Edward Rutherford, William Steel, Gordon Smith, Charles Cox, David Duncan.
Goals: Émile Bongiorni (55), Pierre Flamion (60), Jean Baratte (79)

174.   06.06.1948
BELGIUM v FRANCE   4-2 (1-0)
Stade du Heysel, Brussels
Referee: Dirk Nijs (Netherlands)   Attendance: 52,873
BELGIUM: François Daenen, Léon Aernaudts, Alfons De Buck, Hendrik Coppens, Victor Erroelen, Victor Lemberechts, Henri Govard, Joseph Mermans, Frédéric Chavès d'Aguilar, François Sermon, Léopold Anoul.
Manager: William Joseph Gormlie
FRANCE: Julien Darui, Guy Huguet, Roger Marche, Antoine Cuissard, Jean Grégoire, Jean Prouff, Albert Batteux, Jean Baratte, Émile Bongiorni, Haj Abdelkader Larbi Ben M'barek, Pierre Flamion.   Manager: Gaston Barreau
Goals: Frédéric Chavès d'Aguilar (10, 89), Henri Govard (76), Joseph Mermans (85) / Antoine Cuissard (47), Haj Abdelkader Larbi Ben M'barek (74)

175.   12.06.1948
CZECHOSLOVAKIA v FRANCE   0-4 (0-0)

Letenský Stadion, Praha

Referee: Karel Louis van der Meer (Netherlands)
Attendance: 52,000

CZECHOSLOVAKIA: Vlastimil Havlíček (89 Karel Capek), Karel Senecký, Jozef Marko, Eugen Prosovský, Vlastimil Pokorný, Jozef Karel, Václav Kokstejn, Miloslav Malý, Jaroslav Cejp, Jan Ríha, Jirí Pesek.   Manager: Jan Knobloch

FRANCE: Julien Darui, Guy Huguet, Roger Marche, Jean Prouff, Antoine Cuissard, Louis Hon, Henri Baillot, Albert Batteux, Jean Baratte, Haj Abdelkader Larbi Ben M'barek, Pierre Flamion.   Manager: Gaston Barreau

Goals: A. Batteux (62), Jean Baratte (66, 89), Henri Baillot (74)

176.   17.10.1948
FRANCE v BELGIUM   3-3 (2-1)

Stade Olympique Yves-du-Manoir, Colombes

Referee: Jean Lutz (Switzerland)   Attendance: 55,600

FRANCE: Julien Darui, Guy Huguet, Roger Marche, Jean Prouff, Antoine Cuissard (41 Henri Guérin), Louis Hon, Henri Baillot, Albert Batteux, Jean Baratte, Pierre Sinibaldi, Pierre Flamion.   Manager: Gaston Barreau

BELGIUM: François Daenen (30 Henri Meert), Léon Aernaudts, Hendrik Coppens, Louis Carré, Jules Henriet, Alfred Bertrand, Henri Govard, Joseph Mermans, Frédéric Chavès d'Aguilar, René Thirifays, Léopold Anoul. Manager: William Joseph Gormlie

Goals: Pierre Flamion (9, 50), Jean Baratte (22) / Joseph Mermans (23), Léopold Anoul (52), Frédéric Chavès d'Aguilar (66)

177.   23.04.1949
NETHERLANDS v FRANCE   4-1 (3-1)

De Kuip, Rotterdam

Referee: Laurent Franken (Belgium)   Attendance: 64,000

NETHERLANDS: Frans de Munck, Jeu van Bun, Henk Schijvenaar, Jan van Schijndel, Rinus Terlouw, Arie de Vroet, Piet van Overbeek, Faas Wilkes, Joep Brandes, Theo Timmermans, Abe Lenstra.   Manager: Karel Joseph Kaufman

FRANCE: René Vignal, Marcel Salva, Roger Marche, Antoine Cuissard, Robert Jonquet, Louis Hon, Roger Gabet, Albert Batteux, Jean Baratte, Jean Prouff, Pierre Flamion.   Manager: Gaston Barreau

Goals: Theo Timmermans (6, 10, 33), Faas Wilkes (58) / Jean Baratte (3)

178.   27.04.1949
SCOTLAND v FRANCE   2-0 (1-0)

Hampden Park, Glasgow

Referee: William (Bill) Ling (England)   Attendance: 125,683

SCOTLAND: James Cowan, George Young, Samuel Cox, Robert Evans, William Woodburn, George Aitken, William Waddell, William Thornton, William Houliston, William Steel, Lawrence Reilly.

FRANCE: René Vignal, Marcel Salva, Roger Marche, Robert Jonquet, Roger Mindonnet, Louis Hon, Roger Gabet, Antoine Cuissard, Jean Baratte, Albert Batteux, Pierre Flamion.   Manager: Gaston Barreau

Goals: William Steel (37, 80)

179.   22.05.1949
FRANCE v ENGLAND   1-3 (1-2)

Stade Olympique Yves-du-Manoir, Colombes

Referee: Karel Louis van der Meer (Netherlands)
Attendance: 61,308

FRANCE: René Vignal, André Grillon, Marcel Salva, Robert Jonquet, Roger Mindonnet, Louis Hon, Roger Gabet, Antoine Cuissard, Roger Quenolle, Albert Batteux, Georges Moreel.   Manager: Gaston Barreau

ENGLAND: Bert Williams, Billy Ellerington, Jack Aston, Billy Wright, Neil Franklin, Jimmy Dickinson, Tom Finney, Johnny Morris, Jack Rowley, Wilf Mannion, Jimmy Mullen. Manager: Walter Winterbottom

Goals: Georges Moreel (1) /
Johnny Morris (8, 86), Billy Wright (24)

180.   04.06.1949
FRANCE v SWITZERLAND   4-2 (2-0)

Stade Olympique Yves-du-Manoir, Colombes

Referee: George Reader (England)   Attendance: 33,474

FRANCE: René Vignal, André Grillon, Roger Mindonnet, Louis Hon, Henri Guérin, Jean Grégoire, Henri Baillot, Roger Vandooren, Jean Baratte, Albert Batteux, Jean Grumellon.   Manager: Gaston Barreau

SWITZERLAND: Fritz Jucker, Rudolf Gyger, André Neury, Olivier Eggimann, Roger Bocquet, Robert Ballaman, André Facchinetti, Jean Tamini, Lucien Pasteur (46 René Maillard), Bernard Lanz, Jacques Fatton.   Manager: Karl Rappan

Goals: Henri Baillot (26), Jean Grumellon (30), Jean Baratte (50, 84) / Jacques Fatton (73, 74 pen)

181. 19.06.1949
FRANCE v SPAIN 1-5 (0-3)

Stade Olympique Yves-du-Manoir, Colombes

Referee: Giacomo Bertolio (Italy)   Attendance: 52,217

FRANCE: René Vignal, André Grillon, Roger Mindonnet, Jean Grégoire, Henri Guérin, Louis Hon, Henri Baillot, Albert Batteux, Jean Baratte, Ernest Vaast, Jean Grumellon. Manager: Gaston Barreau

SPAIN: Ignacio "IÑAKI" EIZAGUIRRE Arregui, Vicente ASENSI Albentosa, Francisco ANTÚNEZ Espada, Diego LOZANO Rodríguez, Mariano GONZALVO Falcón (III), Antonio PUCHADES Casanova, Estanislao BASORA Brunet "El Pipo", VENANCIO Pérez García, Telmo Zarraonaindía Montoya "ZARRA", José Luis López PANIZO, Augustín "PIRU" GAÍNZA Vicandi. Manager: Guillermo EIZAGUIRRE Olmos

Goals: Jean Baratte (64 pen) / Estanislao BASORA Brunet "El Pipo" (15, 20, 26), Augustín "PIRU" GAÍNZA Vicandi (65, 84 pen)

182. 09.10.1949   FIFA World Cup Qualification – Group 3
YUGOSLAVIA v FRANCE 1-1 (1-0)

Stadion Jugoslovenska Narodna Armija, Beograd

Referee: Karel Louis van der Meer (Netherlands)
Attendance: 50,000

YUGOSLAVIA: Franjo Sostaric, Branko Stankovic, Ratko Colic, Zlatko Cajkovski, Miodrag Jovanovic, Lajos Jakovetic, Kiril Simonovski, Rajko Mitic, Marko Valok, Stjepan Bobek, Zeljko Cajkovski. Manager: Milorad Arsenijevic

FRANCE: Abderrahman Ibrir, André Frey, Louis Hon, Roger Marche, Jean Prouff, Roger Carré, Pierre Ranzoni, Roger Vandooren, Henri Baillot, Jean Baratte, Jean Grumellon. Manager: Gaston Barreau

Goals: Zeljko Cajkovski (36) / Henri Baillot (55)

183. 30.10.1949   FIFA World Cup Qualification – Group 3
FRANCE v YUGOSLAVIA 1-1 (1-1)

Stade Olympique Yves-du-Manoir, Colombes

Referee: Eugen Adolf Scherz (Switzerland)
Attendance: 53,569

FRANCE: Abderrahman Ibrir, André Frey, Louis Hon, Roger Marche, Jean Prouff, Jean Luciano, Roger Vandooren, André Strappe, Henri Baillot, Jean Baratte, Jean Grumellon. Manager: Gaston Barreau

YUGOSLAVIA: Franjo Sostaric, Ivica Horvat, Branko Stankovic, Zlatko Cajkovski, Miodrag Jovanovic, Predrag Djajic, Branislav Vukosavljevic, Stjepan Bobek, Milos Pajevic, Zeljko Cajkovski, Aleksandar Benko. Manager: Milorad Arsenijevic

Goals: Henri Baillot (8) / Stjepan Bobek (44)

184. 13.11.1949
FRANCE v CZECHOSLOVAKIA 1-0 (1-0)

Stade Olympique Yves-du-Manoir, Colombes

Referee: William H. (Bill) Evans (England)
Attendance: 38,946

FRANCE: Abderrahman Ibrir, Guy Huguet, Roger Marche, Antoine Cuissard, Louis Hon, Jean Luciano, Henri Baillot, Désiré Carré, Jean Baratte, André Strappe, Jean Lechantre. Manager: Gaston Barreau

CZECHOSLOVAKIA: Václav Pavlis, Vladimír Venglár, Jozef Marko (34 Michal Vican), Jirí Rubás, Oldrich Menclík, Michal Benedikovic, Václav Kokstejn, Emil Pazický, Viktor Tegelhoff, Vlastimil Preis, Gejza Simanský. Manager: Alexa Boksay

Goal: Jean Baratte (8 pen)

185. 11.12.1949   FIFA World Cup Qualification – Group 3
FRANCE v YUGOSLAVIA 2-3 (1-1, 2-2) (AET)

Stadio Comunale Artemio Franchi, Firenze (Italy)

Referee: Giovanni Galeati (Italy)   Attendance: 25,000

FRANCE: Abderrahman Ibrir, André Frey, Louis Hon, Roger Marche, Antoine Cuissard, Jean Luciano, Maik Walter, Jean Baratte, Roger Quenolle, Francis Méano, Jean Lechantre. Manager: Gaston Barreau

YUGOSLAVIA: Srdjan Mrkusic, Ivica Horvat, Ratko Colic, Zlatko Cajkovski, Miodrag Jovanovic, Predrag Djajic, Prvoslav Mihajlovic, Rajko Mitic, Vladimir Firm, Stjepan Bobek, Zeljko Cajkovski. Manager: Milorad Arsenijevic

Goals: Maik Walter (13), Jean Luciano (83) / Prvoslav Mihajlovic (12, 84 pen), Zeljko Cajkovski (114)

186. 27.05.1950
FRANCE v SCOTLAND 0-1 (0-0)

Stade Olympique Yves-du-Manoir, Colombes

Referee: Julián Alejandro Arqué Martín (Spain)
Attendance: 35,568

FRANCE: Abderrahman Ibrir, Guy Huguet, Roger Marche, Jean Grégoire, Roger Lamy, Antoine Cuissard, Henri Baillot, André Strappe, Jean Baratte, Jean Grumellon, Georges Dard. Manager: Gaston Barreau

SCOTLAND: James Cowan, George Young, Samuel Cox, John Miller McColl, William Woodburn, Alexander Forbes, Robert Campbell, Allan Brown, Lawrence Reilly, William Steel, William Liddell.

Goal: Allan Brown (69)

187. 04.06.1950
BELGIUM v FRANCE 4-1 (2-1)
Stade du Heysel, Brussels
Referee: Giuseppe Carpani (Italy)   Attendance: 45,006
BELGIUM: Henri Meert, Arsène Vaillant, Jan Van Der Auwera, Louis Carré, Victor Mees, Rik Coppens, Frédéric Chavès d'Aguilar, Joseph Mermans, Albert De Hert, Georges Mordant, Léopold Anoul.   Manager: William Joseph Gormlie
FRANCE: Paul Sinibaldi, André Frey, Roger Marche, Jean Luciano, Jean Swiatek, Jean Belver, Maik Walter, André Strappe, Édouard Kargu, Mustapha Ben M'Barek, Pierre Flamion.   Manager: Gaston Barreau
Goals: Joseph Mermans (6, 63, 83), Georges Mordant (9) / Édouard Kargu (19)

188. 01.11.1950
FRANCE v BELGIUM 3-3 (1-3)
Stade Olympique Yves-du-Manoir, Colombes
Referee: Arthur Edward Ellis (England)   Attendance: 48,788
FRANCE: Abderrahman Ibrir, Manuel Garriga, Roger Marche, Henri Arnaudeau, Roger Lamy, Roger Scotti, André Strappe, Édouard Kargu, Jean Baratte, Pierre Flamion, André Doye.   Manager: Gaston Barreau
BELGIUM: Henri Meert, Arsène Vaillant, Jan Van Der Auwera, Louis Carré, Victor Mees, Victor Lemberechts, Frédéric Chavès d'Aguilar, Joseph Mermans, Albert De Hert, Rik Coppens, Léopold Anoul.   Manager: William Joseph Gormlie
Goals: André Doye (18), J. Baratte (69), Édouard Kargu (87) / Victor Lemberechts (3), Joseph Mermans (17, 36)

189. 10.12.1950
FRANCE v NETHERLANDS 5-2 (3-2)
Stade Olympique Yves-du-Manoir, Colombes
Referee: Louis André Baert (Belgium)   Attendance: 37,468
FRANCE: René Vignal, Guy Huguet, Roger Marche, Pierre Ranzoni, Antoine Cuissard, Henri Arnaudeau, André Strappe, Édouard Kargu, Jean Baratte, Pierre Flamion, André Doye.   Manager: Gaston Barreau
NETHERLANDS: Piet Kraak, Aad de Jong, Henk Schijvenaar, Jan van Schijndel, Rinus Terlouw, Louis Biesbrouck, Frits de Graaf, Cock van der Tuyn, Noud van Melis, Dick Snoek, Mick Clavan.   Manager: Jaap van der Leck
Goals: Pierre Flamion (4, 47), Jean Baratte (29, 49), André Doye (41) / Noud van Melis (34), Cock van der Tuyn (42)

190. 06.02.1951
FRANCE v YUGOSLAVIA 2-1 (1-1)
Parc des Princes, Paris
Referee: Laurent Franken (Belgium)   Attendance: 33,532
FRANCE: Julien Darui, Guy Huguet, Roger Marche, Antoine Cuissard, Robert Jonquet, Henri Arnaudeau, André Strappe, Roger Vandooren, Édouard Kargu, Pierre Flamion, André Doye.   Manager: Gaston Barreau
YUGOSLAVIA: Vladimir Beara, Bozidar Kolakovic, Ratko Colic, Zlatko Cajkovski, Ivica Horvat, Predrag Djajic, Tihomir Ognjanov, Rajko Mitic, Kosta Tomasevic, Stjepan Bobek, Antun Herceg.   Manager: Milorad Arsenijevic
Goals: André Strappe (4), Pierre Flamion (62) / Kosta Tomasevic (14)

191. 12.05.1951
NORTHERN IRELAND v FRANCE 2-2 (1-2)
Windsor Park, Belfast
Referee: Arthur Edward Ellis (England)   Attendance: 24,000
NORTHERN IRELAND: Ted Hinton, Len Graham, Alf McMichael, Danny Blanchflower, Jackie Vernon, Ray Ferris, Billy Bingham, Kevin McGarry, Billy Simpson, Billy Dickson, Johnny McKenna.
FRANCE: Julien Darui, Guy Huguet, Roger Marche, Antoine Cuissard, Robert Jonquet, René Gallice, André Strappe, Antoine Bonifaci, Jean Baratte, Édouard Kargu, Edmond Haan.   Manager: Gaston Barreau
Goals: Ray Ferris (9 pen), Billy Simpson (62) / Jean Baratte (16), Antoine Bonifaci (28)

192. 16.05.1951
SCOTLAND v FRANCE 1-0 (0-0)
Hampden Park, Glasgow
Referee: Reginald Andrew (Reg) Mortimer (England)   Attendance: 75,394
SCOTLAND: James Cowan, George Young, Samuel Cox, James Scoular, William Woodburn, William Redpath, William Waddell, Robert Johnstone, Lawrence Reilly, William Steel, Robert Mitchell.
FRANCE: Stéphane Dakowski, Guy Huguet, Roger Marche, Antoine Bonifaci, Robert Jonquet, Antoine Cuissard, René Alpsteg, André Strappe, Jean Baratte, Édouard Kargu, Edmond Haan.   Manager: Gaston Barreau
Goal: Lawrence Reilly (78)

193. 03.06.1951
ITALY v FRANCE 4-1 (1-1)

Stadio Comunale Luigi Ferraris, Genova

Referee: Jean Lutz (Switzerland)   Attendance: 52,500

ITALY: Giuseppe Casari, Attilio Giovannini, Sergio Cervato, Carlo Annovazzi, Omero Tognon, Arcadio Venturi, Cesarino Cervellati, Giampiero Boniperti, Amedeo Amadei, Benito Lorenzi, Gino Cappello.

FRANCE: Stéphane Dakowski, Guy Huguet, Roger Marche, Antoine Cuissard, Robert Jonquet, Antoine Bonifaci, René Alpsteg, André Strappe, Jean Grumellon, Jean Baratte (13 Édouard Kargu), Edmond Haan.   Manager: Gaston Barreau

Goals: Benito Lorenzi (37, 56), Amedeo Amadei (67), Gino Cappello (87 pen) / Jean Grumellon (34)

194. 03.10.1951
ENGLAND v FRANCE 2-2 (2-2)

Highbury Stadium, London

Referee: John Alexander (Jack) Mowat (Scotland)   Attendance: 57,603

ENGLAND: Bert Williams, Alf Ramsey, Arthur Willis, Billy Wright, Allenby Chilton, Henry Cockburn, Tom Finney, Wilf Mannion, Jackie Milburn, Harold Hassall, Leslie Medley. Manager: Walter Winterbottom

FRANCE: René Vignal, André Grillon, Marcel Salva, Abdelkader Firoud, Robert Jonquet, Antoine Bonifaci, René Alpsteg, Jean Baratte, Jean Grumellon, Pierre Flamion, André Doye.   Manager: Gaston Barreau

Goals: Abdelkader Firoud (4 og), Leslie Medley (32) / André Doye (18), René Alpsteg (19)

195. 14.10.1951
SWITZERLAND v FRANCE 1-2 (0-2)

Stade des Charmilles, Geneva

Referee: Reginald James (Reg) Leafe (England)   Attendance: 33,534

SWITZERLAND: Eugenio Corrodi, André Neury, Roger Bocquet, Walter Fink, Olivier Eggimann, Willi Neukom, Robert Ballaman, René Maillard, Alfred Bickel, Lucien Pasteur, Jacques Fatton.

FRANCE: René Vignal, André Grillon, Marcel Salva, Abdelkader Firoud, Robert Jonquet, Antoine Bonifaci, René Alpsteg, Jean Baratte, André Strappe, André Doye, Jean Grumellon.   Manager: Gaston Barreau

Goals: Robert Ballaman (53) / André Doye (27), Jean Grumellon (34)

196. 01.11.1951
FRANCE v AUSTRIA 2-2 (2-2)

Stade Olympique Yves-du-Manoir, Colombes

Referee: William Ling (England)   Attendance: 61,687

FRANCE: René Vignal, André Grillon, Robert Jonquet, Marcel Salva, Pierre Flamion, Antoine Bonifaci, Abdelkader Firoud, René Alpsteg, Jean Baratte, Jean Grumellon, Thadée Cisowski (10 Marceau Stricanne).   Manager: Gaston Barreau

AUSTRIA: Walter Zeman, Rudolf Röckl, Ernst Happel, Gerhard Hanappi, Ernst Ocwirk, Walter Schleger, Ernst Melchior, Karl Decker (41 Erich Habitzl), Leopold Gernhardt, Ernst Stojaspal, Alfred Körner.   Manager: Walter Nausch

Goals: Jean Grumellon (3, 45) / Alfred Körner (12), Ernst Stojaspal (15)

197. 26.03.1952
FRANCE v SWEDEN 0-1 (0-0)

Parc des Princes, Paris

Referee: Henri Bauwens (Belgium)   Attendance: 35,779

FRANCE: René Vignal, Guy Huguet, Marcel Salva, Abdelkader Firoud, Robert Jonquet, Albert Dubreucq, René Alpsteg, Antoine Bonifaci, Jean Baratte, André Doye, Pierre Flamion.   Manager: Gaston Barreau

SWEDEN: Karl Oskar Svensson, Hans Malmström, Erik Nilsson, Olle Åhlund, Bengt Gustavsson, Gösta Lindh, Egon Jönsson, Karl Gösta Löfgren, Sven-Erik Westerberg, Arne Lundqvist, Gösta Sandberg.   Manager: George Raynor

Goal: Sven-Erik Westerberg (85)

198. 20.04.1952
FRANCE v PORTUGAL 3-0 (1-0)

Stade Olympique Yves-du-Manoir, Colombes

Referee: Alfred (Alf) Bond (England)   Attendance: 35,735

FRANCE: René Vignal, André Jacowski, Roger Marche, Abdelkader Firoud, Robert Jonquet, Antoine Bonifaci, Jean Grumellon (4 René Alpsteg), Jean Baratte, André Strappe, Roger Boury, Léon Deladerrière.   Manager: Gaston Barreau

PORTUGAL: Frederico BARRIGANA, SERAFIM Das NEVES, Ângelo Ferreira CARVALHO, JOAQUIM MACHADO (46 José Maria Carvalho PEDROTO), FÉLIX Assunção Antunes, Fernando Augusto Amaral CAIADO, António JESUS CORREIA, Manuel Soeiro VASQUES, Henrique De Sena BEN DAVID, JOSÉ António Barreto TRAVASSOS, ALBANO Narciso Pereira.
Manager: CÂNDIDO Fernandes Plácido DE OLIVEIRA

Goals: René Alpsteg (15), André Strappe (68, 89)

199. 22.05.1952

BELGIUM v FRANCE 1-2 (1-2)

Stade du Heysel, Brussels

Referee: Paul von Wartburg (Switzerland)
Attendance: 55,485

BELGIUM: Henri Meert, William Saeren, Martin Schroyens, Robert Van Kerkhoven, Louis Carré, Robert Maertens, Joseph Mermans, Léopold Anoul, Rik Coppens, Joseph Givard, José Moës.   Manager: William Joseph Gormlie

FRANCE: René Vignal, André Jacowski, Roger Marche, Abdelkader Firoud, Robert Jonquet, Ferenc Koczur "Ferry", Léon Deladerrière, Jean Baratte, André Strappe, André Doye, Abdelaziz Ben-Tifour.   Manager: Gaston Barreau

Goals: Joseph Mermans (28) /
André Doye (22), Léon Deladerrière (24)

200. 05.10.1952

FRANCE v WEST GERMANY 3-1 (1-1)

Stade Olympique Yves-du-Manoir, Colombes

Referee: William H. (Bill) Evans (England)
Attendance: 56,021

FRANCE: César Ruminski, Lazare Gianessi, Roger Marche, Antoine Bonifaci, Robert Jonquet, Joseph Ujlaki, André Strappe, Raymond Kopa, Thadée Cisowski, Léon Deladerrière, Armand Penverne.   Manager: Gaston Barreau

WEST GERMANY: Toni Turek, Erich Retter, Kurt Borkenhagen, Jupp Posipal, Werner Liebrich, Erich Schanko, Helmut Rahn, Clemens Wientjes, Ottmar Walter (31' Georg Stollenwerk), Bernhard Termath, Fritz Walter.   Manager: Sepp Herberger

Goals: Joseph Ujlaki (4), Thadée Cisowski (81), André Strappe (90) / Ottmar Walter (16)

201. 19.10.1952

AUSTRIA v FRANCE 1-2 (0-2)

Praterstadion, Vienna

Referee: Arthur Edward Ellis (England)   Attendance: 63,000

AUSTRIA: Walter Zeman, Rudolf Röckl, Ernst Happel, Gerhard Hanappi, Karl Koller, Theodor Brinek Jr., Ernst Melchior, Otto Walzhofer, Robert Dienst, Ernst Ocwirk, Alfred Körner.   Manager: Walter Nausch

FRANCE: César Ruminski, Lazare Gianessi, Roger Marche, Antoine Bonifaci, Robert Jonquet, Armand Penverne, Raymond Kopa, Jean Baratte, Thadée Cisowski, André Strappe, Francis Méano.   Manager: Gaston Barreau

Goals: Otto Walzhofer (47 pen) /
Jean Baratte (10), Armand Penverne (26)

202. 11.11.1952

FRANCE v NORTHERN IRELAND 3-1 (2-1)

Stade Olympique Yves-du-Manoir, Colombes

Referee: Klaas Schipper (Netherlands)   Attendance: 52,399

FRANCE: César Ruminski, Lazare Gianessi, Roger Marche, Antoine Bonifaci (32 Jean Baratte), Thadée Cisowski, Armand Penverne, Joseph Ujlaki, André Strappe, Robert Jonquet, Stanislas Curyl, Raymond Kopa.   Manager: Gaston Barreau

NORTHERN IRELAND: Norman Uprichard, Len Graham, Alf McMichael, Danny Blanchflower, Billy Dickson, Frank McCourt, Billy Bingham, Jimmy D'Arcy, Eddie McMorran, Bertie Peacock, Charlie Tully.   Manager: Peter Doherty

Goals: Joseph Ujlaki (30), Raymond Kopa (36, 89) /
Charlie Tully (42)

203. 16.11.1952

REPUBLIC OF IRELAND v FRANCE 1-1 (1-0)

Dalymount Park, Dublin

Referee: Albert Alsteen (Belgium)   Attendance: 40,000

REPUBLIC OF IRELAND: James O'Neill, Seamus Dunne, Thomas Aherne, Peter Farrell, Johnny Carey, Sean Cusack, Johnny Gavin, Arthur Fitzsimons, Sean Fallon, Reg Ryan, Tommy Eglington.   Manager: Dugald (Doug) Livingstone

FRANCE: César Ruminski, Lazare Gianessi, Roger Marche, Ferenc Koczur "Ferry", Robert Jonquet, Armand Penverne, Raymond Kopa, Joseph Ujlaki, André Strappe, Roger Piantoni, Stanislas Curyl.   Manager: Gaston Barreau

Goals: Robert Jonquet (19 og) / Roger Piantoni (67)

204. 25.12.1952

FRANCE v BELGIUM 0-1 (0-1)

Stade Olympique Yves-du-Manoir, Colombes

Referee: William H. (Bill) Evans (England)
Attendance: 38,379

FRANCE: César Ruminski, Lazare Gianessi, Roger Marche, Ferenc Koczur "Ferry", Robert Jonquet, Armand Penverne, Joseph Ujlaki, André Strappe, Raymond Kopa, Roger Piantoni, Léon Deladerrière.   Manager: Gaston Barreau

BELGIUM: Armand Seghers, Henri Dirickx, Alfons Van Brandt, Jan Van Der Auwera, Louis Carré, Jean Mathonet, Rik Coppens, Léopold Anoul, Joseph Mermans, Jean Straetmans, Augustin Janssens.   Manager: William Joseph Gormlie

Goal: Jean Straetmans (6)

205. 14.05.1953
FRANCE v WALES 6-1 (4-1)

Stade Olympique Yves-du-Manoir, Colombes

Referee: José Vieira da Costa (Portugal)   Attendance: 33,020

FRANCE: César Ruminski, Lazare Gianessi, Roger Marche, Antoine Bonifaci, Robert Jonquet, Jean-Jacques Marcel, Joseph Ujlaki, Raymond Kopa, Édouard Kargu, Roger Piantoni, René Gardien.   Manager: Gaston Barreau

WALES: Bill Shortt, Derrick Sullivan, Alf Sherwood, Roy Paul, Ray Daniel, Ron Burgess, Terry Medwin, John Charles, Trevor Ford, Ivor Allchurch, Billy Foulkes.

Goals: René Gardien (10, 33), Raymond Kopa (14, 37), Antoine Bonifaci (73), Joseph Ujlaki (88) / Ivor Allchurch (2)

206. 11.06.1953
SWEDEN v FRANCE 1-0 (1-0)

Råsunda Fotbollstadion, Solna

Referee: Edvin Pedersen (Norway)   Attendance: 35,712

SWEDEN: Karl Oskar Svensson, Lennart Samuelsson, Orvar Bergmark, Sven-Ove Svensson, Sven Hjertsson, Lars Eriksson, Henry Thillberg, Nils-Åke Sandell, Karl Gösta Löfgren, Gösta Sandberg, Gösta Lindh.   Manager: George Raynor

FRANCE: François Remetter, Lazare Gianessi, Roger Marche, Jean-Jacques Marcel, Robert Jonquet, Armand Penverne, Joseph Ujlaki, Édouard Kargu, Raymond Kopa, André Strappe, René Gardien.   Manager: Gaston Barreau

Goal: Nils-Åke Sandell (15)

207. 20.09.1953   FIFA World Cup Qualification – Group 4
LUXEMBOURG v FRANCE 1-6 (1-4)

Stade Municipal, Luxembourg City

Referee: Ernst Dörflinger (Switzerland)   Attendance: 3,000

LUXEMBOURG: Ferdy Lahure, Camille Wagner, Jos Hansen, Jean-Pierre Mertl, Léon Spartz, Michel Reuter, François Muller, Henri Fickinger, Antoine (Spitz) Kohn, Roger Weydert, Paul Kemp.   Manager: Béla Volentik

FRANCE: René Vignal (8 François Remetter), Lazare Gianessi, Robert Jonquet, Roger Marche, Armand Penverne, Raymond Cicci, Léon Glovacki, Pierre Flamion, Raymond Kopa, Édouard Kargu, Roger Piantoni.   Manager: Gaston Barreau

Goals: Antoine (Spitz) Kohn (6) / Roger Piantoni (5), Raymond Kopa (10), Raymond Cicci (41), Léon Glovacki (42), Édouard Kargu (73), Pierre Flamion (88)

208. 04.10.1953   FIFA World Cup Qualification – Group 4
REPUBLIC OF IRELAND v FRANCE 3-5 (0-2)

Dalymount Park, Dublin

Referee: Laurent Franken (Belgium)   Attendance: 45,000

REPUBLIC OF IRELAND: James O'Neill, Seamus Dunne, Thomas Aherne, Peter Farrell, Frank O'Farrell, Tommy Moroney, Con Martin, Reg Ryan, Arthur Fitzsimons, Davy Walsh, Tommy Eglington.
Manager: Alexander Ernest Stevenson

FRANCE: René Vignal, Lazare Gianessi, Robert Jonquet, Roger Marche, Armand Penverne, Jean-Jacques Marcel, Léon Glovacki, Pierre Flamion, Joseph Ujlaki, Raymond Kopa, Roger Piantoni.   Manager: Gaston Barreau

Goals: Reg Ryan (58), Davy Walsh (83), Frank O'Farrell (88) / Léon Glovacki (23), A. Penverne (40), Joseph Ujlaki (50, 69), Pierre Flamion (72)

209. 18.10.1953
YUGOSLAVIA v FRANCE 3-1 (0-1)

Stadion Maksimir, Zagreb

Referee: Carl Erich Steiner (Austria)   Attendance: 40,000

YUGOSLAVIA: Vladimir Beara, Branko Stankovic, Tomislav Crnkovic, Zlatko Cajkovski, Ljubisa Spajic, Vujadin Boskov, Zdravko Rajkov, Todor Veselinovic, Milos Milutinovic (40 Dionizije Dvornic), Bernard Vukas, Branko Zebec.   Manager: Milorad Arsenijevic

FRANCE: René Vignal, René Pleimelding, Roger Marche, Armand Penverne, Robert Jonquet, Jean-Jacques Marcel, Joseph Ujlaki, Léon Glovacki, Raymond Kopa, Pierre Flamion, Roger Piantoni.   Manager: Gaston Barreau

Goals: Todor Veselinovic (47), Zdravko Rajkov (55), Dionizije Dvornic (62) / Jean-Jacques Marcel (44)

210. 11.11.1953
FRANCE v SWITZERLAND 2-4 (1-4)

Stade Olympique Yves-du-Manoir, Colombes

Referee: Arthur Edward Ellis (England)   Attendance: 45,986

FRANCE: René Vignal (22 François Remetter), Lazare Gianessi, Robert Jonquet, Roger Marche, Armand Penverne, Jean-Jacques Marcel, Joseph Ujlaki, Édouard Kargu, Raymond Kopa, Pierre Flamion, Edmond Haan.
Manager: Gaston Barreau

SWITZERLAND: Georges Stuber, André Neury, Roger Bocquet, Willi Kernen, Olivier Eggimann, Charles Casali, Charles Antenen, Roger Vonlanthen, Eugen Meier, Robert Ballaman, Jacques Fatton.   Manager: Karl Rappan

Goals: Joseph Ujlaki (2, 62) / Charles Antenen (9, 16, 36), Jacques Fatton (21)

211. 25.11.1953   FIFA World Cup Qualification – Group 4
FRANCE v REPUBLIC OF IRELAND 1-0 (0-0)
Parc des Princes, Paris

Referee: Lucien (Luc) Van Nuffel (Belgium)
Attendance: 32,265

FRANCE: François Remetter, Ahmed Mihoubi, Lazare Gianessi, Roger Marche, Antoine Cuissard, Jean-Jacques Marcel, André Strappe, Roger Piantoni, Joseph Ujlaki, Abdesselem Ben Mohammed, Léon Deladerrière.   Manager: Gaston Barreau

REPUBLIC OF IRELAND: James O'Neill, Tommy Clinton, Con Martin, Robin Lawler, Eddie Gannon, Peter Farrell, Reg Ryan, Arthur Fitzsimons, Alf Ringstead, Davy Walsh, Tommy Eglington.   Manager: Alexander Ernest Stevenson

Goal: Roger Piantoni (73)

212. 17.12.1953   FIFA World Cup Qualification – Group 4
FRANCE v LUXEMBOURG 8-0 (4-0)
Parc des Princes, Paris

Referee: François Roeykens (Belgium)   Attendance: 20,146

FRANCE: Jean-Pierre Kress, Antoine Pazur, Marius Bruat, Robert Lemaître, Guillaume Bieganski, Abderrahmane Mahjoub, Jean Desgranges, Just Fontaine, Jacques Foix, Célestin Oliver, Jean Vincent.   Manager: Gaston Barreau

LUXEMBOURG: Paul Steffen, Jacques Speck, Camille Wagner, Léon Spartz, Michel Reuter, Nicolas May, Jules Meurisse, Henri Fickinger, Antoine (Spitz) Kohn, Roger Weydert, Paul Kemp.   Manager: Béla Volentik

Goals: Jean Desgranges (2, 88), Jean Vincent (6, 10), Just Fontaine (21, 75, 80), Jacques Foix (57)

213. 11.04.1954
FRANCE v ITALY 1-3 (1-2)
Stade Olympique Yves-du-Manoir, Colombes

Referee: Arthur Edward Ellis (England)   Attendance: 61,382

FRANCE: René Vignal, Lazare Gianessi, Roger Marche, Jean-Jacques Marcel, Robert Jonquet, Armand Penverne, Raymond Kopa, Joseph Ujlaki, Thadée Cisowski, Roger Piantoni, Léon Deladerrière.   Manager: Gaston Barreau

ITALY: Giorgio Ghezzi, Guido Vincenzi, Giovanni Giacomazzi, Maino Neri, Omero Tognon, Fulvio Nesti, Giampiero Boniperti, Egisto Pandolfini, Carlo Galli, Gino Cappello, Amleto Frignani.   Manager: Silvio Piola

Goals: Roger Piantoni (26) /
Egisto Pandolfini (29), Carlo Galli (35, 50)

214. 30.05.1954
BELGIUM v FRANCE 3-3 (3-2)
Stade du Heysel, Brussels

Referee: Vasilije (Vasa) Stefanovic (Yugoslavia)   Att: 54,729

BELGIUM: Leopold Gernaey, Marcel Dries, Alfons Van Brandt, Constant Huysmans, Louis Carré, Victor Mees, Jean Van Steen, Léopold Anoul, Rik Coppens, Marcel De Corte, Joseph Mermans.   Manager: Dugald (Doug) Livingstone

FRANCE: César Ruminski, Daniel Carpentier, Robert Lemaître, Jean-Jacques Marcel, Antoine Cuissard, Abderrahmane Mahjoub, Raymond Kopa, René Dereuddre, André Strappe, Michel Leblond, Jean Vincent.   Manager: Gaston Barreau

Goals: Joseph Mermans (2), Léopold Anoul (5, 8) /
Jean Vincent (7), C. Huysmans (39 og), Raymond Kopa (70)

215. 16.06.1954   FIFA World Cup Final Tournament – Group 1
YUGOSLAVIA v FRANCE 1-0 (1-0)
Stade Olympique de La Pontaise, Lausanne (Switzerland)

Referee: Benjamin Mervyn (Sandy) Griffiths (Wales)
Attendance: 16,000

YUGOSLAVIA: Vladimir Beara, Branko Stankovic, Tomislav Crnkovic, Zlatko Cajkovski, Ivica Horvat, Vujadin Boskov, Milos Milutinovic, Stjepan Bobek, Rajko Mitic, Bernard Vukas, Branko Zebec.

FRANCE: François Remetter, Lazare Gianessi, Robert Jonquet, Raymond Kaelbel, Armand Penverne, Jean-Jacques Marcel, Léon Glovacki, René Dereuddre, Raymond Kopa, André Strappe, Jean Vincent.   Manager: Pierre Pibarot

Goal: Milos Milutinovic (14)

216. 19.06.1954   FIFA World Cup Final Tournament – Group 1
FRANCE v MEXICO 3-2 (1-0)
Stade des Charmilles, Geneva (Switzerland)

Referee: Manuel Asensi Martín (Spain)   Attendance: 19,000

FRANCE: François Remetter, Lazare Gianessi, Raymond Kaelbel, Roger Marche, Jean-Jacques Marcel, Abderrahmane Mahjoub, René Dereuddre, Abdelaziz Ben-Tifour, Raymond Kopa, André Strappe, Jean Vincent.   Manager: Pierre Pibarot

MEXICO: Antonio Félix CARBAJAL Rodríguez, Narciso LÓPEZ Rodríguez, Jorge ROMO Fuentes, Saturnino Paulo MARTINEZ Alvarez, Raúl CÁRDENAS de la Vega, Rafael ÁVALOS Rivas, Juan Alfredo TORRES González, José Alberto NARANJO Rivera, José Luis LAMADRID Cano, Tomás BALCÁZAR González, Raúl ARELLANO Vásquez.   Manager: Antonio LÓPEZ Herranz

Goals: Jean Vincent (19), Raúl CÁRDENAS de la Vega (49og), Raymond Kopa (88 pen) / José Luis LAMADRID Cano (54), Tomás BALCÁZAR González (85)

217. 16.10.1954
WEST GERMANY v FRANCE 1-3 (0-2)

Niedersachsenstadion, Hannover

Referee: Benjamin Mervyn (Sandy) Griffiths (Wales)
Attendance: 86,000

WEST GERMANY: Toni Turek, Herbert Erhardt, Werner Kohlmeyer, Jupp Posipal, Werner Liebrich, Karl Mai, Berni Klodt, Klaus Stürmer, Ottmar Walter, Franz Islacker, Bernhard Termath (22 Uwe Seeler).   Manager: Sepp Herberger

FRANCE: François Remetter, Raymond Kaelbel, Robert Jonquet, Roger Marche, Abderrahmane Mahjoub, Xercès Louis, René Dereuddre, Haj Abdelkader Larbi Ben M'barek (27 Jacques Foix), Pierre Grillet, Raymond Kopa, Jean Vincent.   Manager: Gaston Barreau

Goals: Klaus Stürmer (75) /
Jacques Foix (33, 55), Jean Vincent (36)

218. 11.11.1954
FRANCE v BELGIUM 2-2 (0-1)

Stade Olympique Yves-du-Manoir, Colombes

Referee: Rafael Tamarit Falaguera (Spain)
Attendance: 53,674

FRANCE: François Remetter, Raymond Kaelbel, Roger Marche, Abderrahmane Mahjoub, Robert Jonquet, Xercès Louis, Pierre Grillet, René Dereuddre, Raymond Kopa, Jacques Foix, Jean Vincent.   Manager: Gaston Barreau

BELGIUM: Henri Meert, Marcel Dries, Alfons Van Brandt, Constant Huysmans, Louis Carré, Victor Mees, Victor Lemberechts, Jules Quoilin, Rik Coppens, José Moës, Joseph Mermans.   Manager: Dugald (Doug) Livingstone

Goals: Raymond Kopa (75, 87 pen) /
Robert Jonquet (5 og), Victor Lemberechts (67)

219. 17.03.1955
SPAIN v FRANCE 1-2 (1-1)

Estadio Santiago Bernabéu, Madrid

Referee: Vincenzo Orlandini (Italy)   Attendance: 125,000

SPAIN: Antoni RAMALLETS Simón, Joan SEGARRA Iracheta, Marcos Alonso Imaz "MARQUITOS", Rafael LESMES Bobed (II), Miguel MUÑOZ Mozún, Andrés BOSCH Pujol, Estanislao BASORA Brunet, Luis MOLOWNY Arbelo (40 José Luis ARTETXE Muguire), Eneko ARIETA-Araunabeña Piedra (I), José Héctor RIAL Laguía, Augustín "PIRU" GAÍNZA Vicandi.   Manager: Ramón MELCÓN Bartolomé

FRANCE: François Remetter, Guillaume Bieganski, Roger Marche, Armand Penverne, Robert Jonquet, Xercès Louis, Raymond Kopa, Léon Glovacki, René Bliard, Abderrahmane Mahjoub, Jean Vincent.   Manager: Albert Batteux

Goals: Augustín "PIRU" GAÍNZA Vicandi (11) /
Raymond Kopa (35), Jean Vincent (73)

220. 03.04.1955
FRANCE v SWEDEN 2-0 (1-0)

Stade Olympique Yves-du-Manoir, Colombes

Referee: Giorgio Bernardi (Italy)   Attendance: 34,738

FRANCE: François Remetter, Guillaume Bieganski, Roger Marche, Armand Penverne, Robert Jonquet, Xercès Louis, Maryan Wisniewski, Léon Glovacki, Célestin Oliver, Roger Piantoni, Jean Vincent.   Manager: Albert Batteux

SWEDEN: Karl Oskar Svensson, Nils Håkansson, Orvar Bergmark, Sven-Ove Svensson, Bengt Gustavsson, Sigvard Parling, Kurt Hamrin, Henry Thillberg, John Eriksson, Karl Gösta Löfgren, Gösta Sandberg.   Manager: Rudolf Kock

Goals: Célestin Oliver (36), Léon Glovacki (56)

221. 15.05.1955
FRANCE v ENGLAND 1-0 (1-0)

Stade Olympique Yves-du-Manoir, Colombes

Referee: Emil Karl Schmetzer (West Germany)
Attendance: 54,696

FRANCE: François Remetter, Guillaume Bieganski, Roger Marche, Armand Penverne, Robert Jonquet, Xercès Louis, Joseph Ujlaki, Léon Glovacki, Raymond Kopa, René Bliard, Jean Vincent.   Manager: Albert Batteux

ENGLAND: Bert Williams, Peter Sillett, Roger Byrne, Ron Flowers, Billy Wright, Duncan Edwards, Stanley Matthews, Don Revie, Nat Lofthouse, Dennis Wilshaw, Frank Blunstone.   Manager: Walter Winterbottom

Goal: Raymond Kopa (37 pen)

222. 09.10.1955
SWITZERLAND v FRANCE 1-2 (0-1)

St. Jakob Stadion, Basel

Referee: François Roeykens (Belgium)   Attendance: 54,000

SWITZERLAND: Antonio Permunian, Gilbert Dutoît, Hannes Schmidhauser, Willi Kernen, Marcel Vonlanden, Peter Rösch, Charles Antenen, Eugen Meier, Roger Vonlanthen, Robert Ballaman, Marcel Mauron.

FRANCE: François Remetter, Simon Zimny, Robert Jonquet, Roger Marche, Jean-Jacques Marcel, Abderrahmane Mahjoub, Joseph Ujlaki, Léon Glovacki, Raymond Kopa, Roger Piantoni, Jean Vincent.   Manager: Albert Batteux

Goals: Marcel Mauron (87) /
Raymond Kopa (24 pen), Roger Piantoni (69)

223.   23.10.1955
SOVIET UNION v FRANCE   2-2 (1-1)
Dynamo Stadium, Moscow
Referee: Arthur Edward Ellis (England)   Attendance: 54,000
SOVIET UNION: Boris Razinskiy, Anatoliy Porkhunov, Anatoli Maslyonkin, Mikhail Ogonkov, Yozhef Betsa, Igor Netto, Vladimir Shabrov (50 Boris Tatushin), Eduard Streltsov, Nikita Simonyan, Sergey Salnikov, Anatoliy Ilyin.   Manager: Gavriil Kachalin
FRANCE: François Remetter, Xercés Louis, Robert Jonquet, Roger Marche, Armand Penverne, Jean-Jacques Marcel, Jacques Foix, Léon Glovacki, Raymond Kopa, Roger Piantoni, Jean Vincent (31 René Bliard).   Manager: Albert Batteux
Goals: Eduard Streltsov (43), Nikita Simonyan (46) / Raymond Kopa (29), Roger Piantoni (64)

224.   11.11.1955
FRANCE v YUGOSLAVIA   1-1 (0-1)
Stade Olympique Yves-du-Manoir, Colombes
Referee: Vincenzo Orlandini (Italy)   Attendance: 60,654
FRANCE: François Remetter, Xercés Louis, Roger Marche, Armand Penverne, Robert Jonquet, Jean-Jacques Marcel, Jacques Foix, Léon Glovacki, Raymond Kopa, Roger Piantoni, Abdelaziz Ben-Tifour.   Manager: Albert Batteux
YUGOSLAVIA: Vladimir Beara, Tomislav Crnkovic, Miljan Zekovic, Milan Ljubenovic, Ivica Horvat, Vujadin Boskov, Zdravko Rajkov, Milos Milutinovic, Bernard Vukas, Branko Zebec, Todor Veselinovic.   Manager: Aleksandar Tirnanic
Goals: Roger Piantoni (88) / Todor Veselinovic (25)

225.   25.12.1955
BELGIUM v FRANCE   2-1 (1-0)
Stade du Heysel, Brussels
Referee: Johan (Jan) Bronkhorst (Netherlands)
Attendance: 56,540
BELGIUM: Alfons Dresen, Marcel Dries, Alfons Van Brandt, Constant Huysmans, Louis Carré, Victor Mees, Jef Jurion, Hippolyte van den Bosch, Joseph Mermans, Jean Mathonet, Jean Jadot.   Manager: André Vandeweyer
FRANCE: François Remetter, Xercés Louis, Roger Marche, Armand Penverne, Robert Jonquet, Jean-Jacques Marcel (11 Joseph Telléchéa), Joseph Ujlaki, Léon Glovacki, Raymond Kopa, Roger Piantoni, René Bliard.   Manager: Albert Batteux
Goals: Jean Jadot (43), Hippolyte van den Bosch (76) / Roger Piantoni (63)

226.   15.02.1956
ITALY v FRANCE   2-0 (0-0)
Stadio Comunale Bologna, Bologna
Referee: Leo Lemesic (Yugoslavia)   Attendance: 45,000
ITALY: Giovanni Viola, Ardico Magnini, Sergio Cervato, Giuseppe Chiappella, Francesco Rosetta, Armando Segato, Giampiero Boniperti, Guido Gratton, Giuseppe Virgili, Miguel Montuori, Riccardo Carapellese.   Manager: Alfredo Foni
FRANCE: François Remetter, Xercès Louis, Roger Marche, Armand Penverne, Robert Jonquet, Jean-Jacques Marcel, Jacques Foix, Roger Piantoni, Raymond Kopa, Michel Leblond, René Bliard.   Manager: Albert Batteux
Goals: Riccardo Carapellese (51), Guido Gratton (75)

227.   25.03.1956
FRANCE v AUSTRIA   3-1 (2-0)
Stade Olympique Yves-du-Manoir, Colombes
Referee: Arthur Edward Ellis (England)   Attendance: 42,223
FRANCE: François Remetter, Raymond Kaelbel, Roger Marche, Xercés Louis, Robert Jonquet, Jean-Jacques Marcel, Jean Hédiart, Roger Piantoni, Jacques Foix (29 Léon Deladerrière), Michel Leblond, Jean Vincent.   Manager: Albert Batteux
AUSTRIA: Kurt Schmied, Paul Halla, Franz Swoboda, Ernst Ocwirk, Karl Stotz, Karl Koller, Paul Kozlicek, Theodor Wagner (28 Ernst Kozlicek), Hans Buzek, Gerhard Hanappi, Herbert Grohs.   Managers: Karl Geyer & Josef Molzer
Goals: Michel Leblond (15), Jean Vincent (30), Roger Piantoni (68) / Gerhard Hanappi (49)

228.   07.10.1956
FRANCE v HUNGARY   1-2 (0-0)
Stade Olympique Yves-du-Manoir, Colombes
Referee: Cesare Jonni (Italy)   Attendance: 59,457
FRANCE: François Remetter, Raymond Kaelbel, Roger Marche, Roger Scotti, Robert Jonquet, Jean-Jacques Marcel, Pierre Grillet, Thadée Cisowski, Just Fontaine, Roger Piantoni, Jean Vincent.   Manager: Albert Batteux
HUNGARY: Gyula Grosics, Béla Kárpáti, János Börzsei, Antal Kotász, József Bozsik, Pál Berendi, Károly Sándor, Sándor Kocsis, Nándor Hidegkuti (42 Ferenc Machos), Ferenc Puskás, Zoltán Czibor.   Manager: Márton Bukovi
Goals: Thadée Cisowski (51) /
Ferenc Machos (49), Sándor Kocsis (86)

229. 21.10.1956
FRANCE v SOVIET UNION 2-1 (0-0)

Stade Olympique Yves-du-Manoir, Colombes

Referee: Benjamin Mervyn (Sandy) Griffiths (Wales)
Attendance: 62,145

FRANCE: François Remetter, Raymond Kaelbel, Robert Jonquet, Roger Marche (32 Joseph Tellechéa), Xercès Louis, Jean-Jacques Marcel, Pierre Grillet, Rachid Mekhloufi, Thadée Cisowski, Roger Piantoni, Jean Vincent.
Manager: Albert Batteux

SOVIET UNION: Lev Yashin, Nikolay Tishchenko, Anatoliy Bashashkin, Mikhail Ogonkov, Aleksey Paramonov, Igor Netto, Boris Tatushin, Anatoliy Isaev, Eduard Streltsov, Sergey Salnikov, Vladimir Ryzhkin.   Manager: Gavriil Kachalin

Goals: Joseph Tellechéa (46), Jean Vincent (54) / Anatoliy Isaev (64)

230. 11.11.1956 FIFA World Cup Qualification – Group 2
FRANCE v BELGIUM 6-3 (4-1)

Stade Olympique Yves-du-Manoir, Colombes

Referee: John Holdon (Jack) Clough (England)   Att: 46,049

FRANCE: François Remetter, Raymond Kaelbel, Roger Marche, Xercès Louis, Robert Jonquet, Jean-Jacques Marcel, Maryan Wisniewski, Rachid Mekhloufi, Thadée Cisowski, Roger Piantoni, Jean Vincent.   Manager: Albert Batteux

BELGIUM: Alfons Dresen, Henri Dirickx, Alfons Van Brandt, Victor Mees, Robert Van Kerkhoven, André Van Herpe, Jef Jurion, René Vanderwilt, Maurice Willems, Denis Houf, Richard Orlans.   Manager: André Vandeweyer

Goals: Thadée Cisowski (13, 15, 44, 72, 88), Jean Vincent (18) / Denis Houf (16), Maurice Willems (61, 67)

231. 24.03.1957
PORTUGAL v FRANCE 0-1 (0-0)

Estádio Nacional do Jamor, Oeiras

Referee: Manuel Asensi Martín (Spain)   Attendance: 42,000

PORTUGAL: CARLOS António do Carmo Costa GOMES, VIRGÍLIO Marques MENDES, ÂNGELO Gaspar MARTINS Pereira, JOSÉ MARIA Carvalho PEDROTO, Manuel PASSOS Fernandes, EMÍDIO Da Silva GRAÇA, HERNÂNI Ferreira da Silva, Manuel Soeiro VASQUES, JOSÉ Pinto de Carvalho Santos ÁGUAS, SALVADOR Félix Martins, Domiciano Barrocal Gomes CAVÉM.
Manager: João Joaquim TAVARES DA SILVA

FRANCE: François Remetter, Raymond Kaelbel, Roger Marche, Armand Penverne, Robert Jonquet, Jean-Jacques Marcel, Maryan Wisniewski, Rachid Mekhloufi, Thadée Cisowski, Roger Piantoni, Jean Vincent.
Manager: Albert Batteux

Goal: Roger Piantoni (55)

232. 02.06.1957 FIFA World Cup Qualification – Group 2
FRANCE v ICELAND 8-0 (5-0)

Stade Malakoff, Nantes

Referee: Arthur Edward Ellis (England)   Attendance: 15,080

FRANCE: François Remetter, Raymond Kaelbel, Roger Marche, Armand Penverne, Robert Jonquet, Jean-Jacques Marcel, Saïd Brahimi, René Dereuddre, Célestin Oliver, Roger Piantoni, Jean Vincent.   Manager: Albert Batteux

ICELAND: Helgi Daníelsson, Ólafur Gíslason, Kristinn Gunnlaugsson, Sveinn Teitsson, Halldór Halldórsson, Gudjón Finnbogason, Dagbjartur Grímsson, Ríkhardur Jónsson, Thórdur Thórdarson, Gunnar Gudmannsson, Thórdur Jónsson.   Manager: Alex Wier

Goals: Célestin Oliver (6, 11), Jean Vincent (29, 83), René Dereuddre (36), R. Piantoni (45, 81), Saïd Brahimi (49)

233. 01.09.1957 FIFA World Cup Qualification – Group 2
ICELAND v FRANCE 1-5 (0-2)

Laugardalsvöllur, Reykjavík

Referee: Robert Holly (Bobby) Davidson (Scotland)
Attendance: 8,000

ICELAND: Helgi Daníelsson, Árni Njálsson, Kristinn Gunnlaugsson, Reynir Karlsson, Halldór Halldórsson, Gudjón Finnbogason, Halldór Sigurbjörnsson, Ríkhardur Jónsson, Thórdur Thórdarson, Gunnar Gunnarsson, Thórdur Jónsson.
Manager: Alex Wier

FRANCE: Dominique Colonna, Raymond Kaelbel, Richard Boucher, Armand Penverne, Robert Jonquet, Jean-Jacques Marcel, Maryan Wisniewski, Joseph Ujlaki, Thadée Cisowski, Roger Piantoni, René Bliard.   Manager: Albert Batteux

Goals: Thórdur Jónsson (64) / Thadée Cisowski (29, 32), Joseph Ujlaki (48, 66), Maryan Wisniewski (53)

234. 06.10.1957
HUNGARY v FRANCE 2-0 (1-0)

Népstadion, Budapest

Referee: Leopold Sylvain (Leo) Horn (Netherlands)
Attendance: 94,000

HUNGARY: Gyula Grosics, Sándor Mátrai, Ferenc Sipos, Jenö Dálnoki, József Bozsik, Ferenc Szojka, Károly Sándor, Ferenc Machos, Nándor Hidegkuti, Gusztáv Aspirány, Máté Fenyvesi.

FRANCE: Dominique Colonna, Raymond Kaelbel, André Lerond, Armand Penverne, Mustapha Zitouni, Pierre Cahuzac, Maryan Wisniewski, Joseph Ujlaki, Just Fontaine, Roger Piantoni, Abdelaziz Ben-Tifour.   Manager: Albert Batteux

Goals: Gusztáv Aspirány (45, 66)

235.   27.10.1957   FIFA World Cup Qualification – Group 2
BELGIUM v FRANCE   0-0
Stade du Heysel, Brussels

Referee: Leo Alfred Helge (Denmark)   Attendance: 56,497

BELGIUM: Louis Leysen, Marcel Dries, Alfons Van Brandt, Victor Mees, Jan Nelissen, Jean Mathonet, André Piters, Joseph Givard, Michel Delire, Paul Van Den Berg, Richard Orlans.   Manager: Géza Toldi

FRANCE: Claude Abbès, Raymond Kaelbel, André Lerond, Armand Penverne, Mustapha Zitouni, Célestin Oliver, Saïd Brahimi, Jean-Jacques Marcel, Stéphane Bruey, Michel Leblond, Jean Vincent.   Manager: Albert Batteux

236.   27.11.1957
ENGLAND v FRANCE   4-0 (3-0)
British Empire Exhibition Stadium, London

Referee: Nikolay Latyshev (Soviet Union)
Attendance: 64,349

ENGLAND: Eddie Hopkinson, Don Howe, Roger Byrne, Ronnie Clayton, Billy Wright, Duncan Edwards, Bryan Douglas, Bobby Robson, Tommy Taylor, Johnny Haynes, Tom Finney.   Manager: Walter Winterbottom

FRANCE: Claude Abbès, Mustapha Zitouni, Raymond Kaelbel, René Domingo, Richard Tylinski, Bruno Bollini, Maryan Wisniewski, Joseph Ujlaki, Yvon Douis, Roger Paintoni, Jean Vincent.   Manager: Albert Batteux

Goals: Tommy Taylor (3, 33), Bobby Robson (24, 84)

237.   25.12.1957
FRANCE v BULGARIA   2-2 (1-0)
Parc des Princes, Paris

Referee: Günther Ternieden (West Germany)
Attendance: 38,086

FRANCE: Dominique Colonna, Raymond Kaelbel, André Lerond, Armand Penverne, Robert Jonquet, Pierre Cahuzac, Maryan Wisniewski (36 Rachid Mekhloufi), Yvon Douis, Roger Paintoni, Jean Vincent, Stéphane Bruey.   Manager: Albert Batteux

BULGARIA: Ivan Derventski, Kiril Rakarov, Manol Manolov, Nikola Kovachev, Stefan Bozhkov, Metodi Nestorov, Todor Diev, Hristo Iliev (38 Dimitar Milanov), Panayot Panayotov, Krum Yanev, Ivan Kolev.   Manager: Krum Milev

Goals: Maryan Wisniewski (11), Yvon Douis (56) / Todor Diev (55), Metodi Nestorov (75)

238.   13.03.1958
FRANCE v SPAIN   2-2 (0-1)
Parc des Princes, Paris

Referee: John Holden (Jack) Clough (England)   Att: 37,983

FRANCE: Claude Abbès, Raymond Kaelbel, André Lerond, Armand Penverne, Mustapha Zitouni, Jean-Jacques Marcel, Maryan Wisniewski, Yvon Douis, Just Fontaine, Roger Piantoni, Jean Vincent.   Manager: Albert Batteux

SPAIN: CARMELO Cedrún Ochandategui, Juan Carlos Díaz QUINCOCES (II), Jesús GARAY Vecino, Alberto CALLEJO Román, Juan SANTISTEBAN Troyano, José María ZÁRRAGA Martín, MIGUEL González Pérez, Ladislav (László) KUBALA Stecz, ALFREDO Stéfano DI STÉFANO Laulhé, LUIS SUÁREZ Miramontes, Enrique COLLAR Monterrubio.   Manager: Manuel MEANA Vallina

Goals: Just Fontaine (49), Roger Piantoni (65) / Ladislav (László) KUBALA Stecz (15), LUIS SUÁREZ Miramontes (58)

239.   16.04.1958
FRANCE v SWITZERLAND   0-0
Parc des Princes, Paris

Ref: Pieter Paulus (Piet) Roomer (Netherlands)   Att: 36,019

FRANCE: François Remetter, Raymond Kaelbel, Robert Jonquet, Roger Marche, Jean-Jacques Marcel, Bernard Chiarelli, Maryan Wisniewski, René Bliard, Just Fontaine, Célestin Oliver, Jean Vincent.   Manager: Albert Batteux

SWITZERLAND: Karl Elsener, Hans Weber, Gilbert Fesselet, André Grobéty, Eugen Meier, Heinz Schneiter, Norbert Eschmann, Charles Antenen, Gilbert Rey, Robert Ballaman, Ferdinando Riva (46 Francesco Chiesa).   Manager: Jacques Spagnoli

240.   08.06.1958   FIFA World Cup Final Tournament – Group 2
FRANCE v PARAGUAY   7-3 (2-2)
Norrköpings Idrottspark, Norrköping (Sweden)

Referee: Juan Gardeazábal Garay (Spain)   Att: 16,518

FRANCE: François Remetter, Raymond Kaelbel, André Lerond, Armand Penverne, Robert Jonquet, Jean-Jacques Marcel, Maryan Wisniewski, Just Fontaine, Raymond Kopa, Roger Piantoni, Jean Vincent.   Manager: Albert Batteux

PARAGUAY: Ramon MAYEREGGER Galarza, Eldemiro ARÉVALO, Juan Vicente LEZCANO López, Agustín MIRANDA, Ignacio ACHUCARRO Ayala, Salvador VILLALBA, Juan Bautista AGÜERO Sánchez, Silvio José del Rosario PARODI Rojas, Jorge Lino ROMERO Santa Cruz, Cayetano RÉ Ramírez, Florencio AMARILLA Lacasa.   Manager: Aurelio Ramón GONZÁLEZ Benítez

Goals: Just Fontaine (24, 30, 68), Roger Piantoni (51), Maryan Wisniewski (62), Raymond Kopa (70) Jean Vincent (84) / Florencio AMARILLA Lacasa (21, 43 pen), Jorge Lino ROMERO Santa Cruz (50)

241.   11.06.1958   FIFA World Cup Final Tournament – Group 2

YUGOSLAVIA v FRANCE   3-2 (1-1)

Arosvallen Stadion, Västerås (Sweden)

Referee: Benjamin Mervyn (Sandy) Griffiths (Wales)
Attendance: 12,217

YUGOSLAVIA: Vladimir Beara, Novak Tomic, Tomislav Crnkovic, Dobrosav Krstic, Branko Zebec, Vujadin Boskov, Zdravko Rajkov, Aleksandar Petakovic, Todor Veselinovic, Milos Milutinovic, Dragoslav Sekularac.
Manager: Aleksandar Tirnanic

FRANCE: François Remetter, Raymond Kaelbel, Roger Marche, Armand Penverne, Robert Jonquet, Maryan Wisniewski, André Lerond, Just Fontaine, Raymond Kopa, Roger Piantoni, Jean Vincent.   Manager: Albert Batteux

Goals: Aleksandar Petakovic (16), Todor Veselinovic (63, 87) / Just Fontaine (4, 85)

242.   15.06.1958   FIFA World Cup Final Tournament – Group 2

FRANCE v SCOTLAND   2-1 (2-0)

Eyravallen, Örebro (Sweden)

Referee: Juan Regis Brozzi (Argentina)   Attendance: 13,554

FRANCE: Claude Abbès, Raymond Kaelbel, André Lerond, Armand Penverne, Robert Jonquet, Jean-Jacques Marcel, Maryan Wisniewski, Just Fontaine, Raymond Kopa, Roger Piantoni, Jean Vincent.   Manager: Albert Batteux

SCOTLAND: Billy Brown, Eric Caldow, John Hewie, Eddie Turnbull, Bobby Evans, Dave MacKay, Bobby Collins, Jimmy Murray, Jackie Mudie, Samuel Baird, Stewart Imlach.   Manager: Dawson Walker

Goals: Raymond Kopa (21), Just Fontaine (44) / Samuel Baird (58)

243.   19.06.1958   FIFA World Cup Final Tournament – Quarter-finals

FRANCE v NORTHERN IRELAND   4-0 (1-0)

Norrköpings Idrottspark, Norrköping (Sweden)

Referee: Juan Gardeazábal Garay (Spain)
Attendance: 11,800

FRANCE: Claude Abbès, Raymond Kaelbel, André Lerond, Armand Penverne, Robert Jonquet, Jean-Jacques Marcel, Maryan Wisniewski, Just Fontaine, Raymond Kopa, Roger Piantoni, Jean Vincent.   Manager: Albert Batteux

NORTHERN IRELAND: Harry Gregg, Dick Keith, Alf McMichael, Danny Blanchflower, Willie Cunningham, Billy Cush, Billy Bingham, Tommy Casey, Jackie Scott, Jimmy McIlroy, Peter McParland.   Manager: Peter Doherty

Goals: Maryan Wisniewski (44), Just Fontaine (56, 64), Roger Piantoni (68)

244.   24.06.1958   FIFA World Cup Final Tournament – Semi-finals

BRAZIL v FRANCE   5-2 (2-1)

Råsunda Fotbollstadion, Solna (Sweden)

Referee: Benjamin Mervyn (Sandy) Griffiths (Wales)
Attendance: 27,100

BRAZIL: GILMAR dos Santos Neves, Newton DE SORDI, Hideraldo Luis BELLINI, ORLANDO PEÇANHA de Carvalho, NÍLTON Reis dos SANTOS, José Ely de Miranda "ZITO", Waldir Pereira "DIDÍ", Manoel dos Santos "GARRINCHA", Edvaldo Izídio Neto "VAVÁ", Édison Arantes do Nascimento "PELÉ", Mário Jorge Lobo ZAGALLO.
Manager: VICENTE Ítalo FEOLA

FRANCE: Claude Abbès, Raymond Kaelbel, André Lerond, Armand Penverne, Robert Jonquet, Jean-Jacques Marcel, Maryan Wisniewski, Just Fontaine, Raymond Kopa, Roger Piantoni, Jean Vincent.   Manager: Albert Batteux

Goals: Edvaldo I. Neto "VAVÁ" (2), Waldir Pereira "DIDÍ" (39), Édison Arantes do Nascimento "PELÉ" (53, 64, 76) / Just Fontaine (9), Roger Piantoni (82)

245.   28.06.1958   FIFA World Cup Final Tournament – Third Place play-off

FRANCE v WEST GERMANY   6-3 (3-1)

Ullevi Stadion, Gothenburg (Sweden)

Referee: Juan Regis Brozzi (Argentina)   Attendance: 32,483

FRANCE: Claude Abbès, Raymond Kaelbel, André Lerond, Armand Penverne, Maurice Lafont, Jean-Jacques Marcel, Maryan Wisniewski, Just Fontaine, Raymond Kopa, Yvon Douis, Jean Vincent.   Manager: Albert Batteux

WEST GERMANY: Heinz Kwiatkowski, Georg Stollenwerk, Herbert Erhardt, Karl-Heinz Schnellinger, Heinz Wewers, Horst Szymaniak, Helmut Rahn, Hans Sturm, Alfred Kelbassa, Hans Schäfer, Hans Cieslarczyk.   Manager: Sepp Herberger

Goals: Just Fontaine (15, 36, 77, 89), Raymond Kopa (27 pen), Yvon Douis (50) / Hans Cieslarczyk (18), Helmut Rahn (52), Hans Schäfer (84)

246. 01.10.1958   European Nation's Cup Qualifying – Round of 16
FRANCE v GREECE 7-1 (3-0)
Parc des Princes, Paris

Referee: Gottfried Dienst (Switzerland)   Attendance: 37,590

FRANCE: Dominique Colonna, Raymond Kaelbel, André Lerond, Armand Penverne, Maurice Lafont, Jean-Jacques Marcel, Yvon Douis, Raymond Kopa, Just Fontaine, Thadée Cisowski, Jean Vincent.   Manager: Albert Batteux

GREECE: Savvas Theodoridis, Takis Papoulidis, Kostas Linoxilakis, Mimis Stefanakos, Takis Loukanidis, Kostas Polychroniou, Pavlos Emmanouilidis, Dimitris Theofanis, Ilias Yfantis, Kostas Nestoridis, Yiannis Cholevas.   Manager: Vittorio (Rino) Martini

Goals: Raymond Kopa (23), Just Fontaine (25, 85), Thadée Cisowski (29, 68), Jean Vincent (61, 88) / Ilias Yfantis (47)

247. 05.10.1958
AUSTRIA v FRANCE 1-2 (1-0)
Praterstadion, Vienna

Referee: Cesare Jonni (Italy)   Attendance: 71,000

AUSTRIA: Kurt Schmied, Rudolf Oslansky, Erich Hasenkopf, Gerhard Hanappi, Heinrich Büllwatsch, Karl Koller, Walter Horak, Paul Kozlicek, Erich Hof, Alfred Körner, Herbert Ninaus.   Manager: Josef Molzer

FRANCE: Dominique Colonna, Raymond Kaelbel, André Lerond, Armand Penverne, Maurice Lafont, Jean-Jacques Marcel, Léon Deladerrière, Yvon Douis, Just Fontaine, Thadée Cisowski, Jean Vincent.   Manager: Albert Batteux

Goals: Erich Hof (21) / Léon Deladerrière (54), Just Fontaine (56)

248. 26.10.1958
FRANCE v WEST GERMANY 2-2 (1-1)
Stade Olympique Yves-du-Manoir, Colombes

Referee: Arthur Edward Ellis (England)   Attendance: 50,992

FRANCE: Dominique Colonna (30 Claude Abbès), Raymond Kaelbel, Maurice Lafont, André Lerond, Armand Penverne, Jean-Jacques Marcel, Léon Deladerrière, Yvon Douis, Just Fontaine, Roger Piantoni (42 Thadée Cisowski), Jean Vincent.   Manager: Albert Batteux

WEST GERMANY: Hans Tilkowski, Georg Stollenwerk, Hans Bauer, Alfred (Aki) Schmidt, Herbert Erhardt, Horst Szymaniak, Helmut Rahn, Helmut Haller, Uwe Seeler, Rolf Geiger, Hans Cieslarczyk.   Manager: Sepp Herberger

Goals: Léon Deladerrière (23), Yvon Douis (69 pen) / Helmut Rahn (13), Uwe Seeler (79)

249. 09.11.1958
FRANCE v ITALY 2-2 (1-0)
Stade Olympique Yves-du-Manoir, Colombes

Referee: Juan Gardeazábal Garay (Spain)
Attendance: 58,122

FRANCE: Dominique Colonna, Raymond Kaelbel, Roger Marche, Armand Penverne, Robert Jonquet, André Lerond, Maryan Wisniewski, Yvon Douis, Just Fontaine, Léon Deladerrièrre, Jean Vincent.   Manager: Albert Batteux

ITALY: Lorenzo Buffon, Giuseppe Corradi, Benito Sarti, Mario Bergamaschi, Sergio Cervato, Armando Segato, Gastone Bean, Giampiero Boniperti, Bruno Nicolè, Carlo Galli, Ezio Pascutti.   Manager: Giuseppe Viani

Goals: Jean Vincent (15), Just Fontaine (84) / Bruno Nicolè (57, 65)

250. 03.12.1958   European Nation's Cup Qualifying – Round of 16
GREECE v FRANCE 1-1 (0-0)
Leoforos Alexandras Stadium, Athens

Referee: Vincenzo Orlandini (Italy)   Attendance: 26,000

GREECE: Savvas Theodoridis, Takis Papoulidis, Kostas Linoxilakis, Sotiris Aggelopoulos, Kostas Polychroniou, Giannis Nembidis, Giorgos Sideris, Andreas Papaemmanouil, Ilias Yfantis, Kostas Nestoridis, Stelios Psychos.   Manager: Antonis Migiakis

FRANCE: Claude Abbès, Raymond Kaelbel, Roger Marche, René Ferrier, Bruno Bollini, André Lerond, Maryan Wisniewski, Roland Guillas, Stéphane Bruey, Stanislas Dombeck, Léon Deladerrièrre.   Manager: Albert Batteux

Goals: Roger Marche (85 og) / Stéphane Bruey (71)

251. 01.03.1959
FRANCE v BELGIUM 2-2 (1-1)
Stade Olympique Yves-du-Manoir, Colombes

Referee: John (Jack) Kelly (England)   Attendance: 42,206

FRANCE: Dominique Colonna, Raymond Kaelbel, Roger Marche, Jean-Jacques Marcel, Robert Jonquet, André Lerond (23 Joseph Tellechéa), Maryan Wisniewski, Roland Guillas, Henri Skiba, Édouard Stako, Jean Vincent.   Manager: Albert Batteux

BELGIUM: André Vanderstappen, Edouard Wauters, Henri Thellin, Pierre Hanon, Roland Storme, Martin Lippens, Fernand Goyvaerts, Denis Houf, Jef Jurion, Frits Vanden Boer, André Piters.   Manager: Viktor Havlicek

Goals: Jean Vincent (2, 68) / Martin Lippens (32), André Piters (80)

252. 11.10.1959
BULGARIA v FRANCE 1-0 (0-0)
National Stadium Vasil Levski, Sofia

Referee: Josef Stoll (Austria)   Attendance: 45,000

BULGARIA: Georgi Naydenov, Kiril Rakarov, Manol Manolov, Ivan Dimitrov, Dimitar Largov, Nikola Kovachev, Dimitar Milanov (40 Todor Diev), Stefan Abadjiev, Panayot Panayotov, Dimitar Yakimov, Ivan Kolev.
Manager: Stoyan Ormandzhiev

FRANCE: Dominique Colonna, Raymond Kaelbel, Roger Marche, Armand Penverne, Robert Jonquet, André Lerond, Pierre Grillet, Raymond Kopa, Roger Piantoni (27 Lucien Muller), Jean Vincent, Just Fontaine.
Manager: Albert Batteux

Goal: Ivan Kolev (88)

Sent off: Just Fontaine (89)

253. 11.11.1959
FRANCE v PORTUGAL 5-3 (3-2)
Stade Olympique Yves-du-Manoir, Colombes

Referee: Kenneth George (Ken) Aston (England)
Attendance: 48,111

FRANCE: Dominique Colonna (62 Georges Lamia), Jean Wendling, Roger Marche, Armand Penverne, Robert Jonquet, René Ferrier, Pierre Grillet, Raymond Kopa, Just Fontaine, Lucien Muller, Jean Vincent.   Manager: Albert Batteux

PORTUGAL: ACÚRCIO Alves Carrelo (60 Alberto Da COSTA PEREIRA), Manuel Francisco SERRA, HILÁRIO Rosário da CONCEIÇÃO, FERNANDO Mamede MENDES, ARTUR Lopes dos SANTOS, VICENTE Da Fonseca Lucas, António Fernandes "YAÚCA", Lucas Sebastião Da Fonseca "MATATEU", JOSÉ Pinto de Carvalho Santos ÁGUAS (30 JOSÉ AUGUSTO Pinto de Almeida), Mário Esteves COLUNA, Domiciano Barrocal Gomes CAVÉM.
Manager: JOSÉ MARIA ANTUNES Juniór

Goals: Just Fontaine (3, 54, 58), Pierre Grillet (11), Lucien Muller (22) / Lucas Da Fonseca "MATATEU" (36, 76), Domiciano Barrocal Gomes CAVÉM (41)

254. 13.12.1959   European Nation's Cup Qualifying – Quarter-finals
FRANCE v AUSTRIA 5-2 (3-1)
Stade Olympique Yves-du-Manoir, Colombes

Referee: Manuel Asensi Martín (Spain)   Attendance: 43,775

FRANCE: Georges Lamia, Jean Wendling, Roger Marche, Armand Penverne, Robert Jonquet, René Ferrier, François Heutte, Raymond Kopa, Just Fontaine, Lucien Muller, Jean Vincent.   Manager: Albert Batteux

AUSTRIA: Kurt Schmied, Paul Halla, Karl Nickerl, Gerhard Hanappi, Karl Stotz, Karl Koller, Walter Horak, Helmut Senekowitsch, Horst Nemec, Rudolf Pichler, Karl Höfer.
Manager: Karl Decker

Goals: Just Fontaine (6, 18, 70), Jen Vincent (38, 81) / Walter Horak (40), Rudolf Pichler (65)

255. 17.12.1959
FRANCE v SPAIN 4-3 (3-1)
Parc des Princes, Paris

Referee: Reginald James (Reg) Leafe (England)
Attendance: 38,622

FRANCE: François Remetter, Jean Wendling, Raymond Kaelbel (23 Roger Marche), Lucien Muller, Robert Jonquet, René Ferrier, Roland Guillas, Yvon Douis (52 Bernard Rahis), Just Fontaine, Raymond Kopa, Jean Vincent.
Manager: Albert Batteux

SPAIN: Antoni RAMALLETS Simón, Fernando OLIVELLA Pons, Jesús GARAY Vecino, Martín VERGÉS Massa, Joan SEGARRA Iracheta, José Luis ARTETXE Muguire (20 Enrique MATEOS Mancebo), Ladislav (László) KUBALA Stecz (46 Eulogio MARTÍNEZ Ramiro), ALFREDO Stéfano DI STÉFANO Laulhé, LUIS SUÁREZ Miramontes, Francisco GENTO López, Sigfrido GRACIA Royo.

Goals: L. Muller (27), Just Fontaine (31), Jean Vincent (36), Roger Marche (61) / LUIS SUÁREZ Miramontes (21), Eulogio MARTÍNEZ Ramiro (80), Martín VERGÉS Massa (88)

256. 28.02.1960
BELGIUM v FRANCE 1-0 (1-0)
Stade du Heysel, Brussels

Referee: Gottfried Dienst (Switzerland)   Attendance: 56,257

BELGIUM: Armand Seghers, Edouard Wauters, Guillaume Raskin, Victor Mees, Charles Saeys, Jef Jurion, André Piters, Michel Delire, Léon Ritzen, Frits Vanden Boer, Jean-Marie Letawe.   Manager: Viktor Havlicek

FRANCE: Georges Lamia, Jean Wendling, André Lerond, Lucien Muller, Raymond Kaelbel, René Ferrier, Pierre Grillet, Roland Guillas, Raymond Kopa, Roger Piantoni (40 François Heutte), Jean Vincent.   Manager: Albert Batteux

Goal: André Piters (36)

257. 16.03.1960
FRANCE v CHILE 6-0 (1-0)

Parc des Princes, Paris

Referee: Gérard André Versyp (Belgium)   Att: 36,094

FRANCE: Georges Lamia, Jean Wendling, André Chorda, Georges Peyroche, Raymond Kaelbel, René Ferrier, Pierre Grillet, Lucien Muller, François Heutte, Just Fontaine, Jean Vincent.   Manager: Albert Batteux

CHILE: Raúl Ernesto COLOMA Rivas, Luis Armando EYZAGUIRRE Silva, Raúl Pedro SÁNCHEZ Soya, Sergio Raúl NAVARRO Rodríguez (40 Isaac CARRASCO Rivas), Jorge Fernando LUCO Urzúa, Hernán RODRÍGUEZ Aliste, Mario Eduardo MORENO Burgos, Juan Rodolfo SOTO Mura, Armando Segundo TOBAR Vargas, Leonel Guillermo SÁNCHEZ Lineros, Bernardo Francisco BELLO Gutiérrez. Manager: Fernando RIERA Bauzá

Goals: Raymond Kaelbel (10), Jean Vincent (51), Pierre Grillet (57), Just Fontaine (78, 80), Lucien Muller (82)

258. 27.03.1960   European Nation's Cup Qualifying – Quarter-finals
AUSTRIA v FRANCE 2-4 (1-0)

Praterstadion, Vienna

Referee: Leo Alfred Helge (Denmark)   Attendance: 39,229

AUSTRIA: Rudolf Szanwald, Johann Windisch, Erich Hasenkopf, Gerhard Hanappi, Giuseppe Koschier, Karl Koller, Walter Horak, Paul Kozlicek, Horst Nemec, Wilhelm Huberts, Erich Probst.   Manager: Karl Decker

FRANCE: Georges Lamia, Jean Wendling, Raymond Kaelbel, Bruno Rodzik, René Ferrier, Jean-Jacques Marcel, Pierre Grillet, Lucien Muller, Raymond Kopa, Bernard Rahis, François Heutte.   Manager: Albert Batteux

Goals: Horst Nemec (27), Erich Probst (64) / Jean-Jacques Marcel (46), Bernard Rahis (59), François Heutte (77), Raymond Kopa (83 pen)

259. 06.07.1960   UEFA European Nation's Cup – Semi-finals
FRANCE v YUGOSLAVIA 4-5 (2-1)

Parc des Princes, Paris (France)

Referee: Gaston Grandain (Belgium)   Attendance: 26,370

FRANCE: Georges Lamia, Jean Wendling, Bruno Rodzik, Jean-Jacques Marcel, Robert Herbin, René Ferrier, François Heutte, Lucien Muller, Maryan Wisniewski, Michel Stievenard, Jean Vincent.   Manager: Albert Batteux

YUGOSLAVIA: Milutin Soskic, Vladimir Durkovic, Fahrudin Jusufi, Ante Zanetic, Branko Zebec, Zeljko Perusic, Tomislav Knez, Drazen Jerkovic, Dragoslav Sekularac, Milan Galic, Borivoje Kostic.   Manager: Aleksandar Tirnanic

Goals: Jean Vincent (12), François Heutte (43, 62), Maryan Wisniewski (52) / Milan Galic (11), Ante Zanetic (55), Tomislav Knez (75), Drazan Jerkovic (77, 78)

260. 09.07.1960   UEFA Europaen Nation's Cup – Third Place play-off
CZECHOSLOVAKIA v FRANCE 2-0 (0-0)

Stade Vélodrome, Marseille (France)

Referee: Cesare Jonni (Italy)   Attendance: 9,438

CZECHOSLOVAKIA: Viliam Schrojf, Frantisek Safránek, Ján Popluhár, Ladislav Novák, Josef Masopust, Titus Buberník, Ladislav Pavlovic, Josef Vojta, Pavol Molnár, Vlastimil Bubník, Milan Dolinksý.   Manager: Rudolf Vytlacil

FRANCE: Jean Taillandier, Bruno Rodzik, André Chorda, Jean-Jacques Marcel, Robert Jonquet, Robert Siatka, François Heutte, Yvon Douis, Maryan Wisniewski, Michel Stievenard, Jean Vincent.   Manager: Albert Batteux

Goals: Vlastimil Bubník (58), Ladislav Pavlovic (88)

261. 25.09.1960   FIFA World Cup Qualification – Group 2
FINLAND v FRANCE 1-2 (1-0)

Helsingin Olympiastadion, Helsinki

Referee: Johannes Malka (West Germany)
Attendance: 15,572

FINLAND: Carl-Gustaf Nabb, Reijo Jalava, Antti Nieminen, Olli Heinonen, Veijo Valtonen, Stig Holmqvist, Aulis Rytkönen, Unto Nevalainen, Nils Rikberg, Kai Pahlman, Juhani Peltonen.   Manager: Aatos Lehtonen

FRANCE: Dominique Colonna, Jean Wendling, Bruno Rodzik, Henri Biancheri, Raymond Kaelbel, René Ferrier, Maryan Wisniewski, Joseph Ujlaki, François Heutte, Roland Guillas, Jean Vincent.   Manager: Albert Batteux

Goals: Kai Pahlman (30 pen) / Maryan Wisniewski (63), Joseph Ujlaki (83)

262. 28.09.1960
POLAND v FRANCE 2-2 (1-0)

Stadion Dziesieciolecia Manifestu Lipcowego, Warszawa

Referee: Zivko Bajic (Yugoslavia)   Attendance: 55,000

POLAND: Stanislaw Foltyn, Henryk Szczepanski, Wladyslaw Kawula, Fryderyk Monica, Ryszard Grzegorczyk, Edmund Zientara, Zygmunt Gadecki, Lucjan Brychczy, Marian Norkowski, Ernest Pol, Eugeniusz Faber.
Manager: Jean Prouff

FRANCE: Jean Taillandier, Jean Wendling, Richard Tylinski, Bruno Rodzik, Henri Biancheri, René Ferrier, Yvon Goujon, Joseph Ujlaki, Maryan Wisniewski, Roland Guillas, Jean Vincent.   Manager: Albert Batteux

Goals: Marian Norkowski (43), Eugeniusz Faber (65) / Roland Guillas (84), Maryan Wisniewski (89)

263. 12.10.1960
SWITZERLAND v FRANCE 6-2 (2-1)

St. Jakob Stadion, Basel

Referee: Cesare Jonni (Italy)   Attendance: 37,517

SWITZERLAND: Karl Elsener, Willy Kernen, Heinz Schneiter, André Grobéty, Eugen Meier, Hans Weber, Charles Antenen, Roger Vonlanthen, Josef Hügi, Anton Allemann, Robert Ballaman.   Manager: Karl Rappan

FRANCE: Dominique Colonna, Jean Wendling, Richard Tylinski, Georges Peyroche, Jean-Jacques Marcel, René Ferrier, Julien Stopyra, Joseph Ujlaki, Maryan Wisniewski, Yvon Goujon, Jean Vincent.   Manager: Albert Batteux

Goals: Hans Weber (19), Josef Hügi (42, 61, 65, 80, 89) / Yvon Goujon (18, 87)

264. 30.10.1960
SWEDEN v FRANCE 1-0 (1-0)

Råsunda Fotbollstadion, Solna

Referee: Nikolay Latyshev (Soviet Union)
Attendance: 34,050

SWEDEN: Bengt Nyholm, Orvar Bergmark, Hans Mild, Olle Hellström, Åke Johansson, Torbjörn Jonsson, Gösta Sandberg, Harry Bild, Örjan Martinsson, Rune Börjesson, Lennart Backman.   Manager: Eric Person

FRANCE: Jean Taillandier, Jean Wendling, Guillaume Bieganski, Bruno Rodzik, Lucien Muller, Jean-Jacques Marcel, Maryan Wisniewski, Joseph Ujlaki, Raymond Kopa, Roger Piantoni, Jean Vincent.   Manager: Albert Batteux

Goal: Torbjörn Jonsson (27)

265. 11.12.1960   FIFA World Cup Qualification – Group 2
FRANCE v BULGARIA 3-0 (0-0)

Stade Olympique Yves-du-Manoir, Colombes

Referee: Pietro Bonetto (Italy)   Attendance: 40,690

FRANCE: Pierre Bernard, Jean Wendling, Bruno Rodzik, Jean-Jacques Marcel, Guy Sénac, Guillaume Bieganski, Maryan Wisniewski, Just Fontaine, Yvon Douis, Roger Piantoni, Lucien Cossou.   Manager: Albert Batteux

BULGARIA: Georgi Naydenov, Vasil Metodiev, Manol Manolov, Ivan Dimitrov, Dimitar Largov, Nikola Kovachev, Stefan Abadjiev, Hristo Iliev, Dimitar Yordanov, Dimitar Yakimov, Ivan Kolev.   Manager: Stoyan Ormandzhiev

Goals: Maryan Wisniewski (48), Jean-Jacques Marcel (58), Lucien Cossou (80)

266. 15.03.1961
FRANCE v BELGIUM 1-1 (1-0)

Parc des Princes, Paris

Referee: John (Jack) Kelly (England)   Attendance: 36,072

FRANCE: Pierre Bernard, Jean Wendling, Bruno Rodzik, Guy Sénac, Guillaume Bieganski, Bruno Bollini, Maryan Wisniewski, Jean-Jacques Marcel, Raymond Kopa, Roger Piantoni, Paul Sauvage.   Manager: Albert Batteux

BELGIUM: Guy Delhasse (46 Jean Nicolay), Georges Heylens, Henri Thellin, Pierre Hanon, Émile Lejeune, Martin Lippens, Jef Jurion, Fernand Goyvaerts, Victor Wégria, Denis Houf, Marcel Paeschen.   Manager: Henri Dekens

Goals: Roger Piantoni (3) / Marcel Paeschen (58)

267. 02.04.1961
SPAIN v FRANCE 2-0 (1-0)

Estadio Santiago Bernabéu, Madrid

Referee: Giulio Campanati (Italy)   Attendance: 75,000

SPAIN: José VICENTE Train, Feliciano Muñoz RIVILLA, José Emilio SANTAMARÍA Iglesias, Pedro CASADO Bucho, José María VIDAL Bravo, Enric GENSANA Merola, Justo TEJADA Martínez, Ladislav (László) KUBALA Stecz, ALFREDO Stéfano DI STÉFANO Laulhé, Luis DEL SOL Cascajares, Francisco GENTO López.
Manager: Pedro ESCARTÍN Morán

FRANCE: Pierre Bernard (46 Dominique Colonna), Guillaume Bieganski, Bruno Rodzik, Lucien Muller, François Ludo, Jean-Jacques Marcel, Roland Guillas, Raymond Kopa (31 René Ferrier), Serge Roy, Yvon Douis, Bernard Rahis.   Manager: Albert Batteux

Goals: Enric GENSANA Merola (30), Francisco GENTO (53)

268. 28.09.1961   FIFA World Cup Qualification – Group 2
FRANCE v FINLAND 5-1 (3-1)

Parc des Princes, Paris

Referee: Gottfried Dienst (Switzerland)   Attendance: 17,013

FRANCE: Pierre Bernard, Jean Wendling, Richard Boucher, Lucien Muller, Guillaume Bieganski, André Lerond, Maryan Wisniewski, Jean-Jacques Marcel, Ernest Schultz, Roger Piantoni, Jacques Faivre.   Manager: Albert Batteux

FINLAND: Anders Westerholm, Martti Hyvärinen, Matti Haahti, Unto Nevalainen, Olli Heinonen, Yrjö Pärnänen, Sauli Pietiläinen, Kai Pahlman, Stig Holmqvist, Aulis Rytkönen, Arno Nordlund.   Manager: Aatos Lehtonen

Goals: Jacques Faivre (6, 41), Maryan Wisniewski (12), Roger Piantoni (79), Ernest Schultz (86) / Kai Pahlman (44)

269. 18.10.1961
BELGIUM v FRANCE 3-0 (1-0)
Stade du Heysel, Brussels

Referee: Kevin Howley (England)   Attendance: 11,019

BELGIUM: Jean Nicolay, Yves Baré, Laurent Verbiest, Pierre Hanon, Émile Lejeune, Martin Lippens, Jef Jurion, Paul Van Himst, Roger Claessen, Paul Van Den Berg, Marcel Paeschen. Manager: Arthur Ceuleers

FRANCE: Pierre Bernard, Jean Wendling, Richard Boucher, Jean-Jacques Marcel, André Lerond, Jean Vincent, Raymond Kopa, Mahi Khennane, Maryan Wisniewski, Guy Van Sam, Jacques Faivre.   Manager: Albert Batteux

Goals: Pierre Hanon (18), Paul Van Den Berg (60), Roger Claessen (84)

270. 12.11.1961   FIFA World Cup Qualification – Group 2
BULGARIA v FRANCE 1-0 (0-0)
National Stadium Vasil Levski, Sofia

Referee: Milan Fencl (Czechoslovakia)   Attendance: 55,000

BULGARIA: Georgi Naydenov, Kiril Rakarov, Ivan Dimitrov, Vasil Metodiev, Dimitar Dimov, Nikola Kovachev, Todor Diev, Hristo Iliev, Dimitar Yakimov, Ivan Kolev, Spiro Debarski. Manager: Georgi Pachedzhiev

FRANCE: Pierre Bernard, Jean Wendling, Bruno Rodzik, Maryan Synakowski, André Lerond, René Ferrier, Roland Guillas, Lucien Muller, Mahi Khennane, Maxime Fulgenzy, Georges Peyroche.   Manager: Albert Batteux

Goal: Hristo Iliev (89)

271. 10.12.1961
FRANCE v SPAIN 1-1 (1-0)
Stade Olympique Yves-du-Manoir, Colombes

Referee: John (Jack) Kelly (England)   Attendance: 46,496

FRANCE: Pierre Bernard, Jean Wendling, Maryan Synakowski, André Lerond, Bruno Rodzik, Lucien Muller, René Ferrier, Maryan Wisniewski, Henri Skiba, François Heutte, Guy Van Sam.   Manager: Albert Batteux

SPAIN: José "JOSETXO" ARAQUISTÁIN Arrieta, Vicente PIQUER Mora, José Emilio SANTAMARÍA Iglesias, Vicente MIERA Campos, Ignacio ZOCO Esparza, Enrique Pérez Díaz "PACHÍN", José Antonio ZALDÚA Urdanavia, Luis DEL SOL Cascajares, ALFREDO Stéfano DI STÉFANO Laulhé, FÉLIX RUIZ Gabari, Francisco GENTO López.
Manager: Pedro ESCARTÍN Morán

Goals: François Heutte (13) / FÉLIX RUIZ Gabari (58)

272. 16.12.1961   FIFA World Cup Qualification – Group 2 Play-off
BULGARIA v FRANCE 1-0 (0-0)
Stadio San Siro, Milano (Italy)

Referee: Concetto Lo Bello (Italy)   Attendance: 34,740

BULGARIA: Georgi Naydenov, Kiril Rakarov, Ivan Dimitrov, Vasil Metodiev, Dimitar Dimov, Nikola Kovachev, Todor Diev, Petar Velichkov, Hristo Iliev, Ivan Kolev, Dimitar Yakimov. Manager: Georgi Pachedzhiev

FRANCE: Pierre Bernard, Jean Wendling, Bruno Rodzik, Maryan Synakowski, André Lerond, René Ferrier, Maryan Wisniewski, Lucien Muller, Henri Skiba, François Heutte, Guy Van Sam.   Manager: Albert Batteux

Goal: Dimitar Yakimov (47)

273. 11.04.1962
FRANCE v POLAND 1-3 (1-2)
Parc des Princes, Paris

Referee: Pietro Bonetto (Italy)   Attendance: 19,698

FRANCE: Pierre Bernard, Jean Wendling, Alain Cornu, Bruno Rodzik, Robert Herbin, Héctor De Bourgoing, Casimir Koza (26 Roland Guillas), Raymond Kopa, Théodore Szkudlapski, Ángel Rambert, René Ferrier.
Manager: Albert Batteux

POLAND: Konrad Kornek, Henryk Szczepanski, Stanislaw Oslizlo, Jerzy Wozniak, Jan Kowalski, Ryszard Grzegorczyk, Eugeniusz Faber, Lucjan Brychczy, Norbert Gajda, Ernest Pol, Roman Lentner.   Manager: Ryszard Koncewicz

Goals: Héctor De Bourgoing (24) /
Ernest Pol (33), Roman Lentner (43), Lucjan Brychczy (77)

274. 05.05.1962
ITALY v FRANCE 2-1 (0-1)
Stadio Comunale, Firenze

Referee: Josef Kandlbinder (West Germany)
Attendance: 45,000

ITALY: Lorenzo Buffon, Giacomo Losi, Luigi Radice, Sandro Salvadore, Cesare Maldini, Rino Marchesi, Bruno Mora, Humberto Maschio, José Altafini, Omar Enrique Sívori, Giampaolo Menichelli.
Managers: Giovanni Ferrari & Paolo Mazza

FRANCE: Bruno Ferrero, Jean Wendling, Bruno Rodzik, Maryan Synakowski, André Lerond, Jean-Claude Piumi, Raymond Kopa, Yvon Goujon, Stéphane Bruey (46 Michel Hidalgo), Héctor De Bourgoing, Laurent Robuschi.
Manager: Albert Batteux

Goals: José Altafini (47, 51) / Jean-Claude Piumi (28)

275. 03.10.1962   European Nation's Cup Qualifying – First round
ENGLAND v FRANCE 1-1 (0-1)
Hillsborough Stadium, Sheffield
Referee: Frede Eiving Hansen (Denmark)
Attendance: 35,380
ENGLAND: Ron Springett, Jimmy Armfield, Ray Wilson, Bobby Moore, Maurice Norman, Ron Flowers, Mike Hellawell, Chris Crowe, Ray Charnley, Jimmy Greaves, Alan Hinton.   Manager: Walter Winterbottom
FRANCE: Pierre Bernard, Jean Wendling, Maryan Synakowski, André Lerond, André Chorda, Joseph Bonnel, Yvon Goujon, René Ferrier, Laurent Robuschi, Raymond Kopa, Paul Sauvage.   Manager: Henri Guérin
Goals: Ron Flowers (57 pen) / Yvon Goujon (8)

276. 24.10.1962
WEST GERMANY v FRANCE 2-2 (0-2)
Neckarstadion, Stuttgart
Referee: Friedrich (Fritz) Seipelt (Austria)
Attendance: 75,000
WEST GERMANY: Wolfgang Fahrian (46 Günter Bernard), Fritz Pott, Karl-Heinz Schnellinger, Willi Schulz (43 Heinz Steinmann), Leo Wilden, Stefan Reisch, Uwe Seeler, Jürgen Schütz, Heinz Strehl, Friedhelm (Timo) Konietzka, Wolfgang Solz.   Manager: Sepp Herberger
FRANCE: Georges Lamia, Jean Wendling, Bruno Rodzik, Maryan Synakowski, André Lerond, René Ferrier, Laurent Robuschi, Joseph Bonnel, Yvon Goujon, Édouard Stako, Paul Sauvage.   Manager: Henri Guérin
Goals: Friedhelm (Timo) Konietzka (46), H. Steinmann (82) / Édouard Stako (25), Yvon Goujon (32)

277. 11.11.1962
FRANCE v HUNGARY 2-3 (1-2)
Stade Olympique Yves-du-Manoir, Colombes
Referee: Juan Gardeazábal Garay (Spain)
Attendance: 35,136
FRANCE: Pierre Bernard, Jean Wendling, Maryan Synakowski, André Lerond, Bruno Rodzik, Joseph Bonnel, René Ferrier, Raymond Kopa, Yvon Goujon, Fleury Di Nallo, Paul Sauvage.   Manager: Henri Guérin
HUNGARY: Antal Szentmihályi, Sándor Mátrai, Kálmán Mészöly, Ferenc Sipos, Kálmán Sóvári, János Göröcs, Ernö Solymosi, Károly Sándor, Flórián Albert (24 Gyula Rákosi), Lajos Tichý, Máté Fenyvesi.   Manager: Lajos Baróti
Goals: Fleury Di Nallo (18, 75) / Lajos Tichý (12, 80), Gyula Rákosi (36)

278. 09.01.1963
SPAIN v FRANCE 0-0
Estadio del Club de Fútbal Barcelona, Barcelona
Referee: Jozef Casteleyn (Belgium)   Attendance: 72,000
SPAIN: Salvador SADURNÍ Urpi, Feliciano Muñoz RIVILLA, Luis María ECHEBERRÍA Igartua, Isacio CALLEJA García, Francisco "PAQUITO" García Gómez, Jesús GLARÍA (IV) Jordán, Enrique COLLAR Monterrubio (46 Fernando Rodríguez SERENA), ADELARDO Rodríguez Sánchez, Emilio MOROLLÓN Estébanez, Vicente GUILLOT Fabián, Francisco GENTO López.   Manager: José VILLALONGA Llorente
FRANCE: Pierre Bernard, Jean Wendling, Maryan Synakowski, André Lerond, André Chorda, Joseph Bonnel, Yvon Douis, René Ferrier, Yvon Goujon, Serge Masnaghetti, Paul Sauvage.   Manager: Henri Guérin

279. 27.02.1963   European Nation's Cup Qualifying – First round
FRANCE v ENGLAND 5-2 (3-0)
Parc des Princes, Paris
Referee: Josef Kandlbinder (West Germany)
Attendance: 23,986
FRANCE: Pierre Bernard, Jean Wendling, Maryan Synakowski, André Lerond, Bruno Rodzik, Joseph Bonnel, Yvon Goujon, Robert Herbin, Maryan Wisniewski, Yvon Douis, Lucien Cossou.   Manager: Henri Guérin
ENGLAND: Ron Springett, Jimmy Armfield, Ron Henry, Bobby Moore, Brian Labone, Ron Flowers, John Connelly, Bobby Tambling, Bobby Smith, Jimmy Greaves, Bobby Charlton.   Manager: Alf Ramsey
Goals: Maryan Wisniewski (3, 75), Yvon Douis (32), Lucien Cossou (43, 82) / Bobby Smith (57), Bobby Tambling (74)

280. 17.04.1963
NETHERLANDS v FRANCE 1-0 (0-0)
De Kuip, Rotterdam
Referee: Johannes Malka (West Germany)
Attendance: 41,000
NETHERLANDS: Eddy Pieters Graafland, Guus Haak, Jan Klaassens, Ton Pronk, Piet Ouderland, Fons van Wissen, Rinus Bennaars, Sjaak Swart, Piet Kruiver, Coen Moulijn, Henk Groot.   Manager: Elek Schwartz
FRANCE: Pierre Bernard, Jean Wendling, Maryan Synakowski, André Lerond, Bruno Roznik, Joseph Bonnel, Yvon Douis, Robert Herbin, Maryan Wisniewski, Lucien Cossou, Paul Chillan.   Manager: Henri Guérin
Goal: Henk Groot (73)

281. 28.04.1963
FRANCE v BRAZIL 2-3 (0-1)
Stade Olympique Yves-du-Manoir, Colombes
Referee: Concetto Lo Bello (Italy)   Attendance: 50,000
FRANCE: Georges Carnus, Bruno Roznik, André Lerond, André Chorda, Maryan Synakowski, Robert Herbin, Maryan Wisniewski, Joseph Bonnel, Yvon Douis, Fleury Di Nallo, Lucien Cossou (46 Paul Chillan).   Manager: Henri Guérin
BRAZIL: GILMAR (I) dos Santos Neves, Dejalma dos Santos "DJALMA SANTOS", EDUARDO (I) Barbosa de Albuquerque, ROBERTO DIAS Branco, ALTAIR Gomes Figueiredo, José Ely de Miranda "ZITO", GÉRSON (I) de Oliveira Nunes, MARCOS Pereira Martins, NEY de Oliveira, Édison Arantes do Nascimento "PELÉ", José Macia "PEPE".
Manager: AYMORÉ MOREIRA
Goals: Maryan Wisniewski (70), Fleury Di Nallo (83) / Édison Arantes do Nascimento "PELÉ" (30, 76 pen, 84)

282. 29.09.1963   European Nation's Cup Qualifying – Round of 16
BULGARIA v FRANCE 1-0 (1-0)
National Stadium Vasil Levski, Sofia
Referee: Faruk Talu (Turkey)   Attendance: 25,947
BULGARIA: Georgi Naydenov, Aleksandar Shalamanov, Ivan Dimitrov, Ivan Vutsov, Dobromir Zhechev, Stoyan Kitov, Todor Diev, Petar Velichkov, Georgi Asparuhov, Dimitar Yakimov, Ivan Kolev.   Manager: Béla Volentik
FRANCE: Pierre Bernard, Marcel Adamczyk, André Chorda, Marcel Artélésa, Joseph Bonnel, Yvon Douis, Laurent Robuschi, Pierre Michelin, Lucien Cossou, Théodore Szkudlapski, Jean-Louis Buron.   Manager: Henri Guérin
Goal: Todor Diev (24)

283. 26.10.1963   European Nation's Cup Qualifying – Round of 16
FRANCE v BULGARIA 3-1 (1-0)
Parc des Princes, Paris
Referee: José María Ortiz de Mendíbil (Spain)
Attendance: 32,233
FRANCE: Pierre Bernard, Bruno Rodzik, Pierre Michelin, Marcel Artélésa, André Chorda, Robert Herbin, Yvon Douis, René Ferrier, Georges Lech, Yvon Goujon, Jean-Louis Buron.
Manager: Henri Guérin
BULGARIA: Georgi Naydenov, Vasil Metodiev, Ivan Dimitrov, Dobromir Zhechev, Ivan Vutsov, Petar Velichkov, Stoyan Kitov, Stefan Abadjiev, Georgi Asparukhov, Dimitar Yakimov, Ivan Kolev.   Manager: Béla Volentik
Goals: Yvon Goujon (44, 81), Robert Herbin (78) / Dimitar Yakimov (75)

284. 11.11.1963
FRANCE v SWITZERLAND 2-2 (2-0)
Parc des Princes, Paris
Referee: Arthur Holland (England)   Attendance: 27,350
FRANCE: Pierre Bernard, Bruno Rodzik, Marcel Artélésa, André Chorda, Pierre Michelin, Jean-Claude Piumi, Georges Lech, Robert Herbin, Yvon Goujon, Yvon Douis, Jean-Louis Buron.   Manager: Henri Guérin
SWITZERLAND: René Schneider (42 Karl Elsener), Werner Leimgruber, Heinz Schneiter, Raymond Maffiolo, Rolf Wüthrich, Ely Tacchella, Karl Odermatt, André Bosson, Michel Desbiolles (46 Charly Hertig), Philippe Pottier, Ernst Meyer.
Manager: Karl Rappan
Goals: Jean-Louis Buron (18), Georges Lech (31) / Marcel Artélésa (51 og), André Bosson (75)

285. 25.12.1963
FRANCE v BELGIUM 1-2 (1-2)
Parc des Princes, Paris
Referee: Josef Stoll (Austria)   Attendance: 12,649
FRANCE: Pierre Bernard, Georges Casolari, Marcel Artélésa, Pierre Michelin, André Chorda, Robert Herbin, Lucien Muller, Georges Lech, Yvon Goujon, Serge Masnaghetti, Jean-Louis Buron.   Manager: Henri Guérin
BELGIUM: Jean Nicolay, Georges Heylens, Martin Lippens, Guillaume Raskin, Jean Cornelis, Pierre Hanon, Jef Jurion, Frans Vermeyen, Paul Van Himst, Paul Van Den Berg, Wilfried Puis.   Manager: Arthur Ceuleers
Goals: Serge Masnaghetti (33) / Paul Van Himst (26, 37)

286. 25.04.1964   European Nation's Cup Qualifying – Quarter-final
FRANCE v HUNGARY 1-3 (0-2)
Stade Olympique Yves-du-Manoir, Colombes
Referee: Cesare Jonni (Italy)   Attendance: 35,274
FRANCE: Pierre Bernard, Georges Casolari, Pierre Michelin, Marcel Artélésa, André Chorda, Joseph Bonnel, Robert Herbin, Lucien Muller, Georges Lech, Nestor Combin, Lucien Cossou.
Manager: Henri Guérin
HUNGARY: Antal Szentmihályi, Sándor Mátrai, Kálmán Mészöly, Ferenc Sipos, László Sárosi, János Göröcs, István Nagy, Gyula Rákosi, Máté Fenyvesi, Flórián Albert, Lajos Tichý.
Manager: Lajos Baróti
Goals: Lucien Cossou (73) / Flórián Albert (15), Lajos Tichý (16, 70)

287.   23.05.1964   European Nation's Cup Qualifying – Quarter-final
HUNGARY v FRANCE 2-1 (1-1)

Népstadion, Budapest

Referee: Concetto Lo Bello (Italy)   Attendance: 70,120

HUNGARY: Antal Szentmihályi, Sándor Mátrai, Kálmán Mészöly, Ferenc Sipos, László Sárosi, István Nagy, Gyula Rákosi, Máté Fenyvesi, Károly Sándor, Lajos Tichý, Ferenc Bene.   Manager: Lajos Baróti

FRANCE: Pierre Bernard, Georges Casolari, Marcel Artélésa, Daniel Charles-Alfred, André Chorda, Joseph Bonnel, Édouard Stako, Ángel Rambert, Georges Lech, Nestor Combin, Fleury Di Nallo.   Manager: Henri Guérin

Goals: Ferenc Sipos (24), Ferenc Bene (55) / Nestor Combin (2)

288.   04.10.1964   FIFA World Cup Qualification – Group 3
LUXEMBOURG v FRANCE 0-2 (0-1)

Stade Municipal, Luxembourg City

Referee: Vital Georges Gilbert Loraux (Belgium)   Attendance: 17,536

LUXEMBOURG: René Hoffmann, Ernest Brenner, Jean-Pierre Hoffstetter, François Konter, Fernand Brosius, Louis Pilot, Jean Klein, Paul May, Camille Dimmer, Ady Schmit, Norry Wampach.   Manager: Robert Heinz

FRANCE: Marcel Aubour, Jean Djorkaeff, Marcel Artélésa, Daniel Charles-Alfred, André Chorda, Robert Herbin, René Ferrier, Ángel Rambert, Georges Lech, André Guy, Nestor Combin.   Manager: Henri Guérin

Goals: André Guy (17), Marcel Artélésa (80)

289.   11.11.1964   FIFA World Cup Qualification – Group 3
FRANCE v NORWAY 1-0 (1-0)

Parc des Princes, Paris

Referee: John (Jack) Adair (Northern Ireland)   Attendance: 33,517

FRANCE: Marcel Aubour, Jean Djorkaeff, Marcel Artélésa, Daniel Charles-Alfred, André Chorda, Joseph Bonnel, Robert Herbin, René Ferrier, Georges Lech, André Guy, Ángel Rambert.   Manager: Henri Guérin

NORWAY: Kjell Kaspersen, Roar Johansen, Finn Thorsen, Trygve Andersen, Jack Kramer, Arne Pedersen, Olav Nilsen, Egil Olsen, Erik Johansen, Harald Berg, Finn Seemann.   Manager: Ragnar Larsen

Goal: Ángel Rambert (17)

290.   02.12.1964
BELGIUM v FRANCE 3-0 (1-0)

Stade du Heysel, Brussels

Referee: Rudolf Kreitlein (West Germany)   Attendance: 5,917

BELGIUM: Jean Nicolay, Georges Heylens, Laurent Verbiest, Jean Plaskie, Jean Cornelis, Gérard Sulon, Jef Jurion, Frans Vermeyen, Paul Van Himst, Paul Van Den Berg, Wilfried Puis.   Manager: Arthur Ceuleers

FRANCE: Marcel Aubour, Bernard Bosquier, Marcel Artélésa, Daniel Charles-Alfred, André Chorda, Joseph Bonnel, René Ferrier, Ángel Rambert, Georges Lech, André Guy, Edmond Baraffe.   Manager: Henri Guérin

Goals: Paul Van Himst (16), Frans Vermeyen (76, 87)

291.   24.03.1965
FRANCE v AUSTRIA 1-2 (1-2)

Parc des Princes, Paris

Referee: Franz Geluck (Belgium)   Attendance: 24,206

FRANCE: Pierre Bernard (46 Marcel Aubour), Jean Djorkaeff, Denis Devaux, Robert Péri, Bernard Bosquier, Jacques Simon, Joseph Bonnel, Marcel Loncle, Georges Lech, Daniel Rodighiero, Gérard Hausser.   Manager: Henri Guérin

AUSTRIA: Gernot Fraydl, Paul Halla, Friedrich Kremser, Heinz Binder, Walter Glechner, Ewald Ullmann (26 Gerhard Sturmberger), Horst Hirnschrodt, Walter Seitl, Hans Buzek, Karl Koller, Johann Hörmayer.   Manager: Edi Frühwirth

Goals: Gérard Hausser (28) / Walter Seitl (15), Karl Koller (44)

292.   18.04.1965   FIFA World Cup Qualification – Group 3
YUGOSLAVIA v FRANCE 1-0 (0-0)

Stadion Crvena Zvezda, Beograd

Referee: Dimitris (Taki) Wlachojanis (Austria)   Attendance: 23,906

YUGOSLAVIA: Zlatko Skoric, Vladimir Durkovic, Fahrudin Jusufi, Rudolf Belin, Velibor Vasovic, Vladimir Popovic, Vladimir Lukaric, Slaven Zambata, Ivica Osim, Milan Galic, Josip Skoblar.   Manager: Aleksandar Tirnanic

FRANCE: Marcel Aubour, Jean Djorkaeff, Robert Herbin, Marcel Artélésa, Bernard Bosquier, Jacques Simon, Joseph Bonnel, Marcel Loncle, Georges Lech, Paul Sauvage, Gérard Hausser.   Manager: Henri Guérin

Goal: Milan Galic (59)

293.   03.06.1965
FRANCE v ARGENTINA   0-0
Parc des Princes, Paris

Referee: John Keith (Jack) Taylor (England)
Attendance: 11,931

FRANCE: Marcel Aubour, Jean Djorkaeff, Robert Herbin, Marcel Artélésa, Louis Cardiet, Yves Herbet, Maryan Synakowski, Jacques Simon, Georges Lech, Daniel Rodighiero, Gérard Hausser.   Manager: Henri Guérin

ARGENTINA: Antonio Roma, Jose Manuel Ramos Delgado, Silvio Marzolini, Roberto Oscar Ferreiro, Antonio Ubaldo Rattin, José Rafael Albrecht, José Luis Luna (46 Norberto Santiago Raffo), Alberto Rendo, Daniel Alberto Willington, Alfredo Hugo ROJAS Delinge, Alberto Mario González.   Manager: José María Minella

294.   15.09.1965   FIFA World Cup Qualification – Group 3
NORWAY v FRANCE   0-1 (0-1)
Ullevaal Stadion, Oslo

Referee: Hugh Phillips (Scotland)   Attendance: 31,234

NORWAY: Kjell Kaspersen, Roar Johansen, Finn Thorsen, Sveinung Aarnseth, Edgar Stakset, Arne Pedersen, Arild Gulden, Finn Seemann, Harald Berg, Kai Sjøberg, Erik Johansen.   Manager: Ragnar Larsen

FRANCE: Marcel Aubour, Louis Cardiet, Bernard Bosquier, Marcel Artélésa, André Chorda, Yves Herbet, Maryan Synakowski, Yvon Douis, Nestor Combin, Gérard Hausser, Robert Herbin.   Manager: Henri Guérin

Goal: Nestor Combin (22)

295.   09.10.1965   FIFA World Cup Qualification – Group 3
FRANCE v YUGOSLAVIA   1-0 (0-0)
Parc des Princes, Paris

Referee: Frede Eiving Hansen (Denmark)
Attendance: 35,546

FRANCE: Marcel Aubour, Louis Cardiet, Bernard Bosquier, Robert Budzynski, André Chorda, Yves Herbet, Joseph Bonnel, Marcel Artélésa, Gérard Hausser, Nestor Combin, Philippe Gondet.   Manager: Henri Guérin

YUGOSLAVIA: Milutin Soskic, Vinko Cuzzi, Fahrudin Jusufi, Rudolf Belin, Velibor Vasovic, Josip Zemko, Dzemaludin Musovic, Vojislav Melic, Milan Galic, Dragoslav Sekularac, Dragan Dzajic.   Manager: Aleksandar Tirnanic

Goal: Philippe Gondet (77)

296.   06.11.1965   FIFA World Cup Qualification – Group 3
FRANCE v LUXEMBOURG   4-1 (4-0)
Stade Vélodrome, Marseille

Referee: Daniel María Zariquiegui Izco (Spain)
Attendance: 30,080

FRANCE: Marcel Aubour, Bernard Bosquier, Louis Cardiet, Robert Budzynski, André Chorda, Yves Herbet, Joseph Bonnel, Marcel Artélésa, Gérard Hausser, Nestor Combin, Philippe Gondet.   Manager: Henri Guérin

LUXEMBOURG: Nico Schmitt, Erwin Kuffer, Jean-Pierre Hoffstetter, Fernand Jeitz, Fernand Brosius, François Konter, Jean Klein, Louis Pilot, Ady Schmit, René Schneider, Arno Biewers.   Manager: Robert Heinz

Goals: Philippe Gondet (8, 27), Nestor Combin (11, 38) / Louis Pilot (53)

297.   19.03.1966
FRANCE v ITALY   0-0
Parc des Princes, Paris

Referee: Joseph Hannet (Belgium)   Attendance: 31,795

FRANCE: Marcel Aubour, Bernard Bosquier, André Chorda, Marcel Artélésa, Robert Budzynski, Robert Péri, Edmond Baraffe, Robert Herbin, Philippe Gondet, Jacques Simon, Gérard Hausser.   Manager: Henri Guérin

ITALY: Enrico Albertosi, Tarcisio Burgnich, Giacinto Facchetti, Roberto Rosato, Sandro Salvadore, Giovan Battista Pirovano (46 Giovanni Lodetti), Angelo Domenghini (46 Luigi Meroni), Gianni Rivera, Alessandro Mazzola, Mario Corso, Luigi Riva.   Manager: Edmondo Fabbri

298.   20.04.1966
FRANCE v BELGIUM   0-3 (0-1)
Parc des Princes, Paris

Referee: Daniel Zariquiegui Izco (Spain)
Attendance: 16,664

FRANCE: Marcel Aubour, Bernard Bosquier, Jean Djorkaeff, Marcel Artélésa, Robert Herbin, André Chorda, Joseph Bonnel, Jacques Simon, Edmond Baraffe, Philippe Gondet, Gérard Hausser (46 Bernard Blanchet).   Manager: Henri Guérin

BELGIUM: Jean Nicolay, Georges Heylens, Jean Plaskie, Marcel Lemoine, Jean Cornelis, Pierre Hanon, Frits Vanden Boer, John Thio, Paul Van Himst, Raoul Lambert (46 Jacques Stockman), Wilfried Puis.   Manager: Raymond Goethals

Goals: Raoul Lambert (20), Jacques Stockman (71), John Thio (90)

299.   06.06.1966
SOVIET UNION v FRANCE   3-3 (1-2)

Lenin Central Stadium, Moscow

Referee: Bertil Wilhelm Lööw (Sweden)
Attendance: 102,000

SOVIET UNION: Viktor Bannikov (46 Anzor Kavazashvili), Vladimir Ponomaryov, Albert Shesternyov, Vasiliy Danilov, Valeriy Voronin, Valentin Afonin (46 Viktor Serebryanikov), Slava Metreveli, Yozhef Sabo, Anatoliy Banishevskiy, Eduard Malofeyev (46 Eduard Markarov), Igor Chislenko.   Manager: Nikolay Morozov

FRANCE: Daniel Éon, Jean Djorkaeff, André Chorda, Marcel Artélésa, Robert Budzynski, Bernard Bosquier, Bernard Blanchet, Philippe Gondet, Joseph Bonnel, Gérard Hausser, Robert Herbin.   Manager: Henri Guérin

Goals: Slava Metreveli (26), Anatoliy Banishevskiy (64), Igor Chislenko (66) / Bernard Blanchet (19), Philippe Gondet (21), Joseph Bonnel (78)

300.   13.07.1966   FIFA World Cup Final Tournament – Group 1
FRANCE v MEXICO   1-1 (0-0)

British Empire Exhibition Stadium, London (England)

Referee: Menahem Ashkenazi (Israel)   Attendance: 69,237

FRANCE: Marcel Aubour, Jean Djorkaeff, Robert Budzynski, Marcel Artélésa, Gabriel De Michèle, Bernard Bosquier, Robert Herbin, Joseph Bonnel, Nestor Combin, Philippe Gondet, Gérard Hausser.   Manager: Henri Guérin

MEXICO: Ignacio Francisco CALDERÓN González, Gustavo PEÑA Velazco, Enrique David BORJA García, Arturo CHAIRES Rizo, Magdaleno Diego MERCADO Gutiérrez, Guillermo Alejandro HERNÁNDEZ Sánchez, Gabriel NÚÑEZ Aguirre, Isidoro DÍAZ Mejia, Javier Gonzalo FRAGOSO Rodríguez, Salvador REYES Monteón, Aarón PADILLA Gutiérrez.   Manager: Ignacio TRELLES Campos

Goals: Gérard Hausser (62) / Enrique BORJA García (48)

301.   15.07.1966   FIFA World Cup Final Tournament – Group 1
URUGUAY v FRANCE   2-1 (2-1)

White City Stadium, London (England)

Referee: Dr. Karol Galba (Czechoslovakia)
Attendance: 45,662

URUGUAY: Ladislao MAZURKIEWICZ Iglesias, Horacio Florentín TROCHE Herrera, Jorge Carlos MANICERA Fuentes, Luis Ignacio UBIÑA Olivera, Néstor GONÇÁLVES, Omar CAETANO Otero, Julio César CORTÉS Lagos, Milton VIERA Rivero, José Francisco SASÍA Lugo, Pedro Virgílio ROCHA Franchetti, Domingo Salvador PÉREZ.   Manager: Ondino Leonel VIERA Palaserez

FRANCE: Marcel Aubour, Jean Djorkaeff, Robert Budzynski, Marcel Artélésa, Héctor De Bourgoing, Bernard Bosquier, Jacques Simon, Joseph Bonnel, Yves Herbet, Philippe Gondet, Gérard Hausser.   Manager: Henri Guérin

Goals: Pedro Virgílio ROCHA Franchetti (27), Julio César CORTÉS Lagos (32) / Héctor De Bourgoing (16 pen)

302.   20.07.1966   FIFA World Cup Final Tournament – Group 1
ENGLAND v FRANCE   2-0 (1-0)

British Empire Exhibition Stadium, London (England)

Referee: Arturo Maximo Yamasaki Maldonado (Peru)
Attendance: 98,270

ENGLAND: Gordon Banks, George Cohen, Ray Wilson, Nobby Stiles, Jack Charlton, Bobby Moore, Ian Callaghan, Jimmy Greaves, Bobby Charlton, Roger Hunt, Martin Peters.   Manager: Alf Ramsey

FRANCE: Marcel Aubour, Jean Djorkaeff, Robert Budzynski, Marcel Artélésa, Robert Herbin, Bernard Bosquier, Jacques Simon, Joseph Bonnel, Yves Herbet, Philippe Gondet, Gérard Hausser.   Manager: Henri Guérin

Goals: Roger Hunt (39, 76)

303.   28.09.1966
HUNGARY v FRANCE   4-2 (1-1)

Népstadion, Budapest

Referee: Dimitrios (Taki) Wlachojanis (Austria)
Attendance: 25,000

HUNGARY: Antal Szentmihályi, Benö Káposzta, Sándor Mátrai, Kálmán Mészöly, Kálmán Ihász, Imre Mathesz (66 István Bánkúti), Flórián Albert, Zoltán Varga, Dezsö Molnár, János Farkas, István Korsós.   Manager: Rudolf Illovszky

FRANCE: Georges Carnus, Jean Djorkaeff, Bernard Bosquier, Robert Budzynski, André Chorda, Jean-Claude Suaudeau, Jacques Simon (82 Claude Robin), Georges Lech, Philippe Gondet, Hervé Revelli, Gérard Hausser.   Managers: Jean Snella & José Arribas

Goals: János Farkas (13, 57, 83, 89) / Philippe Gondet (26), Hervé Revelli (58)

304.   22.10.1966   UEFA Euro 1968 Qualifying – Group 7

FRANCE v POLAND   2-1 (1-0)

Parc des Princes, Paris

Referee: Gerhard Schulenburg (West Germany)
Attendance: 23,524

FRANCE: Georges Carnus, Jean Djorkaeff, Claude Robin, Robert Budzynski, André Chorda, Jean-Claude Suaudeau, Jacques Simon, Yves Herbet, Georges Lech, Fleury Di Nallo, Paul Courtin.   Managers: Jean Snella & José Arribas

POLAND: Jan Gomola, Roman Strzalkowski, Jacek Gmoch, Stanislaw Oslizlo, Zygmunt Anczok, Piotr Suski, Ryszard Grzegorczyk, Jerzy Sadek, Wlodzimierz Lubanski, Jan Liberda, Andrzej Jarosik.   Manager: Antoni Brzezanczyk

Goals: Fleury Di Nallo (26), Georges Lech (85) / Ryszard Grzegorczyk (61)

305.   11.11.1966   UEFA Euro 1968 Qualifying – Group 7

BELGIUM v FRANCE   2-1 (0-0)

Stade du Heysel, Brussels

Referee: John Keith (Jack) Taylor (England)
Attendance: 43,404

BELGIUM: Jean Nicolay, Georges Heylens, Pierre Hanon, Jean Plaskie, Yves Baré, Wilfried Van Moer, Jef Jurion, John Thio, Raoul Lambert, Paul Van Himst, Wilfried Puis.   Manager: Raymond Goethals

FRANCE: Georges Carnus, Jean Djorkaeff, Claude Robin, Robert Budzynski, André Chorda, Jacques Simon, Jean-Claude Suaudeau, Bernard Blanchet, Hervé Revelli, Georges Lech, Gérard Hausser.   Managers: Jean Snella & José Arribas

Goals: Paul Van Himst (51, 54) / Georges Lech (67)

306.   26.11.1966   UEFA Euro 1968 Qualifying – Group 7

LUXEMBOURG v FRANCE   0-3 (0-3)

Stade Municipal, Luxembourg City

Referee: Laurens (Lau) van Ravens (Netherlands)
Attendance: 3,465

LUXEMBOURG: Théo Stendebach, Erwin Kuffer, Fernand Jeitz, Mathias Ewen, Jean-Pierre Hoffstetter, Nicolas Hoffmann, François Konter, Edy Dublin, Johny Léonard, Ady Schmit, Josy Kirchens.   Manager: Robert Heinz

FRANCE: Georges Carnus, Jean Djorkaeff, Marcel Artélésa, Bernard Bosquier, André Chorda, Joseph Bonnel, Michel Watteau, Yves Herbet, Hervé Revelli, Georges Lech, Laurent Robuschi.   Managers: Jean Snella & José Arribas

Goals: Yves Herbet (8), Hervé Revelli (40), Georges Lech (41)

307.   22.03.1967

FRANCE v ROMANIA   1-2 (0-1)

Parc des Princes, Paris

Referee: Günter Baumgärtel (West Germany)   Att: 23,769

FRANCE: Daniel Éon (46 Georges Carnus), Jean-Claude Lavaud, Jean-Claude Piumi, Louis Provelli (20 Robert Budzynski), Louis Cardiet, Jean-Pierre Dogliani, Jean-Claude Suaudeau (65 Joseph Bonnel), Bernard Blanchet, Georges Lech, Philippe Gondet, Charly Loubet.
Manager: Just Fontaine

ROMANIA: Mihai Ionescu, Lajos Satmareanu (64 Corneliu Popa), Ion Nunweiller, Dumitru Nicolae, Mihai Mocanu, Laszlo Vasile Gergely, Nicolae Dobrin, Mircea Lucescu, Constantin Fratila, Mircea Dridea, Sorin Avram.
Manager: Ilie Oana

Goals: Jean-Pierre Dogliani (88) / Constantin Fratila (14), Mircea Dridea (76)

308.   03.06.1967

FRANCE v SOVIET UNION   2-4 (2-1)

Parc des Princes, Paris

Referee: Décio Vítor Bentes de Freitas (Portugal)
Attendance: 24,778

FRANCE: Daniel Éon, Gabriel De Michèle, Gilbert Le Chenadec, Jean-Claude Piumi, Louis Cardiet, Jean Deloffre, Bernard Blanchet, Jacques Simon, Philippe Gondet (46 Joseph Bonnel), Charly Loubet, André Guy.   Manager: Just Fontaine

SOVIET UNION: Lev Yashin (85 Anzor Kavazashvili), Valentin Afonin, Albert Shesternyov, Vadim Sosnikhin, Aleksandr Lenyov, Valeriy Voronin, Igor Chislenko (85 Gennadiy Evryuzhikhin), Yozhef Sabo, Fyodor Medvid, Eduard Streltsov, Anatoliy Byshovets (85 Vitaliy Khmelnitskiy).   Manager: Mikhail Yakushin

Goals: Philippe Gondet (12), Jacky Simon (45) / Igor Chislenko (33, 59), Anatoliy Byshovets (48), Eduard Streltsov (80)

309.   17.09.1967   UEFA Euro 1968 Qualifying – Group 7

POLAND v FRANCE   1-4 (1-2)

Stadion Dziesieciolecia Manifestu Lipcowego, Warszawa

Referee: Ferdinand Marschall (Austria)   Attendance: 51,010

POLAND: Hubert Kostka, Pawel Kowalski, Jacek Gmoch, Stanislaw Oslizlo, Zygmunt Anczok, Lucjan Brychczy, Piotr Suski, Eugeniusz Faber, Zygfryd Szoltysik, Wlodzimierz Lubanski, Robert Gadocha.   Manager: Michal Matyas

FRANCE: Marcel Aubour, Jean Djorkaeff, Roland Mitoraj, Bernard Bosquier, Jean Baeza, Henri Michel, Robert Herbin, Yves Herbet, André Guy, Fleury Di Nallo, Charly Loubet.
Manager: Louis Dugauguez

Goals: Lucjan Brychczy (26) / Robert Herbin (13), Fleury Di Nallo (34, 85), André Guy (63)

310. 27.09.1967
WEST GERMANY v FRANCE 5-1 (1-0)

Olympiastadion, West-Berlin

Referee: Fabio Monti (Italy)   Attendance: 80,000

WEST GERMANY: Sepp Maier, Bernd Patzke, Horst-Dieter Höttges, Franz Beckenbauer (67 Gerd Müller), Willi Schulz, Wolfgang Weber, Reinhard Libuda, Hans Siemensmeyer, Uwe Seeler, Wolfgang Overath, Hannes Löhr. Manager: Helmut Schön

FRANCE: Marcel Aubour, Jean Djorkaeff, Claude Quittet, Bernard Bosquier, Jean Baeza, Gilbert Gress, Robert Péri, Jacques Simon (69 Claude Robin), Philippe Gondet, Fleury Di Nallo, Charly Loubet.   Manager: Louis Dugauguez

Goals: Reinhard Libuda (28), Hans Siemensmeyer (47, 58), Gerd Müller (74), Wolfgang Overath (75) / Bernard Bosquier (83)

Sent off: Robert Péri (42)

311. 28.10.1967   UEFA Euro 1968 Qualifying – Group 7
FRANCE v BELGIUM 1-1 (0-1)

Stade Marcel Saupin, Nantes

Referee: Francesco Francescon (Italy)   Attendance: 14,591

FRANCE: Marcel Aubour, Jean Djorkaeff, Claude Quittet, Bernard Bosquier, Jean Baeza, Yves Herbet, Henri Michel, Robert Herbin, Fleury Di Nallo, Hervé Revelli, Charly Loubet. Manager: Louis Dugauguez

BELGIUM: Fernand Boone, Georges Heylens, André Stassart, Jean Plaskie, Jean Cornelis, Pierre Hanon, Nicolas Dewalque, Johan Devrindt, Roger Claessen, Raoul Lambert, Wilfried Puis.   Manager: Raymond Goethals

Goals: Robert Herbin (84) / Roger Claessen (37)

312. 23.12.1967   UEFA Euro 1968 Qualifying – Group 7
FRANCE v LUXEMBOURG 3-1 (1-0)

Parc des Princes, Paris

Referee: Aníbal da Silva Oliveira (Portugal) Attendance: 7,320

FRANCE: Marcel Aubour, Jean Djorkaeff, Claude Quittet, Bernard Bosquier, Jean Baeza, Richard Krawczyk, Henri Michel, Robert Szczepaniak, Charly Loubet, Didier Couécou, Georges Bereta.   Manager: Louis Dugauguez

LUXEMBOURG: René Hoffmann, Erwin Kuffer, Mathias Ewen, Fernand Jeitz, Jean-Pierre Hoffstetter, François Konter, Louis Pilot, Jean Klein, Johny Léonard, Edy Dublin, Ady Schmit.   Manager: Robert Heinz

Goals: Charly Loubet (42, 47, 53) / Jean Klein (85)

313. 06.04.1968   UEFA Euro 1968 Qualifying – Quarter-final
FRANCE v YUGOSLAVIA 1-1 (0-0)

Stade Vélodrome, Marseille

Referee: Erwin Vetter (East Germany)   Attendance: 35,423

FRANCE: Marcel Aubour, Jean Djorkaeff, Claude Quittet, Bernard Bosquier, Jean Baeza, Robert Herbin, Jacques Simon, Charly Loubet, Nestor Combin, Fleury Di Nallo, Georges Bereta.   Manager: Louis Dugauguez

YUGOSLAVIA: Ilija Pantelic, Mirsad Fazlagic, Dragan Holcer, Borivoje Djordjevic, Blagoje Paunovic, Ljubomir Mihajlovic, Dzemaludin Musovic, Ivica Osim, Vahidin Musemic, Dobrivoje Trivic, Dragan Dzajic. Manager: Rajko Mitic

Goals: Fleury Di Nallo (78) / Vahidin Musemic (64)

314. 24.04.1968   UEFA Euro 1968 Qualifying – Quarter-final
YUGOSLAVIA v FRANCE 5-1 (4-1)

Stadion Crvena Zvezda, Beograd

Referee: Paul Schiller (Austria)   Attendance: 47,687

YUGOSLAVIA: Ilija Pantelic, Mirsad Fazlagic, Dragan Holcer, Rudolf Belin, Mladen Ramljak, Ljubomir Mihajlovic, Ilija Petkovic, Dobrivoje Trivic, Vahidin Musemic, Ivica Osim, Dragan Dzajic. Manager: Rajko Mitic

FRANCE: Marcel Aubour, Jean Djorkaeff, Vincent Estève, Claude Quittet, Bernard Bosquier, Jean Baeza, Yves Herbet, Robert Szczepaniak, André Guy, Charly Loubet, Fleury Di Nallo.   Manager: Louis Dugauguez

Goals: Ilija Petkovic (3, 32), Vahidin Musemic (13, 79), Dragan Dzajic (14) / Fleury Di Nallo (33)

315. 25.09.1968
FRANCE v WEST GERMANY 1-1 (0-0)

Stade Vélodrome, Marseille

Referee: José María Ortiz de Mendíbil (Spain) Attendance: 22,355

FRANCE: Georges Carnus, Jean Djorkaeff, Roland Mitoraj, Bernard Bosquier, Jean Baeza (67 Roger Lemerre), Aimé Jacquet, André Betta, Bernard Blanchet (34 Charly Loubet), Hervé Revelli, Robert Szczepaniak, Georges Bereta. Manager: Louis Dugauguez

WEST GERMANY: Sepp Maier, Berti Vogts, Max Lorenz, Willi Schulz, Klaus Fichtel, Ludwig Müller (46 Günter Netzer), Bernd Dörfel, Franz Beckenbauer, Gerd Müller, Wolfgang Overath, Siegfried Held.   Manager: Helmut Schön

Goals: Bernard Bosquier (71) / Wolfgang Overath (87)

316.   17.10.1968

FRANCE v SPAIN   1-3 (1-0)

Stade de Gerland, Lyon

Referee: Aurelio Angonese (Italy)   Attendance: 35,000

FRANCE: Georges Carnus, Jean Djorkaeff, Roland Mitoraj, Bernard Bosquier, Jean Baeza, Aimé Jacquet, Robert Szczepaniak (46 Jacques Simon), Robert Herbin, Bernard Blanchet, André Guy, Georges Bereta.   Manager: Louis Dugauguez

SPAIN: Salvador SADURNÍ Urpi (46 José Angel IRÍBAR Kortajerena), Antonio TORRES García, Francisco CASTELLANO Rodríguez (36 Antonio "TONONO" Alfonso Moreno), Francisco Fernández Rodríguez "GALLEGO" (42 GERMÁN Dévora Ceballos), ELADIO Silvestre Graells, José Martínez Sánchez "PIRRI", MARCIAL Manuel Pina Morales, Pedro María ZABALZA Inda, AMANCIO Amara Varela, José Armando UFARTE Ventoso, LUIS ARAGONÉS Suárez.   Manager: Eduardo TOBA Muíño

Goals: Bernard Blanchet (22) / José Martínez Sánchez "PIRRI" (59), José Armando UFARTE Ventoso (74), LUIS ARAGONÉS Suárez (84)

317.   06.11.1968   FIFA World Cup Qualification – Group 5

FRANCE v NORWAY   0-1 (0-0

Stade de la Meinau, Strasbourg

Referee: Francesco Francescon (Italy)   Attendance: 18,319

FRANCE: Georges Carnus, Jean Djorkaeff, Roger Lemerre, Claude Quittet, Bernard Bosquier, Gilbert Gress (73 Charly Loubet), Robert Szczepaniak (46 André Betta), Bernard Blanchet, André Guy, Georges Bereta, Henri Michel.   Manager: Louis Dugauguez

NORWAY: Svein Bjørn Olsen, Jan Rodvang, Thor Spydevold, Nils Arne Eggen, Arild Mathisen, Trygve Bornø, Olav Nilsen, Karl Johan Johannessen, Ole Dybwad-Olsen, Odd Iversen, Harald Sunde.   Manager: Wilhelm Kment

Goal: Odd Iversen (67)

318.   12.03.1969

ENGLAND v FRANCE   5-0 (1-0)

British Empire Exhibition Stadium, London

Referee: István Zsolt (Hungary)   Attendance: 85,000

ENGLAND: Gordon Banks, Keith Newton, Terry Cooper, Alan Mullery, Jack Charlton, Bobby Moore, Francis Lee, Colin Bell, Geoff Hurst, Martin Peters, Michael O'Grady.   Manager: Alf Ramsey

FRANCE: Georges Carnus, Jean Djorkaeff, Bernard Bosquier, Roger Lemerre, Jean-Paul Rostagni, Joseph Bonnel, Jacques Simon, Henri Michel, Yves Herbet, Charly Loubet, Georges Bereta.   Manager: Georges Boulogne

Goals: Michael O'Grady (33), Geoff Hurst (48 pen, 49, 80 pen), Francis Lee (75)

319.   30.04.1969

FRANCE v ROMANIA   1-0 (0-0)

Parc des Princes, Paris

Referee: Bruno De Marchi (Italy)   Attendance: 18,218

FRANCE: Yves Chauveau, Jacques Novi, Jean Djorkaeff, Roger Lemerre, Jean-Paul Rostagni, Henri Michel, José Broissart, Daniel Horlaville (47 Georges Bereta), Charly Loubet, Hervé Revelli, Jean-Claude Bras.   Manager: Georges Boulogne

ROMANIA: Necula Raducanu, Niculae Lupescu, Bujor Halmageanu, Dan Coe, Augustin Deleanu, Laszlo Vasile Gergely (43 Radu Nunweiller), Cornel Dinu, Constantin Nasturescu, Emerich Dembrovschi, Florea Dumitrache, Mircea Lucescu.   Manager: Angelo Nicolescu

Goal: Henri Michel (80)

320.   10.09.1969   FIFA World Cup Qualification – Group 5

NORWAY v FRANCE   1-3 (0-1)

Ullevaal Stadion, Oslo

Referee: Laurens (Lau) van Ravens (Netherlands)   Attendance: 22,495

NORWAY: Kjell Kaspersen (55 Per Haftorsen), Nils Arne Eggen, Finn Thorsen, Frank Olafsen, Sigbjørn Slinning, Trygve Bornø, Finn Seemann, Ole Dybwad-Olsen, Harald Berg (46 Harry Hestad), Odd Iversen, Roald Jensen.   Manager: Wilhelm Kment

FRANCE: Georges Carnus, Jean Djorkaeff, Jacques Novi, Bernard Bosquier, Jean-Paul Rostagni, Henri Michel, José Broissart, Charly Loubet, Hervé Revelli, Serge Chiesa (46 Jean-Michel Larqué), Jean-Claude Bras.   Manager: Georges Boulogne

Goals: Ole Dybwad-Olsen (90), / Hervé Revelli (9, 48, 76)

321.   15.10.1969   FIFA World Cup Qualification – Group 5

SWEDEN v FRANCE   2-0 (1-0)

Råsunda Fotbollstadion, Solna

Referee: Rudolf (Rudi) Glöckner (East Germany)   Attendance: 51,954

SWEDEN: Ronnie Hellström, Hans Selander, Björn Nordqvist, Kurt Axelsson, Roland Grip, Tommy Svensson, Bosse Larsson, Leif Eriksson (62 Roger Magnusson), Ove Grahn, Ove Kindvall, Örjan Persson.   Manager: Orvar Bergmark

FRANCE: Georges Carnus, Jean Djorkaeff, Jacques Novi, Bernard Bosquier, Jean-Paul Rostagni, José Broissart, Henri Michel, Charly Loubet, Serge Chiesa, Hervé Revelli, Georges Bereta.   Manager: Georges Boulogne

Goals: Ove Kindvall (33 pen, 65)

322. 01.11.1969 FIFA World Cup Qualification – Group 5
FRANCE – SWEDEN 3-0 (3-0)
Parc de Princes, Paris
Referee: David William (Dave) Smith (England)   Attendance: 17,916

FRANCE: Georges Carnus, Jean Djorkaeff, Jacques Novi, Bernard Bosquier, Jean-Paul Rostagni, José Broissart, Henri Michel, Jean-Claude Bras, Charly Loubet, Georges Lech, Georges Bereta.   Manager: Georges Boulogne

SWEDEN: Ronnie Hellström, Björn Ericson, Krister Kristensson, Björn Nordqvist, Roland Grip, Tommy Svensson (14 Göran Nicklasson), Bosse Larsson, Roger Magnusson, Ove Grahn, Tom Turesson, Hans Johansson (46 Ove Eklund). Manager: Orvar Bergmark

Goals: Jean-Claude Bras (37, 43), Jean Djorkaeff (39 pen)

323. 08.04.1970
FRANCE v BULGARIA 1-1 (1-1)
Stade Robert Diochon, Rouen
Referee: Joseph Hannet (Belgium)   Attendance: 22,000

FRANCE: Georges Carnus, Jean Djorkaeff, Jacques Novi, Bernard Bosquier, Jean-Paul Rostagni, José Broissart (60 Jean-Noël Huck), Henri Michel, Jean-Claude Bras, Hervé Revelli, Charly Loubet, Georges Bereta (65 Serge Chiesa). Manager: Georges Boulogne

BULGARIA: Simeon Simeonov, Aleksandar Shalamanov, Ivan Dimitrov, Stefan Aladzhov, Ivan Davidov, Asparuh Nikodimov, Dinko Dermendzhiev, Hristo Bonev, Petar Zhekov, Dimitar Yakimov (74 Petko Petkov), Dimitar Marashliev. Manager: Stefan Bozhkov

Goals: Henri Michel (38) / Petar Zhekov (28)

324. 28.04.1970
FRANCE v ROMANIA 2-0 (2-0)
Stade Auguste Delaune, Reims
Referee: Othmar Huber (Switzerland)   Attendance: 10,929

FRANCE: Georges Carnus, Jean Djorkaeff, Jacques Novi, Bernard Bosquier, Jean-Paul Rostagni, Jean-Claude Bras, Henri Michel, Jean-Noël Huck, Georges Bereta, Hervé Revelli, Charly Loubet. Manager: Georges Boulogne

ROMANIA: Necula Raducanu (46 Stere Adamache), Lajos Satmareanu, Niculae Lopescu, Cornel Dinu, Mihai Mocanu, Radu Nunweiller, Ion Dumitru (46 Nicolae Pescaru), Alexandru Neagu, Flavius Domide (46 Nicolae Dobrin), Florea Dumitrache, Mircea Lucescu. Manager: Angelo Niculescu

Goals: Charly Loubet (10), Jean Djorkaeff (40 pen)

325. 03.05.1970
SWITZERLAND v FRANCE 2-1 (1-0)
St. Jakob Stadion, Basel
Referee: Paul Schiller (Austria)   Attendance: 23,676

SWITZERLAND: Marcel Kunz, Peter Ramseier, Pierre-Albert Chapuisat, Roland Citherlet (24 Anton Weibel), Jean-Paul Loichat, Karl Odermatt, Jakob (Köbi) Kuhn, Walter Balmer, Friedrich Künzli (46 Georges Vuilleumier), Rolf Blättler, Peter Wenger. Manager: René Hüssy

FRANCE: Georges Carnus, Jean Djorkaeff, Jacques Novi, Bernard Bosquier, Jean-Paul Rostagni, Henri Michel, Michel Mézy, Jean-Claude Bras (48 Georges Lech), Charly Loubet (70 Serge Chiesa, 88 Bernard Blanchet), Georges Bereta, Hervé Revelli. Manager: Georges Boulogne

Goals: Rolf Blättler (28, 72) / Hervé Revelli (79)

326. 05.09.1970
FRANCE v CZECHOSLOVAKIA 3-0 (3-0)
Stade du Ray, Nice
Referee: Rudolf Scheurer (Switzerland)   Attendance: 13,418

FRANCE: Georges Carnus, Jean Djorkaeff, Jacques Novi, Bernard Bosquier, Jean-Paul Rostagni, Yves Herbet, Henri Michel, Michel Mézy, Georges Bereta, Philippe Gondet, Charly Loubet (61 Bernard Blanchet).   Manager: Georges Boulogne

CZECHOSLOVAKIA: Ivo Viktor (46 Alexander Vencel), Karol Dobias, Václav Migas, Jirí Novák, Vladimír Hagara, Ivan Hrdlicka (46 Josef Jurkanin), Ján Geleta, Ladislav Kuna, Frantisek Veselý, Ladislav Petrás (46 Milan Albrecht), Juraj Szikora. Manager: Antonín Rýgr

Goals: Philippe Gondet (8), Charly Loubet (13), Bernard Bosquier (42)

327. 07.10.1970
AUSTRIA v FRANCE 1-0 (0-0)
Praterstadion, Vienna
Referee: Ferdinand Biwersi (West Germany)   Attendance: 25,000

AUSTRIA: Friedl Koncilia, Peter Clement (46 Johannes Demantke), Hans Schmidradner, Gerhard Sturmberger, Erich Fak, Josef Hickersberger (76 Eduard Krieger), Norbert Hof, August Starek (46 Johann Ettmayer), Thomas Parits, Wilhelm Kreuz, Helmut Redl.   Manager: Leopold Stastný

FRANCE: Georges Carnus, Jean Djorkaeff, Jacques Novi, Bernard Bosquier, Jean-Paul Rostagni, Yves Herbet (78 Jean-Michel Larqué), Henri Michel, Michel Mézy, Georges Bereta, Philippe Gondet (78 Louis Floch), Charly Loubet (46 Hervé Revelli).   Manager: Georges Boulogne

Goal: Wilhelm Kreuz (49)

328. 11.11.1970 UEFA Euro 1972 Qualifying – Group 2
FRANCE v NORWAY 3-1 (1-0)
Stade de Gerland, Lyon

Referee: António Saldanha Ribeiro (Portugal)
Attendance: 10,357

FRANCE: Georges Carnus, Jean Djorkaeff, Jacques Novi, Bernard Bosquier, Jean-Paul Rostagni, Georges Lech, Henri Michel, Jean-Noël Huck, Michel Mézy, Louis Floch, Charly Loubet.   Manager: Georges Boulogne

NORWAY: Per Haftorsen, Per Pettersen, Finn Thorsen, Arild Hetleøen, Sigbjørn Slinning, Trygve Bornø, Thor Spydevold, Olav Nilsen, Harry Hestad, Egil Olsen, Finn Seemann.
Manager: Øivind Johannessen

Goals: Louis Floch (30), Georges Lech (55), Michel Mézy (63) / Olav Nilsen (79)

329. 15.11.1970
BELGIUM v FRANCE 1-2 (0-0)
Stade du Heysel, Brussels

Referee: Kurt Waldemar Tschenscher (West Germany)
Attendance: 19,937

BELGIUM: Christian Piot, Alfons Bastijns, Nicolas Dewalque, Léon Jeck, Jean Thissen, Wilfried Van Moer, Erwin Vandendaele, Jean Dockx, Léon Semmeling (46 John Thio), Pierre Carteus, Jacques Teugels.
Manager: Raymond Goethals

FRANCE: Georges Carnus, Roger Lemerre, Jacques Novi, Bernard Bosquier, Jean Djorkaeff, Georges Lech, Henri Michel, Jean-Noël Huck, Robert Rico, Louis Floch, Marc Molitor.   Manager: Georges Boulogne

Goals: Wilfried Van Moer (73) / Marc Molitor (50, 77)
Sent off: Roger Lemerre (79)

330. 08.01.1971
ARGENTINA v FRANCE 3-4 (0-1)
Estadio La Bombonera, Buenos Aires

Referee: Roberto Osvaldo Barreiro (Argentina)
Attendance: 4,500

ARGENTINA: José Miguel MARÍN Ocotto, Rubén José Suñé, Roberto Alfredo Perfumo, César Auguste Larraignée, Jorge Omar Carrascosa, Norberto Rubén Madurga, Miguel Alberto Nicolau, Miguel Ángel Tojo (46 Miguel Ángel BRINDISI de Marco), Roberto Artemio Gramajo (46 Ángel Alberto Marcos), Alfredo Domingo Obberti (66 Carlos Alberto Bianchi), Juan Ramón Verón.   Manager: Juan José Pizzuti

FRANCE: Georges Carnus, Jean Djorkaeff, Jacques Novi, Bernard Bosquier, Jean-Paul Rostagni, Jean-Noël Huck, Georges Lech, Michel Mézy, Georges Bereta (82 Yves Herbet), Louis Floch, Charly Loubet (46 Hervé Revelli).
Manager: Georges Boulogne

Goals: Miguel Ángel BRINDISI de Marco (55), Miguel Alberto Nicolau (73), César Auguste Larraignée (90 pen) / Charly Loubet (3), Jean Djorkaeff (50 pen), Georges Lech (64), Hervé Revelli (89)
Sent off: Jacques Novi (81)

331. 12.01.1971
ARGENTINA v FRANCE 2-0 (1-0)
Estadio General San Martín, Mar del Plata

Referee: Arturo Andrés Ithurralde (Argentina)
Attendance: 18,000

ARGENTINA: Miguel Ángel SANTORO Marcore, Rubén José Suñé, Roberto Alfredo Perfumo (.. Miguel Ángel Tojo), César Auguste Larraignée, Jorge Omar Carrascosa, Norberto Rubén Madurga, Miguel Alberto Nicolau, Miguel Ángel BRINDISI de Marco, Ángel Alberto Marcos, Héctor Casimiro Yazalde, Juan Ramón Verón.   Manager: Juan José Pizzuti

FRANCE: Georges Carnus, Jean Djorkaeff, Henri Michel, Bernard Bosquier, Jean-Paul Rostagni, Yves Herbet, Jean-Noël Huck, Georges Lech (75 Marc Molitor), Michel Mézy, Charly Loubet, Georges Bereta (69 Louis Floch).
Manager: Georges Boulogne

Goals: César Auguste Larraignée (4 pen), Norberto Rubén Madurga (75)

332. 17.03.1971
SPAIN v FRANCE 2-2 (0-1)
Estadio Luís Casanova, Valencia

Referee: Aurelio Angonese (Italy)   Attendance: 20,038

SPAIN: José Angel IRÍBAR Kortajerena, Juan Cruz SOL Oria, Francisco Fernández Rodríguez "GALLEGO", Antonio "TONONO" Alfonso Moreno, Antonio Manuel "ANTÓN" Martínez Morales, Enrique Álvarez COSTAS (46 Enrique LORA Millán), José CLARAMUNT Torres, AMANCIO Amara Varela (46 Carlos REXACH Cerdá), Antonio María ARIETA-Araunabeña Piedra (46 Enrique "QUINI" Castro González), José Ignacio CHURRUCA Sistiaga, José Martínez Sánchez "PIRRI".   Manager: Ladislav (László) KUBALA Stecz

FRANCE: Georges Carnus, Jean Djorkaeff, Jacques Novi, Bernard Bosquier, Jean-Paul Rostagni, Henri Michel, Georges Lech, Michel Mézy, Georges Bereta, Hervé Revelli, Charly Loubet (10 Louis Floch).   Manager: Georges Boulogne

Goals: José Martínez Sánchez "PIRRI" (61, 63) / Hervé Revelli (14, 54)

333. 24.04.1971   UEFA Euro 1972 Qualifying – Group 2
HUNGARY v FRANCE 1-1 (0-0)
Népstadion, Budapest
Referee: Joaquim Fernandes dos Campos (Portugal)
Attendance: 45,867

HUNGARY: Ádám Rothermel, Ernö Noskó, Lajos Szücs, Miklós Páncsics, Péter Juhász, László Fazekas, Sándor Zámbó, Flórián Albert, Lajos Kocsis, Ferenc Bene, Mihály Kozma (53 László Karsai).   Manager: József Hoffer

FRANCE: Georges Carnus, Jean Djorkaeff, Roger Lemerre, Francis Camerini, Bernard Bosquier, Jacques Novi, Henri Michel, Georges Lech, Georges Bereta, Hervé Revelli, Fleury Di Nallo (46 Charly Loubet).   Manager: Georges Boulogne

Goals: Lajos Kocsis (70 pen) / Hervé Revelli (64)

334. 08.09.1971   UEFA Euro 1972 Qualifying – Group 2
NORWAY v FRANCE 1-3 (0-2)
Ullevaal Stadion, Oslo
Referee: John Wright Patterson (Scotland)
Attendance: 16,544

NORWAY: Geir Karlsen (81 Svein Bjørn Olsen), Anbjørn Ekeland, Tore Børrehaug, Thor Spydevold, Sigbjørn Slinning, Tom Jacobsen, Jan Christiansen, Egil Olsen, Jan Fuglset, Tom Lund (75 Ola Dybwad-Olsen), Kjetil Hasund.   Manager: Øivind Johannessen

FRANCE: Georges Carnus, Jean Djorkaeff, Jacques Novi, Bernard Bosquier, Jean-Paul Rostagni, Henri Michel, Michel Mézy, Georges Bereta, Bernard Blanchet (76 Georges Lech), Jacques Vergnes, Charly Loubet.
Manager: Georges Boulogne

Goals: Ola Dybwad-Olsen (80) / Jacques Vergnes (33), Charly Loubet (34), Bernard Blanchet (49)

335. 09.10.1971   UEFA Euro 1972 Qualifying – Group 2
FRANCE v HUNGARY 0-2 (0-2)
Stade Olympique Yves-du-Manoir, Colombes
Referee: Gaspart Pintado Viu (Spain)   Attendance: 21,756

FRANCE: Georges Carnus, Jean Djorkaeff, Jacques Novi, Bernard Bosquier, Jean-Paul Rostagni, Georges Lech, Henri Michel, Michel Mézy, Georges Bereta, Charly Loubet (46 Gilbert Gress), Hervé Revelli.   Manager: Georges Boulogne

HUNGARY: István Géczi, Ernö Noskó, Miklós Páncsics, Csaba Vidáts, Péter Juhász, László Fazekas, István Juhász, Lajos Szücs, Sándor Zámbó, Ferenc Bene, Antal Dunai.   Manager: Rudolf Illovszky

Goals: Ferenc Bene (35), Sándor Zámbó (43)

336. 10.11.1971   UEFA Euro 1972 Qualifying – Group 2
FRANCE v BULGARIA 2-1 (0-0)
Stade Marcel Saupin, Nantes
Referee: John Keith (Jack) Taylor (England)
Attendance: 9,405

FRANCE: Georges Carnus, Jean Djorkaeff, Francis Camerini, Jacques Novi, Claude Quittet, Michel Mézy, Bernard Blanchet, Henri Michel, Hervé Revelli (82 Louis Floch), Georges Lech, Charly Loubet.   Manager: Georges Boulogne

BULGARIA: Yordan Filipov, Ivan Zafirov, Dimitar Penev, Stefan Velichkov, Dobromir Zhechev, Bozhil Kolev, Mladen Vasilev, Hristo Bonev, Petko Petkov (85 Georgi Tsvetkov), Georgi Denev, Dinko Dermendzhiev.   Manager: Vasil Spasov

Goals: Georges Lech (64), Charly Loubet (87) / Hristo Bonev (54 pen)

337. 04.12.1971   UEFA Euro 1972 Qualifying – Group 2
BULGARIA v FRANCE 2-1 (0-0)
National Stadium Vasil Levski, Sofia
Referee: Kurt Tschenscher (West Germany)
Attendance: 18,057

BULGARIA: Rumen Goranov (65 Yordan Filipov), Milko Gaydarski, Dimitar Penev, Stefan Velichkov (46 Viktor Yonov), Dobromir Zhechev, Bozhil Kolev, Mladen Vasilev, Hristo Bonev, Petar Zhekov, Atanas Mihaylov, Dinko Dermendzhiev.   Manager: Vasil Spasov

FRANCE: Georges Carnus, Jean Djorkaeff, Marius Trésor, Jacques Novi, Bernard Bosquier, Michel Mézy, Bernard Blanchet, Henri Michel, Georges Lech, Charly Loubet (76 Georges Bereta), Hervé Revelli (60 Louis Floch).
Manager: Georges Boulogne

Goals: Petar Zhekov (47), Atanas Mihaylov (82) / Bernard Blanchet (84)

338. 08.04.1972
ROMANIA v FRANCE 2-0 (1-0)
Stadionul 23 August, Bucharest
Referee: Josip Strmecki (Yugoslavia)   Attendance: 25,000

ROMANIA: Necula Raducanu, Lajos Satmareanu, Nicolae Lupescu, Cornel Dinu, Augustin Deleanu (46 Nicolae Ionescu), Ion Dumitru, Radu Nunweiller, Mircea Lucescu, Emerich Dembrovschi, Mircea Sandu (46 Flavius Domide), Anghel Iordanescu.   Manager: Angelo Niculescu

FRANCE: Georges Carnus, Marius Trésor, Jacques Novi, Bernard Bosquier, Jean-Paul Rostagni, Georges Lech, Henri Michel, Michel Mézy (46 Claude Quittet), Georges Bereta (70 Jean-Michel Larqué), Bernard Blanchet, Louis Floch (70 Marc Molitor).   Manager: Georges Boulogne

Goals: Anghel Iordanescu (16), Cornel Dinu (54)

339. 11.06.1972   Taça Independência 1972 – Group A
C.O.N.C.A.C.A.F. v FRANCE 0-5 (0-1)
Estádio Octávio Mangabeira, Salvador de Bahia (Brazil)
Referee: Kurt Tschenscher (West Germany)
Attendance: 21,422
C.O.N.C.A.C.A.F.: Henri FRANÇILLON, José Luis CRUZ Figueroa (46' Mario VELARDE Valázquez), Miguel Ángel MATAMOROS Morales, Wilner NAZAIRE, José Fernando BULNES Zelaya, Ángel Ramón PAZ Rápalo (25' Francisco FLORES), Philippe VORBÉ, Jean-Claude DÉSIR, Claude BARTHÉLÉMY, Jorge URQUÍA Elvir, Emmanuel SANON.   Managers: Antoine Tassy & Carlos Antonio PADILLA Velásquez
FRANCE: Dominique Baratelli, Jean Djorkaeff, Claude Quittet, Marius Trésor, Jean-Paul Rostagni, Jean-Michel Larqué (46 Georges Lech), Henri Michel, Michel Mézy, Bernard Blanchet (74 Louis Floch), Hervé Revelli, Georges Bereta.   Manager: Georges Boulogne
Goals: Georges Bereta (35), Hervé Revelli (60, 66, 84), José Fernando BULNES (80 og)

340. 15.06.1972   Taça Independência 1972 – Group A
AFRICA v FRANCE 0-2 (0-1)
Estádio Rei Pelé, Maceió (Brazil)
Referee: Rudolf Scheurer (Switzerland)   Attendance: 10,000
AFRICA: Sadok "Attouga" Sassi, Édouard Gnacadja, Miloud Hadefi, Tahar Benferhat, Mohammed Hani Moustafa, Jean-Pierre Tokoto, Hassan Shehata (.. Noël Minga), Ibrahima "Petit" Sory Keita, Laurent D'Dri Pokou, Malik Jabir, Mamadouba Resmu "Maxime" Camara.
Managers: Cheikh Kouyate & Anani Matthia
FRANCE: Dominique Baratelli, Jean Djorkaeff, Claude Quittet, Marius Trésor (78 Jean-Pierre Adams), Jean-Paul Rostagni, Georges Lech, Henri Michel, Michel Mézy, Bernard Blanchet, Hervé Revelli, Georges Bereta (46 Louis Floch).   Manager: Georges Boulogne
Goals: Bernard Blanchet (35), Louis Floch (83)
Sent off: Miloud Hadefi (84)

341. 18.06.1972   Taça Independência 1972 – Group A
COLOMBIA v FRANCE 2-3 (1-2)
Estádio Octávio Mangabeira, Salvador de Bahia (Brazil)
Referee: Ángel Eduardo Pazos Bianchi (Uruguay)
Attendance: 10,000
COLOMBIA: Pedro Antonio ZAPE, Gerardo MONCADA, Jaime RODRÍGUEZ Suarez, Óscar ORTEGA, Jesús María RUBIO, Álvaro CONTRERAS, Alejandro BRAND Quintero, Luis GARCÍA (.. Adolfo José ANDRADE Chaparro), Carlos Alberto LUGO (52 Orlando MESA), Jaime MORÓN León, José Hernando PIÑEROS.   Manager: Toza Veselinovic
FRANCE: Georges Carnus, Jean Djorkaeff, Claude Quittet, Marius Trésor, Jean-François Jodar, Jean-Michel Larqué, Jean-Pierre Adams, Louis Floch (46 Georges Bereta), Marc Molitor (78 Georges Lech), Charly Loubet, Henri Michel.   Manager: Georges Boulogne
Goals: Hernando PIÑEROS (23 pen), Orlando MESA (82) / Charly Loubet (30, 72), Marc Molitor (33 pen)

342. 25.06.1972   Taça Independência 1972 – Group A
ARGENTINA v FRANCE 0-0
Estádio Octávio Mangabeira, Salvador de Bahia (Brazil)
Ref: Armando Nunes Castanheira da Rosa Marques (Brazil)
Attendance: 6,587
ARGENTINA: Miguel Ángel SANTORO Marcore, Enrique Ernesto WOLFF Dos Santos, Osvaldo José Piazza, Ángel Hugo Bargas, Rubén Oswaldo DÍAZ Figueras, Alejandro Estanislao Semenewicz, José Omar Pastoriza, Miguel Ángel Raimondo, Carlos Alberto Bianchi (.. Ernesto Mastrángelo), Rodolfo José FISCHER Eichler, Óscar Tomás MAS Magallán.   Manager: Juan José Pizzuti
FRANCE: Georges Carnus, Jean Djorkaeff, Jean-Pierre Adams, Marius Trésor, Jean-Paul Rostagni, Georges Lech, Henri Michel, Michel Mézy, Bernard Blanchet (75 Louis Floch), Hervé Revelli (84 Charly Loubet), Georges Bereta.   Manager: Georges Boulogne

343. 02.09.1972
GREECE v FRANCE 1-3 (0-0)
Georgios Karaiskakis Stadium, Piraeus
Referee: Fulvio Pieroni (Italy)   Attendance: 10,000
GREECE: Nikos Christidis, Dimitris Dimitriou, Takis Synetopoulos, Apostolos Toskas, Thanasis Aggelis, Kostas Eleftherakis, Charalambos Stavropoulos (78 Spyros Pomonis), Stavros Sarafis, Antonis Antoniadis (65 Kyriakos Apostolidis), Dimitris Domazos, Dimitris Papaioannou.
Manager: Billy Bingham
FRANCE: Georges Carnus, Jean Djorkaeff (46 José Broissart), Jacques Novi, Claude Quittet, Jean-Pierre Adams, Marius Trésor, Georges Lech (46 Charly Loubet), Jean-Michel Larqué, Hervé Revelli, Georges Bereta, Henri Michel.
Manager: Georges Boulogne
Goals: Stavros Sarafis (85) / Henri Michel (67), Hervé Revelli (86), Jean-Michel Larqué (90)

344. 13.10.1972   FIFA World Cup Qualification – Group 9
FRANCE v SOVIET UNION 1-0 (0-0)
Parc des Princes, Paris
Referee: Rudolf Scheurer (Switzerland)   Attendance: 29,746
FRANCE: Georges Carnus, José Broissart, Claude Quittet, Marius Trésor, Jean-Paul Rostagni, Henri Michel, Jean-Pierre Adams, Serge Chiesa (85 Charly Loubet), Hervé Revelli, Jean-Michel Larqué, Georges Bereta. Manager: Georges Boulogne
SOVIET UNION: Yevgeniy Rudakov, Revaz Dzodzuashvili, Murtaz Khurtsilava, Yevgeniy Lovchev, Vladimir Kaplichny, Viktor Kolotov, Levon Ishtoyan (57 Gennadiy Evryuzhikhin), Vyacheslav Semyonov, Vladimir Fedotov, Sergey Olshanskiy, Oleg Blokhin (67 Anatoliy Puzach).
Manager: Aleksandr Ponomaryov
Goal: Georges Bereta (61)

345. 15.11.1972   FIFA World Cup Qualification – Group 9
REPUBLIC OF IRELAND v FRANCE 2-1 (1-0)
Dalymount Park, Dublin
Referee: Kaj Bernhard Rasmussen (Denmark)   Att: 26,511
REPUBLIC OF IRELAND: Alan Kelly, Joe Kinnear, Paddy Mulligan, Tommy McConville, Jimmy Holmes, Eoin Hand, Johnny Giles, Tony Byrne (64 Noel Campbell), Terry Conroy (88 Turlough O'Connor), Ray Treacy, Don Givens.
Manager: Liam Tuohy
FRANCE: Georges Carnus, José Broissart, Claude Quittet, Marius Trésor, Jean-Paul Rostagni, Jean-Noël Huck, Jean-Pierre Adams, Charly Loubet (63 Marc Molitor), Hervé Revelli, Jean-Michel Larqué, Georges Bereta.
Manager: Georges Boulogne
Goals: Terry Conroy (27), Ray Treacy (77) / Jean-Michel Larqué (66)

346. 03.03.1973
FRANCE v PORTUGAL 1-2 (1-1)
Parc des Princes, Paris
Referee: Franz Geluck (Belgium)   Attendance: 45,267
FRANCE: Georges Carnus, José Broissart, Jean-Pierre Adams, Marius Trésor, Jean-Paul Rostagni, Georges Lech, Henri Michel, Michel Mézy (85 Jean-Noël Huck), Georges Bereta, Hervé Revelli, Marc Molitor (75 Louis Floch).
Manager: Georges Boulogne
PORTUGAL: JOSÉ HENRIQUE Rodrigues Marques, ARTUR Manuel Soares CORREIA, HUMBERTO Manuel de Jesus COELHO (10 ANTÓNIO José SIMÕES da Costa), FERNANDO José António FREITAS Alexandrino, ADOLFO António Da Luz CALISTO, António José "TONI" Da Conceiçao Oliveira, ALFREDO Perrulas QUARESMA, Fernando Pascoal Neves "PAVÃO", Manuel Gomes Baptista Tamagnini "NENÉ" (81 António DINIS Joaquim), ABEL Fernando Miglietti (65 ARTUR JORGE Braga de Melo Teixeira), EUSÉBIO Da Silva Ferreira.   Manager: JOSÉ AUGUSTO Pinto De Almeida
Goals: Marc Molitor (36) / EUSÉBIO Da Silva Ferreira (38 pen, 87)

347. 19.05.1973   FIFA World Cup Qualification – Group 9
FRANCE v REPUBLIC OF IRELAND 1-1 (0-0)
Parc des Princes, Paris
Referee: Nicolae (Nicu) Rainea (Romania)
Attendance: 28,405
FRANCE: Georges Carnus, Raymond Domenech, Claude Quittet, Marius Trésor, Jean-Paul Rostagni, Henri Michel, Jean-Pierre Adams, Louis Floch, Hervé Revelli, Jean-Michel Larqué (61 Serge Chiesa), Georges Bereta.
Manager: Georges Boulogne
REPUBLIC OF IRELAND: Alan Kelly, Tommy Carroll (25 John Herrick), Paddy Mulligan, Tommy McConville, Jimmy Holmes, Mick Martin, Eoin Hand, Tony Byrne, Miah Dennehy, Ray Treacy, Don Givens.   Manager: Liam Tuohy
Goals: Serge Chiesa (78) / Mick Martin (83)

348.   26.05.1973   FIFA World Cup Qualification – Group 9
SOVIET UNION v FRANCE   2-0 (0-0)

Lenin Central Stadium, Moscow

Referee: Ferdinand Biwersi (West Germany)
Attendance: 76,604

SOVIET UNION: Yevgeniy Rudakov, Revaz Dzodzuashvili, Murtaz Khurtsilava (75 Vladimir Fedotov), Yevgeniy Lovchev, Vladimir Kaplichny, Yuriy Vasenin, Vladimir Muntyan, Viktor Kuznetsov (60 Sergey Olshanskiy), Arkadiy Andreasyan, Vladimir Onishchenko, Oleg Blokhin.   Manager: Evgeniy Goryanskiy

FRANCE: Dominique Baratelli, José Broissart, Jean-Paul Rostagni, Bernard Gardon, Marius Trésor, Claude Quittet, Louis Floch (46 Michel Mézy), Henri Michel, Hervé Revelli, Serge Chiesa, Georges Bereta.   Manager: Georges Boulogne

Goals: Oleg Blokhin (81), Vladimir Onishchenko (84)

349.   08.09.1973
FRANCE v GREECE   3-1 (1-0)

Parc des Princes, Paris

Referee: Paolo Toselli (Italy)   Attendance: 30,237

FRANCE: Dominique Baratelli, Jean-Claude Osman, Jean-Pierre Adams, Marius Trésor, Pierre Repellini, Roger Jouve, Serge Chiesa, Georges Bereta, Marc Molitor, Bernard Lacombe (57 Marc Berdoll), Christian Sarramagna (77 Daniel Ravier).   Manager: Stefan Kovács

GREECE: Panagiotis Kelesidis, Dimitris Dimitriou, Anthimos Kapsis, Takis Synetopoulos, Thanasis Aggelis, Dimitris Domazos, Kostas Eleftherakis, Stavros Sarafis (46 Christos Terzanidis), Giorgos Koudas, Antonis Antoniadis, Kostantinos Aidiniou (75 Lakis Nikolaou).   Manager: Alketas Panagoulias

Goals: Roger Jouve (9), Marc Berdoli (59), Serge Chiesa (72) / Kostantinos Aidiniou (66)

350.   13.10.1973
WEST GERMANY v FRANCE   2-1 (0-0)

Parkstadion, Gelsenkirchen

Referee: Rudolf Scheurer (Switzerland)   AttendanceL 70,200

WEST GERMANY: Wolfgang Kleff, Horst-Dieter Höttges (46 Bernd Cullmann), Wolfgang Weber, Franz Beckenbauer, Helmut Kremers, Uli Hoeneß, Heinz Flohe, Wolfgang Overath, Jürgen Grabowski, Gerd Müller, Erwin Kremers.   Manager: Helmut Schön

FRANCE: Dominique Baratelli, Dario Grava, Jean-Pierre Adams, Marius Trésor, Pierre Repellini, Henri Michel, Serge Chiesa, Roger Jouve, Georges Bereta, Charly Loubet, Marc Molitor (65 Marc Berdoll).   Manager: Stefan Kovács

Goals: Gerd Müller (55, 59 pen) / Marius Trésor (82)

351.   21.11.1973
FRANCE v DENMARK   3-0 (0-0)

Parc des Princes, Paris

Referee: Heinz Aldinger (West Germany)
Attendance: 22,534

FRANCE: Jean-Paul Bertrand-Demanes, Pierre Repellini, Alain Merchadier, Jean-Pierre Adams, François Bracci, Serge Chiesa (75 Patrick Revelli), Henri Michel, Georges Bereta, Daniel Ravier (80 Claude Papi), Hervé Revelli, Christian Sarramagna.   Manager: Stefan Kovács

DENMARK: Birger Jensen, Johnny Hansen, Helge Vonsyld, Kresten Bjerre, Viggo Jensen (70 Søren Larsen), John Steen Olsen, Ole Bjørnmose (70 Ole Skouboe), Morten Olsen, Flemming Lund, Hans Aabech, Henning Jensen.   Manager: Rudolf Strittich

Goals: Georges Bereta (57), Søren Larsen (78 og), Hervé Revelli (89)

352.   23.03.1974
FRANCE v ROMANIA   1-0 (0-0)

Parc des Princes, Paris

Referee: Bartley John Homewood (England)
Attendance: 20,224

FRANCE: Jean-Paul Bertrand-Demanes, Albert Vanucci, Jean-Pierre Adams, Marius Trésor, François Bracci, Henri Michel, Serge Chiesa, Jean-Marc Guillou, Christian Dalger (57 Patrick Revelli), Hervé Revelli (83 Marc Berdoll), Georges Bereta.   Manager: Stefan Kovács

ROMANIA: Necula Raducanu, Teodor Anghelini, Dumitru Antonescu, Cornel Dinu, Gheorghe Christache, Ilie Balaci (75 Iuliu Hajnal), Aurel Beldeanu, Anghel Iordanescu, Radu Troi (70 Mircea Sandu), Florea Dumitrache, Attila Kun.   Manager: Valentin Stanescu

Goal: Georges Bereta (59)

353.   27.04.1974
CZECHOSLOVAKIA v FRANCE   3-3 (2-2)

Letenský Stadion, Praha

Referee: Günter Männig (East Germany)
Attendance: 12,000

CZECHOSLOVAKIA: Alexander Vencel, Ján Pivarník, Karol Dobias, Anton Ondrus, Zdenek Rygel, Premysl Bicovský (78 Milan Cermák), Ladislav Kuna, Antonín Panenka, Bohumil Veselý, Ján Svehlík, Zdenek Nehoda.   Manager: Václav Jezek

FRANCE: Jean-Paul Bertrand-Demanes, Albert Vanucci, Jean-Pierre Adams (64 Alain Merchadier), Marius Trésor, François Bracci, Jean-Noël Huck, Serge Chiesa, Henri Michel, Jean-Marc Guillou, Bernard Lacombe, Georges Bereta.   Manager: Stefan Kovács

Goals: Ján Pivarník (33), Premysl Bicovský (35), Antonín Panenka (87) / Serge Chiesa (7), Bernard Lacombe (28, 72)

354.   18.05.1974
FRANCE v ARGENTINA 0-1 (0-1)

Parc des Princes, Paris

Ref: Johannes Nicolaas Ignatius (Jan) Keizer (Netherlands)
Attendance: 26,735

FRANCE: Dominique Baratelli, Pierre Repellini, Alain Merchadier (46 Jean-François Jodar), François Bracci, Jean-Noël Huck, Jean-Marc Guillou, Georges Bereta, Jean-Pierre Adams, Marc Molitor, Bernard Lacombe (70 Charly Loubet), Christian Sarramagna.   Manager: Stefan Kovács

ARGENTINA: Daniel Alberto CARNEVALI Spurchesi, Rubén Oscar Glaría (46 Enrique Ernesto WOLFF Dos Santos), Roberto Alfredo Perfumo, Ángel Hugo Bargas, Francisco Pedro Manuel Sá, Miguel Ángel BRINDISI de Marco (61 Enrique Salvador CHAZARRETA Herrera), Roberto Marcelo Telch, Carlos Vicente Squeo, Agustín Alberto Balbuena, Marío Alberto KEMPES Chiodi, René Orlando Houseman (46 Roque Alberto Avallay).   Manager: Vladislao Wenceslao Cap

Goal: Marío Alberto KEMPES Chiodi (22)

355.   07.09.1974
POLAND v FRANCE 0-2 (0-2)

Stadion Olimpijski, Wroclaw

Referee: Erik Fredriksson (Sweden)   Attendance: 25,000

POLAND: Jan Tomaszewski, Antoni Szymanowski, Miroslaw Bulzacki (46 Stanislaw Sobczynski), Henryk Wieczorek, Piotr Drzewiecki, Leslaw Cmikiewicz (46 Zygmunt Maszczyk), Kazimierz Deyna, Józef Kopicera, Grzegorz Lato, Zdzislaw Kapka (76 Marek Kusto), Robert Gadocha.   Manager: Kazimierz Górski

FRANCE: Jean-Paul Bertrand-Demanes, Jean-François Jodar, Jean-Pierre Adams, Marius Trésor, François Bracci, Jean-Noël Huck, Henri Michel (87 Alain Merchadier), Jean-Marc Guillou, Alain Giresse (71 Patrick Revelli), Christian Coste, Georges Bereta.   Manager: Stefan Kovács

Goals: Christian Coste (37), Jean-François Jodar (39)

356.   12.10.1974   UEFA Euro 1976 Qualifying – Group 7
BELGIUM v FRANCE 2-1 (1-1)

Stade du Heysel, Brussels

Referee: Kenneth Howard (Ken) Burns (England)
Attendance: 32,108

BELGIUM: Christian Piot, Gilbert Van Binst, Hugo Broos, Erwin Vandendaele, Maurice Martens, Wilfried Van Moer, Jan Verheyen, Paul Van Himst (71 Jean Dockx), François Van der Elst, Raoul Lambert, Jacques Teugels.
Manager: Raymond Goethals

FRANCE: Dominique Baratelli, Jean-François Jodar, Jean-Pierre Adams, Marius Trésor, François Bracci, Jean-Noël Huck, Henri Michel, Jean-Marc Guillou, Christian Coste, Bernard Lacombe (83 Jean Gallice), Georges Bereta.
Manager: Stefan Kovács

Goals: Maurice Martens (12), François Van der Elst (75) / Christian Coste (16)

357.   16.11.1974   UEFA Euro 1976 Qualifying – Group 7
FRANCE v EAST GERMANY 2-2 (0-1)

Parc des Princes, Paris

Referee: Pablo Augusto Sánchez Ibáñez (Spain)
Attendance: 45,381

FRANCE: Jean-Paul Bertrand-Demanes, Jean-François Jodar, Jean-Pierre Adams, Marius Trésor, François Bracci, Jean-Noël Huck, Henri Michel (68 Christian Synaeghel), Jean-Marc Guillou, Gérard Soler, Christian Coste (46 Jean Gallice), Georges Bereta.   Manager: Stefan Kovács

EAST GERMANY: Jürgen Croy, Hans-Jürgen (Dixie) Dörner, Gerd Kische, Konrad Weise, Siegmar Wätzlich, Reinhard Häfner, Lothar Kurbjuweit, Reinhard Lauck, Hans-Jürgen Kreische (83 Wolfgang Seguin), Jürgen Sparwasser, Martin Hoffmann.   Manager: Georg Buschner

Goals: Jean-Marc Guillou (79), Jean Gallice (89) / Jürgen Sparwasser (25), Hans-Jürgen Kreische (57)

Sent off: Gérard Soler (86)

358.   26.03.1975
FRANCE v HUNGARY 2-0 (0-0)

Parc des Princes, Paris

Referee: Klaus Ohmsen (West Germany)
Attendance: 25,000

FRANCE: René Charrier, Christian López (83 Alain Merchadier), Victor Zvunka, Marius Trésor, François Bracci, Jean-Noël Huck (70 Claude Papi), Jean-Marc Guillou, Henri Michel, Yves Triantafilos, Hervé Revelli (60 Patrick Parizon), Georges Bereta.   Manager: Stefan Kovács

HUNGARY: Ferenc Mészáros, Endre Kolár, László Bálint, Ede Dunai, József Horváth, József Tóth, László Fazekas, Lajos Kocsis, Sándor Pintér, Ferenc Bene, László Nagy (59 András Tóth).   Manager: Ede Moór

Goals: Henri Michel (56), Patrick Parizon (63)

359. 26.04.1975
FRANCE v PORTUGAL 0-2 (0-1)
Stade Olympique Yves-du-Manoir, Colombes
Referee: Hans-Joachim Weyland (West Germany)
Attendance: 24,816

FRANCE: René Charrier (46 Dominique Baratelli), Jean-François Jodar (88 Bernard Boissier), Jean-Pierre Adams, Marius Trésor, François Bracci, Jean-Noël Huck (46 Jean Gallice), Henri Michel, Jean-Marc Guillou, Patrick Parizon, Christian Coste, Georges Bereta (72 Yves Mariot). Manager: Stefan Kovács

PORTUGAL: VÍTOR Manuel Afonso De Oliveira "DAMAS", REBELO Francisco Moreira da Silva, HUMBERTO Manuel de Jesus COELHO, CARLOS Alexandre Fortes ALHINHO, António Monteiro Teixeira de BARROS (88 Minervino José Lopes PIETRA), António José "TONI" Da Conceiçao Oliveira, JOÃO António Ferreira Resende ALVES (79 Adelino De Jesus TEIXEIRA), OCTÁVIO Joaquim Coelho MACHADO, Samuel Ferreira FRAGUITO, Mário Da Silva Mateus "MARINHO" (72 FERNANDO Mendes Soares GOMES), Manuel Gomes Baptista Tamagnini "NENÉ" (46 Mário Jorge MOÍNHOS Matos). Manager: José Maria Carvalho PEDROTO

Goals: Manuel Gomes Baptista Tamagnini "NENÉ" (21), Mário Da Silva Mateus "MARINHO" (64)

360. 25.05.1975   UEFA Euro 1976 Qualifying – Group 7
ICELAND v FRANCE 0-0
Laugardalsvöllur, Reykjavík
Referee: Malcolm Hall Wright (Northern Ireland)
Attendance: 7,613

ICELAND: Sigurdur Dagsson, Gísli Torfason, Jón Pétursson, Marteinn Geirsson, Jóhannes Edvaldsson, Karl Hermannsson (76 Grétar Magnússon), Gudgeir Leifsson, Ásgeir Sigurvinsson, Ólafur Júliusson, Teitur Thórdarson, Matthías Hallgrímsson (55 Ernst Elmar Geirsson). Manager: Tony Knapp

FRANCE: Dominique Baratelli, Christian López, Jean-Pierre Adams, Marius Trésor, François Bracci, Jean Gallice (75 Patrick Parizon), Henri Michel, Jean-Michel Larqué, Jean-Marc Guillou, Marc Berdoll, Georges Bereta. Manager: Stefan Kovács

361. 03.09.1975   UEFA Euro 1976 Qualifying – Group 7
FRANCE v ICELAND 3-0 (1-0)
Stade Marcel Saupin, Nantes
Referee: Albert Victor (Luxembourg)   Attendance: 14,217

FRANCE: Dominique Baratelli, Raymond Domenech, Jean-Pierre Adams, Marius Trésor, François Bracci, Jean-Noël Huck, Henri Michel, Dominique Rocheteau, Marc Molitor (46 Marc Berdoll), Albert Emon, Jean-Marc Guillou. Manager: Stefan Kovács

ICELAND: Árni Stefánsson, Ólafur Sigurvinsson, Jón Pétursson, Marteinn Geirsson, Jóhannes Edvaldsson, Gísli Torfason, Hördur Hilmarsson (61 Karl Thórdarson), Gudgeir Leifsson, Ásgeir Sigurvinsson, Teitur Thórdarson, Matthías Hallgrímsson (75 Ernst Elmar Geirsson). Manager: Tony Knapp

Goals: Jean-Marc Guillou (20, 74), Marc Berdoll (87)

362. 12.10.1975   UEFA Euro 1976 Qualifying – Group 7
EAST GERMANY v FRANCE 2-1 (0-0)
Zentralstadion, Leipzig
Referee: Erik Fredriksson (Sweden)   Attendance: 28,544

EAST GERMANY: Jürgen Croy, Hans-Jürgen (Dixie) Dörner, Gerd Weber, Konrad Weise, Joachim Fritsche, Reinhard Häfner, Hartmut Schade, Reinhard Lauck, Joachim Streich (75 Martin Hoffmann), Peter Ducke, Eberhard Vogel. Manager: Georg Buschner

FRANCE: Dominique Baratelli, Gérard Janvion, Jean-Pierre Adams, Marius Trésor, François Bracci, Henri Michel, Jean Gallice, Jean-Marc Guillou, Dominique Bathenay, Dominique Rocheteau, Albert Emon. Manager: Stefan Kovács

Goals: Joachim Streich (56), Eberhard Vogel (78 pen) / Dominique Bathenay (50)

363. 15.11.1975   UEFA Euro 1976 Qualifying – Group 7
FRANCE v BELGIUM 0-0
Parc des Princes, Paris
Referee: Robert Holley (Bobby) Davidson (Scotland)
Attendance: 35,547

FRANCE: Dominique Baratelli, Raymond Domenech, Charles Orlanducci, Marius Trésor, François Bracci, Jean-Noël Huck (46 Jean-Michel Larqué), Henri Michel, Jean-Marc Guillou, Dominique Rocheteau, Christian Coste (78 Jean Gallice), Albert Emon. Manager: Stefan Kovács

BELGIUM: Christian Piot, Gilbert Van Binst, Erwin Vandendaele, Georges Leekens, Jean Dockx, Julien Cools, Ludo Coeck, Jan Verheyden, René Vandereycken, Roger Van Gool, Raoul Lambert (78 Jacques Teugels). Manager: Raymond Goethals

Sent off: Jean-Michel Larqué (67)

364. 27.03.1976
FRANCE v CZECHOSLOVAKIA 2-2 (1-0)
Parc des Princes, Paris
Referee: Francis Jean Elisa Rion (Belgium)
Attendance: 19,559
FRANCE: Jean-Paul Bertrand-Demanes, Raymond Domenech, Patrice Rio, Marius Trésor, Maxime Bossis, Henri Michel, Michel Platini, Gilles Rampillon (65 Roger Jouve), Gérard Soler (81 Didier Six), Robert Pintenat, Albert Emon. Manager: Michel Hidalgo
CZECHOSLOVAKIA: Ivo Viktor, Pavol Biros (71 Karol Dobias), Anton Ondrus, Ladislav Jurkemik, Koloman Gögh, Jaroslav Pollák, Lubomír Knapp, Miroslav Gajdusek, Marián Masný (46 Ján Svehlík), Ladislav Petrás (46 Jozef Móder), Zdenek Nehoda.   Manager: Václav Jezek
Goals: Gérard Soler (17), Michel Platini (73) / Anton Ondrus (78), Karol Dobias (83)

365. 24.04.1976
FRANCE v POLAND 2-0 (1-0)
Stade Félix Bollaert, Lens
Referee: Ferdinand Biwersi (West Germany)
Attendance: 14,490
FRANCE: Dominique Baratelli, Raymond Domenech, Patrice Rio, Carlos Curbelo, Gérard Farison, Christian Synaeghel, Jean-Michel Larqué, Jean-Marc Guillou (56 Farès Bousdira), Patrick Revelli, Robert Pintenat, Didier Six.
Manager: Michel Hidalgo
POLAND: Stanislaw Burzynski, Antoni Szymanowski, Jerzy Gorgon, Henryk Maculewicz, Henryk Wawrowski, Henryk Kasperczak, Kazimierz Deyna, Zbigniew Boniek, Grzegorz Lato, Andrzej Szarmach, Kazimierz Kmiecik (46 Jan Benigier). Manager: Kazimierz Górski
Goals: Robert Pintenat (13), Patrick Revelli (64)

366. 22.05.1976
HUNGARY v FRANCE 1-0 (0-0)
Népstadion, Budapest
Referee: Franz Wöhrer (Austria)   Attendance: 8,726
HUNGARY: Sándor Gujdár, Zoltán Kereki (46 Péter Török), Attila Kerekes, László Bálint, Sándor Lukács (71 Mihály Kántor), Sándor Pintér (46 András Tóth), Ferenc Csongrádi, László Fazekas, László Fekete, István Magyar, Tibor Nyilasi (46 János Nagy).   Manager: Lajos Baróti
FRANCE: Dominique Baratelli, Gérard Janvion, Patrice Rio, Marius Trésor, Francis Meynieu, Michel Platini, Jean-Michel Larqué, Jean-Marc Guillou (50 Carlos Curbelo), Albert Emon (73 Didier Six), Robert Pintenat, Christian Sarramagna. Manager: Michel Hidalgo
Goal: László Fekete (46)

367. 01.09.1976
DENMARK v FRANCE 1-1 (0-0)
Københavns Idrætspark, Copenhagen
Referee: Lars-Åke Björck (Sweden)   Attendance: 23,100
DENMARK: Benno Larsen, Johnny Hansen, Henning Munk Jensen, Per Røntved, Flemming Ahlberg, Morten Olsen, Heino Hansen, Ole Rasmussen, Ove Flindt-Bjerg, Kurt Hansen (46 Niels-Christian Holmstrøm), Jørgen Kristensen. Manager: Kurt Nielsen
FRANCE: Dominique Baratelli, Gérard Janvion (46 Raymond Domenech), Jean-Pierre Adams, Marius Trésor, Maxime Bossis, Jean-Michel Larqué, Michel Platini, Dominique Bathenay, Dominique Rocheteau, Bernard Lacombe, Didier Six.   Manager: Michel Hidalgo
Goals: Per Røntved (53) / Michel Platini (89)

368. 09.10.1976   FIFA World Cup Qualification – Group 5
BULGARIA v FRANCE 2-2 (1-2)
National Stadium Vasil Levski, Sofia
Referee: Ian Montgomery Davidson Foote (Scotland)
Attendance: 45,000
BULGARIA: Todor Krastev, Nikolay Grancharov, Ivan Tishanski, Tsonyo Vasilev, Borislav Dimitrov (51 Atanas Aleksandrov), Kiril Stankov, Voyn Voynov, Hristo Bonev, Kiril Milanov, Pavel Panov, Georgi Denev (46 Chavdar Tsvetkov). Manager: Hristo Mladenov
FRANCE: Dominique Baratelli, Gérard Janvion, Maxime Bossis, Christian López, Marius Trésor, Dominique Bathenay, Christian Synaeghel, Jean Gallice, Bernard Lacombe, Michel Platini, Didier Six (61 Olivier Rouyer).
Manager: Michel Hidalgo
Goals: Hristo Bonev (45), Pavel Panov (68) / Michel Platini (37), Bernard Lacombe (40)

369. 17.11.1976   FIFA World Cup Qualification – Group 5
FRANCE v REPUBLIC OF IRELAND 2-0 (0-0)
Parc des Princes, Paris
Referee: Dusan Aron Maksimovic (Yugoslavia)
Attendance: 43,437
FRANCE: Dominique Baratelli, Gérard Janvion, Christian López, Marius Trésor, Maxime Bossis, Dominique Bathenay, Michel Platini, Raymond Kéruzoré, Dominique Rocheteau, Bernard Lacombe (71 Olivier Rouyer), Didier Six. Manager: Michel Hidalgo
REPUBLIC OF IRELAND: Mick Kearns, Paddy Mulligan, David O'Leary, Mick Martin, Jimmy Holmes, Gerry Daly, Johnny Giles, Liam Brady, Steve Heighway, Don Givens, Frank Stapleton (63 Mickey Walsh).   Manager: Michael John Giles
Goals: Michel Platini (47), Dominique Bathenay (88)

370. 23.02.1977
FRANCE v WEST GERMANY 1-0 (0-0)

Parc des Princes, Paris

Referee: Pablo Augusto Sánchez Ibáñez (Spain)
Attendance: 43,802

FRANCE: André Rey, Patrick Battiston, Patrice Rio, Christian López, Gérard Janvion, Dominique Bathenay, Michel Platini, Christian Synaeghel (72 Omar Sahnoun), Bernard Lacombe (46 Patrick Revelli), Loïc Amisse (64 Bernard Zénier), Olivier Rouyer.   Manager: Michel Hidalgo

WEST GERMANY: Sepp Maier, Berti Vogts, Peter Nogly, Franz Beckenbauer, Bernard Dietz, Rainer Bonhof, Heinz Flohe, Uli Stielike, Bernd Hölzenbein, Karl-Heinz Rummenigge, Dieter Müller (69 Erich Beer).   Manager: Helmut Schön

Goal: Olivier Rouyer (52)

371. 30.03.1977   FIFA World Cup Qualification – Group 5
REPUBLIC OF IRELAND v FRANCE 1-0 (1-0)

Lansdowne Road, Dublin

Referee: Erich Linemayr (Austria)   Attendance: 48,000

REPUBLIC OF IRELAND: Mick Kearns, Paddy Mulligan, David O'Leary, Mick Martin, Jimmy Holmes, Gerry Daly, Johnny Giles, Liam Brady, Steve Heighway, Ray Treacy, Don Givens.   Manager: Michael John Giles

FRANCE: André Rey, Gérard Janvion, Patrice Rio, Christian López, Thierry Tusseau, Dominique Bathenay, Michel Platini, Christian Synaeghel, Dominique Rocheteau, Bernard Lacombe, Olivier Rouyer.   Manager: Michel Hidalgo

Goal: Liam Brady (11)

372. 23.04.1977
SWITZERLAND v FRANCE 0-4 (0-1)

Stade des Charmilles, Geneva

Referee: Alfred Delcourt (Belgium)   Attendance: 27,600

SWITZERLAND: Hans Küng, Pierre-Albert Chapuisat, Jakob (Köbi) Brechbühl, Lucio Bizzini, Serge Trinchero, Umberto Barberis, Arthur Von Wartburg, René Botteron, Rudolf Elsener, Kurt Müller (74 Peter Risi), Daniel Jeandupeux (62 Claudio Sulser).   Manager: Roger Vonlanthen

FRANCE: André Rey, Christian López, Gérard Janvion, Patrice Rio, Thierry Tusseau, Omar Sahnoun, Michel Platini, Alain Giresse, Dominique Rocheteau, Bruno Baronchelli (46 Olivier Rouyer), Didier Six.   Manager: Michel Hidalgo

Goals: Michel Platini (31), Didier Six (73), Dominique Rocheteau (87), Olivier Rouyer (89)

373. 26.06.1977
ARGENTINA v FRANCE 0-0

Estadio La Bombonera, Buenos Aires

Referee: Edison Pérez Núñez (Peru)   Attendance: 40,000

ARGENTINA: Héctor Rodolfo Baley, Alberto César Tarantini, Daniel Pedro Killer (69 Jorge Mario Olguín), Daniel Alberto Passarella, Jorge Omar Carrascosa, Omar Rubén Larrosa, Américo Rubén Gallego, Julio Ricardo Villa, Pedro Alexis González (46 Osvaldo César Ardiles), Leopoldo Jacinto Luqué (60 Enzo Héctor Trossero), René Orlando Houseman.   Manager: César Luis Menotti

FRANCE: Dominique Baratelli, Patrick Battiston, Patrice Rio, Marius Trésor, Maxime Bossis, Henri Michel (83 Alain Giresse), Omar Sahnoun, Michel Platini, Bruno Baronchelli (64 Jacques Atre "Zimako"), Olivier Rouyer, Loïc Amisse (77 Didier Six).   Manager: Michel Hidalgo

374. 30.06.1977
BRAZIL v FRANCE 2-2 (1-0)

Estádio Jornalista Mário Filho, Rio de Janeiro

Referee: Romualdo Arppi Filho (Brazil)   Attendance: 83,535

BRAZIL: Émerson LEÃO, José "ZÉ" MARIA Rodrigues Alves (62 Orlando Pereira "LELÉ"), LUÍS Edmundo PEREIRA, Edino Nazareth Filho "EDINHO", José RODRIGUES NETO, Antônio Carlos "TONINHO" CEREZO, PAULO ISIDORO de Jesus, Roberto RIVELLINO, Gilberto Alves "GIL", Carlos ROBERTO "DINAMITE" de Oliveira, PAULO CÉSAR Caju Lima.   Manager: CLÁUDIO Pêcego de Moraes COUTINHO

FRANCE: André Rey, Gérard Janvion, Patrice Rio, Marius Trésor, Maxime Bossis, Omar Sahnoun, Michel Platini, Dominique Bathenay, Jacques Atre "Zimako" (59 Olivier Rouyer), Bernard Lacombe, Didier Six.   Manager: Michel Hidalgo

Goals: Edino Nazareth Filho "EDINHO" (30), Carlos ROBERTO "DINAMITE" de Oliveira (51) / Didier Six (52), Marius Trésor (85)

375. 08.10.1977
FRANCE v SOVIET UNION 0-0

Parc des Princes, Paris

Referee: Marcel Van Langenhove (Belgium)   Att: 40,823

FRANCE: André Rey, Gérard Janvion, Patrice Rio, Marius Trésor, Thierry Tusseau, Jean Petit (65 Roger Jouve), Christian Dalger (65 Dominique Rocheteau), Dominique Bathenay, Michel Platini, Marc Berdoll, Didier Six.   Manager: Michel Hidalgo

SOVIET UNION: Yuriy Dehteryov, Anatoliy Konkov, Shota Khinchagashvili, Aleksandr Makhovikov, Aleksandr Bubnov, Sergey Prigoda, Leonid Buryak, Vladimir Bessonov (62 Revaz Chelebadze), Viktor Kolotov, Vladimir Vereemev (60 Aleksandr Minayev), Oleg Blokhin.   Manager: Nikita Simonyan

376. 16.11.1977 FIFA World Cup Qualification – Group 5
FRANCE v BULGARIA 3-1 (1-0)

Parc des Princes, Paris

Referee: Charles George Rainer Corver (Netherlands)   Attendance: 44,860

FRANCE: André Rey, Gérard Janvion, Patrice Rio, Maxime Bossis, Marius Trésor, Dominique Bathenay, Dominique Rocheteau (70 Christian Dalger), Jean-Marc Guillou, Bernard Lacombe, Michel Platini, Didier Six.   Manager: Michel Hidalgo

BULGARIA: Rumen Goranov, Tsonyo Vasilev, Boris Angelov, Georgi Bonev, Kiril Ivkov (46 Chavdar Tsvetkov), Nikolay Arabov, Atanas Aleksandrov, Hristo Bonev, Angel Stankov, Vanyo Kostov, Angel Kolev (54 Voyn Voynov).   Manager: Hristo Mladenov

Goals: Dominique Rocheteau (38), Michel Platini (63), Christian Dalger (90) / Chavdar Tsvetkov (85)

377. 08.02.1978
ITALY v FRANCE 2-2 (2-0)

Stadio San Paolo, Napoli

Referee: Ángel Franco Martínez (Spain)   Attendance: 66,158

ITALY: Dino Zoff, Claudio Gentile, Aldo Maldera, Romeo Benetti, Mauro Bellugi, Gaetano Scirea, Claudio Sala, Marco Tardelli, Francesco Graziani, Giancarlo Antognoni (72 Patrizio Sala), Roberto Bettega (53 Paolino Pulici).   Manager: Enzo Bearzot

FRANCE: André Rey, Gérard Janvion, Maxime Bossis, Patrice Rio (74 Christian López), Marius Trésor, Christian Dalger, Jean-Marc Guillou (46 Henri Michel), Bernard Lacombe, Michel Platini, Olivier Rouyer (29 Albert Gemmrich), Dominique Bathenay.   Manager: Michel Hidalgo

Goals: Francesco Graziani (13 pen, 22) / Dominique Bathenay (51), Michel Platini (81)

378. 08.03.1978
FRANCE v PORTUGAL 2-0 (2-0)

Parc des Princes, Paris

Referee: Alexis Ponnet (Belgium)   Attendance: 42,241

FRANCE: André Rey, Gérard Janvion, Patrice Rio, Christian López (56 Patrick Battiston), Maxime Bossis, Henri Michel, Omar Sahnoun, Alain Giresse, Bruno Baronchelli, Marc Berdoll (75 Loïc Amisse), Didier Six.   Manager: Michel Hidalgo

PORTUGAL: Manuel Galrinho BENTO (46 António José Da Silva BOTELHO), ARTUR Manuel Soares CORREIA, HUMBERTO Manuel de Jesus COELHO, João Gonçalves LARANJEIRA, JOÃO Soares CARDOSO, António José "TONI" Da Conceição Oliveira, CELSO Luís de Matos, JOÃO António Ferreira Resende ALVES, António Luís Alves Ribeiro OLIVEIRA, MANUEL José Tavares FERNANDES (32 Joaquim Arsénio Rodrigues Jardim "SENINHO"), JOSÉ ALBERTO Barroso Machado e COSTA (78 ÓSCAR Vicente Martins DUARTE).   Manager: Júlio Cernadas Pereira "JUCA"

Goals: Bruno Baronchelli (9), Marc Berdoll (40)

379. 01.04.1978
FRANCE v BRAZIL 1-0 (0-0)

Parc des Princes, Paris

Referee: Patrick (Pat) Partridge (England)   Attendance: 46,065

FRANCE: Jean-Paul Bertrand-Demanes, Patrick Battiston (61 François Bracci), Patrice Rio, Christian López, Maxime Bossis, Henri Michel (67 Jean Petit), Jean-Marc Guillou, Bruno Baronchelli, Marc Berdoll, Loïc Amisse (81 Didier Six), Michel Platini.   Manager: Michel Hidalgo

BRAZIL: Émerson LEÃO, Antônio Dias dos Santos "TONINHO BAIANO", José OSCAR Bernardi, João Justino AMARAL dos Santos, Edino Nazareth Filho "EDINHO", Antônio Carlos "TONINHO" CEREZO, Roberto RIVELLINO, José TARCISO de Souza (46 Gilberto Alves "GIL"), Arthur Antunes Coimbra "ZICO", José REINALDO de Lima (61 João Batista NUNES de Oliveira), José Guimarães DIRCEU (II).   Manager: CLÁUDIO Pêcego de Moraes COUTINHO

Goal: Michel Platini (86)

380. 11.05.1978
FRANCE v IRAN 2-1 (1-0)

Stade Municipal de Toulouse, Toulouse

Referee: Augusto Lamo Castillo (Spain)   Attendance: 34,000

FRANCE: Jean-Paul Bertrand-Demanes, Gérard Janvion, Patrice Rio, Marius Trésor (58 Christian López), Maxime Bossis, Henri Michel, Omar Sahnoun (46 Dominique Bathenay), Raymond Kéruzoré, Dominique Rocheteau (46 Didier Six), Bernard Lacombe (58 Marc Berdoll), Albert Gemmrich.   Manager: Michel Hidalgo

IRAN: Nasser Hedjazi, Hassan Nazari, Nasrollah Abdollahi, Hossein Kazerani, Andaranik Eskandarian, Ali Parvin, Ibrahim Ghassimpour, Mohammad Sadeghi, Hassan Nayebagha (53 Behtash Fariba), Hossein Faraki (6 Hassan Rowshan), Ghaffour Djahani (53 Nasser Nouraei).   Manager: Heshmat Mohajerani

Goals: Albert Gemmrich (14), Didier Six (70) / Hassan Rowshan (47)

381. 19.05.1978
FRANCE v TUNISIA 2-0 (0-0)
Stade du Nord, Villeneuve d'Ascq
Referee: Charles George Rainer Corver (Netherlands)
Attendance: 35,000
FRANCE: Jean-Paul Bertrand-Demanes, Gérard Janvion, Patrick Battiston, Patrice Rio (86 François Bracci), Christian López, Jean Petit, Dominique Bathenay, Jean-Marc Guillou (43 Michel Platini), Christian Dalger, Marc Berdoll (63 Bernard Lacombe), Didier Six (46 Olivier Rouyer).
Manager: Michel Hidalgo
TUNISIA: Mokhtar Naili, Mokhtar Dhouib, Mohsen Labidi Jendoubi, Khaled Gasmi, Ali Kaabi, Hammadi Agrebi, Nejib Ghommidh (77 Khemaïs Labidi), Tarak Dhiab, Temime Lahzani, Mohammed Akid (46 Mokhtar Hasni), Abderaouf Ben Aziz (77 Mohammed Nejib Limam). Manager: Abdelmajid Chetali
Goals: Michel Platini (71), Christian Dalger (74)

382. 02.06.1978   FIFA World Cup Final Tournament – Group 1
ITALY v FRANCE 2-1 (1-1)
Estadio Mundialista, Mar del Plata (Argentina)
Referee: Nicolae (Nicu) Rainea (Romania)
Attendance: 42,373
ITALY: Dino Zoff, Claudio Gentile, Antonio Cabrini, Romeo Benetti, Mauro Bellugi, Gaetano Scirea, Franco Causio, Marco Tardelli, Paolo Rossi, Giancarlo Antognoni (46 Renato Zaccarelli), Roberto Bettega.   Manager: Enzo Bearzot
FRANCE: Jean-Paul Bertrand-Demanes, Gérard Janvion, Maxime Bossis, Henri Michel, Patrice Rio, Marius Trésor, Christian Dalger, Jean-Marc Guillou, Bernard Lacombe (75 Marc Berdoll), Michel Platini, Didier Six (76 Olivier Rouyer).
Manager: Michel Hidalgo
Goals: Paolo Rossi (29), Renato Zaccarelli (54) / Bernard Lacombe (1)

383. 06.06.1978   FIFA World Cup Final Tournament – Group 1
ARGENTINA v FRANCE 2-1 (1-0)
Estadio Monumental, Buenos Aires (Argentina)
Referee: Jean Dubach (Switzerland)   Attendance: 71,666
ARGENTINA: Ubaldo Matildo Fillol, Jorge Mario Olguín, Daniel Alberto Passarella, Luis Adolfo Galván, Alberto César Tarantini, Osvaldo César Ardiles, Américo Rubén Gallego, José Daniel Valencia (61 Norberto Osvaldo Alonso, 70 Oscar Alberto Ortíz), René Orlando Houseman, Leopoldo Jacinto Luqué, Mario Alberto Kempes.   Manager: César Luis Menotti

FRANCE: Jean-Paul Bertrand-Demanes (58 Dominique Baratelli), Patrick Battiston, Maxime Bossis, Christian López, Marius Trésor, Henri Michel, Dominique Rocheteau, Dominique Bathenay, Bernard Lacombe, Michel Platini, Didier Six.   Manager: Michel Hidalgo
Goals: Daniel Alberto Passarella (45 pen), Leopoldo Jacinto Luqué (73) / Michel Platini (60)

384. 10.06.1978   FIFA World Cup Final Tournament – Group 1
FRANCE v HUNGARY 3-1 (3-1)
Estadio Mundialista, Mar del Plata (Argentina)
Referee: Arnaldo David Cézar Coelho (Brazil)
Attendance: 23,127
FRANCE: Dominique Dropsy, François Bracci, Jean Petit, Gérard Janvion, Marc Berdoll, Christian López, Marius Trésor, Olivier Rouyer, Dominique Rocheteau (75 Didier Six), Dominique Bathenay, Claude Papi (46 Michel Platini).
Manager: Michel Hidalgo
HUNGARY: Sándor Gujdár, Györö Martos, Zoltán Kereki, László Bálint, József Tóth, László Pusztai, Sándor Zombori, Sándor Pintér, Tibor Nyilasi, András Törőcsik, László Nagy (73 Károly Csapó).   Manager: Lajos Baróti
Goals: Christian López (22), Marc Berdoll (37), Dominique Rocheteau (42) / Sándor Zombori (41)

385. 01.09.1978   UEFA Euro 1980 Qualifying – Group 5
FRANCE v SWEDEN 2-2 (0-0)
Parc des Princes, Paris
Referee: Károly Palotai (Hungary)   Attendance: 44,703
FRANCE: André Rey, Patrick Battiston, Patrice Rio, Christian López, Maxime Bossis, Henri Michel (77 Alain Giresse), Roger Jouve, Dominique Bathenay, Olivier Rouyer, Albert Gemmrich (65 Marc Berdoll), Didier Six.   Manager: Michel Hidalgo
SWEDEN: Ronnie Hellström, Hans Borg, Björn Nordqvist, Ronald Åhman, Håkan Arvidsson, Lennart Larsson, Anders Linderoth, Mats Nordgren, Anders Grönhagen, Thomas Sjöberg (75 Tommy Berggren), Benny Wendt.
Manager: Georg Ericson
Goals: Marc Berdoll (72), Didier Six (85) / Mats Nordgren (54), Anders Grönhagen (89)

386. 07.10.1978   UEFA Euro 1980 Qualifying – Group 5

LUXEMBOURG v FRANCE 1-3 (0-1)

Stade Municipal, Luxembourg City

Referee: Hendrik (Henk) Weerink (Netherlands)
Attendance: 12,650

LUXEMBOURG: Jeannot Moes, Hubert Meunier (62 Aldo Catani), Jean-Louis Margue, Fernand Raths (43 Roger Fandel), Paul Philipp, Gilbert Dresch, Romain Michaux, Gilbert Dussier, Camille Neumann, Nico Rohmann, Carlo Weis.   Manager: Louis Pilot

FRANCE: Dominique Dropsy, Patrick Battiston, Christian López, Marius Trésor, Maxime Bossis, Jean-François Larios (64 Jean Petit), Roger Jouve, Francis Piasecki, Dominique Rocheteau (59 Albert Gemmrich), Bernard Lacombe, Didier Six.   Manager: Michel Hidalgo

Goals: Romain Michaux (74) /
Didier Six (15), Marius Trésor (63), Albert Gemmrich (80)

387. 08.11.1978

FRANCE v SPAIN 1-0 (1-0)

Parc des Princes, Paris

Referee: Walter Eschweiler (West Germany)
Attendance: 37,897

FRANCE: Dominique Dropsy, Patrick Battiston, Léonard Specht, Christian López, Gérard Janvion, Jean Petit, Henri Michel, Francis Piasecki, Dominique Rocheteau (73 Gérard Soler), Pierre Pleimelding (57 Albert Gemmrich), Didier Six. Manager: Michel Hidalgo

SPAIN: MIGUEL ÁNGEL González Suárez, MARCELINO Pérez Ayllón, Miguel "MIGUELI" Bernardo Blanquetti, Antonio OLMO Ramírez, Francisco Javier ESCALZA Ellacuría, Ángel María VILLAR Llona, VICENTE DEL BOSQUE González (46 Daniel SOLSONA Puig), Juan Manuel ASENSI Ripoll (46 Eugenio LEAL Vargas), Juan "JUANITO" Gómez González, Carlos Alonso González "SANTILLANA", José Francisco "TXETXU" ROJO Arroitia (46 Enrique SAURA Gil).   Manager: Ladislav (László) KUBALA Stecz

Goal: Léonard Specht (41)

388. 25.02.1979   UEFA Euro 1980 Qualifying – Group 5

FRANCE v LUXEMBOURG 3-0 (1-0)

Parc des Princes, Paris

Referee: Ronald (Ron) Bridges (Wales)   Attendance: 46,988

FRANCE: Dominique Dropsy, Patrick Battiston, Léonard Specht, Marius Trésor, Maxime Bossis, Jean Petit, Henri Michel, Francis Piasecki (61 Jean-François Larios), Dominique Rocheteau, Marc Berdoll (66 Éric Pécout), Albert Emon.   Manager: Michel Hidalgo

LUXEMBOURG: Jeannot Moes, Hubert Meunier, Jean-Louis Margue, Fernand Raths, Nico Rohmann, Paul Philipp, Carlo Weis (46 Jeannot Reiter), Romain Michaux, Nico Wagner, André Zwally (73 Camille Neumann), Gilbert Dresch.   Manager: Louis Pilot

Goals: Jean Petit (38), Albert Emon (60), Jean-François Larios (78)

389. 04.04.1979   UEFA Euro 1980 Qualifying – Group 5

CZECHOSLOVAKIA v FRANCE 2-0 (0-0)

Tehelné pole, Bratislava

Referee: Heinz Aldinger (West Germany)
Attendance: 48,138

CZECHOSLOVAKIA: Jaroslav Netolicka, Jozef Barmos, Rostislav Vojácek, Anton Ondrus, Koloman Gögh, Ján Kozák, Antonín Panenka, Frantisek Stambachr, Marián Masný, Zdenek Nehoda (56 Ladislav Vízek), Miroslav Gajdusek.   Manager: Jozef Venglos

FRANCE: Dominique Dropsy, Raymond Domenech, Léonard Specht, Christian López, Maxime Bossis, Jean Petit, Michel Platini, Jean-François Larios, Albert Emon, Marc Berdoll, Loïc Amisse.   Manager: Michel Hidalgo

Goals: Antonín Panenka (65 pen), Frantisek Stambachr (72)

390. 02.05.1979

UNITED STATES v FRANCE 0-6 (0-4)

Giants Stadium, East Rutherford

Referee: Marco Antonio Dorantes García (Mexico)
Attendance: 20,591

UNITED STATES: Arnold Mausser (46 David Brcic), Jim Pollihan, Glenn Myernick, Donald Droege, Colin Fowles (8 Tony Crudo), Larry Hulcer, Richard Davis, Boris Bandov (32 Percival van der Beck), Angelo DiBernardo, Greg Villa, Mark Liveric (75 Louis Nanchoff).   Manager: Walter Chyzowych

FRANCE: Dominique Dropsy (46 André Rey), Gérard Janvion, Raymond Domenech, Marius Trésor, Maxime Bossis (80 Patrick Battiston), Jean Petit, Michel Platini, Roger Jouve (71 Jean-François Larios), Olivier Rouyer (46 Didier Six), Bernard Lacombe (65 Marc Berdoll), Loïc Amisse.   Manager: Michel Hidalgo

Goals: Bernard Lacombe (8, 14, 37), Donald Droege (42 og), Loïc Amisse (61), Didier Six (73)

391.   05.09.1979   UEFA Euro 1980 Qualifying – Group 5

SWEDEN v FRANCE 1-3 (1-1)

Råsunda Fotbollstadion, Solna

Referee: Ángel Franco Martínez (Spain)   Attendance: 14,395

SWEDEN: Ronnie Hellström, Mikael Rönnberg, Kent Jönsson, Hans Borg, Ingemar Erlandsson, Olle Nordin, Anders Linderoth, Mats Nordmgren, Anders Grönhagen (76 Jan Svensson), Rutger Backe, Sigvard Johansson. Manager: Georg Ericson

FRANCE: Dominique Dropsy, Patrick Battiston, Léonard Specht, Christian López, Maxime Bossis, Alain Moizan, Michel Platini, Dominique Bathenay, Dominique Rocheteau (55 Jacques Atre "Zimako"), Bernard Lacombe, Loïc Amisse. Manager: Michel Hidalgo

Goals: Rutger Backe (24) / Bernard Lacombe (14), Michel Platini (54), Patrick Battiston (71)

392.   10.10.1979

FRANCE v UNITED STATES 3-0 (3-0)

Parc des Princes, Paris

Referee: Hendrik Johan (Henk) van Ettekoven (Netherlands)   Attendance: 25,000

FRANCE: Dominique Dropsy (46 Philippe Bergerôo), Gérard Janvion, Léonard Specht (46 Marius Trésor), Christian López, Maxime Bossis, Alain Moizan, Michel Platini (42 Jean-François Larios), Dominique Bathenay, Roland Wagner (46 Patrice Lecornu), Bernard Lacombe, Loïc Amisse. Manager: Michel Hidalgo

UNITED STATES: Arnold Mausser (46 Winston DuBose), Doc Lawson, Steve Pecher, Tyrone Keough, Gregory Makowski, Antonio Crudo (46 Percival van der Beck), Boris Bandov, Larry Hulcer (46 Angelo DiBernardo), Ringo Cantillo, Gregory Villa (46' Njego Pesa), Mark Liveric (71 Louis Nanchoff).   Manager: Walter Chyzowych

Goals: Michel Platini (5), Roland Wagner (18), Loïc Amisse (23)

Sent off: Gérard Janvion (88)

393.   17.11.1979   UEFA Euro 1980 Qualifying – Group 5

FRANCE v CZECHOSLOVAKIA 2-1 (0-0)

Parc des Princes, Paris

Referee: Horst Brummeier (Austria)   Attendance: 39,973

FRANCE: Dominique Dropsy, Patrick Battiston, Léonard Specht, Christian López, Maxime Bossis, Jean Petit, Alain Moizan, Gilles Rampillon, Jacques Atre "Zimako", Bernard Lacombe (46 Éric Pécout), Loïc Amisse. Manager: Michel Hidalgo

CZECHOSLOVAKIA: Zdenek Hruska, Jozef Barmos, Ladislav Jurkemik, Anton Ondrus, Koloman Gögh, Ján Kozák, Frantisek Stambachr, Antonín Panenka, Ladislav Vízek, Karel Kroupa (73 Marián Masný), Miroslav Gajdusek. Manager: Jozef Venglos

Goals: Éric Pécout (67), Gilles Rampillon (76) / Ján Kozák (80)

394.   27.02.1980

FRANCE v GREECE 5-1 (2-1)

Parc des Princes, Paris

Referee: José Luis García Carrión (Spain)
Attendance: 29,992

FRANCE: Dominique Dropsy (46 Jean-Luc Ettori), Patrick Battiston, Léonard Specht, Christian López, Thierry Tusseau, Didier Christophe (68 Bernard Genghini), Michel Platini, Dominique Bathenay, Patrice Lecornu (56 Olivier Rouyer), Éric Pécout (46 Yannick Stopyra), Jacques Atre "Zimako". Manager: Michel Hidalgo

GREECE: Vasilis Konstantinou, Giannis Gounaris, Kostas Iosifidis, Anthimos Kapsis, Spyros Livathinos (46 Takis Nikoloudis), Giorgos Foiros, Giannis Damanakis (65 Charalambos Xanthopoulos), Angelos Anastasiadis, Christos Ardizoglou, Giorgos Kostikos (46 Nikos Anastopoulos), Thomas Mavros.   Manager: Alketas Panagoulias

Goals: Dominique Bathenay (7 pen), Michel Platini (37, 62), Didier Christophe (63), Yannick Stopyra (66) / Thomas Mavros (32)

395.   26.03.1980

FRANCE v NETHERLANDS 0-0

Parc des Princes, Paris

Referee: Paolo Casarin (Italy)   Attendance: 41,477

FRANCE: Dominique Dropsy, Gérard Janvion, Léonard Specht, Marius Trésor, Maxime Bossis, Didier Christophe (78 Thierry Tusseau), Michel Platini, Dominique Bathenay (64 Gilles Rampillon), Alain Couriol, Éric Pécout, Didier Six (71 Olivier Rouyer).   Manager: Michel Hidalgo

NETHERLANDS: Piet Schrijvers, Ben Wijnstekers, Luuk Balkestein (46 Willy van de Kerkhof), Ruud Krol, Huub Stevens, Hugo Hovenkamp, Dick Schoenaker, Frans Thijssen, Johnny Rep, Kees Kist (76 Dick Nanninga), Pierre Vermeulen (46 René van de Kerkhof).   Manager: Jan Zwartkruis

396. 23.05.1980
SOVIET UNION v FRANCE 1-0 (0-0)
Lenin Central Stadium, Moscow

Referee: Sándor Kuti (Hungary)   Attendance: 55,000

SOVIET UNION: Rinat Dasayev, Oleg Rodin, Aleksandr Chivadze, Vagiz Khidiyatullin, Oleg Romantsev, Sergey Shavlo, Sergey Andreyev, Vladimir Bessonov, Yuriy Gavrilov, Fyodor Cherenkov, Revaz Chelebadze.   Manager: Konstantin Beskov

FRANCE: Philippe Bergerôo, Gérard Janvion, Maxime Bossis, Léonard Specht, Marius Trésor, Jacques Atre "Zimako", Jean-Amadou Tigana, Didier Christophe, Bernard Lacombe (62 Éric Pécout), Michel Platini, Albert Emon (46 Alain Couriol). Manager: Michel Hidalgo

Goal: Fyodor Cherenkov (83)

397. 11.10.1980   FIFA World Cup Qualification – Group 2
CYPRUS v FRANCE 0-7 (0-4)
Tsirion Athletic Center, Limassol

Referee: Bruno Galler (Switzerland)   Attendance: 9,500

CYPRUS: Giorgos Pantziaras, Andreas Papakostas, Dimitris Kyzas, Kleitos Erotokritou, Stavros Papadopoulos, Nikos Pantziaras, Marios Tsingis, Takis Mavris (46 Stefanos Lysandrou), Sotiris Kaiafas (21 Petros Theophanous), Loizos Mavroudis, Andreas Kissonergis. Manager: Kostas Talianos

FRANCE: Dominique Dropsy, Patrick Battiston, Léonard Specht, Henri Michel, Maxime Bossis, Jean-François Larios, Jean-Amadou Tigana (51 Jean Petit), Michel Platini, Bruno Baronchelli (73 Jacques Atre "Zimako"), Bernard Lacombe, Didier Six.   Manager: Michel Hidalgo

Goals: Bernard Lacombe (4), Michel Platini (14, 23), Jean-François Larios (40 pen, 76 pen), Didier Six (82), Jacques Atre "Zimako" (87)

398. 28.10.1980   FIFA World Cup Qualification – Group 2
FRANCE v REPUBLIC OF IRELAND 2-0 (1-0)
Parc des Princes, Paris

Referee: Augusto Lamo Castillo (Spain)   Attendance: 44,800

FRANCE: Dominique Dropsy, Patrick Battiston, Léonard Specht, Christian López, Maxime Bossis, Jean-François Larios, Jean-Amadou Tigana, Michel Platini (74 Jean Petit), Dominique Rocheteau, Bernard Lacombe (66 Jacques Atre "Zimako"), Didier Six.   Manager: Michel Hidalgo

REPUBLIC OF IRELAND: Gerry Peyton, David Langan, Mark Lawrenson, Kevin Moran, Chris Hughton, Mick Martin (78 Gerry Ryan), Tony Grealish, Liam Brady, Steve Heighway, Frank Stapleton, Michael Robinson.   Manager: Eoin Hand

Goals: Michel Platini (11), Jacques Atre "Zimako" (77)

399. 19.11.1980
WEST GERMANY v FRANCE 4-1 (2-1)
Niedersachsenstadion, Hannover

Referee: Rolf Nyhus (Norway)   Attendance: 62,400

WEST GERMANY: Toni Schumacher, Manfred Kaltz, Bernd Schuster, Karlheinz Förster, Bernard Dietz, Hans-Peter Briegel, Mirko Votava, Hansi Müller, Karl Allgöwer, Horst Hrubesch, Klaus Allofs.   Manager: Jupp Derwall

FRANCE: Dominique Dropsy, Gérard Janvion, Léonard Specht, Christian López, Maxime Bossis, Jean-Amadou Tigana, Jean-François Larios, Michel Platini, Jacques Atre "Zimako", Dominique Rocheteau (60 Olivier Rouyer), Loïc Amisse (79 Didier Six).   Manager: Michel Hidalgo

Goals: Manfred Kaltz (6 pen), Hans-Peter Briegel (31), Horst Hrubesch (62), Klaus Allofs (89) / Jean-François Larios (39 pen)

400. 18.02.1981
SPAIN v FRANCE 1-0 (0-0)
Estadio Vicente Calderón, Madrid

Referee: Carol Jurja (Romania)   Attendance: 18,000

SPAIN: Luis Miguel ARCONADA Echarri, José Antonio CAMACHO Alfaro, Miguel TENDILLO Belenguer, José Ramón ALEXANKO Ventosa, Rafael GORDILLO Vázquez, JOAQUÍN Alonso González (46 Enrique "QUIQUE" RAMOS González), Daniel SOLSONA Puig, Jesús María ZAMORA Ansorena, Juan "JUANITO" Gómez González, Carlos Alonso González "SANTILLANA", Juan José RUBIO Jiménez. Manager: JOSÉ Emilio SANTAMARÍA Iglesias

FRANCE: Jean Castaneda, Gérard Janvion, Léonard Specht, Christian López, Maxime Bossis, Didier Christophe (70 Jean-Amadou Tigana), Jean-François Larios, Michel Platini, Alain Moizan, Bruno Baronchelli (46 Daniel Xuereb), Didier Six.   Manager: Michel Hidalgo

Goal: Juan "JUANITO" Gómez González (86 pen)

401. 25.03.1981   FIFA World Cup Qualification – Group 2
NETHERLANDS v FRANCE 1-0 (0-0)
De Kuip, Rotterdam

Referee: Luigi Agnolin (Italy)   Attendance: 58,000

NETHERLANDS: Piet Schrijvers, Jan Poortvliet, Edo Ophof, Ruud Krol, Hugo Hovenkamp (46 Tscheu La Ling), Frans Thijssen, Jan Peters (65 Huub Stevens), Willy van de Kerkhof, Arnold Mühren, René van de Kerkhof, Johnny Rep. Manager: Kees Rijvers

FRANCE: Dominique Dropsy, Gérard Janvion, Léonard Specht, Christian López, Maxime Bossis, Jean-François Larios, Alain Giresse, Alain Moizan (77 Didier Christophe), Dominique Rocheteau, Bernard Lacombe (63 Jacques Atre "Zimako"), Didier Six.   Manager: Michel Hidalgo

Goal: Arnold Mühren (47)

402.   29.04.1981   FIFA World Cup Qualification – Group 2

FRANCE v BELGIUM   3-2 (3-1)

Parc des Princes, Paris

Referee: Victoriano Sánchez Arminio (Spain)
Attendance: 44,954

FRANCE: Dominique Dropsy, Gérard Janvion, Christian López, Marius Trésor, Maxime Bossis, Jean-Amadou Tigana, Alain Giresse, Bernard Genghini, Gérard Soler (71 Jacques Atre "Zimako"), Dominique Rocheteau, Didier Six. Manager: Michel Hidalgo

BELGIUM: Michel Preud'homme, Eric Gerets, Luc Millecamps (17 Michel De Wolf), Michel Renquin, Walter Meeuws, Wilfried Van Moer, René Vandereycken, Frank Vercauteren (63 René Verheyen), Albert Cluytens, Erwin Vandenbergh, Jan Ceulemans.   Manager: Guy Thys

Goals: Gérard Soler (14, 31), Didier Six (26) / Erwin Vandenbergh (5), Jan Ceulemans (52)

403.   15.05.1981

FRANCE v BRAZIL   1-3 (0-2)

Parc des Princes, Paris

Referee: Gianfranco Menegali (Italy)   Attendance: 47,749

FRANCE: Dominique Dropsy (46 Jean Castaneda), Gérard Janvion, Christian López, Marius Trésor (23 Léonard Specht), Maxime Bossis, Jean-Amadou Tigana, Philippe Anziani (59 Patrick Delamontagne), Alain Moizan, Bernard Genghini, Olivier Rouyer (78 Patrice Lecornu), Didier Six. Manager: Michel Hidalgo

BRAZIL: PAULO SÉRGIO de Oliveira Lima, EDEVALDO de Freitas, José OSCAR Bernardi (78 Edino Nazareth Filho "EDINHO"), Luiz Carlos Ferreira "LUIZINHO", Leovegildo Lins da Gama JÚNIOR, Antônio Carlos "TONINHO" CEREZO, SÓCRATES Brasileiro Sampaio de Souza Vieira de Oliveira (78 VÍTOR Luís Pereira da Silva), Arthur Antunes Coimbra "ZICO", PAULO ISIDORO de Jesus, José REINALDO de Lima (62 Júlio CÉSAR Coelho de Moraes), ÉDER Aleixo de Assis (73 José "ZÉ" SÉRGIO Presti).
Manager: TELÊ SANTANA da Silva

Goals: Didier Six (81) / Arthur Antunes Coimbra "ZICO" (21), José REINALDO de Lima (27), SÓCRATES Brasileiro Sampaio de Souza Vieira de Oliveira (52)

Sent off: Didier Six (90)

404.   09.09.1981   FIFA World Cup Qualification – Group 2

BELGIUM v FRANCE   2-0 (1-0)

Stade du Heysel, Brussels

Referee: Károly Palotai (Hungary)   Attendance: 52,525

BELGIUM: Jean-Marie Pfaff, Michel Renquin, Luc Millecamps, Walter Meeuws, Marc Baecke, Wilfried Van Moer (51 Marc Millecamps), Ludo Coeck, Frank Vercauteren, Alex Czerniatynski, Erwin Vandenbergh, Jan Ceulemans. Manager: Guy Thys

FRANCE: Pierrick Hiard, Gérard Janvion, Philippe Mahut, Christian López, Maxime Bossis, Alain Moizan (60 Yannick Stopyra), Alain Giresse, Jean-François Larios, Jacques Atre "Zimako", Michel Platini, Didier Six.
Manager: Michel Hidalgo

Goals: Alex Czerniatynski (24), Erwin Vandenbergh (83)

405.   14.10.1981   FIFA World Cup Qualification – Group 2

REPUBLIC OF IRELAND v FRANCE   3-2 (3-1)

Lansdowne Road, Dublin

Referee: Rolf Ericsson (Sweden)   Attendance: 53,000

REPUBLIC OF IRELAND: Seamus McDonagh, David Langan, David O'Leary, Kevin Moran, Chris Hughton, Ronnie Whelan, Mick Martin, Mark Lawrenson, Liam Brady, Frank Stapleton (87 Don Givens), Michael Robinson.
Manager: Eoin Hand

FRANCE: Jean Castaneda, Maxime Bossis, Philippe Mahut (69 François Bracci), Christian López, Gérard Janvion, René Girard, Jean-François Larios, Didier Christophe, Michel Platini, Alain Couriol, Bruno Bellone (63 Didier Six). Manager: Michel Hidalgo

Goals: Philippe Mahut (3 og), Frank Stapleton (23), Michael Robinson (40) / B. Bellone (9), Michel Platini (83)

406.   18.11.1981   FIFA World Cup Qualification – Group 2

FRANCE v NETHERLANDS   2-0 (0-0)

Parc des Princes, Paris

Referee: António José da Silva Garrido (Portugal)
Attendance: 44,884

FRANCE: Jean Castaneda, Gérard Janvion, Christian López, Marius Trésor, Maxime Bossis, Alain Giresse, Michel Platini (75 Jean-Amadou Tigana), Bernard Genghini, Dominique Rocheteau, Bernard Lacombe (69 Jacques Atre "Zimako"), Didier Six.   Manager: Michel Hidalgo

NETHERLANDS: Hans van Breukelen, Ben Wijnstekers, Michel van de Korput (72 Tscheu La Ling), Ruud Krol, Jan Poortvliet, John Metgod (46 Simon Tahamata), Jan Peters, Johan Neeskens, Arnold Mühren, Johnny Rep, Cees van Kooten.   Manager: Kees Rijvers

Goals: Michel Platini (52), Didier Six (82)

407. 05.12.1981 FIFA World Cup Qualification – Group 2
FRANCE v CYPRUS 4-0 (2-0)

Parc des Princes, Paris

Referee: Edwin Borg (Malta)   Attendance: 43,437

FRANCE: Jean Castaneda, Gérard Janvion, Christian López, Marius Trésor, Maxime Bossis, Alain Giresse, Jean-Amadou Tigana, Bernard Genghini, Dominique Rocheteau, Bernard Lacombe, Didier Six (63 Bruno Bellone).
Manager: Michel Hidalgo

CYPRUS: Fanos Stylianou, Kostas Miamiliotis, Kleitos Erotokritou, Stefanos Lysandrou, Giorgos Kezos, Filippos Dimitriou, Nikos Pantziaras, Fanis Theophanous, Giannakis Yiangoudakis, Loizos Mavroudis, Foivos Vrahimis.
Manager: Kostas Talianos

Goals: Dominique Rocheteau (25), Bernard Lacombe (29, 82), Bernard Genghini (86)

408. 23.02.1982
FRANCE v ITALY 2-0 (1-0)

Parc des Princes, Paris

Referee: Walter Eschweiler (West Germany)
Attendance: 43,541

FRANCE: Dominique Baratelli, Manuel Amoros, Gérard Janvion (46 Patrick Battiston), Jean-Amadou Tigana, Christian López, Marius Trésor, Gérard Soler, Alain Giresse, Bernard Lacombe (64 Dominique Rocheteau), Michel Platini, Didier Six (66 Daniel Bravo).   Manager: Michel Hidalgo

ITALY: Dino Zoff (46 Ivano Bordon), Claudio Gentile, Antonio Cabrini, Gabriele Oriali, Fulvio Collovati, Gaetano Scirea, Bruno Conti, Marco Tardelli, Roberto Pruzzo, Giuseppe Dossena, Francesco Graziani.   Manager: Enzo Bearzot

Goals: Michel Platini (19), Daniel Bravo (84)

409. 24.03.1982
FRANCE v NORTHERN IRELAND 4-0 (2-0)

Parc des Princes, Paris

Referee: Roger Verhaeghe (Belgium)   Attendance: 34,000

FRANCE: Jean Castaneda, Manuel Amoros, Christian López (68 Patrick Battiston), Marius Trésor, Maxime Bossis, Alain Giresse (76 René Girard), Jean-François Larios, Bernard Genghini, Alain Couriol (75 Gérard Soler), Bruno Bellone, Bernard Zénier.   Manager: Michel Hidalgo

NORTHERN IRELAND: Jim Platt, Jimmy Nicholl, Chris Nicholl, Mal Donaghy, David McCreery (64 Billy Caskey), Martin O'Neill, Sammy McIlroy (64 Derek Spence), Noel Brotherston, Gerry Armstrong, Terry Cochrane (38 Ian Stewart), John O'Neill.   Manager: Billy Bingham

Goals: Bernard Zénier (31), Alain Couriol (45), Jean-François Larios (57 pen), Bernard Genghini (80)

410. 28.04.1982
FRANCE v PERU 0-1 (0-0)

Parc des Princes, Paris

Referee: André Daina (Switzerland)   Attendance: 46,429

FRANCE: Dominique Baratelli, Manuel Amoros, Léonard Specht, Dominique Bathenay, Maxime Bossis, Jean-François Larios (46 Jean-Amadou Tigana), Michel Platini, Bernard Genghini, Alain Couriol (80 Daniel Bravo), Dominique Rocheteau, Bruno Bellone (63 Bernard Zénier).
Manager: Michel Hidalgo

PERU: Ramón QUIROGA Arancibia, Jaime Eduardo DUARTE Huerta, Jorge Andrés OLAECHEA Quijandría, Rubén Toribio DÍAZ Rivas, Miguel Angel GUTIÉRREZ la Rosa, Germán Carlos LEGUÍA Dragó (68 Eduardo Hugo MALÁSQUEZ Maldonado), José Manuel VELÁSQUEZ Castillo, César Augusto CUETO Villa, Julio César URIBE Flores, Guillermo Claudio LA ROSA Laguna, Juan Carlos OBLITAS Saba.   Manager: Lima Elba de Padua "TIM"

Goal: Juan Carlos OBLITAS Saba (82)

411. 14.05.1982
FRANCE v BULGARIA 0-0

Stade de Gerland, Lyon

Referee: Egbert Mulder (Netherlands)   Attendance: 45,000

FRANCE: Jean-Luc Ettori, Manuel Amoros, Philippe Mahut, Marius Trésor, François Bracci, Alain Giresse, Jean-Amadou Tigana, Bernard Genghini (67 Alain Couriol), Daniel Bravo, Bernard Lacombe (77 Yannick Stopyra), Bruno Bellone.
Manager: Michel Hidalgo

BULGARIA: Georgi Velinov, Plamen Nikolov, Veselin Balevski, Blagoy Blangev, Ivan Iliev, Krasimir Bezinski, Radoslav Zdravkov, Tsvetan Yonchev (69 Ayan Sadakov), Grigor Grigorov, Mihail Valchev, Stoycho Mladenov.
Manager: Atanas Parzhelov

412. 02.06.1982
FRANCE v WALES 0-1 (0-0)

Stade Municipal de Toulouse, Toulouse

Referee: Viriato Graça Oliva (Portugal)   Attendance: 26,671

FRANCE: Jean Castaneda, Patrick Battiston, Christian López, Marius Trésor (46 Philippe Mahut), Maxime Bossis, Alain Giresse, Jean-François Larios (64 Jean-Amadou Tigana), Michel Platini, Alain Couriol, Gérard Soler, Didier Six (56 Bruno Bellone).   Manager: Michel Hidalgo

WALES: Dai Davies, Chris Marustik, Paul Price, Byron Stevenson, Joey Jones, Peter Nicholas, Robbie James, Brian Flynn, Ian Walsh (71 Gordon Davies), Ian Rush, Leighton James.   Manager: Mike England

Goal: Ian Rush (55)

413. 16.06.1982   FIFA World Cup Final Tournament – Group 4

ENGLAND v FRANCE 3-1 (1-1)

Estadio de San Mamés, Bilbao (Spain)

Referee: António José da Silva Garrido (Portugal)
Attendance: 44,172

ENGLAND: Peter Shilton, Mick Mills, Kenny Sansom (90 Phil Neal), Phil Thompson, Terry Butcher, Bryan Robson, Steve Coppell, Ray Wilkins, Paul Mariner, Trevor Francis, Graham Rix. Manager: Ron Greenwood

FRANCE: Jean-Luc Ettori, Patrick Battiston, Christian López, Marius Trésor, Maxime Bossis, Jean-François Larios (74 Jean-Amadou Tigana), René Girard, Alain Giresse, Michel Platini, Gérard Soler, Dominique Rocheteau (71 Didier Six). Manager: Michel Hidalgo

Goals: Bryan Robson (1, 67), Paul Mariner (83) / Gérard Soler (24)

414. 21.06.1982   FIFA World Cup Final Tournament – Group 4

FRANCE v KUWAIT 4-1 (2-0)

Nuevo Estadio Municipal José Zorrilla, Valladolid (Spain)

Referee: Miroslav Ivanovich Stupar (Soviet Union)
Attendance: 30,043

FRANCE: Jean-Luc Ettori, Manuel Amoros, Gérard Janvion (61 Christian López), Marius Trésor, Maxime Bossis, Bernard Genghini, Alain Giresse, Michel Platini (81 René Girard), Gérard Soler, Bernard Lacombe, Didier Six.
Manager: Michel Hidalgo

KUWAIT: Ahmad Khodr AL-TARABULSI, Naeem Saad MUBARAK Faraj, Mahboub Juma'a Mahboub MUBARAK, Waleed S. Al-Jasem AL-MUBARAK (78 Hamoud Fleitah AL-SHEMMARI), Sa'ad Mohammad Abdulaziz AL-HOUTI, Abdullah Mohamed H. AL-BULOUSHI, JASEM YAQOUB Sultan Al-Besara, Abdulaziz AL-ANBERI, Abdullah MAYOUF, Faisal AL-DAKHIL, Mohammed Ahmad KARAM (57 Fathi Kameel MATAR Marzouq).
Manager: Carlos Alberto Gomes Parreira

Goals: Bernard Genghini (31), Michel Platini (43), Didier Six (48), Maxime Bossis (89) / Abdullah Mohamed H. AL-BULOUSHI (75)

415. 24.06.1982   FIFA World Cup Final Tournament – Group 4

FRANCE v CZECHOSLOVAKIA 1-1 (0-0)

Nuevo Estadio Municipal José Zorrilla, Valladolid (Spain)

Referee: Paolo Casarin (Italy)   Attendance: 28,000

FRANCE: Jean-Luc Ettori, Manuel Amoros, Marius Trésor, Gérard Janvion, Maxime Bossis, Alain Giresse, Bernard Genghini, Michel Platini, Gérard Soler (87 René Girard), Bernard Lacombe (70 Alain Couriol), Didier Six.
Manager: Michel Hidalgo

CZECHOSLOVAKIA: Karel Stromsík, Jozef Barmos, Jan Fiala, Rostislav Vojácek, Frantisek Stambachr, Libor Radimec, Premysl Bicovský, Tomás Kríz (31 Marián Masný), Zdenek Nehoda, Ladislav Vízek, Petr Janecka (70 Antonín Panenka). Manager: Jozef Venglos

Goals: Didier Six (66) / Antonín Panenka (84 pen)

Sent off: Ladislav Vízek (87)

416. 28.06.1982   FIFA World Cup Final Tournament – Group D

AUSTRIA v FRANCE 0-1 (0-1)

Estadio Vicente Calderón, Madrid (Spain)

Referee: Károly Palotai (Hungary)   Attendance: 37,000

AUSTRIA: Friedl Koncilia, Bernd Krauss, Erich Obermayer, Bruno Pezzey, Josef Degeorgi (46 Ernst Baumeister), Roland Hattenberger, Herbert Prohaska, Reinhold Hintermaier, Kurt Jara (46 Kurt Welzl), Walter Schachner, Hans Krankl.
Managers: Felix Latzke & Georg Schmidt

FRANCE: Jean-Luc Ettori, Patrick Battiston, Marius Trésor, Gérard Janvion, Maxime Bossis, Alain Giresse, Jean-Amadou Tigana, Bernard Genghini (84 René Girard), Gérard Soler, Bernard Lacombe (16 Dominique Rocheteau), Didier Six. Manager: Michel Hidalgo

Goal: Bernard Genghini (39)

417. 04.07.1982   FIFA World Cup Final Tournament – Group D

FRANCE v NORTHERN IRELAND 4-1 (1-0)

Estadio Vicente Calderón, Madrid (Spain)

Referee: Alojzy Jarguz (Poland)   Attendance: 37,000

FRANCE: Jean-Luc Ettori, Manuel Amoros, Marius Trésor, Gérard Janvion, Maxime Bossis, Alain Giresse, Jean-Amadou Tigana, Michel Platini, Bernard Genghini, Gérard Soler (63 Didier Six), Dominique Rocheteau (83 Alain Couriol). Manager: Michel Hidalgo

NORTHERN IRELAND: Pat Jennings, Jimmy Nicholl, Chris Nicholl, Mal Donaghy, John McClelland, David McCreery (86 John O'Neill), Martin O'Neill, Sammy McIlroy, Gerry Armstrong, Norman Whiteside, Billy Hamilton.
Manager: Billy Bingham

Goals: Alain Giresse (33, 81), Dominique Rocheteau (48, 67) / Gerry Armstrong (75)

418. 08.07.1982   FIFA World Cup Final Tournament – Semi-final

WEST GERMANY v FRANCE 3-3 (1-1, 1-1) (AET)

Estadio Ramón Sánchez Pizjuán, Sevilla (Spain)

Referee: Charles George Rainer Corver (Netherlands)
Attendance: 62,440

WEST GERMANY: Toni Schumacher, Manfred Kaltz, Uli Stielike, Karlheinz Förster, Bernd Förster, Wolfgang Dremmler, Paul Breitner, Hans-Peter Briegel (96 Karl-Heinz Rummenigge), Felix Magath (72 Horst Hrubesch), Pierre Littbarski, Klaus Fischer.   Manager: Jupp Derwall

FRANCE: Jean-Luc Ettori, Marius Trésor, Gérard Janvion, Maxime Bossis, Manuel Amoros, Bernard Genghini (52 Patrick Battiston, 62 Christian López), Jean-Amadou Tigana, Michel Platini, Alain Giresse, Dominique Rocheteau, Didier Six.   Manager: Michel Hidalgo

Goals: Pierre Littbarski (18), Karl-Heinz Rummenigge (103), Klaus Fischer (108) /
Michel Platini (26 pen), Marius Trésor (93), Alain Giresse (99)

Penalties: 1-0 Alain Giresse, 1-1 Manfred Kaltz, 2-1 Manuel Amoros, 2-2 Paul Breitner, 3-2 Dominique Rocheteau, Uli Stielike (miss), Didier Six (miss), 3-3 Pierre Littbarski, 4-3 Michel Platini, 4-4 Karl-Heinz Rummenigge, Maxime Bossis (miss), 4-5 Horst Hrubesch.

419. 10.07.1982   FIFA World Cup Final Tournament – Third Place play-off

POLAND v FRANCE 3-2 (2-1)

Estadio José Rico Pérez, Alicante (Spain)

Referee: António José da Silva Garrido (Spain)
Attendance: 28,000

POLAND: Józef Mlynarczyk, Marek Dziuba, Stefan Majewski, Wladyslaw Zmuda, Pawel Janas, Grzegorz Lato, Waldemar Matysik (46 Roman Wójcicki), Janusz Kupcewicz, Andrzej Buncol, Zbigniew Boniek, Andrzej Szarmach. Manager: Antoni Piechniczek

FRANCE: Jean Castaneda, Manuel Amoros, Gérard Janvion (64 Christian López), Marius Trésor, Philippe Mahut, Jean-Amadou Tigana (82 Didier Six), Jean-François Larios, Gérard Soler, René Girard, Bruno Bellone, Alain Couriol.   Manager: Michel Hidalgo

Goals: Andrzej Szarmach (41), Stefan Majewski (44), Janusz Kupcewicz (46) / René Girard (13), Alain Couriol (73)

420. 31.08.1982

FRANCE v POLAND 0-4 (0-1)

Parc des Princes, Paris

Referee: Bruno Galler (Switzerland)   Attendance: 16,000

FRANCE: Jean-Luc Ettori, Manuel Amoros, Gérard Janvion, Marius Trésor, Maxime Bossis (46 Philippe Mahut), Jean-Amadou Tigana, Dominique Bijotat (46 Jean-Marc Ferreri), Bernard Genghini, Gérard Soler, Patrick Delamontagne, Yannick Stopyra (69 Daniel Bravo).   Manager: Michel Hidalgo

POLAND: Jacek Kazimierski, Pawel Janas, Stefan Majewski, Tadeusz Dolny, Jan Jalocha, Andrzej Buncol (78 Miroslaw Okonski), Janusz Kupcewicz, Roman Wójcicki (65 Dariusz Kubicki), Wlodzimierz Ciolek, Wlodzimierz Mazur (46 Dariusz Dziekanowski), Wlodzimierz Smolarek. Manager: Antoni Piechniczek

Goals: Jan Jalocha (28), Janusz Kupcewicz (55, 58), Andrzej Buncol (63 pen)

421. 06.10.1982

FRANCE v HUNGARY 1-0 (0-0)

Parc des Princes, Paris

Referee: Roger Verhaeghe (Belgium)   Attendance: 15,777

FRANCE: Jean Castaneda, Maxime Bossis, Marius Trésor, Philippe Mahut, Thierry Tusseau, Alain Giresse, Jean-Amadou Tigana (79 Alain Couriol), Bernard Genghini (64 Jean-Marc Ferreri), Laurent Roussey (85 Gérard Janvion), Michel Platini, Didier Six (73 Gérard Soler).   Manager: Michel Hidalgo

HUNGARY: Béla Katzirz, Zoltán Péter (85 Gusztáv Kelemen), Attila Kerekes, Imre Garaba, József Tóth, Péter Hannich, József Póczik (68 Károly Csapó), Gyözö Burcsa, Mihály Borostyán (85 László Fazekas), Lázár Szentes (68 András Töröcsik), Gyula Hajszán. Manager: Kálmán Mészöly

Goal: Laurent Roussey (66)

422. 10.11.1982

NETHERLANDS v FRANCE 1-2 (1-1)

De Kuip, Rotterdam

Referee: Roger Schoeters (Belgium)   Attendance: 9,693

NETHERLANDS: Edward Metgod, Ben Wijnstekers, Ronald Spelbos, Michel van de Korput, Peter Boeve, Frank Rijkaard (46 René van der Gijp), Edo Ophof, Michel Valke, Ruud Gullit, Wim Kieft (46 Jurrie Koolhof), Simon Tahamata (57 Jan Wouters).   Manager: Kees Rijvers

FRANCE: Jean-Pierre Tempet, Manuel Amoros, Maxime Bossis, Marius Trésor, Patrick Battiston, Jean-Marc Ferreri, Jean-Amadou Tigana, Luis Fernández, Laurent Roussey (57 Yannick Stopyra), Michel Platini, Jean-Marc Ferratge (68 François Brisson).   Manager: Michel Hidalgo

Goals: Simon Tahamata (6) /
Patrick Battiston (12), Michel Platini (81)

423. 16.02.1983
PORTUGAL v FRANCE 0-3 (0-2)

Estádio Municipal de Guimarães, Guimarães

Referee: Ulrich (Ueli) Nyffenegger (Switzerland)
Attendance: 9,000

PORTUGAL: Manuel Galrinho BENTO, VIRGÍLIO Manuel Bagulho LOPES (64 JOÃO Domingos da Silva PINTO), HUMBERTO Manuel de Jesus COELHO, António José BASTOS LOPES (46 EURICO Monteiro GOMES), JOÃO Soares CARDOSO, CARLOS MANUEL Correia dos Santos, SHÉU Han (46 António Manuel FRASCO Vieira), ANTÓNIO Augusto Gomes de SOUSA, Fernando Albino De Sousa CHALANA, FERNANDO Mendes Soares GOMES, RUI Manuel Trinidade JORDÃO (22 Maurício Zacarias REINALDO Rodrigues Gomes). Manager: Otaviano "OTTO" Martins GLÓRIA

FRANCE: Jean-Pierre Tempet, Patrick Battiston, Philippe Mahut, Maxime Bossis, Manuel Amoros, Alain Giresse, Michel Platini, Luis Fernández (75 Thierry Tusseau), Jean-Marc Ferreri (63 Jean-Amadou Tigana), Yannick Stopyra (80 Dominique Rocheteau), Loïc Amisse. Manager: Michel Hidalgo

Goals: Yannick Stopyra (7, 70), Jean-Marc Ferreri (8)

424. 23.03.1983
FRANCE v SOVIET UNION 1-1 (1-1)

Parc des Princes, Paris

Referee: George Courtney (England)   Attendance: 40,908

FRANCE: Jean-Pierre Tempet, Patrick Battiston, Philippe Mahut (78 Thierry Tusseau), Maxime Bossis, Manuel Amoros, Jean-Marc Ferreri, Luis Fernández, Alain Giresse, Michel Platini (46 Jean-Amadou Tigana), Yannick Stopyra, Loïc Amisse (64 Dominique Rocheteau). Manager: Michel Hidalgo

SOVIET UNION: Rinat Dasayev, Vladimir Bessonov, Sergey Baltacha, Sergey Borovskiy, Anatoliy Demyanenko, Andrey Bal (55 Valeriy Gazzaev), Leonid Buryak (62 Khoren Oganesyan), Sergey Rodionov, Nikolay Larionov, Oleg Blokhin (79 Vadim Evtushenko), Fyodor Cherenkov. Manager: Valeriy Lobanovskyi

Goals: Luis Fernández (42) / Fyodor Cherenkov (29)

425. 23.04.1983
FRANCE v YUGOSLAVIA 4-0 (2-0)

Parc des Princes, Paris

Referee: Aron Schmidhuber (West Germany)
Attendance: 40,881

FRANCE: Jean-Pierre Tempet, Manuel Amoros, Thierry Tusseau, Yvon Le Roux, Maxime Bossis, Luis Fernández, Jean-Amadou Tigana, José Touré (79 Bernard Genghini), Jean-Marc Ferreri (80 Yannick Stopyra), Dominique Rocheteau, Bruno Bellone (66 Didier Six). Manager: Michel Hidalgo

YUGOSLAVIA: Ratko Svilar (80 Tomislav Ivkovic), Jasmin Dzeko, Zvjezdan Cvetkovic, Ismet Hadzic (75 Faruk Hadzibegic), Velimir Zajec, Ljubomir Radanovic, Zlatko Kranjcar (46 Dragan Mance), Aleksandar Trifunovic, Sulejman Halilovic, Mhemed Bazdarevic (46 Marko Mlinaric), Dzevad Secerbegovic (78 Miodrag Jesic). Manager: Todor Veselinovic

Goals: Yvon Le Roux (22), Dominique Rocheteau (32, 47), José Touré (74)

426. 31.05.1983   Fédération Luxembourgeoise de Football 75th Anniversary
BELGIUM v FRANCE 1-1 (1-1)

Stade Municipal, Luxembourg City

Referee: Norbert Rolles (Luxembourg)   Attendance: 5,880

BELGIUM: Jacques Munaron, Eric Gerets, Luc Millecamps, Walter Meeuws, Michel De Wolf, Guy Vandersmissen, Ludo Coeck, Frank Vercauteren, François Van der Elst, Marc Van Der Linden (59 Léo Clijsters), Eddy Voordeckers. Manager: Guy Thys

FRANCE: Jean-Pierre Tempet, Jean-Christophe Thouvenel, Yvon Le Roux, Patrick Battiston, Manuel Amoros, Jean-Claude Lemoult, José Touré, Luis Fernández, Bernard Genghini (86 Philippe Vercruysse), Gérard Soler (64 Yannick Stopyra), Didier Six (64 Bernard Zénier). Manager: Michel Hidalgo

Goals: Eddy Voordeckers (12) / Didier Six (11)

427. 07.09.1983
DENMARK v FRANCE 3-1 (1-1)

Københavns Idrætspark, Copenhagen

Referee: Volker Roth (West Germany)   Attendance: 17,500

DENMARK: Ole Kjær, Ole Rasmussen, Ivan Nielsen, Jan Mølby, Ole Madsen, Allan Simonsen, John Lauridsen, Klaus Berggreen, Søren Lerby, Michael Laudrup (77 John Sivebæk), Kenneth Brylle (68 John Helt). Manager: Sepp Piontek

FRANCE: Joël Bats, Patrick Battiston, Yvon Le Roux, Maxime Bossis, Manuel Amoros, Alain Giresse, Luis Fernández, Michel Platini, Bernard Genghini, Daniel Bravo, Dominique Rocheteau. Manager: Michel Hidalgo

Goals: Michael Laudrup (20, 75), Kenneth Brylle (59) / Michel Platini (26)

428. 05.10.1983
FRANCE v SPAIN 1-1 (0-0)

Parc des Princes, Paris

Referee: Rosario Lo Bello (Italy)   Attendance: 36,628

FRANCE: Joël Bats, William Ayache, Yvon Le Roux, Marius Trésor, Jean-Louis Zanon, Jean-Marc Ferreri, Luis Fernández, Michel Platini (75 Bernard Genghini), Jean-Claude Lemoult, Dominique Rocheteau, Bruno Bellone (85 Alain Couriol).   Manager: Michel Hidalgo

SPAIN: Luis Miguel ARCONADA Echarri, José Ramón NIMO Maldonado (65 Salvador García Puig "SALVA"), Antonio MACEDA Francés, Andoni GOIKOETXEA Olaskoaga (46 Enrique "QUIQUE" RAMOS González), José Antonio CAMACHO Alfaro, Rafael GORDILLO Vázquez, Francisco José GÜERRI Ballarin, Juan Antonio SEÑOR Gomez, Francisco José CARRASCO Hidalgo, Carlos Alonso González "SANTILLANA", MARCOS ALONSO Peña (46 Hipólito RINCÓN Povedano).   Manager: MIGUEL MUÑOZ Mozún

Goals: Dominique Rocheteau (60) / Juan Antonio SEÑOR Gomez (82 pen)

429.   12.11.1983
YUGOSLAVIA v FRANCE 0-0

Stadion Maksimir, Zagreb

Referee: Paolo Casarin (Italy)   Attendance: 15,000

YUGOSLAVIA: Zoran Simovic (46 Tomislav Ivkovic), Zoran Vujovic, Zvjezdan Cvetkovic, Srecko Katanec, Velimir Zajec, Ljubomir Radanovic, Zlatko Vujovic (46 Sulejman Halilovic), Milos Sestic, Safet Susic (79 Dragan Mance), Zlatko Kranjcar (64 Boban Bozovic), Dusan Pesic (46 Dragan Stojkovic).   Manager: Todor Veselinovic

FRANCE: Joël Bats, Manuel Amoros, Maxime Bossis, Yvon Le Roux, Marius Trésor, Luis Fernández, Daniel Bravo, Jean-Amadou Tigana, Dominique Rocheteau (46 Jean-Marc Ferreri), Alain Giresse, Bruno Bellone (63 Daniel Xuereb).   Manager: Michel Hidalgo

430. 29.02.1984
FRANCE v ENGLAND 2-0 (0-0)

Parc des Princes, Paris

Referee: Marcel Van Langenhove (Belgium)   Att: 45,554

FRANCE: Joël Bats, Patrick Battiston (72 Thierry Tusseau), Yvon Le Roux, Maxime Bossis, Manuel Amoros, Alain Giresse, Jean-Amadou Tigana, Luis Fernández, Michel Platini, José Touré, Bruno Bellone (83 Dominique Rocheteau).   Manager: Michel Hidalgo

ENGLAND: Peter Shilton, Michael Duxbury, Kenny Sansom, Sammy Lee (78 John Barnes), Graham Roberts, Terry Butcher, Bryan Robson, Brian Stein (78 Tony Woodcock), Paul Walsh, Glenn Hoddle, Steve Williams.   Manager: Bobby Robson

Goals: Michel Platini (58, 71)

431.   28.03.1984
FRANCE v AUSTRIA 1-0 (0-0)

Parc Lescure, Bordeaux

Referee: Viriato Graça Oliva (Portugal)   Attendance: 23,000

FRANCE: Joël Bats (62 Philippe Bergerôo), Patrick Battiston, Yvon Le Roux, Maxime Bossis, Manuel Amoros, Alain Giresse, Jean-Amadou Tigana, Luis Fernández, Bernard Genghini, Bernard Lacombe (51 Dominique Rocheteau), Bruno Bellone (65 Didier Six).   Manager: Michel Hidalgo

AUSTRIA: Friedl Koncilia (46 Klaus Linderberger), Bernd Krauss, Gerald Messlender, Bruno Pezzey, Josef Degeorgi, Martin Gisinger, Herbert Prohaska, Ernst Baumeister, Gerald Willfurth (69 Andreas Gretschnig), Walter Schachner (69 Peter Pacult), Richard Niederbacher.   Manager: Erich Hof

Goal: Dominique Rocheteau (83)

432. 18.04.1984
FRANCE v WEST GERMANY 1-0 (0-0)

Stade de la Meinau, Strasbourg

Referee: Enzo Barbaresco (Italy)   Attendance: 39,978

FRANCE: Joël Bats, Patrick Battiston, Yvon Le Roux, Maxime Bossis (46 Jean-François Domergue), Manuel Amoros, Luis Fernández, Daniel Bravo, Bernard Genghini, Didier Six, Dominique Rocheteau (68 Philippe Anziani), Bruno Bellone (84 Jean-Marc Ferreri).   Manager: Michel Hidalgo

WEST GERMANY: Toni Schumacher, Bernd Förster, Hans-Günter Bruns, Karlheinz Förster, Hans-Peter Briegel, Wolfgang Rolff (76 Matthias Herget), Lothar Matthäus, Andreas Brehme, Norbert Meier (76 Pierre Littbarski), Karl-Heinz Rummenigge, Rudi Völler.   Manager: Jupp Derwall

Goal: Bernard Genghini (79)

433. 01.06.1984
FRANCE v SCOTLAND 2-0 (2-0)

Stade Vélodrome, Marseille

Referee: Luigi Agnolin (Italy)   Attendance: 21,641

FRANCE: Joël Bats, Patrick Battiston, Yvon Le Roux, Maxime Bossis, Manuel Amoros, Alain Giresse, Jean-Amadou Tigana, Michel Platini, Luis Fernández (67 Bernard Genghini), Bernard Lacombe (46 Daniel Bravo), Bruno Bellone (67 Didier Six).   Manager: Michel Hidalgo

SCOTLAND: Jim Leighton, Richard Gough (67 Charlie Nicholas), Ray Stewart, Willie Miller, Alex McLeish, Maurice Malpas, Gordon Strachan (46 Neil Simpson), John Wark, Steve Archibald, Jim Bett, Mo Johnston.   Manager: Jock Stein

Goals: Alain Giresse (14), Bernard Lacombe (29)

434. 12.06.1984 UEFA European Championship – Group A
FRANCE v DENMARK 1-0 (0-0)
Parc des Princes, Paris (France)
Referee: Volker Roth (West Germany)   Attendance: 47,570
FRANCE: Joël Bats, Patrick Battiston, Yvon Le Roux (60 Jean-François Domergue), Maxime Bossis, Manuel Amoros, Jean-Amadou Tigana, Alain Giresse, Michel Platini, Luis Fernández, Bernard Lacombe, Bruno Bellone.   Manager: Michel Hidalgo
DENMARK: Ole Qvist, Ivan Nielsen, Morten Olsen, Søren Busk, Klaus Berggreen, Frank Arnesen (79 Jesper Olsen), Allan Simonsen (46 John Lauridsen), Jens Jørn Bertelsen, Søren Lerby, Michael Laudrup, Preben Elkjær Larsen.   Manager: Sepp Piontek

Goal: Michel Platini (77)

Sent off: Manuel Amoros (87)

435. 16.06.1984 UEFA European Championship – Group A
FRANCE v BELGIUM 5-0 (3-0)
Stade de la Beaujoire, Nantes (France)
Ref: Robert Bonar (Bob) Valentine (Scotland)   Att: 51,359
FRANCE: Joël Bats, Luis Fernández, Maxime Bossis, Patrick Battiston, Jean-François Domergue, Jean-Amadou Tigana, Bernard Genghini (79 Thierry Tusseau), Alain Giresse, Michel Platini, Bernard Lacombe (65 Dominique Rocheteau), Didier Six.   Manager: Michel Hidalgo
BELGIUM: Jean-Marie Pfaff, Georges Grün, Paul Lambrichts, Walter De Greef, Michel De Wolf, Enzo Scifo (52 René Verheyen), René Vandereycken (46 Ludo Coeck), Jan Ceulemans, Frank Vercauteren, Nico Claesen, Erwin Vandenbergh.   Manager: Guy Thys

Goals: Michel Platini (4, 74 pen, 89), Alain Giresse (33), Luis Fernández (44)

436. 19.06.1984 UEFA European Championship – Group A
FRANCE v YUGOSLAVIA 3-2 (0-1)
Stade Geoffroy Guichard, Saint-Étienne (France)
Referee: André Daina (Switzerland)   Attendance: 47,589
FRANCE: Joël Bats, Patrick Battiston, Jean-François Domergue, Jean-Amadou Tigana, Maxime Bossis, Alain Giresse, Luis Fernández, Jean-Marc Ferreri (77 Daniel Bravo), Dominique Rocheteau (46 Thierry Tusseau), Michel Platini, Didier Six.   Manager: Michel Hidalgo
YUGOSLAVIA: Zoran Simovic, Branko Miljus, Nenad Stojkovic, Ivan Gudelj, Velimir Zajec, Ljubomir Radanovic, Zlatko Vujovic (60 Stjepan Deveric), Dragan Stojkovic, Safet Susic, Mehmed Bazdarevic (84 Srecko Katanec), Milos Sestic.   Manager: Todor Veselinovic

Goals: Michel Platini (59, 61, 76) /
Milos Sestic (31), Dragan Stojkovic (80 pen)

437. 23.06.1984 UEFA European Championship – Semi-final
FRANCE v PORTUGAL 3-2 (1-0, 1-1) (AET)
Stade Vélodrome, Marseille (France)
Referee: Paolo Bergamo (Italy)   Attendance: 54,848
FRANCE: Joël Bats, Patrick Battiston, Yvon Le Roux, Maxime Bossis, Jean-François Domergue, Luis Fernández, Jean-Amadou Tigana, Alain Giresse, Michel Platini, Bernard Lacombe (66 Jean-Marc Ferreri), Didier Six (101 Bruno Bellone).   Manager: Michel Hidalgo
PORTUGAL: Manuel Galrinho BENTO, JOÃO Domingos da Silva PINTO, António José LIMA PEREIRA, EURICO Monteiro GOMES, ÁLVARO Monteiro de Magalhães, António Manuel FRASCO Vieira, JAIME Moreira PACHECO, ANTÓNIO Augusto Gomes de SOUSA (62 Manuel Gomes Baptista Tamagnini "NENÉ"), Fernando Albino De Sousa CHALANA, RUI Manuel Trinidade JORDÃO, DIAMANTINO Manuel Fernandes Miranda (46 FERNANDO Mendes Soares GOMES).   Manager: Fernando da Silva CABRITA

Goals: Jean-François Domergue (25, 115), M. Platini (119) /
RUI Manuel Trinidade JORDÃO (74, 98)

438. 27.06.1984 UEFA European Championship – Final
FRANCE v SPAIN 2-0 (0-0)
Parc des Princes, Paris (France)
Referee: Vojtech Christov (Czechoslovakia)
Attendance: 47,368
FRANCE: Joël Bats, Patrick Battiston (72 Manuel Amoros), Yvon Le Roux, Maxime Bossis, Jean-François Domergue, Alain Giresse, Jean-Amadou Tigana, Luis Fernández, Michel Platini, Bernard Lacombe (80 Bernard Genghini), Bruno Bellone.   Manager: Michel Hidalgo
SPAIN: Luis Miguel ARCONADA Echarri, Santiago URQUIAGA Pérez, Salvador García Puig "SALVA" (84 ROBERTO Fernández Bonillo), Ricardo GALLEGO Redondo, JULIO ALBERTO Moreno Casas (76 Manuel "MANU" SARABIA López), Juan Antonio SEÑOR Gomez, VÍCTOR Muñoz Manrique, José Antonio CAMACHO Alfaro, FRANCISCO Javier LÓPEZ Alfaro, Carlos Alonso González "SANTILLANA", Francisco José CARRASCO Hidalgo.   Manager: MIGUEL MUÑOZ Mozún

Goals: Michel Platini (57), Bruno Bellone (90)

Sent off: Yvon Le Roux (85)

439. 13.10.1984   FIFA World Cup Qualification – Group 4
LUXEMBOURG v FRANCE 0-4 (0-4)

Stade Municipal, Luxembourg City

Referee: Henning Lund-Sørensen (Denmark)
Attendance: 7,982

LUXEMBOURG: John van Rijswijck, Romain Michaux, René Scheuer, Pierre Petry, Hubert Meunier, Laurent Schonckert, Carlo Weis, Gilbert Dresch, Guy Hellers, Robby Langers, Jeannot Reiter.   Manager: Jef Vliers

FRANCE: Joël Bats, Michel Bibard, Patrick Battiston, Maxime Bossis, Manuel Amoros, Alain Giresse, Luis Fernández, Michel Platini (57 Jean-Marc Ferreri), Thierry Tusseau, Yannick Stopyra, François Brisson (73 Philippe Anziani).   Manager: Henri Michel

Goals: Patrick Battiston (2), Michel Platini (12), Yannick Stopyra (24, 32)

440. 21.11.1984   FIFA World Cup Qualification – Group 4
FRANCE v BULGARIA 1-0 (0-0)

Parc des Princes, Paris

Referee: Karl-Heinz Tritschler (West Germany)
Attendance: 42,084

FRANCE: Joël Bats, Michel Bibard, Didier Sénac, Maxime Bossis, Manuel Amoros, Jean-Amadou Tigana, Luis Fernández, Bernard Genghini, Yannick Stopyra (58 José Touré, 84 Thierry Tusseau), Michel Platini, Bruno Bellone.   Manager: Henri Michel

BULGARIA: Borislav Mihaylov, Plamen Nikolov, Nikolay Arabov, Georgi Dimitrov, Aleksandar Markov, Radoslav Zdravkov, Ayan Sadakov, Rusi Gochev, Nasko Sirakov, Bozhidar Iskrenov (46 Zhivko Gospodinov), Stoycho Mladenov (75 Emil Spasov).   Manager: Ivan Vutsov

Goal: Michel Platini (62 pen)

441. 08.12.1984   FIFA World Cup Qualification – Group 4
FRANCE v EAST GERMANY 2-0 (1-0)

Parc des Princes, Paris

Referee: Paolo Casarin (Italy)   Attendance: 43,174

FRANCE: Joël Bats, Michel Bibard, Didier Sénac, Maxime Bossis, Manuel Amoros, Alain Giresse, Jean-Amadou Tigana, Luis Fernández, Michel Platini, Yannick Stopyra (84 Philippe Anziani), Bruno Bellone.   Manager: Henri Michel

EAST GERMANY: Rene Müller, Hans-Jürgen (Dixie) Dörner, Andreas Trautmann, Dirk Stahmann, Matthias Döschner, Jörg Stübner, Rainer Troppa, Matthias Liebers, Wolfgang Steinbach (75 Hans Richter), Ralf Minge (79 Michael Glowatzky), Andreas Thom.   Manager: Bernd Stange

Goals: Yannick Stopyra (32), Philippe Anziani (89)

442. 03.04.1985   FIFA World Cup Qualification – Group 4
YUGOSLAVIA v FRANCE 0-0

Stadion Kosevo, Sarajevo

Referee: Erik Fredriksson (Sweden)   Attendance: 53,500

YUGOSLAVIA: Ranko Stojic, Vlado Capljic, Mirsad Baljic, Ivan Gudelj, Faruk Hadzibegic, Ljubomir Radanovic, Zlatko Vujovic (63 Milko Djurovski), Velimir Zajec, Vahid Halilhodzic, Mehmed Bazdarevic, Milos Sestic (67 Blaz Sliskovic).   Manager: Milos Milutinovic

FRANCE: Joël Bats, Manuel Amoros, William Ayache, Léonard Specht, Patrick Battiston, Luis Fernández (82 Thierry Tusseau), Jean-Amadou Tigana, Alain Giresse, Yannick Stopyra (69 José Touré), Michel Platini, Bruno Bellone.   Manager: Henri Michel

443. 02.05.1985   FIFA World Cup Qualification – Group 4
BULGARIA v FRANCE 2-0 (1-0)

National Stadium Vasil Levski, Sofia

Referee: Brian Robert McGinlay (Scotland)
Attendance: 57,000

BULGARIA: Borislav Mihaylov, Plamen Nikolov, Nikolay Arabov, Georgi Dimitrov, Petar Petrov, Radoslav Zdravkov, Plamen Getov (75 Atanas Pashev), Nasko Sirakov, Ayan Sadakov, Boycho Velichkov (56 Andrey Zhelyazkov), Stoycho Mladenov.   Manager: Ivan Vutsov

FRANCE: Joël Bats, William Ayache, Léonard Specht, Maxime Bossis, Manuel Amoros, José Touré, Jean-Amadou Tigana, Luis Fernández (69 Thierry Tusseau), Michel Platini, Yannick Stopyra, Bruno Bellone.   Manager: Henri Michel

Goals: Georgi Dimitrov (11), Nasko Sirakov (61)

444. 21.08.1985   Artemio Franchi Trophy 1985
FRANCE v URUGUAY 2-0 (1-0)

Parc des Princes, Paris

Referee: Abel Gnecco (Argentina)   Attendance: 20,405

FRANCE: Joël Bats, Maxime Bossis, Michel Bibard, Yvon Le Roux, William Ayache, Luis Fernández, Alain Giresse, Michel Platini, Thierry Tusseau, Dominique Rocheteau, José Touré.   Manager: Henri Michel

URUGUAY: Rodolfo Sergio RODRÍGUEZ Rodríguez, Nelson Daniel GUTIÉRREZ Luongo, Alfonso Darío PEREYRA Bueno, Víctor Hugo DIOGO Silva, Miguel Angel BOSSIO Bastianini, José Alberto BATISTA González, Vénancio Ariel RAMOS Villanueva, Jorge Wálter BARRIOS Balestrasse (77 Mario Daniel SARALEGUI Iriarte), Enzo FRANCÉSCOLI Uriarte, Sergio Rodolfo SANTÍN Spinelli, Wilmar Rubens CABRERA Sappa (77 Gustavo DALTO Calvi).
Manager: Omar Bienvenido BORRÁS Granda

Goals: Dominique Rocheteau (5), José Touré (56)

445. 11.09.1985   FIFA World Cup Qualification – Group 4

EAST GERMANY v FRANCE 2-0 (0-0)

Zentralstadion, Leipzig

Referee: Pietro D'Elia (Italy)   Attendance: 78,000

EAST GERMANY: Rene Müller, Frank Rohde, Ronald Kreer, Carsten Sänger, Uwe Zötzsche, Jörg Stübner, Ralf Minge, Matthias Liebers, Andreas Thom, Ulf Kirsten, Rainer Ernst. Manager: Bernd Stange

FRANCE: Joël Bats, Michel Bibard, Yvon Le Roux, Maxime Bossis, William Ayache, Luis Fernández, Alain Giresse, Michel Platini, Fabrice Poullain (75 Bruno Bellone), José Touré, Dominique Rocheteau.   Manager: Henri Michel

Goals: Rainer Ernst (54), Ronald Kreer (81)

---

446. 30.10.1985   FIFA World Cup Qualification – Group 4

FRANCE v LUXEMBOURG 6-0 (4-0)

Parc des Princes, Paris

Referee: Michal Józef Listkiewicz (Poland)
Attendance: 28,597

FRANCE: Joël Bats, William Ayache, Patrick Battiston, Maxime Bossis (28 Yvon Le Roux), Manuel Amoros, Alain Giresse, Jean-Amadou Tigana, Luis Fernández, José Touré, Michel Platini, Dominique Rocheteau (63 Bruno Bellone).   Manager: Henri Michel

LUXEMBOURG: John van Rijswijck, Hubert Meunier, Marcel Bossi, Gilbert Dresch, Laurent Schonckert, Carlo Weis, Gérard Jeitz (62 Nico Wagner), Guy Hellers, Pierre Hoscheid (80 Théo Scholten), Jean-Paul Girres, Robby Langers. Manager: Paul Philipp

Goals: Dominique Rocheteau (4, 29, 51), José Touré (24), Alain Giresse (36), Luis Fernández (49 pen)

---

447. 16.11.1985   FIFA World Cup Qualification – Group 4

FRANCE v YUGOSLAVIA 2-0 (1-0)

Parc des Princes, Paris

Referee: Alexis Ponnet (Belgium)   Attendance: 45,670

FRANCE: Joël Bats, Manuel Amoros, William Ayache, Yvon Le Roux, Patrick Battiston, Luis Fernández, Jean-Amadou Tigana, Alain Giresse, José Touré, Michel Platini, Dominique Rocheteau (76 Yannick Stopyra).   Manager: Henri Michel

YUGOSLAVIA: Ranko Stojic, Branko Miljus, Mirza Kapetanovic, Ivan Gudelj, Vladimir Vermezovic, Ljubomir Radanovic, Dragan Stojkovic (46 Haris Skoro), Blaz Sliskovic, Milos Bursac, Mehmed Bazdarevic, Zlatko Vujovic. Manager: Milos Milutinovic

Goals: Michel Platini (3, 71)

Sent off: Yvon Le Roux (84) / Ljubomir Radanovic (82)

---

448. 26.02.1986

FRANCE v NORTHERN IRELAND 0-0

Parc des Princes, Paris

Referee: Alphonse Costantin (Belgium)   Attendance: 28,909

FRANCE: Joël Bats, William Ayache (46 Yvon Le Roux), Patrick Battiston, Maxime Bossis, Manuel Amoros, Alain Giresse, Luis Fernández, Thierry Tusseau (65 Jean-Marc Ferreri), Jean-Pierre Papin, Michel Platini, Dominique Rocheteau.   Manager: Henri Michel

NORTHERN IRELAND: Pat Jennings, Jimmy Nicholl, Mal Donaghy, John O'Neill, Alan McDonald, Colin Clarke, David McCreery (80 John McClelland), Sammy McIlroy, Norman Whiteside, Steve Penney (70 Marc Caughey), Jimmy Quinn (80 Gerry Armstrong).   Manager: Billy Bingham

---

449. 26.03.1986

FRANCE v ARGENTINA 2-0 (1-0)

Parc des Princes, Paris

Referee: Franz Gächter (Switzerland)   Attendance: 40,045

FRANCE: Joël Bats, William Ayache, Patrick Battiston (60 Yvon Le Roux), Maxime Bossis, Manuel Amoros, Jean-Amadou Tigana, Luis Fernández, Philippe Vercruysse, Jean-Marc Ferreri, Daniel Xuereb (70 Yannick Stopyra), Bruno Bellone (24 Dominique Rocheteau).   Manager: Henri Michel

ARGENTINA: Ney Alberto PUMPIDO Barrinat, Óscar Alfredo RUGGERI Zocola, Oscar Alfredo Garré, Néstor Rolando Clausen, Sergio Daniel Batista, Daniel Alberto Passarella, Claudio Daniel BORGHI Bidos, Ricardo Omar Giusti, Jorge Luis Burruchaga, Diego Armando MARADONA Franco, Jorge Alberto Francisco VALDANO Castellanos.   Manager: Carlos Salvador Bilardo

Goals: Jean-Marc Ferreri (15), Philippe Vercruysse (80)

Sent off: Claudio Daniel BORGHI Bidos (59)

---

450. 01.06.1986   FIFA World Cup Final Tournament – Group C

CANADA v FRANCE 0-1 (0-0)

Estadio León, León de los Aldama (Mexico)

Referee: Hernán Silva Arce (Chile)   Attendance: 35,748

CANADA: Paul Dolan, Robert Lenarduzzi, Randolph Samuel, Ian Bridge, Bruce Wilson, Paul James (82 Branko Segota), Randolph Ragan, David Norman, Michael Sweeney (55 James Lowery), Carl Valentine, Igor Vrablic.   Manager: Tony Waiters

FRANCE: Joël Bats, Manuel Amoros, Patrick Battiston, Maxime Bossis, Thierry Tusseau, Alain Giresse, Jean-Amadou Tigana, Michel Platini, Luis Fernández, Jean-Pierre Papin, Dominique Rocheteau (70 Yannick Stopyra).   Manager: Henri Michel

Goal: Jean-Pierre Papin (79)

451. 05.06.1986 FIFA World Cup Final Tournament – Group C
FRANCE v SOVIET UNION 1-1 (0-0)
Estadio León, León de los Aldama (Mexico)
Referee: Romualdo Arppi Filho (Brazil) Attendance: 36,540
FRANCE: Joël Bats, Manuel Amoros, William Ayache, Patrick Battiston, Jean-Amadou Tigana, Maxime Bossis, Jean-Pierre Papin (76 Bruno Bellone), Alain Giresse (83 Philippe Vercruysse), Luis Fernández, Michel Platini, Yannick Stopyra.   Manager: Henri Michel
SOVIET UNION: Rinat Dasayev, Vladimir Bessonov, Oleg Kuznetsov, Nikolay Larionov, Anatoliy Demyanenko, Ivan Yaremchuk, Sergey Aleynikov, Pavel Yakovenko (68 Sergey Rodionov), Vasiliy Rats, Aleksandr Zavarov (58 Oleg Blokhin), Igor Belanov.   Manager: Valeriy Lobanovskyi
Goals: Luis Fernández (62) / Vasiliy Rats (53)

452. 09.06.1986 FIFA World Cup Final Tournament – Group C
HUNGARY v FRANCE 0-3 (0-1)
Estadio León, León de los Aldama (Mexico)
Referee: Carlos Alberto da Silva Valente (Portugal)
Attendance: 31,420
HUNGARY: Péter Disztl, Sándor Sallai, Antal Róth, József Kardos, Imre Garaba, Péter Hannich (46 Antal Nagy), László Dajka, Lajos Détári, József Varga, Márton Esterházy, Kálmán Kovács (65 György Bognár).   Manager: György Mezey
FRANCE: Joël Bats, Manuel Amoros, Patrick Battiston, Maxime Bossis, William Ayache, Luis Fernández, Jean-Amadou Tigana, Michel Platini, Alain Giresse, Jean-Pierre Papin (61 Dominique Rocheteau), Yannick Stopyra (71 Jean-Marc Ferreri).   Manager: Henri Michel
Goals: Yannick Stopyra (30), Jean-Amadou Tigana (63), Dominique Rocheteau (84)

453. 17.06.1986 FIFA World Cup Final Tournament – Round of 16
ITALY v FRANCE 0-2 (0-1)
Estadio Olímpico de la Ciudad Universitaria, Mexico City
Referee: Carlos Alfonso Espósito (Argentina) Att: 71,449
ITALY: Giovanni Galli, Giuseppe Bergomi, Antonio Cabrini, Giuseppe Baresi (46 Antonio Di Gennaro), Pietro Vierchowod, Gaetano Scirea, Bruno Conti, Fernando De Napoli, Giuseppe Galderisi (57 Gianluca Vialli), Salvatore Bagni, Alessandro Altobelli.   Manager: Enzo Bearzot
FRANCE: Joël Bats, William Ayache, Manuel Amoros, Luis Fernández (73 Thierry Tusseau), Maxime Bossis, Patrick Battiston, Jean-Amadou Tigana, Alain Giresse, Dominique Rocheteau, Michel Platini (84 Jean-Marc Ferreri), Yannick Stopyra.   Manager: Henri Michel
Goals: Michel Platini (14), Yannick Stopyra (57)

454. 21.06.1986 FIFA World Cup Final Tournament – Quarter-final
BRAZIL v FRANCE 1-1 (1-1, 1-1) (AET)
Estadio Jalisco, Guadalajara (Mexico)
Referee: Ioan Igna (Romania) Attendance: 65,677
BRAZIL: CARLOS Roberto Gallo, JOSIMAR Higino Pereira, JÚLIO CÉSAR da Silva, Edino Nazareth Filho "EDINHO", Cláudio Ibrahim Vaz Leal "BRANCO", ELZO Aloísio Coelho, Ricardo Rogério de Brito "ALEMÃO", Leovegildo Lins da Gama "JÚNIOR" (91 Paulo SILAS do Prado Pereira), SÓCRATES Brasileiro Sampaio de Souza Vieira de Oliveira, Luís Antônio Corrêa da Costa "MÜLLER" (72 Arthur Antunes Coimbra "ZICO"), Antônio de Oliveira Filho "CARECA".   Manager: TELÊ SANTANA da Silva
FRANCE: Joël Bats, Maxime Bossis, Patrick Battiston, Manuel Amoros, Jean-Amadou Tigana, Alain Giresse (84 Jean-Marc Ferreri), Luis Fernández, Michel Platini, Thierry Tusseau, Dominique Rocheteau (101 Bruno Bellone), Yannick Stopyra.   Manager: Henri Michel
Goals: Antônio de Oliveira Filho "CARECA" (18) / Michel Platini (41)
Penalties: SÓCRATES Brasileiro Sampaio de Souza Vieira de Oliveira (missed), 0-1 Yannick Stopyra, 1-1 Ricardo Rogério de Brito "ALEMÃO", 1-2 Manuel Amoros, 2-2 Arthur Antunes Coimbra "ZICO", 2-3 Bruno Bellone, 3-3 Cláudio Ibrahim Vaz Leal "BRANCO", Michel Platini (missed), JÚLIO CÉSAR da Silva (missed), 3-4 Luis Fernández.
Arthur Antunes Coimbra "ZICO" missed a penalty kick (74)

455. 25.06.1986 FIFA World Cup Final Tournament – Semi-final
FRANCE v WEST GERMANY 0-2 (0-1)
Estadio Jalisco, Guadalajara (Mexico)
Referee: Luigi Agnolin (Italy) Attendance: 44,000
FRANCE: Joël Bats, William Ayache, Manuel Amoros, Luis Fernández, Maxime Bossis, Patrick Battiston, Jean-Amadou Tigana, Alain Giresse (72 Philippe Vercruysse), Yannick Stopyra, Michel Platini, Bruno Bellone (66 Daniel Xuereb).   Manager: Henri Michel
WEST GERMANY: Toni Schumacher, Andreas Brehme, Hans-Peter Briegel, Norbert Eder, Karlheinz Förster, Ditmar Jakobs, Wolfgang Rolff, Lothar Matthäus, Karl-Heinz Rummenigge (57 Rudi Völler), Felix Magath, Klaus Allofs.   Manager: Franz Beckenbauer
Goals: Andreas Brehme (8), Rudi Völler (89)

456. 28.06.1986 FIFA World Cup Final Tournament – Third Place play-off

BELGIUM v FRANCE 2-4 (1-2, 2-2) (AET)

Estadio Cuauhtémoc, Heroica Puebla de Zaragoza (Mexico)

Referee: George Courtney (England)   Attendance: 21,500

BELGIUM: Jan-Marie Pfaff, Eric Gerets, Stéphane Demol, Michel Renquin (46 Frank Van der Elst), Georges Grün, Patrick Vervoort, Enzo Scifo (64 Léo Van de Elst), Raymond Mommens, Jan Ceulemans, Daniel Veyt, Nico Claesen. Manager: Guy Thys

FRANCE: Albert Rust, Michel Bibard, Yvon Le Roux (56 Maxime Bossis), Patrick Battiston, Manuel Amoros, Jean-Amadou Tigana (84 Thierry Tusseau), Philippe Vercruysse, Jean-Marc Ferreri, Bernard Genghini, Bruno Bellone, Jean-Pierre Papin.   Manager: Henri Michel

Goals: Jan Ceulemans (11), Nico Claesen (73) / Jean-Marc Ferreri (27), Jean-Pierre Papin (43), Bernard Genghini (104), Manuel Amoros (111 pen)

457. 19.08.1986

SWITZERLAND v FRANCE 2-0 (0-0)

Stade Olympique de La Pontaise, Lausanne

Referee: Karl-Heinz Tritschler (West Gemany)
Attendance: 22,000

SWITZERLAND: Urs Zurbuchen, Jürg Wittwer, Urs Bamert, Martin Weber, Claude Ryf, Christoph Gilli (76 Georges Bregy), Erni Maissen, Heinz Hermann, Thomas Bickel (65 Marco Schällibaum), Beat Sutter, André Halter (46 Dario Zuffi). Manager: Daniel Jeandupeux

FRANCE: Joël Bats, Jean-Christophe Thouvenel, Basile Boli (80 Jean-Pierre Papin), Patrick Battiston, Manuel Amoros (68 Jean-François Domergue), Jean-Marc Ferreri, Dominique Bijotat, Philippe Vercruysse, Fabrice Poullain, Yannick Stopyra, Gérard Buscher (68 Bruno Bellone).   Manager: Henri Michel

Goals: Heinz Hermann (72), Beat Sutter (75)

458. 10.09.1986 UEFA Euro 1988 Qualifying – Group 3

ICELAND v FRANCE 0-0

Laugardalsvöllur, Reykjavík

Referee: Alan Ferguson (Scotland)   Attendance: 13,758

ICELAND: Bjarni Sigurdsson, Ágúst Már Jónsson, Gunnar Gíslason, Sævar Jónsson, Sigurdur Jónsson, Ómar Torfason, Ragnar Margeirsson, Ásgeir Sigurvinsson, Atli Edvaldsson, Arnór Gudjohnsen, Pétur Pétursson. Manager: Sigfried Held

FRANCE: Joël Bats, William Ayache, Basile Boli, Patrick Battiston, Manuel Amoros, Luis Fernández, Jean-Amadou Tigana, Bernard Genghini, Yannick Stopyra, Philippe Vercruysse, Stéphane Paille.   Manager: Henri Michel

459. 11.10.1986 UEFA Euro 1988 Qualifying – Group 3

FRANCE v SOVIET UNION 0-2 (0-0)

Parc des Princes, Paris

Referee: Paolo Casarin (Italy)   Attendance: 40,496

FRANCE: Joël Bats, Manuel Amoros, William Ayache, Basile Boli (87 Philippe Vercruysse), Philippe Jeannol, Luis Fernández, Jean-Marc Ferreri, Jean-Amadou Tigana, Yannick Stopyra, Michel Platini, Jean-Pierre Papin (69 Bruno Bellone). Manager: Henri Michel

SOVIET UNION: Rinat Dasayev, Vladimir Bessonov (31 Vagiz Khidiyatullin), Aleksandr Chivadze, Oleg Kuznetsov, Anatoliy Demyanenko, Vasiliy Rats, Pavel Yakovenko, Aleksandr Zavarov, Sergey Aleynikov, Sergey Rodionov (79 Oleg Blokhin), Igor Belanov.   Manager: Valeriy Lobanovskyi

Goals: Igor Belanov (66), Vasiliy Rats (77)

460. 19.11.1986 UEFA Euro 1988 Qualifying – Group 3

EAST GERMANY v FRANCE 0-0

Zentralstadion, Leipzig

Referee: George Courtney (England)   Attendance: 54,578

EAST GERMANY: Rene Müller, Dirk Stahmann, Detlef Schößler, Frank Rohde, Matthias Döschner, Richard (Rico) Steinmann (62 Hans Richter), Jörg Stübner, Matthias Liebers, Andreas Thom, Ulf Kirsten (77 Matthias Sammer), Frank Pastor.   Manager: Bernd Stange

FRANCE: Joël Bats, William Ayache, Basile Boli, Patrick Battiston, Yvon Le Roux, Manuel Amoros, Jean-Amadou Tigana, Michel Platini, Fabrice Poullain, Yannick Stopyra, Jean-Pierre Papin (83 Bruno Bellone).   Manager: Henri Michel

461. 29.04.1987 UEFA Euro 1988 Qualifying – Group 3

FRANCE v ICELAND 2-0 (1-0)

Parc des Princes, Paris

Referee: Frederick (Fred) McKnight (Northern Ireland)
Attendance: 27,732

FRANCE: Joël Bats, Jean-Christophe Thouvenel, Basile Boli, Jean-François Domergue, Manuel Amoros, José Touré, Luis Fernández, Michel Platini, Gérald Passi, Carmelo Micciche, Yannick Stopyra (67 Jean-Pierre Papin).   Manager: Henri Michel

ICELAND: Bjarni Sigurdsson, Ágúst Már Jónsson, Gunnar Gíslason, Sævar Jónsson, Sigurdur Jónsson, Ómar Torfason, Atli Edvaldsson, Ragnar Margeirsson, Ásgeir Sigurvinsson, Arnór Gudjohnsen, Pétur Pétursson (68 Sigurdur Grétarsson). Manager: Sigfried Held

Goals: Carmelo Micciche (37), Yannick Stopyra (65)

462. 16.06.1987   UEFA Euro 1988 Qualifying – Group 3
NORWAY v FRANCE 2-0 (0-0)

Ullevaal Stadion, Oslo

Referee: Werner Föckler (West Germany)   Attendance: 8,268

NORWAY: Erik Thorstvedt, Hans Herman Henriksen, Terje Kojedal, Anders Giske, Per-Egil Ahlsen, Jan Berg, Per Edmund Mordt, Arve Seland (62 Kjetil Osvold), Jørn Andersen (89 Erik Soler), Tom Sundby, Hallvar Thoresen.
Manager: Tor Røste Fossen

FRANCE: Joël Bats, Jean-Christophe Thouvenel, Basile Boli, Jean-François Domergue, Manuel Amoros, Jean-Marc Ferreri, Jean-Amadou Tigana, Gérald Passi, Fabrice Poullain (80 Patrick Delamontagne), Yannick Stopyra, Carmelo Micciche (75 Philippe Fargeon).   Manager: Henri Michel

Goals: Per Edmund Mordt (73), Jørn Andersen (80)

463. 12.08.1987
WEST GERMANY v FRANCE 2-1 (2-1)

Olympiastadion, West-Berlin

Referee: Henning Lund-Sørensen (Denmark)   Att: 31,217

WEST GERMANY: Eike Immel, Jürgen Kohler, Guido Buchwald (69 Wolfgang Rolff), Hans Pflügler, Andreas Brehme (67 Stefan Reuter), Lothar Matthäus, Uwe Rahn, Hans Dorfner, Rudi Völler (67 Pierre Littbarski), Klaus Allofs, Matthias Herget.   Manager: Franz Beckenbauer

FRANCE: Joël Bats (85 Bruno Martini), Yvon Le Roux, Patrick Battiston, William Ayache, Manuel Amoros, José Touré, Luis Fernández, Fabrice Poullain, Gérald Passi, Jean-Pierre Papin (55 Gérard Buscher), Éric Cantona.
Manager: Henri Michel

Goals: Rudi Völler (4, 9) / Éric Cantona (42)

464. 09.09.1987   UEFA Euro 1988 Qualifying – Group 3
SOVIET UNION v FRANCE 1-1 (0-1)

Lenin Central Stadium, Moscow

Referee: Gerasimos (Makis) Germanakos (Greece)
Attendance: 86,048

SOVIET UNION: Rinat Dasayev, Viktor Losev, Vagiz Khidiyatullin, Oleg Kuznetsov, Vasiliy Rats, Vadym Tyshchenko (46 Igor Belanov), Hennadiy Lytovchenko, Pavel Yakovenko, Sergey Aleynikov, Oleg Protasov, Igor Dobrovolskiy (69 Aleksey Mikhaylichenko).   Manager: Valeriy Lobanovskyi

FRANCE: Joël Bats, Manuel Amoros, William Ayache, Rémy Vogel, Basile Boli, Luis Fernández, Philippe Fargeon (87 Jean-Pierre Papin), José Touré (74 Jean-Philippe Rohr), Yannick Stopyra, Gérald Passi, Fabrice Poullain.
Manager: Henri Michel

Goals: Aleksey Mikhaylichenko (77) / José Touré (13)

465. 14.10.1987   UEFA Euro 1988 Qualifying – Group 3
FRANCE v NORWAY 1-1 (0-0)

Parc des Princes, Paris

Referee: Joaquín Ramos Marcos (Spain)   Attendance: 11,308

FRANCE: Bruno Martini, Luc Sonor, Didier Sénac, Basile Boli, Manuel Amoros, José Touré, Luis Fernández, Philippe Anziani (53 Jean-Marc Ferreri), Dominique Bijotat, Philippe Fargeon, Éric Cantona.   Manager: Henri Michel

NORWAY: Erik Thorstvedt, Hans Herman Henriksen, Terje Kojedal, Rune Bratseth, Anders Giske, Per Edmund Mordt, Kai-Erik Herlovsen (75 Erik Soler), Kjetil Osvold, Tom Sundby, Børre Meinseth, Jan Berg (79 Vegard Skogheim).
Manager: Tord Grip

Goals: Philippe Fargeon (63) / Tom Sundby (79)

466. 18.11.1987   UEFA Euro 1988 Qualifying – Group 3
FRANCE v EAST GERMANY 0-1 (0-0)

Parc des Princes, Paris

Referee: Carlos Alberto da Silva Valente (Portugal)
Attendance: 16,581

FRANCE: Joël Bats, Manuel Amoros, Basile Boli, Sylvain Kastendeuch, Yvon Le Roux, Bruno Germain, Dominique Bijotat (76 Philippe Fargeon), Fabrice Poullain, Bernard Zénier, Éric Cantona, Bruno Bellone.   Manager: Henri Michel

EAST GERMANY: Rene Müller, Ronald Kreer, Dirk Stahmann, Matthias Döschner, Uwe Zötzsche, Hans-Uwe Pilz, Matthias Liebers, Richard (Rico) Steinmann, Ulf Kirsten, Ralf Minge (61 Rainer Ernst), Andreas Thom.
Manager: Bernd Stange

Goal: Rainer Ernst (90)

467. 27.01.1988
ISRAEL v FRANCE 1-1 (0-0)

National Stadium, Ramat Gan

Referee: Allan Gunn (England)   Attendance: 5,000

ISRAEL: Avi Hadad (62 Ofer Fabian), Avi Cohen (II), Avi Cohen, Nir Alon, Igal Hilel, Uri Malmilian, Nir Klinger, Mordechai Ivanir, Daniel Alberto BRAILOVSKY Poliak, Shalom Tikva (89 Moshe Eisenberg), Ronny Rosenthal.
Manager: Miljenko Mihic

FRANCE: Bruno Martini, William Ayache, Yvon Le Roux, Basile Boli, Manuel Amoros, José Touré (77 Jean-Marc Ferreri), Luis Fernández (71 Pascal Despeyroux), Fabrice Poullain, Gérald Passi, Éric Cantona, Bruno Bellone (49 Yannick Stopyra).   Manager: Henri Michel

Goals: Avi Cohen (II) (69) / Yannick Stopyra (60)

468. 02.02.1988   Tournoi de France 1988 Semi-final
FRANCE v SWITZERLAND 2-1 (2-1)

Stade Municipal de Toulouse, Toulouse

Referee: Gérard Biguet (France)   Attendance: 10,348

FRANCE: Bruno Martini, William Ayache (66 Bernard Casoni), Basile Boli, Sylvain Kastenduech, Manuel Amoros, Jean-Marc Ferreri (80 Dominique Bijotat), Pascal Despeyroux, Fabrice Poullain, Yannick Stopyra (71 Jean-Pierre Papin), Philippe Fargeon, Gérald Passi.   Manager: Henri Michel

SWITZERLAND: Martin Brunner, Stefan Marini, Martin Weber, Alain Geiger, Marco Schällibaum, Marcel Koller (78 Blaise Piffaretti), Heinz Hermann, Thomas Bickel, Beat Sutter, Hans-Peter Zwicker (65 Kubilay Türkyilmaz), Christophe Bonvin.   Manager: Daniel Jeandupeux

Goals: Gérald Passi (7), Philippe Fargeon (9) / Beat Sutter (19)

469. 05.02.1988   Tournoi de France 1988 – Final
FRANCE v MOROCCO 2-1 (1-1)

Stade Louis II, Monaco

Referee: Michel Vautrot (France)   Attendance: 10,000

FRANCE: Bruno Martini, Manuel Amoros, Basile Boli (75 Yvon Le Roux), Sylvain Kastenduech, Bernard Casoni, Dominique Bijotat, Fabrice Poullain (52 Luis Fernández), Gérald Passi, Yannick Stopyra (82 Bruno Bellone), Philippe Fargeon, Jean-Marc Ferreri.   Manager: Henri Michel

MOROCCO: Khalil Azmi, Hassan Hirs, Fadel Jilal, Lahcen Ouadani, Abdelmajid Lemriss (76 Hassan Bousselham), Abdelmajid Dolmy, Hassan Benhabicha, Mohammed Lachabi, Moulay El Gharef, Hassan Nader (68 Abdallah Haidamou), Mustapha Kiddi.   Manager: José Mehdi Faría

Goals: Abdelmajid Lemriss (9 og), Yannick Stopyra (49) / Abdelmajid Lemriss (34)

470. 23.03.1988
FRANCE v SPAIN 2-1 (2-1)

Parc Lescure, Bordeaux

Referee: Neil Midgley (England)   Attendance: 14,441

FRANCE: Joël Bats, Luc Sonor, Yvon Le Roux, Sylvain Kastenduech, Manuel Amoros (80 Basile Boli), Dominique Bijotat (85 Marcel Dib), Luis Fernández, Gérald Passi, Jean-Philippe Durand, Jean-Pierre Papin, Éric Cantona.   Manager: Henri Michel

SPAIN: Andoni ZUBIZARRETA Urreta, Miguel Porlán Noguera "CHENDO", Manuel SANCHÍS Hontiyuelo, Miguel TENDILLO Belenguer, Luis María LÓPEZ REKARTE (41 Miquel SOLER Sarasols), Ramón María CALDERÉ del Rey, Ricardo GALLEGO Redondo, José Miguel González Martín del Campo "MÍCHEL", Rafael GORDILLO Vázquez, Emilio BUTRAGUEÑO Santos, José María BAKERO Escudero.   Manager: MIGUEL MUÑOZ Mozún

Goals: Gérald Passi (8), Luis Fernández (26) / Ramón María CALDERÉ del Rey (6)

471. 27.04.1988
NORTHERN IRELAND v FRANCE 0-0

Windsor Park, Belfast

Referee: Keith Cooper (Wales)   Attendance: 6,250

NORTHERN IRELAND: Allen McKnight, Mal Donaghy, Nigel Worthington, Norman Whiteside (41 Jimmy Quinn), Alan McDonald, John McClelland, Danny Wilson, Steve Penney, Colin Clarke (83 Kevin Wilson), Michael O'Neill, Robbie Dennison (48 Kingsley Black).
Manager: Billy Bingham

FRANCE: Bruno Martini, Luc Sonor, Bernard Casoni, Sylvain Kastenduech, Manuel Amoros, Dominique Bijotat, Luis Fernández, Philippe Vercruysse (83 Jean-Marc Ferreri), Jean-Philippe Durand, Yannick Stopyra, Patrice Garande (83 Philippe Fargeon).   Manager: Henri Michel

472. 24.08.1988
FRANCE v CZECHOSLOVAKIA 1-1 (0-0)

Parc des Princes, Paris

Referee: Ildefonso Urízar Azpitarte (Spain)
Attendance: 15,000

FRANCE: Joël Bats, Luc Sonor, Bernard Casoni, Sylvain Kastenduech, Manuel Amoros, Franck Sauzée, Pascal Despeyroux, Gérald Passi (64 Philippe Vercruysse), Bernard Pardo, Jean-Pierre Papin, Stéphane Paille.
Manager: Henri Michel

CZECHOSLOVAKIA: Jan Stejskal, Július Bielik, Václav Nemecek, Jozef Chovanec, Miroslav Kadlec, Lubomír Vlk, Ivan Hasek, Viliam Hýravý, Michal Bílek, Stanislav Griga (75 Günter Bittengel), Milan Luhový (67 Václav Danek).   Manager: Jozef Venglos

Goals: Stéphane Paille (52) / Václav Danek (77)

473. 28.09.1988   FIFA World Cup Qualification – Group 5
FRANCE v NORWAY 1-0 (0-0)

Parc des Princes, Paris

Referee: Günther Habermann (East Germany)
Attendance: 22,000

FRANCE: Joël Bats, Luc Sonor, Bernard Casoni, Basile Boli (63 Sylvain Kastenduech), Manuel Amoros, Marcel Dib, Franck Sauzée, Gérald Passi (76 Stéphane Paille), Daniel Bravo, Jean-Pierre Papin, Daniel Xuereb.
Manager: Henri Michel

NORWAY: Erik Thorstvedt, Hans Herman Henriksen (77 Gunnar Halle), Rune Bratseth, Terje Kojedal, Erland Johnsen, Anders Giske, Kjetil Osvold (81 Tom Gulbrandsen), Sverre Brandhaug, Ørjan Berg, Mini Jakobsen, Gøran Sørloth.   Manager: Ingvar Stadheim

Goal: Jean-Pierre Papin (84 pen)

474.   22.10.1988   FIFA World Cup Qualification – Group 5

CYPRUS v FRANCE   1-1 (0-1)

Makario Stadium, Nicosia

Referee: Emilio Soriano Aladrén (Spain)   Attendance: 2,700

CYPRUS: Giorgos Pantziaras, Giorgos Christodoulou, Andreas Stavrou, Kostas Miamiliotis, Pambos Pittas, Kostas Petsas, Giannakis Yiangoudakis, Floros Nikolaou, Andreas Kantilos, Pavlos Savva, Evagoras Christofi (77 Giannos Ioannou).   Manager: Panikos Iakovou

FRANCE: Joël Bats, Luc Sonor, Bernard Casoni, Basile Boli, Manuel Amoros, Daniel Bravo, Marcel Dib, Franck Sauzée, Gérald Passi (72 Philippe Vercruysse), Jean-Pierre Papin, Daniel Xuereb (80 Stéphane Paille).   Manager: Henri Michel

Goals: Pambos Pittas (78 pen) / Daniel Xuereb (44)

475.   19.11.1988   FIFA World Cup Qualification – Group 5

YUGOSLAVIA v FRANCE   3-2 (1-1)

Stadion Jugoslovenska Narodna Armija, Beograd

Referee: Erik Fredriksson (Sweden)   Attendance: 7,489

YUGOSLAVIA: Tomislav Ivkovic, Vujadin Stanojkovic, Predrag Spasic (54 Goran Juric), Srecko Katanec, Faruk Hadzibegic, Davor Jozic, Dragan Stojkovic, Safet Susic, Borislav Cvetkovic (69 Dejan Savicevic), Mehmed Bazdarevic, Zlatko Vujovic.   Manager: Ivica Osim

FRANCE: Joël Bats, Manuel Amoros, Alain Roche, Basile Boli, Sylvain Kastendeuch, Franck Sauzée, Jean-Marc Ferreri (78 Jean-Pierre Papin), Jean-Amadou Tigana, Stéphane Paille, Marcel Dib, Christian Pérez (68 Daniel Bravo).   Manager: Michel Platini

Goals: P. Spasic (11), Safet Susic (76), Dragan Stojkovic (83) / Christian Pérez (3), Franck Sauzée (68)

476.   07.02.1989

REPUBLIC OF IRELAND v FRANCE   0-0

Dalymount Park, Dublin

Referee: John Walter Lloyd (Wales)   Attendance: 22,000

REPUBLIC OF IRELAND: Pat Bonner, Chris Morris, Mick McCarthy, Paul McGrath, Chris Hughton, Ray Houghton, Ronnie Whelan, Andy Townsend, Liam Brady, Frank Stapleton (76 John Aldridge), Tony Cascarino.   Manager: Jack Charlton

FRANCE: Joël Bats, Sylvain Kastendeuch, Franck Silvestre (73 Alain Roche), Patrick Battiston, Luc Sonor, Manuel Amoros, Laurent Blanc (66 Philippe Vercruysse), Franck Sauzée, Jean-Philippe Durand, Jean-Pierre Papin, Stéphane Paille (46 José Touré).   Manager: Michel Platini

477.   08.03.1989   FIFA World Cup Qualification – Group 5

SCOTLAND v FRANCE   2-0 (1-0)

Hampden Park, Glasgow

Referee: Jirí Stiegler (Czechoslovakia)   Attendance: 65,204

SCOTLAND: Jim Leighton, Richard Gough, Maurice Malpas, Roy Aitken, Alex McLeish, Gary Gillespie, Steve Nicol, Paul McStay, Ally McCoist (69 Brian McClair), Ian Ferguson (56 Gordon Strachan), Mo Johnston.   Manager: Andy Roxburgh

FRANCE: Joël Bats, Manuel Amoros, Franck Silvestre, Luc Sonor, Patrick Battiston, Franck Sauzée, Jean-Philippe Durand (58 Stéphane Paille), Thierry Laurey, Laurent Blanc, Jean-Pierre Papin, Daniel Xuereb (72 Christian Pérez).   Manager: Michel Platini

Goals: Mo Johnston (28, 52)

478.   29.04.1989   FIFA World Cup Qualification – Group 5

FRANCE v YUGOSLAVIA   0-0

Parc des Princes, Paris

Referee: Tullio Lanese (Italy)   Attendance: 39,469

FRANCE: Joël Bats, Manuel Amoros, Patrick Battiston, Luc Sonor, Basile Boli, Laurent Blanc, Franck Sauzée, Jean-Philippe Durand (46 Christophe Cocard), Stéphane Paille, Daniel Xuereb (76 Didier Deschamps), Christian Pérez.   Manager: Michel Platini

YUGOSLAVIA: Tomislav Ivkovic, Vujadin Stanojkovic, Predrag Spasic, Srecko Katanec, Faruk Hadzibegic, Davor Jozic, Zlatko Vujovic (86 Dragoljub Brnovic), Dragan Stojkovic, Zoran Vujovic, Mehmed Bazdarevic, Safet Susic.   Manager: Ivica Osim

479.   16.08.1989

SWEDEN v FRANCE   2-4 (1-0)

Malmö Stadion, Malmö

Referee: Zvi Sharir (Israel)   Attendance; 16,619

SWEDEN: Thomas Ravelli, Roland Nilsson, Glenn Hysén, Peter Larsson, Roger Ljung, Anders Limpar (68 Niclas Larsson-Nyhlén), Glenn Strömberg, Jonas Thern, Joakim Nilsson, Jan Hellström, Mats Magnusson (58 Stefan Lindqvist).   Manager: Olle Nordin

FRANCE: Joël Bats, Manuel Amoros, Yvon Le Roux, Franck Sauzée, Éric Di Meco, Jean-Marc Ferreri (70 Laurent Blanc), Didier Deschamps, Bernard Pardo, Christian Pérez, Jean-Pierre Papin, Éric Cantona.   Manager: Michel Platini

Goals: Jonas Thern (5), Stefan Lindqvist (63) / Éric Cantona (57, 87), Jean-Pierre Papin (61, 83)

480. 05.09.1989   FIFA World Cup Qualification – Group 5

NORWAY v FRANCE 1-1 (0-1)

Ullevaal Stadion, Oslo

Referee: Todor Kolev (Bulgaria)   Attendance: 8,564

NORWAY: Erik Thorstvedt, Gunnar Halle, Terje Kojedal, Rune Bratseth, Stig Inge Bjørnebye, Karl Petter Løken, Sverre Brandhaug (75 Ørjan Berg), Per-Egil Ahlsen, Mini Jakobsen, Jørn Andersen, Jan Åge Fjørtoft (75 Simen Agdestein).   Manager: Ingvar Stadheim

FRANCE: Joël Bats, Manuel Amoros, Éric Di Meco, Yvon Le Roux (56 Franck Silvestre), Franck Sauzée, Bernard Pardo, Didier Deschamps, Christian Pérez, Jean-Marc Ferreri (75 Laurent Blanc), Jean-Pierre Papin, Éric Cantona.   Manager: Michel Platini

Goals: Rune Bratseth (84) / Jean-Pierre Papin (40 pen)

481. 11.10.1989   FIFA World Cup Qualification – Group 5

FRANCE v SCOTLAND 3-0 (1-0)

Parc des Princes, Paris

Referee: Kurt Röthlisberger (Switzerland)   Att: 22,651

FRANCE: Joël Bats, Franck Silvestre, Yvon Le Roux (46 Bernard Casoni), Éric Di Meco, Franck Sauzée, Bernard Pardo, Didier Deschamps, Jean-Philippe Durand, Jean-Marc Ferreri, Christian Pérez (81 Daniel Bravo), Éric Cantona.   Manager: Michel Platini

SCOTLAND: Jim Leighton, Steve Nicol, Richard Gough, Alex McLeish, Maurice Malpas, Roy Aitken, Paul McStay, Gordon Strachan (64 Alan McInally), Murdo MacLeod (76 Jim Bett), Mo Johnston, Ally McCoist.   Manager: Andy Roxburgh

Goals: Didier Deschamps (26), Éric Cantona (63), Steve Nicol (88 og)

Sent off: Éric Di Meco (57)

482. 18.11.1989   FIFA World Cup Qualification – Group 5

FRANCE v CYPRUS 2-0 (1-0)

Stade Municipal de Toulouse, Toulouse

Referee: Valeriy Pavlovich Butenko (Soviet Union)   Attendance: 34,687

FRANCE: Joël Bats, Franck Silvestre, Bernard Casoni, Didier Deschamps, Manuel Amoros, Franck Sauzée, Bernard Pardo, Jean-Marc Ferreri, Christian Pérez (17 Laurent Blanc), Jean-Pierre Papin, Éric Cantona.   Manager: Michel Platini

CYPRUS: Andreas Charitou, Spyros Kastanas, Giorgos Christodoulou, Makis Socratous, Pambos Pittas, Kostas Konstantinou, Floros Nikolaou, Evagoras Christofi, Pavlos Savva, Christos Koliantris, Giannos Ioannou.   Manager: Panikos Iakovou

Goals: Didier Deschamps (25), Laurent Blanc (75)

483. 21.01.1990   Kuwait Tournament 1990

KUWAIT v FRANCE 0-1 (0-0)

Al-Sadaqua Walsalam Stadium, Adiliya Kuwait City

Referee: Ghazi Ali Al Kandi (Kuwait)   Attendance: 5,000

KUWAIT: Samir SAID, Osama HUSSAIN Sultan Abdullah, Fadel MATAR, Bassel ABDEL NABI, Badr MRIFA, Walid BRIKI, Walid AL FLIJ, Wael SULAIMAN Al-Habashi, Badr BATI, Khaled Ali NASSER (80 Mohammed IBRAHIM), Anbar SAID (80 Ahmed AL SALAH).   Manager: OTACÍLIO

FRANCE: Gilles Rousset, Franck Silvestre, Basile Boli, Franck Sauzée, Manuel Amoros, Laurent Blanc, Marcel Dib, Bernard Pardo (46 Didier Deschamps), Rémi Garde, Éric Cantona (46 Jean-Pierre Papin, 77 Éric Di Meco), Pascal Vahirua (46 Jean-Marc Ferreri).   Manager: Michel Platini

Goal: Laurent Blanc (74)

484. 24.01.1990   Kuwait Tournament 1990

FRANCE v EAST GERMANY 3-0 (2-0)

Al-Sadaqua Walsalam Stadium, Adiliya Kuwait City

Referee: Ghazi Ali Al Kandi (Kuwait)   Attendance: 1,500

FRANCE: Bruno Martini, Manuel Amoros (81 Basile Boli), Franck Sauzée (78 Franck Silvestre), Bernard Casoni, Éric Di Meco, Jean-Marc Ferreri (60 Rémi Garde), Bernard Pardo, Didier Deschamps, Éric Cantona, Pascal Vahirua, Laurent Blanc (84 Marcel Dib).   Manager: Michel Platini

EAST GERMANY: Dirk Heyne, Andreas Wagenhaus, Matthias Mauckgsch, Burkhard Reich, Hendrik Herzog, Jörg Stübner (72 Uwe Weidemann), Matthias Sammer (82 Hilmar Weilandt), Dariusz Wosz (46 Marcus Wuckel), Richard (Rico) Steinmann, Ulf Kirsten, Thomas Doll.   Manager: Eduard Geyer

Goals: Éric Cantona (1, 24), Didier Deschamps (73)

485. 28.02.1990

FRANCE v WEST GERMANY 2-1 (1-1)

Stade de la Mosson, Montpellier

Referee: Joaquín Ramos Marcos (Spain)   Attendance: 22,000

FRANCE: Bruno Martini, Manuel Amoros, Basile Boli (49 Laurent Blanc), Bernard Casoni, Éric Di Meco, Bernard Pardo, Rémi Garde, Didier Deschamps, Jean-Pierre Papin, Éric Cantona, Jean-Marc Ferreri (64 Pascal Vahirua).   Manager: Michel Platini

WEST GERMANY: Bodo Illgner, Klaus Augenthaler, Thomas Berthold, Alois Reinhardt, Andreas Brehme, Thomas Häßler, Andreas Möller, Lothar Matthäus, Uwe Bein, Jürgen Klinsmann, Karl-Heinz Riedle (66 Pierre Littbarski).   Manager: Franz Beckenbauer

Goals: Jean-Pierre Papin (43), Éric Cantona (81) / Andreas Möller (36)

486. 28.03.1990
HUNGARY v FRANCE 1-3 (1-1)

Népstadion, Budapest

Referee: Tadeusz Diakonowicz (Poland)   Attendance: 12,000

HUNGARY: István Brockhauser, Tamás Mónos, Attila Pintér, János Palaczky, Géza Mészöly, Zsolt Limperger, Zsolt Máriási, György Bognár (62 József Duró), Kálmán Kovács (62 Róbert Jován), Lajos Détári (79 Tibor Balog), Tamás Petres (52 Pál Fischer).   Manager: Kálmán Mészöly

FRANCE: Bruno Martini, Franck Silvestre, Franck Sauzée (79 Laurent Blanc), Bernard Casoni, Manuel Amoros (46 Jean-Philippe Durand), Bernard Pardo, Luis Fernández (69 Basile Boli), Christian Pérez, Éric Cantona, Philippe Tibeuf (63 Fabrice Divert), Jean-Marc Ferreri.   Manager: Michel Platini

Goals: Attila Pintér (38 pen) /
Éric Cantona (27, 67), Franck Sauzée (70)

487. 15.08.1990
FRANCE v POLAND 0-0

Parc des Princes, Paris

Referee: Neil Midgley (England)   Attendance: 15,919

FRANCE: Bruno Martini, Manuel Amoros (76 Jean-Philippe Durand), Franck Sauzée, Emmanuel Petit, Bernard Casoni, Bernard Pardo, Luis Fernández (46 Basile Boli), Jean-Marc Ferreri (59 Pascal Vahirua), Christian Pérez, Éric Cantona, Jean-Pierre Papin.   Manager: Michel Platini

POLAND: Jaroslaw Bako (46 Józef Wandzik), Piotr Czachowski, Zbigniew Kaczmarek, Dariusz Kubicki, Robert Warzycha, Waldemar Prusik (44 Roman Szewczyk), Ryszard Tarasiewicz, Krzysztof Warzycha (86 Damian Lukasik), Jacek Ziober, Dariusz Dziekanowski (77 Janusz Nawrocki), Jan Furtok.   Manager: Andrzej Strejlau

488. 05.09.1990   UEFA Euro 1992 Qualifying – Group 1
ICELAND v FRANCE 1-2 (0-1)

Laugardalsvöllur, Reykjavík

Referee: David Findlay Taylor Syme (Scotland)
Attendance: 8,388

ICELAND: Bjarni Sigurdsson, Thorgrímur Thráinsson, Atli Edvaldsson, Gudni Bergsson, Sævar Jónsson, Thorvaldur Örlygsson (63 Ragnar Margeirsson), Sigurdur Grétarsson, Pétur Ormslev (63 Rúnar Kristinsson), Ólafur Thórdarson, Arnór Gudjohnsen, Pétur Pétursson.   Manager: Bo Johansson

FRANCE: Bruno Martini, Manuel Amoros, Franck Sauzée, Basile Boli, Bernard Casoni, Laurent Blanc (75 Jean-Philippe Durand), Bernard Pardo, Didier Deschamps, Christian Pérez, Jean-Pierre Papin, Éric Cantona (83 Luis Fernández).   Manager: Michel Platini

Goals: Atli Edvaldsson (85) /
Jean-Pierre Papin (12), Éric Cantona (75)

489. 13.10.1990   UEFA Euro 1992 Qualifying – Group 1
FRANCE v CZECHOSLOVAKIA 2-1 (0-0)

Parc des Princes, Paris

Referee: George Courtney (England)   Attendance: 38,249

FRANCE: Bruno Martini, Basile Boli, Laurent Blanc, Bernard Casoni, Jean-Philippe Durand, Jocelyn Angloma (52 Luis Fernández), Franck Sauzée, Jean-Pierre Papin, Éric Cantona, Pascal Vahirua (84 Franck Silvestre), Didier Deschamps.   Manager: Michel Platini

CZECHOSLOVAKIA: Jan Stejskal, Karel Kula, Miroslav Kadlec, Ján Kocian, Michal Hipp, Lubomír Moravcík, Jozef Chovanec, Lubos Kubík (86 Dusan Tittel), Michal Bílek (83 Ladislav Pecko), Tomás Skuhravý, Ivo Knoflícek.   Manager: Milan Mácala

Goals: Jean-Pierre Papin (59, 82) / Tomás Skuhravý (88)

490. 17.11.1990   UEFA Euro 1992 Qualifying – Group 1
ALBANIA v FRANCE 0-1 (0-1)

Stadiumi Kombëtar Qemal Stafa, Tirana

Referee: Bruno Galler (Switzerland)   Attendance: 12,972

ALBANIA: Anesti Arapi, Lorenc Leskaj (46 Alfred Ferko), Genç Ibro, Skënder Hodja, Artur Lekbello, Arjan Stafa, Hysen Zmijani, Sulejman Demollari, Mirel Josa, Sokol Kushta, Kujtim Majaçi (56 Eduard Kaçaçi).   Manager: Agron Sulaj

FRANCE: Bruno Martini, Basile Boli, Franck Sauzée, Laurent Blanc, Bernard Casoni, Didier Deschamps, Bernard Pardo, Christian Pérez, Philippe Tibeuf (67 David Ginola), Jean-Marc Ferreri, Pascal Vahirua (82 Jocelyn Angloma).   Manager: Michel Platini

Goal: Basile Boli (23)

491.   20.02.1991   UEFA Euro 1992 Qualifying – Group 1
FRANCE v SPAIN   3-1 (1-1)
Parc des Princes, Paris
Referee: Tullio Lanese (Italy)   Attendance: 41,174
FRANCE: Bruno Martini, Manuel Amoros, Basile Boli, Laurent Blanc, Bernard Casoni, Franck Sauzée, Bernard Pardo (51 Luis Fenández), Jean-Philippe Durand, Jean-Pierre Papin, Éric Cantona, Pascal Vahirua (82 Didier Deschamps). Manager: Michel Platini
SPAIN: Andoni ZUBIZARRETA Urreta, Fernando "NANDO" Muñoz García, Enrique "QUIQUE" Sánchez FLORES, Juan Francisco "JUANITO" Rodríguez Herrera, Manuel SANCHÍS Hontiyuelo, José María BAKERO Escudero, Jon Andoni GOIKOETXEA Lasa, José Miguel González Martín del Campo "MÍCHEL", Emilio BUTRAGUEÑO Santos (74 Manuel "MANOLO" Sánchez Delgado), Guillermo AMOR Martínez, Juan VIZCAÍNO Morcillo (60 Miquel SOLER Sarasols). Manager: LUIS SUÁREZ Miramontes
Goals: Franck Sauzée (14), Jean-Pierre Papin (58), Laurent Blanc (77) / José María BAKERO Escudero (10)

492.   30.03.1991   UEFA Euro 1992 Qualifying – Group 1
FRANCE v ALBANIA   5-0 (4-0)
Parc des Princes, Paris
Referee: Einar Halle (Norway)   Attendance: 24,181
FRANCE: Bruno Martini, Manuel Amoros, Laurent Blanc, Basile Boli, Jean-Philippe Durand, Franck Sauzée (73 Didier Deschamps), Luis Fenández, Christophe Cocard, Jean-Pierre Papin, Éric Cantona, Pascal Vahirua (56 Pascal Baills). Manager: Michel Platini
ALBANIA: Blendi Nallbani, Hysen Zmijani, Artur Lekbello, Rudi Vata, Josif Gjergji, Adnan Oçelli, Dashnor Dume, Agim Canaj, Sulejman Demollari, Ermal Tahiri, Ilir Kepa. Manager: Bejkush Birçë
Goals: Franck Sauzée (1, 19), Jean-Pierre Papin (34 pen, 42), Artur Lekbello (81 og)

493.   14.08.1991
POLAND v FRANCE   1-5 (1-2)
Stadion Miejski, Poznan
Referee: Aleksey Nikolaevich Spirin (Soviet Union)
Attendance: 15,000
POLAND: Józef Wandzik (46 Kazimierz Sidorczuk), Piotr Soczynski, Czeslaw Jakolcewicz, Dariusz Kubicki, Andrzej Lesiak, Robert Warzycha (53 Marek Rzepka), Ryszard Tarasiewicz, Piotr Czachowski, Jacek Ziober, Roman Kosecki (70 Dariusz Skrzypczak), Jan Urban. Manager: Andrzej Strejlau
FRANCE: Bruno Martini, Basile Boli, Laurent Blanc, Bernard Casoni (77 Franck Silvestre), Manuel Amoros (72 Rémi Garde), Jocelyn Angloma, Franck Sauzée, Luis Fenández (46 Didier Deschamps), Jean-Philippe Durand (53 Christian Pérez), Jean-Pierre Papin, Amara Simba. Manager: Michel Platini
Goals: Jan Urban (17) / Franck Sauzée (41), Jean-Pierre Papin (43), Amara Simba (68), Laurent Blanc (69), Christian Pérez (77)
Ryszard Tarasiewicz missed a penalty kick (5)

494.   04.09.1991   UEFA Euro 1992 Qualifying – Group 1
CZECHOSLOVAKIA v FRANCE   1-2 (1-0)
Tehelné pole, Bratislava
Referee: Peter Mikkelsen (Denmark)   Attendance: 44,884
CZECHOSLOVAKIA: Ludek Miklosko, Pavel Hapal (78 Ivo Knoflícek), Ján Kocian, Dusan Tittel, Jirí Novotný, Ondrej Kristofík (72 Martin Frýdek), Lubomír Moravcík, Václav Nemecek, Jirí Nemec, Ladislav Pecko, Pavel Kuka. Manager: Milan Mácala
FRANCE: Bruno Martini, Jocelyn Angloma (76 Jean-Philippe Durand), Basile Boli, Laurent Blanc, Bernard Casoni, Manuel Amoros, Franck Sauzée, Didier Deschamps, Christophe Cocard (46 Christian Pérez), Jean-Pierre Papin, Pascal Vahirua. Manager: Michel Platini
Goals: Václav Nemecek (19) / Jean-Pierre Papin (53, 89)

495.   12.10.1991   UEFA Euro 1992 Qualifying – Group 1
SPAIN v FRANCE   1-2 (1-2)
Estadio Benito Villamarín, Sevilla
Referee: Hubert Forstinger (Austria)   Attendance: 9,399
SPAIN: Andoni ZUBIZARRETA Urreta, CRISTÓBAL Parralo Aguilera, ABELARDO Fernández Antuña, Manuel SANCHÍS Hontiyuelo, Roberto SOLOZÁBAL Villanueva (46 EUSEBIO SACRISTÁN Mena), Juan VIZCAÍNO Morcillo, Rafael MARTÍN VÁZQUEZ (73 ÁLVARO Cervera Díaz), Fernando Ruiz HIERRO, Ricardo González BANGO, Manuel "MANOLO" Sánchez Delgado, Emilio BUTRAGUEÑO Santos. Manager: Vicente MIERA Campos
FRANCE: Bruno Martini, Jocelyn Angloma, Basile Boli, Laurent Blanc, Bernard Casoni, Manuel Amoros, Didier Deschamps, Luis Fenández (82 Jean-Philippe Durand), Christian Pérez (63 Rémi Garde), Jean-Pierre Papin, Éric Cantona. Manager: Michel Platini
Goals: ABELARDO Fernández Antuña (34) / Luis Fenández (13), Jean-Pierre Papin (16)

496. 20.11.1991   UEFA Euro 1992 Qualifying – Group 1
FRANCE v ICELAND 3-1 (1-0)
Parc des Princes, Paris

Referee: Erik Fredriksson (Sweden)   Attendance: 27,381

FRANCE: Bruno Martini, Jocelyn Anglona, Laurent Blanc, Bernard Casoni (46 Basile Boli), Manuel Amoros, Didier Deschamps, Luis Fernández (68 Jean-Philippe Durand), Christian Pérez, Amara Simba, Éric Cantona, Pascal Vahirua.   Manager: Michel Platini

ICELAND: Birkir Kristinsson, Gudni Bergsson (81 Sævar Jónsson), Pétur Ormslev, Kristján Jónsson, Valur Valsson, Kristinn Jónsson, Thorvaldur Örlygsson, Arnór Gudjohnsen, Baldur Bjarnason, Gudmundur Torfason (56 Eyjólfur Sverrisson), Sigurdur Grétarsson.   Manager: Ásgeir Elíasson

Goals: Amara Simba (42), Éric Cantona (59, 68) / Eyjólfur Sverrisson (71)

497. 19.02.1992
ENGLAND v FRANCE 2-0 (1-0)
British Empire Exhibition Stadium, London

Referee: Aron Schmidhuber (Germany)   Attendance: 58,723

ENGLAND: Chris Woods, Robert Jones, Stuart Pearce, Martin Keown, Mark Wright, Des Walker, Neil Webb, Geoff Thomas, Nigel Clough, Alan Shearer, David Hirst (46 Gary Lineker).   Manager: Graham Taylor

FRANCE: Gilles Rousset, Jocelyn Anglona, Basile Boli, Laurent Blanc, Bernard Casoni, Manuel Amoros, Didier Deschamps, Luis Fernández (71 Jean-Philippe Durand), Christian Pérez (73 Amara Simba), Éric Cantona, Jean-Pierre Papin.   Managers: Michel Platini & Gérard Houllier

Goals: Alan Shearer (43), Gary Lineker (73)

498. 25.03.1992
FRANCE v BELGIUM 3-3 (2-2)
Parc des Princes, Paris

Referee: Philip Don (England)   Attendance: 25,000

FRANCE: Bruno Martini, Jocelyn Anglona, Basile Boli, Bernard Casoni, Emmanuel Petit (46 Jean-Philippe Durand), Franck Sauzée (62 Manuel Amoros), Didier Deschamps, Christian Pérez, Jean-Pierre Papin, Éric Cantona, Pascal Vahirua (46 Luis Fernández).
Managers: Michel Platini & Gérard Houllier

BELGIUM: Michel Preud'homme, Bertrand Crasson, Georges Grün, Philippe Albert, Vital Borkelmans, Johan Walem, Frank Van der Elst, Luc Nilis (46 Marc Wilmots), Marc Degryse (88 Frank Dauwen), Enzo Scifo, Danny Boffin (58 Bruno Versavel).   Manager: Paul Van Himst

Goals: Jean-Pierre Papin (40 pen, 82), Pascal Vahirua (45) / Philippe Albert (28), Enzo Scifo (44 pen), Marc Wilmots (48)

499. 27.05.1992
SWITZERLAND v FRANCE 2-1 (1-1)
Stade Olympique de La Pontaise, Lausanne

Referee: Alfred Wieser (Austria)   Attendance: 21,000

SWITZERLAND: Stefan Huber, Marc Hottiger, Alain Geiger (39 Dominique Herr), André Egli, Jürg Studer (33 Christophe Ohrel), Georges Bregy, Ciriaco Sforza, Thomas Bickel (71 Alain Sutter), Beat Sutter (88 Adrian Knup), Christophe Bonvin, Stéphane Chapuisat.   Manager: Roy Hodgson),

FRANCE: Bruno Martini, Jocelyn Anglona, Basile Boli (46 Franck Silvestre), Laurent Blanc, Bernard Casoni (46 Emmanuel Petit), Jean-Philippe Durand, Didier Deschamps (46 Luis Fernández), Franck Sauzée (71 Rémi Garde), Christian Pérez (46 Christophe Cocard), Fabrice Divert, Éric Cantona (46 Pascal Vahirua).
Managers: Michel Platini & Gérard Houllier

Goals: Christophe Bonvin (28, 73) / Fabrice Divert (20)

500. 05.06.1992
FRANCE v NETHERLANDS 1-1 (1-1)
Stade Félix Bollaert, Lens

Referee: Hans-Jürgen Weber (Germany)   Attendance: 38,000

FRANCE: Bruno Martini, Jocelyn Anglona (61 Jean-Philippe Durand), Bernard Casoni, Laurent Blanc, Basile Boli, Emmanuel Petit (46 Manuel Amoros), Franck Sauzée (61 Luis Fernández), Didier Deschamps, Jean-Pierre Papin (61 Fabrice Divert), Éric Cantona, Pascal Vahirua (74 Christian Pérez).
Managers: Michel Platini & Gérard Houllier

NETHERLANDS: Hans van Breukelen, Berry van Aerle, Ronald Koeman, Adri van Tiggelen, Aron Winter, Jan Wouters (79 Danny Blind), Dennis Bergkamp (74 Eric Viscaal), Rob Witschge, John van't Schip, Marco van Basten, Bryan Roy (86 Wim Jonk).   Manager: Rinus Michels

Goals: Jean-Pierre Papin (12) / Bryan Roy (18)

501. 10.06.1992   UEFA European Championship – Group 1
SWEDEN v FRANCE 1-1 (1-0)
Råsunda Fotbollstadion, Solna (Sweden)

Referee: Aleksey Nikolaevich Spirin (C.I.S.)
Attendance: 29,680

SWEDEN: Thomas Ravelli, Roland Nilsson, Jan Eriksson, Patrik Andersson, Joachim Björklund, Stefan Schwarz, Klas Ingesson, Jonas Thern, Anders Limpar, Tomas Brolin, Kennet Andersson (74 Martin Dahlin).   Manager: Tommy Svensson

FRANCE: Bruno Martini, Manuel Amoros, Laurent Blanc, Bernard Casoni, Basile Boli, Jocelyn Anglona (68 Luis Fernández), Didier Deschamps, Franck Sauzée, Pascal Vahirua (46 Christian Pérez), Jean-Pierre Papin, Éric Cantona.
Manager: Michel Platini

Goals: Jan Eriksson (25) / Jean-Pierre Papin (59)

502. 14.06.1992   UEFA European Championship – Group 1
ENGLAND v FRANCE 0-0
Malmö Stadion, Malmö (Sweden)
Referee: Sándor Puhl (Hungary)   Attendance: 26,535
ENGLAND: Chris Woods, Martin Keown, Carlton Palmer, Des Walker, Andy Sinton, Trevor Steven, David Batty, David Platt, Stuart Pearce, Gary Lineker, Alan Shearer. Manager: Graham Taylor
FRANCE: Bruno Martini, Manuel Amoros, Basile Boli, Laurent Blanc, Bernard Casoni, Jean-Philippe Durand, Didier Deschamps, Franck Sauzée (46 Jocelyn Angloma), Luis Fernández (74 Christian Pérez), Jean-Pierre Papin, Éric Cantona.   Manager: Michel Platini

503. 17.06.1992   UEFA European Championship – Group 1
DENMARK v FRANCE 2-1 (1-0)
Malmö Stadion, Malmö (Sweden)
Referee: Hubert Forstinger (Austria)   Attendance: 25,673
DENMARK: Peter Schmeichel, John Sivebæk, Kent Nielsen (62 Torben Piechnik), Lars Olsen, Kim Christofte, Henrik Andersen, Henrik Larsen, John (Faxe) Jensen, Brian Laudrup (69 Lars Elstrup), Torben Frank, Flemming Povlsen. Manager: Richard Møller Nielsen
FRANCE: Bruno Martini, Basile Boli, Laurent Blanc, Bernard Casoni, Manuel Amoros, Didier Deschamps, Christian Pérez (81 Christophe Cocard), Jean-Philippe Durand, Jean-Pierre Papin, Éric Cantona, Pascal Vahirua (46 Luis Fernández). Manager: Michel Platini
Goals: Henrik Larsen (8), Lars Elstrup (78) / Jean Pierre Papin (61)

504. 26.08.1992
FRANCE v BRAZIL 0-2 (0-1)
Parc des Princes, Paris
Referee: Frans Van Den Wijngaert (Belgium)   Attendance: 34,428
FRANCE: Bruno Martini, Basile Boli, Alain Roche, William Prunier, Emmanuel Petit (56 Laurent Fournier), Jean-Philippe Durand (64 Franck Sauzée), Laurent Blanc (64 Pascal Vahirua), Didier Deschamps, David Ginola, Christophe Cocard, Jean-Pierre Papin.   Manager: Gérard Houllier
BRAZIL: Cláudio André Mergen TAFFAREL, Jorge Amorim de Oliveira Campos "JORGINHO", RICARDO Roberto Barreto da ROCHA, RICARDO GOMES Raymundo, MAURO da SILVA Gomes, Cláudio Ibrahim Vaz Leal "BRANCO", VALDO Cândido Filho (65 Crizam César de Oliveira Filho "ZINHO"), LUÍS HENRIQUE Pereira Dos Santos (84 Leovegildo Lins da Gama "JÚNIOR"), Antônio de Oliveira Filho "CARECA", RAÍ Souza Vieira de Oliveira, ROMÁRIO de Souza Farias (65 José Roberto Gama de Oliveira "BEBETO").
Manager: CARLOS ALBERTO Gomes PARREIRA
Goals: RAÍ Souza Vieira de Oliveira (43), LUÍS HENRIQUE Pereira Dos Santos (52).

505. 09.09.1992   FIFA World Cup Qualification – Group 6
BULGARIA v FRANCE 2-0 (2-0)
National Stadium Vasil Levski, Sofia
Referee: Sándor Puhl (Hungary)   Attendance: 41,000
BULGARIA: Borislav Mihaylov, Iliyan Kiryakov, Trifon Ivanov, Tsanko Tsvetanov, Nikolay Iliev, Zlatko Yankov, Emil Kostadinov (70 Georgi Yordanov), Hristo Stoichkov, Lyuboslav Penev (78 Stanimir Stoilov), Nasko Sirakov, Krasimir Balakov. Manager: Dimitar Penev
FRANCE: Bruno Martini, Basile Boli, Bernard Casoni, Alain Roche, Emmanuel Petit, Laurent Fournier (61 Laurent Blanc), Franck Sauzée, Didier Deschamps, Pascal Vahirua (64 Jean-Philippe Durand), Jean-Pierre Papin, David Ginola. Manager: Gérard Houllier
Goals: Hristo Stoichkov (21 pen), Krasimir Balakov (29)

506. 14.10.1992   FIFA World Cup Qualification – Group 6
FRANCE v AUSTRIA 2-0 (1-0)
Parc des Princes, Paris
Referee: Vadim Zhuk (Belarus)   Attendance: 39,186
FRANCE: Bruno Martini, Basile Boli, Franck Sauzée, Bernard Casoni, Jean-Luc Sassus, Laurent Fournier (63 Jérôme Gnako), Didier Deschamps, Jean-Philippe Durand, Jean-Pierre Papin, Éric Cantona, Xavier Gravelaine (73 Pascal Vahirua). Manager: Gérard Houllier
AUSTRIA: Franz Wohlfahrt, Wolfgang Feiersinger, Michael Streiter, Manfred Zsak, Robert Wazinger, Peter Stöger (84 Heimo Pfeifenberger), Peter Artner, Andreas Herzog, Michael Baur, Frenkie Schinkels (46 Andreas Ogris), Toni Polster. Manager: Ernst Happel
Goals: Jean-Pierre Papin (3), Éric Cantona (77)
Jean-Pierre Papin missed a penalty kick (82)

507. 14.11.1992   FIFA World Cup Qualification – Group 6

FRANCE v FINLAND 2-1 (2-0)

Parc des Princes, Paris

Referee: Jozef Marko (Czechoslovakia)   Attendance: 28,630

FRANCE: Bruno Martini, Basile Boli, Alain Roche, Bernard Casoni, Bixente Lizarazu, Didier Deschamps, Franck Sauzée, Jean-Philippe Durand (71 Christian Karembeu), Éric Cantona, Jean-Pierre Papin, Xavier Gravelaine (78 Pascal Vahirua).   Manager: Gérard Houllier

FINLAND: Kari Laukkanen, Erik Holmgren, Markku Kanerva, Kari Ukkonen, Erkka Petäjä (86 Jari Kinnunen), Ari Hjelm, Jari Litmanen, Marko Myyry, Petri Järvinen, Kimmo Tarkkio, Mika-Matti Paatelainen (24 Pasi Tauriainen).   Manager: Tommy Lindholm

Goals: Jean-Pierre Papin (18), Éric Cantona (31) / Petri Järvinen (54)

508. 17.02.1993   FIFA World Cup Qualification – Group 6

ISRAEL v FRANCE 0-4 (0-1)

National Stadium, Ramat Gan

Referee: Ryszard Wójcik (Poland)   Attendance: 26,000

ISRAEL: Boni Ginzburg, Felix Halfon, Alon Harazi, Nir Klinger, Ya'acov Hillel, Alon Hazan, Reuven Atar (56 Eli Driks), Tal Banin, Avi Nimni, Ronen Harazi, Ronny Rosenthal.   Manager: Shlomo Scharf

FRANCE: Bernard Lama, Basile Boli, Alain Roche, Laurent Blanc, Bixente Lizarazu (82 Patrice Loko), Franck Sauzée, Paul Le Guen, Didier Deschamps, David Ginola (63 Emmanuel Petit), Jean-Pierre Papin, Éric Cantona.   Manager: Gérard Houllier

Goals: Éric Cantona (27), Laurent Blanc (62, 84), Alain Roche (89)

509. 27.03.1993   FIFA World Cup Qualification – Group 6

AUSTRIA v FRANCE 0-1 (0-0)

Ernst Happel Stadion, Vienna

Referee: John Blankenstein (Netherlands)   Att: 37,837

AUSTRIA: Franz Wohlfahrt, Robert Pecl, Manfred Zsak, Peter Artner, Wolfgang Feiersinger, Harald Cerny, Dietmar Kühbauer, Frenkie Schinkels (71 Andreas Ogris), Andreas Herzog, Toni Polster, Heimo Pfeifenberger.   Manager: Herbert Prohaska

FRANCE: Bernard Lama, Jocelyn Angloma, Alain Roche, Laurent Blanc, Emmanuel Petit, Paul Le Guen, Didier Deschamps, Franck Sauzée (87 Corentin Martins da Silva), Bixente Lizarazu, Jean-Pierre Papin, Xavier Gravelaine (70 Patrice Loko).   Manager: Gérard Houllier

Goal: Jean-Pierre Papin (58)

510. 28.04.1993   FIFA World Cup Qualification – Group 6

FRANCE v SWEDEN 2-1 (1-1)

Parc des Princes, Paris

Referee: Pierluigi Pairetto (Italy)   Attendance: 34,134

FRANCE: Bernard Lama, Jocelyn Angloma, Basile Boli, Laurent Blanc, Emmanuel Petit, Franck Sauzée, Paul Le Guen, Corentin Martins da Silva (89 Bixente Lizarazu), Didier Deschamps, Éric Cantona, David Ginola (46 Pascal Vahirua).   Manager: Gérard Houllier

SWEDEN: Thomas Ravelli, Roland Nilsson, Patrik Andersson, Joachim Björklund, Roger Ljung, Stefan Rehn, Stefan Schwarz, Jonas Thern (26 Pontus Kåmark), Klas Ingesson, Tomas Brolin, Martin Dahlin (67 Stefan Pettersson).   Manager: Tommy Svensson

Goals: Éric Cantona (42 pen, 83) / Martin Dahlin (14)

511. 28.07.1993

FRANCE v RUSSIA 3-1 (3-1)

Stade Michel d'Ornano, Caen

Referee: Alfredo Trentalange (Italy)   Attendance: 20,467

FRANCE: Bruno Martini (46 Bernard Lama), Alain Roche, Emmanuel Petit (80 Xavier Gravelaine), Basile Boli (60 Jean-Luc Dogon), Laurent Blanc, Paul Le Guen, Didier Deschamps, Franck Sauzée (85 Reynald Pedros), Jean-Pierre Papin, Corentin Martins da Silva (64 Bixente Lizarazu), Éric Cantona.   Manager: Gérard Houllier

RUSSIA: Stanislav Cherchesov, Dmitriy Khlestov (46 Dmitriy Popov), Viktor Onopko, Andrey Ivanov, Andrey Kanchelskis, Sergey Gorlukovich, Igor Ledyakhov, Valeriy Karpin (70 Omari Tetradze), Andrey Pyatnitskiy, Sergey Yuran, Dmitriy Radchenko (64 Ilshat Faizulin).   Manager: Pavel Sadyrin

Goals: Franck Sauzée (16), Éric Cantona (20), Jean-Pierre Papin (36 pen) / Laurent Blanc (23 og)

512. 22.08.1993   FIFA World Cup Qualification – Group 6

SWEDEN v FRANCE 1-1 (0-0)

Råsunda Fotbollstadion, Solna

Referee: Aron Schmidhuber (Germany)   Attendance: 30,530

SWEDEN: Thomas Ravelli, Roland Nilsson, Jan Eriksson, Patrik Andersson, Roger Ljung, Stefan Landberg (79 Anders Limpar), Klas Ingesson, Jonas Thern, Pär Zetterberg (68 Stefan Rehn), Martin Dahlin, Tomas Brolin.   Manager: Tommy Svensson

FRANCE: Bernard Lama, Marcel Desailly, Alain Roche, Laurent Blanc, Bixente Lizarazu, Paul Le Guen, Didier Deschamps, Franck Sauzée, Reynald Pedros (80 Pascal Vahirua), Jean-Pierre Papin, Éric Cantona.   Manager: Gérard Houllier

Goals: Martin Dahlin (87) / Franck Sauzée (76)

513.   08.09.1993   FIFA World Cup Qualification – Group 6
FINLAND v FRANCE   0-2 (0-0)

Tampereen Stadion, Tampere

Referee: Stephen John (Steve) Lodge (England)   Attendance: 7,200

FINLAND: Petri Jakonen, Jari Kinnunen, Markku Kanerva, Erkka Petäjä, Anders Eriksson, Jari Litmanen, Janne Lindberg, Kim Suominen (76 Tommi-Björn Paavola), Ari Hjelm, Marko Rajamäki (78 Jukka Ruhanen), Mika-Matti Paatelinen.   Manager: Tommy Lindholm

FRANCE: Bernard Lama, Marcel Desailly, Alain Roche, Laurent Blanc, Emmanuel Petit, Didier Deschamps (88 Vincent Guérin), Paul Le Guen, Franck Sauzée, Corentin Martins da Silva (72 Reynald Pedros), Jean-Pierre Papin, Éric Cantona.   Manager: Gérard Houllier

Goals: Laurent Blanc (47), Jean-Pierre Papin (55 pen)

514.   13.10.1993   FIFA World Cup Qualification – Group 6
FRANCE v ISRAEL   2-3 (2-1)

Parc des Princes, Paris

Referee: Alan Snoddy (Northern Ireland)   Att: 32,700

FRANCE: Bernard Lama, Marcel Desailly, Alain Roche (24 Bixente Lizarazu), Laurent Blanc, Emmanuel Petit, Didier Deschamps, Paul Le Guen, Franck Sauzée, Jean-Pierre Papin, Éric Cantona, David Ginola (86 Youri Djorkaeff).   Manager: Gérard Houllier

ISRAEL: Boni Ginzburg, Felix Halfon (90 Yaakov Schwartz), Alon Harazi, Nir Klinger, Moshe Glam, Alon Hazan, Reuven Atar, Ronny Levy, Avi Nimni (65 Eyal Berkovic), Ronen Harazi, Ronny Rosenthal.   Manager: Shlomo Scharf

Goals: Franck Sauzée (29), David Ginola (39) / Ronen Harazi (21), Eyal Berkovic (84), Reuven Atar (90)

515.   17.11.1993   FIFA World Cup Qualification – Group 6
FRANCE v BULGARIA   1-2 (1-1)

Parc des Princes, Paris

Referee: Leslie William (Les) Mottram (Scotland)   Attendance: 48,402

FRANCE: Bernard Lama, Marcel Desailly, Alain Roche, Laurent Blanc, Emmanuel Petit, Didier Deschamps, Paul Le Guen, Franck Sauzée (81 Vincent Guérin), Reynald Pedros, Jean-Pierre Papin (69 David Ginola), Éric Cantona.   Manager: Gérard Houllier

BULGARIA: Borislav Mihaylov, Emil Kremenliev, Trifon Ivanov, Petar Hubchev, Tsanko Tsvetanov (82 Daniel Borimirov), Yordan Lechkov (82 Petar Aleksandrov), Zlatko Yankov, Krasimir Balakov, Emil Kostadinov, Lyuboslav Penev, Hristo Stoichkov.   Manager: Dimitar Penev

Goals: Éric Cantona (32) / Emil Kostadinov (37, 90)

516.   16.02.1994
ITALY v FRANCE   0-1 (0-1)

Stadio San Paolo, Napoli

Referee: Dr. Markus Merk (Germany)   Attendance: 17,241

ITALY: Gianluca Pagliuca, Antonio Benarrivo, Paolo Maldini, Stefano Eranio, Alessandro Costacurta, Franco Baresi (65 Lorenzo Minotti), Alberigo Evani, Demetrio Albertini, Pierluigi Casiraghi (46 Andrea Silenzi), Roberto Baggio, Giovanni Stroppa (65 Massimiliano Cappioli).   Manager: Arrigo Sacchi

FRANCE: Bernard Lama, Christian Karembeu (73 Jean-Pierre Cyprien), Alain Roche, Marcel Desailly (89 Corentin Martins da Silva), Éric Di Meco, Jérôme Gnako (53 Vincent Guérin), Didier Deschamps, Paul Le Guen, Youri Djorkaeff, Éric Cantona, David Ginola.   Manager: Aimé Jacquet

Goal: Youri Djorkaeff (44)

517.   22.03.1994
FRANCE v CHILE   3-1 (2-1)

Stade de Gerland, Lyon

Referee: Juan Manuel Brito Arceo (Spain)   Attendance: 32,000

FRANCE: Bernard Lama, Jocelyn Angloma, Alain Roche (78 Paul Le Guen), Marcel Desailly (72 Christian Karembeu), Bixente Lizarazu, Didier Deschamps, Jean-Michel Ferri, Youri Djorkaeff (46 Corentin Martins da Silva), Christophe Cocard, Jean-Pierre Papin, David Ginola (46 Pascal Vahirua).   Manager: Aimé Jacquet

CHILE: Nelson Antonio TAPIA Ríos, Daniel Fernando LÓPEZ Rojas, Ronald Hugo FUENTES Núñez, Carlos Alberto FUENTES Ramos, Pedro Fernando JAQUE Gatica, Nelson Rodrigo PARRAGUEZ Riveros, Fabián Raphael ESTAY Silva (82 Lukas Nicolás TUDOR Bakulic), Mario Enrique LEPE González, Raimundo TUPPER Lyon (60 Marcelo Alejandro ÁLVAREZ Rivera), Iván Luis ZAMORANO Zamora, Pedro Alejandro GONZÁLEZ Vera (74 Wilson ROJAS Barrera).   Manager: Mirko Jozic

Goals: Jean-Pierre Papin (8), Youri Djorkaeff (35), Corentin Martins da Silva (51) / Iván Luis ZAMORANO Zamora (11)

518. 26.05.1994   Kirin Cup 1994
AUSTRALIA v FRANCE 0-1 (0-1)
Universiade Memorial Stadium, Kobe (Japan)
Referee: Masayochi Okada (Japan)   Attendance: 16,743
AUSTRALIA: Zeljko Kalac, Tony Vidmar (71 Jason Polak), Mehmet Durakovic, Milan Ivanovic, Alex Tobin, Ned Zelic, Aurelio Vidmar, Paul Wade (83 John Markovski), Carl Veart, Robbie Slater, Jason van Blerck.   Manager: Eddie Thomson
FRANCE: Fabien Barthez, Jocelyn Angloma, Emmanuel Petit, Laurent Blanc, Éric Di Meco, Christian Karembeu, Jean-Michel Ferri, Christophe Dugarry (74 Corentin Martins da Silva), Jean-Pierre Papin, Éric Cantona, David Ginola (74 Reynald Pedros).   Manager: Aimé Jacquet

Goal: Éric Cantona (43)

Jean-Pierre Papin missed a penalty kick (28)

519. 29.05.1994   Kirin Cup 1994
JAPAN v FRANCE 1-4 (0-2)
National Olympic Stadium, Tokyo (Japan)
Ref: Letchmanasamy Kathirveloo (Malaysia)   Att: 48,841
JAPAN: Kazuya Maekawa (46 Kenjo Honnami), Koji Kondo, Masami Ihara, Yoshihiro Natsuka, Teruo Iwamoto (69 Masahiro Endo), Kenta Hasegawa (46 Takafumi Ogura), Tetsuji Hashiratani, Masaaki Sawanobori, Tetsuya Asano (57 Hajime Moriyasu), Hisashi Kurosaki, Kazuyoshi Miura.   Manager: Paulo Roberto FALCÃO
FRANCE: Bernard Lama, Jocelyn Angloma (85 Christian Karembeu), Marcel Desailly, Laurent Blanc, Éric Di Meco (72 Bixente Lizarazu), Didier Deschamps, Paul Le Guen, Youri Djorkaeff (72 Nicolas Ouédec), Jean-Pierre Papin, Éric Cantona, David Ginola.   Manager: Aimé Jacquet

Goals: Takafumi Ogura (79) /
Youri Djorkaeff (16), Jean-Pierre Papin (18),
Hisashi Kurosaki (54 og), David Ginola (56)

520. 17.08.1994
FRANCE v CZECH REPUBLIC 2-2 (0-2)
Parc Lescure, Bordeaux
Referee: Gerd Grabher (Austria)   Attendance: 15,000
FRANCE: Bernard Lama, Bruno N'Gotty, Laurent Blanc, Lilian Thuram, Éric Di Meco, Corentin Martins da Silva (63 Zinédine Zidane), Jocelyn Angloma, Marcel Desailly (24 Jean-Michel Ferri), Éric Cantona, Christophe Dugarry (77 Patrice Loko), David Ginola (46 Bixente Lizarazu).   Manager: Aimé Jacquet
CZECH REPUBLIC: Petr Kouba, Lubos Kubík, Jirí Novotný, Tomás Repka, Daniel Smejkal, Jan Suchopárek, Jirí Nemec (61 Karel Poborský), Václav Nemecek, Radoslav Látal (66 Patrik Berger), Horst Siegl (46 Pavel Kuka), Tomás Skuhravý (82 Petr Samec).   Manager: Dusan Uhrin

Goals: Zinédine Zidane (85, 87) /
Tomás Skuhravý (43), Danile Smejkal (45)

521. 07.09.1994   UEFA Euro 1996 Qualifying – Group 1
SLOVAKIA v FRANCE 0-0
Tehelné pole, Bratislava
Referee: Peter Mikkelsen (Denmark)   Attendance: 14,329
SLOVAKIA: Ladislav Molnár, Tomás Stúpala, Milos Glonek, Marián Zeman, Vladimír Kinder, Róbert Tomaschek, Ondrej Kristofík, Dusan Tittel, Vladislav Zvara (64 Marek Penksa), Lubomír Moravcík, Stefan Rusnák (80 Vladimír Weiss).   Manager: Jozef Venglos
FRANCE: Bernard Lama, Jocelyn Angloma, Éric Di Meco, Alain Roche, Laurent Blanc, Didier Deschamps, Paul Le Guen, Youri Djorkaeff (81 Bixente Lizarazu), Reynald Pedros (64 Christophe Dugarry), David Ginola, Éric Cantona.   Manager: Aimé Jacquet

522. 08.10.1994   UEFA Euro 1996 Qualifying – Group 1
FRANCE v ROMANIA 0-0
Stade Geoffroy Guichard, Saint-Étienne
Referee: Leif Sundell (Sweden)   Attendance: 31,144
FRANCE: Bernard Lama, Jocelyn Angloma, Alain Roche, Laurent Blanc, Bixente Lizarazu, Christian Karembeu, Marcel Desailly, Reynald Pedros, Patrice Loko (83 Christophe Dugarry), Nicolas Ouédec (72 Zinédine Zidane), Éric Cantona.   Manager: Aimé Jacquet
ROMANIA: Bogdan Stelea, Dan Petrescu, Miodrag Belodedici, Tibor Selymes, Ioan Lupescu, Daniel Timofte (72 Marius Lacatus), Gheorghe Popescu, Florin Raducioiu (79 Basarab Nica Panduru), Gheorghe Hagi, Ilie Dumitrescu, Daniel Prodan.   Manager: Anghel Iordanescu

523. 16.11.1994   UEFA Euro 1996 Qualifying – Group 1
POLAND v FRANCE 0-0
Stadion Górnika, Zabrze
Referee: Angelo Amendolia (Italy)   Attendance: 15,400
POLAND: Józef Wandzik, Tomasz Waldoch, Marek Swierczewski, Waldemar Jaskulski, Piotr Swierczewski, Sylwester Czereszewski, Marek Kozminski (29 Jacek Bak), Roman Kosecki, Henryk Baluszynski (83 Dariusz Gesior), Andrzej Juskowiak, Krzysztof Warzycha.   Manager: Henryk Apostel
FRANCE: Bernard Lama, Jocelyn Angloma, Éric Di Meco, Alain Roche, Laurent Blanc, Paul Le Guen, Marcel Desailly, Christian Karembeu, Reynald Pedros (28 Youri Djorkaeff), Nicolas Ouédec (78 Christophe Dugarry), Éric Cantona.   Manager: Aimé Jacquet

Sent off: Christian Karembeu (52)

524. 13.12.1994   UEFA Euro 1996 Qualifying – Group 1

AZERBAIJAN v FRANCE 0-2 (0-1)

Hüseyin Avni Aker Stadyumu, Trabzon (Turkey)

Referee: Rune Pedersen (Norway)   Attendance: 533

AZERBAIJAN: Aleksandr Zhidkov (41 Elkhan Hasanov), Fizuli Allahverdiev, Faig Jabbarov, Emin Agayev, Yashar Vakhabzade, Rasim Abushev, Yunis Hüseynov, Shakhin Diniyev, Arif Asadov (79 Vladislav Kadirov), Velli Kasumov (79 Vidadi Rzayev), Samir Alakbarov.   Manager: Agaselim Mirjavadov

FRANCE: Bernard Lama, Jocelyn Angloma, Éric Di Meco, Alain Roche, Paul Le Guen, Laurent Blanc, Marcel Desailly (71 Jean-Michel Ferri), Reynald Pedros (76 Corentin Martins da Silva), Patrice Loko, Jean-Pierre Papin, Éric Cantona.   Manager: Aimé Jacquet

Goals: Jean-Pierre Papin (24), Patrice Loko (55)

525. 18.01.1995

NETHERLANDS v FRANCE 0-1 (0-1)

Stadion Nieuw Galgenwaard, Utrecht

Referee: Michel Piraux (Belgium)   Attendance: 12,400

NETHERLANDS: Ed de Goey, Stan Valckx, Danny Blind (46 Michael Reiziger), Frank de Boer, Wim Jonk, Aron Winter, Marc Overmars (61 Peter van Vossen), Arthur Numan (77 Edgar Davids), Clarence Seedorf, Michael Mols (54 Pierre van Hooijdonk), Glenn Helder.   Manager: Guus Hiddink

FRANCE: Bernard Lama, Christian Karembeu (87 Lilian Thuram), Éric Di Meco, Jean-Michel Ferri, Marcel Desailly, Laurent Blanc, Paul Le Guen (61 Jocelyn Angloma), Reynald Pedros, Éric Cantona, Patrice Loko, Jean-Pierre Papin (67 Nicolas Ouédec).   Manager: Aimé Jacquet

Goal: Patrice Loko (44)

526. 29.03.1995   UEFA Euro 1996 Qualifying – Group 1

ISRAEL v FRANCE 0-0

National Stadium, Ramat Gan

Referee: James (Jim) McCluskey (Scotland)
Attendance: 39,000

ISRAEL: Boni Ginzburg, Felix Halfon, Alon Harazi, Nir Klinger, Moshe Glam, Eyal Berkovic (64 Itzik Zohar), Alon Hazan, Tal Banin, Haim Revivo, Ronen Harazi, Ronny Rosenthal.   Manager: Shlomo Scharf

FRANCE: Bernard Lama, Jocelyn Angloma, Alain Roche, Laurent Blanc, Éric Di Meco, Marcel Desailly, Corentin Martins da Silva (78 Youri Djorkaeff), Paul Le Guen, Nicolas Ouédec (65 David Ginola), Patrice Loko, Reynald Pedros.   Manager: Aimé Jacquet

527. 26.04.1995   UEFA Euro 1996 Qualifying – Group 1

FRANCE v SLOVAKIA 4-0 (2-0)

Stade de la Beaujoire – Louis Fonteneau, Nantes

Referee: Bernd Heynemann (Germany)   Attendance: 23,910

FRANCE: Bernard Lama, Jocelyn Angloma, Laurent Blanc, Alain Roche, Éric Di Meco, Vincent Guérin, Didier Deschamps, Marcel Desailly, Zinédine Zidane (74 Youri Djorkaeff), David Ginola, Patrice Loko.   Manager: Aimé Jacquet

SLOVAKIA: Ladislav Molnár, Milos Glonek, Tomás Stúpala, Marián Zeman, Vladimír Kinder, Ondrej Kristofík, Róbert Tomaschek (46 Jaroslav Timko), Dusan Tittel, Lubomír Moravcík, Peter Dubovský, Marek Penksa (74 Stefan Maixner).   Manager: Jozef Venglos

Goals: Ondrej Kristofík (27 og), David Ginola (42), Laurent Blanc (58), Vincent Guerín (63)

528. 22.07.1995

NORWAY v FRANCE 0-0

Ullevaal Stadion, Oslo

Referee: Hugo Luijten (Netherlands)   Attendance: 12,030

NORWAY: Erik Thorstvedt, Gunnar Halle (46 Alf-Inge Håland), Henning Berg, Erland Johnsen, Roger Nilsen (64 Ronny Johnsen), Ståle Solbakken, Kjetil Rekdal (87 Kåre Ingebrigtsen), Øyvind Leonhardsen, Mons Ivar Mjelde, Jan Åge Fjørtoft, Jostein Flo.   Manager: Egil Olsen

FRANCE: Bernard Lama, Lilian Thuram, Alain Roche, Laurent Blanc, Bixente Lizarazu, Claude Makélélé, Paul Le Guen (68 Frank Lebœuf), Christophe Cocard (73 Corentin Martins da Silva), Reynald Pedros, Vincent Guérin, Zinédine Zidane (46 Youri Djorkaeff).   Manager: Aimé Jacquet

529. 16.08.1995   UEFA Euro 1996 Qualifying – Group 1

FRANCE v POLAND 1-1 (0-1)

Parc des Princes, Paris

Referee: Manuel Díaz Vega (Spain)   Attendance: 40,426

FRANCE: Bernard Lama, Jocelyn Angloma (65 Christian Karembeu), Lilian Thuram, Frank Lebœuf (69 Youri Djorkaeff), Bixente Lizarazu, Didier Deschamps, Marcel Desailly, Vincent Guérin, Zinédine Zidane, Christophe Dugarry, David Ginola (63 Reynald Pedros).   Manager: Aimé Jacquet

POLAND: Andrzej Wozniak, Tomasz Waldoch, Tomasz Lapinski, Jacek Zielinski, Marek Kozminski, Tomasz Iwan, Piotr Nowak (56 Ryszard Czerwiec), Roman Kosecki (71 Pawel Wojtala), Piotr Swierczewski, Andrzej Juskowiak, Wojciech Kowalczyk (60 Krzysztof Bukalski).   Manager: Henryk Apostel

Goals: Youri Djorkaeff (86) / Andrzej Juskowiak (34)

Sent off: Tomasz Lapinski (55)

530. 06.09.1995   UEFA Euro 1996 Qualifying – Group 1

FRANCE v AZERBAIJAN 10-0 (3-0)

Stade de l'Abbé-Deschamps, Auxerre

Referee: Alfred Micallef (Malta)   Attendance: 13,479

FRANCE: Bernard Lama, Jocelyn Angloma (57 Lilian Thuram), Marcel Desailly, Frank Lebœuf, Bixente Lizarazu, Didier Deschamps, Vincent Guérin, Zinédine Zidane, Youri Djorkaeff, Christophe Dugarry (69 Christophe Cocard), Reynald Pedros (65 David Ginola).   Manager: Aimé Jacquet

AZERBAIJAN: Elkhan Hasanov (36 Nizami Sadikov), Arif Asadov, Igor Getman, Tarlan Ahmadov, Emin Agayev, Rasim Abushev, Yunis Hüseynov, Shakhin Diniyev, Vladislav Kadirov (74 Musviq Huseynov), Makhmud Gurbanov (46 Samir Alakbarov), Vyacheslav Lichkin.
Manager: Agaselim Mirjavadov

Goals: Marcel Desailly (13), Youri Djorkaeff (17, 78), Vincent Guérin (33), Reynald Pedros (49), Frank Lebœuf (54, 74), Christophe Dugarry (65), Zinédine Zidane (72), Christophe Cocard (90).

531. 11.10.1995   UEFA Euro 1996 Qualifying – Group 1

ROMANIA v FRANCE 1-3 (0-2)

Stadionul Steaua, Bucharest

Referee: Pierluigi Pairetto (Italy)   Attendance: 23,200

ROMANIA: Bogdan Stelea, Dan Petrescu, Daniel Prodan, Gheorghe Mihali (46 Danut Lupu), Ioan Lupescu, Gheorghe Popescu, Marius Lacatus, Ilie Dumitrescu (46 Ion Vladoiu), Tibor Selymes, Gheorghe Hagi (63 Basarab Nica Panduru), Dorinel Munteanu.   Manager: Anghel Iordanescu

FRANCE: Fabien Barthez, Jocelyn Angloma, Frank Lebœuf, Marcel Desailly, Éric Di Meco, Didier Deschamps, Vincent Guérin, Christian Karembeu, Zinédine Zidane (84 Lilian Thuram), Youri Djorkaeff (73 Bixente Lizarazu), Christophe Dugarry (63 Mickaël Madar).   Manager: Aimé Jacquet

Goals: Marius Lacatus (52) / Christian Karembeu (29), Youri Djorkaeff (41), Zinédine Zidane (72)

532. 15.11.1995   UEFA Euro 1996 Qualifying – Group 1

FRANCE v ISRAEL 2-0 (0-0)

Stade Michel d'Ornano, Caen

Referee: Gerd Grabher (Austria)   Attendance: 20,822

FRANCE: Bernard Lama, Jocelyn Angloma, Marcel Desailly, Frank Lebœuf, Éric Di Meco (63 Bixente Lizarazu), Christian Karembeu (90 Marc Keller), Didier Deschamps, Vincent Guérin, Zinédine Zidane, Youri Djorkaeff, Mickaël Madar (63 Patrice Loko).   Manager: Aimé Jacquet

ISRAEL: Rafi Cohen, Felix Halfon, Gadi Brumer, Amir Shelach, Moshe Glam, Alon Hazan, Nir Klinger (79 Itzik Zohar), Eyal Berkovic (70 Reuven Atar), Tal Banin, Ronen Harazi (85 Ofer Mizrahi), Ronny Rosenthal.
Manager: Shlomo Scharf

Goals: Youri Djorkaeff (69), Bixente Lizarazu (89)

533. 24.01.1996

FRANCE v PORTUGAL 3-2 (1-2)

Parc des Princes, Paris

Referee: Dermot Gallagher (England)   Attendance: 25,725

FRANCE: Bernard Lama, Jocelyn Angloma (69 Sabri Lamouchi), Marcel Desailly, Frank Lebœuf, Éric Di Meco, Christian Karembeu, Didier Deschamps, Zinédine Zidane, Vincent Guérin (46 Reynald Pedros), Youri Djorkaeff, Patrice Loko (78 Cyrille Pouget).   Manager: Aimé Jacquet

PORTUGAL: Adelino Augusto Graça Barbosa Barros "NENO", Fernando NÉLSON Jesus Vieira Alves (62 JOSÉ Manuel Martins DOMINGUEZ), HÉLDER Marino Rodrigues Cristóvão (83 NUNO "GOMES" Miguel Soares Pereira Ribeiro), JORGE Paulo COSTA Almeida, FERNANDO Manuel Silva COUTO, DIMAS Manuel Marques Teixeira, Carlos Alberto de Oliveira SECRETÁRIO, João Paulo "PAULINHO" Maio dos SANTOS (61 PEDRO Alexandre dos Santos BARBOSA), ANTÓNIO José dos Santos FOLHA (75 Daniel da Cruz Carvalho "DANI"), RUI Manuel César COSTA, PAULO Lourenço Martins ALVES.
Manager: António Luís Alves Ribeiro OLIVEIRA

Goals: Youri Djorkaeff (24, 75), Reynald Pedros (77) / FERNANDO Manuel Silva COUTO (22), RUI COSTA (34)

534. 21.02.1996

FRANCE v GREECE 3-1 (1-1)

Stade des Costières, Nîmes

Referee: Roger Philippi (Luxembourg)   Attendance: 23,454

FRANCE: Bernard Lama, Jocelyn Angloma (46 Frank Lebœuf), Lilian Thuram, Marcel Desailly, Emmanuel Petit (77 Cyrille Pouget), Christian Karembeu, Didier Deschamps, Sabri Lamouchi (70 Pierre Laigle), Youri Djorkaeff (46 Zinédine Zidane), Reynald Pedros, Patrice Loko.
Manager: Aimé Jacquet

GREECE: Elias Atmatsidis, Stratos Apostolakis, Marinos Ouzounidis, Giannis Kalitzakis (70 Kostas Konstantinidis), Mihalis Kasapis, Thodoros Zagorakis (78 Nikos Lyberopoulos), Nikolaos Dabizas, Alexis Alexandris, Zisis Vryzas, Nikos Machlas (71 Demis Nikolaidis), Giorgios Donis (71 Christos Kostis).   Manager: Kostas Polychroniou

Goals: Patrice Loko (30, 47 pen), Zinédine Zidane (49) / Alexiss Alexandris (4)

535. 27.03.1996

BELGIUM v FRANCE 0-2 (0-0)

Stade Roi Baudouin, Brussels

Referee: Fritz Stuchlik (Austria)   Attendance: 24,417

BELGIUM: Filip De Wilde, Régis Génaux, Dirk Medved (46 Gunter Verjans), Pascal Renier, Rudi Smidts, Philippe Albert, Frédéric Peiremans, Danny Boffin (69 Gilles De Bilde), Marc Degryse (46 Michaël Goossens), Enzo Scifo, Luís Airton Oliveira Barosso.   Manager: Paul Van Himst

FRANCE: Bernard Lama, Lilian Thuram (46 Jocelyn Angloma), Alain Roche, Laurent Blanc, Éric Di Meco, Christian Karembeu, Didier Deschamps, Sabri Lamouchi, Corentin Martins da Silva, Reynald Pedros (72 Pierre Laigle), Christophe Dugarry (82 Cyrille Pouget).
Manager: Aimé Jacquet

Goals: Philippe Albert (65 og), Sabri Lamouchi (70)

536. 29.05.1996

FRANCE v FINLAND 2-0 (2-0)

Stade de la Meinau, Strasbourg

Referee: Edgar Steinborn (Germany)   Attendance: 27,156

FRANCE: Bruno Martini, Jocelyn Angloma, Lilian Thuram, Frank Lebœuf, Éric Di Meco (67 Bixente Lizarazu), Vincent Guérin, Sabri Lamouchi (69 Christian Karembeu), Marcel Desailly, Reynald Pedros, Corentin Martins da Silva, Patrice Loko (46 Christophe Dugarry).   Manager: Aimé Jacquet

FINLAND: Antti Niemi, Harri Ylönen, Aki Hyryläinen, Lasse Karjalainen, Antti Heinola, Sami Hyypiä, Kim Suominen, Tommi Grönlund, Jari Litmanen, Sami Väisänen, Joonas Kolkka (81 Jari Jäväjä).   Manager: Jukka Ikäläinen

Goals: Patrice Loko (15), Reynald Pedros (17)

537. 01.06.1996

GERMANY v FRANCE 0-1 (0-1)

Gottlieb Daimler Stadion, Stuttgart

Referee: Ryszard Wójcik (Poland)   Attendance: 53,135

GERMANY: Andreas Köpke, Matthias Sammer, Markus Babbel, Stefan Reuter, Dieter Eilts (46 Steffen Freund), Thomas Helmer, Christian Ziege (83 Mehmet Scholl), Thomas Häßler (46 Mario Basler), Andreas Möller, Fredi Bobic, Jürgen Klinsmann.   Manager: Berti Vogts

FRANCE: Bernard Lama, Christian Karembeu (86 Jocelyn Angloma), Lilian Thuram, Laurent Blanc, Éric Di Meco (66 Bixente Lizarazu), Vincent Guérin (81 Sabri Lamouchi), Didier Deschamps, Marcel Desailly, Youri Djorkaeff, Zinédine Zidane (46 Patrice Loko), Christophe Dugarry (72 Reynald Pedros).   Manager: Aimé Jacquet

Goal: Laurent Blanc (7)

538. 05.06.1996

FRANCE v ARMENIA 2-0 (1-0)

Stade du Nord, Villeneuve d'Ascq

Referee: Alain Hamer (Lucxembourg)   Attendance: 21,486

FRANCE: Bernard Lama, Jocelyn Angloma (46 Lilian Thuram), Laurent Blanc, Bixente Lizarazu, Sabri Lamouchi, Vincent Guérin (46 Christian Karembeu), Didier Deschamps, Marcel Desailly, Youri Djorkaeff (46 Patrice Loko), Zinédine Zidane, Mickaël Madar.   Manager: Aimé Jacquet

ARMENIA: Harutyun Abrahamyan, Ervand Sukiasyan, Vardan Khachatryan, Sargis Hovsepyan, Sargis Hovhannisyan, Hakob Ter-Petrosyan (74 Yervand Krbashyan), Razmik Grigoryan (63 Arsen Avetisyan), Hamlet Mkhitaryan, Aramayis Tonoyan (57 Harutyun Vardanyan), Varazdat Avetisyan, Artur Petrosyan.   Manager: Samvel Darbinyan

Goals: Jocelyn Angloma (16), Mickaël Madar (71)

539. 10.06.1996   UEFA European Championship – Group B

FRANCE v ROMANIA 1-0 (1-0)

St. James' Park, Newcastle upon Tyne (England)

Referee: Hellmut Krug (Germany)   Attendance: 26,323

FRANCE: Bernard Lama, Lilian Thuram, Laurent Blanc, Marcel Desailly, Éric Di Meco (67 Bixente Lizarazu), Christian Karembeu, Didier Deschamps, Vincent Guérin, Zinédine Zidane (79 Alain Roche), Youri Djorkaeff, Christophe Dugarry (67 Patrice Loko).   Manager: Aimé Jacquet

ROMANIA: Bogdan Stelea, Dan Petrescu (77 Iulian Filipescu), Miodrag Belodedici, Tibor Selymes, Gheorghe Mihali, Ioan Lupescu, Gheorghe Popescu, Gheorghe Hagi, Dorinel Munteanu, Marius Lacatus (56 Adrian Ilie), Florin Raducioiu (46 Viorel Moldovan).
Manager: Anghel Iordanescu

Goal: Christophe Dugarry (24)

540. 15.06.1996   UEFA European Championship – Group B

FRANCE v SPAIN 1-1 (0-0)

Elland Road, Leeds (England)

Referee: Vadim Zhuk (Belarus)   Attendance: 35,626

FRANCE: Bernard Lama, Jocelyn Angloma (65 Alain Roche), Laurent Blanc, Marcel Desailly, Christian Karembeu, Bixente Lizarazu, Didier Deschamps, Vincent Guérin (81 Lilian Thuram), Zinédine Zidane, Youri Djorkaeff, Patrice Loko (73 Christophe Dugarry).   Manager: Aimé Jacquet

SPAIN: Andoni ZUBIZARRETA Urreta, Jorge OTERO Bouzas (58 Francisco Miguel Narváez Machón "KIKO"), Rafael ALKORTA Martínez, ABELARDO Fernández Antuña, SERGI Barjuan Esclusa, Fernando Ruiz HIERRO, Juan Manuel "JUANMA" LÓPEZ Martinez, José Luis Pérez CAMINERO, LUIS ENRIQUE Martínez García (54 Javier MANJARÍN Pereda), José Emilio AMAVISCA Gárate, ALFONSO Pérez Muñoz (82 JULIO SALINAS Fernández).
Manager: JAVIER CLEMENTE Lázaro

Goals: Youri Djorkaeff (48) /
José Luis Pérez CAMINERO (87)

541.   18.06.1996   UEFA European Championship – Group B
FRANCE v BULGARIA   3-1 (1-0)

St. James' Park, Newcastle upon Tyne (England)

Referee: Dermot Gallagher (England) (28 Paul Anthony Durkin (England))   Attendance: 26,976

FRANCE: Bernard Lama, Lilian Thuram, Laurent Blanc, Marcel Desailly, Bixente Lizarazu, Christian Karembeu, Didier Deschamps, Vincent Guérin, Zinédine Zidane (62 Reynald Pedros), Youri Djorkaeff, Christophe Dugarry (70 Patrice Loko).   Manager: Aimé Jacquet

BULGARIA: Borislav Mihaylov, Emil Kremenliev, Petar Hubchev, Trifon Ivanov, Tsanko Tsvetanov, Yordan Lechkov, Zlatko Yankov (78 Daniel Borimirov), Ivaylo Yordanov, Krasimir Balakov (82 Georgi Donkov), Hristo Stoichkov, Lyuboslav Penev.   Manager: Dimitar Penev

Goals: Laurent Blanc (21), Lyuboslav Penev (64 og), Patrice Loko (90) / Hristo Stoichkov (69)

542.   22.06.1996   UEFA European Championship – Round of 16
FRANCE v NETHERLANDS   0-0 (AET)

Anfield Road, Liverpool (England)

Referee: Antonio Jesús López Nieto (Spain)
Attendance: 37,456

FRANCE: Bernard Lama, Lilian Thuram, Laurent Blanc, Marcel Desailly, Bixente Lizarazu, Christian Karembeu, Didier Deschamps, Vincent Guérin, Zinédine Zidane, Youri Djorkaeff, Patrice Loko (62 Christophe Dugarry, 80 Reynald Pedros).   Manager: Aimé Jacquet

NETHERLANDS: Edwin van der Sar, Michael Reiziger, Johan de Kock, Danny Blind, Winston Bogarde, Ronald de Boer, Richard Witschge (80 Youri Mulder), Phillip Cocu, Jordi Cruijff (69 Aron Winter), Dennis Bergkamp (60 Clarence Seedorf), Patrick Kluivert.   Manager: Guus Hiddink

Penalties: 1-0 Johan de Kock, 1-1 Zinédine Zidane, 2-1 Ronald de Boer, 2-2 Youri Djorkaeff, 3-2 Patrick Kluivert, 3-3 Bixente Lizarazu, Clarence Seedorf (missed), 3-4 Vincent Guérin, 4-4 Danny Blind, 4-5 Laurent Blanc.

543.   26.06.1996   UEFA European Championship – Semi-final
CZECH REPUBLIC v FRANCE   0-0 (AET)

Old Trafford, Manchester (England)

Referee: Leslie William (Les) Mottram (Scotland)
Attendance: 43,877

CZECH REPUBLIC: Petr Kouba, Karel Rada, Michal Hornák, Miroslav Kadlec, Pavel Novotný, Karel Poborský, Jirí Nemec (84 Lubos Kubík), Václav Nemecek, Pavel Nedved, Radek Drulák (70 Martin Kotulek), Vladimír Smicer (46 Patrik Berger).   Manager: Dusan Uhrin

FRANCE: Bernard Lama, Lilian Thuram (82 Jocelyn Angloma), Laurent Blanc, Alain Roche, Bixente Lizarazu, Sabri Lamouchi (60 Reynald Pedros), Marcel Desailly, Vincent Guérin, Zinédine Zidane, Youri Djorkaeff, Patrice Loko.   Manager: Aimé Jacquet

Penalties: 1-0 Zinédine Zidane, 1-1 Lubos Kubík, 2-1 Youri Djorkaeff, 2-2 Pavel Nedved, 3-2 Bixente Lizarazu, 3-3 Patrik Berger, 4-3 Vincent Guérin, 4-4 Karel Poborský, 5-4 Laurent Blanc, 5-5 Karel Rada, Reynald Pedros (missed), 5-6 Miroslav Kadlec.

544.   31.08.1996
FRANCE v MEXICO   2-0 (0-0)

Parc des Princes, Paris

Referee: Joseph (Joe) Byrne (Republic of Ireland)
Attendance: 20,259

FRANCE: Bernard Lama, Lilian Thuram (88 Sabri Lamouchi), Laurent Blanc, Marcel Desailly (46 Frank Lebœuf), Bixente Lizarazu (79 Vincent Guérin), Christian Karembeu, Didier Deschamps, Reynald Pedros (46 Robert Pirès), Youri Djorkaeff, Nicolas Ouédec (64 Florian Maurice), Patrice Loko (46 Zinédine Zidane).   Manager: Aimé Jacquet

MEXICO: Oswaldo Javier SÁNCHEZ Ibarra (78 José Adolfo RÍOS García), Duilio César Jean Pierre DAVINO Rodríguez (46 Octavio BECERRIL Morales), Luis Claudio SUÁREZ Sánchez, Enrique ALFARO Rojas (78 Juan Francisco PALENCIA Hernández), Jesús Ramón RAMÍREZ Ceseña (71 José de Jesús ARELLANO Alcocer), Alberto García ASPE Mena, Joaquín Alberto DEL OLMO Blanco, Raúl Rodrigo LARA Tovar (65 Cuauhtémoc BLANCO Bravo), Germán VILLA Castañeda (86 Francisco Javier GÓMEZ Hernandez), Pável PARDO Segura, Luis Alejandro García POSTIGO Dias (69 Ricardo PELÁEZ Linares).   Manager: Bora Milutinovic

Goals: Nicolas Ouédec (49), Youri Djorkaeff (53)

Sent off: Frank Lebœuf (88)

545. 09.10.1996
FRANCE v TURKEY 4-0 (2-0)

Parc des Princes, Paris

Referee: Jorge Emanuel Monteiro Coroado (Portugal)   Attendance: 28,611

FRANCE: Fabien Barthez, Christian Karembeu, Laurent Blanc, Alain Goma, Lilian Thuram (77 Martin Djétou), Didier Deschamps, Sabri Lamouchi (23 Vincent Candela), Reynald Pedros (66 Franck Gava), Zinédine Zidane, Youri Djorkaeff, Patrice Loko (72 Robert Pirès).   Manager: Aimé Jacquet

TURKEY: Rüstü Reçber, Recep Çetin, Alpay Özalan, Bülent Korkmaz, Abdullah Ercan, Ogün Temizkanoglu, Tolunay Kafkas (73 Erkan Avseren), Ünal Karaman (36 Oguz Çetin), Arif Erdem (46 Saffet Sancakli), Hakan Sükür (63 Mehmet Özdilek), Celil Sagir (61 Serdar Toprakstepe).   Manager: Mustafa Denizli

Goals: Laurent Blanc (33), Reynald Pedros (35), Youri Djorkaeff (51), Robert Pirès (83)

546. 09.11.1996
DENMARK v FRANCE 1-0 (1-0)

Parken, Copenhagen

Referee: Roy Helge Olsen (Norway)   Attendance: 10,645

DENMARK: Peter Schmeichel, Jacob Laursen (41 Søren Colding), Marc Rieper, Jakob Friss-Hansen, Jan Heintze, Thomas Helveg, Per Frandsen (69 Peter Nielsen), Allan Nielsen, Michael Schjønberg, Per Pedersen (76 Søren Andersen), Peter Møller (63 Miklos Molnar).   Manager: Bo Johansson

FRANCE: Fabien Barthez, Lilian Thuram, Bruno N'Gotty, Marcel Desailly, Vincent Candela (74 Pierre Laigle), Christian Karembeu, Didier Deschamps, Zinédine Zidane (80 Marc Keller), Reynald Pedros (46 Robert Pirès), Youri Djorkaeff, Corentin Martins da Silva (62 Patrice Loko).   Manager: Aimé Jacquet

Goal: Per Pedersen (19)

547. 22.01.1997
PORTUGAL v FRANCE 0-2 (0-1)

Estádio Primeiro de Maio, Braga

Referee: José Núñez Manrique (Spain)   Attendance: 40,000

PORTUGAL: VÍTOR Manuel Martins BAÍA, SÉRGIO Paulo Marceneiro da CONCEIÇÃO, FERNANDO Manuel Silva COUTO, HÉLDER Marino Rodrigues Cristóvão (46 JORGE Paulo COSTA Almeida), DIMAS Manuel Marques Teixeira (69 Jorge Paulo CADETE Santos Reis), OCEANO Andrade da Cruz (21 DOMINGOS José Paciência Oliveira), PAULO Jorge Gomes BENTO, RUI Manuel César COSTA (46 Ricardo Manuel Andrade e Silva SÁ PINTO), João Paulo "PAULINHO" Maio dos SANTOS, LUÍS Filipe Madeira Caeiro FIGO (46 Nuno Fernando Gonçalves da Rocha "CAPUCHO"), JOÃO Manuel VIEIRA PINTO.
Manager: ARTUR JORGE Braga de Melo Teixeira

FRANCE: Fabien Barthez, Lilian Thuram, Laurent Blanc, Marcel Desailly, Pierre Laigle, Christian Karembeu, Didier Deschamps (63 Bruno N'Gotty), Ibrahim Ba (63 Youri Djorkaeff), Zinédine Zidane, Robert Pirès (79 Patrick Blondeau), Christophe Dugarry (79 Patrice Loko).   Manager: Aimé Jacquet

Goals: Didier Deschamps (10), Ibrahim Ba (62)

548. 26.02.1997
FRANCE v NETHERLANDS 2-1 (0-1)

Parc des Princes, Paris

Referee: Ryszard Wójcik (Poland)   Attendance: 35,331

FRANCE: Bernard Lama, Lilian Thuram, Laurent Blanc, Marcel Desailly, Bixente Lizarazu (87 Vincent Candela), Patrick Vieira (78 Bruno N'Gotty), Christian Karembeu, Pierre Laigle (33 Robert Pirès), Ibrahim Ba (79 Patrice Loko), Zinédine Zidane, Christophe Dugarry.
Manager: Aimé Jacquet

NETHERLANDS: Edwin van der Sar, Michael Reiziger, Jaap Stam, Frank de Boer, Arthur Numan, Wim Jonk, Ronald de Boer, Dennis Bergkamp, Patrick Kluivert, Clarence Seedorf (73 Marc Overmars), Phillip Cocu (79 Giovanni van Bronckhorst).   Manager: Jan Rab

Goals: Robert Pirès (75), Patrice Loko (83) /
Dennis Bergkamp (3)

549.   02.04.1997
FRANCE v SWEDEN 1-0 (1-0)

Parc des Princes, Paris

Referee: Marnix Sandra (Belgium)   Attendance: 34,514

FRANCE: Fabien Barthez, Lilian Thuram (65 Patrick Blondeau), Laurent Blanc, Marcel Desailly, Vincent Candela, Claude Makélélé, Patrick Vieira (63 Martin Djétou), Ibrahim Ba (79 Marc Keller), Zinédine Zidane (56 Franck Gava), Youri Djorkaeff, Christophe Dugarry (56 Patrice Loko). Manager: Aimé Jacquet

SWEDEN: Thomas Ravelli, Roland Nilsson (56 Gary Sundgren), Joachim Björklund, Patrik Andersson, Teddy Lucic, Niclas Alexandersson (46 Stefan Schwarz), Pär Zetterberg, Jesper Blomqvist (66 Henrik Larsson), Andreas Andersson, Martin Dahlin (59 Jörgen Pettersson), Kennet Andersson.   Manager: Tommy Svensson

Goal: Youri Djorkaeff (44 pen)

550.   03.06.1997   Tournoi de France 1997
FRANCE v BRAZIL 1-1 (0-1)

Stade de Gerland, Lyon

Referee: Kim Milton Nielsen (Denmark)
Attendance: 28,193

FRANCE: Fabien Barthez, Vincent Candela, Laurent Blanc, Marcel Desailly (67 Lilian Thuram), Bixente Lizarazu, Christian Karembeu (15 Patrick Vieira), Didier Deschamps, Zinédine Zidane, Ibrahim Ba, Florian Maurice, Robert Pirès (46 Marc Keller).   Manager: Aimé Jacquet

BRAZIL: Cláudio André Mergen TAFFAREL, Marcos Evangelista de Moraes "CAFÚ", Vagno CÉLIO do Nascimento SILVA, ALDAIR Nascimento Santos (88 Marcelo GONÇALVES Costa Lopes), ROBERTO CARLOS da Silva, Carlos Caetano Bledorn Verri "DUNGA", MAURO da SILVA Gomes, LEONARDO Nascimento de Araújo, GIOVANNI Silva de Oliveira (73 Djalma Feitosa Dias "DJALMINHA"), ROMÁRIO de Souza Farias (79 Arílson de Paula Nunes "PAULO NUNES"), RONALDO Luís Nazário de Lima. Manager: Jorge MÁRIO Lobo ZAGALLO

Goals: Marc Keller (59) / ROBERTO CARLOS da Silva (22)

551.   07.06.1997   Tournoi de France 1997
FRANCE v ENGLAND 0-1 (0-0)

Stade de la Mosson, Montpellier

Referee: Said Belqola (Morocco)   Attendance: 21,331

FRANCE: Fabien Barthez, Lilian Thuram, Laurent Blanc, Bruno N'Gotty, Pierre Laigle (83 Bixente Lizarazu), Patrick Vieira, Didier Deschamps, Marc Keller, Youri Djorkaeff, Christophe Dugarry (76 Zinédine Zidane), Nicolas Ouédec (63 Patrice Loko).   Manager: Aimé Jacquet

ENGLAND: David Seaman, Gary Neville, Gareth Southgate, Sol Campbell, David Batty (46 Paul Ince), Graeme Le Saux, Phil Neville, David Beckham (76 Rob Lee), Paul Gascoigne, Ian Wright (80 Teddy Sheringham), Alan Shearer. Manager: Glenn Hoddle

Goal: Alan Shearer (86)

552.   11.06.1997   Tournoi de France 1997
FRANCE v ITALY 2-2 (1-0)

Parc des Princes, Paris

Referee: Antonio Jesús López Nieto (Spain)
Attendance: 23,137

FRANCE: Lionel Charbonnier, Lilian Thuram, Frank Lebœuf, Marcel Desailly (85 Bruno N'Gotty), Bixente Lizarazu, Didier Deschamps, Christian Karembeu (66 Patrick Vieira), Ibrahim Ba, Zinédine Zidane, Christophe Dugarry, Florian Maurice (64 Youri Djorkaeff).   Manager: Aimé Jacquet

ITALY: Gianluca Pagliuca, Alessandro Nesta, Alessandro Costacurta (46 Stefano Torrisi), Fabio Cannavaro, Paolo Maldini, Attilio Lombardo, Angelo Di Livio, Roberto Di Matteo, Gianfranco Zola (55 Christian Panucci), Pierluigi Casiraghi (77 Christian Vieri), Alessandro Del Piero. Manager: Cesare Maldini

Goals: Zinédine Zidane (12), Youri Djorkaeff (73) / Pierluigi Casiraghi (61), Alessandro Del Piero (90 pen)

553.   11.10.1997
FRANCE v SOUTH AFRICA 2-1 (0-1)

Stade Félix Bollaert, Lens

Referee: Roger Philippi (Luxembourg)   Attendance: 29,677

FRANCE: Lionel Letizi, Lilian Thuram, Laurent Blanc, Marcel Desailly, Vincent Candela (73 Pierre Laigle), Didier Deschamps, Emmanuel Petit (31 Alain Boghossian), Youri Djorkaeff (78 Ibrahim Ba), Robert Pirès (46 Zinédine Zidane), Stéphane Guivarc'h, Thierry Henry.   Manager: Aimé Jacquet

IVORY COAST: Andre Arendse, Sizwe Motaung, Lucas Radebe, Neil Tovey, Willem Jackson, Eric Tinkler (74 Clinton Larsen), John Moeti, John Moshoeu (89 Benedict (Benny) McCarthy), Helman Mkhalele (64 Isaac Shai), Shaun Bartlett (79 Mark Williams), Philemon Masinga. Manager: Clive Barker

Goals: Stéphane Guivarc'h (53), Ibrahim Ba (83) / Shaun Bartlett (40)

554.   12.11.1997
FRANCE v SCOTLAND 2-1 (1-1)
Stade Geoffroy Guichard, Saint-Étienne
Referee: Antonio Jesús López Nieto (Spain)
Attendance: 19,514
FRANCE: Fabien Barthez, Lilian Thuram, Laurent Blanc, Marcel Desailly, Pierre Laigle (79 Vincent Candela), Didier Deschamps, Emmanuel Petit (73 Alain Boghossian), Ibrahim Ba (79 Franck Gava), Zinédine Zidane, Lilian Laslandes (71 Youri Djorkaeff), Stéphane Guivarc'h.   Manager: Aimé Jacquet
SCOTLAND: Neil Sullivan, Craig Burley, Tommy Boyd (79 Tosh McKinlay), Colin Calderwood, David Weir (76 Matt Elliott), Christian Dailly, Kevin Gallacher (83 Simon Donnelly), Billy McKinlay, Gordon Durie (89 David Hopkin), Gary McAllister, John Collins.   Manager: Craig Brown
Goals: Pierre Laigle (35), Youri Djorkaeff (77 pen) / Gordon Durie (36)

555.   28.01.1998
FRANCE v SPAIN 1-0 (1-0)
Stade de France, Saint-Denis
Referee: Urs Meier (Switzerland)   Attendance: 78,836
FRANCE: Fabien Barthez, Lilian Thuram, Laurent Blanc, Marcel Desailly, Ibrahim Ba (62 Robert Pirès), Didier Deschamps (62 Vincent Candela), Alain Boghossian, Bernard Diomède, Zinédine Zidane, Youri Djorkaeff (90+5 Frank Lebœuf), Stéphane Guivarc'h (74 David Trézéguet).   Manager: Aimé Jacquet
SPAIN: Andoni ZUBIZARRETA Urreta, Juan Carlos AGUILERA Martín, ABELARDO Fernández Antuña, Miguel Ángel NADAL Homar, Rafael ALKORTA Martínez, SERGI Barjuan Esclusa (59 Roberto RÍOS Patus), Joseba ETXEBERRIA Lizardi (53 JORDI LARDÍN Cruz), Guillermo AMOR Martínez (80 FERNANDO Sánchez Cipitria), LUIS ENRIQUE Martínez García, RAÚL González Blanco (73 Juan Antonio PIZZI Torroja), ALFONSO Pérez Muñoz.   Managers: José Antonio CAMACHO Alfaro & JAVIER CLEMENTE Lázaro
Goal: Zinédine Zidane (20)

556.   25.02.1998
FRANCE v NORWAY 3-3 (2-1)
Stade Vélodrome, Marseille
Referee: Jan Willem Wegereef (Netherlands)
Attendance: 47,124
FRANCE: Fabien Barthez, Lilian Thuram, Laurent Blanc, Marcel Desailly, Robert Pirès, Didier Deschamps, Alain Boghossian, Bernard Diomède, Youri Djorkaeff, Zinédine Zidane (62 Claude Makélélé), Stéphane Guivarc'h (62 David Trézéguet).   Manager: Aimé Jacquet
NORWAY: Frode Grodås, Alf-Inge Håland, Henning Berg, Claus Lundekvam, Stig Inge Bjørnebye, Petter Rudi (46 Vidar Riseth), Bent Skammelsrud, Frank Strandli (85 Egil Østenstad), Lars Bohinen (79 Vegard Heggem), Tore André Flo, Erik Mykland.   Manager: Egil Olsen
Goals: Laurent Blanc (23), Zinédine Zidane (28), Marcel Desailly (90) / Frank Strandli (13 pen), Tore André Flo (68), Vegard Heggem (89)

557.   25.03.1998
RUSSIA v FRANCE 1-0 (1-0)
Dynamo Stadium, Moscow
Referee: Igor Yaremchuk (Ukraine)   Attendance: 7,000
RUSSIA: Aleksandr Filimonov, Dmitriy Khlestov, Yuriy Nikiforov (67 Yuri Kovtun), Igor Chugaynov, Igor Yanovski, Andrey Kanchelskis (46 Dmitriy Khokhlov), Dmitriy Alenichev, Viktor Onopko, Aleksey Gerasimenko, Sergey Yuran (76 Yevgeni Kharlachyov), Igor Kolyvanov.   Manager: Boris Ignatyev
FRANCE: Lionel Letizi, Lilian Thuram, Frank Lebœuf, Marcel Desailly, Didier Deschamps (46 Alain Boghossian), Emmanuel Petit (46 Vincent Candela), Christian Karembeu (63 Marc Keller), Sabri Lamouchi (74 Robert Pirès), Youri Djorkaeff, Stéphane Guivarc'h, Bernard Diomède.   Manager: Aimé Jacquet
Goal: Sergey Yuran (2)

558.   22.04.1998
SWEDEN v FRANCE 0-0
Råsunda Fotbollstadion, Solna
Referee: Graham Poll (England)   Attendance: 14,018
SWEDEN: Magnus Hedman, Teddy Lucic, Joachim Björklund, Pontus Kåmark, Patrik Andersson (46 Johan Mjällby), Stefan Schwarz, Håkan Mild (77 Jörgen Pettersson), Henrik Larsson, Pär Zetterberg (46 Daniel Andersson), Jesper Blomqvist, Andreas Andersson.   Manager: Tommy Söderberg
FRANCE: Bernard Lama, Lilian Thuram, Laurent Blanc, Martin Djétou, Bixente Lizarazu, Didier Deschamps (68 Patrick Vieira), Christian Karembeu, Sabri Lamouchi, Zinédine Zidane (46 Robert Pirès), Christophe Dugarry (46 Youri Djorkaeff), Nicolas Anelka (67 David Trézéguet).   Manager: Aimé Jacquet

559.   27.05.1998   King Hassan II Tournament 1998
FRANCE v BELGIUM   1-0 (0-0)

Stade Mohamed V, Casablanca (Morocco)

Referee: Mohamed Guezzaz (Morocco)   Attendance: 70,000

FRANCE: Fabien Barthez, Lilian Thuram, Laurent Blanc, Marcel Desailly, Bixente Lizarazu, Didier Deschamps, Emmanuel Petit, Zinédine Zidane, Robert Pirès (61 Thierry Henry), Youri Djorkaeff (46 Christophe Dugarry), Stéphane Guivarc'h.   Manager: Aimé Jacquet

BELGIUM: Filip De Wilde, Bertrand Crasson, Lorenzo Staelens, Gordan Vidovic, Philippe Léonard (73 Danny Boffin), Frank Van der Elst, Marc Wilmots, Luís Airton Oliveira Barosso, Luc Nilis (87 Mbo Mpenza), Philippe Clement (88 Eric Deflandre), Nico Van Kerckhoven (51 Glen De Boeck).   Manager: Georges Leekens

Goal: Zinédine Zidane (64)

560.   29.05.1998   King Hassan II Tournament 1998
MOROCCO v FRANCE   2-2 (1-1)

Stade Mohamed V, Casablanca (Morocco)

Referee: Idrissa Seck (Senegal)   Attendance: 65,000

MOROCCO: Abdelkader El Brazi, Lahcen Abrami, Youssef Rossi, Smahi Triki, Abdelkrim El Hadrioui (46 Abdelilah Saber), Gharib Amzine, Saïd Chiba, Rachid Azzouzi (66 Abderrahim Ouakili), Youssef Chippo (66 Jamal Sellami), Salaheddine Bassir (78 Ali El Khattabi), Abdeljalil Hadda.   Manager: Henri Michel

FRANCE: Bernard Lama, Vincent Candela, Frank Lebœuf, Laurent Blanc, Alain Boghossian, Didier Deschamps (46 Patrick Vieira), Christian Karembeu, Zinédine Zidane (61 Youri Djorkaeff), Thierry Henry, Bernard Diomède (76 Robert Pirès), Christophe Dugarry (68 David Trézéguet).   Manager: Aimé Jacquet

Goals: Salaheddin Bassir (9, 64) / Laurent Blanc (24), Youri Djorkaeff (74)

Penalties: 1-0 Abderrahim Ouakili, 1-1 Laurent Blanc, 2-1 Smahi Triki, 2-2 Frank Lebœuf, 3-2 Abdelilah Saber, 3-3 David Trezeguet, 4-3 Abdeljalil Hadda, 4-4 Robert Pirès, 5-4 Gharib Amzine, 5-5 Patrick Vieira, Lahcen Abrami (miss), Youri Djorkaeff (miss), 6-5 Youssef Rossi, Vincent Candela (miss)

561.   05.06.1998

FINLAND v FRANCE   0-1 (0-0)

Helsingin Olympiastadion, Helsinki

Referee: Konrad Plautz (Austria)   Attendance: 21,619

FINLAND: Antti Niemi, Harri Ylönen, Sami Hyypiä, Tomi Kinnunen, Aarno Turpeinen, Aki Riihilahti, Juha Reini (86 Kari Rissanen), Joonas Kolkka, Jarkko Wiss, Mika-Matti Paatelainen, Jonatan Johansson (68 Simo Valakari).   Manager: Richard Møller Nielsen

FRANCE: Fabien Barthez, Lilian Thuram (69 Christian Karembeu), Laurent Blanc, Marcel Desailly, Bixente Lizarazu, Didier Deschamps, Emmanuel Petit, Zinédine Zidane (89 Robert Pirès), Youri Djorkaeff, Christophe Dugarry (77 Bernard Diomède), Stéphane Guivarc'h (75 David Trézéguet).   Manager: Aimé Jacquet

Goal: David Trezeguet (83)

562.   12.06.1998   FIFA World Cup Final Tournament – Group C
FRANCE v SOUTH AFRICA   3-0 (1-0)

Stade Vélodrome, Marseille (France)

Referee: Marcio Resende de Freitas (Brazil)   Attendance: 55,077

FRANCE: Fabien Barthez, Lilian Thuram, Laurent Blanc, Marcel Desailly, Bixente Lizarazu, Didier Deschamps, Emmanuel Petit (73 Alain Boghossian), Zinédine Zidane, Youri Djorkaeff (82 David Trézéguet), Stéphane Guivarc'h (26 Christophe Dugarry), Thierry Henry.   Manager: Aimé Jacquet

IVORY COAST: Hans Vonk, Mark Fish, Pierre Issa, Willem Jackson, David Nyathi, Lucas Radebe, Quinton Fortune, Brendan Augustine (56 Helman Mkhalele), Philemon Masinga, Benedict (Benny) McCarthy (89 Shaun Bartlett), John Moshoeu.   Manager: Philippe Troussier

Goals: Christophe Dugarry (34), Pierre Issa (78 og), Thierry Henry (90)

563.   18.06.1998   FIFA World Cup Final Tournament – Group C
FRANCE v SAUDI ARABIA   4-0 (1-0)

Stade de France, Saint-Denis (France)

Referee: Arturo Brizio Carter (Mexico)   Attendance: 75,000

FRANCE: Fabien Barthez, Bixente Lizarazu, Marcel Desailly, Laurent Blanc, Lilian Thuram, Alain Boghossian, Zinédine Zidane, Didier Deschamps, Thierry Henry (78 Robert Pirès), Bernard Diomède (58 Youri Djorkaeff), Christophe Dugarry (29 David Trézéguet).   Manager: Aimé Jacquet

SAUDI ARABIA: Mohammed Abdulaziz AL-DEAYEA, Mohammed Shiliya AL-JAHANI (76 Ahmed Douki AL-DOSARI), Mohammed Saleh AL-KHILAIWI, Abdullah Sulaiman ZIBROMAWI, Hussein Omar Abdulghani AL-SULAIMANI, Ibrahim Suwayed AL-SHAHRANI, Fuad Anwar AMIN, Khamis Al Owairan AL-DOSARI, Hamzah Hagoo SALEH, Sami Abdullah AL-JABER, Saeed AL-OWAIRAN (33 Ibrahim Maatar AL-HARBI, 63 Khalid Mossaed AL-MUWALID).   Manager: CARLOS ALBERTO Gomes PARREIRA

Goals: Thierry Henry (36, 77), David Trézéguet (69), Bixente Lizarazu (85)

Sent off: Zinédine Zidane (71) / Mohammed Saleh AL-KHILAIWI (19)

564. 24.06.1998   FIFA World Cup Final Tournament – Group C

FRANCE v DENMARK 2-1 (1-1)

Stade de Gerland, Lyon (France)

Referee: Pierluigi Collina (Italy)   Attendance: 39,100

FRANCE: Fabien Barthez, Christian Karembeu, Frank Lebœuf, Marcel Desailly, Vincent Candela, Emmanuel Petit (65 Alain Boghossian), Patrick Vieira, Bernard Diomède, Robert Pirès (72 Thierry Henry), Youri Djorkaeff, David Trézéguet (86 Stéphane Guivarc'h).   Manager: Aimé Jacquet

DENMARK: Peter Schmeichel, Jacob Laursen (46 Søren Colding), Marc Rieper, Jes Høgh, Jan Heintze, Martin Jørgensen (55 Ebbe Sand), Thomas Helveg, Allan Nielsen, Michael Laudrup, Michael Schjønberg, Brian Laudrup (75 Stig Tøfting).   Manager: Bo Johansson

Goals: Youri Djorkaeff (13 pen), Emmanuel Petit (56) / Michael Laudrup (42 pen)

565. 28.06.1998   FIFA World Cup Final Tournament – Round of 16

FRANCE v PARAGUAY 1-0 (0-0, 0-0) (AET)

Stade Félix Bollaert, Lens (France)

Referee: Ali Mohamed Bujsaim (UA Emirates)
Attendance: 41,275

FRANCE: Fabien Barthez, Bixente Lizarazu, Laurent Blanc, Marcel Desailly, Lilian Thuram, Youri Djorkaeff, Didier Deschamps, Emmanuel Petit (70 Alain Boghossian), Thierry Henry (65 Robert Pirès), Bernard Diomède (77 Stéphane Guivarc'h), David Trézéguet.   Manager: Aimé Jacquet

PARAGUAY: José Luis Félix CHILAVERT González, Francisco Javier ARCE Rolón, Carlos Alberto GAMARRA Pavón, Celso Rafael AYALA Gavilán, Pedro Alcides SARABIA Achucarro, Roberto Miguel ACUÑA Cabello, Julio César ENCISO Ferreira, Carlos Humberto PAREDES Monges (75 Denis Ramón CANIZA Acuña), Miguel Ángel BENÍTEZ Pavón, José Saturnino CARDOZO Otazú (91 Arístides Fabián ROJAS Aranda), Jorge Luis CAMPOS Velasquez (56 Julio César YEGROS Torres).   Manager: Paulo César CARPEGGIANI

Goal: Laurent Blanc (114 golden goal)

566. 03.07.1998   FIFA World Cup Final Tournament – Quarter-final

ITALY v FRANCE 0-0 (AET)

Stade de France, Saint-Denis (France)

Referee: Hugh Dallas (Scotland)   Attendance: 77,000

ITALY: Gianluca Pagliuca, Fabio Cannavaro, Alessandro Costacurta, Giuseppe Bergomi, Paolo Maldini, Francesco Moriero, Dino Baggio (53 Demetrio Albertini), Luigi Di Biagio, Gianluca Pessotto (90 Angelo Di Livio), Christian Vieri, Alessandro Del Piero (67 Roberto Baggio).
Manager: Cesare Maldini

FRANCE: Fabien Barthez, Lilian Thuram, Laurent Blanc, Marcel Desailly, Bixente Lizarazu, Didier Deschamps, Emmanuel Petit, Youri Djorkaeff, Christian Karembeu (65 Thierry Henry), Zinédine Zidane, Stéphane Guivarc'h (65 David Trézéguet).   Manager: Aimé Jacquet

Penalties: 1-0 Zinédine Zidane, 1-1 Roberto Baggio, Bixente Lizarazu (missed), Demetrio Albertini (missed), 2-1 David Trézéguet, 2-2 Alessandro Costacurta, 3-2 Thierry Henry, 3-3 Christian Vieri, 4-3 Laurent Blanc, Luigi Di Biagio (missed)

567. 08.07.1998   FIFA World Cup Final Tournament – Semi-final

FRANCE v CROATIA 2-1 (0-0)

Stade de France, Saint-Denis (France)

Referee: José María García-Aranda Encinar (Spain)
Attendance: 76,000

FRANCE: Fabien Barthez, Bixente Lizarazu, Laurent Blanc, Lilian Thuram, Didier Deschamps, Youri Djorkaeff (74 Frank Lebœuf), Christian Karembeu (31 Thierry Henry), Zinédine Zidane, Marcel Desailly, Emmanuel Petit, Stéphane Guivarc'h (69 David Trézéguet).   Manager: Aimé Jacquet

CROATIA: Drazen Ladic, Dario Simic, Robert Jarni, Igor Stimac, Zvonimir Soldo, Slaven Bilic, Aljosa Asanovic, Mario Stanic (89 Robert Prosinecki), Davor Suker, Zvonimir Boban (65 Silvio Maric), Goran Vlaovic.
Manager: Miroslav Blazevic

Goals: Lilian Thuram (47, 69) / Davor Suker (46)

Sent off: Laurent Blanc (76)

568. 12.07.1998   FIFA World Cup Final Tournament – Final

BRAZIL v FRANCE 0-3 (0-2)

Stade de France, Saint-Denis (France)

Referee: Said Belqola (Morocco)   Attendance: 75,000

BRAZIL: Cláudio André Mergen TAFFAREL, Marcos Evangelista de Moraes "CAFÚ", Raimundo Ferreira Ramos JÚNIOR "BAIANO", ALDAIR Nascimento Santos, ROBERTO CARLOS da Silva, Carlos CÉSAR SAMPAIO Campos (74 EDMUNDO Alves de Souza Neto), Carlos Caetano Bledorn Verri "DUNGA", RIVALDO Vito Borba Ferreira, LEONARDO Nascimento de Araújo (46 DENÍLSON de Oliveira), RONALDO Luís Nazário de Lima, José Roberto da Gama de Oliveira "BEBETO".   Manager: Jorge MÁRIO Lobo ZAGALLO

FRANCE: Fabien Barthez, Lilian Thuram, Frank Lebœuf, Marcel Desailly, Bixente Lizarazu, Didier Deschamps, Emmanuel Petit, Youri Djorkaeff (76 Patrick Vieira), Christian Karembeu (57 Alain Boghossian), Zinédine Zidane, Stéphane Guivarc'h (66 Christophe Dugarry).   Manager: Aimé Jacquet

Goals: Zinédine Zidane (27, 45), Emmanuel Petit (90)

Sent off: Marcel Desailly (68)

569. 19.08.1998
AUSTRIA v FRANCE 2-2 (1-1)

Ernst Happel Stadion, Vienna

Referee: Mario van der Ende (Netherlands)
Attendance: 44,000

AUSTRIA: Michael Konsel (21 Franz Wohlfahrt), Wolfgang Feiersinger, Peter Schöttel, Anton Pfeffer, Markus Schopp (46 Martin Hiden), Dietmar Kühbauer (46 Peter Stöger), Roman Mählich, Hannes Reinmayr (79 Heimo Pfeifenberger), Arnold Wetl (79 Günther Neukirchner), Ivica Vastic, Mario Haas (73 Christian Mayrleb). Manager: Herbert Prohaska

FRANCE: Bernard Lama, Bixente Lizarazu (46 Vincent Candela), Lilian Thuram, Frank Lebœuf (79 Alain Goma), Alain Boghossian, Christian Karembeu, Didier Deschamps (46 Frédéric Déhu), Tony Vairelles, Lilian Laslandes (81 Florian Maurice), Zinédine Zidane (46 Youri Djorkaeff), Thierry Henry (65 Robert Pirès). Manager: Roger Lemerre

Goals: Mario Haas (42), Ivica Vastic (76 pen) / Lilian Laslandes (16), Alain Boghossian (84)

570. 05.09.1998   UEFA Euro 2000 Qualifying – Group 4
ICELAND v FRANCE 1-1 (1-1)

Laugardalsvöllur, Reykjavík

Referee: Eric Achille Blareau (Belgium)   Attendance: 10,382

ICELAND: Birkir Kristinsson, Eyjólfur Sverrisson, Lárus Sigurdsson, Pétur Marteinsson, Hermann Hreidarsson, Audun Helgason, Helgi Kolvidsson, Rúnar Kristinsson, Thórdur Gudjónsson, Arnar Gunnlaugsson (69 Stefán Thórdarson), Ríkhardur Dadason. Manager: Gudjón Thórdarson

FRANCE: Fabien Barthez, Christian Karembeu, Bixente Lizarazu, Lilian Thuram, Frank Lebœuf, Youri Djorkaeff, Didier Deschamps, Christophe Dugarry (67 Thierry Henry), Lilian Laslandes, Zinédine Zidane, Robert Pirès. Manager: Roger Lemerre

Goals: Ríkhardur Dadason (32) / Christophe Dugarry (35)

571. 10.10.1998   UEFA Euro 2000 Qualifying – Group 4
RUSSIA v FRANCE 2-3 (1-2)

Grand Sports Arena of the Luzhniki Olympic Complex, Moscow

Referee: Pietro Ceccarini (Italy)   Attendance: 20,989

RUSSIA: Sergey Ovchinnikov, Dmitriy Khlestov, Viktor Onopko, Yevgeniy Varlamov, Igor Yanovski, Valeriy Karpin, Dmitriy Alenichev (70 Sergey Semak), Yegor Titov, Aleksandr Mostovoy, Andrey Tikhonov, Vladimir Beschastnykh (60 Aleksey Gerasimenko). Manager: Anatoliy Byshovets

FRANCE: Bernard Lama, Lilian Thuram, Laurent Blanc, Bixente Lizarazu, Marcel Desailly, Emmanuel Petit (46 Alain Boghossian), Didier Deschamps, Youri Djorkaeff (54 Patrick Vieira), Zinédine Zidane, Nicolas Anelka (86 Tony Vairelles), Robert Pirès. Manager: Roger Lemerre

Goals: Igor Yanovski (45), Aleksandr Mostovoy (55) / Nicolas Anelka (13), Robert Pirès (28), Alain Boghossian (81)

Laurent Blanc missed a penalty kick (90)

572. 14.10.1998   UEFA Euro 2000 Qualifying – Group 4
FRANCE v ANDORRA 2-0 (0-0)

Stade de France, Saint-Denis

Referee: Dani Koren (Israel)   Attendance: 75,416

FRANCE: Bernard Lama, Vincent Candela, Frank Lebœuf, Laurent Blanc, Bixente Lizarazu, Youri Djorkaeff (81 Alain Boghossian), Didier Deschamps, Tony Vairelles, David Trézéguet (67 Nicolas Anelka), Zinédine Zidane, Christophe Dugarry (67 Robert Pirès). Manager: Roger Lemerre

ANDORRA: Jesús Luis Álvarez de Eulate Güergue "KOLDO", Francesc Javier RAMÍREZ Palomo (80 Julià "JULI" SÁNCHEZ Soto), José Manuel García Luena "TXEMA", ÁNGEL MARTÍN García, Antoni "TONI" LIMA Solá, ILDEFONS LIMA Solà, AGUSTI POL Pérez, ÓSCAR SONEJEE Masand, JESÚS Julián LUCENDO Heredia (85 Manuel "MANOLO" JIMÉNEZ Soria), JUSTO RUÍZ González, EMILIANO GONZÁLEZ Arqués. Manager: MANOEL MILUIR Macedo Cunha

Goals: Vincent Candela (54), Youri Djorkaeff (59)

573. 20.01.1999
FRANCE v MOROCCO 1-0 (0-0)

Stade Vélodrome, Marseille

Referee: Alain Hamer (Luxembourg)   Attendance: 46,756

FRANCE: Fabien Barthez, Lilian Thuram, Laurent Blanc (46 Frank Lebœuf), Marcel Desailly, Vincent Candela, Didier Deschamps (46 Emmanuel Petit), Alain Boghossian, Zinédine Zidane (67 Nicolas Anelka), Youri Djorkaeff, Christophe Dugarry (46 Robert Pirès), Florian Maurice. Manager: Roger Lemerre

MOROCCO: Driss Benzekri, Abdelilah Saber, Youssef Rossi, Noureddine Naybet, Abdelkrim El Hadrioui (46 Lahcen Abrami), Saïd Chiba (46 Adil Ramzi), Tahar El Khalej, Mustapha Hadji, Youssef Chippo (79 Jamal Sellami), Salaheddine Bassir, Abdeljalil Hadda (84 Rachid Rokki). Manager: Henri Michel

Goal: Youri Djorkaeff (47)

574. 10.02.1999
ENGLAND v FRANCE 0-2 (0-0)
British Empire Exhibition Stadium, London
Referee: Hellmut Heinz Krug (Germany)   Att: 74,111
ENGLAND: David Seaman (46 Nigel Martyn), Lee Dixon (72 Rio Ferdinand), Tony Adams, Martin Keown (85 Paul Scholes), Graeme Le Saux, David Beckham, Paul Ince, Jamie Redknapp (86 Jason Wilcox), Darren Anderton, Michael Owen (64 Andy Cole), Alan Shearer.   Manager: Howard Wilkinson
FRANCE: Fabien Barthez, Lilian Thuram, Marcel Desailly, Laurent Blanc (46 Frank Lebœuf), Bixente Lizarazu, Robert Pirès (46 Christophe Dugarry), Emmanuel Petit, Didier Deschamps (90 Vincent Candela), Zinédine Zidane, Youri Djorkaeff (83 Patrick Vieira), Nicolas Anelka (84 Sylvain Wiltord).   Manager: Roger Lemerre

Goals: Nicolas Anelka (69, 76)

575. 27.03.1999   UEFA Euro 2000 Qualifying – Group 4
FRANCE v UKRAINE 0-0
Stade de France, Saint-Denis
Referee: Günter Benkö (Austria)   Attendance: 78,519
FRANCE: Fabien Barthez, Lilian Thuram, Bixente Lizarazu, Emmanuel Petit (78 Alain Boghossian), Laurent Blanc, Youri Djorkaeff, Didier Deschamps, Marcel Desailly, Nicolas Anelka, Robert Pirès (84 Vikash Dhorasoo), Christophe Dugarry (69 Sylvain Wiltord).   Manager: Roger Lemerre
UKRAINE: Oleksandr Shovkovskiy, Oleh Luzhny, Volodymyr Mykytyn, Oleksandr Holovko, Vladyslav Vashchuk, Andriy Gusin (86 Viktor Skrypnyk), Serhiy Popov, Serhiy Kovalyov (55 Vitaliy Kosovskiy), Serhiy Skachenko (69 Yuriy Maksymov), Andriy Shevchenko, Serhiy Rebrov. Manager: József Szabó

576. 31.03.1999   UEFA Euro 2000 Qualifying – Group 4
FRANCE v ARMENIA 2-0 (2-0)
Stade de France, Saint-Denis
Referee: Giorgos Bikas (Greece)   Attendance: 78,852
FRANCE: Fabien Barthez, Lilian Thuram (79 Christian Karembeu), Marcel Desailly, Laurent Blanc, Didier Deschamps, Patrick Vieira, Youri Djorkaeff (69 Robert Pirès), Alain Boghossian, Nicolas Anelka, Sylvain Wiltord, Christophe Dugarry (46 David Trézéguet).   Manager: Roger Lemerre
ARMENIA: Roman Berezovsky, Ervand Sukiasyan (39 Vardan Khachatryan), Arthur Mkrtchyan, Harutyun Vardanyan, Sargis Hovsepyan, Sargis Hovhannisyan, Artur Petrosyan, Arthur Voskanyan (77 Aram Hayrapetyan), Albert Sargsyan, Armen Shahgeldyan (53 Tigran Yesayan), Karapet Mikaelyan.   Manager: Souren Barseghyan

Goals: Sylvain Wiltord (2), Christophe Dugarry (45)

577. 05.06.1999   UEFA Euro 2000 Qualifying – Group 4
FRANCE v RUSSIA 2-3 (0-1)
Stade de France, Saint-Denis
Referee: Paul Anthony Durkin (England)
Attendance: 78,288
FRANCE: Fabien Barthez, Vincent Candela (88 Robert Pirès), Lilian Thuram, Emmanuel Petit, Laurent Blanc, Youri Djorkaeff (90 Alain Boghossian), Didier Deschamps, Marcel Desailly, Nicolas Anelka, Sylvain Wiltord, Christophe Dugarry (57 Patrick Vieira).   Manager: Roger Lemerre
RUSSIA: Aleksandr Filimonov, Dmitriy Khlestov, Viktor Onopko, Aleksey Smertin, Yevgeniy Varlamov, Sergey Semak (59 Vladimir Beschastnykh), Valeriy Karpin, Aleksandr Mostovoy (25 Dmitriy Khokhlov), Yegor Titov, Andrey Tikhonov (71 Ilya Tsymbalar), Aleksandr Panov. Manager: Oleg Romantsev

Goals: Emmanuel Petit (47), Sylvain Wiltord (53) / Aleksandr Panov (37, 74), Valeriy Karpin (86)

578. 09.06.1999   UEFA Euro 2000 Qualifying – Group 4
ANDORRA v FRANCE 0-1 (0-0)
Estadio Olímpico de Montjuïc, Barcelona (Spain)
Referee: Michael Ross (Northern Ireland)
Attendance: 7,600
ANDORRA: Jesús Luis Álvarez de Eulate Güergue "KOLDO", AGUSTI POL Pérez, Antoni "TONI" LIMA Solá, ILDEFONS LIMA Solà, José Manuel García Luena "TXEMA" (70 ROBERTO JONÁS Alonso Martínez), Francesc Javier RAMÍREZ Palomo, ÓSCAR SONEJEE Masand, JUSTO RUÍZ González, Manuel "MANOLO" JIMÉNEZ Soria (89 GENÍS GARCÍA Iscla), JESÚS Julián LUCENDO Heredia (77 ÁNGEL MARTÍN García), EMILIANO GONZÁLEZ Arqués. Manager: DAVID RODRIGO Lo
FRANCE: Ulrich Ramé, Christian Karembeu, Frank Lebœuf, Marcel Desailly, Vincent Candela, Alain Boghossian, Emmanuel Petit (56 Patrick Vieira), Sylvain Wiltord, Vikash Dhorasoo (61 Robert Pirès), Christophe Dugarry, Nicolas Anelka.   Manager: Roger Lemerre

Goal: Frank Lebœuf (86 pen)

Sent off: Antoni "TONI" LIMA Solá (86) / Christophe Dugarry (24)

579. 18.08.1999
NORTHERN IRELAND v FRANCE 0-1 (0-0)

Windsor Park, Belfast

Referee: William (Willie) Young (Scotland)
Attendance: 11,804

NORTHERN IRELAND: Maik Taylor (46 Tommy Wright), Aaron Hughes, Mark Williams, Barry Hunter, Jon McCarthy, Kevin Horlock, Neil Lennon, Steve Lomas, Peter Kennedy (74 Keith Gillespie), Iain Dowie (55 James Quinn), Michael Hughes.   Manager: Lawrie McMenemy

FRANCE: Fabien Barthez, Lilian Thuram, Laurent Blanc, Marcel Desailly (65 Frank Lebœuf), Bixente Lizarazu (56 Vincent Candela), Alain Boghossian, Patrick Vieira (83 Frédéric Déhu), Jean Micoud, Robert Pirès, Lilian Laslandes (76 Tony Vairelles), Sylvain Wiltord (56 Laurent Robert).   Manager: Roger Lemerre

Goal: Lilian Laslandes (67)

580. 04.09.1999   UEFA Euro 2000 Qualifying – Group 4
UKRAINE v FRANCE 0-0

Olimpiysky National Sports Complex, Kyiv

Referee: Hugh Dallas (Scotland)   Attendance: 70,000

UKRAINE: Oleksandr Shovkovskiy, Oleh Luzhny, Serhiy Popov, Oleksandr Holovko, Vladyslav Vashchuk, Yuriy Dmytrulin (46 Volodymyr Mykytyn), Andriy Gusin (81 Eduard Tsykhmeystruk), Yuriy Maksymov (67 Serhiy Kovalyov), Vitaliy Kosovskiy, Andriy Shevchenko, Serhiy Rebrov.   Manager: József Szabó

FRANCE: Fabien Barthez, Lilian Thuram, Bixente Lizarazu, Christian Karembeu, Patrick Vieira, Laurent Blanc, Youri Djorkaeff (68 Robert Pirès), Didier Deschamps, Marcel Desailly, Nicolas Anelka (52 Lilian Laslandes), Zinédine Zidane.   Manager: Roger Lemerre

581. 08.09.1999   UEFA Euro 2000 Qualifying – Group 4
ARMENIA v FRANCE 2-3 (1-1)

Hrazdan Stadium, Yerevan

Referee: Atanas Uzunov (Bulgaria)   Attendance: 14,500

ARMENIA: Roman Berezovsky, Arthur Mkrtchyan, Vardan Khachatryan, Sargis Hovsepyan, Romik Khachatryan (74 Artur Kocharyan), Tigran Yesayan, Tigran Petrosyan, Hayk Harutyunyan (64 Razmik Grigoryan), Albert Sargsyan, Armen Shahgeldyan, Karapet Mikaelyan (67 Marcelo Devani).   Manager: Souren Barseghyan

FRANCE: Fabien Barthez, Lilian Thuram, Laurent Blanc, Marcel Desailly, Bixente Lizarazu, Christian Karembeu, Zinédine Zidane (72 Frédérik Déhu), Didier Deschamps, Youri Djorkaeff, Lilian Laslandes, Sylvain Wiltord (62 Laurent Robert).   Manager: Roger Lemerre

Goals: Karapet Mikaelyan (6), Armen Shahgeldyan (90 pen) / Youri Djorkaeff (44 pen), Zinédine Zidane (66), Lilian Laslandes (74)

Sent off: Frédérik Déhu (89)

582. 09.10.1999   UEFA Euro 2000 Qualifying – Group 4
FRANCE v ICELAND 3-2 (2-0)

Stade de France, Saint-Denis

Referee: Bernd Reinhold Gerhard Heynemann (Germany)
Attendance: 78,381

FRANCE: Bernard Lama, Lilian Thuram, Laurent Blanc, Marcel Desailly, Bixente Lizarazu, Didier Deschamps, Alain Boghossian (90 Patrick Vieira), Zinédine Zidane, Youri Djorkaeff, Lilian Laslandes (64 David Trézéguet), Sylvain Wiltord (83 Tony Vairelles).   Manager: Roger Lemerre

ICELAND: Birkir Kristinsson, Audun Helgason, Lárus Sigurdsson, Eyjólfur Sverrisson, Pétur Marteinsson (81 Helgi Kolvidsson), Hermann Hreidarsson, Brynjar Gunnarsson, Rúnar Kristinsson, Thórdur Gudjónsson, Ríkhardur Dadason (53 Eidur Gudjohnsen), Helgi Sigurdsson (65 Heidar Helguson).   Manager: Gudjón Thórdarson

Goals: Ríkhardur Dadason (18 og), Youri Djorkaeff (38), David Trezéguet (71) /
Eyjólfur Sverrisson (48), Brynjar Gunnarsson (56)

583. 13.11.1999
FRANCE v CROATIA 3-0 (0-0)

Stade de France, Sain-Denis

Referee: Lubos Michel (Slovakia)   Attendance: 74,167

FRANCE: Stéphane Porato, Lilian Thuram, Frank Lebœuf, Marcel Desailly, Vincent Candela, Alain Boghossian (73 Frédéric Déhu), Patrick Vieira, Johan Micoud (85 Didier Deschamps), Zinédine Zidane (46 Youri Djorkaeff), Robert Pirès (59 Tony Vairelles), Stéphane Guivarc'h (46 Florian Maurice).   Manager: Roger Lemerre

CROATIA: Zeljko Pavlovic, Stjepan Tomas, Igor Stimac (62 Boris Zivkovic), Zvonimir Soldo, Tomislav Rukavina (77 Daniel Saric), Zvonimir Boban (85 Niko Kovac), Robert Jarni, Mario Stanic, Aljosa Asanovic, Davor Suker, Alen Boksic.   Manager: Miroslav Blazevic

Goals: Robert Pirès (46), F. Maurice (67), Tony Vairelles (74)

584. 23.02.2000

FRANCE v POLAND 1-0 (0-0)

Stade de France, Saint-Denis

Referee: Kyros Vasaras (Greece)   Attendance: 74,341

FRANCE: Fabien Barthez, Lilian Thuram, Marcel Desailly, Laurent Blanc (46 Frank Lebœuf), Bixente Lizarazu, Youri Djorkaeff (74 Tony Vairelles), Didier Deschamps, Zinédine Zidane, Emmanuel Petit (57 Patrick Vieira), Sylvain Wiltord (57 Robert Pirès), David Trézéguet.   Manager: Roger Lemerre

POLAND: Jerzy Dudek, Tomasz Klos, Tomasz Waldoch, Jacek Bak, Michal Zewlakow (64 Tomasz Hajto), Tomasz Iwan (73 Tomasz Wieszczycki), Jacek Krznówek (90+1 Tomasz Kielbowicz), Piotr Swierczewski, Marcin Zewlakow (56 Pawel Kryszalowicz), Piotr Reiss (85 Tomasz Rzasa), Bartosz Karwan.   Manager: Jerzy Engel

Goal: Zinédine Zidane (87)

585. 29.03.2000

SCOTLAND v FRANCE 0-2 (0-0)

Hampden Park, Glasgow

Referee: Rune Pedersen (Norway)   Attendance: 48,157

SCOTLAND: Neil Sullivan, Paul Ritchie (46 Steven Pressley), Christian Dailly, Paul Telfer (67 Allan Johnston), Barry Ferguson, Don Hutchison, Colin Cameron (46 Neil McCann), Kevin Gallacher (78 Mark Burchill), Billy Dodds, Callum Davidson, Colin Hendry.   Manager: Craig Brown

FRANCE: Ulrich Ramé, Lilian Thuram, Marcel Desailly, Laurent Blanc, Bixente Lizarazu, Didier Deschamps (60 Patrick Vieira), Emmanuel Petit, Ludovic Giuly (46 Sylvain Wiltord), Youri Djorkaeff (46 Johan Micoud), Christophe Dugarry (71 Robert Pirès), Thierry Henry.   Manager: Roger Lemerre

Goals: Sylvain Wiltord (53), Thierry Henry (88)

586. 26.04.2000

FRANCE v SLOVENIA 3-2 (0-2)

Stade de France, Saint-Denis

Referee: Abderrahim Larjoune (Morocco)   Att: 59,652

FRANCE: Fabien Barthez, Lilian Thuram, Frank Lebœuf, Laurent Blanc, Bixente Lizarazu, Didier Deschamps (63 Emmanuel Petit), Patrick Vieira, Zinédine Zidane, Robert Pirès (63 Tony Vairelles), Thierry Henry (46 David Trézéguet), Christophe Dugarry (46 Johan Micoud).   Manager: Roger Lemerre

SLOVENIA: Mladen Dabanovic, Amir Karic (64 Marinko Galic), Mladen Rudonja, Darko Milanic, Zeljko Milinovic, Aleksander Knavs, Dzoni Novak (89 Sasa Gajser), Ales Ceh, Saso Udovic (57 Milan Osterc), Zlatko Zahovic, Miran Pavlin (64 Zoran Pavlovic).   Manager: Srecko Katanec

Goals: David Trézéguet (62, 90+5), Laurent Blanc (77) / Zeljko Milinovic (3), Saso Udovic (10)

587. 28.05.2000

CROATIA v FRANCE 0-2 (0-1)

Stadion Maksimir, Zagreb

Referee: Fritz Stuchlik (Austria)   Attendance: 10,079

CROATIA: Drazen Ladic (8 Zeljko Pavlovic), Robert Kovac (46 Daniel Saric), Igor Stimac, Dario Simic, Niko Kovac, Mario Stanic (89 Stanko Bubalo), Aljosa Asanovic (58 Krunoslav Jurcic), Robert Jarni, Davor Suker, Alen Boksic (46 Jurica Vucko), Zvonimir Soldo.   Manager: Miroslav Blazevic

FRANCE: Fabien Barthez, Lilian Thuram, Marcel Desailly, Laurent Blanc (75 Frank Lebœuf), Bixente Lizarazu, Didier Deschamps, Emmanuel Petit (46 Patrick Vieira), Robert Pirès (46 David Trézéguet), Zinédine Zidane (82 Vincent Candela), Sylvain Wiltord, Thierry Henry (60 Johan Micoud).   Manager: Roger Lemerre

Goals: Robert Pirès (23), David Trézéguet (70)

588. 04.06.2000   King Hassan II Tournament 2000 – Semi-final

FRANCE v JAPAN 2-2 (0-1)

Stade Mohamed V, Casablanca (Morocco)

Referee: Abderrahim Larjoune (Morocco)
Attendance: 30,000

FRANCE: Fabien Barthez, Lilian Thuram, Laurent Blanc, Marcel Desailly (67 Frank Lebœuf), Bixente Lizarazu, Robert Pirès (46 Youri Djorkaeff), Didier Deschamps (46 Patrick Vieira), Zinédine Zidane (89 Thierry Henry), Emmanuel Petit, David Trézéguet (76 Nicolas Anelka), Sylvain Wiltord (46 Christophe Dugarry).   Manager: Roger Lemerre

JAPAN: Seigo Narazaki, Ryuzo Morioka, Naoki Matsuda, Go Oiwa, Shunsuke Nakamura (67 Atsuhiro Miura), Teruyoshi Ito, Hidetoshi Nakata, Junichi Inamoto, Hiroshi Nanami, Hiroaki Morishima, Akinori Nishizawa (90 Atsushi Yanagisawa).   Manager: Philippe Troussier

Goals: Zinédine Zidane (61), Youri Djorkaeff (75) / Hiroaki Morishima (34), Akinori Nishizawa (70)

Penalties: 1-0 Hidetoshi Nakata, 1-1 Youri Djorkaeff, 2-1 Atsuhiro Miura, 2-2 Nicolas Anelka, Junichi Inamoto (missed), 2-3 Thierry Henry, Hiroshi Nanami (missed), 2-4 Frank Lebœuf.

589. 06.06.2000 King Hassan II Tournament 2000 – Final

MOROCCO v FRANCE 1-5 (0-1)

Stade Mohamed V, Casablanca (Morocco)

Referee: Ali Mohamed Bujsaim (UA Emirates)
Attendance: 57,000

MOROCCO: Khalid Fouhami, Youssef Mariana, Talal El Kharkouri, Noureddine Naybet, Youssef Safri, Bouchaib M'Barkhi (63 Abdelfettah El Khattari), Mourad Hdiouad, Lahcen Abrami, Othmane El Assas, Salaheddine Bassir, Hicham Zerouali.   Manager: Henry Kasperczak

FRANCE: Bernard Lama, Christian Karembeu, Frank Lebœuf, Marcel Desailly, Vincent Candela, Patrick Vieira, Youri Djorkaeff (61 Zinédine Zidane), Johan Micoud (67 Didier Deschamps), Christophe Dugarry (87 Sylvain Wiltord), Nicolas Anelka, Thierry Henry (74 Emmanuel Petit).   Manager: Roger Lemerre

Goals: Talal El Kharkouri (66) / Thierry Henry (27), Youri Djorkaeff (56 pen), Christophe Dugarry (79), Nicolas Anelka (83), Sylvain Wiltord (90)

590. 11.06.2000 UEFA European Championship – Group D

FRANCE v DENMARK 3-0 (1-0)

Jan Breydelstadion, Brugge (Belgium)

Referee: Günter Benkö (Austria)   Attendance: 28,100

FRANCE: Fabien Barthez, Lilian Thuram, Bixente Lizarazu, Laurent Blanc, Youri Djorkaeff (58 Patrick Vieira), Didier Deschamps, Marcel Desailly, Nicolas Anelka (82 Sylvain Wiltord), Zinédine Zidane, Thierry Henry, Emmanuel Petit. Manager: Roger Lemerre

DENMARK: Peter Schmeichel, Michael Schjønberg, René Henriksen, Jan Heintze, Allan Nielsen, Jesper Grønkjær, Jon Dahl Tomasson (79 Mikkel Beck), Ebbe Sand, Søren Colding, Stig Tøfting (72 Thomas Gravesen), Morten Bisgaard (72 Martin Jørgensen).   Manager: Bo Johansson

Goals: Laurent Blanc (16), Thierry Henry (64), Sylvain Wiltord (90+2)

591. 16.06.2000 UEFA European Championship – Group D

CZECH REPUBLIC v FRANCE 1-2 (1-1)

Jan Breydelstadion, Brugge (Belgium)

Referee: Graham Poll (England)   Attendance: 27,243

CZECH REPUBLIC: Pavel Srnícek, Karel Rada, Tomás Repka, Petr Gabriel (46 Milan Fukal), Karel Poborský, Pavel Nedved, Radek Bejbl (49 Vratislav Lokvenc), Tomás Rosický (62 Marek Jankulovski), Jirí Nemec, Jan Koller, Vladimír Smicer.   Manager: Jozef Chovanec

FRANCE: Fabien Barthez, Lilian Thuram, Vincent Candela, Laurent Blanc, Patrick Vieira, Didier Deschamps, Marcel Desailly, Nicolas Anelka (55 Christophe Dugarry), Zinédine Zidane, Thierry Henry (89 Sylvain Wiltord), Emmanuel Petit (46 Youri Djorkaeff).   Manager: Roger Lemerre

Goals: Karel Poborský (35 pen) / Thierry Henry (7), Youri Djorkaeff (60)

592. 21.06.2000 UEFA European Championship – Group D

FRANCE v NETHERLANDS 2-3 (2-1)

Amsterdam ArenA, Amsterdam (Netherlands)

Referee: Anders Frisk (Sweden)   Attendance: 44,000

FRANCE: Bernard Lama, Vincent Candela, Patrick Vieira (90 Didier Deschamps), Robert Pirès, Sylvain Wiltord (80 Nicolas Anelka), Marcel Desailly, Johan Micoud, Frank Lebœuf, Christian Karembeu, David Trézéguet, Christophe Dugarry (68 Youri Djorkaeff).   Manager: Roger Lemerre

NETHERLANDS: Sander Westerveld, Jaap Stam, Frank de Boer, Arthur Numan, Boudewijn Zenden, Phillip Cocu, Edgar Davids, Paul Bosvelt, Patrick Kluivert (60 Roy Makaay), Dennis Bergkamp (78 Aron Winter), Marc Overmars (89 Peter van Vossen).   Manager: Frank Rijkaard

Goals: Christophe Dugarry (8), David Trézéguet (31) / P. Kluivert (14), Frank de Boer (51), Boudewijn Zenden (59)

593. 25.06.2000 UEFA European Championship – Quarter-final

SPAIN v FRANCE 1-2 (1-2)

Jan Breydelstadion, Brugge (Belgium)

Referee: Pierluigi Collina (Italy)   Attendance: 26,614

SPAIN. José Santiago CAÑIZARES Ruiz, Miguel Ángel "MÍCHEL" SALGADO Fernández, Agustín ARANZÁBAL Alkorta, Josep "PEP" GUARDIOLA i Sala, ABELARDO Fernández Antuña, IVÁN HELGUERA Bujía (77 GERARD López Segú), Pedro Manuel MUNITIS Álvarez (73 Joseba ETXEBERRIA Lizardi), RAÚL González Blanco, ALFONSO Pérez Muñoz, Gaizka MENDIETA Zabala (57 Ismael URZÁIZ Aranda), Francisco Manuel "PACO" JÉMEZ Martín.   Manager: José Antonio CAMACHO Alfaro

FRANCE: Fabien Barthez, Lilian Thuram, Bixente Lizarazu, Patrick Vieira, Laurent Blanc, Youri Djorkaeff, Didier Deschamps, Marcel Desailly, Zinédine Zidane, Thierry Henry (81 Nicolas Anelka), Christophe Dugarry.   Manager: Roger Lemerre

Goals: Gaizka MENDIETA Zabala (38 pen) / Zinédine Zidane (32), Youri Djorkaeff (44)

RAÚL González Blanco missed a penalty kick (90)

594.   28.06.2000   UEFA European Championship – Semi-final
PORTUGAL v FRANCE 1-2 (1-0, 1-1) (AET)

Stade Roi Baudouin, Brussels (Belgium)

Referee: Günter Benkö (Austria)   Attendance: 47,000

PORTUGAL: VÍTOR Manuel Martins BAÍA, JORGE Paulo COSTA Almeida, José Luís da Cruz VIDIGAL (61 PAULO Jorge Gomes BENTO), FERNANDO Manuel Silva COUTO, LUÍS Filipe Madeira Caeiro FIGO, RUI Manuel César COSTA (78 JOÃO Manuel VIEIRA PINTO), SÉRGIO Paulo Marceneiro da CONCEIÇÃO, DIMAS Manuel Marques Teixeira (90+1 RUI JORGE de Sousa Dias Macedo de Oliveira), ABEL Luís da Silva Costa XAVIER, Francisco José Rodrigues da Costa "COSTINHA", NUNO "GOMES" Miguel Soares Pereira Ribeiro. Manager: HUMBERTO Manuel de Jesus COELHO

FRANCE: Fabien Barthez, Lilian Thuram, Laurent Blanc, Marcel Desailly, Bixente Lizarazu, Patrick Vieira, Didier Deschamps, Zinédine Zidane, Emmanuel Petit (87 Robert Pirès), Thierry Henry (105 David Trézéguet), Nicolas Anelka (72 Sylvain Wiltord).   Manager: Roger Lemerre

Goals: NUNO "GOMES" Miguel Soares Pereira Ribeiro (19) / Thierry Henry (51), Zinédine Zidane (117 pen) Golden goal

Sent off: NUNO "GOMES" (116)

595.   02.07.2000   UEFA European Championship – Final
FRANCE v ITALY 2-1 (0-0, 1-1) (AET)

De Kuip, Rotterdam (Netherlands)

Referee: Anders Frisk (Sweden)   Attendance: 48,200

FRANCE: Fabien Barthez, Lilian Thuram, Laurent Blanc, Bixente Lizarazu (86 Robert Pirès), Didier Deschamps, Marcel Desailly, Patrick Vieira, Youri Djorkaeff (76 David Trézéguet), Christophe Dugarry (58 Sylvain Wiltord), Thierry Henry, Zinédine Zidane.   Manager: Roger Lemerre

ITALY: Francesco Toldo, Paolo Maldini, Demetrio Albertini, Fabio Cannavaro, Marco Delvecchio (86 Vincenzo Montella), Luigi Di Biagio (66 Massimo Ambrosini), Stefano Fiore (53 Alessandro Del Piero), Mark Iuliano, Alessandro Nesta, Gianluca Pessotto, Francesco Totti.   Manager: Dino Zoff

Goals: Sylvain Wiltord (90+4), David Trézéguet (103 Golden goal) / Marco Delvecchio (55)

596.   16.08.2000   Childrens Charity Friendly
FRANCE v F.I.F.A. 5-1 (2-0)

Stade Vélodrome, Marseille

Referee: Mohamed Guezzaz (Morocco)   Attendance: 58,016

FRANCE: Fabien Barthez (46 Ulrich Ramé), Laurent Blanc (51 Frank Lebœuf), Vincent Candela, Marcel Desailly, Bixente Lizarazu (74 Christian Karembeu), Emmanuel Petit (46 Robert Pirès), Didier Deschamps (61 Patrick Vieira), Zinédine Zidane, Christophe Dugarry, Thierry Henry (46 Youri Djorkaeff), David Trézéguet (51 Nicolas Anelka).   Manager: Roger Lemerre

F.I.F.A.: Andreas Köpke (46 Jacques Songo'o), Samuel Kuffour (58 Ciro Ferrara), ALDAIR Nascimento dos Santos (58 Frank Verlaat), Carlos Caetano Bledorn Verri "DUNGA" (61' José "ZÉ" ELIAS Moedim Júnior), Aron Winter (46 Zoubeir Beya), Su Maozhen (46 Geremi Njitap), Roberto Baggio, Hidetoshi Nakata (46 Saliou Lassisi), Pierre Njanka (46 Khalid Al-Muwallad), Rigobert Song (46 Pablo Thiam), Taribo West (46 Yoo Sang-Cheol).
Managers: CARLOS QUIEROZ & Jozef Venglos

Goals: David Trézéguet (11, 26, 46), Robert Pirès (55), Nicolas Anelka (76) / Roberto Baggio (79 pen)

597.   02.09.2000
FRANCE v ENGLAND 1-1 (0-0)

Stade de France, Saint-Denis

Referee: Juan Ansuátegui Roca (Spain)   Attendance: 76,318

FRANCE: Bernard Lama, Bixente Lizarazu, Marcel Desailly, Laurent Blanc (59 Frank Lebœuf), Lilian Thuram (80 Vincent Candela), Didier Deschamps (59 Patrick Vieira), Emmanuel Petit, Zinédine Zidane (65 Robert Pirès), Youri Djorkaeff, Thierry Henry (73 David Trézéguet), Nicolas Anelka (46 Sylvain Wiltord).   Manager: Roger Lemerre

ENGLAND: David Seaman, Sol Campbell, Tony Adams (46 Gareth Southgate), Martin Keown, Gareth Barry, Darren Anderton (69 Kieron Dyer), David Beckham, Dennis Wise, Nick Barmby (83 Steve McManaman), Paul Scholes (77 Michael Owen), Andy Cole.   Manager: Kevin Keegan

Goals: Emmanuel Petit (64) / Michael Owen (86)

598.   04.10.2000

FRANCE v CAMEROON   1-1 (1-1)

Stade de France, Saint-Denis

Referee: Michel Piraux (Belgium)   Attendance: 63,704

FRANCE: Lionel Letizi (59 Richard Dutruel), Lilian Thuram, Marcel Desailly, Frank Lebœuf, Bixente Lizarazu (56 Claude Makélélé), Emmanuel Petit, Patrick Vieira, Johan Micoud (75 Martin Djétou), Sylvain Wiltord (67 Ludovic Giuly), Thierry Henry, David Trézéguet (56 Laurent Robert).
Manager: Roger Lemerre

CAMEROON: Alioum Boukar, Rigobert Song, Raymond Kalla, Pierre Njanka, Patrice Abanda (32 Nicolas Alnoudji), Geremi Njitap, Salomon Olembé (88 Modeste M'Bami), Marc-Vivien Foé, Pierre Womé (66 Bill Tchato), Samuel Eto'o (82 Joseph-Désiré Job), Patrick M'Boma (66 Bernard Tchoutang).
Manager: Pierre Lechantre

Goals: Sylvain Wiltord (19) / Patrick M'Boma (44)

599.   07.10.2000

SOUTH AFRICA v FRANCE   0-0

Ellis Park Stadium, Johannesburg

Referee: Jelas Ntebu Masole (Botswana)   Attendance: 37,000

IVORY COAST: Hans Vonk, Mark Fish, Bradley Carnell, Frank Schoeman, Pierre Issa, Quinton Fortune, Thabo Mngomeni, Dumisa Ngobe, Delron Buckley (52 Sibusiso Zuma), Shaun Bartlett, Benedict (Benny) McCarthy (79 Godfrey Sapula).
Manager: CARLOS Manuel Brito Leal QUEIROZ

FRANCE: Ulrich Ramé, Lilian Thuram (32 Ludovic Giuly), Frank Lebœuf (59 Philippe Christanval), Marcel Desailly, Christian Karembeu, Martin Djétou (75 Emmanuel Petit), Patrick Vieira, Claude Makélélé, Sylvain Wiltord (46 Thierry Henry), Nicolas Anelka (66 David Trézéguet), Laurent Robert.
Manager: Roger Lemerre

600.   15.11.2000

TURKEY v FRANCE   0-4 (0-3)

Besiktas Jimnastik Kubülü Inönü Stadi, Istanbul

Referee: Georgios Borovilos (Greece)   Attendance: 9,000

TURKEY: Rüstü Reçber (46 Ömer Çatkiç), Bülent Korkmaz, Ogün Temizkanoglu, Emre Belözoglu (67 Ergün Penbe), Fatih Akyel, Okan Buruk (76 Tamer Tuna), Suat Kaya (46 Tayfur Havutçu), Muzzy Izzet (36 Mehmet Polat), Fatih Tekke (46 Ümit Karan), Hakan Ünsal, Ahmet Dursun.
Manager: Senol Günes

FRANCE: Fabien Barthez, Marcel Desailly, Frank Lebœuf, Lilian Thuram (78 Willy Sagnol), Vincent Candela, Patrick Vieira (31 Claude Makélélé), Emmanuel Petit (69 Martin Djétou), Zinédine Zidane (63 Frédéric Déhu), Johan Micoud, David Trézéguet (81 Steve Marlet), Sylvain Wiltord (57 Laurent Robert).   Manager: Roger Lemerre

Goals: David Trézéguet (14), Sylvain Wiltord (23), Johan Micoud (43), Laurent Robert (74).

601.   27.02.2001

FRANCE v GERMANY   1-0 (1-0)

Stade de France, Saint-Denis

Referee: Alfredo Trentalange (Italy)   Attendance: 77,929

FRANCE: Fabien Barthez, Willy Sagnol (59 Bixente Lizarazu), Marcel Desailly (76 Mikaël Silvestre), Frank Lebœuf, Vincent Candela, Emmanuel Petit, Patrick Vieira, Zinédine Zidane (83 Claude Makélélé), Christophe Dugarry, Sylvain Wiltord (54 Robert Pirès), Nicolas Anelka (59 Thierry Henry).   Manager: Roger Lemerre

GERMANY: Oliver Kahn, Christian Wörns, Jens Jeremies, Thomas Linke, Marko Rehmer (81 Torsten Frings), Dietmar Hamann (46 Oliver Neuville), Carsten Ramelow, Michael Ballack, Marco Bode (90 Christian Ziege), Mehmet Scholl, Carsten Jancker (67 Oliver Bierhoff).   Manager: Rudi Völler

Goal: Zinédine Zidane (26)

602.   24.03.2001

FRANCE v JAPAN   5-0 (2-0)

Stade de France, Saint-Denis

Referee: Dieter Schoch (Switzerland)   Attendance: 77,888

FRANCE: Ulrich Ramé, Vincent Candela, Frank Lebœuf (35 Mikaël Silvestre), Marcel Desailly, Bixente Lizarazu (81 Christian Karembeu), Sabri Lamouchi, Robert Pirès (58 Johan Micoud), Emmanuel Petit (46 Patrick Vieira), Zinédine Zidane, Christophe Dugarry (52 Sylvain Wiltord), Thierry Henry (52 David Trézéguet).   Manager: Roger Lemerre

JAPAN: Seigo Narazaki, Toshihiro Hattori (78 Koji Nakata), Naoki Matsuda, Ryuzo Morioka (72 Yuji Nakazawa), Tomokazu Myojin (46 Naohiro Takahara), Hiroshi Nanami, Hidetoshi Nakata, Shunsuke Nakamura (67 Atsuhiro Miura), Teruyoshi Ito, Akinori Nishizawa (69 Shoji Jo), Junichi Inamoto (69' Shigeyoshi Mochizuki).
Manager: Philippe Troussier

Goals: Zinédine Zidane (9 pen), Thierry Henry (13), Sylvain Wiltord (55), David Trézéguet (62, 68)

603. 28.03.2001
SPAIN v FRANCE 2-1 (1-0)

Estadio de Mestalla, Valencia

Referee: Lutz Michael Fröhlich (Germany)
Attendance: 35,500

SPAIN: José Santiago CAÑIZARES Ruiz, Fernando Ruiz HIERRO, Miguel Ángel NADAL Homar, SERGI Barjuan Esclusa, MANUEL PABLO García Díaz, IVÁN HELGUERA Bujía (63 Rubén BARAJA Vegas), Gaizka MENDIETA Zabala (88 Joseba ETXEBERRIA Lizardi), RAÚL González Blanco, Josep "PEP" GUARDIOLA i Sala, Pedro Manuel MUNITIS Álvarez (71 VICENTE Rodríguez Guillén), Fernando MORIENTES Sánchez (81 Javier "JAVI" MORENO Valera). Manager: José Antonio CAMACHO Alfaro

FRANCE: Lionel Letizi, Christian Karembeu, Mikaël Silvestre, Marcel Desailly, Bixente Lizarazu, Claude Makélélé (58 Robert Pirès), Patrick Vieira (77 David Trézéguet), Emmanuel Petit, Zinédine Zidane (62 Johan Micoud), Christophe Dugarry (46 Sylvain Wiltord), Thierry Henry. Manager: Roger Lemerre

Goals: IVÁN HELGUERA Bujía (38), Fernando MORIENTES Sánchez (47) / David Trézéguet (84)

604. 25.04.2001
FRANCE v PORTUGAL 4-0 (3-0)

Stade de France, Saint-Denis

Referee: Hellmut Heinz Krug (Germany)
Attendance: 78,832

FRANCE: Fabien Barthez, Lilian Thuram (71 Vincent Candela), Marcel Desailly, Mikaël Silvestre, Bixente Lizarazu, Robert Pirès, Patrick Vieira (62 Claude Makélélé), Emmanuel Petit (86 Willy Sagnol), Zinédine Zidane (46 Youri Djorkaeff), Sylvain Wiltord (55 David Trézéguet), Thierry Henry. Manager: Roger Lemerre

PORTUGAL: Joaquim Manuel Sampaio da Silva "QUIM", ABEL Luís da Silva Costa XAVIER (51 HÉLDER Marino Rodrigues Cristóvão), JORGE Manuel Almeida Gomes de ANDRADE, FERNANDO Manuel Silva COUTO, Fernando NÉLSON Jesus Vieira Alves, FERNANDO José da Silva Freitas MEIRA, RUI JORGE de Sousa Dias Macedo de Oliveira (36 Luís BOA MORTE Pereira, 87 NUNO "GOMES" Miguel Soares Pereira Ribeiro), RUI Fernando da Silva Calapez Pereira BENTO (43 SIMÃO Pedro Fonseca Sabrosa), SÉRGIO Paulo Marceneiro da CONCEIÇÃO, LUÍS Filipe Madeira Caeiro FIGO, Pedro Miguel Carreiro Resendes "PAULETA". Manager: ANTÓNIO Luís Alves Ribeiro OLIVEIRA

Goals: Sylvain Wiltord (16), Mikaël Silvestre (32), Thierry Henry (34), Youri Djorkaeff (80)

605. 30.05.2001   FIFA Confederations Cup 2001 – Group A
FRANCE v SOUTH KOREA 5-0 (3-0)

Daegu World Cup Stadium, Daegu (Republic of Korea)

Referee: Gamal Mahmoud Ahmed El Ghandour (Egypt)
Attendance: 61,500

FRANCE: Ulrich Ramé, Willy Sagnol, Bixente Lizarazu, Marcel Desailly, Mikaël Silvestre, Éric Carrière, Robert Pirès (84 Olivier Dacourt), Patrick Vieira, Christophe Dugarry (74 Youri Djorkaeff), Steve Marlet (67 Sylvain Wiltord), Nicolas Anelka.   Manager: Roger Lemerre

SOUTH KOREA: Lee Woon-Jae, Choi Sung-Yong, Song Jong-Gook, Hong Myung-Bo, Kim Tae-Young (76 Ha Seok-Joo), Lee Min-Sung, Yoo Sang-Cheol, Lee Young-Pyo (46 Hwang Seon-Hong), Park Ji-Sung, Ko Jong-Soo (71 Ahn Hyo-Yeon), Seol Ki-Hyun. Manager: Guus Hiddink

Goals: S. Marlet (9), Patrick Vieira (19), Nicolas Anelka (34), Youri Djorkaeff (80), Sylvain Wiltord (90+2)

606. 01.06.2001   FIFA Confederations Cup 2001 – Group A
AUSTRALIA v FRANCE 1-0 (0-0)

Daegu World Cup Stadium, Daegu (Republic of Korea)

Referee: Carlos Alberto Batrés González (Guatemala)
Attendance: 38,513

AUSTRALIA: Mark Schwarzer, Tony Vidmar, Tony Popovic, Craig Moore, Kevin Muscat, Stan Lazaridis, Josip Skoko (78 Mark Bresciano), Paul Okon, Steve Corica, Clayton Zane (87 John Aloisi), Brett Emerton. Manager: Frank Farina

FRANCE: Grégory Coupet, Zoumana Camara, Frank Lebœuf, Nicolas Gillet, Jérémie Bréchet, Christian Karembeu, Olivier Dacourt (74 Robert Pirès), Sylvain Wiltord, Youri Djorkaeff (87 Patrick Vieira), Laurent Robert, Frédéric Née (71 Nicolas Anelka).   Manager: Roger Lemerre

Goal: Clayton Zane (59)

Sent off: Frank Lebœuf (78)

607. 03.06.2001   FIFA Confederations Cup 2001
– Group A
FRANCE v MEXICO 4-0 (1-0)

Ulsan Munsu Football Stadium, Ulsan (Republic of Korea)

Referee: Ali Mohamed Bujsaim (UAE)   Attendance: 28,864

FRANCE: Mickaël Landreau, Marcel Desailly, Mikaël Silvestre, Bixente Lizarazu, Willy Sagnol, Patrick Vieira, Éric Carrière, Robert Pirès (85 Olivier Dacourt), Sylvain Wiltord (77 Youri Djorkaeff), Steve Marlet (64 Laurent Robert), Nicolas Anelka.   Manager: Roger Lemerre

MEXICO: Oswaldo Javier SÁNCHEZ Ibarra, Luis Claudio SUÁREZ Sánchez, Duilio César Jean Pierre DAVINO Rodríguez, Marco Antonio RUÍZ Garcia (64 Joaquín REYES Chávez), José David RANGEL Torres, Pável PARDO Segura, Octavio VALDÉZ Martínez, Cesáreo VICTORINO Mungaray (76 Juan Pablo RODRÍGUEZ Guerrero), Víctor RUÍZ del Valle, José Manuel ABUNDIS Sandoval, Antonio DE NIGRIS Guajardo (46 Jared Francisco BORGETTI Echavarría).   Manager: Enrique Maximiliano MEZA Salinas

Goals: Sylvain Wiltord (9), Éric Carrière (63, 84), Robert Pirès (72)

608. 07.06.2001   FIFA Confederations Cup 2001
– Semi-final
FRANCE v BRAZIL 2-1 (1-1)

Suwon World Cup Stadium, Suwon (Republic of Korea)

Referee: Gamal Mahmoud Ahmed El Ghandour (Egypt)
Attendance: 34,527

FRANCE: Ulrich Ramé, Willy Sagnol, Bixente Lizarazu, Marcel Desailly, Frank Lebœuf, Robert Pirès, Patrick Vieira, Christian Karembeu, Youri Djorkaeff (61 Éric Carrière), Sylvain Wiltord (87 Laurent Robert), Nicolas Anelka.   Manager: Roger Lemerre

BRAZIL: Nelson de Jesus da Silva "DIDA", José Marcelo Ferreira ZÉ MARIA", Lucimar da Silva Ferreira "LÚCIO", José EDMÍLSON Gomes de Moraes, Leonardo Lourenço Bastos "LÉO", LÉOMAR Leiria, FÁBIO ROCHEMBACK, RAMÓN Menezes Hubner, CARLOS MIGUEL da Silva Júnior (68 ROBERT da Silva Almeida), WASHINGTON Stécanela Cerqueira, LEANDRO Câmara do Amaral (56 Marcos André Batista dos Santos "VAMPETA").   Manager: ÉMERSON LEÃO

Goals: Robert Pirès (7), Marcel Desailly (54) /
RAMÓN Menezes Hubner (29)

609. 10.06.2001   FIFA Confederations Cup 2001
– Final
JAPAN v FRANCE 0-1 (0-1)

International Stadium, Yokohama (Japan)

Referee: Ali Mohamed Bujsaim (UAE)   Attendance: 65,335

JAPAN: Yoshikatsu Kawaguchi, Naoki Matsuda, Ryuzo Morioka, Koji Nakata, Kazuyuki Toda, Teruyoshi Ito, Shinji Ono (59 Tatsuhiko Kubo), Yasuhiro Hato, Junichi Inamoto (46 Atsuhiro Miura), Akinori Nishizawa (74 Masashi Nakayama), Hiroaki Morishima.   Manager: Philippe Troussier

FRANCE: Ulrich Ramé, Christian Karembeu, Marcel Desailly, Frank Lebœuf, Bixente Lizarazu, Patrick Vieira, Robert Pirès, Youri Djorkaeff (64 Éric Carrière), Sylvain Wiltord, Nicolas Anelka, Steve Marlet (57 Laurent Robert).
Manager: Roger Lemerre

Goal: Patrick Vieira (29)

610. 15.08.2001
FRANCE v DENMARK 1-0 (1-0)

Stade de la Beaujoire – Louis Fonteneau, Nantes

Referee: Thomas Michael (Mike) McCurry (Scotland)
Attendance: 36,548

FRANCE: Fabien Barthez, Lilian Thuram, Frank Lebœuf, Marcel Desailly, Bixente Lizarazu (81 Vincent Candela), Patrick Vieira (73 Willy Sagnol), Emmanuel Petit, Sylvain Wiltord (56 Steve Marlet), Zınédıne Zıdane, Robert Pırès (64 Johan Micoud), Thierry Henry (56 David Trézéguet).
Manager: Roger Lemerre

DENMARK: Thomas Sørensen, Stig Tøfting, René Henriksen, Martin Laursen (74 Steven Lustü), Jan Heintze, Thomas Helveg, Thomas Gravesen (46 Peter Nielsen), Jesper Grønkjær (81 Brian Steen Nielsen), Jon Dahl Tomasson (46 Jan Michaelsen), Dennis Rommedahl, Ebbe Sand (17 Marc Nygaard).   Manager: Morten Olsen

Goal: Robert Pirès (13)

611. 01.09.2001
CHILE v FRANCE 2-1 (1-0)
Estadio Nacional de Chile, Ñuñoa
Referee: Daniel Orlando Giménez (Argentina)
Attendance: 66,384
CHILE: Sergio Bernabé VARGAS Buscalia (73 Nelson Antonio TAPIA Ríos), Francisco Ulises ROJAS Rojas, Pedro Antonio REYES González, Jorge Francisco VARGAS Palacios, Mauricio Fernando AROS Bahamondes (69 Rodrigo Antonio PÉREZ Albornoz), Ricardo Francisco ROJAS Trujillo (78 Luis Alberto FUENTES Rodríguez), Pablo Manuel GALDAMES Díaz, Clarence Williams ACUÑA Donoso, Rodrigo Álvaro TELLO Valenzuela (83 Esteban Andrés VALENCIA Bascuñán), Reinaldo Marcelino NAVIA Amador (60 Cristián Antonio MONTECINOS González), Iván Luis ZAMORANO Zamora (88 Claudio Patricio NÚÑEZ Camaño).
Manager: Pedro GARCÍA Barros
FRANCE: Ulrich Ramé, Lilian Thuram (87 Willy Sagnol), Marcel Desailly (46 Frank Lebœuf), Mikaël Silvestre, Bixente Lizarazu, Patrick Vieira (63 Claude Makélélé), Emmanuel Petit, Sylvain Wiltord (46 Thierry Henry), Zinédine Zidane, Robert Pirès (69 Steve Marlet), David Trézéguet.
Manager: Roger Lemerre

Goals: Pablo Manuel GALDAMES Díaz (4), Reinaldo Marcelino NAVIA Amador (51) / David Trézéguet (74)

612. 06.10.2001
FRANCE v ALGERIA 4-1 (3-1)
Stade de France, Saint-Denis
Referee: António Manuel Perdigão Silva (Portugal)
Attendance: 78,421
FRANCE: Fabien Barthez, Lilian Thuram, Frank Lebœuf (46 Mikaël Silvestre), Marcel Desailly, Vincent Candela, Patrick Vieira, Emmanuel Petit (57 Sylvain Wiltord), Zinédine Zidane (46 Youri Djorkaeff), Robert Pirès, Thierry Henry (58 Claude Makélélé), David Trézéguet. Manager: Roger Lemerre
ALGERIA: Hichem Mezaïr, Slimane Raho, Mehdi Meniri, Mohamed Bradja, Moulay Haddou, Yazid Mansouri, Omar Belbey, Nasrédine Kraouche (56 Mounir Zeghdoud), Djamel Belmadi (53' Rafik Saïfi), Abdelhafid Tasfaout (66 Rachid Djebaili), Farid Ghazi.
Managers: Rabah Madjer & Mircea Radulescu

Goals: Vincent Candela (20), Emmanuel Petit (32), Thierry Henry (41), Robert Pirès (55) / Djamel Belmadi (45)
The match was abandoned after 75 minutes due to a pitch invasion.

613. 11.11.2001
AUSTRALIA v FRANCE 1-1 (1-0)
Melbourne Cricket Ground, Melbourne
Referee: Simon Micallef (Australia)   Attendance: 53,173
AUSTRALIA: Mark Schwarzer, Shaun Murphy, Craig Moore, Kevin Muscat (58 John Aloisi), Tony Vidmar, Brett Emerton, Josip Skoko (73 Mark Bresciano), Paul Okon, Stan Lazaridis, Harry Kewell, Mark Viduka. Manager: Frank Farina
FRANCE: Fabien Barthez, Marcel Desailly (83 Mikaël Silvestre), Frank Lebœuf, Vincent Candela, Robert Pirès, Patrick Vieira, Christian Karembeu, Zinédine Zidane (81 Alain Boghossian), Claude Makélélé (66 Éric Carrière), Christophe Dugarry (57 Sylvain Wiltord), David Trézéguet (66 Nicolas Anelka). Manager: Roger Lemerre

Goals: Craig Moore (43) / David Trézéguet (49)

614. 13.02.2002
FRANCE v ROMANIA 2-1 (2-0)
Stade de France, Saint-Denis
Referee: Dick van Egmond (Netherlands)
Attendance: 77,144
FRANCE: Ulrich Ramé, Marcel Desailly, Philippe Christanval, Lilian Thuram, Vincent Candela, Patrick Vieira (46 Alain Boghossian), Emmanuel Petit (46 Claude Makélélé), Robert Pirès, Christophe Dugarry (59 Sylvain Wiltord), Zinédine Zidane (71 Éric Carrière), Thierry Henry (71 David Trézéguet). Manager: Roger Lemerre
ROMANIA: Bogdan Lobont, Cosmin Contra (86 Flavius Stoican), Gheorghe Popescu, Cristian Chivu, Mirel Radoi, Dorinel Munteanu, Razvan Rat (46 Florin Soava), Adrian Mutu (76 Laurentiu Rosu), Tiberiu Ghioane, Viorel Moldovan (71 Daniel Pancu), Adrian Ilie (46 Ionel Ganea).
Manager: Anghel Iordanescu

Goals: Patrick Vieira (1), Emmanuel Petit (26) / Ionel Ganea (88)

615.　27.03.2002

FRANCE v SCOTLAND　5-0　(4-0)

Stade de France, Saint-Denis

Referee:　Jacek Granat (Poland)　　Attendance:　76,961

FRANCE:　Fabien Barthez, Frank Lebœuf (64 Philippe Christanval), Marcel Desailly (46 Mikaël Silvestre), Vincent Candela (57 Christian Karembeu), Bixente Lizarazu, Patrick Vieira (46 Claude Makélélé), Emmanuel Petit, Sylvain Wiltord (57 Steve Marlet), Zinédine Zidane (81 Youri Djorkaeff), Thierry Henry, David Trézéguet (74 Éric Carrière).
Manager:　Roger Lemerre

SCOTLAND:　Neil Sullivan, David Weir, Christian Dailly, Dominic Matteo, Stephen Crainey, Paul Lambert, Colin Cameron (46 Gary Holt, 73 Jackie McNamara), Stephen Crawford (63 Steven Thompson), Neil McCann, Dougie Freedman (46 Scott Gemmill), Gary Caldwell.
Manager:　Berti Vogts

Goals:　Zinédine Zidane (12), David Trézéguet (21, 42), Thierry Henry (31), Steve Marlet (88)

616.　17.04.2002

FRANCE v RUSSIA　0-0

Stade de France, Saint-Denis

Referee:　Michael Anthony (Mike) Riley (England)
Attendance:　78,294

FRANCE:　Fabien Barthez, Bixente Lizarazu (78 Vincent Candela), Marcel Desailly, Frank Lebœuf (46 Philippe Christanval), Lilian Thuram, Emmanuel Petit (61 Alain Boghossian), Patrick Vieira, Zinédine Zidane, Youri Djorkaeff (61 Steve Marlet), Thierry Henry, Nicolas Anelka (82 Johan Micoud).　Manager:　Roger Lemerre

RUSSIA:　Ruslan Nigmatullin, Vyacheslav Dayev, Viktor Onopko, Dmitriy Sennikov, Yuriy Nikiforov, Aleksey Smertin, Marat Izmaylov, Aleksandr Mostovoy, Yegor Titov, Valeriy Karpin, Vladimir Beschastnykh (66 Dmitriy Sychev).
Manager:　Oleg Romantsev

617.　18.05.2002

FRANCE v BELGIUM　1-2　(1-1)

Stade de France, Saint-Denis

Referee:　Valentin Ivanov (Russia)　　Attendance:　79,056

FRANCE:　Ulrich Ramé, Bixente Lizarazu (46 Vincent Candela), Marcel Desailly, Frank Lebœuf, Lilian Thuram (46 Willy Sagnol), Emmanuel Petit, Patrick Vieira, Youri Djorkaeff (46 Johan Micoud), Christophe Dugarry, David Trézéguet (46 Djibril Cissé), Sylvain Wiltord (80 Alain Boghossian).
Manager:　Roger Lemerre

BELGIUM:　Geert De Vlieger, Jacky Peeters (63 Eric Deflandre), Glen De Boeck, Daniel Van Buyten, Marc Wilmots, Nico Van Kerckhoven, Mbo Mpenza (46 Wesley Sonck), Johan Walem (80 Gaëtan Englebert), Timmy Simons (74 Yves Vanderhaeghe), Bart Goor (46 Danny Boffin), Gert Verheyen.
Manager:　Robert Waseige

Goals:　Timmy Simons (40 og) /
Glen De Boeck (20), Marc Wilmots (90+1)

618.　26.05.2002

SOUTH KOREA v FRANCE　2-3　(2-1)

Suwon World Cup Stadium, Suwon

Referee:　Masayochi Okada (Japan)　　Attendance:　43,000

SOUTH KOREA:　Kim Byung-Ji, Choi Jin-Cheol (63 Choi Sung-Yong), Lee Young-Pyo, Hong Myung-Bo (63 Lee Min-Sung), Song Jong-Gook, Kim Nam-Il (46 Lee Eul-Yong), Yoo Sang-Cheol, Park Ji-Sung (76 Yoon Jung-Hwan), Choi Tae-Uk, Seol Ki-Hyun, Hwang Seon-Hong (46 Choi Yong-Soo).
Manager:　Guus Hiddink

FRANCE:　Fabien Barthez, Lilian Thuram (46 Vincent Candela), Frank Lebœuf, Marcel Desailly (73 Mikaël Silvestre), Bixente Lizarazu (82 Willy Sagnol), Emmanuel Petit, Patrick Vieira (78 Claude Makélélé), Zinédine Zidane (37 Sylvain Wiltord), Youri Djorkaeff (66 Djibril Cissé), Thierry Henry (46 Christophe Dugarry), David Trézéguet.
Manager:　Roger Lemerre

Goals:　Park Ji-Sung (24), Seol Ki-Hyun (38) /
David Trézéguet (16), C. Dugarry (53), Frank Lebœuf (89)

619.　31.05.2002　FIFA World Cup Final Tournament – Group A

FRANCE v SENEGAL　0-1　(0-1)

Seoul World Cup Stadium, Seoul (Republic of Korea)

Referee:　Ali Mohamed Bujsaim (UAE)　　Attendance:　62,561

FRANCE:　Fabien Barthez, Lilian Thuram, Bixente Lizarazu, Patrick Vieira, Frank Lebœuf, Youri Djorkaeff (59 Christophe Dugarry), Marcel Desailly, Sylvain Wiltord (81 Djibril Cissé), Thierry Henry, Emmanuel Petit, David Trézéguet.
Manager:　Roger Lemerre

SENEGAL:　Tony Sylva, Omar Daf, Papa Malick Diop, Aliou Cissé, Khalilou Fadiga, El-Hadji Diouf, Lamine Diatta, Moussa N'Diaye, Salif Diao, Ferdinand Coly, Papa Bouba Diop.
Manager:　Bruno Metsu

Goal:　Papa Bouba Diop (30)

620. 06.06.2002 FIFA World Cup Final Tournament – Group A
FRANCE v URUGUAY 0-0

Asiad Main Stadium, Busan (Republic of Korea)

Referee: Felipe de Jesús Ramos Rizo (Mexico)
Attendance: 38,287

FRANCE: Fabien Barthez, Lilian Thuram, Frank Lebœuf (16 Vincent Candela), Bixente Lizarazu, Patrick Vieira, Marcel Desailly, David Trézéguet (81 Djibril Cissé), Emmanuel Petit, Sylvain Wiltord (90+3 Christophe Dugarry), Johan Micoud, Thierry Henry.   Manager: Roger Lemerre

URUGUAY: Héctor Fabián CARINI Hernández, Daniel Alejandro LEMBO Betancor, Paolo Ronald MONTERO Iglesias, Pablo Gabriel GARCÍA Pérez, Darío Octavio RODRÍGUEZ Peña (72 Gianni Bismark GUIGOU Martínez), Gustavo Antonio VARELA Rodríguez, Darío Dobray SILVA Pereira (60 Gerardo Federico MAGALLANES González), Washington Sebastián ABREU Gallo, Gonzalo SORONDO Amaro, Cléver Marcelo ROMERO Silva (71 Gonzalo DE LOS SANTOS da Rosa), Álvaro Alexandre RECOBA Rivero. Manager: Víctor Haroldo PÚA Sosa

Sent off: Thierry Henry (26)

621. 11.06.2002 FIFA World Cup Final Tournament – Group A
DENMARK v FRANCE 2-0 (1-0)

Incheon Munhak Stadium, Incheon (Republic of Korea)

Referee: Vítor Manuel Melo Pereira (Portugal)
Attendance: 48,100

DENMARK: Thomas Sørensen, Stig Tøfting (79 Brian Steen Nielsen), René Henriksen, Martin Laursen, Thomas Helveg, Thomas Gravesen, Jon Dahl Tomasson, Martin Jørgensen (46 Jesper Grønkjær), Niclas Jensen, Christian Poulsen (76 Kasper Bøgelund), Dennis Rommedahl.   Manager: Morten Olsen

FRANCE: Fabien Barthez, Lilian Thuram, Vincent Candela, Bixente Lizarazu, Sylvain Wiltord (83 Youri Djorkaeff), Claude Makélélé, Marcel Desailly, Christophe Dugarry (54 Djibril Cissé), Zinédine Zidane, David Trézéguet, Patrick Vieira (71 Johan Micoud).   Manager: Roger Lemerre

Goals: Dennis Rommedahl (22), Jon Dahl Tomasson (67)

622. 21.08.2002
TUNISIA v FRANCE 1-1 (1-1)

Stade du 7 Novembre, Radès

Referee: Cosimo Bolognino (Italy)   Attendance: 59,223

TUNISIA: Ali Boumnijel, Hatem Trabelsi, Khaled Badra, Radhi Jaïdi, Hamdi Marzouki, Jawar Mnari (58 Oussama Sellami), Hassen Gabsi (71 Imed Mhebhebi), José Clayton (71 Tarek Thabet), Slim Ben Achour, Mourad Melki (54 Lassaâd Ouertani), Ali Zitouni (73 Mohamed Selliti). Manager: Youssef Zouaoui

FRANCE: Grégory Coupet, Philippe Christanval, Vincent Candela (63 Jérémie Bréchet), Willy Sagnol (46 Emmanuel Petit), Lilian Thuram (75 Bruno Cheyrou), Mikaël Silvestre (46 Marcel Desailly), Éric Carrière (46 Patrick Vieira), Zinédine Zidane, Claude Makélélé, Thierry Henry (46 Steve Marlet), Sidney Govou (63 Djibril Cissé).   Manager: Jacques Santini

Goals: Ali Zitouni (39) / Mikaël Silvestre (19)

623. 07.09.2002 UEFA Euro 2004 Qualifying – Group 1
CYPRUS v FRANCE 1-2 (1-1)

G.S.P. Stadium, Strovolos

Referee: Herbert Fandel (Germany)   Attendance: 11,898

CYPRUS: Nikos Panayiotou, Giorgos Theodotou, Petros Konnafis, Akis Ioakim, Demetris Daskalakis (68 Michalis Michael), Panagiotis Spyrou, Kostas Kaiafas, Nikos Nikolaou (74 Marios Agathokleous), Giannis Okkas, Rainer Rauffmann (63 Giasoumis Giasoumi), Marinos Satsias. Manager: Momcilo Vukotic

FRANCE: Grégory Coupet, Philippe Christanval, Marcel Desailly, Lilian Thuram, Mikaël Silvestre, Patrick Vieira, Zinédine Zidane, Claude Makélélé, Steve Marlet (70 Sidney Govou), Sylvain Wiltord (81 Olivier Kapo), Djibril Cissé. Manager: Jacques Santini

Goals: Giannis Okkas (14) /
Djibril Cissé (39), Sylvain Wiltord (52)

624. 12.10.2002 UEFA Euro 2004 Qualifying – Group 1
FRANCE v SLOVENIA 5-0 (2-0)

Stade de France, Saint-Denis

Referee: Kim Milton Nielsen (Denmark)
Attendance: 77,619

FRANCE: Fabien Barthez, William Gallas, Marcel Desailly, Lilian Thuram (84 Willy Sagnol), Mikaël Silvestre, Patrick Vieira, Zinédine Zidane, Claude Makélélé, Thierry Henry, Steve Marlet (80 Sidney Govou), Sylvain Wiltord (87 Bruno Cheyrou).   Manager: Jacques Santini

SLOVENIA: Marko Simeunovic, Amir Karic (88 Suad Filekovic), Fabijan Cipot, Goran Sukalo, Aleksandar Radosavljevic (67 Anton Zlogar), Ermin Siljak, Zlatko Zahovic, Miran Pavlin, Sasa Gajser, Sebastjan Cimirotic (46 Nastja Ceh), Muamer Vigdalic.   Manager: Bojan Prasnikar

Goals: Patrick Vieira (10), Steve Marlet (35, 64), Sylvain Wiltord (79), Sidney Govou (86)

Sent off: Sasa Gajser (90+1)

625. 16.10.2002   UEFA Euro 2004 Qualifying – Group 1
MALTA v FRANCE   0-4 (0-2)

Ta'Qali National Stadium, Attard

Referee: Alexandru Dan Tudor (Romania)
Attendance: 9,748

MALTA: Mario Muscat, David Carabott, Darren Debono (87 Miguel Mifsud), Brian Said, Luke Dimech, Jeffrey Chetcuti, Stefan Giglio, Gilbert Agius, Joe Brincat (69 George Mallia), Chucks Nwoko (46 Daniel Bogdanovic), Michael Mifsud.   Manager: Sigfried Held

FRANCE: Fabien Barthez, William Gallas (84 Philippe Mexès), Marcel Desailly, Lilian Thuram, Mikaël Silvestre, Patrick Vieira (70 Olivier Dacourt), Zinédine Zidane, Claude Makélélé, Thierry Henry (78 Éric Carrière), Steve Marlet, Sylvain Wiltord.   Manager: Jacques Santini

Goals: Thierry Henry (25, 36), Sylvain Wiltord (59), Éric Carrière (85)

626. 20.11.2002
FRANCE v YUGOSLAVIA   3-0 (1-0)

Stade de France, Saint-Denis

Referee: Eduardo Jesús Iturralde González (Spain)
Attendance: 59,958

FRANCE: Fabien Barthez, Lilian Thuram (80 Benoît Pedretti), William Gallas, Marcel Desailly (46 Philippe Mexès), Jérémie Bréchet (14 Mikaël Silvestre), Claude Makélélé (54 Sylvain Wiltord), Emmanuel Petit, Éric Carrière (85 Ludovic Giuly), Olivier Kapo, Steve Marlet, Thierry Henry (75 Daniel Moreira).   Manager: Jacques Santini

YUGOSLAVIA: Dragoslav Jevric, Nemanja Vidic, Sinisa Mihajlovic (61 Dejan Stefanovic), Marjan Markovic, Mladen Krstajic (85 Milan Dudic), Ivica Dragutinovic, Predrag Djordjevic (51 Ognjen Koroman), Igor Duljaj (68 Goran Trobok), Dejan Stankovic (71 Branko Boskovic), Mateja Kezman, Darko Kovacevic (46 Savo Milosevic).   Manager: Dejan Savicevic

Goals: Éric Carrière (11, 49), Olivier Kapo (69)

627. 12.02.2003
FRANCE v CZECH REPUBLIC   0-2 (0-1)

Stade de France, Saint-Denis

Referee: Wolfgang Stark (Germany)   Attendance: 57,354

FRANCE: Ulrich Ramé, Lilian Thuram, William Gallas, Marcel Desailly, Bixente Lizarazu (76 Mikaël Silvestre), Claude Makélélé (46 Patrick Vieira), Emmanuel Petit (76 Benoît Pedretti), Sylvain Wiltord (46 Robert Pirès), Zinédine Zidane, Steve Marlet (46 David Trézéguet), Thierry Henry (68 Djibril Cissé).   Manager: Jacques Santini

CZECH REPUBLIC: Petr Cech, René Bolf, Tomás Ujfalusi, Marek Jankulovski (89 Adam Petrous), Karel Poborský (77 Tomás Hübschman), Tomás Galásek (73 Patrik Gedeon), Tomás Rosický (56 Richard Dostálek), Jan Koller (56 Milan Baros, 79 Vratislav Lokvenc), Vladimír Smicer (17 Stepán Vachousek), Pavel Nedved, Zdenek Grygera.
Manager: Karel Brückner

Goals: Zdenek Grygera (7), Milan Baros (61)

628. 29.03.2003   UEFA Euro 2004 Qualifying – Group 1
FRANCE v MALTA   6-0 (2-0)

Stade Félix Bollaert, Lens

Referee: Emil Bozinovski (Macedonia)   Attendance: 40,775

FRANCE: Fabien Barthez, Lilian Thuram (66 Willy Sagnol), William Gallas, Mikaël Silvestre, Bixente Lizarazu, Benoît Pedretti, Claude Makélélé, Sylvain Wiltord (74 Sidney Govou), Zinédine Zidane, David Trézéguet, Thierry Henry (81 Jérôme Rothen).   Manager: Jacques Santini

MALTA: Mario Muscat, Carlo Mamo (72 Jeffrey Chetcuti), Simon Vella, Brian Said, Ian Ciantar, Daniel Bogdanovic (61 Noel Turner), George Mallia, Luke Dimech, David Carabott, Chucks Nwoko, Michael Mifsud.   Manager: Sigfried Held

Goals: Sylvain Wiltord (37), Thierry Henry (39, 54), Zinédine Zidane (57 pen, 80), David Trézéguet (71)

629. 02.04.2003   UEFA Euro 2004 Qualifying – Group 1
ISRAEL v FRANCE   1-2 (1-2)

Stadio Renzo Barbera, Palermo (Italy)

Referee: Graham Barber (England)   Attendance: 2,455

ISRAEL: Dudu Aouate, Alon Harazi, Arik Benado, Tal Ben Haim, Adoram Keisi, Omri Afek, Tal Banin (74 Yossi Benayoun), Amir Turgeman (46 Michael Zandberg), Idan Tal (56 Walid Badir), Yossi Abukasis, Haim Revivo.
Manager: Avram Grant

FRANCE: Fabien Barthez, Lilian Thuram, William Gallas, Mikaël Silvestre, Bixente Lizarazu, Patrick Vieira, Claude Makélélé, Sylvain Wiltord (66 Sidney Govou), Zinédine Zidane, David Trézéguet (73 Djibril Cissé), Thierry Henry.
Manager: Jacques Santini

Goals: Omri Afek (2) /
David Trézéguet (23), Zinédine Zidane (45+1)

630. 30.04.2003

FRANCE v EGYPT 5-0 (3-0)

Stade de France, Saint-Denis

Referee: Massimo Busacca (Switzerland)
Attendance: 54,554

FRANCE: Fabien Barthez, Bixente Lizarazu, William Gallas, Olivier Dacourt, Robert Pirès (66 Jérôme Rothen), Marcel Desailly (74 Philippe Mexès), Willy Sagnol, Djibril Cissé (81 Mikaël Silvestre), Sylvain Wiltord (71 Daniel Moreira), Thierry Henry (57 Olivier Kapo), Benoît Pedretti.
Manager: Jacques Santini

EGYPT: Ahmed Fathi Essam El Hadary, Ahmed Fathi, Abdel Zaher El Sakka, Beshir El Tabei, Tarek El Sayed (72 Tarek El Said), Ahmed Hassan, Hossam Ghaly (75 Hazem Emam), Ayman Abd El Aziz, Hany Saïd, Ahmed Hossam, Gamal Hamza (46 Mohamed Gouda).   Manager: Mohsen Saleh

Goals: Thierry Henry (25, 34), Robert Pirès (45+1), Djibril Cissé (62), Oliver Kapo (78)

631. 18.06.2003   FIFA Confederations Cup 2003 – Group A

FRANCE v COLOMBIA 1-0 (1-0)

Stade de Gerland, Lyon (France)

Referee: Lucílio Cardoso Cortez Batista (Portugal)
Attendance: 38,541

FRANCE: Grégory Coupet, Bixente Lizarazu, Philippe Mexès, Marcel Desailly, Lilian Thuram, Olivier Dacourt, Benoît Pedretti, Olivier Kapo (61 Robert Pirès), Sylvain Wiltord, Djibril Cissé (77 Sidney Govou), Thierry Henry (84 Steve Marlet).   Manager: Jacques Santini

COLOMBIA: Óscar Eduardo CÓRDOBA Arce, Gonzalo MARTÍNEZ Caicedo (90+3 Gerardo Enrique VALLEJO Matute), Mario Alberto YEPES Díaz, Iván Ramiro CÓRDOBA Sepúlveda, Gerardo Alberto BEDOYA Múnera, Giovanni Andrés HERNÁNDEZ Soto, Rubén Darío VELÁSQUEZ Bermúdez, Jorge Enrique LÓPEZ Caballero, Jairo Leonard PATIÑO Rosero (66 Eudalio Eulises ARRIAGA Blandón), Víctor Hugo ARISTIZÁBAL Posada, Elson Evelio BECERRA Vaca.   Manager: Francisco MATURANA García

Goal: Thierry Henry (39 pen)

632. 20.06.2003   FIFA Confederations Cup 2003 – Group A

FRANCE v JAPAN 2-1 (1-0)

Stade Geoffroy Guichard, Saint-Étienne (France)

Referee: Mark Alexander Shield (Australia)
Attendance: 33,070

FRANCE: Fabien Barthez, Jean-Alain Boumsong, William Gallas, Olivier Dacourt (58 Benoît Pedretti), Robert Pirès, Mikaël Silvestre, Jérôme Rothen (67 Sylvain Wiltord), Willy Sagnol, Steve Marlet (80 Thierry Henry), Ousmane Dabo, Sidney Govou.   Manager: Jacques Santini

JAPAN: Seigo Narazaki, Junichi Inamoto (73 Koji Nakata), Hidetoshi Nakata, Yoshito Okubo, Shunsuke Nakamura (80 Mitsuo Ogasawara), Alessandro Santos "ALEX", Tsuneyasu Miyamoto, Yasuhito Endo, Naohiro Takahara, Keisuke Tsuboi, Nobuhisa Yamada.
Manager: Arthur Antunes Coimbra "ZICO"

Goals: Robert Pirès (42 pen), Sidney Govou (66) / Shunsuke Nakamura (59)

Sent off: Willy Sagnol (90+1)

633. 22.06.2003   FIFA Confederations Cup 2003 – Group A

FRANCE v NEW ZEALAND 5-0 (2-0)

Stade de France, Saint-Denis (France)

Referee: Masoud Moradi (Iran)   Attendance: 36,842

FRANCE: Mickaël Landreau, Philippe Mexès, Bixente Lizarazu, Marcel Desailly, Lilian Thuram, Ludovic Giuly, Sylvain Wiltord (76 Robert Pirès), Olivier Kapo, Benoît Pedretti (68 Ousmane Dabo), Thierry Henry (74 Steve Marlet), Djibril Cissé.   Manager: Jacques Santini

NEW ZEALAND: Michael Utting, Chris Zoricich (73 Duncan Oughton), Daniel Hay (81 Scott Smith), Ryan Nelsen, Gerard Davis, Raffaele De Gregorio, Simon Elliott, Mark Burton (69' Chris Jackson), Noah Hickey, Vaughan Coveny, Chris Bouckenooghe.   Manager: Mick Waitt

Goals: O. Kapo (17), Thierry Henry (20), Djibril Cissé (71), Ludovic Giuly (90+2), Robert Pirès (90+4)

634. 26.06.2003 FIFA Confederations Cup 2003 – Semi-final

FRANCE v TURKEY 3-2 (3-1)

Stade de France, Saint-Denis (France)

Referee: Jorge Luis Larrionda Pietrafesa (Uruguay)
Attendance: 41,195

FRANCE: Grégory Coupet, William Gallas, Lilian Thuram, Benoît Pedretti, Olivier Dacourt, Robert Pirès (69 Olivier Kapo), Marcel Desailly, Sylvain Wiltord (77 Ludovic Giuly), Thierry Henry, Mikaël Silvestre, Sidney Govou (66 Djibril Cissé). Manager: Jacques Santini

TURKEY: Rüstü Reçber (36 Ömer Çatkiç), Ibrahim Üzülmez, Bülent Korkmaz, Fatih Akyel, Alpay Özalan, Ergün Penbe, Gökdeniz Karadeniz, Selçuk Sahin (85 Volkan Arslan), Yildiray Bastürk (81 Necati Ates), Okan Yilmaz, Tuncay Sanli. Manager: Senol Günes

Goals: Thierry Henry (11), Robert Pirès (26), S. Wiltord (43) / Gökdeniz Karadeniz (42), Tuncay Sanli (48)

635. 29.06.2003 FIFA Confederations Cup 2003 – Final

CAMEROON v FRANCE 0-1 (0-0, 0-0) (AET)

Stade de France, Saint-Denis (France)

Referee: Valentin Valentinovich Ivanov (Russia)
Attendance: 51,985

CAMEROON: Idriss Carlos Kameni, Jean-Joël Perrier-Doumbé, Lucien Mettomo, Rigobert Song, Thimothée Atouba, Geremi Njitap, Eric Djemba-Djemba, Valéry Mézague (91 Achille Emaná), Modeste M'Bami, Pius N'Diefi (67 Samuel Eto'o), Mohamadou Idrissou. Manager: Winfried Schäfer

FRANCE: Fabien Barthez, Willy Sagnol (76 Lilian Thuram), William Gallas, Marcel Desailly, Bixente Lizarazu, Ludovic Giuly, Benoît Pedretti, Olivier Dacourt (90 Olivier Kapo), Sylvain Wiltord (65 Robert Pirès), Djibril Cissé, Thierry Henry. Manager: Jacques Santini

Goal: Thierry Henry (97 Golden goal)

636. 20.08.2003

SWITZERLAND v FRANCE 0-2 (0-1)

Stade de Genève, Lancy

Referee: Paul Allaerts (Belgium)   Attendance: 30,000

SWITZERLAND: Jörg Stiel (46 Pascal Zuberbühler), Rémo Meyer, Stéphane Henchoz, Murat Yakin (46 Marco Zwyssig), Bruno Berner, Fabio Celestini (77 Raphaël Wicky), Johann Vogel (86 Mario Cantaluppi), Patrick Müller (77 Benjamin Huggel), Ricardo Cabanas, Alexander Frei, Stéphane Chapuisat (46 Milaim Rama). Manager: Jakob (Köbi) Kuhn

FRANCE: Fabien Barthez, Lilian Thuram (61 Willy Sagnol), Marcel Desailly (77 Jean-Alain Boumsong), Mikaël Silvestre, Bixente Lizarazu, Sylvain Wiltord (70 Djibril Cissé), Patrick Vieira (46 Benoît Pedretti), Olivier Dacourt (84 Ousmane Dabo), Zinédine Zidane (70 Ludovic Giuly), David Trézéguet (61 Robert Pirès), Thierry Henry (46 Steve Marlet). Manager: Jacques Santini

Goals: Sylvain Wiltord (12), Steve Marlet (54)

637. 06.09.2003 UEFA Euro 2004 Qualifying – Group 1

FRANCE v CYPRUS 5-0 (3-0)

Stade de France, Saint-Denis

Referee: Leslie John Irvine (Northern Ireland)
Attendance: 50,132

FRANCE: Fabien Barthez, Lilian Thuram (65 Willy Sagnol), Marcel Desailly, Mikaël Silvestre, Bixente Lizarazu, Patrick Vieira (71 Olivier Dacourt), Claude Makélélé, Robert Pirès, Sylvain Wiltord, Thierry Henry (78 Steve Marlet), David Trézéguet. Manager: Jacques Santini

CYPRUS: Nikos Panayiotou, Nikos Nikolaou, Giorgos Theodotou, Nicolas Georgiou, Petros Konnafis (46 Akis Ioakim), Stelios Okkaridis, Marinos Satsias, Kostas Kaiafas, Panayiotis Engomitis (59 Michalis Michael), Giannis Okkas, Michalis Konstantinou (67 Giasoumis Giasoumi). Manager: Momcilo Vukotic

Goals: David Trézéguet (7, 80), Sylvain Wiltord (19, 40), Thierry Henry (59)

638. 10.09.2003 UEFA Euro 2004 Qualifying – Group 1

SLOVENIA v FRANCE 0-2 (0-1)

Centralni Stadion Bezigrad, Ljubljana

Referee: Domenico Messina (Italy)   Attendance: 8,500

SLOVENIA: Marko Simeunovic, Fabijan Cipot, Amir Karic, Muamer Vugdalic (83 Matej Snofl), Aleksander Knavs, Goran Sukalo (55 Adem Kapic), Nastja Ceh, Ermin Siljak, Zlatko Zahovic (65 Sebastjan Cimirotic), Miran Pavlin, Milenko Acimovic. Manager: Bojan Prasnikar

FRANCE: Fabien Barthez, Bixente Lizarazu, Marcel Desailly, Mikaël Silvestre, Lilian Thuram, Claude Makélélé, Patrick Vieira, Sylvain Wiltord (76 Willy Sagnol), Zinédine Zidane (79 Robert Pirès), Thierry Henry, David Trézéguet (69 Olivier Dacourt). Manager: Jacques Santini

Goals: David Trézéguet (10), Olivier Dacourt (71)
Sent off: Claude Makélélé (67)

639. 11.10.2003   UEFA Euro 2004 Qualifying – Group 1
FRANCE v ISRAEL 3-0 (3-0)
Stade de France, Saint-Denis

Referee: Cosimo Bolognino (Italy)   Attendance: 57,009

FRANCE: Fabien Barthez, Bixente Lizarazu, Jean-Alain Boumsong, Lilian Thuram, Anthony Réveillère, Olivier Dacourt, Benoît Pedretti, Robert Pirès (85 Ludovic Giuly), Zinédine Zidane, Thierry Henry (77 Djibril Cissé), David Trézéguet (85 Steve Marlet).   Manager: Jacques Santini

ISRAEL: Nir Davidovich, Alon Harazi, Arik Benado, Shimon Gershon, Adoram Keisi, Walid Badir (76 Kfir Udi), Oren Zeitouni (89 Pini Balili), Michael Zandberg (46 Yossi Abukasis), Yossi Benayoun, Idan Tal, Haim Revivo. Manager: Avram Grant

Goals: Thierry Henry (9), David Trézéguet (24), Jean-Alain Boumsong (43)

640.   15.11.2003
GERMANY v FRANCE 0-3 (0-1)
Arena AufSchalke, Gelsenkirchen

Referee: Stefano Farina (Italy)   Attendance: 53,574

GERMANY: Oliver Kahn, Arne Friedrich, Jens Nowotny (76 Marko Rehmer), Christian Wörns, Andreas Hinkel, Frank Baumann (71 Fabian Ernst), Jens Jeremies, Bernd Schneider (67 Paul Freier), Michael Ballack, Fredi Bobic (67 Miroslav Klose), Kevin Kurányi.   Manager: Rudi Völler

FRANCE: Grégory Coupet, Willy Sagnol (61 William Gallas), Lilian Thuram, Mikaël Silvestre, Bixente Lizarazu, Olivier Dacourt, Claude Makélélé, Zinédine Zidane, Robert Pirès (73 Sylvain Wiltord), Thierry Henry, David Trézéguet (81 Sidney Govou).   Manager: Jacques Santini

Goals: Thierry Henry (21), David Trézéguet (55, 81)

641.   18.02.2004
BELGIUM v FRANCE 0-2 (0-1)
Stade Roi Baudouin, Brussels

Referee: Mark Halsey (England)   Attendance: 43,160

BELGIUM: Geert De Vlieger (46 Frédéric Herpoel), Eric Deflandre (85 Olivier De Cock), Vincent Kompany, Timmy Simons, Jelle Van Damme, Mbo Mpenza (69 Émile Mpenza), Philippe Clement, Walter Baseggio (85 Roberto Bisconti), Peter Van der Heyden (54 Tom Soetaers), Thomas Buffel (85 Thomas Chatelle), Wesley Sonck (88 Luigi Pieroni). Manager: Aimé Anthuenis

FRANCE: Fabien Barthez, Mikaël Silvestre (46 Bixente Lizarazu), Marcel Desailly, Lilian Thuram, William Gallas (85 Jean-Alain Boumsong), Olivier Dacourt (18 Claude Makélélé), Patrick Vieira (62 Jérôme Rothen), Zinédine Zidane (77 Olivier Kapo), Sidney Govou (46 Robert Pirès), Louis Saha (85 Philippe Mexès), Péguy Luyindula (62 Steve Marlet). Manager: Jacques Santini

Goals: Sidney Govou (45+1), Louis Saha (76)

642.   31.03.2004
NETHERLANDS v FRANCE 0-0
De Kuip, Rotterdam

Referee: Wolfgang Stark (Germany)   Attendance: 47,000

NETHERLANDS: Edwin van der Sar, Mario Melchiot, John Heitinga, Phillip Cocu, Boudewijn Zenden, Andy van der Meijde (89 Paul Bosvelt), Mark van Bommel (46 Wesley Sneijder), Edgar Davids, Rafael van der Vaart (67 Nigel de Jong), Marc Overmars, Roy Makaay (67 Pierre van Hooijdonk)   Manager: Dick Advocaat

FRANCE: Fabien Barthez, Willy Sagnol, Lilian Thuram (69 William Gallas), Marcel Desailly, Bixente Lizarazu (58 Mikaël Silvestre), Claude Makélélé (58 Benoît Pedretti), Olivier Dacourt, Ludovic Giuly (46 Bruno Cheyrou), Johan Micoud, Sidney Govou (46 Thierry Henry), David Trézéguet (69 Péguy Luyindula).   Manager: Jacques Santini

643.   20.05.2004   FIFA 100th Anniversary Match
FRANCE v BRAZIL 0-0
Stade de France, Saint-Denis

Referee: Manuel Enrique Mejuto González (Spain)   Attendance: 79,334

FRANCE: Grégory Coupet, William Gallas, Jean-Alain Boumsong, Marcel Desailly (46 Bernard Mendy), Lilian Thuram, Robert Pirès (46 Sylvain Wiltord), Patrick Vieira, Zinédine Zidane (68 Olivier Kapo), Claude Makélélé, Thierry Henry, David Trézéguet.   Manager: Jacques Santini

BRAZIL: Nelson de Jesus da Silva "DIDA", Marcos Evangelista de Moraes "CAFÚ", Ânderson Luiz da Silva "LUISÃO", Cristiano Marques Gomes "CRIS", ROBERTO CARLOS da Silva, José EDMÍLSON Gomes de Moraes, Antônio Augusto Ribeiro Reis Júnior "JUNINHO PERNAMBUCANO" (80 JÚLIO César BAPTISTA), Ricardo Izecson Santos Leite "KAKÁ" (46 Alexsandro de Souza "ALEX"), José "ZÉ" ROBERTO da Silva Júnior (46 Eduardo César Daudi Gaspar "EDU DRACENA"), Ronaldo de Assis Moreira "RONALDINHO GAÚCHU", RONALDO Luís Nazário de Lima.   Manager: CARLOS ALBERTO Gomes PARREIRA

644.   28.05.2004
FRANCE v ANDORRA   4-0 (1-0)

Stade de la Mosson, Montpellier

Referee: Mourad Daami (Tunisia)   Attendance: 27,753

FRANCE: Grégory Coupet, Willy Sagnol, William Gallas, Marcel Desailly (70 Lilian Thuram), Mikaël Silvestre, Patrick Vieira (46 Bixente Lizarazu), Benoît Pedretti, Sylvain Wiltord, Louis Saha (70 David Trézéguet), Steve Marlet (79 Jean-Alain Boumsong), Robert Pirès.   Manager: Jacques Santini

ANDORRA: Jesús Luis Álvarez de Eulate Güergue "KOLDO", Francesc Javier RAMÍREZ Palomo (86 JORDI ESCURA Aixas), José Manuel García Luena "TXEMA", Julià "JULI" FERNÁNDEZ Ariza (75 Manuel "MANOLO" JIMÉNEZ Soria), Antoni "TONI" LIMA Solá (90+3 ALEX RODRÍGUEZ Medina), ILDEFONS LIMA Solà, ANTONI Miguel SIVERA Peris, MARC PUJOL Pons (90 GENÍS GARCÍA Iscla), Julià "JULI" SÁNCHEZ Soto (81 Gabriel "GABI" RIERA Lancha), JOSEP Manel AYALA Díaz (57 ROBERTO JONÁS Alonso Martínez), JUSTO RUÍZ González (65 ÓSCAR SONEJEE Masand).   Manager: DAVID RODRIGO Lo

Goals: Sylvain Wiltord (44, 55), Louis Saha (68), Steve Marlet (74)

645.   06.06.2004
FRANCE v UKRAINE   1-0 (0-0)

Stade de France, Saint-Denis

Referee: Darko Ceferin (Slovenia)   Attendance: 66,646

FRANCE: Fabien Barthez, William Gallas (76 Willy Sagnol), Lilian Thuram, Mikaël Silvestre, Bixente Lizarazu, Claude Makélélé (83 Benoît Pedretti), Patrick Vieira, Robert Pirès (83 Sylvain Wiltord), Zinédine Zidane, Louis Saha (76 Steve Marlet), Thierry Henry.   Manager: Jacques Santini

UKRAINE: Oleksandr Shovkovskiy, Mykhaylo Starostyak (71 Ruslan Bidnenko), Andriy Rusol, Sergey Fedorov (78 Vyacheslav Checher), Volodymyr Yezerskyi, Andriy Nesmachniy, Anatoliy Tymoshchuk (90 Oleh Venhlinskyi), Oleh Shelayev, Oleh Husyev (61 Serhiy Rebrov), Ruslan Rotan (84 Serhiy Nazarenko), Andriy Vorobey (69 Oleksandr Kosyrin).   Manager: Oleg Blokhin

Goal: Zinédine Zidane (88)

646.   13.06.2004   UEFA European Championship – Group B
FRANCE v ENGLAND   2-1 (0-1)

Estádio do Sport Lisboa e Benfica, Lisboa (Portugal)

Referee: Dr. Markus Merk (Germany)   Attendance: 62,487

FRANCE: Fabien Barthez, Bixente Lizarazu, Mikaël Silvestre (79 Willy Sagnol), Lilian Thuram, William Gallas, Claude Makélélé (90+4 Olivier Dacourt), Patrick Vieira, Robert Pirès (76 Sylvain Wiltord), Zinédine Zidane, David Trézéguet, Thierry Henry.   Manager: Jacques Santini

ENGLAND: David James, Gary Neville, Ashley Cole, Steven Gerrard, Ledley King, Sol Campbell, David Beckham, Paul Scholes (76 Emile Heskey), Wayne Rooney (76 Owen Hargreaves), Michael Owen (69 Darius Vassell), Frank Lampard.   Manager: Sven-Göran Eriksson

Goals: Zinédine Zidane (90+1, 90+3 pen) / Frank Lampard (38)

David Beckham missed a penalty kick (72)

647.   17.06.2004   UEFA European Championship – Group B
CROATIA v FRANCE   2-2 (0-1)

Estádio Dr. Magalhães Pessoa, Leiria (Portugal)

Referee: Kim Milton Nielsen (Denmark)   Attendance: 29,160

CROATIA: Tomislav Butina, Dario Simic, Robert Kovac, Igor Tudor, Josip Simunic, Nenad Bjelica (68 Jerko Leko), Niko Kovac, Djovani Roso, Milan Rapaic (86 Ivica Mornar), Dado Prso, Tomo Sokota (72 Ivica Olic).   Manager: Otto Baric

FRANCE: Fabien Barthez, William Gallas (81 Willy Sagnol), Marcel Desailly, Lilian Thuram, Mikaël Silvestre, Olivier Dacourt (79 Benoît Pedretti), Patrick Vieira, Zinédine Zidane, Sylvain Wiltord (70 Robert Pirès), David Trézéguet, Thierry Henry.   Manager: Jacques Santini

Goals: Milan Rapaic (49 pen), Dado Prso (54) / Igor Tudor (22 og), David Trézéguet (64)

648.   21.06.2004   UEFA European Championship – Group B
SWITZERLAND v FRANCE   1-3 (1-1)

Estádio Cidade de Coimbra, Coimbra (Portugal)

Referee: Lubos Michel (Slovakia)   Attendance: 28,111

SWITZERLAND: Jörg Stiel, Stéphane Henchoz (86 Ludovic Magnin), Murat Yakin, Patrick Müller, Christoph Spycher, Ricardo Cabanas, Johann Vogel, Raphaël Wicky, Daniel Gygax (86 Milaim Rama), Hakan Yakin (60 Benjamin Huggel), Johan Vonlanthen.   Manager: Jakob (Köbi) Kuhn

FRANCE: Fabien Barthez, Willy Sagnol (46 William Gallas, 90+2 Jean-Alain Boumsong), Lilian Thuram, Mikaël Silvestre, Bixente Lizarazu, Claude Makélélé, Patrick Vieira, Robert Pirès, Zinédine Zidane, David Trézéguet (75 Louis Saha), Thierry Henry.   Manager: Jacques Santini

Goals: Johan Vonlanthen (26) / Zinédine Zidane (20), Thierry Henry (76, 84)

649. 25.06.2004 UEFA European Championship – Quarter-final
FRANCE v GREECE 0-1 (0-0)
Estádio José Alvalade, Lisboa

Referee: Anders Frisk (Sweden)   Attendance: 45,390

FRANCE: Fabien Barthez, William Gallas, Mikaël Silvestre, Lilian Thuram, Bixente Lizarazu, Claude Makélélé, Olivier Dacourt (72 Sylvain Wiltord), Robert Pirès (79 Jérôme Rothen), Zinédine Zidane, Thierry Henry, David Trézéguet (72 Louis Saha).   Manager: Jacques Santini

GREECE: Antonis Nikopolidis, Giourkas Seitaridis, Panagiotis Fyssas, Traianos Dellas, Michalis Kapsis, Kostas Katsouranis, Angelos Basinas (84 Vasilios Tsiartas), Theodoros Zagorakis, Giorgios Karagounis, Demis Nikolaidis (61 Vasilios Lakis), Angelos Charisteas.   Manager: Otto Rehhagel

Goal: Angelos Charisteas (65)

650. 18.08.2004
FRANCE v BOSNIA & HERZEGOVINA 1-1 (1-1)
Stade de la Route de Lorient, Rennes

Referee: Douglas (Dougie) McDonald (Scotland)
Attendance: 26,527

FRANCE: Fabien Barthez, William Gallas, Sébastien Squillaci (46 Gaël Givet), Éric Abidal, Bernard Mendy, Rio Mavuba (46 Sidney Govou), Benoît Pedretti, Patrice Évra (46 Robert Pirès), Péguy Luyindula, Thierry Henry (46 Djibril Cissé), Jérôme Rothen.   Manager: Raymond Domenech

BOSNIA & HERZEGOVINA: Kenan Hasagic, Hasan Salihamidzic, Branimir Bajic, Sasa Papac, Nermin Sabic (46 Emir Spahic), Zlatan Bajramovic (59 Vladan Grujic), Ivica Grlic, Mirsad Beslija, Elvir Bolic (23 Zvjezdan Misimovic), Sergej Barbarez (46 Asim Sehic), Elvir Baljic (90+1 Gradimir Crnogorac).   Manager: Blaz Sliskovic

Goals: Péguy Luyindula (7) / Ivica Grlic (37)

Thierry Henry missed a penalty kick (18)

651. 04.09.2004 FIFA World Cup Qualification – Group 4
FRANCE v ISRAEL 0-0
Stade de France, Saint-Denis

Referee: Renatus Hendrikus Johannes (René) Temmink (Netherlands)   Attendance: 43,526

FRANCE: Grégory Coupet, Gaël Givet, Sébastien Squillaci, William Gallas, Patrice Évra, Bernard Mendy (57 Ludovic Giuly), Claude Makélélé, Patrick Vieira, Jérôme Rothen (66 Robert Pirès), Louis Saha, Thierry Henry.
Manager: Raymond Domenech

ISRAEL: Nir Davidovich, Omri Afek (71 Ravid Gazal), Tal Ben Haim, Klemi Saban, Arik Benado, Yigal Antebi (13 Adoram Keisi), Walid Badir, Idan Tal, Yaniv Katan, Yossi Benayoun (80 Avi Nimni), Omer Galan.
Manager: Avram Grant

652. 08.09.2004 FIFA World Cup Qualification – Group 4
FAROE ISLANDS v FRANCE 0-2 (0-1)
Tórsvøllur, Tórshavn

Referee: Craig Alexander Thomson (Scotland)   Att: 5,917

FAROE ISLANDS: Jákup Mikkelsen, Súni Olsen, Pól Thorsteinsson, Jón Rói Jacobsen, Óli Johannesen, Rógvi Jacobsen (75 Andrew av Fløtum), Julian Johnsson, Claus Bech Jørgensen (82 Atli Danielsen), Fródi Benjaminsen, Jákup á Borg, Jónhard Frederiksberg (68 John Petersen).   Manager: Henrik Larsen

FRANCE: Grégory Coupet, Patrice Évra, Gaël Givet, Sébastien Squillaci, William Gallas, Benoît Pedretti, Patrick Vieira, Robert Pirès, Ludovic Giuly, Thierry Henry (64 Vikash Dhorasoo), Louis Saha (9 Djibril Cissé).
Manager: Raymond Domenech

Goals: Ludovic Giuly (32), Djibril Cissé (73)

Sent off: Patrick Vieira (65)

653. 09.10.2004 FIFA World Cup Qualification – Group 4
FRANCE v REPUBLIC OF IRELAND 0-0
Stade de France, Saint-Denis

Referee: Arturo Daudén Ibáñez (Spain)   Attendance: 78,863

FRANCE: Fabien Barthez, Mikaël Silvestre, Gaël Givet, Sébastien Squillaci, William Gallas, Olivier Dacourt (64 Alou Diarra), Rio Mavuba, Robert Pirès, Sylvain Wiltord, Djibril Cissé (82 Sidney Govou), Thierry Henry.
Manager: Raymond Domenech

REPUBLIC OF IRELAND: Shay Given, Andy O'Brien, Steve Finnan, John O'Shea, Stephen Carr, Kenny Cunningham, Kevin Kilbane, Roy Keane, Damien Duff, Clinton Morrison (40 Andy Reid), Robbie Keane.   Manager: Brian Kerr

654. 13.10.2004 FIFA World Cup Qualification – Group 4
CYPRUS v FRANCE 0-2 (0-1)
G.S.P. Stadium, Strovolos

Referee: Claus Bo Larsen (Denmark)   Attendance: 3,319

CYPRUS: Nikos Panayiotou, Loizos Kakoyiannis, Marinos Satsias, Marios Elia, Stelios Okkaridis, Stavros Georgiou (82 Giasoumis Giasoumi), Elias Charalambous, Nikos Nikolaou (76 Lambros Lambrou), Kostas Charalambidis (56 Konstantinos Makridis), Giannis Okkas, Michalis Konstantinou.   Manager: Momcilo Vukotic

FRANCE: Fabien Barthez, Mikaël Silvestre, Gaël Givet, Sébastien Squillaci, William Gallas, Patrick Vieira, Olivier Dacourt (90+1 Alou Diarra), Robert Pirès (46 Daniel Moreira), Sylvain Wiltord, Thierry Henry, Péguy Luyindula (66 Patrice Évra).   Manager: Raymond Domenech

Goals: Sylvain Wiltord (38), Thierry Henry (72)

655.   17.11.2004
FRANCE v POLAND 0-0
Stade de France, Saint-Denis
Referee: Olegário Manuel Bártolo Faustino Benquerença (Portugal)   Attendance: 50,480
FRANCE: Mickaël Landreau, Willy Sagnol, Sébastien Squillaci (46 Gaël Givet), Jean-Alain Boumsong, William Gallas, Benoît Pedretti, Patrick Vieira, Florent Malouda (46 Patrice Évra), Ludovic Giuly (26 Sidney Govou), Thierry Henry, Louis Saha (65 Camel Meriem).
Manager: Raymond Domenech
POLAND: Jerzy Dudek, Marcin Baszczynski, Tomasz Hajto (46 Tomasz Klos), Jacek Bak, Tomasz Rzasa (56 Michal Zewlakow), Kamil Kosowski (90 Damian Gorawski), Radoslaw Kaluzny, Miroslaw Szymkowiak (66 Sebastian Mila), Jacek Krzynówek (90+2 Arkadiusz Radomski), Maciej Zurawski, Tomasz Frankowski (82 Grzegorz Rasiak).
Manager: Pawel Janas

656.   09.02.2005
FRANCE v SWEDEN 1-1 (1-1)
Stade de France, Saint-Denis
Referee: Julián Rodríguez Santiago (Spain)   Att: 56,923
FRANCE: Grégory Coupet, Jonathan Zebina (68 Éric Abidal), Sébastien Squillaci, Gaël Givet, William Gallas, Patrick Vieira, Benoît Pedretti, Vikash Dhorasoo, Ludovic Giuly (68 Camel Meriem), Thierry Henry, David Trézéguet.
Manager: Raymond Domenech
SWEDEN: Andreas Isaksson, Alexander Östlund, Olof Mellberg, Teddy Lucic (76 Petter Hansson), Erik Edman, Tobias Linderoth (76 Daniel Andersson), Christian Wilhelmsson (87 Anders Andersson), Anders Svensson, Fredrik Ljungberg (46 Niclas Alexandersson), Marcus Allbäck (63 Kim Källström), Markus Rosenberg.
Manager: Lars Lagerbäck
Goals: David Trézéguet (36) / Fredrik Ljungberg (11)

657.   26.03.2005   FIFA World Cup Qualification – Group 4
FRANCE v SWITZERLAND 0-0
Stade de France, Saint-Denis
Referee: Massimo De Santis (Italy)   Attendance: 79,373
FRANCE: Fabien Barthez, Willy Sagnol, Jean-Alain Boumsong, Gaël Givet, William Gallas, Benoît Pedretti, Patrick Vieira, Vikash Dhorasoo (59 Camel Meriem), Ludovic Giuly, David Trézéguet, Sylvain Wiltord (82 Sidney Govou).
Manager: Raymond Domenech
SWITZERLAND: Pascal Zuberbühler, Philipp Degen, Philippe Senderos, Patrick Müller, Christoph Spycher, Daniel Gygax (90+2 Stéphane Henchoz), Johann Lonfat (29 Benjamin Huggel), Johann Vogel, Reto Ziegler (69 Ludovic Magnin), Ricardo Cabanas, Alexander Frei.
Manager: Jakob (Köbi) Kuhn

658.   30.03.2005   FIFA World Cup Qualification – Group 4
ISRAEL v FRANCE 1-1 (0-0)
National Stadium, Ramat Gan
Referee: Dr. Markus Merk (Germany)   Attendance: 32,150
ISRAEL: Dudu Aouate, Klemi Saban, Shimon Gershon, Tal Ben Haim, Adoram Keisi, Walid Badir, Avi Nimni, Idan Tal (67 Omri Afek), Yossi Benayoun, Pini Balili, Yaniv Katan.
Manager: Avram Grant
FRANCE: Fabien Barthez, William Gallas, Gaël Givet, Jean-Alain Boumsong, Willy Sagnol, Alou Diarra, Patrick Vieira, Benoît Pedretti, Florent Malouda, Sylvain Wiltord (90+2 Vikash Dhorasoo), David Trézéguet.
Manager: Raymond Domenech
Goals: Walid Badir (83) / David Trézéguet (50)
Sent off: David Trézéguet (56)

659.   31.05.2005
FRANCE v HUNGARY 2-1 (2-0)
Stade Municipal Saint-Symphorien, Metz
Referee: Paul Allaerts (Belgium)   Attendance: 26,186
FRANCE: Grégory Coupet, Anthony Réveillère, William Gallas (82 Sébastien Squillaci), Jean-Alain Boumsong, Éric Abidal, Vikash Dhorasoo (65 Rio Mavuba), Benoît Pedretti, Jérôme Rothen, Sylvain Wiltord (59 Sidney Govou), Florent Malouda, Djibril Cissé (75 Ludovic Giuly).
Manager: Raymond Domenech
HUNGARY: Gábor Király (46 Márton Fülöp), László Bodnár, Zoltán Balog, Péter Stark, Vilmos Vanczák, Zoltán Gera (46 Ákos Takács), Gábor Vincze (46 Norbert Tóth), Tamás Hajnal, Szabolcs Huszti, Ottó Vincze (46 Zsolt Bárányos), Imre Szabics (46 Zsombor Kerekes).   Manager: Lothar Matthäus
Goals: Djibril Cissé (10), Florent Malouda (35) / Zsombor Kerekes (78)

660.   17.08.2005
FRANCE v IVORY COAST 3-0 (1-0)
Stade de la Mosson, Montpellier
Referee: Paolo Bertini (Italy)   Attendance: 31,457
FRANCE: Grégory Coupet, Willy Sagnol, Jean-Alain Boumsong, Lilian Thuram (23 Sébastien Squillaci), William Gallas, Claude Makélélé (89 Alou Diarra), Vikash Dhorasoo, Sylvain Wiltord (80 David Trézéguet), Florent Malouda (71 Jérôme Rothen, Zinédine Zidane, Thierry Henry (71 Djibril Cissé).   Manager: Raymond Domenech
IVORY COAST: Jean-Jacques Tizié, Marc Kpolo Zoro (46 Emmanuel Eboué), Cyril Domoraud, Kolo Touré, Arthur Boka, Didier Zokora (70 Guy Demel), Gilles Yapi-Yapo, Bonaventura Kalou (46 Ndri Romaric), Siaka Tiéné (46 Emerse Faé), Aruna Dindane, Didier Drogba (78 Bakari Koné).
Manager: Henri Michel
Goals: William Gallas (28), Zinédine Zidane (62), Thierry Henry (66)

661. 03.09.2005 FIFA World Cup Qualification – Group 4
FRANCE v FAROE ISLANDS 3-0 (2-0)
Stade Félix Bollaert, Lens
Referee: Jaroslav Jára (Czech Republic)   Attendance: 40,126
FRANCE: Grégory Coupet, Willy Sagnol, Lilian Thuram (77 Sébastien Squillaci), Jean-Alain Boumsong, William Gallas, Claude Makélélé, Patrick Vieira, Zinédine Zidane (58 Vikash Dhorasoo), Florent Malouda, Djibril Cissé, Thierry Henry (67 Sylvain Wiltord).   Manager: Raymond Domenech
FAROE ISLANDS: Jákup Mikkelsen, Súni Olsen, Óli Johannesen, Jón Rói Jacobsen, Mortan ür Hørg (56 Christian Høgni Jacobsen), Claus Bech Jørgensen (76 Hedin á Lakjuni), Fródi Benjaminsen, Ingi Højsted, Jákup á Borg, Andrew av Fløtum, Todi Jónsson (67 Rógvi Jacobsen).
Manager: Henrik Larsen
Goals: Djibril Cissé (13, 76), Súni Olsen (18 og)

662. 07.09.2005 FIFA World Cup Qualification – Group 4
REPUBLIC OF IRELAND v FRANCE 0-1 (0-0)
Lansdowne Road, Dublin
Referee: Herbert Fandel (Germany)   Attendance: 36,000
REPUBLIC OF IRELAND: Shay Given, John O'Shea, Stephen Carr, Richard Dunne, Kenny Cunningham, Kevin Kilbane (79 Ian Harte), Roy Keane, Andy Reid, Clinton Morrison (79 Gary Doherty), Damien Duff, Robbie Keane.   Manager: Brian Kerr
FRANCE: Grégory Coupet, Willy Sagnol (90 Gaël Givet), Jean-Alain Boumsong, Lilian Thuram, William Gallas, Claude Makélélé, Patrick Vieira, Vikash Dhorasoo, Zinédine Zidane (70 Florent Malouda), Sylvain Wiltord, Thierry Henry (76 Djibril Cissé).   Manager: Raymond Domenech
Goal: Thierry Henry (68)

663. 08.10.2005 FIFA World Cup Qualification – Group 4
SWITZERLAND v FRANCE 1-1 (0-0)
Stade de Suisse, Bern
Referee: Terje Hauge (Norway)   Attendance: 31,400
SWITZERLAND: Pascal Zuberbühler, Philipp Degen, Patrick Müller, Philippe Senderos, Ludovic Magnin, Tranquillo Barnetta (90+1 Valon Behrami), Johann Vogel, Raphael Wicky (83 Mauro Lustrinelli), Ricardo Cabanas, Alexander Frei, Johan Vonlanthen (60 Daniel Gygax).
Manager: Jakob (Köbi) Kuhn
FRANCE: Grégory Coupet, Anthony Réveillère, Lilian Thuram, Jean-Alain Boumsong, William Gallas, Patrick Vieira, Claude Makélélé, Vikash Dhorasoo (46 Djibril Cissé), Zinédine Zidane, Florent Malouda (90+1 Sidney Govou), Sylvain Wiltord.   Manager: Raymond Domenech
Goals: Ludovic Magnin (79) / Djibril Cissé (52)

664. 12.10.2005 FIFA World Cup Qualification – Group 4
FRANCE v CYPRUS 4-0 (3-0)
Stade de France, Saint-Denis
Referee: Wolfgang Stark (Germany)   Attendance: 78,864
FRANCE: Grégory Coupet, Willy Sagnol, Lilian Thuram, Jean-Alain Boumsong, William Gallas, Patrick Vieira (25 Alou Diarra), Vikash Dhorasoo, Zinédine Zidane, Sylvain Wiltord (60 Ludovic Giuly), Sidney Govou (90+3 Franck Jurietti), Djibril Cissé.   Manager: Raymond Domenech
CYPRUS: Michalis Morfis, Marios Elia, Loukas Louka, Lambros Lambrou, Alexandros Garpozis (46 Christos Marangos), Kostas Charalambidis, Konstantinos Makridis (81 Marios Nikolaou), Elias Charalambous, Eustathios Aloneftis, Simos Krassas, Giasoumis Giasoumi (63 Petros Filaniotis).
Manager: Angelos Anastasiadis
Goals: Zinédine Zidane (29), Sylvain Wiltord (32), Vikash Dhorasoo (44), Ludovic Giuly (84)

665. 09.11.2005
FRANCE v COSTA RICA 3-2 (0-2)
Stade Dillon, Fort-de-France (Martinique)
Referee: Gilberto Alcalá Piñeda (Mexico)
Attendance: 16,216
FRANCE: Fabien Barthez, William Gallas, Lilian Thuram, Gaël Givet (71 Jérôme Rothen), Éric Abidal (14 Anthony Réveillère), Alou Diarra, Vikash Dhorasoo, Florent Malouda, Sylvain Wiltord (64 Sidney Govou), Nicolas Anelka (71 Djibril Cissé), Thierry Henry.   Manager: Raymond Domenech
COSTA RICA: José Francisco PORRAS Hidalgo, Harold WALLACE McDonald (63 Christián BOLAÑOS Navarro), Luis Antonio MARÍN Murillo, Leonardo GONZÁLEZ Arce (84 Carlos Eduardo CASTRO Mora), Carlos Gerardo HERNÁNDEZ Valverde (63 Roy Anthony MYERS Francos), Douglas Esteban SEQUEIRA Solano (87 Pablo Andrés SALAZAR Sánchez), Jervis DRUMMOND Johnson, Wálter CENTENO Corea, Danny Alberto FONSECA Bravo, Rónald GÓMEZ Gómez, Álvaro Alberto SABORÍO Chacón (74 Bryan Jafet RUIZ González).
Manager: Alexandre GUIMARÃES Borges
Goals: Nicolas Anelka (49), Djibril Cissé (80), T. Henry (87) / Álvaro Alberto SABORÍO Chacón (14), Danny Alberto FONSECA Bravo (41)

666. 12.11.2005

FRANCE v GERMANY 0-0

Stade de France, Saint-Denis

Referee: Stephen Graham (Steve) Bennett (England)
Attendance: 58,889

FRANCE: Grégory Coupet, Anthony Réveillère, Lilian Thuram, Jean-Alain Boumsong, William Gallas, Willy Sagnol, Claude Makélélé, Vikash Dhorasoo (75 Alou Diarra), Florent Malouda (69 Jérôme Rothen), Thierry Henry (46 Nicolas Anelka), David Trézéguet (69 Djibril Cissé). Manager: Raymond Domenech

GERMANY: Jens Lehmann, Arne Friedrich, Per Mertesacker, Robert Huth, Marcell Jansen, Sebastian Deisler (46 Bastian Schweinsteiger), Torsten Frings, Michael Ballack, Bernd Schneider (76 Tim Borowski), Miroslav Klose, Lukas Podolski (83 Kevin Kurányi).   Manager: Jürgen Klinsmann

667. 01.03.2006

FRANCE v SLOVAKIA 1-2 (0-0)

Stade de France, Saint-Denis

Referee: Craig Alexander Thomson (Scotland)
Attendance: 56,273

FRANCE: Fabien Barthez, Willy Sagnol, Lilian Thuram, Jean-Alain Boumsong, Mikaël Silvestre (62 Éric Abidal), Alou Diarra, Patrick Vieira, Vikash Dhorasoo, Zinédine Zidane (46 Florent Malouda), Nicolas Anelka (46 Sylvain Wiltord), David Trézéguet (46 Thierry Henry).
Manager: Raymond Domenech

SLOVAKIA: Lubos Hajdúch, Radoslav Zabavník (90+1 Peter Petrás), Martin Skrtel, Ján Durica, Marek Cech, Matej Krajcík (78 Jozef Valachovic), Balázs Borbély, Martin Jakubko (70 Mário Bicák), Peter Hlinka (86 Ivan Hodúr), Filip Holosko (60 Szilárd Németh), Róbert Vittek (88 Kamil Kopúbek).
Manager: Dusan Galis

Goals: Sylvain Wiltord (73 pen) /
Szilárd Németh (62), Jozcf Valachovic (81)

Jozef Valachovic missed a penalty kick (80)

668. 27.05.2006

FRANCE v MEXICO 1-0 (1-0)

Stade de France, Saint-Denis

Referee: Mourad Daami (Tunisia)   Attendance: 78,819

FRANCE: Fabien Barthez, Éric Abidal, William Gallas (46 Mikaël Silvestre), Lilian Thuram (50 Jean-Alain Boumsong), Willy Sagnol, Claude Makélélé (48 Alou Diarra), Patrick Vieira (46 Sylvain Wiltord), Florent Malouda, Zinédine Zidane (52 Vikash Dhorasoo), Djibril Cissé, David Trézéguet (74 Franck Ribéry).   Manager: Raymond Domenech

MEXICO: Oswaldo Javier SÁNCHEZ Ibarra, Luis Claudio SUÁREZ Sánchez (66 Francisco Javier "MAZA" RODRÍGUEZ Pinedo), Carlos Arnoldo SALCIDO Flores, Rafael MÁRQUEZ Álvarez (74 Gerardo TORRADO Díez de Bonilla), Ricardo OSORIO Mendoza, Pável PARDO Segura, Jared Francisco BORGETTI Echavarría (67 José de Jesus ARELLANO Alcócer), Guillermo Luis FRANCO Farquarson (46 Omar BRAVO Tordecillas), Gonzalo PINEDA Reyes (46 Ramón Heriberto Cortez MORALES Higuera), José Antonio CASTRO González, Luis Ernesto PÉREZ Gómez (46 Antonio Naelson Matías "ZINHA").
Manager: Ricardo Antonio LA VOLPE Guarchioni

Goal: Florent Malouda (45+1)

669. 31.05.2006

FRANCE v DENMARK 2-0 (1-0)

Stade Félix Bollaerts, Lens

Referee: Alan Kelly (Republic of Ireland)
Attendance: 39,000

FRANCE: Fabien Barthez, Éric Abidal (82 Mikaël Silvestre), William Gallas, Lilian Thuram, Willy Sagnol (89 Pascal Chimbonda), Claude Makélélé, Patrick Vieira, Florent Malouda, Zinédine Zidane (66 Franck Ribéry), Thierry Henry (79 Djibril Cissé), Louis Saha (57 Sylvain Wiltord).
Manager: Raymond Domenech

DENMARK: Jesper Christiansen, Brian Priske, Thomas Helveg, Per Krøldrup (64 Lars Jacobsen), Jan Kristiansen (77 Allan Jespen), Christian Poulsen, Thomas Gravesen, Daniel Jensen (72 Søren Larsen), Michael Silberbauer, Jon Dahl Tomasson (86 Kenneth Pérez), Martin Jørgensen.
Manager: Morten Olsen

Goals: Thierry Henry (13), Sylvain Wiltord (76 pen)

670. 07.06.2006

FRANCE v CHINA 3-1 (1-0)

Stade Geoffroy Guichard, Saint-Étienne

Referee: Carlos Megía Dávila (Spain)   Attendance: 34,147

FRANCE: Fabien Barthez, Willy Sagnol, Lilian Thuram, William Gallas, Éric Abidal, Claude Makélélé, Patrick Vieira (75 Franck Ribéry), Florent Malouda, Zinédine Zidane, Djibril Cissé (13 David Trézéguet, 84 Sylvain Wiltord), Thierry Henry.
Manager: Raymond Domenech

CHINA: Li Leilei, Xu Yunlong, Zhang Yaokun, Ji Mingyi, Cao Yang (88 Zhang Yonghai), Gao Lin (31 Hao Junmin, 75 Wang Yun), Wang Yun, Zhao Junzhe (69 Jiang Kun), Zhao Xuri, Tao Wei (80 Li Tie), Zheng Zhi, Han Peng (60 Dong Fangzhuo).
Manager: Guanghu Zu

Goals: David Trézéguet (30), Wang Yun (90 og), Thierry Henry (90+2) / Zheng Zhi (69 pen)

671.　13.06.2006　FIFA World Cup Final Tournament – Group G
FRANCE v SWITZERLAND 0-0
Gottlieb Daimler Stadion, Stuttgart (Germany)

Referee: Valentin Valentinovitch Ivanov (Russia)　　Att: 52,000

FRANCE: Fabien Barthez, Willy Sagnol, Lilian Thuram, William Gallas, Éric Abidal, Claude Makélélé, Patrick Vieira, Zinédine Zidane, Franck Ribéry (70 Louis Saha), Sylvain Wiltord (84 Vikash Dhorasoo), Thierry Henry.　Manager: Raymond Domenech

SWITZERLAND: Pascal Zuberbühler, Philipp Degen, Patrick Müller (75 Johan Djourou), Philippe Senderos, Ludovic Magnin, Tranquillo Barnetta, Johann Vogel, Ricardo Cabanas, Raphael Wicky (81 Xavier Margairaz), Alexander Frei, Marco Streller (57 Daniel Gygax).　Manager: Jakob (Köbi) Kuhn

672.　18.06.2006　FIFA World Cup Final Tournament – Group G
FRANCE v SOUTH KOREA 1-1 (1-0)
Zentralstadion, Leipzig (Germany)

Referee: Benito Armando Archundia Téllez (Mexico)
Attendance: 43,000

FRANCE: Fabien Barthez, Willy Sagnol, Lilian Thuram, William Gallas, Éric Abidal, Claude Makélélé, Patrick Vieira, Florent Malouda (87 Vikash Dhorasoo), Zinédine Zidane (90+1 David Trézéguet), Sylvain Wiltord (59 Franck Ribéry), Thierry Henry.　Manager: Raymond Domenech

SOUTH KOREA: Lee Woon-Jae, Kim Young-Chul, Kim Dong-Jin, Choi Jin-Cheol, Lee Young-Pyo, Kim Nam-Il, Lee Ho (69 Kim Sang-Sik), Lee Eul-Yong (46 Seol Ki-Hyun), Lee Chun-Soo (72 Ahn Jung-Hwan), Cho Jae-Jin, Park Ji-Sung. Manager: Dick Advocaat

Goals: Thierry Henry (9) / Park Ji-Sung (81)

673.　23.06.2006　FIFA World Cup Final Tournament – Group G
TOGO v FRANCE 0-2 (0-0)
RheinEnergieStadion, Cologne (Germany)

Referee: Jorge Luis Larrionda Pietrafesa (Uruguay)
Attendance: 45,000

TOGO: Kossia Agassa, Daré Nibombé, Jean-Paul Abalo Dosseh, Massamesso Tchangai, Moustapha Salifou, Yao Junior Sènaya, Chérif Touré Mamam (59 Adekanmi Olufade), Yao Aziawanou, Mohamed Kader Coubadja, Richmond Forson, Emmanuel Adebayor (75 Thomas Dossevi).
Manager: Otto Pfister

FRANCE: Fabien Barthez, Willy Sagnol, Lilian Thuram, William Gallas, Mikaël Silvestre, Claude Makélélé, Patrick Vieira (80 Alou Diarra), Florent Malouda (73 Sylvain Wiltord), Franck Ribéry (76 Sidney Govou), Thierry Henry, David Trézéguet.　Manager: Raymond Domenech

Goals: Patrick Vieira (55), Thierry Henry (61)

674.　27.06.2006　FIFA World Cup Final Tournament – Round of 16
SPAIN v FRANCE 1-3 (1-1)
A.W.D. Arena, Hannover (Germany)

Referee: Roberto Rosetti (Italy)　　Attendance: 43,000

SPAIN: IKER CASILLAS Fernández, SERGIO RAMOS García, PABLO IBÁÑEZ Tébar, Carles PUYOL í Saforcada, MARIANO Andrés PERNÍA Molina, Xabier "XABI" ALONSO Olano, Xavier "XAVI" Hernández i Creus (72 MARCOS Antônio SENNA da Silva), Francesc "CESC" FÀBREGAS i Soler, RAÚL González Blanco (54 LUIS Javier GARCÍA Sanz), FERNANDO José TORRES Sanz, DAVID VILLA Sánchez (54 JOAQUÍN Sánchez Rodríguez).　Manager: Luis ARAGONÉS Suárez

FRANCE: Fabien Barthez, Willy Sagnol, Lilian Thuram, William Gallas, Éric Abidal, Claude Makélélé, Patrick Vieira, Zinédine Zidane, Franck Ribéry, Florent Malouda (74 Sidney Govou), Thierry Henry (88 Sylvain Wiltord). Manager: Raymond Domenech

Goals: DAVID VILLA Sánchez (28 pen) / Franck Ribéry (41), Patrick Vieira (83), Zinédine Zidane (90+2)

675.　01.07.2006　FIFA World Cup Final Tournament – Quarter-final
BRAZIL v FRANCE 0-1 (0-0)
Commerzbank Arena, Frankfurt am Main (Germany)

Referee: Luis Medina Cantalejo (Spain)　　Attendance: 48,000

BRAZIL: Nelson de Jesus da Silva "DIDA", Marcos Evangelista de Moraes "CAFÚ" (76 Cícero João de Cézare "CICINHO"), Lucimar da Silva Ferreira "LÚCIO", JUAN Silveira dos Santos, ROBERTO CARLOS da Silva, GILBERTO Aparecido da SILVA, José "ZÉ" ROBERTO da Silva Júnior, Antônio Augusto Ribeiro Reis Júnior "JUNINHO PERNAMBUCANO" (64 ADRIANO Leite Ribeiro), Ricardo Izecson Santos Leite "KAKÁ" (79 Robson de Souza "ROBINHO"), Ronaldo de Assis Moreira "RONALDINHO GAÚCHU", RONALDO Luís Nazário de Lima.　Manager: CARLOS ALBERTO Gomes PARREIRA

FRANCE: Fabien Barthez, Willy Sagnol, Lilian Thuram, William Gallas, Éric Abidal, Claude Makélélé, Patrick Vieira, Franck Ribéry (77 Sidney Govou), Zinédine Zidane, Florent Malouda (81 Sylvain Wiltord), Thierry Henry (86 Louis Saha). Manager: Raymond Domenech

Goal: Thierry Henry (57)

676. 05.07.2006   FIFA World Cup Final Tournament – Semi-final
PORTUGAL v FRANCE 0-1 (0-1)
Allianz Arena, München (Germany)

Referee: Jorge Luis Larrionda Pietrafesa (Uruguay)
Attendance: 66,000

PORTUGAL: RICARDO Alexandre Martins Soares Pereira, Luís MIGUEL Brito Garcia Monteiro (62 PAULO Renato Rebocho FERREIRA), FERNANDO José da Silva Freitas MEIRA, RICARDO Alberto Silveira de CARVALHO, NUNO Jorge Pereira da Silva VALENTE, Francisco José Rodrigues da Costa "COSTINHA" (75 HÉLDER Manuel Marques POSTIGA), Nuno Ricardo de Oliveira Ribeiro "MANICHE", LUÍS Filipe Madeira Caeiro FIGO, Anderson Luís de Souza "DECO", CRISTIANO RONALDO dos Santos Aveiro, Pedro Miguel Carreiro Resendes "PAULETA" (68 SIMÃO Pedro Fonseca Sabrosa).   Manager: Luiz Felipe SCOLARI

FRANCE: Fabien Barthez, Willy Sagnol, Lilian Thuram, William Gallas, Éric Abidal, Claude Makélélé, Patrick Vieira, Franck Ribéry (72 Sidney Govou), Zinédine Zidane, Florent Malouda (69 Sylvain Wiltord), Thierry Henry (85 Louis Saha).   Manager: Raymond Domenech

Goal: Zinédine Zidane (33 pen)

677. 09.07.2006   FIFA World Cup Final Tournament – Final
ITALY v FRANCE 1-1 (1-1, 1-1) (AET)
Olympiastadion, Berlin (Germany)

Referee: Horacio Marcelo Elizondo (Argentina)
Attendance: 69,000

ITALY: Gianluigi Buffon, Gianluca Zambrotta, Fabio Cannavaro, Marco Materazzi, Fabio Grosso, Mauro Camoranesi (86 Alessandro Del Piero), Gennaro Gattuso, Andrea Pirlo, Simone Perrotta (61 Daniele De Rossi), Francesco Totti (61 Vincenzo Iaquinta), Luca Toni. Manager: Marcello Lippi

FRANCE: Fabien Barthez, Willy Sagnol, Lilian Thuram, William Gallas, Éric Abidal, Claude Makélélé, Patrick Vieira (56 Alou Diarra), Zinédine Zidane, Florent Malouda, Franck Ribéry (100 David Trézéguet), Thierry Henry (107 Sylvain Wiltord).   Manager: Raymond Domenech

Goals: Marco Materazzi (19) / Zinédine Zidane (7 pen)

Penalties: 1-0 Andrea Pirlo, 1-1 Sylvain Wiltord, 2-1 Marco Materazzi, David Trézéguet (missed), 3-1 Daniele De Rossi, 3-2 Éric Abidal, 4-2 Ales. Del Piero, 4-3 Willy Sagnol, 5-3 Fabio Grosso

Sent off: Zinédine Zidane (110)

678. 16.08.2006
BOSNIA & HERZEGOVINA v FRANCE 1-2 (1-1)
Olimpijski Stadion Asim Ferhatovic Hase, Sarajevo

Referee: Dr. Franz-Xaver Wack (Germany)
Attendance: 35,000

BOSNIA & HERZEGOVINA: Kenan Hasagic, Dzemal Berberovic, Muhamed Konjic (4 Emir Spahic), Zlatan Bajramovic (79 Vule Trivunovic), Sasa Papac, Vedin Music, Sergej Barbarez (59 Zlatan Muslimovic), Hasan Salihamidzic (46 Admir Vladavic), Vladan Grujic (65 Ivica Grlic), Zvjezdan Misimovic (84 Ivan Jolic), Mladen Bartolovic (74 Mirko Hrgovic).   Manager: Blaz Sliskovic

FRANCE: Grégory Coupet, Éric Abidal, Jean-Alain Boumsong (59 Gaël Givet), William Gallas, Willy Sagnol, Patrick Vieira, Rio Mavuba, Florent Malouda (53 Sylvain Wiltord), Franck Ribéry (69 Julien Faubert), Thierry Henry, Louis Saha.   Manager: Raymond Domenech

Goals: Sergej Barbarez (16) / William Gallas (41), Julien Faubert (90+1)

679. 02.09.2006   UEFA Euro 2008 Qualifying – Group B
GEORGIA v FRANCE 0-3 (0-2)
Boris Paichadze National Stadium, Tbilisi

Referee: Jan Willem Wegereef (Netherlands)
Attendance: 53,500

GEORGIA: Grigol Chanturia, Kakhaber Aladashvili (37 Ilia Kandelaki), Zurab Khizanishvili, Malkhaz Asatiani, Gogita Gogua, Jaba Kankava, Levan Kobiashvili, Davit Mujiri, Aleksandr Iashvili (46 Dato Kvirkvelia), Shota Arveladze, Giorgi Demetradze (81 Zurab Menteshashvili).   Manager: Klaus Toppmöller

FRANCE: Grégory Coupet, Willy Sagnol, William Gallas, Lilian Thuram, Éric Abidal, Patrick Vieira, Claude Makélélé (58 Rio Mavuba), Florent Malouda, Franck Ribéry (69 Sidney Govou), Thierry Henry, Louis Saha (86 Sylvain Wiltord).   Manager: Raymond Domenech

Goals: F. Malouda (7), Louis Saha (16), Thierry Henry (46)

680.   06.09.2006   UEFA Euro 2008 Qualifying – Group B

FRANCE v ITALY 3-1 (2-1)

Stade de France, Saint-Denis

Referee: Herbert Fandel (Germany)   Attendance: 78,831

FRANCE: Grégory Coupet, Éric Abidal, Lilian Thuram, William Gallas, Willy Sagnol, Claude Makélélé, Patrick Vieira, Florent Malouda, Franck Ribéry (88 Louis Saha), Sidney Govou (75 Sylvain Wiltord), Thierry Henry.   Manager: Raymond Domenech

ITALY: Gianluigi Buffon, Gianluca Zambrotta, Fabio Cannavaro, Andrea Barzagli, Fabio Grosso, Franco Semioli (54 Davide Di Michele), Gennaro Gattuso, Andrea Pirlo, Simone Perrotta, Antonio Cassano (73 Filippo Inzaghi), Alberto Gilardino (87 Daniele De Rossi).   Manager: Roberto Donadoni

Goals: Sidney Govou (2, 55), Thierry Henry (17) / Alberto Gilardino (20)

681.   07.10.2006   UEFA Euro 2008 Qualifying – Group B

SCOTLAND v FRANCE 1-0 (0-0)

Hampden Park, Glasgow

Referee: Massimo Busacca (Switzerland)   Att: 50,456

SCOTLAND: Craig Gordon, Christian Dailly, Graham Alexander, David Weir, Barry Ferguson, Darren Fletcher, Gary Caldwell, James McFadden (71 Garry O'Connor), Paul Hartley, Lee McCulloch (57 Gary Teale), Steven Pressley.   Manager: Walter Smith

FRANCE: Grégory Coupet, Éric Abidal, Jean-Alain Boumsong, Lilian Thuram, Willy Sagnol, Claude Makélélé, Patrick Vieira, Florent Malouda, Franck Ribéry (74 Sylvain Wiltord), Thierry Henry, David Trézéguet (62 Louis Saha).   Manager: Raymond Domenech

Goal: Gary Caldwell (67)

682.   11.10.2006   UEFA Euro 2008 Qualifying – Group B

FRANCE v FAROE ISLANDS 5-0 (2-0)

Stade Auguste Bonal, Montbéliard

Referee: Sorin Corpodean (Romania)   Attendance: 19,314

FRANCE: Mickaël Landreau, Willy Sagnol (78 François Clerc), Lilian Thuram, William Gallas, Julien Escudé, Jérémy Toulalan, Patrick Vieira, Franck Ribéry, Florent Malouda, Thierry Henry (61 Nicolas Anelka), Louis Saha (61 David Trézéguet).   Manager: Raymond Domenech

FAROE ISLANDS: Jákup Mikkelsen, Atli Danielsen, Vagnur Mortensen, Fróði Benjaminsen, Marni Djurhuus, Jákup á Borg (88 Jónhard Frederiksberg), Pauli Hansen (47 Kári Nielsen), Mikkjal Thomassen, Símun Samuelsen, Rógvi Jacobsen, Christian Høgni Jacobsen.   Manager: Jógvan Martin Olsen

Goals: Louis Saha (1), Thierry Henry (22), Nicolas Anelka (76), David Trézéguet (78, 84)

683.   15.11.2006

FRANCE v GREECE 1-0 (1-0)

Stade de France, Saint-Denis

Referee: Dr. Franz-Xaver Wack (Germany) (46 Volker Wezel (Germany))   Attendance: 63,680

FRANCE: Grégory Coupet, Éric Abidal (46 Patrice Évra), William Gallas, Lilian Thuram, Willy Sagnol (46 François Clerc), Claude Makélélé (46 Alou Diarra), Patrick Vieira, Florent Malouda, Sylvain Wiltord, Thierry Henry, Louis Saha (46 Nicolas Anelka).   Manager: Raymond Domenech

GREECE: Antonis Nikopolidis, Traianos Dellas (66 Giannis Goumas), Michalis Kapsis, Kostas Katsouranis, Sotirios Kyrgiakos, Panagiotis Fyssas (62 Panagiotis Lagos), Stelios Giannakopoulos (46 Theofanis Gekas), Angelos Basinas (86 Alexandros Tziolis), Giorgios Karagounis (77 Pantelis Kafes), Giorgios Samaras, Giannis Amanatidis (46 Nikos Liberopoulos).   Manager: Otto Rehhagel

Goal: Thierry Henry (26)

684.   07.02.2007

FRANCE v ARGENTINA 0-1 (0-1)

Stade de France, Saint-Denis

Referee: Damir Skomina (Slovenia)   Attendance: 79,862

FRANCE: Grégory Coupet, Éric Abidal, Sébastien Squillaci, Julien Escudé, Willy Sagnol (46 François Clerc), Claude Makélélé (88 Djibril Cissé), Patrick Vieira, Florent Malouda (46 Sidney Govou), Franck Ribéry, Thierry Henry, David Trézéguet (72 Nicolas Anelka).   Manager: Raymond Domenech

ARGENTINA: Roberto Carlos Abbondanzieri, Gabriel Alejandro Milito, Gabriel Iván Heinze, Nicolás Andrés Burdisso, Roberto Fabián Ayala, Javier Adelmar Zanetti, Luis Óscar "Lucho" González (78 Jonás Manuel Gutiérrez), Fernando Rubén Gago, Esteban Matías Cambiasso Deleau, Javier Pedro Saviola Fernández (84 Sergio Leonel "Kun" Agüero del Castillo), Hernán Jorge Crespo (78 Diego Alberto Milito).   Manager: Alfredo (Alfio) Rubén Basile Moreno

Goal: Javier Saviola (15)

685. 24.03.2007   UEFA Euro 2008 Qualifying – Group B
LITHUANIA v FRANCE 0-1 (0-0)
Steponas Darius ir Stasys Girenas Stadionas, Kaunas
Referee: Howard Melton Webb (England)   Attendance: 8,000
LITHUANIA: Zydrūnas Karcemarskas, Arūnas Klimavicius, Andrius Skerla, Tomas Zvirgzdauskas, Gediminas Paulauskas, Deividas Semberas, Igoris Morinas (82 Ricardas Beniusis), Mantas Savenas (77 Mindaugas Kalonas), Tomas Danilevicius, Robertas Poskus (86 Tomas Radzinevicius), Marius Stankevicius.   Manager: Algimantas Liubinskas
FRANCE: Grégory Coupet, Éric Abidal, William Gallas, Lilian Thuram, Willy Sagnol, Claude Makélélé, Jérémy Toulalan, Lassana Diarra, Florent Malouda (89 Abou Diaby), Sidney Govou (62 Djibril Cissé), Nicolas Anelka.
Manager: Raymond Domenech
Goal: Nicolas Anelka (73)

686. 28.03.2007
FRANCE v AUSTRIA 1-0 (0-0)
Stade de France, Saint-Denis
Referee: Athanasios Briakos (Greece)   Attendance: 68,403
FRANCE: Grégory Coupet, François Clerc, Philippe Mexès (46 Éric Abidal), Lilian Thuram (46 William Gallas), Julien Escudé, Lassana Diarra, Rio Mavuba, Abou Diaby (78 Frédéric Piquionne), Samir Nasri (70 Florent Malouda), Djibril Cissé (46 Karim Benzema), Nicolas Anelka.
Manager: Raymond Domenech
AUSTRIA: Jürgen Macho, Andreas Ibertsberger (59 Joachim Standfest), Martin Hiden, Martin Stranzl, Christian Fuchs, Andreas Ivanschitz, René Aufhauser, Thomas Prager (90 Yüksel Sariyar), Christoph Leitgeb (83 Cem Atan), Roland Linz (82 Mario Haas), Sanel Kuljic (69 Ronald Gërçaliu).
Manager: Josef Hickersberger
Goal: Karim Benzema (53)

687. 02.06.2007   UEFA Euro 2008 Qualifying – Group B
FRANCE v UKRAINE 2-0 (0-0)
Stade de France, Saint-Denis
Referee: Luis Medina Cantalejo (Spain)   Attendance: 80,051
FRANCE: Grégory Coupet, Éric Abidal, William Gallas, Lilian Thuram, François Clerc, Claude Makélélé, Jérémy Toulalan, Samir Nasri (81 Lassana Diarra), Florent Malouda, Franck Ribéry, Nicolas Anelka (76 Djibril Cissé).
Manager: Raymond Domenech
UKRAINE: Oleksandr Shovkovskiy, Andriy Nesmachnyi, Volodymyr Yezerskyi (78 Evgeniy Levchenko), Andriy Rusol, Dmytro Chygrynskiy, Oleksiy Gai, Anatoliy Tymoshchuk, Oleh Husyev, Taras Mykhalyk, Maksim Kalinichenko (64 Ruslan Rotan), Andriy Voronin (72 Andriy Vorobey).
Manager: Oleg Blokhin
Goals: Franck Ribéry (57), Nicolas Anelka (71)

688. 06.06.2007   UEFA Euro 2008 Qualifying – Group B
FRANCE v GEORGIA 1-0 (1-0)
Stade de l'Abbé-Deschamps, Auxerre
Referee: Lucílio Cardoso Cortez Batista (Portugal)
Attendance: 21,000
FRANCE: Mickaël Landreau, Éric Abidal, William Gallas, Lilian Thuram, François Clerc, Claude Makélélé, Jérémy Toulalan, Florent Malouda (65 Djibril Cissé), Samir Nasri, Franck Ribéry (90+5 Sidney Govou), Nicolas Anelka (90+3 Karim Benzema).   Manager: Raymond Domenech
GEORGIA: Giorgi Lomaia, Zurab Khizanishvili, Otar Khizaneishvili, Kakha Kaladze, Zaali Eliava (62 Otar Martsvaladze), Dato Kvirkvelia, Aleksandr Iashvili, Vladimer Burduli, Mate Ghvinianidze, Lasha Salukvadze (12 Davit Mujiri), Jaba Kankava (89 Giorgi Shashiashvili).
Manager: Klaus Toppmöller
Goal: Samir Nasri (33)

689. 22.08.2007
SLOVAKIA v FRANCE 0-1 (0-1)
Stadión Antona Malatinského, Trnava
Referee: Igor Vyacheslavovich Egorov (Russia)
Attendance: 13,164
SLOVAKIA: Stefan Senecký, Majej Krajcík (84 Milos Brezinský), Maros Klimpl, Ján Durica, Marián Had (67 Igor Zofcák), Marek Hamsík (85 Zdeno Strba), Stanislav Sesták (46 Samuel Slovák), Marek Sapara (72 Ján Kozák), Marek Cech, Marek Mintál (46 Filip Holosko), Róbert Vittek.
Manager: Ján Kocian
FRANCE: Mickaël Landreau, Patrice Évra, Éric Abidal, Philippe Mexès (88 Jean-Alain Boumsong), François Clerc (63 Bacary Sagna), Claude Makélélé, Patrick Vieira (59 Jérémy Toulalan), Florent Malouda, Franck Ribéry (73 Samir Nasri), Nicolas Anelka, Thierry Henry (84 Karim Benzema).
Manager: Raymond Domenech
Goal: Thierry Henry (38)

690. 08.09.2007   UEFA Euro 2008 Qualifying – Group B
ITALY v FRANCE 0-0
Stadio Giuseppe Meazza, Milano

Referee: Lubos Michel (Slovakia)   Attendance: 81,200

ITALY: Gianluigi Buffon, Massimo Oddo, Fabio Cannavaro, Andrea Barzagli, Gianluca Zambrotta, Mauro Germán Camoranesi Serra (58 Simone Perrotta), Gennaro Gattuso, Andrea Pirlo, Daniele De Rossi, Alessandro Del Piero (83 Antonio Di Natale), Filippo Inzaghi (65 Cristiano Lucarelli).   Manager: Roberto Donadoni

FRANCE: Mickaël Landreau, Lassana Diarra, Lilian Thuram, Julien Escudé, Éric Abidal, Franck Ribéry (87 Jérémy Toulalan), Patrick Vieira, Claude Makélélé, Florent Malouda, Nicolas Anelka, Thierry Henry.   Manager: Raymond Domenech

691. 12.09.2007   UEFA Euro 2008 Qualifying – Group B
FRANCE v SCOTLAND 0-1 (0-0)
Parc des Princes, Paris

Referee: Konrad Plautz (Austria)   Attendance: 43,342

FRANCE: Mickaël Landreau, Lassana Diarra, Lilian Thuram, Julien Escudé, Éric Abidal (77 Karim Benzema), Claude Makélélé, Patrick Vieira (69 Samir Nasri), Florent Malouda, Franck Ribéry, Nicolas Anelka, David Trézéguet.   Manager: Raymond Domenech

SCOTLAND: Craig Gordon, Alan Hutton, Graham Alexander, Stephen McManus, David Weir, Barry Ferguson, Darren Fletcher (26 Stephen Pearson), Lee McCulloch, James McFadden (75 Garry O'Connor), Scott Brown, Paul Hartley.   Manager: Alex McLeish

Goal: James McFadden (64)

692. 13.10.2007   UEFA Euro 2008 Qualifying – Group B
FAROE ISLANDS v FRANCE 0-6 (0-2)
Tórsvøllur, Tórshavn

Referee: Gabriele Rossi (San Marino)   Attendance: 1,980

FAROE ISLANDS: Jákup Mikkelsen, Jón Rói Jacobsen, Rógvi Jacobsen, Fródi Benjaminsen, Mikkjal Thomassen (78 Rókur Jespersen), Símun Samuelsen (86 Andrew av Fløtum), Christian Høgni Jacobsen, Christian Lamhauge Holst, Einar Tróndargjógv Hansen, Hjalgrím Elttør (46 Bergur Midjord), Súni Olsen.   Manager: Jógvan Martin Olsen

FRANCE: Mickaël Landreau, Bacary Sagna, Lilian Thuram, Éric Abidal, Patrice Évra, Claude Makélélé (72 Lassana Diarra), Jérémy Toulalan, Franck Ribéry (62 Hatem Ben Arfa), Jérôme Rothen, Nicolas Anelka (46 Karim Benzema), Thierry Henry.   Manager: Raymond Domenech

Goals: Nicolas Anelka (7), Thierry Henry (8), Karim Benzema (49, 79), Jérôme Rothen (64), Hatem Ben Arfa (90+3)

693. 17.10.2007   UEFA Euro 2008 Qualifying – Group B
FRANCE v LITHUANIA 2-0 (0-0)
Stade de la Beaujoire – Lousi Fonteneau, Nantes

Referee: Viktor Kassai (Hungary)   Attendance: 36,650

FRANCE: Mickaël Landreau, Éric Abidal, William Gallas, Lilian Thuram, Lassana Diarra (70 Hatem Ben Arfa), Jérémy Toulalan, Claude Makélélé, Florent Malouda, Franck Ribéry, Karim Benzema, Thierry Henry.   Manager: Raymond Domenech

LITHUANIA: Zydrūnas Karcemarskas, Arūnas Klimavicius, Andrius Skerla, Tomas Zvirgzdauskas, Ignas Dedura, Aurimas Kucys (84 Andrius Velicka), Audrius Ksanavicius (77 Tadas Labukas), Igoris Morinas, Mindaugas Kalonas (63 Mantas Savenas), Tomas Danilevicius, Edgaras Jankauskas.   Manager: Algimantas Liubinskas

Goals: Thierry Henry (79, 81)

694. 16.11.2007
FRANCE v MOROCCO 2-2 (1-1)
Stade de France, Saint-Denis

Referee: Ruud Bossen (Netherlands)   Attendance: 78,000

FRANCE: Mickaël Landreau, Patrice Évra, William Gallas (46 Éric Abidal), Lilian Thuram (64 Sébastien Squillaci), François Clerc, Claude Makélélé (46 Jérémy Toulalan), Lassana Diarra, Samir Nasri, Jérôme Rothen (81 Mathieu Flamini), Sidney Govou (75 Hatem Ben Arfa), Karim Benzema (63 Nicolas Anelka).   Manager: Raymond Domenech

MOROCCO: Nadir Lamyaghri, Elamine Erbate, Abdeslam Ouaddou, Youssef Safri, Badr El Kaddouri, Youssef Hadji (83 Jaouad Zairi), Abdelkarim Kissi (46 Nourdin Boukhari), Houssine Kharja (46 Abderrahman Kabous), Mickaël Chrétien Basser, Tarik Sektioui (74 Youssef Mokhtari), Marouane Chamakh (66 Soufiane Alloudi).   Manager: Henry Michel

Goals: Sidney Govou (15), Samir Nasri (75) / Tarik Sektioui (8), Youssef Mokhtari (84)

695.   21.11.2007   UEFA Euro 2008 Qualifying – Group B
UKRAINE v FRANCE   2-2 (1-2)
Olimpiysky National Sports Complex, Kyiv
Referee: Tom Henning Øvrebø (Norway)   Attendance: 7,800
UKRAINE: Andriy Pyatov, Oleksandr Romanchuk (81 Volodymyr Yezerskyi), Sergey Fedorov, Anatoliy Tymoshchuk, Andriy Shevchenko, Oleh Husyev (90+1 Artem Milevskyi), Andriy Voronin (85 Oleh Shelayev), Ruslan Rotan, Vladyslav Vashchuk, Oleksiy Gai, Oleksandr Grytsay.
Manager: Oleg Blokhin
FRANCE: Sébastien Frey, François Clerc, Lilian Thuram, William Gallas, Éric Abidal, Lassana Diarra, Claude Makélélé, Franck Ribéry (89 Hatem Ben Arfa), Sidney Govou, Karim Benzema (46 Samir Nasri), Thierry Henry.
Manager: Raymond Domenech
Goals: Andriy Voronin (14), Andriy Shevchenko (47) / Thierry Henry (20), Sidney Govou (34)

696.   06.02.2008
SPAIN v FRANCE   1-0 (0-0)
Estadio La Rosaleda, Málaga
Referee: Tony Asumaa (Finland)   Attendance: 29,000
SPAIN: IKER CASILLAS Fernández, SERGIO RAMOS García (46 ÁNGEL Domingo López Ruano, 74 Juan Gutiérrez Moreno "JUANITO"), RAÚL ALBIOL Tortajada, Carlos MARCHENA López (46 PABLO IBÁÑEZ Tébar), Joan CAPDEVILA i Méndez, Xavier "XAVI" Hernández i Creus, David ALBELDA Aliqués (62 Xabier "XABI" ALONSO Olano), Francesc "CESC" FÀBREGAS i Soler, Andrés INIESTA Luján, ALBERT RIERA Ortega (46 DAVID VILLA Sánchez), FERNANDO José TORRES Sanz (22 Daniel "DANI" González GÜIZA).
Manager: Luis ARAGONÉS Suárez
FRANCE: Grégory Coupet, Willy Sagnol, William Gallas, Lilian Thuram (46 Julien Escudé), Éric Abidal, Patrick Vieira (82 Hatem Ben Arfa), Jérémy Toulalan, Lassana Diarra, Florent Malouda, Nicolas Anelka (60 Karim Benzema), Thierry Henry.   Manager: Raymond Domenech
Goal: Joan CAPDEVILA i Méndez (80)

697.   26.03.2008
FRANCE v ENGLAND   1-0 (1-0)
Stade de France, Saint-Denis
Referee: Florian Meyer (Germany)   Attendance: 78,500
FRANCE: Grégory Coupet, Éric Abidal, William Gallas, Lilian Thuram, François Clerc, Jérémy Toulalan, Claude Makélélé, Florent Malouda, Franck Ribéry, David Trézéguet (63 Sidney Govou), Nicolas Anelka (79 Djibril Cissé).
Manager: Raymond Domenech

ENGLAND: David James, Wes Brown (63 Glen Johnson), Ashley Cole, Owen Hargreaves, Rio Ferdinand, John Terry (46 Joleon Lescott), David Beckham (63 David Bentley), Gareth Barry, Wayne Rooney (46 Michael Owen), Steven Gerrard (46 Peter Crouch), Joe Cole (46 Stewart Downing).
Manager: Fabio Capello
Goal: Franck Ribéry (32 pen)

698.   27.05.2008
FRANCE v ECUADOR   2-0 (0-0)
Stade des Alpes, Grenoble
Referee: Paul Allaerts (Belgium)   Attendance: 20,000
FRANCE: Sébastien Frey (46 Steve Mandanda), Willy Sagnol (74 François Clerc), Lilian Thuram, Julien Escudé (46 Patrice Évra), Éric Abidal, Alou Diarra (46 Mathieu Flamini), Lassana Diarra, Samir Nasri, Hatem Ben Arfa (78 Florent Malouda), Nicolas Anelka, Djibril Cissé (46 Bafétimbi Gomis).
Manager: Raymond Domenech
ECUADOR: Marcelo Ramón ELIZAGA Ferrero, Omar Andrés DE JESUS Borja, Iván Jacinto HURTADO Angulo, Carlos Ernesto CASTRO Cadena, Isaac Bryan MINA Arboleda, Mario David QUIROZ Villón (63 Félix Alexander BORJA Valencia), José Luis CORTÉZ Arroyo, Segundo Alejandro CASTILLO Nazareno, Walter Orlando AYOVÍ Corozo, Luis Antonio VALENCIA Mosquera, Carlos Vicente TENORIO Medina (86 Felipe Salvador CAICEDO Corozo).
Manager: Sixto Rafael VIZUETE Toapanta
Goals: Bafétimbi Gomis (59, 86)

699.   31.05.2008
FRANCE v PARAGUAY   0-0
Stade Municipal de Toulouse, Toulouse
Referee: Pedro Proença Oliveira Alves Garcia (Portugal)
Attendance: 33,418
FRANCE: Grégory Coupet, François Clerc, Sébastien Squillaci, Jean-Alain Boumsong, Patrice Évra, Jérémy Toulalan (71 Samir Nasri), Claude Makélélé (46 Lassana Diarra), Franck Ribéry (46 Sidney Govou), Florent Malouda, Karim Benzema (63 Nicolas Anelka), Thierry Henry (46 Bafétimbi Gomis).   Manager: Raymond Domenech
PARAGUAY: Justo Wilmar VILLAR Viceros, Denis Ramón CANIZA Acuña, Paulo César DA SILVA Barrios, Darío Anastacio VERÓN Maldonado, Pedro Juan BENÍTEZ Dominguez, Edgar Osvaldo BARRETO Cáceres (89 Carlos Humberto PAREDES Monges), Víctor Javier CÁCERES Centurión (83 Jonathan SANTANA Gehre), Sergio Daniel AQUINO (42 Marcelo Alejandro ESTIGARRIBIA Balmori), Aureliano TORRES Román, Roque Luis SANTA CRUZ Cantero (57 Óscar René CARDOZO Marín), Nelson Antonio HAEDO Valdez (69 Dante Rafael LÓPEZ Fariña).
Manager: Gerardo Daniel MARTINO Capiglioni

700.   03.06.2008
FRANCE v COLOMBIA   1-0 (1-0)
Stade de France, Saint-Denis

Referee: Michael Leslie (Mike) Dean (England)
Attendance: 79,727

FRANCE: Grégory Coupet, Éric Abidal, William Gallas, Lilian Thuram, Willy Sagnol, Claude Makélélé, Jérémy Toulalan, Florent Malouda, Franck Ribéry (76 Samir Nasri), Karim Benzema (65 Lassana Diarra), Thierry Henry (76 Nicolas Anelka).   Manager: Raymond Domenech

COLOMBIA: Agustín JULIO Castro, Rubén Dario BUSTOS Torres, Cristián Eduardo ZAPATA Valencia, Wálter José MORENO Arco, Pablo Estifer ARMERO (56 Elvis Manuel GONZÁLEZ Rosendo), Carlos Alberto SÁNCHEZ Moreno (81 Stalin MOTTA Vaquiro), José Antonio AMAYA Pardo, Giovanni Andres HERNÁNDEZ Soto (65 Macnelly TORRES Berrío), Juan Carlos ESCOBAR Rodríguez (81 Fredy Alejandro GUARÍN Vasquez), Radamel FALCAO García Zárate (58 Roberto POLO Guete), Edixon PEREA Valencia (88 Carmelo Enrique VALENCIA Chaverra).
Manager: Jorge Luis PINTO Afanador

Goal: Franck Ribéry (23 pen)

701.   09.06.2008   UEFA European Championship – Group C
ROMANIA v FRANCE   0-0
Letzigrund, Zürich (Switzerland)

Referee: Manuel Enrique Mejuto González (Spain)
Attendance: 30,585

ROMANIA: Bogdan Lobont, Cosmin Contra, Gabriel Tamas, Dorin Goian, Razvan Rat, Razvan Cocis (64 Paul Codrea), Mirel Radoi (90+3 Nicolae Dica), Cristian Chivu, Banel Nicolita, Daniel Niculae, Adrian Mutu (78 Marius Niculae). Manager: Victor Piturca

FRANCE: Grégory Coupet, Éric Abidal, William Gallas, Lilian Thuram, Willy Sagnol, Claude Makélélé, Jérémy Toulalan, Florent Malouda, Franck Ribéry, Nicolas Anelka (72 Bafétimbi Gomis), Karim Benzema (77 Samir Nasri).   Manager: Raymond Domenech

702.   13.06.2008   UEFA European Championship – Group C
NETHERLANDS v FRANCE   4-1 (1-0)
Stade de Suisse, Bern (Switzerland)

Referee: Herbert Fandel (Germany)   Attendance: 30,777

NETHERLANDS: Edwin van der Sar, Khalid Boulahrouz, André Ooijer, Joris Mathijsen, Giovanni van Bronckhorst, Dirk Kuijt (55 Robin van Persie), Nigel de Jong, Rafael van der Vaart (78 Wilfred Bouma), Orlando Engelaar (46 Arjen Robben), Wesley Sneijder, Ruud van Nistelrooy.
Manager: Marco van Basten

FRANCE: Grégory Coupet, Patrice Évra, William Gallas, Lilian Thuram, Willy Sagnol, Claude Makélélé, Jérémy Toulalan, Florent Malouda (60 Bafétimbi Gomis), Franck Ribéry, Sidney Govou (75 Nicolas Anelka), Thierry Henry.   Manager: Raymond Domenech

Goals: Dirk Kuijt (9), Robin van Persie (59), A. Robben (72), Wesley Sneijder (90+2) / Thierry Henry (71)

703.   17.06.2008   UEFA European Championship – Group C
FRANCE v ITALY   0-2 (0-1)
Letzigrund, Zürich (Switzerland)

Referee: Lubos Michel (Slovakia)   Attendance: 30,585

FRANCE: Grégory Coupet, Patrice Évra, Éric Abidal, William Gallas, François Clerc, Claude Makélélé, Jérémy Toulalan, Franck Ribéry (9 Samir Nasri, 26 Jean-Alain Boumsong), Sidney Govou (66 Nicolas Anelka), Thierry Henry, Karim Benzema.   Manager: Raymond Domenech

ITALY: Gianluigi Buffon, Gianluca Zambrotta, Christian Panucci, Giorgio Chiellini, Fabio Grosso, Gennaro Gattuso (82 Alberto Aquilani), Andrea Pirlo (55 Massimo Ambrosini), Daniele De Rossi, Simone Perrotta (64 Mauro Germán Camoranesi Serra), Antonio Cassano, Luca Toni.
Manager: Roberto Donadoni

Goals: Andrea Pirlo (25 pen), Daniele De Rossi (62)
Sent off: Éric Abidal (24)

704.   20.08.2008   Jubileumslandskamp 1958-2008
SWEDEN v FRANCE   2-3 (1-1)
Ullevi Stadion, Gothenburg

Referee: Frederikus Johannes (Eric) Braamhaar (Netherlands)   Attendance: 23,263

SWEDEN: Andreas Isaksson, Olof Mellberg (70 Max von Schlebrügge), Daniel Majstorovic, Petter Hansson, Mikael Nilsson (62 Fredrik Stoor), Daniel Andersson (83 Samuel Holmén), Kim Källström, Anders Svensson, Christian Wilhelmsson (46 Oscar Wendt), Henrik Larsson (62 Marcus Berg), Markus Rosenberg.   Manager: Lars Lagerbäck

FRANCE: Steve Mandanda, Bacary Sagna, Philippe Mexès, William Gallas, Patrice Évra, Jérémy Toulalan (90+3 Yoann Gourcuff), Lassana Diarra, Sidney Govou, Florent Malouda (70 Alou Diarra), Karim Benzema, Thierry Henry.   Manager: Raymond Domenech

Goals: Henrik Larsson (5), Kim Källström (84 pen) / Karim Benzema (18), Sidney Govou (61, 77)

705.   06.09.2008   FIFA World Cup Qualification – Group 7
AUSTRIA v FRANCE 3-1 (2-0)

Ernst Happel Stadion, Vienna

Referee: Claus Bo Larsen (Denmark)   Attendance: 48,000

AUSTRIA: Alexander Manninger, György Garics, Sebastian Prödl, Martin Stranzl, Emanuel Pogatetz, René Aufhauser, Paul Scharner, Martin Harnik (90 Joachim Standfest), Andreas Ivanschitz (81 Christoph Leitgeb), Christian Fuchs, Marc Janko (89 Stefan Maierhofer).   Manager: Karel Brückner

FRANCE: Steve Mandanda, Bacary Sagna (70 Yoann Gourcuff), William Gallas, Philippe Mexès, Patrice Évra, Lassana Diarra, Jérémy Toulalan, Samir Nasri (80 Nicolas Anelka), Sidney Govou, Karim Benzema, Thierry Henry.   Manager: Raymond Domenech

Goals: Marc Janko (8), René Aufhauser (41), Andreas Ivanschitz (73 pen) / Sidney Govou (61)

706.   10.09.2008   FIFA World Cup Qualification – Group 7
FRANCE v SERBIA 2-1 (0-0)

Stade de France, Saint-Denis

Referee: Olegário Manuel Bartolo Faustino Benquerença (Portugal)   Attendance: 53,027

FRANCE: Steve Mandanda, Bacary Sagna, William Gallas, Éric Abidal, Gaël Clichy, Jérémy Toulalan, Lassana Diarra, Sidney Govou (82 Alou Diarra), Yoann Gourcuff (90+4 Mathieu Flamini), Karim Benzema (46 Nicolas Anelka), Thierry Henry.   Manager: Raymond Domenech

SERBIA: Vladimir Stojkovic, Branislav Ivanovic, Nemanja Vidic, Mladen Krstajic, Zoran Tosic, Dejan Stankovic (4 Gojko Kacar), Zdravko Kuzmanovic, Ivan Ergic (56 Nikola Zigic), Bosko Jankovic, Miralem Sulejmani (69 Milos Krasic), Marko Pantelic.   Manager: Radomir Antic

Goals: Thierry Henry (54), Nicolas Anelka (64) / Branislav Ivanovic (76)

707.   11.10.2008   FIFA World Cup Qualification – Group 7
ROMANIA v FRANCE 2-2 (2-1)

Stadionul Farul, Constanta

Referee: Frank De Bleeckere (Belgium)   Attendance: 12,800

ROMANIA: Bogdan Lobont, George Ogararu, Gabriel Tamas, Dorin Goian, Razvan Rat, Razvan Cocis, Gabriel Muresan, Cristian Chivu, Florentin Petre (75 Gigel Bucur), Ciprian Marica, Adrian Mutu (75 Florin Costea).
Manager: Victor Piturca

FRANCE: Steve Mandanda, Patrice Évra, Éric Abidal, Jean-Alain Boumsong, Bacary Sagna, Alou Diarra, Jérémy Toulalan, Florent Malouda (38 Karim Benzema), Yoann Gourcuff, Franck Ribéry (90+1 Jimmy Briand), Thierry Henry.   Manager: Raymond Domenech

Goals: Florentin Petre (6), Dorin Goian (17) / Franck Ribéry (36), Yoann Gourcuff (69)

708.   14.10.2008
FRANCE v TUNISIA 3-1 (1-1)

Stade de France, Saint-Denis

Referee: Anton Genov (Bulgaria)   Attendance; 74,564

FRANCE: Steve Mandanda, Gaël Clichy, Jean-Alain Boumsong, Éric Abidal, Rod Fanni, Alou Diarra, Jérémy Toulalan, Yoann Gourcuff (80 Jimmy Briand), Franck Ribéry (46 Hatem Ben Arfa), Karim Benzema (69 Florent Sinama-Pongolle), Thierry Henry (84 Florent Malouda).   Manager: Raymond Domenech

TUNISIA: Aymen Mathlouthi, Anis Boussaïdi, Yassine Mikari, Saïf Ghezal, Karim Haggui, Radhouène Felhi (85 Mohamed Ali Nafkha), Houcine Ragued (73 Oussama Darragui), Wissem Ben Yahia (64 Anis Boujelbene), Fahid Ben Khalfallah (90+2 Majdi Mosrati), Tijani Belaïd (68 Hichem Essifi), Issam Jemâa (76 Chaouki Ben Saada).   Manager: Humberto Manuel de Jesus Coelho

Goals: Thierry Henry (40, 48), Karim Benzema (58) / Issam Jemâa (30)

709.   19.11.2008
FRANCE v URUGUAY 0-0

Stade de France, Saint-Denis

Referee: Cyril Zimmermann (Switzerland)
Attendance: 79,666

FRANCE: Hugo Lloris, Rod Fanni, William Gallas, Philippe Mexès, Petrice Évra, Patrick Vieira (46 Alou Diarra), Jérémy Toulalan, Yoann Gourcuff (72 Samir Nasri), Franck Ribéry (58 Karim Benzema), Thierry Henry (72 Jimmy Briand), Nicolas Anelka (46 Steve Savidan).   Manager: Raymond Domenech

URUGUAY: Héctor Fabián CARINI Hernández, Bruno Ramón SILVA Barone, Diego Alfredo LUGANO Moreno, Diego Roberto GODÍN Leal (18 Carlos Adrián VALDEZ Suárez), José Martín CÁCERES Silva, Victorio Maximiliano PEREIRA Páez, Walter Alejandro GARGANO Guevara, Álvaro Daniel PEREIRA Barragán (71 Mathías Adolfo CARDACCIO Alaguich), Cristian Gabriel RODRÍGUEZ Barotti (82 Vicente Martín SÁNCHEZ Bragunde), Luis Alberto SUÁREZ Díaz (69 Washington Sebastián ABREU Gallo), Diego Martín FORLÁN Corazo (46 Edinson Roberto CAVANI Gómez).   Manager: Óscar Washington TABÁREZ Sclavo

710. 11.02.2009
FRANCE v ARGENTINA 0-2 (0-1)
Stade Vélodrome, Marseille
Referee: Hans Jonas Eriksson (Sweden)   Attendance: 60,000
FRANCE: Steve Mandanda, Bacary Sagna, Philippe Mexès, William Gallas, Éric Abidal, Jérémy Toulalan, Lassana Diarra, Yoann Gourcuff, Franck Ribéry, Thierry Henry, Nicolas Anelka (65 Karim Benzema).   Manager: Raymond Domenech
ARGENTINA: Juan Pablo Carrizo, Javier Adelmar Zanetti, Martín Gastón Demichelis, Gabriel Iván Heinze, Emiliano Ramiro Papa, Maximiliano Rubén "Maxi" Rodríguez (82 Marcos Alberto Angeleri), Javier Alejandro Mascherano, Fernando Rubén Gago, Jonás Manuel Gutiérrez, Lionel Andrés Messi Cuccittini, Sergio Leonel "Kun" Agüero del Castillo (82 Carlos Alberto Tévez).
Manager: Diego Armando Maradona Franco
Goals: Jonás Manuel Gutiérrez (41), Lionel Andrés Messi (83)

711. 28.03.2009   FIFA World Cup Qualification – Group 7
LITHUANIA v FRANCE 0-1 (0-0)
Steponas Darius ir Stasys Girenas Stadionas, Kaunas
Referee: Frederikus Johannes (Eric) Braamhaar (Netherlands)   Attendance: 8,700
LITHUANIA: Zydrūnas Karcemarskas, Deividas Semberas, Andrius Skerla, Ignas Dedura, Arūnas Klimavicius, Edgaras Cesnauskis (84 Saulius Mikoliūnas), Darvydas Sernas, Mantas Savenas (66 Kestutis Ivaskevicius), Mindaugas Panka (81 Robertas Poskus), Deividas Cesnauskis, Tomas Danilevicius.
Manager: José Júlio de Carvalho Peyroteo Martins Couceiro
FRANCE: Steve Mandanda, Bacary Sagna, Sébastien Squillaci, William Gallas, Patrice Évra, Jérémy Toulalan, Lassana Diarra, Yoann Gourcuff (78 Samir Nasri), Franck Ribéry, Thierry Henry, Péguy Luyindula (64 Karim Benzema).
Manager: Raymond Domenech
Goal: Franck Ribéry (67)

712. 01.04.2009   FIFA World Cup Qualification – Group 7
FRANCE v LITHUANIA 1-0 (0-0)
Stade de France, Saint-Denis
Referee: Howard Melton Webb (England)
Attendance: 79,543
FRANCE: Steve Mandanda, Bacary Sagna, Sébastien Squillaci, William Gallas, Patrice Évra, Alou Diarra, Lassana Diarra, Yoann Gourcuff (57 Karim Benzema), Franck Ribéry, Péguy Luyindula (69 André-Pierre Gignac), Thierry Henry.
Manager: Raymond Domenech
LITHUANIA: Zydrūnas Karcemarskas, Vidas Alunderis, Andrius Skerla, Marius Zaliūkas, Arūnas Klimavicius, Deividas Semberas, Saulius Mikoliūnas (65 Edgaras Cesnauskis), Darvydas Sernas, Linas Pilibaitis (82 Andrius Velicka), Mindaugas Kalonas (59 Mantas Savenas), Tomas Danilevicius.
Manager: José Júlio de Carvalho Peyroteo Martins Couceiro
Goal: Franck Ribéry (76)

713. 02.06.2009
FRANCE v NIGERIA 0-1 (0-1)
Stade Geoffroy Guichard, Saint-Étienne
Referee: Matthew Dyer (South Africa)   Attendance: 18,000
FRANCE: Steve Mandanda, Patrice Évra, Julien Escudé, Sébastien Squillaci, Rod Fanni, Alou Diarra (46 Jérémy Toulalan), Patrick Vieira, Loïc Rémy, Franck Ribéry (70 Sidney Govou), Nicolas Anelka (46 André-Pierre Gignac), Karim Benzema (46 Yoann Gourcuff).
Manager: Raymond Domenech
NIGERIA: Vincent Enyeama, Sam Sodje (60 Obinna Nwaneri), Dele Adeleye, Olubayo Adefemi, Elderson Echiéjilé, Seyi Olofinjana, Kalu Uche (71 Dickson Etuhu), Peter Odemwingie, Nwankwo Kanu (46 Mohamed Yusuf), Joseph Akpala (74 Victor Obinna), Ikechukwu Uche.
Manager: Shuaibu Amodu
Goal: Joseph Akpala (32)

714. 05.06.2009
FRANCE v TURKEY 1-0 (1-0)
Stade de Gerland, Lyon
Referee: Manuel Gräfe (Germany)   Attendance: 41,044
FRANCE: Hugo Lloris, Bacary Sagna, Jean-Alain Boumsong, Philippe Mexès, Éric Abidal, Lassana Diarra, Jérémy Toulalan, Yoann Gourcuff, Florent Malouda (59 Franck Ribéry), Nicolas Anelka (59 Sidney Govou), Karim Benzema (46 André-Pierre Gignac).   Manager: Raymond Domenech
TURKEY: Volkan Demirel, Sabri Sarioglu (84 Ibrahim Kas), Gökhan Zan, Hakan Balta (86 Caner Erkin), Ibrahim Üzülmez, Tuncay Sanli, Mehmet Topal (74 Sercan Yildirim), Nuri Sahin, Arda Turan (79 Yusuf Simsek), Mevlüt Erdinç (42 Eren Güngör), Halil Altintop (46 Semih Sentürk).
Manager: Fatih Terim
Goal: Karim Benzema (38 pen)
Sent off: Ibrahim Üzülmez (37)

715. 12.08.2009   FIFA World Cup Qualification – Group 7

FAROE ISLANDS v FRANCE 0-1 (0-1)

Tórsvøllur, Tórshavn

Referee: Michalis Koukoulakis (Greece)   Attendance: 2,974

FAROE ISLANDS: Jákup Mikkelsen, Jónas Thór Næs, Jóhan Davidsen, Atli Danielsen (42 Jann Ingi Petersen), Egil á Bø, Atli Gregersen, Fródi Benjaminsen, Símun Samuelsen, Súni Olsen (84 Jákup á Borg), Christian Lamhauge Holst (28 Jóan Símun Edmundsson), Bogi Løkin.   Manager: Brian Kerr

FRANCE: Hugo Lloris, Bacary Sagna, William Gallas, Julien Escudé, Patrice Évra, Lassana Diarra, Jérémy Toulalan, Yoann Gourcuff, Florent Malouda (65 Franck Ribéry), Nicolas Anelka, André-Pierre Gignac.   Manager: Raymond Domenech

Goal: André-Pierre Gignac (42)

716. 05.09.2009   FIFA World Cup Qualification – Group 7

FRANCE v ROMANIA 1-1 (0-0)

Stade de France, Saint-Denis

Referee: Ivan Bebek (Croatia)   Attendance: 78,209

FRANCE: Hugo Lloris, Bacary Sagna, William Gallas, Julien Escudé, Patrice Évra, Jérémy Toulalan, Lassana Diarra, Yoann Gourcuff (73 Karim Benzema), Thierry Henry, Nicolas Anelka, André-Pierre Gignac (57 Franck Ribéry).   Manager: Raymond Domenech

ROMANIA: Danut Coman, Vasile Maftei, Mirel Radoi, Cristian Chivu, Razvan Rat, Ion Bogdan Mara (61 Mihai Roman (I)), Iulian Apostol, Tiberiu Ghioane, Maximilian Nicu (77 Gigel Bucur), Romeo Surdu (86 Paul Codrea), Ciprian Marica.   Manager: Razvan Lucescu

Goals: Thierry Henry (48) / Julien Escudé (56 og)

717. 09.09.2009   FIFA World Cup Qualification – Group 7

SERBIA v FRANCE 1-1 (1-1)

Stadion Crvena Zvezda, Beograd

Referee: Roberto Rosetti (Italy)   Attendance: 49,456

SERBIA: Vladimir Stojkovic, Branislav Ivanovic, Ivan Obradovic, Aleksandar Lukovic, Nemanja Vidic, Nenad Milijas (71 Zdravko Kuzmanovic), Gojko Kacar (46 Milos Ninkovic), Milos Krasic, Milan Jovanovic (74 Danko Lazovic), Nikola Zigic, Dejan Stankovic.   Manager: Radomir Antic

FRANCE: Hugo Lloris, Bacary Sagna, William Gallas, Éric Abidal, Patrice Évra, Jérémy Toulalan, Lassana Diarra, Yoann Gourcuff (86 Alou Diarra), Thierry Henry (77 Franck Ribéry), Nicolas Anelka, André-Pierre Gignac (12 Steve Mandanda goalkeeper).   Manager: Raymond Domenech

Goals: Nenad Milijas (13 pen) / Thierry Henry (36)

Sent off: Danko Lazovic (89) / Hugo Lloris (9)

718. 10.10.2009   FIFA World Cup Qualification – Group 7

FRANCE v FAROE ISLANDS 5-0 (2-0)

Stade du Roudourou, Guingamp

Referee: Robert Malek (Poland) (77 Pawel Gil (Poland))   Attendance: 16,755

FRANCE: Steve Mandanda, Patrice Évra, Éric Abidal, William Gallas, Bacary Sagna, Lassana Diarra, Jérémy Toulalan (61 Moussa Sissoko), Sidney Govou (62 Florent Malouda), Thierry Henry, Nicolas Anelka, André-Pierre Gignac (73 Karim Benzema).   Manager: Raymond Domenech

FAROE ISLANDS: Jákup Mikkelsen, Jann Ingi Petersen (64 Jónas Thór Næs), Jóhan Davidsen, Atli Gregersen, Egil á Bø, Rógvi Jacobsen (80 Andreas Lava Olsen), Fródi Benjaminsen, Atli Danielsen, Súni Olsen (90 Brian Olsen), Christian Høgni Jacobsen, Bogi Løkin.   Manager: Brian Kerr

Goals: André-Pierre Gignac (34, 39), William Gallas (52), Nicolas Anelka (86), Karim Benzema (88)

719. 14.10.2009   FIFA World Cup Qualification – Group 7

FRANCE v AUSTRIA 3-1 (2-0)

Stade de France, Saint-Denis

Referee: Pedro Proença Oliveira Alves Garcia (Portugal)   Attendance: 78,098

FRANCE: Hugo Lloris, Gaël Clichy, Julien Escudé, Sébastien Squillaci, Rod Fanni, Alou Diarra, Moussa Sissoko, Florent Malouda, Sidney Govou, Thierry Henry (50 André-Pierre Gignac), Karim Benzema (79 Bafétimbi Gomis).   Manager: Raymond Domenech

AUSTRIA: Helge Payer (46 Christian Gratzei), Paul Scharner, Jürgen Patocka, Aleksandar Dragovic, Christian Fuchs (80 David Alaba), Veli Kavlak, Julian Baumgartlinger, Yasin Pehlivan, Jakob Jantscher, Stefan Maierhofer (46 Erwin Hoffer), Marc Janko.   Manager: Dietmar Constantini

Goals: Karim Benzema (17), Thierry Henry (26 pen), André-Pierre Gignac (66) / Marc Janko (48)

720. 14.11.2009 FIFA World Cup Qualification – Play-off

REPUBLIC OF IRELAND v FRANCE 0-1 (0-0)

Croke Park, Dublin

Referee: Dr. Felix Brych (Germany)   Attendance: 74,103

REPUBLIC OF IRELAND: Shay Given, Sean St Ledger, John O'Shea, Richard Dunne, Kevin Kilbane, Keith Andrews, Glenn Whelan, Damien Duff (76 Aiden McGeady), Liam Lawrence (80 Stephen Hunt), Kevin Doyle (71 Leon Best), Robbie Keane.   Manager: Giovanni Trapattoni

FRANCE: Hugo Lloris, Bacary Sagna, William Gallas, Éric Abidal, Patrice Évra, Lassana Diarra, Alou Diarra, Yoann Gourcuff, Thierry Henry, Nicolas Anelka, André-Pierre Gignac (90+1 Florent Malouda).   Manager: Raymond Domenech

Goal: Ncolas Anelka (72)

721. 18.11.2009 FIFA World Cup Qualification – Play-off

FRANCE v REPUBLIC OF IRELAND 1-1 (0-1, 0-1) (AET)

Stade de France, Saint-Denis

Referee: Martin Hansson (Sweden)   Attendance: 79,145

FRANCE: Hugo Lloris, Patrice Évra, Julien Escudé (9 Sébastien Squillaci), William Gallas, Bacary Sagna, Alou Diarra, Lassana Diarra, Yoann Gourcuff (87 Florent Malouda), Thierry Henry, Nicolas Anelka, André-Pierre Gignac (57 Sidney Govou).   Manager: Raymond Domenech

REPUBLIC OF IRELAND: Shay Given, Sean St Ledger, John O'Shea (67 Paul McShane), Richard Dunne, Glenn Whelan (63 Darron Gibson), Liam Lawrence (107 Aiden McGeady), Kevin Kilbane, Damien Duff, Keith Andrews, Robbie Keane, Kevin Doyle.   Manager: Giovanni Trapattoni

Goals: William Gallas (103) / Robbie Keane (33)

722. 03.03.2010

FRANCE v SPAIN 0-2 (0-2)

Stade de France, Saint-Denis

Referee: Craig Alexander Thomson (Scotland)
Attendance: 79,021

FRANCE: Hugo Lloris, Bacary Sagna, Michaël Ciani, Julien Escudé, Patrice Évra, Lassana Diarra, Jérémy Toulalan, Yoann Gourcuff, Franck Ribéry (74 Florent Malouda), Thierry Henry (64 Sidney Govou), Nicolas Anelka (77 Djibril Cissé).   Manager: Raymond Domenech

SPAIN: IKER CASILLAS Fernández, SERGIO RAMOS García, Carles PUYOL í Saforcada (46 RAÚL ALBIOL Tortajada), Gerard PIQUÉ i Bernabéu, Álvaro ARBELOA Coca, Sergio BUSQUETS i Burgos, Xabier "XABI" ALONSO Olano (63 MARCOS Antônio SENNA da Silva), Andrés INIESTA Luján (63 JESÚS NAVAS González), DAVID Josué Jiménez SILVA (80 Daniel "DANI" González GÜIZA), DAVID VILLA Sánchez (46 FERNANDO José TORRES Sanz), Francesc "CESC" FÀBREGAS i Soler (46 Xavier "XAVI" Hernández i Creus).   Manager: Vicente DEL BOSQUE González

Goals: DAVID VILLA (21), SERGIO RAMOS García (45+1)

723. 26.05.2010

FRANCE v COSTA RICA 2-1 (1-1)

Stade Félix Bollaert, Lens

Ref: Vladislav Yuryevich Bezborodov (Russia)   Att: 37,539

FRANCE: Steve Mandanda, Bacary Sagna, William Gallas (46 Sébastien Squillaci), Éric Abidal, Patrice Évra, Jérémy Toulalan (46 Alou Diarra), Yoann Gourcuff, Florent Malouda (77 Abou Diaby), Sidney Govou (65 Mathieu Valbuena), Franck Ribéry (84 André-Pierre Gignac), Nicolas Anelka (46 Thierry Henry).   Manager: Raymond Domenech

COSTA RICA: Keylor Antonio NAVAS Gamboa, Gonzalo SEGARES González, Douglas Estebán SEQUEIRA Solano, Júnior Enrique DÍAZ Campbell, Micheal Francisco BARRANTES Rojas, Randall AZOFEIFA Corrales, Josué Isaac MARTÍNEZ Areas (42 Winston Antonio PARKS Tifet), Marcos Danilo UREÑA Porras (75 Diego Alonso ESTRADA Valverde), Roy Alexander MYRIE Medrano (65 Cristian Esteban GAMBOA Luna), Carlos Gerardo HERNÁNDEZ Valverde (56 Christián BOLAÑOS Navarro), Bryan Jafet RUIZ González (90 Diego Josué MADRIGAL Ulloa).
Manager: Rónald Alfonso GONZÁLEZ Brenes

Goals: Douglas Estebán SEQUEIRA Solano (22 og), Mathieu Valbuena (83) / Carlos Gerardo HERNÁNDEZ (11)

724. 30.05.2010

TUNISIA v FRANCE 1-1 (1-0)

Stade du 7 Novembre, Radès

Referee: Adel El Raay (Libya)   Attendance: 26,000

TUNISIA: Aymen Mathlouthi (46 Hamdi Kasraoui), Ammar Jemal, Bilel Ifa, Yassine Mikari (85 Mehdi Meriah), Karim Haggui, Fahid Ben Khalfallah, Mehdi Nafti (71 Houcine Ragued), Youssef Msakni (63 Youssef Mouihbi), Khaled Korbi, Issam Jemâa (77 Yacine Chikhaoui), Oussama Darragui (59 Selim Ben Achour).   Manager: Sami Trabelsi

FRANCE: Hugo Lloris, Patrice Évra (64 Gaël Clichy), Éric Abidal (46 Marc Planus), William Gallas (63 Sébastien Squillaci), Bacary Sagna, Jérémy Toulalan, Florent Malouda, Yoann Gourcuff (64 Abou Diaby), Franck Ribéry (46 Thierry Henry), Sidney Govou (75 Djibril Cissé), Nicolas Anelka (63 André-Pierre Gignac).   Manager: Raymond Domenech

Goals: Issam Jemâa (6) / William Gallas (62)

725. 04.06.2010

FRANCE v CHINA 0-1 (0-0)

Stade Michel Volnay, Saint-Pierre (Réunion)

Referee: Pedro Proença Oliveira Alves Garcia (Portugal)   Attendance: 10,403

FRANCE: Hugo Lloris, Bacary Sagna (46 Anthony Réveillère), William Gallas, Éric Abidal, Patrice Évra, Jérémy Toulalan, Yoann Gourcuff, Florent Malouda (62 Abou Diaby), Sidney Govou (71 Mathieu Valbuena), Nicolas Anelka (6 Thierry Henry), Franck Ribéry (63 André-Pierre Gignac).   Manager: Raymond Domenech

CHINA: Cheng Zeng, Qiang Wang, Wei Du (46 Xuepeng Li), Hanchao Yu, Peng Cui (80 Xu Yang), Zhuoxiang Deng (73 Jianye Liu), Jian Liu, Lei Bai (61 Yang He), Hao Rong, Bo Qu (46' Hai Yu), Lin Gao (51 Ting Zhu).   Manager: Hongbo Gao

Goal: Zhuoxiang Deng (68)

726. 11.06.2010   FIFA World Cup Final Tournament – Group A

URUGUAY v FRANCE 0-0

Cape Town Stadium, Cape Town (South Africa)

Referee: Yuichi Nishimura (Japan)   Attendance: 64,100

URUGUAY: Néstor Fernando MUSLERA Micol, Mauricio Bernardo VICTORINO Dansilio, Diego Alfredo LUGANO Moreno, Diego Roberto GODÍN Leal, Victorio Maximiliano PEREIRA Páez, Diego Fernando PÉREZ Aguado (88 Sebastián EGUREN Ledesma), Egidio Raúl ARÉVALO Ríos, Álvaro Daniel PEREIRA Barragán, Ignacio María GONZÁLEZ Gatti (63 Marcelo Nicolás LODEIRO Benítez), Luis Alberto SUÁREZ Díaz (73 Washington Sebastián ABREU Gallo), Diego Martín FORLÁN Corazo.   Manager: Óscar Washington TABÁREZ Sclavo

FRANCE: Hugo Lloris, Bacary Sagna, William Gallas, Patrice Évra, Éric Abidal, Abou Diaby, Jérémy Toulalan, Yoann Gourcuff (75 Florent Malouda), Sidney Govou (85 André-Pierre Gignac), Franck Ribéry, Nicolas Anelka (72 Thierry Henry).   Manager: Raymond Domenech

Sent off: Marcelo Nicolás LODEIRO Benítez (81)

727. 17.06.2010   FIFA World Cup Final Tournament – Group A

FRANCE v MEXICO 0-2 (0-0)

Peter Mokaba Stadium, Polokwane (South Africa)

Referee: Khalil Ibrahim Al Ghamdi (Saudi Arabia)   Attendance: 35,370

FRANCE: Hugo Lloris, Bacary Sagna, William Gallas, Éric Abidal, Patrice Évra, Abou Diaby, Jérémy Toulalan, Sidney Govou (69 Mathieu Valbuena), Franck Ribéry, Florent Malouda, Nicolas Anelka (46 André-Pierre Gignac).   Manager: Raymond Domenech

MEXICO: Óscar PÉREZ Rojas, Francisco Javier "MAZA" RODRÍGUEZ Pinedo, Rafael MÁRQUEZ Álvarez, Héctor Alfredo MORENO Herrera, Ricardo OSORIO Mendoza, Efraín JUÁREZ Valdez (55 Javier HERNÁNDEZ Balcazar), Gerardo TORRADO Díez de Bonilla, Carlos Arnoldo SALCIDO Flores, Guillermo Luis FRANCO Farquarson (62 Cuauhtémoc Bravo BLANCO), Giovani Alex DOS SANTOS Ramírez, Carlos Alberto VELA Garrido (31 Pablo Edson BARRERA Acosta).   Manager: Javier AGUIRRE Onandía

Goals: Javier HERNÁNDEZ Balcazar (64), Cuauhtémoc Bravo BLANCO (79 pen)

728. 22.06.2010   FIFA World Cup Final Tournament – Group A

FRANCE v SOUTH AFRICA 1-2 (0-2)

Free State Stadium, Bloemfontein (South Africa)

Referee: Óscar Julián Ruiz Acosta (Colombia)   Attendance: 39,415

FRANCE: Hugo Lloris, Gaël Clichy, Sébastien Squillaci, William Gallas, Bacary Sagna, Abou Diaby, Alou Diarra (82 Sidney Govou), Franck Ribéry, Yoann Gourcuff, André-Pierre Gignac (46 Florent Malouda), Djibril Cissé (55 Thierry Henry).   Manager: Raymond Domenech

IVORY COAST: Moeneeb Josephs, Anele Ngoncga (55 Siboniso Gaxa), Aaron Mokoena, Bongani Khumalo, Tsepo Masilela, Steven Pienaar, MacBeth Sibaya, Thanduyise Khuboni (78 Teko Modise), Siphiwe Tshabalala, Katlego Mphela, Bernard Parker (68 Siyabonga Nomvethe).   Manager: Carlos Alberto Gomes Parreira

Goals: Florent Malouda (70) /
Bongani Khumalo (20), Katlego Mphela (37)

Sent off: Yoann Gourcuff (26)

729. 11.08.2010

NORWAY v FRANCE 2-1 (0-0)

Ullevaal Stadion, Oslo

Referee: Carlos Velasco Carballo (Spain)   Attendance: 15,165

NORWAY: Jon Knudsen, Tom Høgli, Kjetil Wæhler (46 Vadim Demidov), Brede Hangeland, John Arne Riise, Erik Huseklepp, Bjørn Helge Riise (87 Per Ciljan Skjelbred), Henning Hauger (90 Ruben Yttergård Jenssen), Christian Grindheim (62 Jan Gunnar Solli), Morten Gamst Pedersen, Mohammed Abdellaoue (46 Espen Ruud).   Manager: Egil Olsen

FRANCE: Stéphane Ruffier, Aly Cissokho, Philippe Mexès, Adil Rami, Rod Fanni, Yann M'Vila (74 Yohan Cabaye), Charles N'Zogbia (46 Lassana Diarra), Moussa Sissoko (46 Hatem Ben Arfa), Samir Nasri (79 Jimmy Briand), Guillaume Hoarau (61 Karim Benzema), Loïc Rémy (46 Jérémy Ménez).   Manager: Laurent Blanc

Goals: Erik Huseklepp (51, 71) / Hatem Ben Arfa (48)

730. 03.09.2010 UEFA Euro 2012 Qualifying – Group D
FRANCE v BELARUS 0-1 (0-0)
Stade de France, Saint-Denis
Referee: William (Willie) Collum (Scotland)   Att: 76,395
FRANCE: Hugo Lloris, Bacary Sagna, Adil Rami, Philippe Mexès, Gaël Clichy, Abou Diaby, Yann M'Vila, Florent Malouda, Jérémy Ménez (69 Louis Saha, 80 Kévin Gameiro), Guillaume Hoarau, Loïc Rémy (34 Mathieu Valbuena). Manager: Laurent Blanc
BELARUS: Yuri Zhevnov, Igor Shitov, Aleksandr Martinovich, Sergey Omelyanchuk, Aleksandr Yurevich, Aleksandr Kulchiy, Jan Tigorev, Vyatcheslav Hleb (89 Anton Putila), Aliaksandr Hleb, Vitaliy Kutuzov (75 Sergey Kislyak), Vitaliy Rodionov (85 Sergey Kornilenko). Manager: Bernd Stange
Goal: Sergey Kislyak (86)

731. 07.09.2010 UEFA Euro 2012 Qualifying – Group D
BOSNIA & HERZEGOVIA v FRANCE 0-2 (0-0)
Olimpijski Stadion Asim Ferhatovic – Hase, Sarajevo
Referee: Dr. Felix Brych (Germany)   Attendance: 28,000
BOSNIA & HERZEGOVINA: Kenan Hasagic, Emir Spahic, Elvir Rahimic (74 Ermin Zec), Miralem Pjanic, Zvjezdan Misimovic, Edin Dzeko, Safet Nadarevic, Vedad Ibisevic (74 Sanel Jahic), Senad Lulic, Senijad Ibricic, Mensur Mujdza. Manager: Safet Susic
FRANCE: Hugo Lloris, Bacary Sagna, Adil Rami, Philippe Mexès, Gaël Clichy, Yann M'Vila, Alou Diarra, Abou Diaby, Florent Malouda (80 Blaise Matuidi), Mathieu Valbuena, Karim Benzema. Manager: Laurent Blanc
Goals: Karim Benzema (72), Florent Malouda (78)

732. 09.10.2010 UEFA Euro 2012 Qualifying – Group D
FRANCE v ROMANIA 2-0 (0-0)
Stade de France, Saint-Denis
Referee: Pedro Proença Oliveira Alves Garcia (Portugal) Attendance: 79,299
FRANCE: Hugo Lloris, Anthony Réveillère, Adil Rami, Philippe Mexès, Gaël Clichy, Alou Diarra, Yann M'Vila, Mathieu Valbuena (68 Loïc Rémy), Florent Malouda, Samir Nasri (74 Yoann Gourcuff), Karim Benzema (86 Dimitri Payet). Manager: Laurent Blanc
ROMANIA: Costel Pantilimon, Cristian Sapunaru, Gabriel Tamas, Cristian Chivu, Razvan Rat, Ianis Zicu (46 Ciprian Deac), Mirel Radoi, George Florescu, Razvan Cocis (87 Mihai Roman (I)), Bogdan Stancu, Daniel Niculea (63 Ciprian Marica). Managers: Razvan Lucescu & Cosmin Contra
Goals: Loïc Rémy (83), Yoann Gourcuff (90+3)

733. 12.10.2010 UEFA Euro 2012 Qualifying – Group D
FRANCE v LUXEMBOURG 2-0 (1-0)
Stade Municipal Saint-Symphorien, Metz
Referee: Matej Jug (Slovenia)   Attendance: 24,710
FRANCE: Hugo Lloris, Gaël Clichy, Philippe Mexès, Adil Rami, Anthony Réveillère, Abou Diaby, Alou Diarra, Yoann Gourcuff, Florent Malouda (63 Samir Nasri), Karim Benzema (63 Dimitri Payet), Guillaume Hoarau (73 Loïc Rémy). Manager: Laurent Blanc
LUXEMBOURG: Jonathan Joubert, Tom Schnell, Eric Hoffmann, Guy Blaise, Mario Mutsch, Tom Laterza (69 Jeff Strasser), Ben Payal, René Peters, Gilles Bettmer (84 Daniël da Mota), Charles Leweck, Aurélien Joachim (53 Joël Kitenge). Manager: Luc Holtz
Goals: Karim Benzema (22), Yoann Gourcuff (76)
Sent off: René Peters (54)

734. 17.11.2010
ENGLAND v FRANCE 1-2 (0-1)
Wembley Stadium, London
Referee: Claus Bo Larsen (Denmark)   Attendance: 85,495
ENGLAND: Ben Foster, Phil Jagielka, Kieran Gibbs (72 Stephen Warnock), Steven Gerrard (84 Peter Crouch), Rio Ferdinand (46 Micah Richards), Joleon Lescott, Theo Walcott (46 Adam Johnson), Jordan Henderson, Andy Carroll (72 Jay Bothroyd), Gareth Barry (46 Ashley Young), James Milner. Manager: Fabio Capello
FRANCE: Hugo Lloris, Éric Abidal, Philippe Mexès (46 Mamadou Sakho), Adil Rami, Bacary Sagna (87 Anthony Réveillère), Yann M'Vila, Yoann Gourcuff (85 Guillaume Hoarau), Samir Nasri, Florent Malouda (77 Dimitri Payet), Mathieu Valbuena (68 Alou Diarra), Karim Benzema (67 Loïc Rémy). Manager: Laurent Blanc
Goals: Peter Crouch (86) / Karim Benzema (16), Mathieu Valbuena (55)

735. 09.02.2011
FRANCE v BRAZIL 1-0 (0-0)
Stade de France, Saint-Denis
Referee: Wolfgang Stark (Germany)   Attendance: 79,712
FRANCE: Hugo Lloris, Bacary Sagna, Adil Rami, Philippe Mexès, Éric Abidal, Yann M'Vila (59 Abou Diaby), Alou Diarra, Yoann Gourcuff (85 Yohan Cabaye), Jérémy Ménez (69 Loïc Rémy), Florent Malouda, Karim Benzema (85 Kévin Gameiro).   Manager: Laurent Blanc
BRAZIL: JÚLIO CÉSAR Soares de Espíndola, Daniel "DANI" ALVES da Silva, THIAGO Emiliano SILVA, DAVID LUIZ Moreira Marinho, ANDRÉ Clarindo dos SANTOS, LUCAS Pezzini LEIVA, ELÍAS Mendes Trindade (89 ANDRÉ Felipe Ribeiro de Souza), RENATO Soares de Oliveira AUGUSTO (58 JÁDSON Rodrigues da Silva), Ânderson HERNANES de Carvalho Viana Lima, Robson de Souza "ROBINHO" (70 SANDRO Raniere Guimarães Cordeiro), Alexandre "PATO" Rodrigues da Silva (85 Givanildo Vieira de Souza "HULK"). Manager: Luiz Antonio Venker "MANO" MENEZES
Goal: Karim Benzema (54)
Sent off: Ânderson HERNANES de Carvalho Viana Lima (40)

736. 25.03.2011   UEFA Euro 2012 Qualifying – Group D
LUXEMBOURG v FRANCE 0-2 (0-1)
Stade Josy Barthel, Luxembourg City
Referee: Tom Harald Hagen (Norway)   Attendance: 8,052
LUXEMBOURG: Jonathan Joubert, Guy Blaise, Eric Hoffmann, Tom Schnell, Charles Leweck (90 Jacques Plein), Gilles Bettmer, Ben Payal, Aurélien Joachim, Tom Laterza (54 Massimo Martino), Mario Mutsch, Lars Krogh Gerson (71 Daniël da Mota). Manager: Luc Holtz
FRANCE: Hugo Lloris, Bacary Sagna, Adil Rami, Philippe Mexès, Patrice Évra, Yoann Gourcuff, Yann M'Vila, Samir Nasri, Franck Ribéry, Florent Malouda, Karim Benzema. Manager: Laurent Blanc
Goals: Philippe Mexès (28), Yoann Gourcuff (72)

737. 29.03.2011
FRANCE v CROATIA 0-0
Stade de France, Saint-Denis
Referee: Alan Kelly (Republic of Ireland)
Attendance: 55,000
FRANCE: Hugo Lloris, Anthony Réveillère, Adil Rami (90+3 Mamadou Sakho), Philippe Mexès, Gaël Clichy, Alou Diarra, Blaise Matuidi (87 Yann M'Vila), Jérémy Ménez (60 Loïc Rémy), Samir Nasri (88 Yoann Gourcuff), Florent Malouda (59 Franck Ribéry), Karim Benzema (74 Kévin Gameiro). Manager: Laurent Blanc

CROATIA: Vedran Runje (46 Stipe Pletikosa), Vedran Corluka, Dejan Lovren, Josip Simunic, Darijo Srna (80 Domagoj Vida), Ognjen Vukojevic, Luka Modric, Niko Kranjcar, Danijel Pranjic (24 Ivan Strinic, 46 Ivan Rakitic), Ivan Perisic (71 Mladen Petric), Nikica Jelavic (56 Nikola Kalinic). Manager: Slaven Bilic

738. 03.06.2011   UEFA Euro 2012 Qualifying – Group D
BELARUS v FRANCE 1-1 (1-1)
Dynama Stadium, Minsk
Referee: David Fernández Borbalán (Spain)
Attendance: 26,500
BELARUS: Sergey Veremko, Igor Shitov, Aleksandr Martinovich, Dmitriy Verkhovtsov, Maksim Bordachev, Sergey Omelyanchuk, Jan Tigorev, Tsimafei Kalachev (90 Vyatcheslav Hleb), Anton Putila (86 Sergey Kislyak), Vitaliy Trubilo, Andrey Voronkov. Manager: Bernd Stange
FRANCE: Hugo Lloris, Bacary Sagna, Adil Rami, Mamadou Sakho, Éric Abidal, Alou Diarra, Abou Diaby (73 Loïc Rémy), Florent Malouda, Franck Ribéry, Samir Nasri, Karim Benzema. Manager: Laurent Blanc
Goals: Éric Abidal (20 og) / Florent Malouda (22)

739. 06.06.2011
UKRAINE v FRANCE 1-4 (0-0)
Donbas Arena, Donetsk
Referee: Mark Clattenburg (England)   Attendance: 15,000
UKRAINE: Andriy Pyatov, Vasiliy Kobin, Anatoliy Tymoshchuk, Oleksandr Kucher (33 Yevhen Khacheridi), Oleh Husyev (74 Igor Khudobyak), Andriy Voronin (60 Artem Milevskiy), Vyacheslav Shevchuk, Ruslan Rotan, Sergiy Nazarenko (62 Denis Kozhanov), Marko Devic (69 Yevhen Seleznyov), Mikola Ishchenko. Manager: Oleg Blokhin
FRANCE: Steve Mandanda, Anthony Réveillère, Younès Kaboul, Mamadou Sakho (76 Éric Abidal), Patrice Évra, Yohan Cabaye (76 Marvin Martin), Yann M'Vila, Blaise Matuidi (76 Abou Diaby), Loïc Rémy (64 Franck Ribéry), Kévin Gameiro (64 Karim Benzema), Jérémy Ménez (64 Florent Malouda). Manager: Laurent Blanc
Goals: Anatoliy Tymoshchuk (53) / Kévin Gameiro (58), Marvin Martin (87, 90+2), Younès Kaboul (89)

740. 09.06.2011
POLAND v FRANCE 0-1 (0-1)
Stadion Wojska Polskiego imienia Marszalka Józefa Pilsudskiego, Warszawa
Referee: Björn Kuipers (Netherlands)   Attendance: 31,000
POLAND: Wojciech Szczesny, Lukasz Piszczek, Grzegorz Wojtkowiak, Tomasz Jodlowiec, Jakub Wawrzyniak, Jakub Blaszczykowski (87 Pawel Brozek), Dariusz Dudka, Rafal Murawski, Ludovic Obraniak (88 Szymon Pawlowski), Adrian Mierzejewski (79 Adam Matuszczyk), Robert Lewandowski.   Manager: Franciszek Smuda
FRANCE: Cédric Carrasso, Bacary Sagna, Younès Kaboul (27 Adil Rami), Éric Abidal, Patrice Évra, Yohan Cabaye (46 Abou Diaby), Alou Diarra (46 Yann M'Vila), Marvin Martin, Mathieu Valbuena (73 Florent Malouda), Charles N'Zogbia (73 Loïc Rémy), Guillaume Hoarau (78 Kévin Gameiro). Manager: Laurent Blanc
Goal: Tomasz Jodlowiec (12 og)

741. 10.08.2011
FRANCE v CHILE 1-1 (1-0)
Stade de la Mosson, Montpellier
Referee: Stuart Steven Attwell (England)
Attendance: 30,000
FRANCE: Hugo Lloris, Bacary Sagna (80 Anthony Réveillère), Younès Kaboul, Éric Abidal, Gaël Clichy, Yann M'Vila, Marvin Martin (78 Blaise Matuidi), Samir Nasri (65 Yohan Cabaye), Loïc Rémy, Florent Malouda (65 Jérémy Ménez), Karim Benzema (65 Kévin Gameiro). Manager: Laurent Blanc
CHILE: Claudio Andrés BRAVO Muñoz, Pablo Andrés CONTRERAS Fica (89 Gonzalo Alejandro JARA Reyes), Waldo Alonso PONCE Carrizo, Arturo Erasmo VIDAL Pardo, Mauricio Aníbal ISLA Isla, Carlos Emilio CARMONA Tello (85 Marco Andrés ESTRADA Quinteros), Gary Alexis MEDEL Soto (46 Felipe Ignacio SEYMOUR Dobud), Luis Antonio JIMÉNEZ Garces (46 Alexis Alejandro SÁNCHEZ Sánchez), Jorge Luis VALDIVIA Toro, Jean André Emanuel BEAUSEJOUR Coliqueo (79 Fabián Ariel ORELLANA Valenzuela), Diego Iván RUBIO Köstner (64 Nicolás Andrés CÓRDOVA San Cristóbal). Manager: Claudio Daniel BORGHI Bidos
Goals: Loïc Rémy (19) /
Nicolás Andrés CÓRDOVA San Cristóbal (76)

742. 02.09.2011   UEFA Euro 2012 Qualifying – Group D
ALBANIA v FRANCE 1-2 (0-2)
Stadiumi Kombëtar Qemal Stafa, Tirana
Referee: Aleksey Nikolaev (Russia)   Attendance: 15,600
ALBANIA: Samir Ujkani, Kristi Vangjeli, Armend Dallku, Lorik Cana, Debatik Çurri (24 Altin Lala), Ansi Agolli, Ervin Bulku (70 Elis Bakaj), Ervin Skela (46 Jahmir Hyka), Admir Teli, Hamdi Salihi, Erjon Bogdani.   Manager: Josip Kuze
FRANCE: Hugo Lloris, Patrice Évra, Anthony Réveillère, Éric Abidal, Younès Kaboul, Franck Ribéry, Samir Nasri, Yann M'Vila, Alou Diarra, Karim Benzema, Florent Malouda (82 Marvin Martin).   Manager: Laurent Blanc
Goals: Erjon Bogdani (46) /
Karim Benzema (11), Yann M'Vila (18)

743. 06.09.2011   UEFA Euro 2012 Qualifying – Group D
ROMANIA v FRANCE 0-0
Arena Nationala, Bucharest
Referee: Howard Melton Webb (England)
Attendance: 49,137
ROMANIA: Ciprian Tatarusanu, Razvan Rat, Vlad Chiriches, Alexandru Bourceanu, Costin Lazar (43 Bogdan Stancu), Ciprian Marica (90 Gigel Bucur), Cristian Tanase, Dorin Goian, Banel Nicolita, Srgian Luchin, Razvan Cocis. Managers: Victor Piturca & Cosmin Contra
FRANCE: Hugo Lloris, Bacary Sagna, Patrice Évra, Éric Abidal, Adil Rami, Yohan Cabaye (75 Samir Nasri), Franck Ribéry, Mathieu Valbuena (71 Loïc Rémy), Karim Benzema, Marvin Martin, Yann M'Vila.   Manager: Laurent Blanc

744. 07.10.2011   UEFA Euro 2012 Qualifying – Group D
FRANCE v ALBANIA 3-0 (2-0)
Stade de France, Saint-Denis
Referee: Michalis Koukoulakis (Greece)   Attendance: 65,239
FRANCE: Hugo Lloris, Mathieu Debuchy, Patrice Évra (46 Anthony Réveillère), Adil Rami, Younès Kaboul, Yohan Cabaye (47 Marvin Martin), Bafétimbi Gomis (79 Djibril Cissé), Samir Nasri, Florent Malouda, Yann M'Vila, Loïc Rémy. Manager: Laurent Blanc
ALBANIA: Samir Ujkani, Andi Lila, Kristi Vangjeli, Armend Dallku, Lorik Cana, Klodian Duro, Gilman Lika (81 Sabien Lilaj), Hamdi Salihi, Gjergj Muzaka (74 Ahmed Januzi), Jahmir Hyka (63 Elis Bakaj), Odise Roshi. Manager: Josip Kuze
Goals: Florent Malouda (11), Loïc Rémy (38), Anthony Réveillère (68)

745.   11.10.2011   UEFA Euro 2012 Qualifying – Group D
FRANCE v BOSNIA & HERZEGOVINA   1-1   (0-1)
Stade de France, Saint-Denis

Referee: Craig Alexander Thomson (Scotland)
Attendance: 78,357

FRANCE: Hugo Lloris, Patrice Évra, Éric Abidal, Adil Rami, Yohan Cabaye (61 Marvin Martin), Samir Nasri, Anthony Réveillère, Jérémy Ménez, Florent Malouda (61 Kévin Gameiro), Yann M'Vila, Loïc Rémy (82 Alou Diarra).   Manager: Laurent Blanc

BOSNIA & HERZEGOVINA: Kenan Hasagic (46 Asmir Begovic), Emir Spahic, Elvir Rahimic, Miralem Pjanic, Zvjezdan Misimovic, Edin Dzeko, Mensur Mujdza (61 Darko Maletic), Senad Lulic, Haris Medunjanin (71 Adnan Zahirovic), Boris Pandza, Sasa Papac.   Manager: Safet Susic

Goals: Samir Nasri (78 pen) / Edin Dzeko (40)

746.   11.11.2011
FRANCE v UNITED STATES   1-0   (0-0)
Stade de France, Saint-Denis

Referee: Michalis Koukoulakis (Greece)   Attendance: 70,018

FRANCE: Hugo Lloris, Mathieu Debuchy, Adil Rami, Laurent Koscielny, Jérémy Mathieu, Yann M'Vila (60 Maxime Gonalons), Alou Diarra, Franck Ribéry (63 Loïc Rémy), Jérémy Ménez, Kévin Gameiro (59 Olivier Giroud), Karim Benzema (63 Marvin Martin).   Manager: Laurent Blanc

UNITED STATES: Tim Howard, Daniel Williams (70 Fabian Johnson), Carlos Bocanegra, Clarence Goodson, Brek Shea (71 DaMarcus Beasley), Steven Cherundolo, Clint Dempsey, Kyle Beckerman (66 Jermaine Jones), Maurice Edu (77 Edson Buddle), Jozy Altidore, Timothy Chandler.   Manager: Jürgen Klinsmann

Goal: Loïc Rémy (72)

747.   15.11.2011
FRANCE v BELGIUM   0-0
Stade de France, Saint-Denis

Referee: César Muñiz Fernández (Spain)
Attendance: 52,825

FRANCE: Hugo Lloris, Éric Abidal, Anthony Réveillère, Mamadou Sakho, Adil Rami, Franck Ribéry (72 Florent Malouda), Yohan Cabaye, Yann M'Vila (42 Maxime Gonalons), Marvin Martin, Karim Benzema (72 Jérémy Ménez), Loïc Rémy (72 Olivier Giroud).   Manager: Laurent Blanc

BELGIUM: Thibaut Courtois, Vincent Kompany, Daniel Van Buyten, Thomas Vermaelen, Toby Alderweireld, Timmy Simons, Marouane Fellaini, Axel Witsel, Eden Hazard, Moussa Dembélé (62 Nacer Chadli), Jelle Vossen (70 Kevin Mirallas).   Manager: Georges Leekens

748.   29.02.2012
GERMANY v FRANCE   1-2   (0-1)
Weserstadion, Bremen

Referee: Paolo Tagliavento (Italy)   Attendance: 37,800

GERMANY: Tim Wiese, Jérôme Boateng, Dennis Aogo, Mats Hummels, Holger Badstuber (46 Benedikt Höwedes), Mesut Özil, Sami Khedira (70 Lars Bender), Toni Kroos, Marco Reus (70 Claudemir Jerônimo Barreto "CACAU"), Miroslav Klose (46 Mario Gómez), André Schürrle (45 Thomas Müller).   Manager: Joachim Löw

FRANCE: Hugo Lloris, Éric Abidal, Mathieu Debuchy, Philippe Mexès, Adil Rami, Franck Ribéry (46 Jérémy Ménez), Mathieu Valbuena (68 Morgan Amalfitano), Samir Nasri, Yohan Cabaye (62 Alou Diarra), Yann M'Vila (62 Florent Malouda), Olivier Giroud (76 Louis Saha).   Manager: Laurent Blanc

Goals: Claudemir Jerônimo Barreto "CACAU" (90+1) / Olivier Giroud (21), Florent Malouda (69)

749.   27.05.2012
FRANCE v ICELAND   3-2   (0-2)
Stade du Hainaut, Valenciennes

Referee: Sébastien Delférière (Belgium)   Attendance: 20,580

FRANCE: Steve Mandanda, Mathieu Debuchy, Adil Rami, Philippe Mexès, Patrice Évra, Yohan Cabaye (59 Alou Diarra), Yoann Gourcuff (75 Franck Ribéry), Samir Nasri (60 Marvin Martin), Hatem Ben Arfa (59 Olivier Giroud), Jérémy Ménez (75 Mathieu Valbuena), Karim Benzema (59 Florent Malouda).   Manager: Laurent Blanc

ICELAND: Hannes Halldórsson, Hallgrímur Jónasson, Kári Árnason, Ragnar Sigurdsson, Hjörtur Valgardsson (58 Ari Skúlason), Birkir Bjarnason, Eggert Jónsson (65 Helgi Danielsson), Aron Gunnarsson, Gylfi Sigurdsson, Rúrik Gíslason (76 Jóhann Gudmundsson), Kolbeinn Sigthórsson (46 Eyjólfur Hédinsson).   Manager: Lars Lagerbäck

Goals: M. Debuchy (51), Franck Ribéry (85), Adil Rami (87) / Birkir Bjarnason (28), Kolbeinn Sigthórsson (34)

750. 31.05.2012

FRANCE v SERBIA 2-0 (2-0)

Stade Auguste Delaune, Reims

Referee: Knut Kircher (Germany)   Attendance: 18,000

FRANCE: Hugo Lloris, Anthony Réveillère, Laurent Koscielny, Philippe Mexès (72 Adil Rami), Gaël Clichy, Yohan Cabaye (60 Marvin Martin), Yann M'Vila (7 Alou Diarra), Florent Malouda (76 Hatem Ben Arfa), Karim Benzema (61 Olivier Giroud), Franck Ribéry (61 Jérémy Ménez), Samir Nasri.   Manager: Laurent Blanc

SERBIA: Zeljko Brkic, Branislav Ivanovic, Nikola Maksimovic, Slobodan Rajkovic, Pavle Ninkov, Ljubomir Fejsa (60 Ivan Radovanovic), Nemanja Matic (60 Srdjan Mijailovic), Filip Mladenovic (60 Aleksandar Kolarov), Dusan Tadic (80 Nemanja Tomic), Bosko Jankovic (75 Darko Lazovic), Stefan Scepovic.   Manager: Sinisa Mihajlovic

Goals: Franck Ribéry (11), Florent Malouda (15)

751. 05.06.2012

FRANCE v ESTONIA 4-0 (2-0)

MMArena, Le Mans

Referee: Liran Liany (Israel)   Attendance: 23,500

FRANCE: Hugo Lloris, Patrice Évra, Philippe Mexès, Adil Rami, Mathieu Debuchy, Alou Diarra (65 Laurent Koscielny), Franck Ribéry (65 Marvin Martin), Florent Malouda (73 Olivier Giroud), Yohan Cabaye (51 Mathieu Valbuena), Samir Nasri (73 Hatem Ben Arfa), Karim Benzema (74 Jérémy Ménez).   Manager: Laurent Blanc

ESTONIA: Sergei Pareiko, Enar Jääger, Taavi Rähn, Ragnar Klavan, Taijo Teniste (46 Dmitri Kruglov), Sander Puri, Aleksandr Dmitrijev, Konstantin Vassiljev, Tarmo Kink (68 Ats Purje), Henrik Ojamaa (61 Kaimar Saag), Andres Oper (67 Vladimir Voskoboinikov).   Manager: Tarmo Rüütli

Goals: Franck Ribéry (25), Karim Benzema (37, 47), Jérémy Ménez (90+1)

752. 11.06.2012   UEFA European Championship – Group D

FRANCE v ENGLAND 1-1 (1-1)

Donbas Arena, Donetsk (Ukraine)

Referee: Nicola Rizzoli (Italy)   Attendance: 47,400

FRANCE: Hugo Lloris, Mathieu Debuchy, Patrice Évra, Philippe Mexès, Adil Rami, Alou Diarra, Florent Malouda (85 Marvin Martin), Franck Ribéry, Samir Nasri, Yohan Cabaye (84 Hatem Ben Arfa), Karim Benzema.   Manager: Laurent Blanc

ENGLAND: Joe Hart, Ashley Cole, John Terry, Glen Johnson, Joleon Lescott, Steven Gerrard, Ashley Young, James Milner, Scott Parker (78 Jordan Henderson), Alex Oxlade-Chamberlain (77 Jermain Defoe), Danny Welbeck (90+1 Theo Walcott).   Manager: Roy Hodgson

Goals: Samir Nasri (39) / Joleon Lescott (30)

753. 15.06.2012   UEFA European Championship – Group D

UKRAINE v FRANCE 0-2 (0-0)

Donbass Arena, Donetsk (Ukraine)

Referee: Björn Kuipers (Netherlands)   Attendance: 48,000

UKRAINE: Andriy Pyatov, Taras Mikhalik, Evgen Selin, Yevhen Khacheridi, Oleh Husyev, Sergiy Nazarenko (60 Artem Milevskiy), Anatoliy Tymoshchuk, Yevhen Konoplyanka, Andriy Shevchenko, Andriy Voronin (46 Marko Devic), Andrey Yarmolenko (68 Aleksandr Aliyev).   Manager: Oleg Blokhin

FRANCE: Hugo Lloris, Mathieu Debuchy, Gaël Clichy, Philippe Mexès, Adil Rami, Alou Diarra, Franck Ribéry, Jérémy Ménez (73 Marvin Martin), Samir Nasri, Yohan Cabaye (68 Yann M'Vila), Karim Benzema (76 Olivier Giroud).   Manager: Laurent Blanc

Goals: Jérémy Ménez (53), Yohan Cabaye (56)

754. 19.06.2012   UEFA European Championship – Group D

SWEDEN v FRANCE 2-0 (0-0)

Olimpiysky National Sports Complex, Kyiv (Ukraine)

Referee: Pedro Proença Oliveira Alves Garcia (Portugal)   Attendance: 63,010

SWEDEN: Andreas Isaksson, Olof Mellberg, Jonas Olsson, Martin Olsson, Andreas Granqvist, Kim Källström, Anders Svensson (78 Samuel Holmén), Emir Bajrami (46 Christian Wilhelmsson), Ola Toivonen (78 Pontus Wernbloom), Sebastian Larsson, Zlatan Ibrahimovic.   Manager: Erik Hamrén

FRANCE: Hugo Lloris, Mathieu Debuchy, Gaël Clichy, Philippe Mexès, Adil Rami, Alou Diarra, Franck Ribéry, Samir Nasri (77 Jérémy Ménez), Hatem Ben Arfa (59 Florent Malouda), Yann M'Vila (83 Olivier Giroud), Karim Benzema.   Manager: Laurent Blanc

Goals: Zlatan Ibrahimovic (54), Sebastian Larsson (90+1)

755. 23.06.2012 UEFA European Championship – Quarter-final
SPAIN v FRANCE 2-0 (1-0)
Donbass Arena, Donetsk (Ukraine)
Referee: Nicola Rizzoli (Italy)   Attendance: 47,000
SPAIN: IKER CASILLAS Fernández, SERGIO RAMOS García, Álvaro ARBELOA Coca, Gerard PIQUÉ i Bernabéu, JORDI ALBA Ramos, Francesc "CESC" FÀBREGAS i Soler (67 FERNANDO José TORRES Sanz), Andrés INIESTA Luján (84 Santiago "SANTI" CAZORLA González), Xabier "XABI" ALONSO Olano, Xavier "XAVI" Hernández i Creus, DAVID Josué Jiménez SILVA (65 PEDRO Eliezer Rodríguez Ledesma), Sergio BUSQUETS i Burgos.
Manager: Vicente DEL BOSQUE González
FRANCE: Hugo Lloris, Anthony Réveillère, Mathieu Debuchy (64 Jérémy Ménez), Gaël Clichy, Adil Rami, Laurent Koscielny, Florent Malouda (65 Samir Nasri), Franck Ribéry, Yohan Cabaye, Yann M'Vila (79 Olivier Giroud), Karim Benzema.
Manager: Laurent Blanc
Goals: Xabier "XABI" ALONSO Olano (19, 90+1 pen)

756. 15.08.2012
FRANCE v URUGUAY 0-0
Stade Océane, Le Havre
Referee: Daniele Orsato (Italy)   Attendance: 25,178
FRANCE: Hugo Lloris, Mathieu Debuchy (28 Christophe Jallet), Patrice Évra, Mamadou Sakho, Mapou Yanga-Mbiwa, Franck Ribéry, Rio Mavuba (46 Étienne Capoue), Mathieu Valbuena (75 Jimmy Briand), Maxime Gonalons, Karim Benzema (63 Marvin Martin), Olivier Giroud (75 Bafétimbi Gomis).   Manager: Didier Deschamps
URUGUAY: Néstor Fernando MUSLERA Micol, Victorio Maximiliano "Maxi" PEREIRA Páez, Mauricio Bernardo VICTORINO Dansilio, Diego Alfredo LUGANO Moreno, Diego Roberto GODÍN Leal, Álvaro Daniel PEREIRA Barragán, Diego Fernando PÉREZ Aguado (86 Sebastián EGUREN Ledesma), Walter Alejandro GARGANO Guevara (64 Álvaro Rafael GONZÁLEZ Luengo), Cristian Gabriel RODRÍGUEZ Barotti, Diego Martín FORLÁN Corazo (89 Sebastián Bruno FERNÁNDEZ Miglierina), Washington Sebastián ABREU Gallo.   Manager: Óscar Washington TABÁREZ Sclavo

757. 07.09.2012 FIFA World Cup Qualification – Group I
FINLAND v FRANCE 0-1 (0-1)
Helsingin Olympiastadion, Helsinki
Referee: Craig Alexander Thomson (Scotland)   Att: 35,111
FINLAND: Lukás Hrádecký, Kari Arkivuo, Markus Halsti, Niklas Moisander, Joona Toivio, Roman Eremenko, Tim Sparv, Kasper Hämäläinen (78 Njazi Kuqi), Përparim Hetemaj (65 Alexei Eremenko), Alexander Ring, Teemu Pukki.
Manager: Mika-Matti "Mixu" Paatelainen

FRANCE: Hugo Lloris, Anthony Réveillère, Patrice Évra, Mamadou Sakho, Mapou Yanga-Mbiwa, Franck Ribéry (89 Bafétimbi Gomis), Rio Mavuba, Jérémy Ménez (63 Mathieu Valbuena), Yohan Cabaye (73 Blaise Matuidi), Abou Diaby, Karim Benzema.   Manager: Didier Deschamps
Goal: Abou Diaby (20)

758. 11.09.2012 FIFA World Cup Qualification – Group I
FRANCE v BELARUS 3-1 (0-0)
Stade de France, Saint-Denis
Referee: Hüseyin Göçek (Turkey)   Attendance: 52,552
FRANCE: Hugo Lloris, Mapou Yanga-Mbiwa, Patrice Évra, Christophe Jallet, Mamadou Sakho, Yohan Cabaye (75 Blaise Matuidi), Franck Ribéry (90+1 Jérémy Ménez), Étienne Capoue, Olivier Giroud (61 Mathieu Valbuena), Rio Mavuba, Karim Benzema.   Manager: Didier Deschamps
BELARUS: Sergey Veremko, Aleksandr Martinovich, Artem Radkov, Renan Bressan (46 Aleksandr Kulchiy), Sergey Kislyak, Anton Putila, Denis Polyakov, Dmitriy Verkhovtsov (70 Sergey Balanovich), Maksim Bordachev, Vitaliy Rodionov (62 Sergey Kornilenko), Stanislav Dragun.
Manager: Georgiy Kondratiev
Goals: Étienne Capoue (49), Christophe Jallet (68), Franck Ribéry (80) / Anton Putila (72)
Sergey Kornilenko missed a penalty kick (72)

759. 12.10.2012
FRANCE v JAPAN 0-1 (0-0)
Stade de France, Saint-Denis
Referee: William (Willie) Collum (Scotland)
Attendance: 60,205
FRANCE: Hugo Lloris, Mathieu Debuchy (46 Christophe Jallet), Gaël Clichy, Mamadou Sakho, Laurent Koscielny, Jérémy Ménez (67 Franck Ribéry), Blaise Matuidi (46 Clément Chantôme, 74 Bafétimbi Gomis), Étienne Capoue (67 Maxime Gonalons), Karim Benzema (46 Mathieu Valbuena), Olivier Giroud, Moussa Sissoko.   Manager: Didier Deschamps
JAPAN: Eiji Kawashima, Hiroki Sakai (86 Atsuto Uchida), Maya Yoshida, Yasuyuki Konno, Yuto Nagatomo, Makoto Hasebe (62 Hajime Hosogai), Yasuhito Endo, Hiroshi Kiyotake, Shinji Kagawa, Kengo Nakamura (62 Takashi Inui), Mike Havenaar (86 Hideto Takahashi).
Manager: Alberto Zaccheroni
Goal: Shinji Kagawa (88)

760. 16.10.2012 FIFA World Cup Qualification – Group I
SPAIN v FRANCE 1-1 (1-0)
Estadio Vicente Calderón, Madrid
Referee: Dr. Felix Brych (Germany)   Attendance: 46,825
SPAIN: IKER CASILLAS Fernández, SERGIO RAMOS García, Álvaro ARBELOA Coca (50 Juan Francisco "JUANFRAN" Torres Belén), JORDI ALBA Ramos, Andrés INIESTA Luján (74 FERNANDO José TORRES Sanz), Xavier "XAVI" Hernández i Creus, Francesc "CESC" FÀBREGAS i Soler, PEDRO Eliezer Rodríguez Ledesma, Xabier "XABI" ALONSO Olano, Sergio BUSQUETS i Burgos, DAVID Josué Jiménez SILVA (13 Santiago "SANTI" CAZORLA González). Manager: Vicente DEL BOSQUE González
FRANCE: Hugo Lloris, Mathieu Debuchy, Patrice Évra, Mamadou Sakho, Laurent Koscielny, Yohan Cabaye, Franck Ribéry, Blaise Matuidi, Jérémy Ménez (68 Moussa Sissoko), Maxime Gonalons (57 Mathieu Valbuena), Karim Benzema (88 Olivier Giroud).   Manager: Didier Deschamps
Goals: SERGIO RAMOS García (25) / Olivier Giroud (90+4)
Francesc "CESC" FÀBREGAS missed a penalty kick (42)

761. 14.11.2012
ITALY v FRANCE 1-2 (1-1)
Stadio Ennio Tardini, Parma
Referee: Alberto Undiano Mallenco (Spain)   Att: 19,665
ITALY: Salvatore Sirigu, Andrea Barzagli (46 Leonardo Bonucci), Giorgio Chiellini, Federico Balzaretti, Riccardo Montolivo (50 Alessandro Florenzi), Christian Maggio, Claudio Marchisio (50 Emanuele Giaccherini), Antonio Candreva (70 Sebastian Giovinco), Marco Verratti (51 Andrea Pirlo), Mario Barwuah Balotelli, Stephan Kareem El Shaarawy (73 Alessandro Diamanti).   Manager: Cesare Claudio Prandelli
FRANCE: Hugo Lloris, Mathieu Debuchy (46 Anthony Réveillère), Patrice Évra, Mamadou Sakho, Laurent Koscielny, Franck Ribéry (63 Jérémy Ménez), Blaise Matuidi, Mathieu Valbuena (72 Yoann Gourcuff), Moussa Sissoko (90+1 Benoît Trémoulinas), Étienne Capoue (83 Maxime Gonalons), Olivier Giroud (63 Bafétimbi Gomis).   Manager: Didier Deschamps
Goals: Stephan Kareem El Shaarawy (35) / Mathieu Valbuena (37), Bafétimbi Gomis (68)

762. 06.02.2013
FRANCE v GERMANY 1-2 (1-0)
Stade de France, Saint-Denis
Referee: Paolo Mazzoleni (Italy)   Attendance: 75,000
FRANCE: Hugo Lloris, Bacary Sagna, Patrice Évra, Mamadou Sakho, Laurent Koscielny (46 Adil Rami), Franck Ribéry, Blaise Matuidi (46 Étienne Capoue), Mathieu Valbuena (86 Jérémy Ménez), Yohan Cabaye, Moussa Sissoko (80 Olivier Giroud), Karim Benzema.   Manager: Didier Deschamps
GERMANY: René Adler, Philipp Lahm, Per Mertesacker, Benedikt Höwedes, Mats Hummels, Mesut Özil, Sami Khedira, Ilkay Gündogan, Mario Gómez (57 Toni Kroos), Lukas Podolski (68 André Schürrle), Thomas Müller (89 Lars Bender).   Manager: Joachim Löw
Goals: Mathieu Valbuena (44) / Thomas Müller (51), Sami Khedira (74)

763. 22.03.2013 FIFA World Cup Qualification – Group I
FRANCE v GEORGIA 3-1 (1-0)
Stade de France, Saint-Denis
Referee: Ivan Bebek (Croatia)   Attendance: 71,147
FRANCE: Hugo Lloris, Raphaël Varane, Gaël Clichy, Mamadou Sakho, Christophe Jallet, Franck Ribéry (78 Jérémy Ménez), Mathieu Valbuena (66 Loïc Rémy), Blaise Matuidi (67 Moussa Sissoko), Olivier Giroud, Karim Benzema, Paul Pogba.   Manager: Didier Deschamps
GEORGIA: Giorgi Loria, Guram Kashia, Aleksandr Amisulashvili, Zurab Khizanishvili, Aleksandr Kobakhidze, Murtaz Daushvili, David Targamadze (84 Nikoloz Gelashvili), Jano Ananidze (46 Levan Kenia), Mate Vatsadze (74 Vladimer Dvalishvili), Dato Kvirkvelia, Ucha Lobjanidze.   Manager: Temuri Ketsbaia
Goals: Olivier Giroud (45+1), Mathieu Valbuena (47), Franck Ribéry (61) / Aleksandr Kobakhidze (71)

764. 26.03.2013 FIFA World Cup Qualification – Group I
FRANCE v SPAIN 0-1 (0-0)
Stade de France, Saint-Denis
Referee: Viktor Kassai (Hungary)   Attendance: 78,329
FRANCE: Hugo Lloris, Patrice Évra, Raphaël Varane, Yohan Cabaye (70 Jérémy Ménez), Christophe Jallet (90+2 Olivier Giroud), Laurent Koscielny, Franck Ribéry, Mathieu Valbuena, Karim Benzema (82 Moussa Sissoko), Blaise Matuidi, Paul Pogba.   Manager: Didier Deschamps
SPAIN: VÍCTOR VALDÉS i Arribas, Ignacio "NACHO" MONREAL Eraso, SERGIO RAMOS García, Gerard PIQUÉ i Bernabéu, Álvaro ARBELOA Coca, Andrés INIESTA Luján (90+3 Juan Manuel MATA García), DAVID VILLA Sánchez (61 JESÚS NAVAS González), Xavier "XAVI" Hernández i Creus, PEDRO Eliezer Rodríguez Ledesma (76 Francesc "CESC" FÀBREGAS i Soler), Xabier "XABI" ALONSO Olano, Sergio BUSQUETS i Burgos.   Manager: Vicente DEL BOSQUE González
Goal: PEDRO Eliezer Rodríguez Ledesma (58)
Sent off: Paul Pogba (78)

765.   05.06.2013
URUGUAY v FRANCE   1-0 (0-0)
Estadio Centenario, Montevideo
Referee: Antonio Javier Arias Alvarenga (Paraguay)
Attendance: 20,000

URUGUAY: Néstor Fernando MUSLERA Micol, Diego Alfredo LUGANO Moreno (46 Andrés SCOTTI Ponce de León), Victorio Maximiliano "Maxi" PEREIRA Páez, José Martín CÁCERES Silva, Álvaro Daniel PEREIRA Barragán (71 Cristian Gabriel RODRÍGUEZ Barotti), Sebastián COATES Nión, Walter Alejandro GARGANO Guevara, Egídio Raúl ARÉVALO Ríos (46 Sebastián EGUREN Ledesma), Marcelo Nicolás LODEIRO Benítez (46 Gastón Exequiel RAMÍREZ Pereyra), Diego Martín FORLÁN Corazo (46 Luis Alberto SUÁREZ Díaz), Edinson Roberto CAVANI Gómez (66 Abel Mathias HERNÁNDEZ Platero).
Manager: Óscar Washington TABÁREZ Sclavo

FRANCE: Steve Mandanda, Bacary Sagna, Benoît Trémoulinas, Laurent Koscielny, Eliaquim Mangala, Blaise Matuidi (76 Yohan Cabaye), Mathieu Valbuena (67 Clément Grenier), Yoann Gourcuff (58 Alexandre Lacazette), Étienne Capoue (67 Josuha Guilavogui), Dimitri Payet, Olivier Giroud (58 Bafétimbi Gomis).   Manager: Didier Deschamps

Goal: Luis Alberto SUÁREZ Díaz (50)

766.   09.06.2013
BRAZIL v FRANCE   3-0 (0-0)
Arena do Grêmio, Porto Alegre
Referee: Víctor Hugo Carrillo Casanova (Peru)
Attendance: 51,643

BRAZIL: JÚLIO CÉSAR Soares de Espíndola, Daniel "DANI" ALVES da Silva, THIAGO Emiliano de SILVA, DAVID LUIZ Moreira Marinho, MARCELO Vieira da Silva Júnior, LUIZ GUSTAVO Dias (81 Ânderson HERNANES de Carvalho Viana Lima), José Paulo Bezzera Júnior "PAULINHO" (87 Bonfim Costa Santos DANTE), OSCAR dos Santos Emboaba Júnior (65 FERNANDO Lucas Martins), Frederico "FRED" Chaves Guedes (71 "JÔ" João Alves de Assis Silva), Givanildo Vieira de Souza "HULK" (65 LUCAS Rodrigues Moura da Silva), NEYMAR da Silva Santos Junior (89 BERNARD Anicio Caldeira Duarte).   Manager: Luiz Elena Felipe SCOLARI

FRANCE: Hugo Lloris, Jérémy Mathieu, Mathieu Debuchy, Mamadou Sakho, Adil Rami, Blaise Matuidi (70 Clément Grenier), Mathieu Valbuena (70 Alexandre Lacazette), Yohan Cabaye (82 Bafétimbi Gomis), Dimitri Payet, Josuha Guilavogui, Karim Benzema (70 Olivier Giroud).   Manager: Didier Deschamps

Goals: OSCAR dos Santos Emboaba Júnior (54), Ânderson HERNANES de Carvalho Viana Lima (85), LUCAS Rodrigues Moura da Silva (90+3 pen)

767.   14.08.2013
BELGIUM v FRANCE   0-0
Stade Roi Baudouin, Brussels
Referee: Craig Alexander Thomson (Scotland)   Att: 41,773

BELGIUM: Thibaut Courtois, Vincent Kompany, Daniel Van Buyten (77 Nicolas Lombaerts), Sébastien Pocognoli (80 Jelle Van Damme), Toby Alderweireld, Marouane Fellaini, Axel Witsel, Eden Hazard (74 Dries Mertens), Kevin De Bruyne (85 Moussa Dembélé), Nacer Chadli (71 Kevin Mirallas), Romelu Lukaku (60 Christian Benteke).   Manager: Marc Wilmots

FRANCE: Hugo Lloris, Éric Abidal, Bacary Sagna, Gaël Clichy, Laurent Koscielny, Franck Ribéry, Mathieu Valbuena (74 Clément Grenier), Josuha Guilavogui, Geoffrey Kondogbia (63 Étienne Capoue), Dimitri Payet (63 Samir Nasri), Karim Benzema (73 Olivier Giroud).   Manager: Didier Deschamps

768.   06.09.2013   FIFA World Cup Qualification – Group I
GEORGIA v FRANCE   0-0
Boris Paichadzis Sakhelobis Dinamo Arena, Tbilisi
Referee: Firat Aydinus (Turkey)   Attendance: 26,360

GEORGIA: Giorgi Loria, Ucha Lobjanidze, Gia Grigalava, Guram Kashia, Aleksandr Amisulashvili, Akaki Khubutia, Jaba Kankava, Aleksandr Kobakhidze (60 Tornike Grigalashvili), Nikoloz Gelashvili (79 Vladimer Dvalishvili), Jano Ananidze (69 David Targamadze), Tornike Gorgiashvili.
Manager: Temur Ketsbaia

FRANCE: Hugo Lloris, Bacary Sagna, Éric Abidal, Patrice Évra, Laurent Koscielny, Josuha Guilavogui (78 Samir Nasri), Franck Ribéry, Mathieu Valbuena, Moussa Sissoko, Olivier Giroud, Karim Benzema (62 André-Pierre Gignac).   Manager: Didier Deschamps

769.   10.09.2013   FIFA World Cup Qualification – Group I
BELARUS v FRANCE   2-4 (1-0)
Central Stadium, Gomel
Referee: Daniele Orsato (Italy)   Attendance: 12,203

BELARUS: Sergey Veremko, Stanislav Dragun (71 Edgar Olekhnovich), Aleksandr Martinovich, Aliaksandr Hleb, Anton Putila, Sergey Balanovich, Jan Tigorev (83 Renan Bressan), Dmitriy Verkhovtsov (77 Vitaliy Rodionov), Maksim Bordachev, Egor Filipenko, Tsimafei Kalachev.
Manager: Georgiy Kondratiev

FRANCE: Hugo Lloris, Éric Abidal, Bacary Sagna, Gaël Clichy, Laurent Koscielny, Mathieu Valbuena (90+3 Josuha Guilavogui), Franck Ribéry (80 Moussa Sissoko), Blaise Matuidi, Olivier Giroud, Dimitri Payet (68 Samir Nasri), Paul Pogba.   Manager: Didier Deschamps

Goals: Egor Filipenko (32), Tsimafei Kalachev (57) / Franck Ribéry (47 pen, 64), Samir Nasri (71), Paul Pogba (73)

770. 11.10.2013
FRANCE v AUSTRALIA 6-0 (4-0)

Parc des Princes, Paris

Referee: Artur Manuel Ribeiro Soares Dias (Portugal)
Attendance: 40,710

FRANCE: Hugo Lloris, Éric Abidal (46 Mamadou Sakho), Mathieu Debuchy, Patrice Évra (64 Gaël Clichy), Raphaël Varane, Franck Ribéry (63 Mathieu Valbuena), Samir Nasri, Yohan Cabaye (82 Moussa Sissoko), Paul Pogba (63 Blaise Matuidi), Loïc Rémy, Olivier Giroud (46 Karim Benzema). Manager: Didier Deschamps

AUSTRALIA: Mitchell Langerak, Lucas Neill, Luke Wilkshire (69 Mathew Leckie), David Carney (46 Jason Davidson), Rhys Williams, Mark Bresciano, Tim Cahill (79 Joshua Kennedy), Mile Jedinak, Matt McKay, Robbie Kruse (46 Nikita Rukavytsya), James Holland. Manager: Holger Osieck

Goals: Franck Ribéry (8 pen), Olivier Giroud (16, 27), Y. Cabaye (29), Mathieu Debuchy (47), Karim Benzema (51)

771. 15.10.2013   FIFA World Cup Qualification – Group I
FRANCE v FINLAND 3-0 (1-0)

Stade de France, Saint-Denis

Referee: Michalis Koukoulakis (Greece)   Attendance: 70,156

FRANCE: Hugo Lloris, Éric Abidal, Mathieu Debuchy, Patrice Évra, Laurent Koscielny, Franck Ribéry, Mathieu Valbuena, Samir Nasri (71 Loïc Rémy), Blaise Matuidi (70 Yohan Cabaye), Paul Pogba, Olivier Giroud (81 Karim Benzema). Manager: Didier Deschamps

FINLAND: Niki Mäenpää, Petri Pasanen, Veli Lampi, Roman Eremenko, Përparim Hetemaj, Teemu Pukki (86 Timo Furuholm), Kari Arkivuo, Markus Halsti, Teemu Tainio (64 Joona Toivio), Alexander Ring, Kasper Hämäläinen (79 Riku Riski). Manager: Mika-Matti "Mixu" Paatelainen

Goals: Franck Ribéry (8), Joona Toivio (76 og), Karim Benzema (87)

772. 15.11.2013   FIFA World Cup Qualification – Play-off
UKRAINE v FRANCE 2-0 (0-0)

Olimpiysky National Sports Complex, Kyiv

Referee: Cüneyt Çakir (Turkey)   Attendance: 67,732

UKRAINE: Andriy Pyatov, Oleksandr Kucher, Vyacheslav Shevchuk, Artem Fedetskyi, Yevhen Khacheridi, Ruslan Rotan, Edmar (76 Roman Bezus), Taras Stepanenko, Yevhen Konoplyanka (90+2 Oleh Husyev), Andrey Yarmolenko, Roman Zozulya (86 Yevhen Seleznyov). Manager: Mykhaylo Fomenko

FRANCE: Hugo Lloris, Éric Abidal, Mathieu Debuchy, Patrice Évra, Laurent Koscielny, Franck Ribéry, Blaise Matuidi, Samir Nasri (80 Mathieu Valbuena), Paul Pogba, Loïc Rémy (62 Moussa Sissoko), Olivier Giroud (70 Karim Benzema). Manager: Didier Deschamps

Goals: Roman Zozulya (61), Andrey Yarmolenko (83 pen)

Sent off: Oleksandr Kucher (90+5) / L. Koscielny (90+1)

773. 19.11.2013   FIFA World Cup Qualification – Play-off
FRANCE v UKRAINE 3-0 (2-0)

Stade de France, Saint-Denis

Referee: Damir Skomina (Slovenia)   Attendance: 77,098

FRANCE: Hugo Lloris, Mathieu Debuchy (78 Bacary Sagna), Patrice Évra, Mamadou Sakho, Raphaël Varane, Franck Ribéry, Blaise Matuidi, Mathieu Valbuena, Yohan Cabaye, Paul Pogba, Karim Benzema (82 Olivier Giroud). Manager: Didier Deschamps

UKRAINE: Andriy Pyatov, Vyacheslav Shevchuk, Vitaliy Mandzyuk, Yaroslav Rakitskiy, Yevhen Khacheridi, Ruslan Rotan, Edmar, Yevhen Konoplyanka, Andrey Yarmolenko, Roman Zozulya (76 Yevhen Seleznyov), Roman Bezus (64 Oleh Husyev). Manager: Mykhaylo Fomenko

Goals: Mamadou Sakho (22, 72), Karim Benzema (34)

Sent off: Yevhen Khacheridi (47)

774. 05.03.2014
FRANCE v NETHERLANDS 2-0 (2-0)

Stade de France, Saint-Denis

Referee: Martin Atkinson (England)   Attendance: 78,292

FRANCE: Hugo Lloris, Mathieu Debuchy (87 Bacary Sagna), Patrice Évra (46 Lucas Digne), Eliaquim Mangala, Raphaël Varane, Blaise Matuidi, Mathieu Valbuena (63 Franck Ribéry), Yohan Cabaye, Paul Pogba (81 Moussa Sissoko), Karim Benzema (81 Olivier Giroud), Antoine Griezmann (68 Loïc Rémy). Manager: Didier Deschamps

NETHERLANDS: Jasper Cillessen, Ron Vlaar, Gregory van der Wiel, Daley Blind (52 Karim Rekik), Bruno Martins Indi, Wesley Sneijder (72 Davy Klaassen), Kevin Strootman (39 Stijn Schaars), Jordy Clasie, Quincy Promes, Robin van Persie, Jean-Paul Boëtius (72 Memphis Depay). Manager: Louis van Gaal

Goals: Karim Benzema (32), Blaise Matuidi (41)

775. 27.05.2014
FRANCE v NORWAY 4-0 (1-0)
Stade de France, Saint-Denis
Referee: Padraigh Sutton (Republic of Ireland)   Attendance: 75,000

FRANCE: Stéphane Ruffier, Mathieu Debuchy, Patrice Évra (46 Moussa Sissoko), Mamadou Sakho, Laurent Koscielny, Blaise Matuidi (74 Rio Mavuba), Mathieu Valbuena (70 Clément Grenier), Yohan Cabaye (80 Rémy Cabella), Paul Pogba (46 Lucas Digne), Olivier Giroud, Antoine Griezmann (65 Loïc Rémy).   Manager: Didier Deschamps

NORWAY: Ørjan Nyland, Brede Hangeland, Tom Høgli, Martin Linnes (90+1 Stian Ringstad), Alexander Tettey (72 Anders Konradsen), Ruben Yttergård Jenssen (57 Daniel Braaten), Håvard Nordtveit, Tarik Elyounoussi (72 Valon Berisha), Stefan Johansen, Joshua King (63 Håvard Nielsen), Mats Møller Dæhli (77 Jone Samuelsen).   Manager: Per-Mathias Høgmo

Goals: Paul Pogba (15), Olivier Giroud (51, 69), Loïc Rémy (67)

776. 01.06.2014
FRANCE v PARAGUAY 1-1 (0-0)
Allianz Riviera, Nice
Referee: Carlos Clos Gómez (Spain)   Attendance: 35,200

FRANCE: Hugo Lloris, Bacary Sagna, Patrice Évra, Mamadou Sakho (46 Eliaquim Mangala), Laurent Koscielny, Blaise Matuidi (64 Clément Grenier), Yohan Cabaye (46 Rio Mavuba), Paul Pogba, Loïc Rémy (64 Antoine Griezmann), Olivier Giroud, Mathieu Valbuena (72 Moussa Sissoko).   Manager: Didier Deschamps

PARAGUAY: Antony Domingo SILVA Cano, Luis Carlos CARDOZO Espillaga (75 Derlis Ricardo ORUÉ Acevedo), Miguel Angel Ramón SAMUDIO, Danilo Fabián ORTÍZ Soto, Ramón David CORONEL Gómez (70 José Ariel NÚÑEZ Portelli), Junior Osmar Ignacio ALONSO Mujica, David Ariel MENDIETA Chávez (42 Jorge Luis ROJAS Meza), Víctor Javier CÁCERES Centurión, Fidencio OVIEDO Domínguez (89 Silvio Gabriel TORALES Giménez), Óscar David ROMERO Villamayor (77 Derlis Alberto GONZÁLEZ Galeano), Roque Luis SANTA CRUZ Cantero (65 Jorge Daniel BENÍTEZ Guillen).   Manager: Víctor GENES

Goals: Antoine Griezmann (82) / Víctor Javier CÁCERES Centurión (89)

777. 08.06.2014
FRANCE v JAMAICA 8-0 (3-0)
Stade Pierre-Mauroy, Villeneuve d'Ascq
Referee: Felix Zwayer (Germany)   Attendance: 49,900

FRANCE: Hugo Lloris, Mathieu Debuchy (46 Bacary Sagna), Patrice Évra, Mamadou Sakho, Raphaël Varane, Blaise Matuidi (72 Paul Pogba), Mathieu Valbuena (80 Loïc Rémy), Yohan Cabaye (59 Rio Mavuba), Moussa Sissoko, Olivier Giroud (71 Antoine Griezmann), Karim Benzema (86 Morgan Schneiderlin).   Manager: Didier Deschamps

JAMAICA: Jacomeno Barrett, Lloyd Doyley, Wes Morgan, Adrian Mariappa, Kemar Lawrence (46 Hughan Gray), Joel Grant, Rodolph Austin, Nicholas Beckett (46 Romario Campbell), Chris Humphrey (64 Ramil Sheriff), Simon Dawkins (85 John-Ross Edwards), Michael Seaton (64 Dicoy Williams).   Manager: Winfried Schäfer

Goals: Yohan Cabaye (17), Blaise Matuidi (21, 66), Karim Benzema (37, 63), Olivier Giroud (53), Antoine Griezmann (77, 89)

778. 15.06.2014   FIFA World Cup Final Tournament – Group E
FRANCE v HONDURAS 3-0 (1-0)
Estádio José Pinheiro Borda, Porto Alegre (Brazil)
Referee: Sandro Meira Ricci (Brazil)   Attendance: 42,991

FRANCE: Hugo Lloris, Mathieu Debuchy, Patrice Évra, Raphaël Varane, Mamadou Sakho, Blaise Matuidi, Mathieu Valbuena (78 Olivier Giroud), Yohan Cabaye (65 Rio Mavuba), Paul Pogba (56 Moussa Sissoko), Karim Benzema, Antoine Griezmann.   Manager: Didier Deschamps

HONDURAS: Noel Eduardo VALLADARES Bonilla, Brayan Antonio BECKELES, Víctor Salvador BERNÁRDEZ Blanco (46 Osman Danilo CHÁVEZ Guity), Maynor Alexis FIGUEROA Róchez, Emilio Arturo IZAGUIRRE Giron, Andy Aryel NÁJAR Rodríguez (58 Jorge Aarón CLAROS Juárez), Wilson Roberto PALACIOS Suazo, Luis Fernando GARRIDO Garrido, Roger Aníbal ESPINOZA Ramírez, Carlo Yaír COSTLY Molina, Jerry Ricardo BENGTSON Bodden (46 Óscar Boniek GARCÍA Ramírez).   Manager: Luis Fernando SUÁREZ Guzman

Goals: Karim Benzema (45 pen, 72), Noel Eduardo VALLADARES Bonilla (48 og)

Sent off: Wilson Roberto PALACIOS Suazo (43)

779. 20.06.2014   FIFA World Cup Final Tournament – Group E
SWITZERLAND v FRANCE 2-5 (0-3)
Complexo Esportivo Cultural Professor Octávio Mangabeira, Salvador (Brazil)
Referee: Björn Kuipers (Netherlands)   Attendance: 51,003
SWITZERLAND: Diego Benaglio, Johan Djourou, Stephan Lichtsteiner, Steve von Bergen (9 Philippe Senderos), Ricardo Rodríguez, Valon Behrami (46 Blerim Dzemaili), Gökhan Inler, Xherdan Shaqiri, Granit Xhaka, Admir Mehmedi, Haris Seferovic (69 Josip Drmir).   Manager: Ottmar Hitzfeld
FRANCE: Hugo Lloris, Mathieu Debuchy, Patrice Évra, Mamadou Sakho (66 Laurent Koscielny), Raphaël Varane, Blaise Matuidi, Mathieu Valbuena (82 Antoine Griezmann), Yohan Cabaye, Moussa Sissoko, Karim Benzema, Olivier Giroud (63 Paul Pogba).   Manager: Didier Deschamps
Goals: Blerim Dzemaili (81), Granit Xhaka (87) / O. Giroud (17), Blaise Matuidi (18), Mathieu Valbuena (40), Karim Benzema (67), Moussa Sissoko (73)

Karim Benzema missed a penalty kick (32)

780. 25.06.2014   FIFA World Cup Final Tournament – Group E
ECUADOR v FRANCE 0-0
Estádio Jornalista Mário Filho, Rio de Janeiro (Brazil)
Referee: Noumandiez Doué (Ivory Coast)
Attendance: 73,749
ECUADOR: Alexander DOMÍNGUEZ Carabalí, Jorge Daniel GUAGUA Tamayo, Frickson Rafael ERAZO Vivero, Juan Carlos PAREDES Reasco, Christian Fernando NOBOA Tello (89 Felipe Salvador CAICEDO Corozo), Jefferson Antonio MONTERO Vite (63 Alex Renato IBARRA Mina), Walter Orlando AYOVÍ Corozo, Tilson Oswaldo MINDA Suscal, Michael Antonio ARROYO Mina (82 Alex Gabriel Eduardo ACHILIER Zurita), Luis Antonio VALENCIA Mosquera, Enner Remberto VALENCIA Lastra.
Manager: Reinaldo RUEDA Rivera
FRANCE: Hugo Lloris, Bacary Sagna, Mamadou Sakho (61 Raphaël Varane), Laurent Koscielny, Lucas Digne, Blaise Matuidi (67 Olivier Giroud), Moussa Sissoko, Morgan Schneiderlin, Paul Pogba, Karim Benzema, Antoine Griezmann (79 Loïc Rémy).   Manager: Didier Deschamps
Sent off: Luis Antonio VALENCIA Mosquera (50)

781. 30.06.2014   FIFA World Cup Final Tournament – Round of 16
FRANCE v NIGERIA 2-0 (0-0)
Estádio Nacional de Brasília Mané Garrincha, Brasília (Brazil)
Referee: Mark Geiger (United States)   Attendance: 67,882
FRANCE: Hugo Lloris, Mathieu Debuchy, Patrice Évra, Laurent Koscielny, Raphaël Varane, Blaise Matuidi, Mathieu Valbuena (90+4 Moussa Sissoko), Yohan Cabaye, Paul Pogba, Karim Benzema, Olivier Giroud (62 Antoine Griezmann).
Manager: Didier Deschamps
NIGERIA: Vincent Enyeama, Efe Ambrose, Joseph Ikpo Yobo, Juwon Oshaniwa, Kenneth Omeruo, Ahmed Musa, Ogenyi Onazi (59 Reuben Shalu Gabriel), John Obi Mikel, Victor Moses (89 Uche Nwofor), Emmanuel Emenike, Peter Odemwingie.   Manager: Stephen Keshi
Goals: Paul Pogba (79), Joseph Ikpo Yobo (90+1 og)

782. 04.07.2014   FIFA World Cup Final Tournament – Quarter-final
FRANCE v GERMANY 0-1 (0-1)
Estádio Jornalista Mário Filho, Rio de Janeiro (Brazil)
Referee: Néstor Fabián Pitana (Argentina)
Attendance: 74,240
FRANCE: Hugo Lloris, Mathieu Debuchy, Patrice Évra, Mamadou Sakho (72 Laurent Koscielny), Raphaël Varane, Blaise Matuidi, Mathieu Valbuena (85 Olivier Giroud), Yohan Cabaye (73 Loïc Rémy), Paul Pogba, Karim Benzema, Antoine Griezmann.   Manager: Didier Deschamps
GERMANY: Manuel Neuer, Philipp Lahm, Jérôme Boateng, Benedikt Höwedes, Mats Hummels, Bastian Schweinsteiger, Mesut Özil (83 Mario Götze), Sami Khedira, Miroslav Klose (69 André Schürrle), Thomas Müller, Toni Kroos (90+2 Christoph Kramer).   Manager: Joachim Löw
Goal: Mats Hummels (12)

783. 04.09.2014

FRANCE v SPAIN 1-0 (0-0)

Stade de France, Saint-Denis

Referee: Alain Bieri (Switzerland)   Attendance: 79,132

FRANCE: Hugo Lloris, Mathieu Debuchy, Patrice Évra (68 Lucas Digne), Mamadou Sakho, Raphaël Varane, Blaise Matuidi (68 Yohan Cabaye), Mathieu Valbuena (75 Rémy Cabella), Moussa Sissoko (78 Morgan Schneiderlin), Paul Pogba, Karim Benzema, Antoine Griezmann (58 Loïc Rémy). Manager: Didier Deschamps

SPAIN: David DE GEA Quintana, SERGIO RAMOS García, César AZPILICUETA Tanco, MIKEL SAN JOSÉ Domínguez, Daniel "DANI" CARVAJAL Ramos, Francesc "CESC" FÀBREGAS i Soler (68 PEDRO Eliezer Rodríguez Ledesma), RAÚL GARCÍA Escudero (58 DAVID Josué Jiménez SILVA), Sergio BUSQUETS i Burgos (46 Ander ITURRASPE Derteano), Jorge Resurrección Merodio "KOKE", DIEGO da Silva COSTA (67 Francisco "PACO" ALCÁCER García), Santiago "SANTI" CAZORLA González (78 Francisco Román Alarcón Suárez "ISCO"). Manager: Vicente DEL BOSQUE González

Goal: Loïc Rémy (73)

784. 07.09.2014

SERBIA v FRANCE 1-1 (0-1)

Stadion Patizana, Beograd

Referee: Wolfgang Stark (Germany)   Attendance: 12,500

SERBIA: Vladimir Stojkovic, Branislav Ivanovic, Aleksandar Kolarov, Stefan Mitrovic, Matija Nastasic, Nemanja Matic, Zoran Tosic, Nemanja Gudelj (60 Zdravko Kuzmanovic), Filip Djordjevic (75 Aleksandar Mitrovic), Dusan Tadic (61 Filip Djuricic), Lazar Markovic (86 Adem Ljajic).   Manager: Dick Advocaat

FRANCE: Hugo Lloris, Jérémy Mathieu, Bacary Sagna, Lucas Digne, Raphaël Varane, Yohan Cabaye, Moussa Sissoko (82 Mathieu Valbuena), Morgan Schneiderlin, Rémy Cabella (62 Alexandre Lacazette), Loïc Rémy (62 Karim Benzema), Paul Pogba (74 Blaise Matuidi).   Manager: Didier Deschamps

Goals: Aleksandar Kolarov (80) / Paul Pogba (14)

785. 11.10.2014

FRANCE v PORTUGAL 2-1 (1-0)

Stade de France, Saint-Denis

Referee: Szymon Marciniak (Poland)   Attendance: 79,000

FRANCE: Steve Mandanda, Bacary Sagna, Patrice Évra, Eliaquim Mangala, Raphaël Varane, Blaise Matuidi, Mathieu Valbuena (58 Dimitri Payet), Yohan Cabaye (71 Moussa Sissoko), Paul Pogba, Karim Benzema (89 André-Pierre Gignac), Antoine Griezmann (84 Morgan Schneiderlin). Manager: Didier Deschamps

PORTUGAL: RUI Pedro dos Santos PATRÍCIO, Képler Laveran Lima Ferreira "PEPE", BRUNO Eduardo Regufe ALVES (46 RICARDO Alberto Silveira de CARVALHO), ELISEU Pereira dos Santos, CÉDRIC Ricardo Alves SOARES, TIAGO Cardoso Mendes (68 Ederzito António "ÉDER" Macedo Lopes), Luís Carlos Almeida da Cunha "NANI" (68 RICARDO Andrade QUARESMA Bernardo), JOÃO Filipe Iria Santos MOUTINHO, ANDRÉ Filipe Tavares GOMES (46 WILLIAM Silva de CARVALHO), CRISTIANO RONALDO dos Santos Aveiro (76 JOÃO MÁRIO Naval da Costa Eduardo), Daniel Miguel "DANNY" Alves Gomes (84 Adelino André Vieira Freitas "VIEIRINHA").
Manager: FERNANDO Manuel Fernandes da Costa SANTOS

Goals: Karim Benzema (3), Paul Pogba (69) / RICARDO Andrade QUARESMA Bernardo (76 pen)

786. 14.10.2014

ARMENIA v FRANCE 0-3 (0-1)

Republican Vazgen Sargsyan Stadium, Yerevan

Referee: István Kovács (Romania)   Attendance: 6,000

ARMENIA: Roman Berezovsky (61 Gevorg Kasparov), Robert Arzumanyan, Varazdat Haroyan, Artem Simonyan (69 Rumyan Hovsepyan), Artur Yedigaryan (58 Artak Dashyan), Marcos Pizzelli (82 Aleksandr Karapetyan), Levon Hayrapetyan, Kamo Hovhannisyan, Taron Voskanyan, Artur Sarkisov (65 Hovhannes Hambartzumyan), Karlen Mkrtchyan (90+1 Norair Aslanyan).   Manager: Bernard Challandes

FRANCE: Steve Mandanda, Christophe Jallet, Jérémy Mathieu, Lucas Digne, Raphaël Varane, Blaise Matuidi (46 Paul Pogba), Moussa Sissoko (60 Antoine Griezmann), Morgan Schneiderlin, Dimitri Payet (60 Rémy Cabella), Loïc Rémy (73 Mathieu Valbuena), André-Pierre Gignac (87 Karim Benzema).   Manager: Didier Deschamps

Goals: Loïc Rémy (7), André-Pierre Gignac (55 pen), Antoine Griezmann (83)

787. 14.11.2014

FRANCE v ALBANIA 1-1 (0-1)

Stade de la Route de Lorient, Rennes

Referee: Miroslav Zelinka (Czech Republic)
Attendance: 26,527

FRANCE: Hugo Lloris, Christophe Jallet, Lucas Digne (70 Layvin Kurzawa), Raphaël Varane, Mapou Yanga-Mbiwa, Paul Pogba, Yohan Cabaye (59 Antoine Griezmann), Moussa Sissoko (80 Morgan Schneiderlin), Mathieu Valbuena (85 Dimitri Payet), Karim Benzema, Alexandre Lacazette (69 André-Pierre Gignac).   Manager: Didier Deschamps

ALBANIA: Etrit Berisha, Elseid Hysaj, Ansi Agolli, Mërgim Mavraj, Ledian Memushaj, Lorik Cana, Andi Lila (85 Emiljano Vila), Burim Kukeli (90+2 Ervin Bulku), Amir Abrashi (69 Arlind Ajeti), Ermir Lenjani (76 Herolind Shala), Sokol Çikalleshi (90+3 Bekim Balaj).   Manager: Gianni De Biasi

Goals: Antoine Griezmann (73) / Mërgim Mavraj (40)

788. 18.11.2014
FRANCE v SWEDEN 1-0 (0-0)
Stade Vélodrome, Marseille

Referee: Jesús Gil Manzano (Spain)   Attendance: 55,000

FRANCE: Steve Mandanda, Bacary Sagna, Eliaquim Mangala, Layvin Kurzawa (78 Lucas Digne), Raphaël Varane, Mathieu Valbuena (68 Alexandre Lacazette), Josuha Guilavogui (86 Maxime Gonalons), Dimitri Payet (61 Moussa Sissoko), André-Pierre Gignac (68 Karim Benzema), Antoine Griezmann, Paul Pogba.   Manager: Didier Deschamps

SWEDEN: Andreas Isaksson, Andreas Granqvist, Pierre Bengtsson (46 Oscar Wendt), Pontus Jansson, Emil Krafth, Kim Källström (46 Albin Ekdal), Erkan Zengin (67 Branimir Hrgota), Sebastian Larsson, Alexander Kacaniklic (86 Emil Forsberg), Nabil Bahoui (46 Jimmy Durmaz), Isaac Kiese Thelin (67 John Guidetti).   Manager: Erik Hamrén

Goal: Raphaël Varane (83)
Karim Benzema missed a penalty kick (86)

789. 26.03.2015
FRANCE v BRAZIL 1-3 (1-1)
Stade de France, Saint-Denis

Referee: Nicola Rizzoli (Italy)   Attendance: 81,338

FRANCE: Steve Mandanda, Bacary Sagna, Patrice Évra, Mamadou Sakho, Raphaël Varane, Blaise Matuidi (84 Olivier Giroud), Mathieu Valbuena (82 Dimitri Payet), Moussa Sissoko (74 Geoffrey Kondogbia), Morgan Schneiderlin, Karim Benzema, Antoine Griezmann (74 Nabil Fekir).   Manager: Didier Deschamps

BRAZIL: JEFFERSON de Oliviera Galvão, João MIRANDA de Souza Filho, FILIPE LUÍS Kasmirski, THIAGO Emiliano de SILVA, DANILO Luiz da Silva, WILLIAN Borges da Silva (83 DOUGLAS COSTA de Souza), LUIZ GUSTAVO Dias (90 Fernando Luis Roza "FERNANDINHO"), ELÍAS Mendes Trindade (90+2 MARCELO Vieira da Silva Júnior), OSCAR dos Santos Emboaba Júnior (86 JOSEF de Souza Dias), NEYMAR da Silva Santos Júnior, ROBERTO FIRMINO Barbosa de Oliveira (88 LUIZ ADRIANO de Souza da Silva).   Manager: Carlos Caetano Bledorn Verri "DUNGA"

Goals: Raphaël Varane (21) /
OSCAR dos Santos Emboaba Júnior (40), NEYMAR da Silva Santos Júnior (57), LUIZ GUSTAVO Dias (69)

790. 29.03.2015
FRANCE v DENMARK 2-0 (2-0)
Stade Geoffroy Guichard, Saint-Étienne

Referee: Ivan Kruzliak (Slovakia)   Attendance: 38,458

FRANCE: Stéphane Ruffier, Christophe Jallet (89 Bacary Sagna), Benoît Trémoulinas, Laurent Koscielny, Raphaël Varane, Geoffrey Kondogbia (60 Josuha Guilavogui), Dimitri Payet (82 Mathieu Valbuena), Olivier Giroud, Alexandre Lacazette (71 Blaise Matuidi), Antoine Griezmann (60 Nabil Fekir), Morgan Schneiderlin (82 Kurt Zouma).   Manager: Didier Deschamps

DENMARK: Kasper Schmeichel, Simon Kjær, Lars Jacobsen, Daniel Wass (46 Simon Poulsen), Nicolai Boilesen (46 Anders Christiansen), Michael Krohn-Dehli, Christian Eriksen (83 Lasse Schöne), Lasse Vibe (58 Nicolai Jørgensen), Nicklas Bendtner, Erik Sviatchenko (77 Kian Hansen), William Kvist (88 Thomas Delaney).   Manager: Morten Olsen

Goals: Alexandre Lacazette (14), Olivier Giroud (38)

791. 07.06.2015
FRANCE v BELGIUM 3-4 (0-2)
Stade de France, Saint-Denis

Referee: Marijo Strahonja (Croatia)   Attendance: 70,000

FRANCE: Hugo Lloris, Bacary Sagna, Benoît Trémoulinas, Laurent Koscielny, Raphaël Varane, Yohan Cabaye (46 Dimitri Payet), Blaise Matuidi, Mathieu Valbuena (73 Nabil Fekir), Moussa Sissoko, Olivier Giroud (80 Paul-Georges Ntep), Antoine Griezmann (46 Alexandre Lacazette).   Manager: Didier Deschamps

BELGIUM: Thibaut Courtois, Jan Vertonghen, Nicolas Lombaerts, Toby Alderweireld, Jason Denayer (85 Leander Dendoncker), Marouane Fellaini (77 Nacer Chadli), Axel Witsel (81 Moussa Dembélé), Radja Nainggolan, Eden Hazard, Dries Mertens (59 Yannick Carrasco), Christian Benteke (59 Romelu Lukaku).   Manager: Marc Wilmots

Goals: M. Valbuena (53), Nabil Fekir (89), D. Payet (90+1) / Marouane Fellaini (17, 42), Radja Nainggolan (50), Eden Hazard (54 pen)

792. 13.06.2015

ALBANIA v FRANCE 1-0 (1-0)

Elbasan Arena, Elbasan

Referee: Halis Özkahya (Turkey)   Attendance: 12,000

ALBANIA: Etrit Berisha, Lorik Cana, Andi Lila (18 Ledian Memushaj), Elseid Hysaj, Arlind Ajeti, Naser Aliji, Odise Roshi (64 Armando Sadiku), Ermir Lenjani (56 Valdet Rama), Ergys Kaçe (80 Bekim Balaj), Migjen Basha (72 Sabien Lilaj), Sokol Çikalleshi (88 Arbnor Fejzullahu).   Manager: Gianni De Biasi

FRANCE: Hugo Lloris, Christophe Jallet (72 Bacary Sagna), Patrice Évra, Mamadou Sakho, Raphaël Varane, Maxime Gonalons (59 Mathieu Valbuena), Geoffrey Kondogbia, Dimitri Payet (46 Paul Pogba), Olivier Giroud (46 Nabil Fekir), Alexandre Lacazette, Antoine Griezmann (59 Paul-Georges Ntep).   Manager: Didier Deschamps

Goal: Ergys Kaçe (43)

793. 04.09.2015

PORTUGAL v FRANCE 0-1 (0-0)

Estádio José Alvalade, Lisboa

Ref: Danny Desmond Makkelie (Netherlands)   Att: 39,853

PORTUGAL: RUI Pedro dos Santos PATRÍCIO, RICARDO Alberto Silveira de CARVALHO (27 JOSÉ Miguel da Rocha FONTE), Képler Laveran Lima Ferreira "PEPE", ELISEU Pereira dos Santos, Luís Carlos Almeida da Cunha "NANI", ADRIEN Sebastién Perruchet SILVA (61 MIGUEL Luís Pinto VELOSO), Adelino André Vieira Freitas "VIEIRINHA" (61 CÉDRIC Ricardo Alves SOARES), DANILO Luís Hélio Pereira (85 BERNARDO Mota Veiga de Carvalho e SILVA), CRISTIANO RONALDO dos Santos Aveiro (67 RICARDO Andrade QUARESMA Bernardo), Ederzito António "ÉDER" Macedo Lopes, JOÃO MÁRIO Naval da Costa Eduardo (79 Daniel Miguel "DANNY" Alves Gomes).   Manager: FERNANDO Manuel Fernandes da Costa SANTOS

FRANCE: Hugo Lloris, Bacary Sagna, Patrice Évra, Laurent Koscielny, Raphaël Varane, Blaise Matuidi, Yohan Cabaye (46 Morgan Schneiderlin), Moussa Sissoko (79 Mathieu Valbuena), Paul Pogba, Nabil Fekir (14 Antoine Griezmann, 88 Olivier Giroud), Karim Benzema (74 Anthony Martial).   Manager: Didier Deschamps

Goal: Mathieu Valbuena (85)

794. 07.09.2015

FRANCE v SERBIA 2-1 (2-1)

Nouveau Stade de Bordeaux, Bordeaux

Referee: Artur Manuel Ribeiro Soares Dias (Portugal)   Attendance: 43,500

FRANCE: Hugo Lloris, Bacary Sagna (46 Mathieu Debuchy), Benoît Trémoulinas, Eliaquim Mangala, Raphaël Varane, Blaise Matuidi (46 Geoffrey Kondogbia), Mathieu Valbuena (76 Anthony Martial), Morgan Schneiderlin, Paul Pogba, Olivier Giroud (62 Karim Benzema), Antoine Griezmann (90 Moussa Sissoko).   Manager: Didier Deschamps

SERBIA: Predrag Rajkovic, Branislav Ivanovic, Ivan Obradovic, Nenad Tomovic, Uros Spajic (89 Milos Kosanovic), Ljubomir Fejsa (82 Radosav Petrovic), Nemanja Matic, Dusan Tadic (56 Filip Kostic), Nemanja Gudelj (56 Adem Ljajic), Lazar Markovic (58 Zoran Tosic), Aleksandar Mitrovic (76 Petar Skuletic).   Manager: Radovan Curcic

Goals: Blaise Matuidi (9, 25) / Aleksandar Mitrovic (39)

795. 08.10.2015

FRANCE v ARMENIA 4-0 (1-0)

Allianz Riviera, Nice

Referee: Slavko Vincic (Slovenia)   Attendance: 32,136

FRANCE: Hugo Lloris, Patrice Évra, Mamadou Sakho, Raphaël Varane, Bacary Sagna, Blaise Matuidi (63 Morgan Schneiderlin), Lassana Diarra, Yohan Cabaye (77 Moussa Sissoko), Antoine Griezmann (87 Alexandre Lacazette), Mathieu Valbuena (62 Anthony Martial), Karim Benzema (81 Olivier Giroud).   Manager: Didier Deschamps

ARMENIA: Gevorg Kasparov, Henrikh Mkhitaryan (60 Marcos Pizzelli), Gaël Andonian, Taron Voskanyan, Gevorg Ghazaryan (66 Norair Aslanyan), Artur Sarkisov (54 Aras Özbiliz), Kamo Hovhannisyan (61 Vardan Poghosyan), Artur Yuspashyan, Hovhannes Hambartzumyan (70 David Manoyan), Levon Hayrapetyan, Karlen Mkrtchyan (80 Artak Grigoryan).   Manager: Sargis Hovsepyan

Goals: Antoine Griezmann (35), Yohan Cabaye (55), Karim Benzema (77, 79)

796. 11.10.2015

DENMARK v FRANCE 1-2 (0-2)

Telia Parken, Copenhagen

Referee: Hans Jonas Eriksson (Sweden)   Attendance: 18,145

DENMARK: Kasper Schmeichel, Daniel Agger (85 Jannik Vestergaard), Simon Kjær (73 Erik Sviatchenko), Lars Jacobsen, Riza Durmisi, Michael Krohn-Dehli (56 Nicolai Jørgensen), Jakob Poulsen (46 Pierre-Emile Højbjerg), William Kvist, Christian Eriksen (61 Yussuf Poulsen), Nicklas Bendtner, Martin Braithwaite (69 Pione Sisto).   Manager: Morten Olsen

FRANCE: Steve Mandanda, Christophe Jallet, Eliaquim Mangala, Lucas Digne, Raphaël Varane (46 Kurt Zouma), Blaise Matuidi, Moussa Sissoko, Morgan Schneiderlin, Olivier Giroud (73 Alexandre Lacazette), Antoine Griezmann (78 Mathieu Valbuena), Anthony Martial (88 Yohan Cabaye).   Manager: Didier Deschamps

Goals: Erik Sviatchenko (90+1) / Olivier Giroud (4, 6)

797. 13.11.2015
FRANCE v GERMANY 2-0 (1-0)
Stade de France, Saint-Denis

Referee: Antonio Miguel Mateu Lahoz (Spain)
Attendance: 78,000

FRANCE: Hugo Lloris, Bacary Sagna, Patrice Évra, Laurent Koscielny, Raphaël Varane, Blaise Matuidi (86 Yohan Cabaye), Lassana Diarra (80 Morgan Schneiderlin), Paul Pogba, Olivier Giroud (68 André-Pierre Gignac), Antoine Griezmann (80 Hatem Ben Arfa), Anthony Martial (69 Kingsley Coman).
Manager: Didier Deschamps

GERMANY: Manuel Neuer, Jérôme Boateng (46 Shkodran Mustafi), Mats Hummels, Jonas Hector (34 Emre Can), Antonio Rüdiger, Matthias Ginter (79 Kevin Volland), Bastian Schweinsteiger, Sami Khedira (61 Ilkay Gündogan), Julian Draxler (61 Leroy Sané), Mario Gómez, Thomas Müller.
Manager: Joachim Löw

Goals: Olivier Giroud (45+1), André-Pierre Gignac (86)

798.   17.11.2015
ENGLAND v FRANCE 2-0 (1-0)
Wembley Stadium, London

Referee: Hans Jonas Eriksson (Sweden)   Attendance: 79,223

ENGLAND: Joe Hart (46 Jack Butland), Kieran Gibbs, Eric Dier, Nathaniel Clyne, Gary Cahill, John Stones, Ross Barkley (79 Jonjo Shelvey), Dele Alli (88 Phil Jones), Raheem Sterling (68 Adam Lallana), Wayne Rooney, Harry Kane (80 Ryan Bertrand).   Manager: Roy Hodgson

FRANCE: Hugo Lloris, Laurent Koscielny, Lucas Digne, Raphaël Varane, Bacary Sagna, Yohan Cabaye (57 Lassana Diarra), Hatem Ben Arfa (46 Kingsley Coman), Morgan Schneiderlin (82 Moussa Sissoko), Blaise Matuidi (46 Paul Pogba), André-Pierre Gignac (57 Olivier Giroud), Anthony Martial (68 Antoine Griezmann).
Manager: Didier Deschamps

Goals: Dele Alli (39), Wayne Rooney (48)

799.   25.03.2016
NETHERLANDS v FRANCE 2-3 (0-2)
Amsterdam ArenA, Amsterdam

Referee: Felix Zwayer (Germany)   Attendance: 46,103

NETHERLANDS: Jasper Cillessen, Jeffrey Bruma, Joël Veltman, Jetro Willems (78 Patrick van Aanholt), Virgil van Dijk (46 Ibrahim Afelley), Daley Blind, Wesley Sneijder (37 Riechedly Bazoer), Jordy Clasie (46 Memphis Depay), Davy Klaassen (76 Georginio Wijnaldum), Quincy Promes, Luuk de Jong (81 Vincent Janssen).   Manager: Danny Blind

FRANCE: Steve Mandanda, Christophe Jallet, Patrice Évra (46 Lucas Digne), Laurent Koscielny, Raphaël Varane, Blaise Matuidi, Dimitri Payet, Lassana Diarra (46 N'Golo Kanté), Olivier Giroud (73 André-Pierre Gignac), Antoine Griezmann (46 Anthony Martial), Paul Pogba (87 Moussa Sissoko).
Manager: Didier Deschamps

Goals: Luuk de Jong (47), Ibrahim Affelay (86) /
A. Griezmann (6), Olivier Giroud (13), Blaise Matuidi (88)

800.   29.03.2016
FRANCE v RUSSIA 4-2 (2-0)
Stade de France, Saint-Denis

Referee: Craig Alexander Thomson (Scotland)
Attendance: 65,000

FRANCE: Hugo Lloris, Patrice Évra (46 Jérémy Mathieu, 54 Lucas Digne), Bacary Sagna, Mamadou Sakho, Raphaël Varane, N'Golo Kanté, Paul Pogba (69 Moussa Sissoko), André-Pierre Gignac (79 Olivier Giroud), Lassana Diarra, Anthony Martial (46 Kingsley Coman), Antoine Griezmann (63 Dimitri Payet).   Manager: Didier Deschamps

RUSSIA: Igor Akinfeev (46 Yuriy Lodygin), Aleksey Berezutskiy, Oleg Kuzmin, Yuriy Zhirkov (69 Igor Smolnikov), Aleksandr Golovin (80 Denis Glushakov), Roman Shirokov (70 Pavel Mamaev), Aleksandr Kokorin (80 Fedor Smolov), Artem Dzyuba, Vasiliy Berezutskiy, Alan Dzagoev, Oleg Shatov (88 Aleksandr Samedov).   Manager: Leonid Slutskiy

Goals: N'Golo Kanté (9), André-Pierre Gignac (38), Dimitri Payet (64), Kingsley Coman (76) /
Aleksandr Kokorin (56), Yuriy Zhirkov (68)

801.   30.05.2016
FRANCE v CAMEROON 3-2 (2-1)
Stade de la Beaujoire – Louis Fonteneau, Nantes

Referee: Simon Lee Evans (Wales)   Attendance: 37,000

FRANCE: Hugo Lloris, Patrice Évra, Laurent Koscielny, Adil Rami, Bacary Sagna, Blaise Matuidi, Lassana Diarra (46 N'Golo Kanté), Paul Pogba (65 Moussa Sissoko), Olivier Giroud (65 André-Pierre Gignac), Dimitri Payet, Kingsley Coman (76 Yohan Cabaye).   Manager: Didier Deschamps

CAMEROON: Fabrice Ondoa, Allan Nyom, Adolphe Teikeu, Ambroise Oyongo, Aurélien Chedjou (80 Mohammed Djetei), Georges Mandjeck (69 Clinton N'Jie), Eyong Enoh (46 Sébastien Siani), Edgar Salli (46 Eric Maxim Choupo-Moting), Vincent Aboubakar (71 Anatole Abang), Karl Toko Ekambi (76 Franck Kom), Jacques Zoua.   Manager: Hugo Broos

Goals: Blaise Matuidi (20), Olivier Giroud (41), D. Payet (90) / Vincent Aboubakar (22), Eric Maxim Choupo-Moting (87)

802.   04.06.2016

FRANCE v SCOTLAND 3-0 (3-0)

Stade Municipal Saint-Symphorien, Longeville-lès-Metz

Referee: Sébastien Delférière (Belgium)   Attendance: 25,057

FRANCE: Hugo Lloris, Bacary Sagna, Patrice Évra (83 Lucas Digne), Adil Rami, N'Golo Kanté (88 Moussa Sissoko), Blaise Matuidi (69 Yohan Cabaye), Paul Pogba, Laurent Koscielny, Dimitri Payet (46 Anthony Martial), Kingsley Coman (46 Antoine Griezmann), Olivier Giroud (63 André-Pierre Gignac).   Manager: Didier Deschamps

SCOTLAND: David Marshall, Andrew Robertson (46 Charlie Mulgrew), Russell Martin, Grant Hanley, Gordon Greer, Robert Snodgrass (66 Stephen Kingsley), Matt Ritchie, James McArthur (84 Barrie McKay), Shaun Maloney (46 Ikechi Anya), Darren Fletcher, Steven Fletcher (58 Steven Naismith).   Manager: Gordon Strachan

Goals: Olivier Giroud (8, 35), Laurent Koscielny (39)

803.   10.06.2016   UEFA European Championship – Group A

FRANCE v ROMANIA 2-1 (0-0)

Stade de France, Saint-Denis (France)

Referee: Viktor Kassai (Hungary)   Attendance: 75,113

FRANCE: Hugo Lloris, Bacary Sagna, Laurent Koscielny, Adil Rami, Patrice Évra, Blaise Matuidi, N'Golo Kanté, Paul Pogba (77 Anthony Martial), Antoine Griezmann (66 Kingsley Coman), Dimitri Payet (90+2 Moussa Sissoko), Olivier Giroud.   Manager: Didier Deschamps

ROMANIA: Ciprian Tatarusanu, Cristian Sapunaru, Dragos Grigore, Vlad Chiriches, Razvan Rat, Ovidiu Hoban, Mihail Pintilii, Nicolae Stanciu (72 Alexandru Chipciu), Adrian Popa (82 Gabriel Torje), Florin Andone (61 Denis Alibec), Bogdan Stancu.   Manager: Anghel Iordanescu

Goals: Olivier Giroud (57), Dimitri Payet (89) / Bogdan Stancu (65 pen)

804.   15.06.2016   UEFA European Championship – Group A

FRANCE v ALBANIA 2-0 (0-0)

Stade Vélodrome, Marseille (France)

Referee: William (Willie) Collum (Scotland)   Att: 67,354

FRANCE: Hugo Lloris, Bacary Sagna, Patrice Évra, Adil Rami, Laurent Koscielny, Blaise Matuidi, Dimitri Payet, N'Golo Kanté, Olivier Giroud (77 André-Pierre Gignac), Anthony Martial (46 Paul Pogba), Kingsley Coman (68 Antoine Griezmann).   Manager: Didier Deschamps

ALBANIA: Etrit Berisha, Elseid Hysaj, Ansi Agolli, Mërgim Mavraj, Ermir Lenjani, Arlind Ajeti (85 Freddie Veseli), Burim Kukeli (74 Taulant Xhaka), Andi Lila (71 Odise Roshi), Amir Abrashi, Ledian Memushaj, Armando Sadiku.   Manager: Gianni De Biasi

Goals: Antoine Griezmann (90), Dimitri Payet (90+6)

805.   19.06.2016   UEFA European Championship – Group A

SWITZERLAND v FRANCE 0-0

Stade Pierre-Mauroy, Villeneuve d'Ascq (France)

Referee: Damir Skomina (Slovenia)   Attendance: 45,616

SWITZERLAND: Yann Sommer, Johan Djourou, Stephan Lichtsteiner, Ricardo Rodríguez, Fabian Schär, Valon Behrami, Blerim Dzemaili, Xherdan Shaqiri (79 Gélson Fernandes), Granit Xhaka, Admir Mehmedi (86 Michael Lang), Breel Embolo (74 Haris Seferovic).   Manager: Vladimir Petkovic

FRANCE: Hugo Lloris, Bacary Sagna, Patrice Évra, Adil Rami, Laurent Koscielny, Yohan Cabaye, Moussa Sissoko, Paul Pogba, André-Pierre Gignac, Antoine Griezmann (77 Blaise Matuidi), Kingsley Coman (63 Dimitri Payet).   Manager: Didier Deschamps

806.   26.06.2016   UEFA European Championship – Round of 16

FRANCE v REPUBLIC OF IRELAND 2-1 (0-1)

Parc Olympique Lyonnais, Décines-Charpieu (France)

Referee: Nicola Rizzoli (Italy)   Attendance: 56,279

FRANCE: Hugo Lloris, Bacary Sagna, Patrice Évra, Adil Rami, Laurent Koscielny, Blaise Matuidi, Dimitri Payet, Paul Pogba, N'Golo Kanté (46 Kingsley Coman, 90+3 Moussa Sissoko), Olivier Giroud (73 André-Pierre Gignac), Antoine Griezmann.   Manager: Didier Deschamps

REPUBLIC OF IRELAND: Darren Randolph, Séamus Coleman, Stephen Ward, Richard Keogh, Shane Duffy, James McCarthy (71 Wes Hoolahan), James McClean (68 John O'Shea), Robbie Brady, Jeff Hendrick, Shane Long, Daryl Murphy (65 Jon Walters).   Manager: Martin O'Neill

Goals: Antoine Griezmann (58, 61) / Robbie Brady (2 pen)

Sent off: Shane Duffy (66)

807.   03.07.2016   UEFA European Championship – Quarter-final

FRANCE v ICELAND 5-2 (4-0)

Stade de France, Saint-Denis (France)

Referee: Björn Kuipers (Netherlands)   Attendance: 76,833

FRANCE: Hugo Lloris, Bacary Sagna, Patrice Évra, Laurent Koscielny (72 Eliaquim Mangala), Samuel Umtiti, Blaise Matuidi, Dimitri Payet (80 Kingsley Coman), Moussa Sissoko, Paul Pogba, Olivier Giroud (60 André-Pierre Gignac), Antoine Griezmann.   Manager: Didier Deschamps

ICELAND: Hannes Halldórsson, Ragnar Sigurdsson, Birkir Sævarsson, Ari Skúlason, Birkir Bjarnason, Kári Árnason (46 Sverrir Ingi Ingason), Aron Gunnarsson, Jóhann Gudmundsson, Gylfi Sigurdsson, Kolbeinn Sigthórsson (83 Eidur Gudjohnsen), Jón Bödvarsson (46 Alfred Finnbogason).   Managers: Lars Lagerbäck & Heimir Hallgrímsson

Goals: Olivier Giroud (12, 59), Paul Pogba (20), D. Payet (43), A. Griezmann (45) / K. Sigthórsson (56), Birkir Bjarnason (84)

808. 07.07.2016   UEFA European Championship – Semi-final
GERMANY v FRANCE 0-2 (0-1)
Stade Vélodrome, Marseille (France)
Referee: Nicola Rizzoli (Italy)   Attendance: 64,078
GERMANY: Manuel Neuer, Jérôme Boateng (61 Shkodran Mustafi), Benedikt Höwedes, Jonas Hector, Bastian Schweinsteiger (79 Leroy Sané), Mesut Özil, Toni Kroos, Emre Can (67 Mario Götze), Julian Draxler, Joshua Kimmich, Thomas Müller.   Manager: Joachim Löw
FRANCE: Hugo Lloris, Bacary Sagna, Patrice Évra, Laurent Koscielny, Samuel Umtiti, Blaise Matuidi, Dimitri Payet (71 N'Golo Kanté), Moussa Sissoko, Paul Pogba, Olivier Giroud (78 André-Pierre Gignac), Antoine Griezmann (90+2 Yohan Cabaye).   Manager: Didier Deschamps
Goals: Antoine Griezmann (45+2 pen, 72)

809. 10.07.2016   UEFA European Championship – Final
PORTUGAL v FRANCE 1-0 (0-0, 0-0) (AET)
Stade de France, Saint-Denis (France)
Referee: Mark Clattenburg (England)   Attendance: 75,868
PORTUGAL: RUI Pedro dos Santos PATRÍCIO, Képler Laveran Lima Ferreira "PEPE", JOSÉ Miguel da Rocha FONTE, CÉDRIC Ricardo Alves SOARES, RAPHAËL Adenilo José GUERREIRO, Luís Carlos Almeida da Cunha "NANI", ADRIEN Sebastién Perruchet SILVA (66 JOÃO Filipe Iria Santos MOUTINHO), WILLIAM Silva de CARVALHO, JOÃO MÁRIO Naval da Costa Eduardo, CRISTIANO RONALDO dos Santos Aveiro (25 RICARDO Andrade QUARESMA Bernardo), RENATO Júnior Luz SANCHES (79 Ederzito António "ÉDER" Macedo Lopes).
Manager: FERNANDO Manuel Fernandes da Costa SANTOS
FRANCE: Hugo Lloris, Bacary Sagna, Patrice Évra, Laurent Koscielny, Samuel Umtiti, Blaise Matuidi, Dimitri Payet (58 Kingsley Coman), Moussa Sissoko (110 Anthony Martial), Paul Pogba, Olivier Giroud (78 André-Pierre Gignac), Antoine Griezmann.   Manager: Didier Deschamps
Goal: Ederzito António "ÉDER" Macedo Lopes (109)

810. 01.09.2016
ITALY v FRANCE 1-3 (1-2)
Stadio San Nicola, Bari
Referee: Björn Kuipers (Netherlands)   Attendance: 39,000
ITALY: Gianluigi Buffon (46 Gianluigi Donnarumma), Andrea Barzagli (46 Riccardo Montolivo), Giorgio Chiellini, Davide Astori, Mattia De Sciglio (58 Alessandro Florenzi), Daniele De Rossi (46 Daniele Rugani), Marco Parolo, Antonio Candreva, Giacomo Bonaventura (66 Marco Verratti), Graziano Pellè, Éder Citadin Martins (74 Andrea Belotti).
Manager: Gian Piero Ventura
FRANCE: Steve Mandanda, Layvin Kurzawa (90+2 Lucas Digne), Laurent Koscielny (83 Samuel Umtiti), Raphaël Varane, Djibril Sidibé, Blaise Matuidi (63 Moussa Sissoko), N'Golo Kanté, Paul Pogba, Anthony Martial (46 Dimitri Payet), Olivier Giroud (46 André-Pierre Gignac), Antoine Griezmann (63 Ousmane Dembélé).
Manager: Didier Deschamps
Goals: Graziano Pellè (21) / Anthony Martial (17), Olivier Giroud (28), Layvin Kurzawa (81)

811. 06.09.2016   FIFA World Cup Qualification – Group A
BELARUS v FRANCE 0-0
Borisov Arena, Borisov
Referee: Ovidiu Alin Hategan (Romania)
Attendance: 12,920
BELARUS: Andrey Gorbunov, Sergey Politevich, Denis Polyakov, Mikhail Sivakov, Maksim Bordachev, Ihar Stasevich (69 Sergey Krivets), Tsimafei Kalachev, Ivan Maevski, Nikita Korzun, Mikhail Gordeychuk (85 Maksim Volodko), Nikolay Signevich (81 Sergey Kornilenko).
Manager: Aleksandr Khatskevich
FRANCE: Steve Mandanda, Layvin Kurzawa, Laurent Koscielny, Raphaël Varane, Djibril Sidibé, Paul Pogba, N'Golo Kanté, Moussa Sissoko (69 Ousmane Dembélé), Anthony Martial (57 Dimitri Payet), Olivier Giroud (83 Kévin Gameiro), Antoine Griezmann.   Manager: Didier Deschamps

812. 07.10.2016   FIFA World Cup Qualification – Group A
FRANCE v BULGARIA 4-1 (3-1)
Stade de France, Saint-Denis
Referee: Luca Banti (Italy)   Attendance: 65,475
FRANCE: Hugo Lloris, Layvin Kurzawa, Laurent Koscielny, Raphaël Varane, Bacary Sagna (27 Djibril Sidibé), Blaise Matuidi, Paul Pogba, Dimitri Payet, Antoine Griezmann (83 Nabil Fekir), Moussa Sissoko, Kévin Gameiro (72 André-Pierre Gignac).   Manager: Didier Deschamps
BULGARIA: Vladislav Stoyanov, Zhivko Milanov, Aleksandar Aleksandrov, Strahil Popov, Dimitar Pirgov, Ivelin Popov (68 Aleksandar Tonev), Svetoslav Dyakov, Mihail Aleksandrov (76 Todor Nedelev), Georgi Milanov, Georgi Kostadinov, Marcelo Nascimento da Costa "MARCELINHO" (62 Dimitar Rangelov).   Manager: Petar Hubchev
Goals: Kévin Gameiro (23, 59) Dimitri Payet (26), Antoine Griezmann (38) / Mihail Aleksandrov (6 pen)

813.   10.10.2016   FIFA World Cup Qualification – Group A
NETHERLANDS v FRANCE 0-1 (0-1)
Amsterdam ArenA, Amsterdam

Referee: Damir Skomina (Slovenia)   Attendance: 50,220

NETHERLANDS: Maarten Stekelenburg, Rick Karsdorp, Jeffrey Bruma, Virgil van Dijk, Daley Blind, Kevin Strootman, Davy Klaassen, Georginio Wijnaldum (62 Bas Dost), Vincent Janssen, Davy Pröpper (84 Jetro Willems), Quincy Promes (16 Memphis Depay).   Manager: Danny Blind

FRANCE: Hugo Lloris, Djibril Sidibé, Layvin Kurzawa, Laurent Koscielny, Raphaël Varane, Paul Pogba, Dimitri Payet (67 Anthony Martial), Kévin Gameiro (79 André-Pierre Gignac), Moussa Sissoko, Blaise Matuidi, Antoine Griezmann (90+3 N'Golo Kanté).   Manager: Didier Deschamps

Goal: Paul Pogba (30)

814.   11.11.2016   FIFA World Cup Qualification – Group A
FRANCE v SWEDEN 2-1 (0-0)
Stade de France, Saint-Denis

Referee: Milorad Mazic (Serbia)   Attendance: 78,000

FRANCE: Hugo Lloris, Patrice Évra, Raphaël Varane, Djibril Sidibé, Laurent Koscielny, Moussa Sissoko, Paul Pogba, Dimitri Payet, Olivier Giroud, Blaise Matuidi, Antoine Griezmann (88 N'Golo Kanté).   Manager: Didier Deschamps

SWEDEN: Robin Olsen, Victor Lindelöf, Andreas Granqvist, Ludwig Augustinsson, Emil Forsberg, Albin Ekdal (66 Oscar Hiljemark), John Guidetti (73 Isaac Kiese Thelin), Jakob Johansson, Emil Krafth, Ola Toivonen, Jimmy Durmaz (87 Pontus Jansson).   Manager: Janne Andersson

Goals: Paul Pogba (57), Dimitri Payet (65) / Emil Forsberg (54)

815.   15.11.2016
FRANCE v IVORY COAST 0-0
Stade Bollaert-Delelis, Lens

Referee: Radu Marian Petrescu (Romania)   Att: 35,000

FRANCE: Benoît Costil, Lucas Digne, Adil Rami, Raphaël Varane (46 Laurent Koscielny), Djibril Sidibé (69 Sébastien Corchia), Adrien Rabiot (78 Thomas Lemar), N'Golo Kanté, Paul Pogba (46 Moussa Sissoko), Dimitri Payet, Ousmane Dembélé (46 Nabil Fekir), Kévin Gameiro (63 Olivier Giroud).   Manager: Didier Deschamps

IVORY COAST: Sylvain Gbohouo, Lamine Koné, Adama Traoré, Serge Aurier, Serge Wilfried Kanon, Sereso Geoffroy Gonzaroua Dié (86 Victorien Angban), Max-Alain Gradel (86 Nicolas Pépé), Cheick Doukouré (68 Ismaël Tiémoko Diomandé), Franck Yannick Kessié, Salomon Armand Magloire Kalou, Jonathan Kodjia (68 Giovanni-Guy Yann Sio).   Manager: Michel Dussuyer

816.   25.03.2017   FIFA World Cup Qualification – Group A
LUXEMBOURG v FRANCE 1-3 (1-2)
Stade Josy Barthel, Luxembourg City

Referee: Andris Treimanis (Latvia)   Attendance: 8,000

LUXEMBOURG: Anthony Moris (21 Ralph Schon), Maxime Chanot, Kevin Malget, Chris Philipps, Lars Krogh Gerson, Christopher Martins Pereira, Daniël da Mota (81 Gerson Rodrigues), Stefano Bensi, Mario Mutsch (62 Florian Bohnert), Laurent Jans, Aurélien Joachim.   Manager: Luc Holtz

FRANCE: Hugo Lloris, Samuel Umtiti, Laurent Koscielny, Djibril Sidibé (62 Christophe Jallet), Benjamin Mendy, Blaise Matuidi (83 Adrien Rabiot), Ousmane Dembélé, N'Golo Kanté, Dimitri Payet (78 Kylian Mbappé), Antoine Griezmann, Olivier Giroud.   Manager: Didier Deschamps

Goals: Aurélien Joachim (34 pen) / Olivier Giroud (28, 77), Antoine Griezmann (37 pen)

817.   28.03.2017
FRANCE v SPAIN 0-2 (0-0)
Stade de France, Saint-Denis

Referee: Felix Zwayer (Germany)   Attendance: 76,419

FRANCE: Hugo Lloris, Christophe Jallet, Laurent Koscielny, Layvin Kurzawa, Samuel Umtiti, N'Golo Kanté, Corentin Tolisso (80 Thomas Lemar), Adrien Rabiot (46 Tiemoué Bakayoko), Kévin Gameiro (80 Ousmane Dembélé), Kylian Mbappé (65 Olivier Giroud), Antoine Griezmann.   Manager: Didier Deschamps

SPAIN: David DE GEA Quintana, SERGIO RAMOS García, Gerard PIQUÉ i Bernabéu, JORDI ALBA Ramos (86 Ignacio "NACHO" MONREAL Eraso), Daniel "DANI" CARVAJAL Ramos, Andrés INIESTA Luján (52 THIAGO Alcântara do Nascimento), Sergio BUSQUETS i Burgos, Francisco Román Alarcón Suárez "ISCO" (53 DAVID Josué Jiménez SILVA), Jorge Resurrección Merodio "KOKE" (74 ANDER HERRERA Agüera), PEDRO Eliezer Rodríguez Ledesma (67 GERARD DEULOFEU Lázaro), Álvaro Borja MORATA Martín (84 IAGO ASPAS Juncal).   Manager: Julen LOPETEGUI Agote

Goals: DAVID Josué Jiménez SILVA (68 pen), GERARD DEULOFEU Lázaro (77)

818. 02.06.2017
FRANCE v PARAGUAY 5-0 (2-0)
Roazhon Park, Rennes

Referee: Artur Manuel Ribeiro Soares Dias (Portugal)
Attendance: 28,256

FRANCE: Hugo Lloris, Benjamin Mendy (67 Lucas Digne), Samuel Umtiti, Laurent Koscielny, Djibril Sidibé, Blaise Matuidi, Paul Pogba (46 N'Golo Kanté), Dimitri Payet (46 Thomas Lemar), Ousmane Dembélé (46 Moussa Sissoko), Antoine Griezmann (80 Florian Thauvin), Olivier Giroud (73 Alexandre Lacazette).   Manager: Didier Deschamps

PARAGUAY: Antony Domingo SILVA Cano, Juan Gabriel PATIÑO Martinez (46 Miguel Angel Ramón SAMUDIO), Gustavo Raúl GÓMEZ Portillo, Bruno Amilcar VALDEZ Rojas, Junior Osmar Ignacio ALONSO Mujica, Juan Manuel ITURBE Arévalos (46 Ivan Rodrigo RAMÍREZ Segovia), Víctor Hugo AYALA Núñez (63 Christian Fabián PAREDES Maciel), Juan José AGUILAR Orzusa, Óscar David ROMERO Villamayor (77 Richard Darío FRANCO Escobar), Edgar Milciades BENÍTEZ Santander (46 Sergio Ismael DÍAZ Velázquez), Federico Javier SANTANDER Mereles (58 Jorge Daniel BENÍTEZ Guillen).   Manager: Francisco Javier ARCE Rolón

Goals: Olivier Giroud (6, 13, 69), Moussa Sissoko (76), Antoine Griezmann (77)

819. 09.06.2017   FIFA World Cup Qualification – Group A
SWEDEN v FRANCE 2-1 (1-1)
Friends Arena, Solna

Referee: Martin Atkinson (England)   Attendance: 48,783

SWEDEN: Robin Olsen, Mikael Lustig, Victor Lindelöf, Andreas Granqvist, Ludwig Augustinsson, Albin Ekdal (77 Sebastian Larsson), Marcus Berg (89 John Guidetti), Emil Forsberg, Jakob Johansson, Ola Toivonen, Jimmy Durmaz (76 Viktor Claesson).   Manager: Janne Andersson

FRANCE: Hugo Lloris, Benjamin Mendy, Raphaël Varane, Djibril Sidibé, Laurent Koscielny, Paul Pogba, Antoine Griezmann (76 Kylian Mbappé), Olivier Giroud, Dimitri Payet (76 Thomas Lemar), Moussa Sissoko, Blaise Matuidi.   Manager: Didier Deschamps

Goals: Jimmy Durmaz (43), Ola Toivonen (90+3) / Olivier Giroud (37)

820. 13.06.2017
FRANCE v ENGLAND 3-2 (2-1)
Stade de France, Saint-Denis

Referee: Davide Massa (Italy)   Attendance: 79,000

FRANCE: Hugo Lloris, Djibril Sidibé (89 Christophe Jallet), Raphaël Varane, Samuel Umtiti, Benjamin Mendy (21 Lucas Digne), Paul Pogba, Thomas Lemar, N'Golo Kanté, Ousmane Dembélé, Olivier Giroud (52 Laurent Koscielny), Kylian Mbappé.   Manager: Didier Deschamps

ENGLAND: Tom Heaton (46 Jack Butland), Gary Cahill, Ryan Bertrand (46 Kyle Walker), Raheem Sterling, Kieran Trippier (76 Adam Lallana), John Stones, Alex Oxlade-Chamberlain, Phil Jones (82 Aaron Cresswell), Dele Alli, Eric Dier, Harry Kane.   Manager: Gareth Southgate

Goals: Samuel Umtiti (22), Djibril Sidibé (43), Ousmane Dembélé (78) / Harry Kane (9, 48 pen)

Sent off: Raphaël Varane (47)

821. 31.08.2017   FIFA World Cup Qualification – Group A
FRANCE v NETHERLANDS 4-0 (1-0)
Stade de France, Saint-Denis

Referee: Gianluca Rocchi (Italy)   Attendance: 79,551

FRANCE: Hugo Lloris, Djibril Sidibé, Layvin Kurzawa, Samuel Umtiti, Thomas Lemar, Kingsley Coman (80 Alexandre Lacazette), N'Golo Kanté, Paul Pogba, Laurent Koscielny, Olivier Giroud (75 Kylian Mbappé), Antoine Griezmann (89 Nabil Fekir).   Manager: Didier Deschamps

NETHERLANDS: Jasper Cillessen, Timothy Fosu-Mensah, Stefan de Vrij, Wesley Hoedt, Daley Blind, Kevin Strootman, Georginio Wijnaldum, Wesley Sneijder (46 Tonny Vilhena), Quincy Promes, Arjen Robben, Vincent Janssen (64 Robin van Persie).   Manager: Dick Advocaat

Goals: Antoine Griezmann (14), Thomas Lemar (73, 88), Kylian Mbappé (90+1)

Sent off: Kevin Strootman (61)

822. 03.09.2017   FIFA World Cup Qualification – Group A
FRANCE v LUXEMBOURG 0-0
Stade Municipal de Toulouse, Toulouse

Referee: Aleksandar Stavrev (Macedonia)   Att: 31,177

FRANCE: Hugo Lloris, Laurent Koscielny, Djibril Sidibé, Layvin Kurzawa, Samuel Umtiti, Paul Pogba, Thomas Lemar, N'Golo Kanté, Olivier Giroud (60 Alexandre Lacazette), Kylian Mbappé (59 Kingsley Coman), Antoine Griezmann (81 Nabil Fekir).   Manager: Didier Deschamps

LUXEMBOURG: Jonathan Joubert, Mathias Jänisch, Kevin Malget, Chris Philipps, Laurent Jans, Aldin Skenderovic, Christopher Martins Pereira, Olivier Thill, Daniël da Mota (59 Danel Sinani), Vincent Thill (59 Gerson Rodrigues), David Turpel (87 Dwayn Holter).   Manager: Luc Holtz

823. 07.10.2017   FIFA World Cup Qualification – Group A
BULGARIA v FRANCE   0-1 (0-1)

National Stadium Vasil Levski, Sofia

Referee: Antonio Miguel Mateu Lahoz (Spain)
Attendance: 12,921

BULGARIA: Plamen Iliev, Stanislav Manolev (87 Ivaylo Dimitrov), Nikolay Bodurov, Petar Zanev, Vasil Bozhikov, Strahil Popov, Georgi Kostadinov, Simeon Slavchev, Todor Nedelev, Spas Delev, Andrey Galabinov (48 Bozhidar Kraev). Manager: Petar Hubchev

FRANCE: Hugo Lloris, Djibril Sidibé, Lucas Digne, Raphaël Varane, Samuel Umtiti, Blaise Matuidi, N'Golo Kanté (34 Adrien Rabiot), Corentin Tolisso, Alexandre Lacazette (76 Dimitri Payet), Antoine Griezmann, Kylian Mbappé (84 Olivier Giroud).   Manager: Didier Deschamps

Goal: Blaise Matuidi (3)

824. 10.10.2017   FIFA World Cup Qualification – Group A
FRANCE v BELARUS   2-1 (2-1)

Stade de France, Saint-Denis

Referee: Halis Özkahya (Turkey)   Attendance: 74,037

FRANCE: Hugo Lloris, Lucas Digne, Samuel Umtiti, Raphaël Varane, Djibril Sidibé, Thomas Lemar (83 Dimitri Payet), Blaise Matuidi, Corentin Tolisso, Kingsley Coman (61 Kylian Mbappé), Olivier Giroud, Antoine Griezmann (78 Moussa Sissoko).   Manager: Didier Deschamps

BELARUS: Sergey Chernik, Sergey Politevich, Sergey Matveichyk, Aleksey Yanushkevich (46 Aleksandr Sachivko), Maksim Volodko, Ihar Stasevich, Stanislav Dragun, Nikita Korzun (79 Artem Bykov), Yuri Kovalev (65 Maksim Skavysh), Aleksandr Karnitskiy, Anton Saroka.
Manager: Igor Kriushenko

Goals: Antoine Griezmann (27), Olivier Giroud (33) / Anton Saroka (44)

825. 10.11.2017
FRANCE v WALES   2-0 (1-0)

Stade de France, Saint-Denis

Referee: Manuel Jorge Neves Moreira de Sousa (Portugal)
Attendance: 50,000

FRANCE: Steve Mandanda, Layvin Kurzawa, Samuel Umtiti, Laurent Koscielny, Christophe Jallet (46 Benjamin Pavard), Kingsley Coman (73 Anthony Martial), Blaise Matuidi, Corentin Tolisso (46 Steven N'Zonzi), Kylian Mbappé (84 Florian Thauvin), Antoine Griezmann (63 Nabil Fekir), Olivier Giroud (73 Alexandre Lacazette).
Manager: Didier Deschamps

WALES: Wayne Hennessey, Chris Gunter, Neil Taylor, James Chester, Ashley Williams, Ben Davies (63 Ben Woodburn), Joe Allen, Joe Ledley (64 Ethan Ampadu), Aaron Ramsey, Andy King (64 David Brooks), Sam Vokes (83 Tom Lawrence).
Manager: Chris Coleman

Goals: Antoine Griezmann (18), Olivier Giroud (71)

826. 14.11.2017
GERMANY v FRANCE   2-2 (0-1)

RheinEnergieStadion, Cologne

Referee: Cüneyt Çakir (Turkey)   Attendance: 36,948

GERMANY: Kevin Trapp, Mats Hummels (46 Antonio Rüdiger), Marvin Plattenhardt, Niklas Süle, Mesut Özil, Sami Khedira (75 Sebastian Rudy), Toni Kroos, Ilkay Gündogan (65 Mario Götze), Emre Can (83 Lars Stindl), Julian Draxler, Timo Werner (85 Sandro Wagner).   Manager: Joachim Löw

FRANCE: Steve Mandanda, Christophe Jallet (64 Benjamin Pavard), Lucas Digne (82 Layvin Kurzawa), Raphaël Varane, Samuel Umtiti, Blaise Matuidi (64 Steven N'Zonzi), Corentin Tolisso, Adrien Rabiot, Alexandre Lacazette (76 Antoine Griezmann), Anthony Martial, Kylian Mbappé.
Manager: Didier Deschamps

Goals: Timo Werner (56), Lars Stindl (90+3) / Alexandre Lacazette (33, 71)

827. 23.03.2018
FRANCE v COLOMBIA   2-3 (2-1)

Stade de France, Saint-Denis

Referee: Adrien Jaccottet (Switzerland)   Attendance: 78,000

FRANCE: Hugo Lloris, Djibril Sidibé, Lucas Digne (76 Lucas Hernández), Raphaël Varane, Samuel Umtiti, Thomas Lemar, Blaise Matuidi (65 Paul Pogba), N'Golo Kanté, Olivier Giroud (73 Wissam Ben Yedder), Antoine Griezmann (83 Florian Thauvin), Kylian Mbappé (66 Ousmane Dembélé).
Manager: Didier Deschamps

COLOMBIA: David OSPINA Ramírez, Santiago ARIAS Naranjo, Yerry Fernando MINA González, Davinson SÁNCHEZ Mina, Frank Yusty FABRA Palacios, Luís Fernando MURIEL Fruito (77 José Heriberto IZQUIERDO Jero), Carlos Alberto SÁNCHEZ Moreno, James David RODRÍGUEZ Rubio (83 Juan Fernando QUINTERO Paniagua), Abel Enrique AGUILAR Tapias (67 Jefferson Andrés LERMA Solís), Andrés Mateus URIBE Villa (90 Wilmar Enrique BARRIOS Teherán), Radamel FALCAO García Zárate (68 Duván Esteban ZAPATA Banguero).   Manager: José Nestor Pekerman

Goals: Olivier Giroud (11), Thomas Lemar (26) / Luis Muriel (28), Radamel FALCAO García Zárate (62), Juan Fernando QUINTERO Paniagua (85 pen)

828. 27.03.2018
RUSSIA v FRANCE 1-3 (0-1)
Saint Petersburg Stadium, Saint Petersburg
Referee: Gediminas Mazeika (Lithuania)
Attendance: 51,165
RUSSIA: Andrey Lunev, Fedor Kudryashov (83 Denis Cheryshev), Vladimir Granat, Yuriy Zhirkov (46 Konstantin Rausch), Roman Neustädter, Aleksandr Samedov (46 Igor Smolnikov), Alan Dzagoev (54 Anton Miranchuk), Aleksandr Yerokhin (76 Anton Shvets), Aleksey Miranchuk (67 Anton Zabolotnyi), Fedor Smolov, Aleksandr Golovin. Manager: Stanislav Cherchesov
FRANCE: Hugo Lloris, Laurent Koscielny, Samuel Umtiti (80 Presnel Kimpembe), Lucas Hernández, Benjamin Pavard, Paul Pogba, N'Golo Kanté (66 Corentin Tolisso), Anthony Martial (58 Antoine Griezmann), Ousmane Dembélé (72 Olivier Giroud), Adrien Rabiot (81 Blaise Matuidi), Kylian Mbappé (86 Thomas Lemar). Manager: Didier Deschamps
Goals: Fedor Smolov (68) / Kylian Mbappé (40, 83), Paul Pogba (49)

829. 28.05.2018
FRANCE v REPUBLIC OF IRELAND 2-0 (2-0)
Stade de France, Saint-Denis
Referee: Georgi Kabakov (Bulgaria)   Attendance: 72,000
FRANCE: Steve Mandanda, Benjamin Mendy (63 Lucas Hernández), Samuel Umtiti (64 Presnel Kimpembe), Adil Rami, Djibril Sidibé (82 Benjamin Pavard), Blaise Matuidi, Steven N'Zonzi, Corentin Tolisso (77 Paul Pogba), Nabil Fekir (64 Antoine Griezmann), Olivier Giroud, Kylian Mbappé (77 Ousmane Dembélé). Manager: Didier Deschamps
REPUBLIC OF IRELAND: Colin Doyle, Séamus Coleman, Kevin Long (80 Shaun Williams), Shane Duffy, Derrick Williams (82 Matt Doherty), Alan Browne (59 Harry Arter), Declan Rice, Jon Walters (59 David Meyler), Shane Long (70 Alan Judge), James McClean, Callum O'Dowda (70 Graham Burke). Manager: Martin O'Neill
Goals: Olivier Giroud (40), Nabil Fekir (43)

830. 01.06.2018
FRANCE v ITALY 3-1 (2-1)
Allianz Riviera, Nice
Referee: Anthony Taylor (England)   Attendance: 35,006
FRANCE: Hugo Lloris, Adil Rami, Samuel Umtiti, Lucas Hernández (62 Benjamin Mendy), Benjamin Pavard, Paul Pogba (86 Steven N'Zonzi), N'Golo Kanté, Corentin Tolisso (77 Blaise Matuidi), Antoine Griezmann (77 Olivier Giroud), Ousmane Dembélé (71 Thomas Lemar), Kylian Mbappé (83 Florian Thauvin). Manager: Didier Deschamps
ITALY: Salvatore Sirigu, Leonardo Bonucci, Danilo D'Ambrosio (74 Alessandro Florenzi), Mattia De Sciglio, Mattia Caldara, Jorge Luiz Frello Filho "Jorginho" (78 Giacomo Bonaventura), Mario Barwuah Balotelli (86 Andrea Belotti), Lorenzo Pellegrini (66 Bryan Cristante), Rolando Mandragora, Domenico Berardi (74 Lorenzo Insigne), Federico Chiesa (88 Davide Zappacosta). Manager: Roberto Mancini
Goals: Samuel Umtiti (8), Antoine Griezmann (29 pen), Ousmane Dembélé (63) / Leonardo Bonucci (36)

831. 09.06.2018
FRANCE v UNITED STATES 1-1 (0-1)
Groupama Stadium, Décines-Charpieu
Referee: William (Willie) Collum (Scotland)
Attendance: 58,241
FRANCE: Hugo Lloris, Djibril Sidibé (74 Benjamin Pavard), Raphaël Varane, Benjamin Mendy (66 Lucas Hernández), Samuel Umtiti, Blaise Matuidi (58 Corentin Tolisso), Paul Pogba, N'Golo Kanté, Olivier Giroud (58 Ousmane Dembélé), Antoine Griezmann (69 Nabil Fekir), Kylian Mbappé (88 Thomas Lemar). Manager: Didier Deschamps
UNITED STATES: Zack Steffen, Shaq Moore (74 DeAndre Yedlin), Cameron Carter-Vickers, Matt Miazga (57 Erik Palmer-Brown), Tim Parker, Antonee Robinson (82 Jorge Villafaña), Tyler Adams, Will Trapp, Weston McKennie, Julian Green (70 Joe Corona), Bobby Wood (74 Josh Sargent). Manager: Dave Sarachan
Goals: Kylian Mbappé (78) / Julian Green (44)

832. 16.06.2018   FIFA World Cup Final Tournament – Group C
FRANCE v AUSTRALIA 2-1 (0-0)
Kazan Arena, Kazan (Russia)
Referee: Andrés Ismael Cunha Soca (Uruguay)
Attendance: 41,279
FRANCE: Hugo Lloris, Raphaël Varane, Samuel Umtiti, Lucas Hernández, Benjamin Pavard, Paul Pogba, N'Golo Kanté, Corentin Tolisso (78 Blaise Matuidi), Antoine Griezmann (70 Olivier Giroud), Ousmane Dembélé (70 Nabil Fekir), Kylian Mbappé. Manager: Didier Deschamps
AUSTRALIA: Mathew Ryan, Joshua Risdon, Trent Sainsbury, Mark Milligan, Aziz Behich, Mathew Leckie, Mile Jedinak, Aaron Mooy, Robbie Kruse (84 Daniel Arzani), Tom Rogic (72 Jackson Irvine), Andrew Nabbout (64 Tomi Juric). Manager: Bert van Marwijk
Goals: Antoine Griezmann (58 pen), Paul Pogba (81) / Mile Jedinak (60 pen)

833. 21.06.2018   FIFA World Cup Final Tournament – Group C

FRANCE v PERU 1-0 (1-0)

Ekaterinburg Arena, Yekaterinburg (Russia)

Referee: Mohammed Abdulla Hassan Mohamed (UAE)
Attendance: 32,789

FRANCE: Hugo Lloris, Raphaël Varane, Samuel Umtiti, Lucas Hernández, Benjamin Pavard, Blaise Matuidi, Paul Pogba (89 Steven N'Zonzi), N'Golo Kanté, Olivier Giroud, Antoine Griezmann (80 Nabil Fekir), Kylian Mbappé (75 Ousmane Dembélé).   Manager: Didier Deschamps

PERU: Pedro David GALLESE Quiróz, Luís Jan Piers ADVÍNCULA Castrillón, Christian Guillermo Martín RAMOS Garagay, Alberto Junior RODRÍGUEZ Valdelomar (45+1 Anderson SANTAMARÍA Bardales), Miguel Angel TRAUCO Saavedra, André Martín CARRILLO Díaz, Pedro Jesús AQUINO Sánchez, Christian Alberto CUEVA Bravo (82 Raúl Mario RUIDÍAZ Misitich), Édison Michael FLORES Peralta, Victor Yoshimar YOTÚN Flores (45+1 Jefferson Agustin FARFÁN Guadalupe), José Paolo GUERRERO Gonzales.
Manager: Ricardo Alberto GARECA Nardi

Goal: Kylian Mbappé (34)

834. 26.06.2018   FIFA World Cup Final Tournament – Group C

DENMARK v FRANCE 0-0

Grand Sports Arena of the Luzhniki Olympic Complex, Moscow (Russia)

Referee: Sandro Meira Ricci (Brazil)   Attendance: 78,011

DENMARK: Kasper Schmeichel, Simon Kjær, Mathias "Zanka" Jørgensen, Henrik Dalsgaard, Jens Stryger Larsen, Christian Eriksen, Andreas Christensen, Thomas Delaney (90+2 Lukas Lerager), Martin Braithwaite, Andreas Cornelius (75 Kasper Dolberg), Pione Sisto (60 Viktor Fischer).
Manager: Åge Hareide

FRANCE: Steve Mandanda, Djibril Sidibé, Raphaël Varane, Presnel Kimpembe, Lucas Hernández (50 Benjamin Mendy), Steven N'Zonzi, Thomas Lemar, N'Golo Kanté, Olivier Giroud, Antoine Griezmann (68 Nabil Fekir), Ousmane Dembélé (78 Kylian Mbappé).   Manager: Didier Deschamps

835. 30.06.2018   FIFA World Cup Final Tournament – Round of 16

FRANCE v ARGENTINA 4-3 (1-1)

Kazan Arena, Kazan (Russia)

Referee: Alireza Faghani (Iran)   Attendance: 42,873

FRANCE: Hugo Lloris, Raphaël Varane, Samuel Umtiti, Lucas Hernández, Benjamin Pavard, Blaise Matuidi (75 Corentin Tolisso), Paul Pogba, N'Golo Kanté, Olivier Giroud, Antoine Griezmann (83 Nabil Fekir), Kylian Mbappé (89 Florian Thauvin).   Manager: Didier Deschamps

ARGENTINA: Franco Armani, Gabriel Iván Mercado, Nicolás Hernán Otamendi, Faustino Marcos Alberto Rojo (46 Federico Julián Fazio), Nicolás Alejandro Tagliafico, Javier Alejandro Mascherano, Enzo Nicolás Pérez (66 Sergio Leonel Agüero del Castillo), Éver Maximiliano David Banega, Ángel Fabián Di María, Cristian David Pavón (75 Maximiliano Eduardo Meza), Lionel Andrés Messi Cuccitini.
Manager: Jorge Luis Sampaoli Moya

Goals: Antoine Griezmann (13 pen), Benjamin Pavard (57), Kylian Mbappé (64, 68) / Ángel Fabián Di María (41), Gabriel Iván Mercado (48), Sergio Leonel Agüero del Castillo (90+3)

836. 06.07.2018   FIFA World Cup Final Tournament – Quarter-final

URUGUAY v FRANCE 0-2 (0-1)

Nizhny Novgorod Stadium, Nizhny Novgorod (Russia)

Referee: Néstor Fabián Pitana (Argentina)   Att: 43,319

URUGUAY: Néstor Fernando MUSLERA Micol, José Martín CÁCERES Silva, Diego Roberto GODÍN Leal, José María GIMÉNEZ de Vargas, Diego Sebastián LAXALT Suárez, Matías VECINO Falero, Lucas Sebastian Di Pascua TORREIRA, Nahitan Michel NÁNDEZ Acosta (73 Jonathan Matías URRETAVISCAYA da Luz), Rodrigo BENTANCUR Colmán (59 Cristian Gabriel RODRÍGUEZ Barotti), Cristhian Ricardo STUANI Curbelo (59 Maximiliano GÓMEZ González), Luis Alberto SUÁREZ Díaz.
Manager: Óscar Washington TABÁREZ Sclavo

FRANCE: Hugo Lloris, Raphaël Varane, Samuel Umtiti, Lucas Hernández, Benjamin Pavard, Paul Pogba, N'Golo Kanté, Corentin Tolisso (80 Steven N'Zonzi), Olivier Giroud, Antoine Griezmann (90+3 Nabil Fekir), Kylian Mbappé (88 Ousmane Dembélé).   Manager: Didier Deschamps

Goals: Raphaël Varane (40), Antoine Griezmann (61)

837. 10.07.2018   FIFA World Cup Final Tournament – Semi-final

FRANCE v BELGIUM 1-0 (0-0)

Saint Petersburg Stadium, Saint Petersburg (Russia)

Referee: Andrés Ismael Cunha Soca (Uruguay)
Attendance: 64,286

FRANCE: Hugo Lloris, Raphaël Varane, Samuel Umtiti, Lucas Hernández, Benjamin Pavard, Blaise Matuidi (86 Corentin Tolisso), Paul Pogba, N'Golo Kanté, Olivier Giroud (84 Steven N'Zonzi), Antoine Griezmann, Kylian Mbappé.
Manager: Didier Deschamps

BELGIUM: Thibaut Courtois, Vincent Kompany, Jan Vertonghen, Toby Alderweireld, Moussa Dembélé (60 Dries Mertens), Marouane Fellaini (80 Yannick Carrasco), Axel Witsel, Nacer Chadli (90+1 Michy Batshuayi), Eden Hazard, Kevin De Bruyne, Romelu Lukaku.
Manager: ROBERTO MARTÍNEZ Montoliú

Goal: Samuel Umtiti (51)

838.   15.07.2018   FIFA World Cup Final Tournament – Final
FRANCE v CROATIA 4-2 (2-1)

Grand Sports Arena of the Luzhniki Olympic Complex, Moscow (Russia)

Referee: Néstor Fabián Pitana (Argentina)   Att: 78,011

FRANCE: Hugo Lloris, Raphaël Varane, Samuel Umtiti, Lucas Hernández, Benjamin Pavard, Blaise Matuidi (73 Corentin Tolisso), Paul Pogba, N'Golo Kanté (55 Steven N'Zonzi), Olivier Giroud (81 Nabil Fekir), Antoine Griezmann, Kylian Mbappé.   Manager: Didier Deschamps

CROATIA: Danijel Subasic, Domagoj Vida, Ivan Strinic (82 Marko Pjaca), Dejan Lovren, Sime Vrsaljko, Luka Modric, Ivan Rakitic, Ivan Perisic, Marcelo Brozovic, Mario Mandzukic, Ante Rebic (71 Andrej Kramaric).   Manager: Zlatko Dalic

Goals: M. Mandzukic (18 og), Antoine Griezmann (38 pen), Paul Pogba (59), Kylian Mbappé (65) /
Ivan Perisic (28), Mario Mandzukic (69)

839.   06.09.2018   UEFA Nations League – Group A1
GERMANY v FRANCE 0-0

Allianz Arena, München

Referee: Daniele Orsato (Italy)   Attendance: 67,485

GERMANY: Manuel Neuer, Jérôme Boateng, Mats Hummels, Antonio Rüdiger, Matthias Ginter, Joshua Kimmich, Toni Kroos, Leon Goretzka (66 Ilkay Gündogan), Thomas Müller, Marco Reus (83 Leroy Sané), Timo Werner.   Manager: Joachim Löw

FRANCE: Alphonse Aréola, Raphaël Varane, Samuel Umtiti, Lucas Hernández, Benjamin Pavard, Blaise Matuidi (86 Corentin Tolisso), Paul Pogba, N'Golo Kanté, Olivier Giroud (66 Ousmane Dembélé), Antoine Griezmann (80 Nabil Fekir), Kylian Mbappé.   Manager: Didier Deschamps

840.   09.09.2018   UEFA Nations League – Group A1
FRANCE v NETHERLANDS 2-1 (1-0)

Stade de France, Saint-Denis

Referee: Alberto Undiano Mallenco (Spain)
Attendance: 76,452

FRANCE: Alphonse Aréola, Raphaël Varane, Samuel Umtiti, Lucas Hernández (62 Benjamin Mendy), Benjamin Pavard, Blaise Matuidi, Paul Pogba, N'Golo Kanté, Olivier Giroud (89 Ousmane Dembélé), Antoine Griezmann (81 Steven N'Zonzi), Kylian Mbappé.   Manager: Didier Deschamps

NETHERLANDS: Jasper Cillessen, Daley Blind, Virgil van Dijk, Kenny Tete (82 Daryl Janmaat), Matthijs de Ligt, Ryan Babel (88 Luuk de Jong), Georginio Wijnaldum, Davy Pröpper, Frenkie de Jong, Memphis Depay, Quincy Promes (76 Ruud Vormer).   Manager: Ronald Koeman

Goals: Kylian Mbappé (14), Olivier Giroud (74) /
Ryan Babel (67)

841.   11.10.2018
FRANCE v ICELAND 2-2 (0-2)

Stade du Roudourou, Guingamp

Referee: Tiago Bruno Lopes Martins (Portugal)   Att: 17,000

FRANCE: Hugo Lloris, Lucas Digne, Raphaël Varane (46 Kurt Zouma), Presnel Kimpembe, Benjamin Pavard, Steven N'Zonzi, Paul Pogba (67 Tanguy NDombèlé), Olivier Giroud, Florian Thauvin (59 Thomas Lemar), Antoine Griezmann (60 Kylian Mbappé), Ousmane Dembélé (67 Dimitri Payet).   Manager: Didier Deschamps

ICELAND: Rúnar Rúnarsson (46 Hannes Halldórsson), Ragnar Sigurdsson, Birkir Sævarsson (81 Jón Fjóluson), Hólmar Eyjólfsson, Birkir Bjarnason, Kári Árnason, Jóhann Gudmundsson (71 Victor Pálsson), Rúnar Sigurjónsson, Arnór Ingvi Traustason (59 Kolbeinn Sigthórsson), Alfred Finnbogason (46 Albert Gudmundsson), Gylfi Sigurdsson (80 Rúrik Gíslason).   Managers: Erik Hamrén

Goals: Hólmar Eyjólfsson (86 og), Kylian Mbappé (90 pen) /
Birkir Bjarnason (30), Kári Árnason (58)

842.   16.10.2018   UEFA Nations League – Group A1
FRANCE v GERMANY 2-1 (0-1)

Stade de France, Saint-Denis

Referee: Milorad Mazic (Serbia)   Attendance: 77,300

FRANCE: Hugo Lloris, Raphaël Varane, Presnel Kimpembe, Lucas Hernández, Benjamin Pavard, Blaise Matuidi, Paul Pogba, N'Golo Kanté (90+4 Steven N'Zonzi), Olivier Giroud, Antoine Griezmann (90+1 Tanguy NDombèlé), Kylian Mbappé (86 Ousmane Dembélé).
Manager: Didier Deschamps

GERMANY: Manuel Neuer, Mats Hummels, Niklas Süle, Matthias Ginter (83 Julian Brandt), Joshua Kimmich, Thilo Kehrer, Toni Kroos, Nico Schulz, Serge Gnabry (88 Thomas Müller), Timo Werner, Leroy Sané (75 Julian Draxler).   Manager: Joachim Löw

Goals: Antoine Griezmann (62, 80 pen) / Toni Kroos (14 pen)

843.   16.11.2018   UEFA Nations League – Group A1
NETHERLANDS v FRANCE 2-0 (1-0)

De Kuip, Rotterdam

Referee: Anthony Taylor (England)   Attendance: 44,366

NETHERLANDS: Jasper Cillessen, Daley Blind, Virgil van Dijk, Denzel Dumfries, Matthijs de Ligt, Ryan Babel (90+2 Nathan Aké), Georginio Wijnaldum (89 Tonny Vilhena), Marten de Roon, Frenkie de Jong, Memphis Depay, Steven Bergwijn (86 Quincy Promes).   Manager: Ronald Koeman

FRANCE: Hugo Lloris, Lucas Digne, Raphaël Varane, Presnel Kimpembe, Steven N'Zonzi (81 Tanguy NDombèlé), Blaise Matuidi (65 Moussa Sissoko), Benjamin Pavard, N'Golo Kanté, Olivier Giroud (65 Ousmane Dembélé), Antoine Griezmann, Kylian Mbappé.   Manager: Didier Deschamps

Goals: G. Wijnaldum (44), Memphis Depay (90+6 pen)

844. 20.11.2018
FRANCE v URUGUAY 1-0 (0-0)

Stade de France, Saint-Denis

Referee: Damir Skomina (Slovenia)   Attendance: 70,000

FRANCE: Hugo Lloris, Mamadou Sakho (46 Presnel Kimpembe), Adil Rami, Ferland Mendy, Benjamin Pavard, Blaise Matuidi (62 Steven N'Zonzi), N'Golo Kanté, Tanguy NDombèlé (71 Nabil Fekir), Antoine Griezmann (90+3 Moussa Sissoko), Kylian Mbappé (36 Florian Thauvin), Olivier Giroud (80 Alassane Pléa).   Manager: Didier Deschamps

URUGUAY: Martín Nicolás CAMPAÑA Delgado, Mathías Sebastián SUÁREZ Suárez, Bruno MÉNDEZ Cittadini, José Martín CÁCERES Silva, Rodrigo BENTANCUR Colmán, Matías VECINO Falero, Federico Santiago VALVERDE Dipetta (60 Giorgian Daniel DE ARRASCAETA Benedetti), Lucas Sebastian Di Pascua TORREIRA (74 Jonathan Javier RODRÍGUEZ Portillo), Diego Sebastián LAXALT Suárez, Luis Alberto SUÁREZ Díaz, Edinson Roberto Gómez CAVANI. Manager: Óscar Washington TABÁREZ Sclavo

Goal: Olivier Giroud (52 pen)

845. 22.03.2019   Euro 2020 Qualifying – Group H
MOLDOVA v FRANCE 1-4 (0-3)

Stadionul Zimbru, Chisinau

Referee: Aleksandar Stavrev (North Macedonia)
Attendance: 10,042

MOLDOVA: Alexei Koselev, Ion Jardan, Veaceslav Posmac, Oleg Reabciuk, Eugeniu Cebotaru, Artur Ionita, Alexandru Antoniuc (73 Vladimir Ambros), Radu Gînsari, Catalin Carp, Eugeniu Cociuc (46 Artiom Rozgoniuc), Ion Nicolaescu (59 Vitalie Damascan).
Managers: Alexandru Spiridon & Engin Firat

FRANCE: Hugo Lloris, Layvin Kurzawa, Raphaël Varane, Samuel Umtiti, Benjamin Pavard, Paul Pogba, N'Golo Kanté, Blaise Matuidi (73 Florian Thauvin), Antoine Griezmann (73 Thomas Lemar), Kylian Mbappé, Olivier Giroud (81 Nabil Fekir).   Manager: Didier Deschamps

Goals: Vladimir Ambros (89) / Antoine Griezmann (24), Raphaël Varane (27), Olivier Giroud (36), Kylian Mbappé (87)

846. 25.03.2019   Euro 2020 Qualifying – Group H
FRANCE v ICELAND 4-0 (1-0)

Stade de France, Saint-Denis

Referee: István Kovács (Romania)   Attendance: 64,538

FRANCE: Hugo Lloris, Layvin Kurzawa (85 Presnel Kimpembe), Raphaël Varane, Samuel Umtiti, Benjamin Pavard, Blaise Matuidi, Paul Pogba, N'Golo Kanté (80 Thomas Lemar), Olivier Giroud (90 Moussa Sissoko), Antoine Griezmann, Kylian Mbappé.   Manager: Didier Deschamps

ICELAND: Hannes Halldórsson, Ragnar Sigurdsson, Birkir Sævarsson (84 Ari Skúlason), Hördur Magnússon, Sverrir Ingi Ingason, Birkir Bjarnason, Kári Árnason, Aron Gunnarsson, Rúnar Sigurjónsson (57 Arnór Ingvi Traustason), Gylfi Sigurdsson, Albert Gudmundsson (62 Alfred Finnbogason). Manager: Erik Hamrén

Goals: Samuel Umtiti (12), Olivier Giroud (68), Kylian Mbappé (78), Antoine Greizmann (84)

847. 08.06.2019
FRANCE v BOLIVIA 2-0 (2-0)

Stade de la Beaujoire – Louis Fonteneau, Nantes

Referee: Alberto Undiano Mallenco (Spain)
Attendance: 35,228

FRANCE: Alphonse Aréola, Lucas Digne (79 Ferland Mendy), Raphaël Varane, Samuel Umtiti (89 Kurt Zouma), Benjamin Pavard (46 Léo Dubois), Paul Pogba, Thomas Lemar (66 Kingsley Coman), Tanguy NDombèlé (66 Blaise Matuidi), Antoine Griezmann, Florian Thauvin, Kylian Mbappé (46 Wissam Ben Yedder).   Manager: Didier Deschamps

BOLIVIA: Carlos Emilio LAMPE Porras, Diego BEJARENO Ibáñez (85 Saúl TORRES Rojas), Luis Fernando HAQUIN López, Adrián Johnny JUSINO Cerruto (89 José María CARRASCO Sanguino), Marvin Orlando BEJARENO Jiménez, Alejandro Saúl CHUMACERO Bracamonte (81 Diego Horacio WAYAR Cruz), Leonel JUSTINIANO Arauz, Samuel GALINDO Suheiro (46 Fernando Javier SAUCEDO Pereyra), Erwin Mario SAAVEDRA Flores (66 Roberto Carlos FERNÁNDEZ Toro), Raúl CASTRO Peñaloza (73 Henry VACA Urquiza), Marcelo MORENO Martins.
Manager: Eduardo Andrés VILLEGAS Camara

Goals: Thomas Lemar (5), Antoine Griezmann (43)

848. 08.06.2019   Euro 2020 Qualifying – Group H
TURKEY v FRANCE 2-0 (2-0)

Konya Büyükşehir Torku Arena, Konya

Referee: Damir Skomina (Slovenia)   Attendance: 36,783

TURKEY: Fehmi Mert Günok, Hasan Ali Kaldirim, Kaan Ayhan, Zeki Çelik, Mahmut Tekdemir, Merih Demiral, Dorukhan Toköz (90 Abdülkadir Ömür), Irfan Can Kahveci (80 Ozan Tufan), Burak Yilmaz, Kenan Karaman, Cengiz Ünder (85 Yusuf Yazici).   Manager: Senol Günes

FRANCE: Hugo Lloris, Lucas Digne (46 Ferland Mendy), Raphaël Varane, Samuel Umtiti, Benjamin Pavard, Blaise Matuidi (46 Kingsley Coman), Moussa Sissoko, Paul Pogba, Olivier Giroud (72 Wissam Ben Yedder), Antoine Griezmann, Kylian Mbappé.   Manager: Didier Deschamps

Goals: Kaan Ayhan (30), Cengiz Ünder (40)

849. 11.06.2019   Euro 2020 Qualifying – Group H
ANDORRA v FRANCE 0-4 (0-3)
Estadi Nacional, Andorra la Vella

Referee: Fran Jovic (Croatia)   Attendance: 3,187

ANDORRA: JOSEP Antoni GÓMES Moreira, ILDEFONS LIMA Solà, MARC VALES González, MOISÉS SAN NICOLÁS Schellens, MARC REBÉS Ruiz, Jesús "TXUS" RUBIO Gómez, MAX LLOREVA González-Adrio, JOAN CERVÓS Moro (81 VÍCTOR RODRÍGUEZ Soria), MÁRCIO VIEIRA de Vasconcelos, JORDI ALÁEZ Peña (85 Julià "JULI" SÁNCHEZ Soto), Alexandre "ÀLEX" MARTÍNEZ Palau (58 JORDI RUBIO Gómez).   Manager: Jesús Luis Álvarez de Eulate Güergue "KOLDO"

FRANCE: Hugo Lloris, Kurt Zouma, Clément Lenglet, Léo Dubois, Ferland Mendy, Paul Pogba, Tanguy NDombèlé (64 Moussa Sissoko), Antoine Griezmann, Wissam Ben Yedder (73 Olivier Giroud), Florian Thauvin (81 Thomas Lemar), Kylian Mbappé.   Manager: Didier Deschamps

Goals: Kylian Mbappé (11), Wissam Ben Yedder (30), Florian Thauvin (45+1), Kurt Zouma (60)

850. 07.09.2019   Euro 2020 Qualifying – Group H
FRANCE v ALBANIA 4-1 (2-0)
Stade de France, Saint-Denis

Referee: Jesús Gil Manzano (Spain)   Attendance: 77,655

FRANCE: Hugo Lloris, Raphaël Varane, Clément Lenglet, Lucas Hernández (80 Lucas Digne), Benjamin Pavard, Blaise Matuidi, Thomas Lemar (84 Nabil Fekir), Corentin Tolisso, Olivier Giroud, Antoine Griezmann, Kingsley Coman (77 Jonathan Ikoné).   Manager: Didier Deschamps

ALBANIA: Thomas Strakosha, Mërgim Mavraj, Elseid Hysaj, Berat Djimsiti, Ardian Ismajli, Amir Abrashi (73 Taulant Xhaka), Odise Roshi, Keidi Bare, Bekim Balaj (62 Sokol Çikalleshi), Myrto Uzuni, Ylber Ramadani (53 Klaus Gjasula).   Manager: Edoardo Reja

Goals: Kingsley Coman (8, 68), Olivier Giroud (27), Jonathan Ikoné (85) / Sokol Çikalleshi (90 pen)

Antoine Griezmann missed a penalty kick (37)

851. 10.09.2019   Euro 2020 Qualifying – Group H
FRANCE v ANDORRA 3-0 (1-0)
Stade de France, Saint-Denis

Referee: Mykola Oleksandrovych Balakin (Ukraine)   Attendance: 55,383

FRANCE: Hugo Lloris, Lucas Digne, Raphaël Varane, Clément Lenglet, Léo Dubois, Moussa Sissoko, Corentin Tolisso, Jonathan Ikoné (63 Thomas Lemar), Olivier Giroud (72 Wissam Ben Yedder), Antoine Griezmann, Kingsley Coman (85 Nabil Fekir).   Manager: Didier Deschamps

ANDORRA: JOSEP Antoni GÓMES Moreira, ILDEFONS LIMA Solà, MARC VALES González, MOISÉS SAN NICOLÁS Schellens, MARC REBÉS Ruiz, Jesús "TXUS" RUBIO Gómez, MAX LLOREVA González-Adrio, JOAN CERVÓS Moro, MÁRCIO VIEIRA de Vasconcelos (86 Sergio "SERGI" MORENO Marín), CRISTIAN MARTÍNEZ Alejo "KIKI" (69 JORDI ALÁEZ Peña), LUDIVIC CLEMENTE Garcés "LUDO" (79 JORDI RUBIO Gómez).
Manager: Jesús Luis Álvarez de Eulate Güergue "KOLDO"

Goals: Kingsley Coman (18), Clément Lenglet (52), Wissam Ben Yedder (90+1)

Antoine Griezmann missed a penalty kick (28)

852. 11.10.2019   Euro 2020 Qualifying – Group H
ICELAND v FRANCE 0-1 (0-0)
Laugardalsvöllur, Reykjavík

Referee: Gianluca Rocchi (Italy)   Attendance: 9,719

ICELAND: Hannes Halldórsson, Kári Árnason, Ragnar Sigurðsson, Ari Skúlason, Birkir Bjarnason, Rúnar Sigurjónsson (73 Alfred Finnbogason), Jóhann Gudmundsson (16 Jón Bödvarsson), Gylfi Sigurdsson, Victor Pálsson, Arnór Ingvi Traustason (81 Arnór Sigurdsson), Kolbeinn Sigthórsson
Manager: Erik Hamrén

FRANCE: Steve Mandanda, Lucas Digne, Raphaël Varane, Clément Lenglet, Benjamin Pavard, Blaise Matuidi, Moussa Sissoko, Corentin Tolisso, Olivier Giroud (78 Wissam Ben Yedder), Antoine Griezmann, Kingsley Coman (88 Jonathan Ikoné).   Manager: Didier Deschamps

Goal: Olivier Giroud (66 pen)

853. 14.10.2019   Euro 2020 Qualifying – Group H
FRANCE v TURKEY 1-1 (0-0)
Stade de France, Saint-Denis

Referee: Dr. Felix Brych (Germany)   Attendance: 72,154

FRANCE: Steve Mandanda, Raphaël Varane, Clément Lenglet, Lucas Hernández, Benjamin Pavard, Blaise Matuidi (77 Thomas Lemar), Moussa Sissoko, Corentin Tolisso, Antoine Griezmann, Wissam Ben Yedder (72 Olivier Giroud), Kingsley Coman (87 Jonathan Ikoné).
Manager: Didier Deschamps

TURKEY: Fehmi Mert Günok, Zeki Çelik (53 Kaan Ayhan), Merih Demiral, Çaglar Söyüncü, Umut Meras, Mahmut Tekdemir, Okay Yokuslu (46 Hakan Çalhanoglu), Irfan Can Kahveci, Ozan Tufan (81 Cenk Tosun), Burak Yilmaz, Kenan Karaman.   Manager: Senol Günes

Goals: Olivier Giroud (76) / Kaan Ayhan (82)

854.   14.11.2019   Euro 2020 Qualifying – Group H
FRANCE v MOLDOVA   2-1 (1-1)

Stade de France, Saint-Denis

Referee: Gediminas Mazeika (Lithuania)
Attendance: 64,367

FRANCE: Steve Mandanda, Lucas Digne, Raphaël Varane, Clément Lenglet, Benjamin Pavard, N'Golo Kanté, Corentin Tolisso, Olivier Giroud, Antoine Griezmann, Kingsley Coman (88 Thomas Lemar), Kylian Mbappé.
Manager: Didier Deschamps

MOLDOVA: Alexei Koselev, Igor Armas, Ion Jardan (68 Dinu Graur), Veaceslav Posmac, Artur Craciun, Artur Ionita, Radu Gînsari (74 Nicolae Milinceanu), Vadim Rata (81 Artur Patras), Eugeniu Cociuc, Catalin Carp, Sergiu Platica.
Manager: Engin Firat

Goals: Raphaël Varane (35), Olivier Giroud (79 pen) / Vadim Rata (9)

855.   17.11.2019   Euro 2020 Qualifying – Group H
ALBANIA v FRANCE   0-2 (0-2)

Air Albania Stadium, Tirana

Referee: Slavko Vincic (Slovenia)   Attendance: 19,228

ALBANIA: Etrit Berisha, Ermir Lenjani (46 Odise Roshi), Freddie Veseli, Elseid Hysaj (82 Lorenc Trashi), Berat Djimsiti, Kastriot Dermaku, Klaus Gjasula, Kristi Qose (46 Ledian Memushaj), Keidi Bare, Bekim Balaj, Rey Manaj.
Manager: Edoardo Reja

FRANCE: Steve Mandanda, Raphaël Varane, Benjamin Mendy (75 Lucas Digne), Clément Lenglet, Presnel Kimpembe, Léo Dubois (88 Benjamin Pavard), Moussa Sissoko, Corentin Tolisso, Olivier Giroud, Antoine Griezmann, Wissam Ben Yedder (85 Nabil Fekir).
Manager: Didier Deschamps

Goals: Corentin Tolisso (9), Antoine Griezmann (30)

856.   05.09.2020   UEFA Nations League – Group A3
SWEDEN v FRANCE   0-1 (0-1)

Friends Arena, Solna

Referee: Szymon Marciniak (Poland)   Attendance: 0

SWEDEN: Robin Olsen, Pierre Bengtsson (88 Ken Sema), Mikael Lustig, Pontus Jansson, Victor Lindelöf, Sebastian Larsson (70 Dejan Kulusevski), Albin Ekdal, Emil Forsberg, Kristoffer Olsson, Marcus Berg, Robin Quaison (77 John Guidetti).   Manager: Janne Andersson

FRANCE: Hugo Lloris, Lucas Digne, Raphaël Varane, Presnel Kimpembe, Léo Dubois (88 Ferland Mendy), Dayot Upamecano, N'Golo Kanté, Adrien Rabiot, Olivier Giroud (90+2 Steven N'Zonzi), Antoine Griezmann, Kylian Mbappé (77 Anthony Martial).   Manager: Didier Deschamps

Goal: Kylian Mbappé (41)

Antoine Griezmann missed a penalty kick (90).

857.   08.09.2020   UEFA Nations League – Group A3
FRANCE v CROATIA   4-2 (2-1)

Stade de France, Saint-Denis

Referee: Ovidiu Alin Hategan (Romania)   Attendance: 0

FRANCE: Hugo Lloris, Clément Lenglet, Ferland Mendy, Lucas Hernández, Dayot Upamecano, Moussa Sissoko, Steven N'Zonzi, N'Golo Kanté (63 Eduardo Camavinga), Wissam Ben Yedder (63 Olivier Giroud), Anthony Martial, Antoine Griezmann (78 Nabil Fekir).   Manager: Didier Deschamps

CROATIA: Dominik Livakovic, Dejan Lovren, Duje Caleta-Car, Dario Melnjak, Filip Uremovic (57 Domagoj Vida), Ivan Perisic (66 Mario Pasalic), Marcelo Brozovic, Mateo Kovacic, Nikola Vlasic, Andrej Kramaric, Ante Rebic (46 Josip Brekalo).
Manager: Zlatko Dalic

Goals: A. Griezmann (43), Dominik Livakovic (45+1 og), Dayot Upamecano (65), Olivier Giroud (77 pen) / Dejan Lovren (17), Josip Brekalo (55)

858.   07.10.2020
FRANCE v UKRAINE   7-1 (4-0)

Stade de France, Saint-Denis

Referee: Andris Treimanis (Latvia)   Attendance: 1,000

FRANCE: Steve Mandanda (46 Mike Maignan), Lucas Digne, Clément Lenglet, Benjamin Pavard, Dayot Upamecano (46 Raphaël Varane), Steven N'Zonzi, Corentin Tolisso, Houssem Aouar (59 Antoine Griezmann), Eduardo Camavinga (59 Paul Pogba), Olivier Giroud (73 Wissam Ben Yedder), Anthony Martial (46 Kylian Mbappé).   Manager: Didier Deschamps

UKRAINE: Georgiy Bushchan, Bogdan Mykhaylichenko (46 Eduardo Sobol), Vitaliy Mykolenko (46 Yevhen Cheberko), Illya Zabarnyi, Yevhen Konoplyanka, Yevhen Makarenko (62 Volodymyr Shepelyev), Igor Kharatin, Ruslan Malinovskyi (46 Viktor Tsygankov), Mykola Shaparenko, Oleksandr Zubkov (71 Roman Bezus), Andriy Yarmolenko (62 Roman Yaremchuk).   Manager: Andriy Shevchenko

Goals: Eduardo Camavinga (9), Olivier Giroud (24, 34), Vitali Mykolenko (39 og), Corentin Tolisso (65), Kylian Mbappé (82), Antoine Griezmann (89) / Viktor Tsygankov (53)

859. 11.10.2020   UEFA Nations League – Group A3
FRANCE v PORTUGAL 0-0
Stade de France, Saint-Denis

Referee: Carlos del Cerro Grande (Spain)   Attendance: 1,000

FRANCE: Hugo Lloris, Raphaël Varane, Presnel Kimpembe, Lucas Hernández, Benjamin Pavard, Paul Pogba, N'Golo Kanté, Adrien Rabiot, Olivier Giroud (74 Anthony Martial), Antoine Griezmann, Kylian Mbappé (84 Kingsley Coman). Manager: Didier Deschamps

PORTUGAL: RUI Pedro dos Santos PATRÍCIO, Képler Laveran Lima Ferreira "PEPE", RAPHAËL Adenilo José GUERREIRO (89 JOÃO Pedro Cavaco CANCELO), NÉLSON Cabral SEMEDO "Nelsinho", RÚBEN Santos Gato Alves DIAS, DANILO Luís Hélio Pereira, BRUNO Miguel Borges FERNANDES (80 RENATO Júnior Luz SANCHES), BERNARDO Mota Veiga de Carvalho e SILVA (61 DIOGO José Teixeira da Silva "JOTA"), CRISTIANO RONALDO dos Santos Aveiro, JOÃO FÉLIX Sequeira (89 Francisco António Machado Mota Castro TRINCÃO), WILLIAM Silva de CARVALHO (88 JOÃO Filipe Iria Santos MOUTINHO). Manager: FERNANDO Manuel Fernandes da Costa SANTOS

860. 14.10.2020   UEFA Nations League – Group A3
CROATIA v FRANCE 1-2 (0-1)
Stadion Maksimir, Zagreb

Referee: Björn Kuipers (Netherlands)   Attendance: 6,266

CROATIA: Dominik Livakovic, Domagoj Vida, Dejan Lovren, Borna Barisic, Filip Uremovic, Luka Modric, Milan Badelj (46 Mateo Kovacic), Mario Pasalic (46 Josip Brekalo), Nikola Vlasic (80 Andrej Kramaric), Ivan Perisic (78 Domagoj Bradaric), Bruno Petkovic (61 Ante Budimir). Manager: Zlatko Dalic

FRANCE: Hugo Lloris, Lucas Digne (82 Lucas Hernández), Raphaël Varane, Clément Lenglet, Ferland Mendy, Steven N'Zonzi, Adrien Rabiot (74 Paul Pogba), Anthony Martial (62 Kingsley Coman), Kylian Mbappé, Corentin Tolisso (63 Eduardo Camavinga), Antoine Griezmann (83 Olivier Giroud). Manager: Didier Deschamps

Goals: Nikola Vlasic (65) /
Antoine Griezmann (8), Kylian Mbappé (79)

861. 11.11.2020
FRANCE v FINLAND 0-2 (0-2)
Stade de France, Saint-Denis

Referee: Nikola Popov (Bulgaria)   Attendance: 0

FRANCE: Steve Mandanda, Lucas Digne, Kurt Zouma, Clément Lenglet (80 Raphaël Varane), Léo Dubois (71 Ruben Aguilar), Moussa Sissoko, Steven N'Zonzi, Paul Pogba (57 N'Golo Kanté), Olivier Giroud (57 Anthony Martial), Wissam Ben Yedder (57 Antoine Griezmann), Marcus Thuram. Manager: Didier Deschamps

FINLAND: Jesse Joronen, Juhani Ojala (66 Joona Toivio), Daniel O'Shaughnessy, Leo Väisänen (75 Paulus Arajuuri), Niko Hämäläinen, Rasmus Schüller (80 Teemu Pukki), Joni Kauko, Onni Valakari (75 Robert Taylor), Rasmus Karjalainen (67 Glen Kamara), Ilmari Niskanen (67 Nikolai Alho), Marcus Forss. Manager: Markku Kanerva

Goals: Marcus Forss (28), Onni Valakari (31)

862. 14.11.2020   UEFA Nations League – Group A3
PORTUGAL v FRANCE 0-1 (0-0)
Estadio do Sport Lisboa e Benfica, Lisboa

Referee: Tobias Stieler (Germany)   Attendance: 0

PORTUGAL: RUI Pedro dos Santos PATRÍCIO, JOSÉ Miguel da Rocha FONTE, JOÃO Pedro Cavaco CANCELO, RAPHAËL Adenilo José GUERREIRO, RÚBEN Santos Gato Alves DIAS, DANILO Luís Hélio Pereira (84 SÉRGIO Miguel Relvas de OLIVEIRA), WILLIAM Silva de CARVALHO (56 DIOGO José Teixeira da Silva "JOTA"), BRUNO Miguel Borges FERNANDES (72 JOÃO Filipe Iria Santos MOUTINHO), CRISTIANO RONALDO dos Santos Aveiro, BERNARDO Mota Veiga de Carvalho e SILVA (71 Francisco António Machado Mota Castro TRINCÃO), JOÃO FÉLIX Sequeira (84 João Paulo Dias Fernandes "PAULINHO").
Manager: FERNANDO Manuel Fernandes da Costa SANTOS

FRANCE: Hugo Lloris, Raphaël Varane, Presnel Kimpembe, Lucas Hernández, Benjamin Pavard, Paul Pogba, N'Golo Kanté, Adrien Rabiot, Antoine Griezmann, Anthony Martial (78 Olivier Giroud), Kingsley Coman (59 Marcus Thuram). Manager: Didier Deschamps

Goal: N'Golo Kanté (54)

863. 17.11.2020   UEFA Nations League – Group A3
FRANCE v SWEDEN 4-2 (2-1)
Stade de France, Saint-Denis

Referee: Aleksey Kulbakov (Belarus)   Attendance: 0

FRANCE: Hugo Lloris, Presnel Kimpembe, Raphaël Varane (46 Kurt Zouma), Lucas Hernández (46 Lucas Digne), Benjamin Pavard, Moussa Sissoko, Paul Pogba, Adrien Rabiot (78 Steven N'Zonzi), Olivier Giroud (84 Kingsley Coman), Marcus Thuram (57 Kylian Mbappé), Antoine Griezmann. Manager: Didier Deschamps

SWEDEN: Robin Olsen, Pierre Bengtsson, Mikael Lustig (67 Emil Krafth), Marcus Danielsson, Victor Lindelöf (66 Filip Helander), Viktor Claesson (66 Robin Quaison), Kristoffer Olsson, Dejan Kulusevski, Marcus Berg (86 Alexander Isak), Emil Forsberg, Sebastian Larsson (87 Jens Cajuste). Manager: Janne Andersson

Goals: Olivier Giroud (16, 59), Benjamin Pavard (36), Kingsley Coman (90+5) / Viktor Claesson (4), R. Quaison (88)